The History and Narrative Reader

Are historians story-tellers? Is it possible to tell true stories about the past? These are two of the central questions addressed in this comprehensive collection of writings about the philosophy, theory and methodology of history. By drawing together seminal texts from philosophers and historians, this volume presents the great debate on the narrative character of history from the 1960s to the present day.

The History and Narrative Reader combines theory with practice to offer a unique overview which illuminates the practical implications of these philosophical debates for the writing of history. The editor's introduction gives a succinct survey of the subject to support the readings. The collection explores the role of narrative in:

* historical understanding
* human action
* linguistics and structure
* the practice of history.

This volume includes the work of F. R. Ankersmit, David Carr, Lawrence Stone, Hayden White, Margaret Somers, William Cronon, W. H. Dray and Frederick Olafson making *The History and Narrative Reader* a practical and philosophical guide to the history and narrative debate. A detailed bibliography and a glossary of key concepts mean this collection will be an invaluable resource for students of historical theory and methodology.

Geoffrey Roberts is Statutory Lecturer in History at University College Cork. He is author of *The Unholy Alliance: Stalin's Pact with Hitler* (1989), *The Soviet Union and the Origins of the Second World War* (1995) and *The Soviet Union in World Politics, 1945–1991* (1998).

The

History and

Narrative Reader

Edited by

Geoffrey Roberts

London and New York

First published 2001
by Routledge
11 New Fetter Lane, London EC4P 4EE

Simultaneously published in the USA and Canada
by Routledge
29 West 35th Street, New York, NY 10001

Routledge is an imprint of the Taylor & Francis Group

Typeset in Perpetua and Bell Gothic by
Florence Production Ltd, Stoodleigh, Devon
Index compiled by Indexing Specialists, Hove, East Sussex
Printed and bound in Great Britain by
TJ International Ltd, Padstow, Cornwall

British Library Cataloguing in Publication Data
A catalogue record for this book is available from the British Library

Library of Congress Cataloging-in-Publication Data
The history and narrative reader / [edited by] Geoffrey Roberts.
    p. cm.
    Includes bibliographical references and index.
    1. History–Philosophy. 2. Historiography–History. 3. Narration (Rhetoric)
    I. Roberts, Geoffrey, 1952–
    D16.8 .H6244 2001
    901–dc21   00-069040

ISBN 0–415–23248–1 (hbk)
ISBN 0–415–23249–x (pbk)

This one is for Ronnie

Contents

Acknowledgements

The author and publishers wish to thank the following for their permission to reproduce copyright material:

"On the Nature and Role of Narrative in History" and "Narrative and Historical Realism" by W. H. Dray by permission of Brill publishers; "Narrative and Historical Understanding" (original title "The Historical Understanding") by W. B. Gallie in *History and Theory* (1964), pp. 149–72, 193–8 by permission of Blackwell publishers; "A Note on History as Narrative" by M. Mandelbaum, *History and Theory* vol. 6 (1967), pp. 411–19, © Wesleyan University and reprinted by permission of Blackwell publishers; "Mandelbaum on Historical Narrative" by R. G. Ely in *History and Theory*, vol. 8, no. 2 (1969) pp. 275–83, © Wesleyan University and reprinted by permission of Blackwell Publishers; "The Dialectic of Action" by F. A. Olafson (original title "Narrative History", Chapter 4 of his *The Dialectic of Action*, pp. 133–4, 144–88) by permission of the author and The University of Chicago Press; "The Structure of Narrative" by M. C. Lemon from his *The Discipline of History and the History of Thought*, pp. 42–3, 51–72, 77–8, by permission of the author and Routledge publishers; "Geoffrey Elton: History and Human Action" by Geoffrey Roberts first appeared as "Geoffrey Elton and the Philosophy of History" in *The Historian*, no. 57 (1998), reproduced by permission of the publishers, © 1998 The Historical Association; "Narrative and the Real World" by D. Carr in *History and Theory*, pp. 117–31, (1986) by permission of Blackwell publishers; "Telling it Like it Was" by A. P. Norman in *History and Theory*, pp. 119–35, (1991) by permission of Blackwell publishers; D. Carr, "Getting the Story Straight" from J. Topolski (ed.) *Historiography Between Modernism and Postmodernism*, reprinted by permission of Rodopi publishers; "Narrative Form as a Cognitive Instrument" by L. O. Mink in R. H. Canary and H. Kozicki (eds), *The Writing of History*, pp. 41–62, 129–34, 141–7, © 1978, reprinted by permission of The University of Wisconsin Press; "Interpretation, History and Narrative" by N. Carroll in *The Monist*, vol. 73, reprinted by permission of the publishers; "Six Theses on Narrativist Philosophy of History" by F. R. Ankersmit in his *History and Tropology: The Rise and Fall of Metaphor*, © 1994 The

nd reprinted by permission of the University
istory to Problem-Oriented History" by F.
pp. 55–67, reprinted by permission of The
of Narrative" by L. Stone in *Past and Present*,
vival of Narrative" by E. J. Hobsbawm in
printed by permission of Oxford University
Revival of Narrative" in his *New Perspectives*
ed by permission of Blackwell publishers
y Park: The Pennsylvania State University
ia State University. Reproduced by per-
and How: Narrative Openings in Donald
war in *Canadian Historical Review*, 62: 3
ission of University of Toronto Press
ity and Social Action: Rethinking English
in *Social Science History*, 16: 4 (1992).
, Social Science History Association. All rights reserved. Reprinted by permission of Duke University Press; "Historical Emplotment and the Problem of Truth"
by H. White, pp. 37–53 from *Probing the Limits of Representation*, S. Friedlander (ed.),
Cambridge, Mass.: Harvard University Press, reprinted by permission of the pub-
lisher, © 1992 by the President and Fellows of Harvard College; "International
History, Theory and the Origins of the Second World War" by P. Finney, in
Rethinking History, 1 (1998), pp. 357–79 reprinted by permission of Taylor & Francis
Ltd, 11 New Fetter Lane, London, EC4P 4EE; "A Place for Stories: Nature, History
and Narrative" by W. Cronon from the March 1992 issue of the *Journal of American
History*, pp. 1347–74, reprinted by permission of the author and the Organization
of American Historians.

Note: Most of the above texts have been reproduced in their entirety, but the text
and/or notes of some pieces have been abridged.

Every effort has been made to obtain permission to reproduce copyright material.
If any proper acknowledgement has not been made, we would invite copyright
holders to inform us of the oversight.

And now, some personal acknowledgements: Arthur J. Presswell, a colleague in
NALGO Education Department in the 1980s, for giving me a set of bound volumes
of *History and Theory*; Charles Reynolds, whose books on the theory of international
politics first made me think about history in a new way; Tim Weston, for philosophical conversations over many years, and for lending me his copy of Hayden
White's *The Content of the Form*; Ken Dewar, whose article on Creighton inspired
the idea of a volume of readings on history and narrative; Heather McCallum, for
encouraging me to take on a project of this kind, and who in the last days of her
reign at Routledge secured the contract; my colleagues in the Department of History
at University College Cork, who have taught me much about diverse ways of doing
history; and, last but not least, Celia Watson for her critical scrutiny and editorial
correction of my own contributions to this book.

The book is dedicated to my late brother.

Introduction
The history and narrative
debate, 1960–2000

■   Geoffrey Roberts

Introduction

THIS BOOK IS ABOUT the most important and central debate in the philosophy of history since the 1960s: the extent to which the discipline of history is essentially a narrative mode of knowing, understanding, explaining and reconstructing the past. This introduction will summarize that debate, provide a context for the various readings, and indicate avenues for further study and research. I will conclude by raising some important issues that require further consideration.

The book has six sections. In the first section on *Narrative and Historical Understanding* the focus is on the 1960s debate on historical narrative as a mode of explanation. This debate began a key discussion between those who saw historical narratives as proto-scientific explanations of the past that could be formally analyzed, and those who emphasized the role of narratives in enhancing historical understanding and intelligibility.

The second section on *Narrative and Human Action* features the work of those philosophers and historians who emphasize that historical narratives are stories of action and that it is the account of human action in narrative terms that makes historical studies meaningful, interesting and significant explanations of the human past.

The third section entitled *Narrative and Historical Realism* explores the view that the reason why historians construct stories about the past is that this reflects life, consciousness and human existence which have a narrative character and constitution.

Section four on *Narrative History and the Linguistic Turn* is concerned with the argument that the construction of historical narrative is driven by linguistic forms and that historians' stories are, to a large degree, literary and fictional accounts of the past.

In the fifth section on *Narrative and Structure* the subject is what relationship there is between narrating the past and providing accounts of the structure of events and of structural change.

Finally, the sixth section of the book on *Narrative and the Practice of History* is devoted to detailed but theoretically-informed studies of historical narration in a diversity of historiographical domains — Canadian History, Labor History, Holocaust History, International History, and Environmental History.

Most of the contributors to the book are philosophers or theorists rather than historians, but it is by no means only aimed at those mainly interested in philosophy. As an historian myself, my interest in the philosophy of history is ultimately practical — in how philosophical and theoretical debates can contribute to a better understanding of the past and to researching and writing history. Most historians most of the time think and write narrative. Because of that, the discussion among philosophers about the narrative character of historical writings is a most illuminating theoretical debate.

What the contributors to this book have in common is that they treat what most historians mostly do — write stories about the past — as a serious enterprise worthy of sustained philosophical and theoretical exploration. Their analyses and conclusions concerning the theory and philosophy of narrative history differ considerably. But most argue that narrative history is a legitimate form of knowledge, at least on a par with other approaches to the study of the past, and constitutes a discipline as theoretically and philosophically sophisticated as any other in the human and social sciences.

"Historians have always told stories," as Lawrence Stone put it (#18)[1], but it was not until the 1960s that philosophers began to pay serious attention to the contents and forms of historical narratives. Narrative was not entirely neglected in the philosophy of history[2] but the few treatments that did exist tended to be overshadowed by traditional philosophical debates about problems of objectivity, explanation and causation in historical study.[3] The shift towards a focus on narrative in the philosophy of history was partly the result of some significant contributions to the discussion by the likes of White, Danto, Dray, Gallie and others featured in this volume; partly because other debates had seemingly exhausted themselves and were becoming repetitive; and partly because philosophers began to pay more attention to the detailed content and character of actual historical writings rather than focusing on an idealized or formalized version of what explanatory, causal or "objective" statements about the past should look like.

There was a certain irony about this growing philosophical interest in narrative history since it came at a time of what Paul Ricoeur subsequently called the "eclipse of narrative" in the discipline itself.[4] He was referring to the predominant influence of various types of social scientific conceptualizing and theorizing in historiography in the 1960s and 1970s. The proponents of these new historiographic trends derided traditional historical storytelling as old fashioned, counterposed so-called analytical history to narrative history, and lauded the search for the grand structures, forces and causes of history. One advocate of the new, social science-oriented history was Lawrence Stone.[5] But, as his contribution to this volume shows, by the late 1970s Stone was celebrating "the revival of narrative" and contrasting the flexibility and indeterminism of narrative history with the rigidity and determinism of social scientific history.

In reality, the eclipse of narrative was mostly an illusory effect of the transitory prominence of certain schools and fashions within history (the French Annales school, various types of Marxism, quantitative history, the new social history in Britain, the United States, Germany and elsewhere).[6] It was also connected to the fact that many of those who wrote about historiographical and theoretical issues tended, like Stone, to endorse the so-called new history.[7] Stone's divination of the return of narrative to prominence in the 1970s was somewhat exaggerated, but by the 1980s and 1990s the defenders of narrative history were competing on much more equal terms with the continuing advocates of non-narrative, structuralist history.[8] Indeed, among the philosophers, the ground had decisively shifted in favor of the so-called narrativists – those who considered that what was distinctive about the discipline of history was its storytelling character.[9]

Narrative and historical understanding

The book begins with the 1960s debate on the nature and role of narrative in history, conducted mainly in the pages of the journal *History and Theory*, which had begun publication at the beginning of the decade.[10] As W. H. Dray explains in his survey of the debate (#1)[11] there were two strands in this early discussion of history and narrative. The first was represented by Morton White[12] and Arthur Danto[13] whose accounts of historical narrative grew out of debates on explanation and causation in history. White argued that historical narratives consisted of series of explanatory statements which traced the causal sequences and connections of past events. For Danto it was the logical structure of "narrative sentences" which distinguished historical narration from other forms of explanation – sentences which linked the contemporaneous descriptions of past events with subsequent knowledge of historical outcomes. But perhaps more important was the crucial general insight about historiography that their work pointed to: that the typical mode of explanation employed by historians was narrative. Ask an historian to explain something and they will usually tell you a story. The story will not just describe what happened but in the course of the narrative provide an explanation of the how and the why of past events. Further, that explanatory content is not readily detachable from the narrative. The story is the explanation and the validation of the explanation is embedded in the very structure of the narrative.

One of the implications of the idea that narrative is *the* historical mode of explanation is that in order to grasp the explanatory content of historical writings readers of history texts have to be able to comprehend the story in which it is embedded. This was the argument of W. B. Gallie (#2) the progenitor of the second strand of the 1960s debate on narrative who said that fundamental to historical understanding was the ability of readers to follow a story – that is the capacity to follow a sequence of human experiences, actions and contingencies across time.

An oft-repeated criticism of Gallie was that narratives are constructed before they are read and that before a story is written a process of historical inquiry takes place. Louis Mink, for example, argued that Gallie "cannot throw light on historical inquiry, since the historian does not follow a narrative but constructs it, and constructing a narrative backwards . . . is quite different from following a narrative forward."[14] Actually, historians are readers as well as constructors of narratives, not least their own stories. Constructing a narrative is a constant process of following one's own story forward (even when the outcome is well-known and clearcut). Gallie's description of the process of following a story is commensurate with the process of writing one. Moreover, the process of historical inquiry does not end when the writing begins nor does constructing a narrative begin only when the research ends. What Gallie calls the capacity for historical understanding is a necessary attribute of researching and writing narratives as well as reading them.

Gallie summarized his position as being "the claim that history is a species of the genus Story."[15] Not unnaturally, such a radical stance was not without its critics. One of the most prominent critics at the time was Maurice Mandelbaum (#3) who argued that historians don't just tell stories of linear sequences of actions; they also describe and analyze the context and circumstances of historical events. In his 1977 book Mandelbaum elaborated this argument, noting that narration was only one form in which historians presented the results of their research. Alternative forms included *explanatory* accounts (which identify the *factors* responsible for past occurrences) and *interpretative* accounts (which concentrate on portraying the *background* to subsequent developments).[16]

In a contribution to the debate between Gallie, Mandelbaum and others Richard G. Ely (#4) pointed out that historical narratives invariably contain descriptions and analyses of the background to the human action being narrated. Moreover, "it is a characteristic feature of the historical study of human projects and human achievements that . . . historians link together their descriptions of purposeful human accounts with their descriptions of the circumstances under which such actions were performed." Ely's focus on the *human action* content of historical accounts was commensurate with Gallie's emphasis that the stories followed by readers were narratives of action and that it was precisely the human content of these narratives that made them comprehensible.

Narrative and human action

The centrality of the connection between narrative and human action is the theme of section two of this book. It begins with a substantial extract (#5) from Frederick Olafson's *The Dialectic of Action*, published in 1979.[17] Olafson's argument in this book was presaged in an important article published in *Theory and History* in 1970. The article was in fact a late contribution to the debate on narrative sparked off by the writings of White and Danto.[18] In it Olafson drew attention to the pervasive presence in historiography of "action sentences" and "action-concepts" which, he argued, denoted the common, thematic interest of historians in human action.

In his later book Olafson went much further, arguing that "human actions are the primary events with which the historian deals" and that "historical narrative is to be understood as the reconstruction of a sequence of human actions within which one action and its consequences become the premise for a succeeding action and so on." This dynamic unfolding of sequences of action was for Olafson the "dialectic of action" – a descriptor, it should be noted, not simply of narrative representations but of the historical process itself.

Olafson's other major theme was that human consciousness and its practical expression in action was teleological – that is, purposeful, goal-directed and intelligible. It was this "rational structure of action" that, he said, provided the connectivity and continuity of the successive episodes of the dialectic of action. Historical narratives in attempting to reconstruct action, display a similar content and structure, which is particularly apparent in the effort to interpret and mirror the perceptions, motivations, calculations and goals of human agents engaged in transforming the practical fields of action in which they operate.

The Dialectic of Action is arguably the most comprehensive and compelling philosophical defense of traditional narrative history. The only really comparable text is a book by the British intellectual historian, M. C. Lemon, published in 1995.[19] Like Olafson, Lemon proceeds from an individualist, action-based ontology to argue that central to the discipline of history is the narration of human conduct. Lemon's theme in the extract reproduced here (#6) is the question of what makes the order of a narrative meaningful and intelligible. One part of Lemon's answer overlaps with Olafson's notion of the dialectic of action and concerns the role played in the creation of the changes and continuities identified in a historical narrative of the responses of human agents to situations (in particular the reasons for action in given circumstances). Another part of Lemon's answer revolves around the argument that human reality itself is a world of "story-objects" or "events," by which he means human-generated sequences of occurrences which constitute a unity or narrative identity. In Lemon's view narratives not only explain, they *explicate* "meaningful overall entities" – existent narrative entities or identities which are discovered and articulated by historians. The story-objects that constitute the human world are far from all being distinct or easily identifiable or even definable. But an important clue to both their existence and significance is the awareness and capabilities that individuals show in comprehending the "events" displayed by historians – including big ones like wars and revolutions. Lemon summarizes: "we are 'story-perceiving' beings; one of the characteristics of the world is that it generates stories, that is, 'story-objects'." As we shall see shortly, Lemon is not alone in promoting this notion of a narrativist ontology of the human world.

Unlike some philosophers Lemon is not shy of telling historians what they ought o do as well as dissecting what they actually do:

> Firstly, the historian cannot construct (narrative) histories of natural events . . . Secondly, the historian should not people his [or her] narrative with pseudo-human agents such as animals, angels, ghosts, or gods. Neither, thirdly, should [s]he exploit abstract agents, such as "the spirit

of liberty," "imperialism," "racialism," or "the Enlightenment." It is only in a manner of speaking that, for example, "nationalism" can do anything, respond to circumstances, or initiate different situations ... analysis confirms and encourages what is still for many historians a preference for concentrating upon the actions of individuals in constructing their narratives. The fact is, they *must* do so in order to locate and sustain intelligible continuity in the real world.[20]

The kind of arguments developed by Gallie, Olafson, Lemon and others were, naturally, highly congenial to narrative historians. Historians, however, generally prefer to write narratives than to write about them. So explicit comment by historians on the philosophical debate on narrative is notable mainly for its absence. Two exceptions were Geoffrey Elton (#7) and J. H. Hexter (#8). Elton and Hexter implicitly shared the ontological individualism and actionism of the philosophical defenders of narrative history. Both prescribed the writing of history in the form of narrative (and practiced the art themselves). Above all, the two historians took a pragmatic and practical approach to problems of narrative construction and validation. Their arguments on narrative by no means lacked theoretical content and sophistication but ultimately their defense of traditional practices and approaches was that narrative history *worked*. Historical accounts which narrate the past, they argued, do produce useful knowledge and understanding of the human world that has gone before – or so it seems to common sense. Elton and Hexter's adherence to a pragmatic attitude to the evaluation of narratives foreshadowed the 1980s turn in the philosophy of history away from what Raymond Martin called the "conceptual approach" towards the "empirical approach" i.e. an examination of the terms within which historians themselves assess and validate historical writings.[21]

Narrative and historical realism

Both Elton and Hexter subscribed to a version of "historical realism" – the that historical narratives attempt (and often succeed) to tell us what really hap in the past. One of the most prominent philosophical defenders of this co sense proposition has been David Carr, whose exploration of the relationship historical narrative and the narrativity of time and action has attracted able attention since the publication in 1986 of his book on *Time, Nar History*.[22]

As set out in the summary-article reproduced here (#9) Carr's that historical writings take the form of narrative because their co is the practical narrativity of human agents acting within time. Hu time, experience life, and act in the world in a narratively structure just historians' stories that have beginnings, middles and ends. Life and lived is like that, too. Nor are historians the only story-tell pants in practical narrativity are constantly telling themselves about life and their lives. Such narrative consciousness not only is constitutive of selfhood, of personal identity. The past that historians address, argues Carr, is a pre-storied human reality. Moreover, it is not only individuals who tell themselves stories, who are "constantly striving . . . to occupy the story-tellers' position with respect to their [own] lives." Various collectivities, what Carr calls "we" groups also exhibit narrativity. Narrative historians relate the stories and actions of groups, organizations, communities, nations and states as well as those of individuals.[23]

Dray in his review of Carr's work (#10) poses the question: "suppose an historian goes beyond what was consciously lived as such by the original agents: what is the epistemological status of the account he gives?" Dray's point has been made by other commentators as well.[24] Carr's analysis works best in relation to historical accounts which focus on the reconstruction of the contemporaneous narratives of agents themselves, and charts the action and forward movement of those agents through time. But historians also tell their own stories about the action of those with whom they are dealing. Carr's philosophical treatment of the narrativity of life may validate the narrative form of those stories but what about the *truth* of their content? A cognate point is made by Andrew P. Norman (#11) who distinguishes between the "discursive form" and the "semantic content" of historical accounts. Discursivity in the form of narrative structure does not guarantee the truth of a historical account and nor does the absence of narrativity in past actuality necessarily mean that a story told about it does not contain truth.

In a retrospective assessment of the discussion of his work (#12) Carr accepts that a general demonstration of the narrative ontology of historical reality is no guarantee of the truth of particular narratives: establishing the truth is more a matter of epistemology than ontology. Carr also accepts that historians tell their own stories (and thereby add to the stock of narratives that compose historical reality) as well as telling those of the historical agents themselves. Indeed, commenting on "history's distinctive cognitive advantage, that of hindsight," Carr notes:

> The historian's retrospective stance permits her (sic) to view the self-descriptions and practical narratives behind historical actions in light of their actual outcomes. The ironic disparity between the envisioned or intended and the actual consequences of an action is practically the historian's stock-in-trade.

As far as the issue of epistemological validation is concerned, Carr's solution is not dissimilar to Andrew Norman's. The truth-content (or not) of narratives is established discursively on a case-by-case basis. Carr stresses, in particular, the intersubjective context of the discussion and assessment of particular narratives. Ultimately, it is the activities of the cognitive community of historians, with its scholarly traditions, practices and values, that acts as the safeguard of historical truth. Carr concludes: "rather than speaking in abstract terms . . . we can . . . make more sense of history's capacity and obligation to truth-telling by considering it in concrete terms as the activity of getting the story straight."

Carr's conclusion, however, does raise some rather large questions about the procedures and criteria applied by historians evaluating historical accounts. Providing answers to those questions is beyond the scope of this book[25], but one general point in support of Carr's anti-foundational and anti-epistemological stance will be made. According to Raymond Martin:

> The overriding explanatory objective of historians is to show that their explanations are better than competing explanations, and they attempt to do this by arguing both *for* their explanations and *against* competing explanations.[26]

Martin's point applies to narrative, too. Typically, the evaluative discourse of historians revolves around points of comparison designed to show the ways in which one narrative is better than, or an improvement upon, other narratives. The pragmatic object of the exercise is not so much the production of truth but the writing of the best story that evidence and argument warrants.

The work of Gallie, Olafson, Lemon and Carr represents what might loosely be called the *phenomenological turn* in the philosophical debate about history and narrative.[27] Whatever their differences of philosophical taste and inclination, all four shared an existentialist standpoint in which everyday perceptions and experiences of historical reality is a crucial informant of the theorization of narrative. By contrast, the fourth section of the reader focuses on contributors to the so-called *linguistic turn* in the philosophy of history.[28] The focus of this trend in the discussion is on the consequences which arise from the use of particular linguistic forms in the construction of narrative.

Narrative history and the linguistic turn

Louis O. Mink (#13) is often seen as the pivotal figure in the developing philosophical discussion on history and narrative. In a series of important essays published in the 1960s and 1970s[29] Mink broke the ground that was to be more firmly and radically occupied by the likes of Hayden White and F. R. Ankersmit. In the first place, Mink was an early proponent of the view that narrative was central to the historical enterprise. In 1962 he argued:

> The significant conclusions of historical arguments are embedded or incorporated in the narrative structure of historical writing itself; they are not propositions for which history provides an array of evidence, but the specific way in which the evidence is discursively ordered.[30]

Mink insisted, too, that "narrative is a typical if not universal historiographical form." Moreover,

> it is a form in which the results of historical enquiry are *directly* reported. It is the narrative history *itself* which claims to be a contribution to

knowledge, not something else which the narrative history merely popu-
larizes or organizes. The claim of a narrative history is that its *structure*
is a contribution to knowledge, not just a literary artifice for the presentation of a series of factual descriptions.[31]

For Mink, narrative was a "mode of comprehension"[32] or, as he puts it in his
contribution to this book, a "cognitive instrument," a means of seeing and understanding things together, in a unity. "The cognitive function of narrative form,"
he argued "is not just to relate a succession of events but to body forth an ensemble
of interrelationships of many different kinds as a single whole." In historical
discourse this ensemble of interrelationships is said to *represent* a part of past actuality. But, says Mink, narrative is a "product of imaginative construction, which
cannot defend its claim to truth by any accepted procedure of argument or authen-
tification." Elsewhere, Mink puts the issue this way:

> Historical actuality has, we may presume, its own complex structure
> (or lack of it); narrative has another ... It could be no more than a
> lucky accident if the structure of the narrative ever successfully repre-
> sented the structure of historical actuality; but even worse, no one could
> possibly know whether it did, since to do so would require *comparing*
> the two and thus would require knowing the structure of historical actu-
> ality in itself independently of *any* representation of it. But this is
> impossible.[33]

Mink's dilemma about structure, shared by other narrativist philosophers[34], is,
arguably, one of his own making. The claim that narrative form itself *represents*
the reality of the structure of the past is not one made by narrative historians.
Indeed, it is doubtful that narrative history "represents" the past at all; rather
narratives *present* aspects of the past, albeit often summarily and partially. The
purpose of that presentation is not narrative mimicry of historical actuality but the
demonstration and *display* of the answer to questions of the what, why, how and
who of past events. Ironically, this alternative formulation of the cognitive function of narrative parallels is, it seems to me, Mink's own gloss on R.G. Collingwood's
concept of historical enquiry and narrative as a critical process of questions and
answers. According to Mink, paraphrasing Collingwood, "what results from the
historian's series of questions and answers is not a theoretical explanation but a
narrative. ... The narrative is not a story supported by evidence, but the statement
of the evidence itself, organized in narrative form so that it jointly constitutes the
unique answer to specific questions."[35]

That historians typically choose to write stories posing and answering the questions that interest them reflects the narrativity that they perceive in past actuality.
Aspects of this narrativity are reproduced in the historical story – a procedure
buttressed by the narrative ontology proposed by Carr, Olafson, Lemon and others.

"Stories are not lived but told" was one of Mink's most striking catchphrases.
Life, he argued:

has no beginnings, middles, or ends; there are meetings, but the start of an affair belongs to the story we tell ourselves later, and there are partings, but final partings only in the story. There are hopes, plans, battles and ideas, but only in retrospective stories are hopes unfulfilled, plans miscarried, battles decisive, and ideas seminal ... We do not dream or remember in narrative ... but tell stories which weave together the separate images of recollection ... So it seems truer to say [pace Barbara Hardy that narrative is "a primary act of mind transferred to art from life"] that narrative qualities are transferred from art to life.[36]

The argument that historical narration is primarily an act of telling, not of discovery, is a major theme of the writings of Hayden White.[37] In the first of his two essays printed in this volume (#14), he characterizes historical narratives as "verbal fictions, the contents of which are as much invented as found and the forms of which have more in common with their counterparts in literature than they have with those in sciences." The source of the invention of the verbal fiction which constitutes a historical narrative is, according to White, "emplotment" – the choice of plot structure by the historian. In order to endow past events with a meaning and order understood by both writer and reader the historian selects a story form or type – romance, tragedy, comedy, satire or epic. White's point is that this configuration of the past does not derive from events themselves but from a choice of pre-existing emplotment strategies imposed on the past by the historian. Like Mink, White sees historical narrative as a representational structure but also as "metaphorical statements which suggest a relation of similitude between such events and processes and the story types that we conventionally use to endow the events of our lives with culturally sanctioned meanings."

In his review and critique of White, Noel Carroll (#16) reiterates the argument of Carr and others that stories *are* lived as well as told. Carroll points out, too, that while narratives are invented by historians in the sense that they are made, that does not mean they are *made-up* in the fictional sense. Carroll also deploys the actionist argument that much of the unity and cohesiveness of narrative derives from the practical, deliberative activity of the human agents who are the subject of the story. In response to White's concept of pre-existing plot structures, Carroll argues that perhaps not all historical narratives fall into the identified categories. Further, "assessing the empirical accuracy of White's theory of generic emplotment would be very difficult – not because there would be so many narratives to consider, but because White's characterization of his generic models is so vague." Indeed, it is difficult to think of anything in human experience that could not be subsumed under categories of tragedy, satire, romance, comedy and epic. Maybe historians emplot the past in they way they do not because of the availability of literary forms but because life is like that.[38]

The other great figure in the linguistic variant of the narrativist philosophy of history is Dutch philosopher F. R. Ankersmit. The reading reproduced here (#15) is a self-summary of his book *Narrative Logic*, published in 1983.[39] Although highly informative, it is a dense and often opaque text. But much of what he says has a familiar ring to it. Ankersmit's treatment of the issue of the retrospectivity of the language of historical narratives is reminiscent of Arthur Danto's analysis of narrative sentences. Because historians deal with unintended consequences, argues Ankersmit, the language they use to interpret historical outcomes is their own, or at least not that of the historical agents themselves who, by definition, have no knowledge of the unintended outcomes of their action. A linguistic distance is created between historians and their subjects. Most important, in describing, analyzing and interpreting these unintended consequences from their own vantage point historians create their own meanings which are then incorporated into the narrative. "Historical narrative, like metaphor, is the birthplace of meaning," says Ankersmit. Further, bringing Mink to mind, Ankersmit states that "interpretations strive for the unity that is characteristic of things." This point can be linked with Ankersmit's version of the narrative-as-representation argument. Narratives, he says, contain not just numerous individual descriptive statements of the past but a "picture of the past."[40] This picture or iconic impression of the past is created by the selection of evidence and statements the historian makes in composing their narrative. Since the past is gone it is, of course, impossible to assess the accuracy of the picture (or unity) presented in the historian's narrative. Those who attempt to tie the composition of the picture to contemporary perceptions and identifications fail because "the language of the unintended consequences is the language of interpretation" and because there is a difference between "the historian's perspective and that of the historical agent."

Ankersmit's argument about retrospectivity has considerable force but underestimates the efforts of historians to overcome the potentially distorting effects of hindsight on the story they seek to tell. There are two points here. First, while it is true that the historian's point of view adds meaning to the description and interpretation of the past, this does not in itself make a narrative inaccurate or inadequate. Second, while narratives do constitute a unity and much effort is invested by historians in creating continuity, coherence and closure[41], the source of that unity is not necessarily structural or retrospective. As Mink himself argued: "surprises, contingencies, and fortuitous events are of the essence of stories; to follow a story is to follow a series of events across a series of contingencies to a conclusion . . . the unity of the story is provided by the sense of alternative possible outcomes."[42] Possibility, surely, is a function of human agency. The best narratives are precisely those that stick as closely as possible to the position and point of view of those who make the future.[43]

Narrative and structure

The fifth section of this book shifts the perspective away from the ongoing philosophical debate about narrative and history to a point of view located within historiography itself.

Among historians there always have been staunch supporters of narrative and purist proponents of some form of social scientific structuralist history. A third group has sought to negotiate its way through and between these extremes by advocating a "weak" variety of what sociologists call "structuration"[44] – a historiography in which accounts of action and agency are combined with analyses of the causal efficacy of structures, institutions and other kinds of "objective" contexts and conditions. Such an approach is typical not only of the readings presented in this section of the book but of many standard primers on historical methodology.[45]

François Furet's article (#17) was first published in 1975 and reflects the moment of the apparent "eclipse of narrative" noted above. Furet favors what he calls "problem-oriented history" rather than narrative but is nevertheless concerned about the problems of a drift away from narrative towards a supposedly more scientific history. Furet's version of structuration is a problem-oriented history in which "interpretation is basically the analysis of the objective and subjective mechanisms by which a probable pattern of collective behaviour – the very one revealed by data analysis – is embodied in individual behaviour in a given period." He concludes: "history will probably always oscillate between the art of narrative, conceptual understanding, and the rigor of proofs; but if its proofs are more solid and its concepts more explicit, knowledge will stand to gain and narrative will have nothing to lose."[46]

Lawrence Stone's famous article (#18), which we have already cited, reflects a different moment, when it seemed that structuralist history was losing its hegemony in historiography. Stone suggests various political and intellectual reasons why this had happened and concludes: "if I am right in my diagnosis, the movement to narrative by the 'new historians' marks the end of an era: the end of the attempt to produce a coherent scientific explanation of change in the past." Stone doesn't wholeheartedly embrace the new narrative trend, and is careful to distance himself from old-style traditional narrative historians (especially "antiquarian empiricists"), but he is evidently enthusiastic about the philosophic shift in focus from "circumstances" to "man," as he puts it. Eric Hobsbawm, in his response to Stone (#19), writes from a Marxist perspective, and resists the individualist, particularist drift of Stone's argument. But even he sees nothing inherently wrong with viewing the world through a microscope as well as a telescope. However, for Hobsbawm "the event, the individual, even the recapture of some mood or way of thinking of the past, are not ends in themselves, but the means of illuminating some wider question, which goes far beyond the particular story and its characters."

Peter Burke (#20) attempts to steer a middle course between individualism and structuralism, posing the problem of "making a narrative thick enough to deal not only with the sequence of events and the conscious actions of the actors in these events, but also with structures . . . whether these structures act as a brake on events or as an accelerator." Burke's solutions include "micronarrative" (detailed local narratives which reveal the operation of structures and institutions); "multivocality" (narration from different points of view); and the "backward" narration of events. Burke's discussion is very illuminating but it is difficult to resist the comment that much of what he prescribes, so-called traditional narrative historians have always done.

The theme of Edgar Kiser (#21) is the growth of narrativist approaches among historical sociologists – a group traditionally concerned with the writing of large-scale structuralist history in which human agency is only a secondary feature. As Kiser notes, the narration of particular events over time with a central role ascribed to human agency can pinpoint the actual causal mechanisms and micro-foundations of large-scale historical change. A second theme of Kiser's is the utility of combining traditional narration with rational choice theory – a mode of analysis derived from economics and political science.[47] More generally, Kiser's contribution illustrates that interest in narrative is not restricted to historians, philosophers and literary theorists. Indeed, in recent years there has been the development of a significant *narrative turn* in a range of human and social sciences.[48] The eclipse of narrative has, it seems, been transformed into a new dawn, and not only in history.

Narrative and the practice of history

The final section of the reader is devoted to detailed studies of historical narrative.[49] In his contribution (#22) the Canadian historian, Kenneth Dewar, distinguishes between "discourse" – the order of telling – and "story" – the postulated real order of the past as recorded in the evidence. He then goes on to show how particular beginnings in the writings of Canadian historian Donald Creighton "initiate particular ways of ordering a discourse." Dewar also examines Creighton's treatment of chronology and, noting the way temporality is manipulated by the narrator, concludes that "rather than ordering the discourse, chronology underlies it."

Another of Dewar's themes is the question of narrative unity, as raised by Mink, among others. Again, Dewar examines Creighton's writings in detail to arrive at the following conclusion:

> Conditions and circumstances, setting and character, and human actions, intentions and experiences may all be elements of a story rendered as narrative. Yet they are seen together in manifold relationships – spatial, temporal, explanatory, genetic, and so on – by means of a discursive form constructed by the teller.

Dewar's formulation, it seems to me, makes a valuable contribution to this particular discussion because it retains the notion of a narrative constituting a totality or a whole, whilst avoiding the problems arising from concepts of narrative "structure" and "representation."

Margaret Somers' (#23) topic is the history of the English working class as treated by social and labor historians of various political persuasions. Her substantive conclusion is that the history of "class-formation" in England would be better served by a narrative approach than by the predominant analytical or structuralist approaches. Her general argument is that despite appearances these latter types of history rest on an implicit "master-narrative" (or "Great Story," to use Berkhofer's terminology[50]) — one that is "denarrativized" i.e. "abstracted into a general model of the relationship between industrialization, proletarianization, the birth of class society, and the expected behavioural response of the working classes." The problem with denarrativized models is that they obscure the role of narrativity in constituting the social identity of the English working class. According to Somers "it is through narrativity that we come to know, understand, and make sense of the social world, and it is through narratives and narrativity that we constitute our social identities." Moreover, "narrativity is a condition of social being, social consciousness, social action, institutions and structures ... [and] the narrative dimension of identities presumes that action can be intelligible only if we recognise the one or many ontological and public narratives in which actors identify themselves."

Hayden White's essay on the historiography of the Holocaust (#24) is among the most controversial of his interventions in the debate on narrative and history. What has particularly provoked the ire of the critics is White's questioning of the role of facticity in assessing the validity of narratives of the Holocaust.[51] White's theme is the familiar one that the facts of the past are transformed into narrative by their emplotment in a generic story pattern. The facts may set limits to the type of narrative created by emplotment but they do not direct which particular story should be told. White illustrates his argument by reference to an account by Andreas Hillgruber of the fighting retreat of the German army on the Eastern Front in 1944–5. Hillgruber controversially cast his account as a tragic story in which the Germany army heroically defends the German people against the barbaric threat of the invading Red Army. White comments: "Hillgruber's suggestion for the emplotment of the history of the eastern front during the winter of 1944–5 indicates the ways in which a specific plot type (tragedy) can simultaneously determine the kinds of events to be featured in any story that can be told about them and provide a pattern for the assignment of the roles that can possibly be played by the agents and agencies inhabiting the scene."

As White's example shows, generic story patterns do figure in historical narratives, although often implicitly, and do have the kind of impact he ascribes to them. But how important are such emplotments? No doubt politically and ideologically Hillgruber's choice of the tragic story form is of the utmost importance. But as a historical narrative what matters about Hillgruber's story are the answers he provides to the question of why the Germans fought on in the way they did despite the enormous losses they suffered and despite staring defeat in the face. Hillgruber's answers might, as many argue, be wrong and his interpretations subject to political and ideological distortion. But in any event the validity of the contents of his narrative can be assessed by the application of conventional historians' criteria regarding accuracy, adequacy, facticity, evidentiality, plausibility and so on. The same general point applies to the historiography of the Holocaust. What interests historians (or at least *this* historian) about this Holocaust literature is the presentation and demonstration of evidence, arguments and interpretations which help us explain and understand how and why millions of Jews were killed by the Nazis and their allies.

In his essay White takes issue with those who favor literal (i.e. plain) not figural (i.e. metaphorical) representations of the Holocaust. Figural representations of the Holocaust abound, including historical ones. But arguably what is impressive about the mainstream historical discussion of the Holocaust is the extent to which historians really have succeeded in telling us how it actually was; by no means completely, definitively, or incontestably, but sufficiently to warrant the claim that even such an apparently inexplicable event as the Holocaust is not beyond historical imagination and reconstruction.[52]

Patrick Finney's article (#25) centers on the historical debate on the origins of World War II. Despite being written from an avowedly postmodernist perspective the article is partly a recapitulation of some very old relativist themes.[53] Historical narratives, we are told, reflect, variously, shifting present-day concerns, cultural concepts and ideological forces, personal and political prejudices. "The postmodern turn within history critically entails a loss of disciplinary innocence, a realization that historians have always been involved in fabricating subjective ideological constructs, interested representations rather than neutral constructs of the past . . . we have become aware that our engagement with the past is always mediated by subjective representations, that we can have no access to the past except through the sedimented layers of the previous textualisations."

More novel is Finney's exposure of the rhetorical devices that historians use to persuade readers of the force of their argument – including some of the rhetoric deployed in my own writings! Finney's call for "a more reflexive historiography" is welcome but perhaps underestimates the reflexive activity in which historians do engage, which is not always fully reflected in their texts. Most historians are very alive to their subjective contexts and dispositions. It could hardly be otherwise given the nature of their subject-matter. It would be a poor historian indeed who, dealing with the passions, prejudices, and perspectives of people in the past, was unaware of his or her own. Nor is there much pretence about the tactics of persuasion that historians deploy in their narratives. Yet for most part historians continue to insist that the stories they tell are "true." Elsewhere I have expressed the view that "narrative history is a way of life" for most historians, that narrative is lived by them as well as their subjects, and that it seems eminently sensible to most people to apply to the study of the past the practical procedures and presuppositions of action that work well enough for "Everyman" in the present.[54]

The final contribution by the environmental historian William Cronon (#26) is about as reflexive as it gets. Written under the impact of narrativist philosophy, the article explores competing narratives of the Great Plains of North America. Cronon has his own story to tell about this historiography, one which doesn't escape his reflexive attention:

> And what of my own story here? What kind of tale have I been telling about Great Plains history? My most visible narrative has of course been a story about storytellers who express their own times and political visions. Each told tales that embodies the values of a particular community. Each tried to be true to the "facts" as they then appeared.

Each looked back to earlier storytellers. Accommodating them when possible and trying to demonstrate their inadequacy when this was necessary to the success of the newer story. The result was a sequence of contesting stories. . . . But the meaning of my story about stories also reflects that other, more personal, narrative, the one about my struggle to accommodate the lessons of critical theory without giving in to relativism.

Cronon's characterization of the evolution of writings on the Great Plains typifies most, if not, all historiography. Grappling with facts and values, with other stories and times as well as one's own is part of the everyday experience of trying to construct narrative history. Cronon's explicit personal intellectual engagement with problems of theory and relativism is not so common. But, as this volume seeks to demonstrate, the further spread of such a philosophical ethos among historians would not go amiss. The practice of narrative history can only gain from theoretical reflection.

Conclusion

In conclusion, here are some points for further discussion.

First, comes the question of the definition of "narrative" and of "story." In this introduction the terms have been used interchangeably to mean simply an account of a connected sequence of human happenings. But as various contributors to this book show, more elaborate definitions are possible, including ones which seek to differentiate between story and narrative.

Second, is the issue of how widely applicable is the narrative debate to the discipline of history as a whole. While large tracts of historical writing fall into the category of narrative history, many other well-established types of history resist such categorization. If history is essentially a narrativist discipline what is the status of analytical, thematic, structuralist and other non-narrative historical writings? One response is to deny the status "historical" to any account that doesn't deal substantially with human-induced change over a period of time. This is often linked to the argument that it is not subject-matter (the past) that defines the discipline of history but the "historical" treatment of that subject-matter. Another response is that of the postmodernists who point out that much ostensibly non-narrative history is implicitly founded on a grand story or metanarrative, indispensable to the intelligibility of the knowledge it seeks to convey. Others argue that to deny the appellation "history" to non-narrative accounts of the past is not to demean the validity of those accounts or to underestimate their important contribution to understanding the past.

Third is the problem of narrative unity, which has surfaced at a number points in this introduction. Stories, good ones anyway, do cohere and convey integrity and completeness. Is that a function of narrative structure (Mink, White); the teleological structure of action (Olafson, Lemon); the narrative identity of past lives and events (Carr, Lemon); or of the discursive form of texts (Norman)? Or is narrative unity a function of the way narratives are read (which takes us back to Gallie's contribution)?

Fourth is the issue of what role hindsight and retrospectivity play in the construction of narratives. In his contribution Dewar shows that where the historian chooses to begin a story has a significant impact on the order of telling (or discourse) of the narrative. To what extent does the same point apply to the ending of a story – that is, does the way the end of the story is seen retrospectively direct the order of telling as well, including, perhaps, the crucial decision on where to begin?

Fifth are the issues raised by the structure and agency debate in the social sciences. Narrative history is allied to the individualist side of that debate and to those who emphasize the role of conscious action in the creation of social structures and institutions.[55] At the same time, most narrative historians are plainly not *methodological* individualists. Their stories deal as much with collective actors as with individual ones, contain as much description, analysis and portrayal of context as the reconstructions of the perceptions of individual persons.

Finally we come to the question of truth. Beyond the question of the validity of narrative form lies the question of assessing the accuracy, adequacy and appositeness of the contents of historians' stories. The postmodernists urge that the truth of historical narratives is not a matter of fact but of values. Others seek to re-direct attention back to the traditional philosophical discussion about "objectivity" in the study of history. The pragmatists, it seems, are content to leave the matter to historians themselves on the grounds that, theoretically impoverished though it may be, a discipline that has produced such a vast and impressive body of knowledge cannot be entirely misguided in its efforts to produce true accounts of the human past.

Notes

1   In this connection see also R. Aron, "Thucydides and the Historical Narrative" in his *Politics and History*, Transaction Books: New York, 1978.

2   For example: R. G. Collingwood, *The Idea of History*, rev. edn Oxford University Press, 1994. For a rare, perhaps unique, discussion of Collingwood's views on narrative see W.H. Dray, *History as Re-Enactment: R. G. Collingwood's Idea of History*, Clarendon Press: Oxford, 1995, pp. 311–15.

3   See W. H. Walsh, *An Introduction to the Philosophy of History*, London, 1951; P. Gardner, *The Nature of Historical Explanation*, Oxford University Press: Oxford, 1952; and W. H. Dray, *Philosophy of History*, Prentice-Hall, 1964. R.F. Atkinson's 1970s textbook, *Knowledge and Explanation in History*, Macmillan: London, 1978 does deal with the narrative issue but the treatment is secondary to more traditional philosophical concerns.

4   P. Ricoeur, *Time and Narrative*, vol.1, University of Chicago Press, 1985, pp. 95ff. On Ricoeur's contribution to the history and narrative debate see David Carr's review of vol. 1 of *Temps et Récit* in *History and Theory*, vol. 23, no. 3, 1984.

5   L. Stone, "History and the Social Sciences in the Twentieth Century" in his *The Past and the Present Revisited*, rev. edn, Routledge: London, 1987.

6   For an overview see G. G. Iggers, *Historiography in the Twentieth Century*, Wesleyan University Press, 1997, part II.

7   For example, P. Burke, *History and Social Theory*, Polity Press: London, 1992. (This book was first published in 1980).

8   A prominent contemporary defender of a social scientific-type approach is Christopher Lloyd. See, in particular his *The Structures of History*, Blackwell: Oxford, 1993. Also: A. Callinicos, *Making History: Agency, Structure and Change in Social Theory*, Polity Press: London, 1987 and *Theories and Narratives*, Polity Press: London, 1995. As the title indicates the latter text focuses on the history and narrative debate. The fact that Callinicos, a Marxist philosopher, chose to make such an intervention is indicative of the shifting terrain of the theoretical debate on the nature of history.

9   One sign of that shift has been the attention devoted to narrative and narrative-related issues in the textbook literature on historical theory and philosophy. See for example M. Stanford, *A Companion to the Study of History*, Blackwell: Oxford, 1994. However, by no means all philosophers have gone along with the narrative turn. For example: C. Behan McCullagh, *The Truth of History*, Routledge: London, 1998.

10   On the role of History and Theory in fostering the debate on narrative see R. T. Vann's highly-informative, "Turning Linguistic: History and Theory" and "History and Theory, 1960–1975" in F. Ankersmit and H. Kellner (eds), *A New Philosophy of History*, Reaktion Books: London, 1995.

11   An alternative survey to that of Dray is L.O. Mink, "Philosophical Analysis and Historical Understanding," *Review of Metaphysics*, June 1968. Reprinted in L. O. Mink, *Historical Understanding*, Cornell University Press: Ithaca, 1987.

12   M. White, *Foundations of Historical Knowledge*, Greenwood Press: Connecticut, 1965. See also White's contribution and the subsequent discussion in S. Hook (ed.), *Philosophy and History: A Symposium*, New York University Press, 1963.

13   A. C. Danto, *Narration and Knowledge*, Columbia University Press, 1985. This book contains the text of *Analytical Philosophy of History*, first published in 1965, together with other essays by Danto. See also his "The Decline and Fall of the Analytical Philosophy of History" in Ankersmit and Kellner, *A New Philosophy of History*.

14   Mink, *Historical Understanding*, p. 175.

15   W. B. Gallie, *Philosophy and Historical Understanding*, Chatto & Windus: London, 1964, p. 66.

16   M. Mandelbaum, *The Anatomy of Historical Knowledge*, The Johns Hopkins University Press: Baltimore, 1977, Chapter 2.

17   For reviews of the book see W. H. Dray's in *History and Theory* in 1981 and S. Bann, "Towards a Critical Historiography: Recent Work in the Philosophy of History," *Philosophy*, 56, 1981. Also: Stanford, *A Companion to the Study of History*, Chapter 4 for a textbook that makes extensive use of Olafson.

18   F. A. Olafson, "Narrative History and the Concept of Action," *History and Theory*, vol. 9, no. 3, 1970.

19   M. C. Lemon, *The Discipline of History and the History of Thought*, Routledge: London, 1995.

20   Ibid., pp. 81–3.

21   R. Martin, *The Past Within Us: An Empirical Approach to Philosophy of History*, Princeton University Press: Princeton, NJ, 1989. Martin is concerned in this text with problems of explanation and causation but his distinction and argument applies

to narrative as well. See also: C. Lorenz, "Historical Knowledge and Historical Reality: A Plea for 'Internal Realism'," *History and Theory*, vol. 33, no. 3, 1994 and M. Bevir, "Objectivity in History", *History and Theory*, vol. 33, no. 3, 1994.

22   D. Carr, *Time, Narrative and History*, Indiana University Press: Bloomington, 1986.

23   This aspect of Carr's work is given much more detailed treatment in *Time, Narrative and History*. See all his "Cogitamus Ergo Sumus: The Intentionality of the First-Person Plural," *The Monist*, vol. 69, no. 4, 1986.

24   See in particular Noël Carroll's review of Carr's book in *History and Theory*, vol. 27, no. 3, 1988. Also: P. A. Roth, "The Object of Understanding" in H. H. Kogler & K. R. Stueber, *Empathy and Agency*, Westview Press: Boulder, Col., 2000 and A.P. Fell, "Epistemological and Ontological Queries Concerning David Carr's *Time, Narrative and History*," *Philosophy of the Social Sciences*, vol. 22, no. 3, 1992.

25   A good philosophical guide to the evaluative principles and procedures deployed by historians is C. Behan McCullagh, *The Truth of History*. See also McCullagh's, *Justifying Historical Descriptions*, Cambridge University Press: Cambridge, 1984.

26   Martin, *The Past Within Us*, p. 31.

27   In this connection see L. Shiner, "A Phenomenological Approach to Historical Knowledge," *History and Theory*, vol. 8, no. 2, 1969.

28   See B. Fay, "The Linguistic Turn and Beyond in Contemporary Theory of History" in B. Fay, P. Pomper & R.T. Vann (eds), *History and Theory: Contemporary Reading*, Blackwell: Oxford, 1998.

29   The essays are collected in Mink, *Historical Understanding*.

30   Ibid., p. 12.

31   Ibid., p. 168.

32   "History and Fiction as Modes of Comprehension," essay reprinted in ibid., and in Fay *et. al. History and Theory*.

33   "The Theory of Practice: Hexter's Historiography" in B.C. Malament (ed.), *After the Reformation: Essays in Honor of J.H. Hexter*, Manchester University Press: Manchester, 1980, p. 19.

34   Cf. Hayden White: "I will consider the historical text as what it most manifestly is – that is, a verbal structure in the form of a narrative prose discourse that *purports to be a model or icon of past structures and processes in the interests of explaining what they were by representing them*" (emphasis added). *Metahistory*, The Johns Hopkins University Press: Baltimore, 1973, p. 2.

35   "Collingwood's Dialectic of History" in Mink, *Historical Understanding*, p. 283.

36   Fay *et. al.*, *History and Theory*, p. 135.

37   As well as *Metahistory*, there are White's collected articles in *Tropics of Discourse* (1978), *The Content of the Form* (1987) and *Figural Realism* (1999) – all published by The Johns Hopkins University Press: Baltimore.

38   The literature on White is extensive. Some of the best summaries may be found in the work of his British followers: A. Munslow, *Deconstructing History* (1997) and *The Routledge Companion to Historical Studies* (2000) and Keith Jenkins, *On "What is History?"* (1995) and *Why History?* (1999) – all published by Routledge: London. An important developer of many of White's themes is H. Kellner, *Language and Historical Representation: Getting the Story Crooked*, University of Wisconsin Press: Madison, Wisc. 1989. For an overview of the impact of White see R. T. Vann, "The Reception of Hayden White," *History and Theory*, vol. 37, no. 2, 1998. For another good critique see C. Lorenz, "Can Histories Be True? Narrativism, Positivism and the 'metaphorical turn'," *History and Theory*, vol. 37, no. 3, 1998.

39   *Narrative Logic: A Semantic Analysis of the Historian's Language*, Martinus Nijhoff: The Hague, 1983. Ankersmit's essays are collected in *History and Tropology*, University of California Press: Berkeley, 1994. For sympathetic summaries see the works of Jenkins, Kellner and Munslow cited in n. 38 above. For critiques see C. Behan McCullagh's review of *Narrative Logic* in *History and Theory*, vol. 23, 1984 and J. H. Zammito, "Ankersmit's Postmodernist Historiography: The Hyperbole of 'Opacity'," *History and Theory*, vol. 37, no. 3, 1998.

40   See F. R. Ankersmit, "Reply to Professor Zagorin," *History and Theory*, vol. 29, no. 3, 1990. Elsewhere Ankersmit uses a different terminology – "narrative substances," "narrative proposal" – to mean much the same thing.

41   This is one of the major themes of Kellner, *Language and Historical Representation*. But cf. J. L. Gorman's comment in his review of Kellner: "I wish to affirm my broad agreement with Kellner's position: I think that he is right when he says that historians use rhetorical strategies to overcome the fragmentation of the historical record and organize the result into a single vision. I think he is right to demand that we read the story 'crooked,' that is, understand that the straightness of any story is a rhetorical invention.... But it is one thing to hold that the 'straightness' of a story is rhetorical invention, and another to hold that 'straightness' of history itself is such an invention." (*History and Theory*, vol. 30, no. 3, 1991).

42   Mink, *Historical Understanding*, p. 133.

43   "Counter-factual" or alternative history is treated in N. Ferguson (ed.), *Virtual History*, Picador: London, 1997 and G. Hawthorn, *Plausible Worlds: Possibility and Understanding in History and the Social Sciences*, Cambridge University Press: Cambridge, 1991.

44   A concept developed by the British sociologist Antony Giddens – whose work has been the subject of extensive discussion in sociology and other disciplines. See A. Giddens, *Central Problems in Social Theory: Action, Structure and Contradiction in Social Analysis*, Macmillan: London, 1977.

45   For example, the various editions of J. Tosh, *The Pursuit of History*, Longman: London, 1984, 1991, 1999 and A. Marwick, *The Nature of History*, Macmillan: London, 1970, 1981, 1989. See also: R. J. Evans, *In Defence of History*, Granta Books: London, 1997; B. Bailyn, "The Challenge of Modern Historiography," *American Historical Review*, vol. 87, 1982; and M. Phillips, "The Revival of Narrative: Thoughts on a Current Historiographical Debate," *The University of Toronto Quarterly*, vol. 53, 1983–4. The latter two articles are American and Canadian equivalents of Stone's "The Revival of Narrative."

46   Furet's article is subjected to a detailed, critical analysis by W. H. Dray, "Narrative versus Analysis in History," *Philosophy of the Social Sciences*, vol. 15, 1985.

47   See also: B. Hindess, *Choice, Rationality and Social Theory*, Unwin Hyman: London, 1988.

48   See, *inter alia*, J. Bruner, "The Narrative Construction of Reality," *Critical Inquiry* 18, 1991; P. A. Roth, "How Narratives Explain," *Social Research*, vol. 56, no. 2, 1989; A. Sayer, "The 'New' Regional Geography and Problems of Narrative," *Environment and Planning D: Society and Space*, vol. 7, 1989; and C. Steyaert and R. Bouwen, "Telling Stories of Entrepreneurship – Towards a Narrative-Contextual Epistemology for Entrepreneurial Studies" in R. Donckels and A. Miettinen (eds), *Entrepreneurship and SME Research*, Ashgate: Aldershot, 1997. (I am grateful to Celia Weston for the latter reference).

49   Classic book-length studies of narrative from the metatheoretical point of view include

White, *Metahistory*; A. Rigney, *The Rhetoric of Historical Representation: Three Narratives of the French Revolution*, Cambridge University Press: Cambridge, 1990; and S. Bann, *The Clothing of Clio: A Study of the Representation of History in Nineteenth-Century Britain and France*, Cambridge University Press: Cambridge, 1984.

50 R. F. Berkhofer, *Beyond the Great Story: History as Text and Discourse*, Harvard University Press: Cambridge, Mass., 1995. In this important summary text Berkhofer explores several other examples of master-narratives in historiography.

51 White's essay was first published in S. Friedlander (ed.), *Probing the Limits of Representation: Nazism and the "Final Solution,"* Harvard University Press: Cambridge, Mass., 1992. The collection also includes a number of highly critical commentaries on White.

52 For a relevant survey of the Holocaust literature see M. Marrus, *The Holocaust in History*, Penguin: London, 1987.

53 For a recent counter-relativist counterblast see C. Behan McCullagh, "Bias in Historical Description, Interpretation and Explanation," *History and Theory*, vol. 39, no. 1, 2000.

54 See G. Roberts, "Narrative History as a Way of Life," *Journal of Contemporary History*, vol. 31, 1996. "Everyman" is, of course, a reference to Carl Becker's "Everyman His Own Historian," *American Historical Review*, vol. 37, no. 2, 1932. For a narrativist alternative to Finney's account of war origins narration see H. Suganami, "Narratives of War Origins and Endings," *Millennium*, vol. 26, no. 3, 1997. Finney's characterization of my work as systematically marginalizing "historiography" is a little unfair. The book in question is full of references to the relevant historiography, and not just in the Introduction. Of course, my account and use of this historiography is different from Finney's. My purpose was not to expose the political, ideological and cultural influences bearing down on the historiography, but (a) to construct a better narrative than my predecessor and (b) to contribute to the creation of a new post-coldwar narrative framework for discussion of the USSR and the origins of World War II. That new framework now exists – thus providing another narrative terrain for Finney and others to explore.

55 In this connection see C. Campbell, *The Myth of Social Action*, Cambridge University Press: Cambridge, 1996 and A. King, "The Accidental Derogation of the Lay Actor: A Critique of Gidden's Concept of Structure," *Philosophy of the Social Sciences*, vol. 30, no. 3, 2000.

PART ONE

Narrative and historical understanding

Chapter 1

W. H. Dray

ON THE NATURE AND ROLE OF NARRATIVE IN HISTORY

I

THE QUESTION OF THE EXTENT to which an examination of narration is central to the analysis of history as a form of inquiry or a type of knowledge has received a good deal of attention from philosophers of late. It has been held that history simply *is* narrative; or that it is *essentially* narrative; or that *one form* of history, at any rate, and perhaps the most important one, narrates. It has been held, too, that it is through narration that historians achieve whatever is specifically historical about historical understanding; or that historical explanations get their distinctive structure by reason of their occurring in the course of historical narratives. It has even been held that narratives can themselves be explanatory in a special way; or that narrative is per se a form of explanation, if not indeed *self*-explanatory. Claims such as these have added interest to recent attempts to clarify the "logic" of historical narrative – although, as Mink has remarked, there has been a certain amount of skepticism, too, as to whether narrative is the sort of thing which could very well be said to have a "logic" of its own.[1]

Whether they talked the language of "logic" and "structure" or not, those philosophers who have emphasized the centrality of narration in history have not failed to generate opposition to their claims. Thus, it has been argued against them that narratives, by their very nature, preclude satisfactory explanation of the events which occur in them, and that they necessarily oversimplify the past in characteristic ways.[2] It has also been held that attention to the narrative aspect of historical works diverts the philosopher's attention from those features of history which make it a form of inquiry or knowledge, rather than a form of art, or even of entertainment.[3] The narrative, it has been claimed, is just a way in which historians often "write up" what they have discovered in the course of historical inquiry proper.

In this essay I shall try to thread my way through some of the chief issues, arguments, and positions centering upon the question of the relation of historiography to narration. My own general position will be that the narrativists – among whom White, Gallie, and Danto have been especially prominent — have made fresh and illuminating contributions to the contemporary philosophical discussion of historiography. My quarrels with them will be chiefly on points of detail. I regret that in trying to make this clear, I shall sometimes seem to be going over ground which Mink, especially, has already traversed. I regret it the more because he has done it with an *élan* which I cannot hope to match, and with a thesis that I have no great inclination to attack.

II

Let me look first, although not at great length, at the question of the necessary connection, if any, between the very ideas of history and of narration. For, at times, a necessary connection does seem to be asserted by some of the narrativists. According to Gallie, for example, history is "a species of the genus Story;" and because of this, the idea of historical narrative is "logically prior" to almost all other questions of critical philosophy of history.[4] According to Danto, all history "presupposes" narrative, the story form providing the historian with an organizing scheme just as theory provides one for the scientist.[5] Morton White is more cautious, saying only that narrative is "the typical form of discourse employed by the historian."[6] But Glenn Morrow, commenting favorably on White's view, declares roundly that "history is narration;"[7] and A. R. Louch has placed himself similarly among the extreme narrativists with the claim that narrative techniques are "essential to the business of historical explanation," not just an "incidental, stylistic feature."[8] Even Maurice Mandelbaum, who has recently expressed some of the most serious misgivings about philosophical accounts of history as narrative, has been shown by a critic to have earlier implicitly equated historical description with historical narration.[9]

If we interpret the claims of the extreme narrativists as implying that no work which fails to have the overall organization of a narrative is a work of history, then their position is surely untenable. As Rolf Gruner has reminded readers of *History and Theory*, the "cross-sectional" or "portrait of an age" variety of historiography is a perfectly respectable one.[10] To use his own example, it would be strange to have to say that Huizinga's *The Waning of the Middle Ages* is not a work of history because it lacks an overall narrative form of organization. For it is clearly not a work of social science: it is not intended to exemplify or test any general theory. Narrativists, of course, often advance a somewhat more limited and seemingly more plausible thesis. They insist only that narrative histories are the principal, essential, or more important of historical works. Thus Gallie sometimes says only that the "key members" of that "family of researches" called history are narratives.[11] But on what grounds could it be said that the non-narrative works are merely "ancillary"? Gallie himself offers none.

I can think of only two likely reasons for asserting Gallie's conclusion, neither of them adequate. The first is the argument that non-narrative histories "presuppose" narrative ones. It might be claimed, for example, that the very notion of the Middle Ages is meaningless without some background conception of a transition from the ancient to the modern world — the kind of thing it would require a narrative to delineate. Just as a "still" might be said to have no meaning *as a still* without reference to a moving picture, so a cross-sectional slice of historical development might be said to require reference to the development from which it was abstracted. But a similar argument could surely be elaborated for the converse conclusion: that narrative history presupposes the cross-sectional sort. As Mandelbaum has pointed out in this connection, any attempt to stick to *pure* narrative history runs into methodological problems.[12] A narrative history that never pauses for a cross-sectional "breather" becomes progressively harder to follow; and the need to preface an historical narrative by a sketch of the context in which the action develops is also commonly acknowledged. I think that Mandelbaum is correct in representing the needs of continuing narrative and of adequate description and explanation as to some extent pulling in opposite ways in historical reconstruction. I doubt, therefore, that we shall find good reasons in this direction for regarding narrative histories as more fundamental than cross-sectional ones.

A second argument for the narrativist conclusion might be sought in some variation on the familiar claim that all historical works must ultimately be regarded as contributing to history-in-the-large. And history-in-the-large, or universal history, it might be argued, necessarily extends through time, so that a narrative treatment of it might seem to be required. Now I would agree that, in some important sense, every history is offered as a putative contribution to universal history, and comes under judgment as such. As Collingwood put it, the unity of the historical world, the existence of "one history," is a *presupposition* of historical inquiry[13] — something which might perhaps be compared to the presupposition of physical scientists that the laws of nature form a single system. But the sense in which this is true is not the one required by the narrativist argument. The sense in which all history might constitute one universal history is not the same as the sense in which it might yield one super-story, whether of the heady sort constructed by speculative philosophers like Hegel, or the more mundane but still linear kind traced by world historians like H. G. Wells. It is not a presupposition of every historical work that there exists a final narrative account of history-in-the-large to be discovered. What is required is only that every account, narrative or otherwise, be consistent with all the rest.

There are nevertheless two points which might be noted on behalf of the narrativists before leaving the untenable claim that all history, or even every important work of history, narrates. The first is that, although there may be works of history which lack the narrative form, we do not usually call these "histories." And when one looks at the examples typically cited by narrativists, it seems clear enough that it is histories they were primarily interested in. Morton White is quite explicit about this: what he has to say about the "logic of narration," he tells us, is to be taken as applying only to those works which offer the history of some continuing central subject, such as a nation or a society.[14] The second and related point is that, even if it is both possible and desirable to write non-narrative works of history, we have to recognize that both narrative histories and historical works which at least contain narrative elements do exist. They are facts of historiography; and facts, as well as necessities, sometimes require philosophical explication.

If the question is seriously raised whether it is at all important for historians to write histories, a narrativist could perhaps point out, for a start, that people commonly ask questions of historians which can only be answered naturally by a narrative — questions like "How did that come about?" or "What consequences followed from that?" Or he could involve himself — as Gallie almost does at some points — in such deeper philosophical issues as the importance for a human sense of identity of a consciousness of the past under narrative forms — especially, although not exclusively, the past which one regards as peculiarly one's own. But these are not the questions I propose to pursue further here. I shall proceed on the assumption that the construction of narratives is an admissible and prominent, although not universal, aspect of historiography. And I shall ask what historians can hope to achieve through it.

III

One recurring answer to the question what historical narration can achieve is "explanation." And this often seems to mean more than just that historical narrative may *contain* explanations. Narrative itself, according to Louch, affords a "distinct kind of explanation."[15] When ideally formulated, Gallie declares, a narrative is *self-explanatory*.[16] Danto, too, claims that historical narrative is itself "a form of explanation;"[17] and he apparently intends this in a strong sense which would imply that "non-explanatory narrative" is somehow an incoherent or contradictory notion. This becomes clear in the way he treats a well-known distinction, earlier drawn by W. H. Walsh (following Croce) between "plain" narrative or chronicle, which would tell us no more than what exactly happened in the past, and "significant" narrative, which would also explain to us why it did.[18] Danto attacks this distinction as expressing a complete misunderstanding of the nature of narrative in history. It may be helpful for our examination of narrativism as a whole if I try to show why I find this position of Danto's unconvincing.

Danto's central point is that by a narrative we mean much more than simply a list of disconnected facts set forth in chronological order. In some sense, those facts have to constitute a "story." And by implication, at least, Danto seems to agree with Mandelbaum, White, and others that this requires at least their being *about* something; the story must have what White called a "central subject."[19] The kinds of central subject which characteristically interest historians are often suggested by the titles of their books: they are such things as the developments and declines of social movements and institutions, reigns, wars, revolutions, climates of opinion, and the like. In some cases, the notion of a central subject may be as loose as "what happened to the English in the nineteenth century." But even this would impose a degree of unity, a kind of structure, upon what would otherwise be just a miscellaneous collection of facts, and it would yield a principle of relevance for their selection and rejection.

Now Danto may be right that, at any rate in the indicated and quite minimal sense, a narrative would have to have a degree of connectedness to be a narrative at all. I am not quite sure myself that it would always have to have this precise kind: it may well be that other sorts of connectedness would sometimes be sufficient to sustain a narrative even where nothing that could plausibly be called a continuous subject could be identified. But let us suppose that a central subject would invariably be needed. It seems clear that this would still not ensure that all narratives were "significant" in the sense which interests Walsh; it would still not require their showing *why* what happened in their central subject happened. The requirement of a central subject might provide a basis for distinguishing between narratives and mere chronological reports of just anything at all. But it would not exclude the possibility of distinguishing between explanatory and non-explanatory narratives.

A quite different argument for refusing a distinction between plain and significant narrative, and one which does concern itself with significance in the explanatory sense, has been advanced at least tentatively by Danto, who points out that historians have to *establish* or *argue for* the facts they narrate.[20] This, if nothing else, Danto maintains, will guarantee that what they eventually report about a central subject will be more than a disconnected series of facts about it. The argument here is reminiscent of a famous paradox, cryptically propounded by Collingwood in *The Idea of History*: the claim that when the historian truly knows *what* happened he necessarily knows already *why* it happened.[21] On one quite natural interpretation of Collingwood's paradox, what he is telling us is that the very process of reasoning through which the historian must go in order to establish historical facts requires him at the same time to understand why they occurred; and although Danto's conception of historical reasoning is different from Collingwood's, since it is basically Hempelian, or "scientistic," I think that he can be read as making an analogous claim. And I think that both of them are clearly wrong.

In Danto's case, the claim seems to rest at least partly on the role in historical thinking which he assigns to what he calls "conceptual evidence."[22] Historians may use their knowledge of human affairs to argue, not just from evidence which receives no mention as such in their final narrative accounts, but also from other details of the narrative itself. One of the ways of certifying the facts of a narrative *as* facts, in other words, is to represent them as having been necessitated by other constituent facts of the story being told. And this would represent them as *explicable* by reference to those other facts.

In so far as Danto's point is simply one about a type of verification open to historians, I have no objection to offer. But I fail to see the relevance of this point for the question whether narrative is, as such, as form of explanation. The possibility of a degree of internal verification does not show that a narrative could not be entirely non-explanatory, while still meeting the requirements of being a narrative at all. There seems to be nothing incoherent or logically impossible about the notion of setting forth a series of facts about a central subject, none of which explains any of the others — a notion which other narrativists, like White, have used to clarify the sense in which they think actual historical narratives, by contrast with their so-called "entailed chronicles," may sometimes be explanatory. Danto may be right to maintain that we can never establish the occurrence of a given event without establishing "connections between this event and other events in the past."[23] The point is that such other events need not be *in the narrative*.

A third objection offered by Danto is open to a combination of the sorts of objection which have been urged against the first two, although this time it is indeed a logical or structural feature of narrative, rather than a methodological point about the verification of its constituent facts, which is called to our attention. Historical narration — and indeed all narration, Danto points out — characteristically makes use of a distinctive type of descriptive statement.[24] An example, for an historian writing about the events leading up to the outbreak of war in 1914, might be: "And so, at Sarajevo, the first shot of the First World War was fired." Such a statement, although about an event at one time, refers forward, not just to something envisaged by the historical agents involved, but to the actual subsequent course of events. It is a judgment which could be regarded as typically historical, since it introduces a kind of retrospective intelligibility into the account of what happened. And it clearly does this by *connecting* facts or events at different times.

Danto's discussion of the role and implications of "narrative sentences," as he calls them, is intrinsically interesting and important — certainly one of the more fruitful and original theoretical ideas in recent philosophizing about history. It is hard to see, however, that it provides us, any more than do the preceding arguments, with a rationale for saying that narrative is itself a form of explanation. First, the use of such sentences is not necessary for the construction of narrative. Doubtless a narrative will be *more* intelligible or significant if it employs such devices; but one which abjures them, possibly attempting to represent the past entirely from the standpoint of the participants, is so far from being inconceivable that it in fact represents the ideal of all those conceptions of historiography which lay stress on its being a re-enactment of past experience. Second, the connections asserted by narrative sentences where they *are* employed need not be explanatory ones; they at any rate need not be explanatory in the sense of showing why the directly referenced (i.e. earlier) event happened. The point of a narrative sentence is not to show why something came about, but to show what its significance was. And third, although the significance of an event with respect to a later one *may* be located in the fact that the earlier explains the later, this is surely not necessarily the case. The shooting at Sarajevo can be judged as the *beginning* of the First World War without also being judged its *cause*. Danto's "narrative sentences" do show how assertions of connectedness may enter quite surreptitiously into historical accounts. But they hardly require us to conclude that narrative is itself a form of explanation.

Danto sometimes argues, quite independently of any role he assigns to narrative sentences, that there simply could not be a narrative which was "plain" in the sense of failing to indicate causes and consequences. Since he agrees that there is a difference between saying that Napoleon lost at Waterloo and saying why he did, the point does not seem to be the utterly implausible one that we couldn't narrate without *mentioning* causes and consequences. It seems to be rather that taking all the causal statements out of a narrative would not necessarily take all the implied causal significance out of it. A narrative, Danto maintains, is "a way of organizing things;"[25] and there is more to the narrative way of organizing than the reference of every detail to a central subject. A narrative of such a subject, it seems, claims implicitly to select what is important about it, and to order what it selects in such a way that the importance, if not stated, is at least shown. An account loses story status if it gets submerged in inconsequential details.

I think that Danto is on sound ground in insisting that the notion of recounting important facts, from the standpoint of some interest or other, is part of what is involved in the idea of narrative. But I cannot follow him in regarding consequential importance as indispensable. Danto puts his position very strongly. Every narrative, he declares, "spells out the consequence of some set of events."[26] And again: "If an earlier event is not significant [in this sense] with regard to a later event in a story, it does not belong in that story."[27] These claims appear to me to be mistaken. They are at any rate not entailed by the general admission that historical narratives must select what is important. For as Danto himself conceded, there is a variety of ideas of importance at work in historical thinking; indeed, Morton White has found no difficulty in distinguishing *seven* such, all different from Danto's notion of what is "consequential."[28] To take a single example: events may sometimes deserve a place in an historical narrative simply because of their intrinsic human interest. This is not to suggest that any actual historical narrative will get very far with this conception of importance alone; but then, actual historical narratives are, as Donagan has put it, "characteristically" explanatory.[29] Our question, however, is whether the very concept of narration or story-telling requires the kind of causal interconnection which would allow Danto to deny the intelligibility of Walsh's distinction. Once again, I fail to see that he has shown this.

A scattering of further arguments can be found in Danto's writings, but none of them calls for any lengthy consideration. We are reminded, for example, that some descriptions are "very nearly" explanations.[30] That is true, but not to the point. We are asked to note that historians would not normally establish a fact without "presupposing" a narrative, and that facts which are established will probably eventually enter into some narrative.[31] This may also be true, but it is similarly irrelevant. We are told that a narrative that failed to explain would "very likely" turn out to be little more than a mere list, and hence no narrative at all.[32] But this ignores the possibility of other modes of organization than the explanatory one. Danto even argues, against Walsh, that since an explanatory narrative must say what exactly happened, and since the complete description of what exactly happened will include the explanatory connections between facts – these also being facts – the distinction between plain and significant narrative must disappear.[33] But Walsh did not mean by "plain" narrative just *any* account that told what exactly happened; he meant one that did *only* this. And a plain narrative would surely not have to give a "complete description" in Danto's special sense of telling everything that was true about its subject, including, perhaps, all those connectional truths that it would require narrative sentences to express.

IV

For the reasons indicated, I think that Walsh is right to distinguish between plain and significant narrative. I think that the distinction between history and chronicle remains similarly viable: a useful device for the philosophical analysis of historiography. But whether these distinctions are recognized or not, it is usually agreed that historical narratives can be, and (if there is any choice) ought to be, explanatory. It is often thought, too, that narratives constitute the specifically historical way of explaining something. Ask an historian for an explanation, Danto observes, and he will "spontaneously offer us a narrative."[34] What the historian understands, writes Mink, is communicated in "the necessarily narrative style of one-thing-after-another."[35] Whether there is anything logically or structurally distinctive about such explanation is a matter about which there is less agreement. According to Robert Stover, for example, there is no "fundamental scheme of intelligibility peculiar to the narrative form itself."[36] Yet narrativists often speak as if they think there is. The questions I now want to raise are therefore what sorts of narratives are explanatory, and by virtue of what structure or logical form. This may also give us a basis for deciding whether there is anything distinctive about a narrative explanation.

Narrativist literature yields a number of accounts of what, in its skeletal structure at least, an explanatory narrative in history would be like. I should like to note and comment on several of these accounts beginning with one proposed by Morton White.[37] As indicated earlier, White distinguishes between an explanatory narrative and a mere chronicle on the principle that in the latter no causal assertions would occur. He therefore finds the explanatory efficacy of a narrative entirely in the causal connections it traces. A very simple case of explanatory narrative, according to White, would go somewhat as follows: The King of England died, which led the Queen to grieve, which led the Princess to worry, and so on. A corresponding chronicle, or plain narrative, would go: The King of England died, and then the Queen grieved, and then the Princess began to worry, and so on. More formally, White says, what makes an historical account explanatory is its reiterated claim that what was true of its central subject at one time was the cause of what was true of it at a later time. Perhaps the sense in which White's example concerns states of a central subject may be thought a trifle thin. But as an account of the family problems of the royal house of England it might be allowed barely to fall under this notion.

White's account of explanatory narrative sets up as the ideal for historical understanding the model of a *causal chain*. And it may well be felt that this is a pretty unrealistic requirement. White is aware of this. He concedes that a high degree of what he calls "causal integrability" will seldom be achieved by actual histories.[38] The degree of understanding they attain can nevertheless be measured only against this ideal: White can offer us no other. What is especially strange about this is the fact that White's own full account of what he called "the logic of historical narration" contains elements which virtually *guarantee* the non-achievement of this very ideal.[39] What I have in mind particularly is his avowed "pluralism" about the principles on which facts may justifiably find a place in an historical narrative – the various concepts of importance already referred to.

What makes a narrative a history of its subject at all, White says, is its claim to be composed, in the first instance, of "basic" facts about that subject, which have been selected on appropriate principles of interest and importance.[40] The basic facts of a history of the United States, he suggests (and his intention is purely illustrative), might consist of the Revolution, the Civil War, the First World War, the Depression, and the Second World War. It is around such salient facts as these that an eventual narrative history of the American nation will be composed. Logically quite separate from this *history-constituting* act of selection, however, is what might be called the *explanation-injecting* feature of narrative construction: the attempt to account causally for, and to indicate the consequential significance of, all those facts which have status as basic ones. This explanatory task involves the selection of still further facts, called by White "derivative" ones, on the ground that they are causes and consequences of those chosen as basic.[41]

But why should we expect the product of two operations such as these to be a narrative which is causally integrated – i.e. one in which, as in White's lugubrious history of the English royal house, every event mentioned (save the first and last) is both consequence of the preceding one and cause of the next? There is no reason at all to expect this, if the basic facts of a history are selectable, as for White they quite clearly are, on principles which are logically unrelated to the overall purpose of constructing a causal chain. The demands of causal integrability, and of what White (in an Herodotean moment) sums up as "memorability,"[42] would coincide only by some kind of miracle. And this is not just because, as White himself laments, "interesting facts, like interesting people, may have boring antecedents and boring offspring."[43] Doubtless there are causal chains to be discovered in history, and the analysis of their structure is a legitimate and somewhat neglected philosophical exercise. There may even be histories which take causal chains as their central subjects. But it is hard to see, if we can find any plausible alternative, why we should represent such chains as formulating a logical paradigm for historical explanation. Certainly there will be few explanatory narratives if we do.

An alternative account of what makes an historical narrative explanatory, although still basically a causal one, is in fact offered by Arthur Danto.[44] Danto's conception of the causal pattern itself is less restrictive than White's. The way *he* thinks of an explanatory sequence developing could be illustrated something like this: Because the commander noticed that the enemy line was wavering, he ordered the cavalry to advance; because the cavalry had to traverse an open space raked by cross-fire, it was unable to penetrate the enemy position; because enemy reinforcements arrived before it was possible to regroup, the chance of a quick decision was lost. Here again we have something which could be called a causal series; but it is not a causal chain in the sense explicated by White. For causes now enter the series, as it were, from the outside. To put it less figuratively, what is called a cause at each stage is itself left unexplained, although it explains the relevant change in the state of the central subject at that stage. Where White could be said to offer a causal chain model of explanatory narrative, Danto's might more appropriately be referred to as a model of *causal input*.

One interesting feature of Danto's analysis is his insistence that, strictly speaking, it is not a final event or state which the historian explains, but the process of change which it terminates. Thus, at the second stage of the series just noted, what is explained is the transmutation of the cavalry from a state of splendid potency to one of decimated inconsequence. What explains that change – the cause of it – is the intervening cross-fire. On the basis of this sort of analysis, Danto represents an historical cause as invariably a middle in a beginning-middle-end structure – a narrative, in other words.[45] He therefore argues, in the end, not only that all historical narratives are explanatory, but also that all causal explanations in history are narrational. The causal question itself is seen as narrative-generating.

If I have difficulties with Danto's account of the structure of a causal input narrative, they are on comparatively minor points. The first, which has been noted by Michael Scriven, is the apparent dependence of this account on the assumption that historians, in seeking causal explanations, are invariably concerned with accounting for *changes*.[46] No doubt they generally are; but they sometimes ask also why things remained the same; and it is not clear how Danto's ingenious argument connecting causes with story-middles would fare in such cases. Another difficulty lies in what seems to me a very misleading way in which Danto repeatedly puts his doctrine in contrasting it with the standard Hempelian theory of explanation. The Hempelians, he says, in their anxiety to cast all explanation into the form of a deductive argument, incorrectly assigned the initial state of explained changes to the historian's *explanans*. But "the earlier event," Danto objects, "is part of what has to be accounted for;" "both the beginning *and* the end are part of the *explanandum*."[47] This could wrongly give the impression that Danto thought that a causal middle explained the *existence* of the initial state, which, of course, it doesn't. But the problem may be no more than one of unhappy formulation.

The real difficulty with Danto's account, from the standpoint of our present concerns (and one which it shares with White's), is that no sufficient argument is in fact offered for concluding that an historical narrative will be explanatory only if it offers causal explanation. White in effect *defines* explanatory narrative so that its explanatoriness is necessarily causal. Danto does not; but his chief efforts are directed towards showing that causal explanations generate narrative rather than the converse. Although more accommodating that White's, Danto's model must still appear highly prescriptive when taken to the details of historical work – Danto himself had to concede that actual narratives include a considerable amount of what he called "narratively inert information."[48] We must still ask, therefore, whether historical narrative cannot also be explanatory in other ways.

V

The third account I want to look at is that of W. B. Gallie, who claims unequivocally that further alternatives are possible.[49] Gallie's theory of explanatory narrative, however, is much more difficult to summarize, even with respect to its central idea, than the models of causal chain and causal input. For one thing, it brings together a number of ideas, not all of which seem to be equally relevant for a contrast with the causal models. Gallie also makes contrast difficult by refusing to speak directly of "narrative explanations," or even of "explanatory narratives." What we properly call explanations in historical work, he says, are normally given at those points where an historical narrative becomes difficult to follow.[50] Explanations are intrusive, correctional; an ideally intelligible narrative would have no need for them. However, since Gallie does hold that the narrative form is the vehicle of what he prefers to call the "historical understanding," and since the accounts he gives of explanations represent them, characteristically, as simply re-establishing a type of intelligibility which good historical narratives have as a matter of course, it does not seem to me that we would misrepresent him seriously if we said that what he offers is an account of what makes a narrative explanatory. Indeed, as already noted, he sometimes himself slips into speaking of narratives as *self*-explanatory; and he talks from time to time of the need for *explicit* explanations, as if the rest of a narrative could be regarded as *implicitly* explanatory.[51]

If Gallie is asked for a general account of what a self-explanatory narrative is like, his reply goes something like this: It consists of a sequence of incidents, actions, states of affairs, and the like, which catch our interest sufficiently to make us want to follow them to some vaguely indicated but unpredictable conclusion, and whose relationship to each other is such that we can accept them in succession, however surprising and unprecedented, as plausible and relevant developments of the theme or subject-matter under consideration. Just as Danto might expect an occasional link or two in an explanatory series to manifest a tighter relationship than that of causal input – perhaps the causal chain relationship – so Gallie would not rule out the possibility of occasional connections in a narrative being of a tighter sort than those suggested by the general description just given. But his claim is that the links of an explanatory narrative do not need to be any tighter than the latter to be intelligible. An explanatory narrative, as he sometimes puts it, can incorporate "contingencies." His account might thus be referred to as the *followable contingency* model.[52]

Mink, especially, would probably have qualms about my use of the word "model" here. And his own suspicion that, in the approach of an extreme narrativist like Gallie, we shall find nothing strictly analogous to the logical schemas of a White or a Danto, may well appear to be vindicated by the very summary which I have just sketched. Mink calls attention to the degree to which Gallie concerns himself with extra-logical criteria of historical narration and of story-telling generally; and rightly so. Nevertheless, I think that something like a competing theory of the so-called "logic of narration" can usefully be extracted from what Gallie has to say. As at least a preliminary move towards extracting it, I should like to make a few remarks about several structural ideas which I believe to be central to Gallie's view of explanatory narrative. These ideas all seem to me, in various ways, to bring him into logical conflict with the claims of the causal models.

The first is the idea of contingency itself. Mink has said that Gallie is "stoutly phenomenological" about this, attending more to the nature of the *experience* of being confronted with a surprising turn of affairs – and the experience, often enough, of a naive or ignorant reader at that – than with anything like an objective relationship.[53] And Gallie certainly encourages such interpretations, both in the detailed account he gives of the requirements for "followable narrative," and in such general complaints as that his predecessors have made of critical philosophy of history just "so many exercises in applied logic."[54] But at several crucial points he makes it clear that, in his view, an intelligible historical event or sequence can be contingent in the strong sense of being *unpredictable in principle*, unpredictable even "after the fact," because not deducible from antecedents and laws.[55] Unlike science, Gallie maintains, history lacks the "fundamental aim" of removing all the contingency from its subject-matter. This *could*, of course, be interpreted as meaning that historians are generally satisfied with half-doing the explanatory job. I take it rather to mean that, although in the ordinary case the question simply won't arise, historical understanding is such that a concomitant assertion of *real* contingency would not necessarily undermine it. And this, I think, is right.

Gallie nevertheless concedes that the contingent and unpredictable is unintelligible per se.[56] Thus although contingencies are "intellectually acceptable" as items in an historical narrative, they contribute nothing to its intelligibility unless further criteria are satisfied.[57] One such criterion that bulks large in Gallie's account is being a necessary condition of some other items of the history – and this is the second structural idea I want to note. According to Gallie, the necessary condition relationship provides "the main bond of logical continuity in any story;" it gives it its "logical texture" or "ground of intelligibility."[58] This doctrine is reminiscent of Gallie's earlier work on the alleged similarities between explanations in history and in the genetic sciences.[59] And now, as then, it is important to notice that there are in fact two different ways in which necessary condition relationships are seen as introducing intelligibility into a narrative.

There is, first, the way a story gains in intelligibility when we see it as having the kind of continuity — a third structural idea — which is fully discernible only when we consider earlier episodes from the standpoint of later ones.[60] A contingency which is unintelligible per se, Gallie says, can become intelligible through its having made a contribution to the development which a history is concerned to trace. To achieve this status, he avers, it need not have been a cause; it need only have been a condition but for which the development would not have continued. What Gallie envisages here, it should be noted, is the necessary condition itself achieving intelligibility, and thereby contributing to the intelligibility of the narrative as a whole. What he is talking about, in other words, is not "explanatoriness" but "significance." The chief gap in Gallie's account at this point, as in his earlier work, is his not saying clearly whether every condition which is retrospectively seen to have been a necessary one for what follows thereby achieves historical significance, or whether only some such conditions do. If only some (which is more likely), then we need to know how the significant ones are discriminated.

The other way in which the necessary condition relationship may be thought to underwrite historical understanding is, of course, the necessary condition's being taken as explaining what it was necessary for. We may well ask, again, whether *everything* that a condition was necessary for would be explained by it. But this time Gallie offers us at least the beginnings of an answer. The sorts of non-causal explanatory connections which he generally mentions — and these constitute the fourth and fifth of Gallie's structural ideas — are between what people in fact do and conditions which provide them with reasons and opportunities for acting in those ways, the historian presumably applying whatever limiting criteria are generally accepted in the language of practice for calling antecedent necessary conditions "reasons" or "opportunities." Even when we would claim no more about certain antecedent conditions than that they "evoked," "occasioned," or "made possible," what was done, Gallie maintains, they may nevertheless enable us to understand its being done.[61] He goes on to commend various non-Hempelians for having formulated views of explanation in terms of agents' reasons or "the logic of the situation," which, he says, highlight concepts which are ideally suited to incorporation into an explanatory narrative.

Does Gallie recognize still a sixth structural idea — some notion of purposive order? This may perhaps seem to be suggested by such dicta as that historical understanding is a "teleologically guided form of attention,"[62] or that a story's conclusion, although usually unpredictable, nevertheless "guides our interest almost from the start," pulling us forward "almost against our will."[63] One might object that the actual conclusion could hardly do this if, while we are reading an historical account, we don't know what the conclusion will be; and Gallie (probably wrongly) seems to think we usually don't know this. But he often appears to be telling us, in any case, that a "presentiment" of a conclusion, or a sense of "possible" conclusions, would do just as well.[64] I am myself inclined to write off most of this – along with much else that Gallie has to say about the role of interest, directed feelings, and emotional involvement – as belonging to what Mink calls the "rhetoric" of history.[65] If anything structural is being hinted at by such language, the five ideas already elicited, especially the idea of retrospective continuity, seem already to have made Gallie's legitimate point. Few stories which historians would bother to tell would fail to emphasize the relevance of earlier conditions which were necessary for what eventuated. In that sense, but surely not in any stronger one, a "teleological order" could generally be expected.

It might be added that Gallie is occasionally tempted to develop the notion of explanation by necessary condition (of whatever further-specifiable kind) into chain-like analogues of the causal models. Thus he tells us at one point that a series in which each incident was seen to be a necessary condition of the one following would clearly be a self-explanatory one.[66] If such a series were indeed his ideal of explanatory narrative, then although its individual sequences would be logically different from those of the causal chain, the whole construction might well encounter the same difficulties about integrability that White's model did. The causal input model would provide a more likely analogue for the ideal he might be expected to recognize: indeed, for all Danto knows, any number of his inputs may themselves be contingent. But even this, as a *general* requirement, would hardly square with the flexibility that Gallie often displays about what can be incorporated into an intelligible narrative. His minimal demand seems to accept the possibility, at least periodically, of *sheer* contingencies. We can follow a narrative through and across contingencies, he insists, provided they do not preclude further relevant developments.[67] The element of contingency in history, he adds, can be expected to match that experienced in life.

Notes

1   "History and Fiction as Modes of Comprehension," *New Literary History*, 1, 1969–70, pp. 541–58.
2   See, for example, M. Mandelbaum, "A Note on History as Narrative," *History and Theory*, 6, 1967, pp. 416–17.
3   Ibid., p. 414.
4   *Philosophy and the Historical Understanding*, New York: Schocken Books, 1964, p. 66.
5   *Analytical Philosophy of History*, Cambridge: The University Press, 1965, pp. 137, 142.
6   *Foundations of Historical Understanding*, New York: Harper & Row, 1965, p. 4.
7   "Comments on White's 'Logic of Historical Narration'" in S. Hook, ed., *Philosophy and History*, New York: New York University Press, 1963, p. 286.
8   "History as Narrative," *History and Theory*, 8, 1969, p. 54.
9   See R. Gruner, "Mandelbaum on Historical Narrative," *History and Theory*, 8, 1969, p. 287, n. 9.
10 Ibid., p. 284.
11 *Philosophy and the Historical Understanding*, p. 71.
12 "A Note on History as Narrative," p. 417.

13   *The Idea of History*, Oxford: The Clarendon Press, 1946, p. 246. But see also Gallie, *Philosophy and the Historical Understanding*, pp. 56–9.
14   *Foundations of Historical Knowledge*, p. 221.
15   "History as Narrative," p. 58.
16   *Philosophy and the Historical Understanding*, p. 108.
17   *Analytical Philosophy of History*, pp. 141, 251.
18   *An Introduction to Philosophy of History*, 3rd edn, London: Hutchinson, 1967, pp. 18, 32–4, 61. See also his " 'Plain' and 'Significant' Narrative in History," *The Journal of Philosophy*, 55, 1958, pp. 479–84. Danto discusses both statements, *Analytical Philosophy of History*, pp. 116–42.
19   *Analytical Philosophy of History*, pp. 235–6.
20   Ibid., pp. 140–1.
21   *The Idea of History*, p. 214.
22   *Analytical Philosophy of History*, pp. 122, 125.
23   Ibid., p. 140.
24   Ibid., chap. 8.
25   Ibid., p. 140.
26   Ibid., p. 138.
27   Ibid., p. 134.
28   Ibid., pp. 238ff.
29   Review of *Analytical Philosophy of History*, *History and Theory*, 6, 1967, p. 432.
30   *Analytical Philosophy of History*, p. 130.
31   Ibid., pp. 140, 142.
32   Ibid., p. 130.
33   Ibid., pp. 140–1.
34   Ibid., p. 201. See also p. 11.
35   "The Autonomy of Historical Understanding" in W. H. Dray, ed., *Philosophical Analysis and History*, New York: Harper & Row, 1966, p. 188.
36   *The Nature of Historical Thinking*, Chapel Hill: University of North Carolina Press, 1967, p. 70.
37   *Foundations of Historical Knowledge*, pp. 221ff. For a clear contrast between White's and Danto's models, and some further comments, see R. G. Ely, "Mandelbaum on Historical Narrative," *History and Theory*, 8, 1969, pp. 276–9.
38   *Foundations of Historical Knowledge*, pp. 224, 239.
39   Ibid., p. 219, n. 1. For his pluralism see pp. 257ff.
40   Ibid., p. 231.
41   Ibid., pp. 232–7.
42   Ibid., pp. 256, 266. I owe the point to D. R. Newman's "Significance in History," thesis submitted for the M.A. degree at the University of Toronto in 1968.
43   Ibid., p. 239.
44   *Analytical Philosophy of History*, chap. 11.
45   Ibid., pp. 235–7.
46   Review of *Analytical Philosophy of History*, *The Journal of Philosophy*, 63, 1966, p. 504.
47   *Analytical Philosophy of History*, pp. 234, 235.
48   Ibid., p. 251.
49   *Philosophy and the Historical Understanding*, chaps. 2–5.
50   Ibid., pp. 22, 89, 105, 110.
51   Ibid., pp. 22, 23.

52 Ibid., pp. 29–30, 32, 96ff.
53 "Philosophical Analysis and Historical Understanding," *Reviewing of Metaphysics*, 21, 1968, p. 684.
54 *Philosophy and the Historical Understanding*, p. 19.
55 Ibid., pp. 88, 91–2.
56 Ibid., p. 41.
57 Ibid., p. 31.
58 Ibid., p. 27.
59 "Explanations in History and the Genetic Sciences," in P. Gardiner, ed., *Theories of History*, Glencoe, Ill.: The Free Press, 1959, esp. pp. 387–8.
60 *Philosophy and the Historical Understanding*, pp. 33, 40–1, 43, 106.
61 Ibid., pp. 22, 26.
62 Ibid., pp. 38, 64.
63 Ibid., pp. 22, 28.
64 Ibid., pp. 25, 42, 67.
65 "Philosophical Analysis and Historical Understanding," p. 686.
66 *Philosophy and the Historical Understanding*, p. 109.
67 Ibid., pp. 29, 67.

Chapter 2

W. B. Gallie

NARRATIVE AND HISTORICAL UNDERSTANDING

Introduction

THE STARTING POINT OF THIS STUDY is the claim of Dilthey, Weber, Collingwood, and others that historical study aims at a kind of understanding quite different from that which is characteristic of the natural sciences. I sympathize with this claim, but I find most previous expositions of it distressingly weak and unpersuasive. I have two main objections to these accounts. In the first place, with hardly an exception, they persistently confuse delineations and analyses of historical understanding with the problem of its vindication, the problem of how historical theses should be tested, and of how the subjective bias of particular writers should be overcome. It is with the first of these problems alone that this study is concerned; and by considering it in isolation from the problem of vindication we can the more easily see how scrappy and ineffective previous work upon it has been. But more particularly, I find it astonishing that no critical philosopher of history has as yet offered us a clear account of what it is to follow or to construct a historical narrative. And yet, I am convinced, such an account is essential to any successful answers to more complicated questions regarding either the nature or the vindication of historical thinking. The effects of this omission are, I maintain, as great as those that we might expect if in philosophies of science we were to find no discussion of measurement or of controlled observation.

In urging that the question of historical narrative is prior to all other questions with which critical philosophers of history have struggled, I am not suggesting that this idea is itself simple or easy to grasp. On the contrary, its complexity is of a kind that is likely to irritate and repel minds nursed and exercised on relatively safe, long-cultivated philosophical topics. To approach it is rather like looking for one's bearings in a fairly familiar country, but from a new viewpoint from which many well-known features re-appear, only in new relations, as if in the wrong order, certainly not according to the book. This difficulty is a result of that bias in our philosophical tradition, from Plato to the present day, in favor of theoretical knowledge, i.e. knowledge admitting of universal statements and of being set out in systematic form. Given the accepted terminologies and characteristic presumptions of that tradition, it is virtually impossible to describe convincingly the most basic and familiar things that historians and readers of history are always doing – but doing without bothering to analyze or to justify what they are doing. Because of this difficulty I shall approach the question of what a historical narrative is, and what it means to follow such a narrative, indirectly; and making use of a time-honoured scientific device, I shall replace my original questions, to begin with, by the logically much simpler and more general questions, "What is a story?" and "What does it mean to follow a story?"

I What is a story?

What is a story? And what does it mean to follow a story? At the common-sense level we might answer:

1. Every story describes a sequence of actions and experiences of a number of people, real or imaginary. These people are usually presented in some characteristic human situation, and are then shown either changing it or reacting to changes which affect that situation from outside. As these changes and the characters' reactions to them accumulate, they commonly reveal hitherto hidden aspects of the original situation and of the characters: they also give rise to a predicament, calling for urgent thought and action from one or more of the main characters. The predicament is usually sustained and developed in various ways that bring out its significance for the main characters. Whether or not the main characters respond successfully to the predicament, their response to it, and the effects of their response upon the other people concerned, bring the story to within sight of its conclusion.

2. Following a story is, at one level, a matter of understanding words, sentences, paragraphs, set out in order. But at a much more important level it means to understand the successive actions and thoughts and feelings of certain described characters with a peculiar directness, and to be pulled forward by this development almost against our will: we commonly appreciate, without needing to articulate to ourselves, many of the reasons and motives and interests upon which the story's development up towards its climax depends. It is only when things become complicated and difficult – when in fact it is no longer possible to *follow* them – that we require an explicit explanation of what the characters are doing and why. But the more skilful the story-teller, the rarer will be the intrusion of such explicit explanations. Ideally, a story should be self-explanatory, even when following the story as a whole requires us to correct (in the light of later developments) the natural and in a sense appropriate ways in which we first followed and accepted its earlier stages. An equally important facet of the experience is that we follow – or, we might better say, are pulled along by – the characters of the story, as if they were real individuals. It goes without saying that these characters must first be presented and described in general terms, so that we can know the kind of people that they are. Thus we both recognize them as types and are interested in them as individuals; but it is in the latter spirit that we follow their actions.

It might be objected that this idea of story is too vague to admit of useful general discussion, and that one could find exceptions to all my suggested generalizations – most obviously in those stories, from Tristram Shandy to shaggy dog stories, whose point depends on breaking the usual rules or patterns of story-telling. But these exceptions prove the existence of some rules which are commonly, if not strictly or universally, exemplified in stories. And it is these rules – or rather some philosophically illuminating facets of them – that I am going to discuss. The above provisional, and as far as possible philosophically non-committal, answers may therefore be usefully borne in mind as a rough sketch-map of the area that we shall be discussing, although in fact I shall work with only a few of the phrases which they contain, in particular "following," "interest," and "conclusion."

To begin with the last of these. What kind of conclusion does a story arrive at? My starting-point is the truism or near-truism that the conclusion of a story is essentially a different kind of conclusion from that which is synonymous with "statement proved" or "result deduced or predicted." The conclusion of any worth-while story is not something that can be deduced or predicted, nor even something that can be seen at a later stage to have been theoretically or ideally predictable on the basis of what had been revealed at some earlier stage. A story always contains some surprises: as a rule it makes use of coincidences, unforeseeable recognitions and revelations, and other fortuitous, happy or unhappy, events. Admittedly, these events should never offend our sense of what is possible, or even of what is acceptable, in the circumstances supposed. Nevertheless the conclusion of a good story – a conclusion which we wait for eagerly – is not something that could have been or should have been foreseen.

The relevant implication of this point can be introduced by means of the following considerations. First, we can imagine almost any good story being presented, and probably ruined, as either a cautionary tale or as the illustration of a moral homily. Let us consider the latter more extreme case. In the homily the persons and early incidents of the story will be introduced somewhat in the manner of instantial or factual premises from which, in conjunction with appropriate wise saws and moral principles, the conclusion of the story – the exemplification of the appropriate moral lesson – can be deduced. But in this process the conclusion will of course have lost all its virtue *as the conclusion of a story*. Inevitably it will have become a foregone conclusion, possibly to be assimilated with moral profit, but certainly not to be awaited with eagerness and excitement. Clearly, therefore, the sense of "following" – following *to* a conclusion – that applies to stories is of an altogether different kind from the sense of following an argument so that we see that its conclusion *follows*.

Second, it is worth recalling that we sometimes compare people, especially children, in respect of their capacities to follow stories – with more or less quickness, comprehensiveness and insight. Now different levels of skill in this respect presumably depend in part upon having had the right kind of training and experience. But what sort of training and experience would here be relevant? Training in "guessing the end" of story after story? Surely not. We can, to be sure, imagine a game – "guessing the end of the story" – being used, no doubt for good educational reasons, in the teaching of young children. And presumably in becoming skilful at guessing the ends of different stories, a child would be displaying (and

cultivating) a certain generalizing power: he would be developing a kind of knowledge of human nature — as revealed in the kinds of story that he has come across
to date. But the crucial sign that a child is good at following stories is that he can
follow developments or volte-face of a kind that he and his fellows have never
met before and that other children (more restricted by their experience of more
nearly foreseeable conclusions in other stories) just cannot "get" or "take." Good
"end-guessers," in the game supposed, would not necessarily be "good followers,"
though they might well be, and vice versa. Just as in real life good prophets are
not necessarily good historians, and vice versa.

While stressing this point we can perfectly well admit that there are many developments in every story which indeed can be predicted: routine developments such
as are easily telescoped into a single phrase since they can almost be taken for
granted; or developments which, although materially important for the story's
result, are so obviously foreseeable that they cannot contribute in any way to its
dramatic value. We can go further, and admit that often, in reading or listening
to a story, we may have a powerful presentiment about its conclusion. But such
presentiments, in story-reading as in real life, are very seldom predictions in the
sense of conclusions drawn from explicit evidence. The truth is rather that the
whole style and set-up of the story often makes it clear from the outset that its
conclusion is bound to take either of two forms: either the lovers will or will not
be re-united; the lost child will or will not be rescued; and so on. Indeed it may
well be that the author intends that we shall feel from early on that some particular love-story cannot end in any normal happiness. We know this about Clym
Yeobright and Eustacia, or about Meaulnes and Yvonne de Galais, even before they
meet. Yet we follow their story with no less interest, eager to have our presentiment specified and articulated, rather than to have it verified.

We should notice here that perhaps of greater importance for stories than the
predictability relation between events is the converse relation which enables us to
see, not indeed that some earlier event necessitated a later one, but that a later
event required, as its necessary condition, some earlier one. More simply, almost
every incident in a story requires, as a necessary condition of its intelligibility, its
acceptability, some indication of the kind of event or context which occasioned or
evoked it, or, at the very least, made it possible. This relation, rather than the
predictability of certain events given the occurrence of others, is the main bond of
logical continuity in any story. In particular, this relation obtains and plays an
evidently crucial role, whenever clues laid down early in a story are made use of
later to establish guilt or identity or what-not, and indeed whenever an important
revelation, by speech or deed, is evoked by some earlier information or question
or command. In these cases what happens is intelligible, we see how and in a sense
see why it happened; but it is not necessarily, and indeed not usually, predictable.
And on this score the logical texture, the ground of the intelligibility, of stories
matches exactly with that of everyday life.

What I have claimed with regard to the conclusion of any story — that in the typical
case we come to it, wait for it, follow the story through and up to it as something
unpredictable yet in its own way intelligible and acceptable — seems to me to be

equally true of every main interim outcome, every main pivot or watershed, in any story. Whenever we accept an "And so it turned out that . . ." we are accepting something in much the same sense that we will accept the story's conclusion when we come to it. We could therefore, if we wished, speak of following a story through a sequence of interim conclusions to a final conclusion.

We can confirm this by recalling the kinds of criticism of a story that we make or hear made on other than purely aesthetic grounds. For instance, its conclusion is said to be far-fetched, ill-prepared, obviously manufactured, unconvincing, and so on. But criticisms such as these could for the most part be just as applicable to any defective link or pivotal scene, any main halt or watershed in the development of a story. From the point of view of intelligibility and acceptability, or in respect of the way that it makes the story followable, every main interim outcome in a story is thus on all fours with the actual conclusion.

Further confirmation of this point can be got by noticing a kind of ambiguity in the idea of the conclusion of a story. We apply the idea of a conclusion, in this connection, sometimes with aesthetic considerations uppermost in our minds, whereas at other times what we have chiefly in mind is the kind of understanding that we reach at the end of a story. From the former point of view the conclusion of a story is the point at which it ought to stop, to obtain its optimum artistic effect; from the latter point of view it is the point at which we accept that last "And so it turned out that . . ." with which our understanding of the action is completed. Usually, indeed, these two ways of regarding or assessing a story's conclusion are equivalent: the right place for a story to stop is the place at which fullest understanding of what happened in it has been achieved. But there is nothing necessary about this coincidence. There are cases in which our final understanding – certain final revelations perhaps – are of too violent or overwhelming or ecstatic a nature to provide an aesthetically suitable stopping-place. So we have the well-known devices of the subdued ending in minor key or the epilogue. In other cases the final moment of understanding is of a kind that defies verbal description: it has been left *beyond* the story's concluding sentence. It would be banal to describe the eventual happiness of Tom Jones and his Sophia; while the last loneliness of condemned or dying men is, by both logical and psychological necessity, indescribable. These considerations help us to appreciate that, from a logical point of view, the final point at which we accept an "And so it turned out that . . ." is of the same general character as all the previous points at which we accept or have followed what has happened so far in the story.

Yet there is something else to be said about the conclusion of a story which distinguishes it from all incidents, halts, outcomes, watersheds that we pass on the way to it. Without being predicted, and often without being even vaguely foreseen, the conclusion of a story nevertheless guides our interest almost from the start. Admittedly, when we are first introduced to the main characters of a story and begin, so to speak, to live in them and with them, we are willing to go with them, to follow them, in almost any direction. They interest us, and all we ask is "What will happen to them now?" and "What will happen to them next?" But very soon these questions are replaced by one that expresses a much more serious concern, namely: "How will things turn out for them *in the end?*." Our hopes and wishes have become involved in their imaginary fortunes. We must hear whether it went well or ill for them in the end – in whatever sense of end applies to their story. Thus the conclusion of a story is the main focus of our interest even before we know what the conclusion is going to be. And it is chiefly in terms of the conclusion – eagerly awaited as we read forward and accepted at the story's end – that we feel and appreciate the unity of a story. Its other episodes and incidents will of course have contributed to that unity; indeed they will have prepared for and contributed to the acceptability of the conclusion. But there is a sense, to be examined in detail later, in which the influence of the conclusion is here predominant.

Putting together the main points in our discussion so far, we thus reach the idea of following a story towards its conclusion through a sequence of incidents and outcomes which are, from the standpoint of reader and audience, acceptable yet unpredictable. Now in any worthwhile story this unpredictability is not something entirely subjective to the audience – a function of their slow-wittedness or the result of artful tricks of concealment played by the narrator. It would be a poor story whose surprising dénouement depended simply upon the author's holding back certain crucial facts until the very last moment. In all good stories the factor of contingency matches that which we feel to be part and parcel of daily life. For example the author brings two very strong personalities face to face: how they will react to one another is anyone's guess. Yet we find ourselves accepting the author's account, however much it may at first surprise us, and, if he knows his business, we shall find it progressively more acceptable as the story advances, no matter how many further unpredictable twists and turns its development may involve. Or again some outlandish disaster – or windfall – strikes a character in a story. Our feeling is that anything might happen – he might go off in any direction. Yet here again, not only do we follow in the direction which the story-teller indicates, no matter how surprising it may be, but we find, as we look back from the story's later stages or its conclusion, that this direction was all the time entirely in character.

These are the familiar unquestionable facts of the experiences of following a story. We follow a story through or across contingencies – accidents, coincidences, unpredictable events of all kinds; yet the story's general direction and continuous advance towards its final conclusion somehow succeed in rendering these contingencies acceptable.

II Story and history

Following a story, we have seen, is a teleologically guided form of attention. We are pulled along by our sympathies towards a promised yet always open conclusion, across any number of contingent, surprising events, but always on the assumption that these do not divert us hopelessly from the vaguely promised end. Can this analysis of story help us to articulate what is peculiar to historical understanding? I believe that it can. But evidently this claim presupposes an answer to two prior questions. First, is an element of story or narrative essential to all history? And second, assuming that our answer to the first question is Yes, then what is the place and function of narrative vis-à-vis other features or aspects of works of history, such as the discussions, analyses, and explanations that they contain? The first of these questions is our immediate concern for the present section; the second will occupy us in sections III and IV below. But before embarking on either question it is essential to remove one all too familiar cause of misunderstanding.

We must bear in mind that an immense variety of literary productions and contributions — books, articles, discussion notes, etc. in which are expressed thoughts of the most varied forms, styles, and intentions — are today bracketed under the rubric History. So true is this that any sane essay in the methodology of history would probably have to begin from an examination of the principles of historical bibliography. But for our broad purposes, I think it fair to take it for granted that a great deal of historical literature is ancillary to or parasitic upon history of a more central and substantial kind. As examples of ancillary history I have in mind not only the production of lists, accounts, diary jottings, and the like as evidence for or against some accepted conclusion as to some historical matter of fact, but the kind of book or article which sets itself the modest purpose of filling in the background to certain major and already deeply studied events, and again the ever-increasing amount of discussion between leading historians as to the proper or most profitable line of approach to and interpretation of different topics and periods. It seems to me quite clear and certain that historical contributions and discussions of these kinds *are* ancillary to the kind of history that interests us all most (historians themselves included): namely histories which treat of some major achievement — or failure — of men living and working together, in societies or nations or any other lastingly organized groups. Examples are the unification — or disintegration — of an empire; the rise or fall of a party; some crucial invention — or what held back its discovery for decades or perhaps centuries; the achievement of some great legal or moral reform; the dissemination of some religious or philosophical idea; the origin, flowering and decline of a great artistic style. Conning over the most famous works of history, one can easily find titles to match these general headings.

But can such central and admittedly most important works of history be considered as primarily narratives? Do we not rather find that in them all manner of elements and aspects of story have been excised or flattened out; so that in place of dramatic and heroic national or religious myth we are being offered a highly complicated yet rationally explained and acceptable unfolding of this or that society or institution or idea or creed? This is obviously true of the kind of history that is intended to debunk earlier traditional accounts. But is it not largely true of all serious histories? Are they not so many fights against the parochialism and the crude personification which seem to be endemic in our everyday thinking about our past and present affairs? The causes which serious historians attribute are in the main massive and impersonal, but for that reason perhaps more easily calculable, than the personal motives and intentions by which we commonly explain human actions: they may be terrifying, they may often act with a fearful justice, but seldom with that dramatic rightness and clear poetic justice which is characteristic of stories. History offends against both romance and simplicity: typically its accounts of important events are more complicated and yet more natural than our traditional stories or our all-too-human expectations would have led us to believe.

All this may be granted, and still it can be maintained that narrative is the form which expresses what is basic to and characteristic of historical understanding.

Granted that every genuine work of history is also a work of reason, of judgment, of hypothesis, of explanation; nevertheless every genuine work of history displays two features which strongly support the claim that history is a species or special application of the genus Story. To appreciate, and in a proper sense to use a book or a chapter of history means to read it *through*; to follow it through; to follow it in the light of its promised or adumbrated conclusion through a succession of contingencies, and not simply to be interested in what resulted, in what came out and counted in the end. Broadly speaking the sciences, e.g. sociology and economics, are particularly interested in results in this sense, and rightly so since it is results that prove their laws and hypotheses right or wrong. The systematic sciences do not claim to give us a followable account of what actually happened in any natural or social process; rather they offer us idealizations or simplified models of what must have happened at certain phases of the process if certain experimental results are to be intelligible. But history, like all stories and all imaginative literature, is as much a journey as an arrival, as much an approach as a result. Second, every genuine work of history is read in this way because its subject-matter is felt to be worth following — through contingencies, accidents, set-backs, and all the multifarious details of its development. And what does this mean if not that its subject-matter is of compelling human interest, that we must hear more and more fully and accurately what certain people really did and failed to do, even if the story of their achievements and failures has to be told in mainly abstract terms that are sadly remote from the lost feelings and gestures and acts of the actual participants?

But against these defenses of our claim that history is essentially story, a second objection can be pressed. Can it seriously be maintained that all works of history — of history of the kind that interests us all — display the kind of unity that is characteristic of story? Do we in all cases follow them as wholes, as complex unities of human action and reaction developing, through no matter how many complications and delays, to some kind of culmination, to some long awaited, to some promised or adumbrated end? Is it not obvious that most histories do not center and emanate from particular individuals and groups of individuals, but rather run through successive groups and generations of individuals, dropping them with complete indifference once they have served their part in a development about whose total character and eventual significance they may have remained ignorant or indifferent? More simply, are not the subjects of most history books too large to allow them to be treated as stories? Either they cover too long a period — histories of England, say, or of the Papacy or of human technology; or else they deal with so many different peoples or other groups — as in histories of wars and alliances, for instance; or else they deal with such abstract features of some relatively short-term period, that appreciation of individual effort and aim is almost impossible, e.g. histories of Allied plans and policies regarding coal or merchant shipping in World War II.

If taken in one way, this objection is easily met. Many serious and important historical works are not real unities. We could say of them, as Ranke said harshly of his own first book: all this is still histories, it is not yet history. And the obvious inference would be that such books, despite the important materials and the valuable individual judgments and descriptions that they contain, must be considered failures: failures, that is, from the point of view of presenting as a followable unity the great theme which they sought to bring to life in a single work.

But this way of meeting the above objection misses what is really important in it: namely, its challenge to us to vindicate the claim that every successful work of history (of the kind that interests us all) must be followable, as a unity, in the way that a story is. For this purpose two considerations from the side of story are, I think, particularly pertinent. First, many of the world's greatest and most moving stories are, so to speak, transpersonal in exactly the way that the objection mentions. Think of the Orestes cycle, for example, with its theme of recurrent inter-family guilt and revenge, or the story that runs from Abraham through Isaac and Jacob to Joseph. Such themes require not simply a group of dramatically opposed characters, but a succession, perhaps generation after generation, of characters who are related at every stage by the gradual working out of a great unifying idea. But second, we may recall from our discussion in Section I that the conclusion of any story can be regarded either from the aesthetic standpoint or from the standpoint of understanding the story's development and that our judgments about the conclusion of a given story may well differ according to which of these two standpoints we are adopting. Thus the event which we would all count as the conclusion of the story, inasmuch as it serves as the focus and goal of our interest, may not in fact occupy the last chapter or paragraph of the story: there may be an epilogue, or the final act may be left entirely untold. We can now go further than this and add that, when we reach what we would naturally take to be a story's conclusion from the point of view of understanding its development, we may quite possibly find the story-teller intervening to tell us that this seeming conclusion is merely an interim halt, a re-starting place for further developments within a larger narrative whole. This is what happens in effect in those multi-sequelled popular novels that theoretically might go on for ever. But something rather like it is found in a form of serious literature, lying halfway between story and history, namely the saga. A saga is not simply a succession of stories, most of them believed to be true, and linked together by the fact that the heroes of the successive stories were ancestors of the original audience, and that the stories are usually set out in chronological order. There is also usually an overlap of certain dominant interests from one part to the next. There is always unfinished business — if only the business of keeping the peace in the next generation — waiting to be taken up in the next book of the saga.

Now it might be suggested that the kind of unity that we find in successful works of history shows a partial analogy both with the kind of unity which is characteristic of saga, and with that which is illustrated in the tales of Orestes and of Jacob. All history is, like saga, basically a narrative of events in which human thought and action play a predominant part. But most historical themes tend to run beyond the interests, plans, lives, and works of any one group or generation of men. History, as we have remarked, seems to run past individuals, using them perhaps for a little while and dropping them without any compunction when once their usefulness is exhausted. On the other hand we know, to quote Marx, that men make history: history is made up of human actions within the world and of nothing else. Both these aspects of life are perfectly conveyed by the great sagas. But equally all history — at least all history of the kind that interests us all — expresses and is in a way delimited by the influence of what Ranke quaintly called "the ideas," meaning by this such dominant trends as can give shape to the aims and actions of successive generations, and which we can see mounting to some kind of culmination. It would not be difficult to obtain general agreement as to the "ideas" that find expression in, for example, *The Peloponnesian War*, *The Annals*, *The Decline and Fall of the Roman Empire*, *The Papacy*, and *The Waning of the Middle Ages*. The outstanding question is whether appreciation of such "ideas" can somehow be brought under, or brought into organic connection with, the act of following a narrative.

A trend or tendency is something that we see gradually disclosed through a succession of events; it is something that belongs to the events which we are following and no others; it is, so to speak, a pattern-quality of those particular events. It would thus seem that our appreciation of any historical trend must depend upon, or be a resultant of, our following a particular narrative, a narrative of events which happen to be arranged in such a way that, roughly speaking, they move in some easily described relation to some fixed point of reference. To be sure our appreciation of any such trend is in its way a kind of intellectual feat: it requires us to stand back a little and reflect upon the progress of the narrative that we have been reading. But this is just as true of many of the subtler indications of motive or influence which a complex narrative may contain. Again, a trend may of course admit of explanation in terms of laws which hold universally of the kinds of ingredient elements which enter into it. But in itself, and simply as a recognized pattern-quality of a succession of events, a trend is neither a law nor a manifest instance of any law. It is something recognized in and through the development of this particular set of events. And when these events are of a kind that make up or can be expressed as a story, then it seems reasonable to regard the trend itself as an aspect or facet of the story in question, and not as an explanatory factor that has been dragged into the narrative, so to speak, from outside. On these grounds it could be maintained that what Ranke called "the ideas" can perfectly well be accommodated under the notion of narrative.

What, then, does the word "history" mean? I would claim that it stands for a wide family or syndrome of researches and writings, the key members of which always contain narratives of past human actions. These narratives are followable or intelligible in the same general way that all stories are. Of course, to be historical a narrative must rest upon evidence, i.e. it must deal with events that can be shown to have actually happened at roughly assignable dates and places. A historical narrative, furthermore, will usually succeed in making its subject-matter more intelligible to its readers (who are usually presumed to have some vague acquaintance with it) by showing its interconnections with other relevant historical evidences and results. These characteristics of history are commonplace enough, and agreement with regard to them does little to illuminate the kind of understanding which works of history communicate. Nevertheless, this preliminary review of the relationship between story and history was necessary before we could ask how the defining characteristics of story, as disclosed by our discussion in section I, can be applied to the special case of history. In turning to this question we shall be facing the main problems of the historical understanding.

III The historical understanding

If it is true that in the physical sciences there is always a theory, it is no less true that in historical research there is always a story. In the former case there is always a provisional theory which guides experimental researches, even though these will lead to its replacement; in the latter case there is always an initial story that acts as provisional guiding thread to the successive assessments, interpretations and criticisms which lead the historian to his final judgment as to what the story really was, or as to what actually happened.

This characteristic situation of the historian is to some extent matched by that of his readers; and the nearer to being ideally prepared and intelligent his readers are, the more perfect the matching becomes. Typically, the reader of a work of history will know the broad course of the events which it covers and something of their consequences for later history. No matter how remote from here and now the events described may be, he must at least know (or believe) that they led ultimately into one of those main streams of history whose waves are still beating the shores of today and tomorrow. This initial appreciation directs and sustains his interest as he reads, but it is compatible with his receiving any number of jolts to his previous beliefs or natural expectations as to what "ought to happen" at this or that point in the narrative. To read a genuine work of history intelligently is thus to receive a lesson in liberation from inborn prejudices and provincial brashness. But in the experience of reading, one's critical powers are not called out only against one's former self. An essential part of accepting a historian's analyses and judgments is that one shall be ready to question, to probe and to criticize them. How else can one come genuinely to accept them for what they are – as one man's serious contribution, on the evidence available to him, to the ideally acceptable account of the events in question?

There are apparent exceptions to this general position; for example, records and memoirs of explorations and adventures in parts of the world which were – anyhow to the book's first readers – hitherto entirely unknown. Imagine the state of mind of the first readers of certain chapters of Raleigh's or Dampier's or Bougainville's accounts of their voyages. What they read and followed must have had for them all the glorious improbability of a boy's adventure-book. The only obvious links with the familiar, commonly accepted facts were that the expedition left some known port in accordance with orders at such and such a date and returned to another so many years later. But, oddly enough, this kind of exception only serves to substantiate, to bring out the general validity, of our account of the characteristic situation of the historian and his readers. It is fatally easy, if one reads the Tahiti chapters of Bougainville's narrative, to slip from reading them historically into reading them as a sheer story: the scenes are so brilliant, the incidents so compelling, the passions involved so inevitable and yet so unheard of, the whole story bathed in a freshness such as we associate with dream or imagination, but which here is due to a kind of irresponsibility that attached to the circumstances – which were such as could obtain once only and never again. To read such pages as history is difficult, because this means reading them as a narrative that is accepted as broadly true on the grounds of the evidence supplied and of the apparent correctness of its explanations and their coherence with the rest of our relevant historical knowledge. Let the critical, doubting, questioning, assessing attitude of mind lapse – or rise – into the sheer joy of following an absorbing narrative, and the historical mind has passed into the land of story, and is heading hard towards the land of dreams.

IV Explanations in history

Historical understanding is the exercise of the capacity to follow a story, where the story is known to be based on evidence and is put forward as a sincere effort to get at *the* story so far as the evidence and the writer's general knowledge and intelligence allow. And to follow a historical narrative always requires the acceptance, from time to time, of explanations which have the effect of enabling one to follow further when one has got stuck, or to follow more perceptively and confidently when one's vision was becoming blurred or one's credulity taxed beyond patience.

This, I maintain, is the essential role of explanations in history: they are essentially aids to the basic capacity or attitude of following, and only in relation to this capacity can they be correctly assessed and construed.

Chapter 3

Maurice Mandelbaum

A NOTE ON HISTORY
AS NARRATIVE

AMONG PHILOSOPHERS OF HISTORY it has recently been claimed with increasing frequency that if we are to understand what historians actually do, we should examine what features are characteristic of *narratives*, and should consider the manner in which a narrative may be said to explain the events included within it. As examples of this view Gallie, Danto, and Morton White may be cited.[1] Earlier forms of a similar tendency are to be found in Dray's continuous series model of explanation, in W. H. Walsh's account of history as "significant narrative," and in certain aspects of the theories of Croce and of Collingwood.[2] To be sure, the positions of Gallie, of Danto, and of White differ from one another in various respects, and even more important differences exist between their views and those of Croce and of Collingwood. I shall not attempt to deal with these differences; what is here of concern to me is what I take to be a characteristic mark of recent theoretical writings concerning historiography.

In the present note I wish to challenge the belief that historical inquiry and historical writing are essentially matters of constructing stories, narratives, or connected chronicles – terms, which, in the present context, I shall take as designating a single concept or a cluster of inseparable concepts. My argument will not be based on the fact that there are instances of historical inquiry which fail to conform to the characterization of history as narrative; for example, that there are monographic studies which are not organized as narrative structures. I shall not rely on that argument since an opponent might claim that such studies are merely adjuncts to "history proper," rather than being instances of it. My contention will be more radical. I shall hold that even in those cases in which it *is* the aim of the historian to construct an historical account in which the precise sequence of occurrences does provide an essential framework for his account, he is not engaging in an activity which is best represented by the model of telling a story. Typically, the person who tells a story may be *inventing* what he tells us, or he may be *recounting* what he already knows, or he may be inventing what he does not know about matters which he is recounting; but he is not in any case engaged in an *inquiry* which aims to establish what did in fact occur. However, it is surely the historian's task to discover facts and relationships which are not already known to him, and which are not invented by him. We expect historians to engage in research, to weigh alternative possibilities, and to marshal evidence in favor of one rather than another of these possibilities. As a consequence, in judging the merits of historiographical works we use standards other than the standards of interest and intelligibility which are, according to recent discussions of historiography, the primary bases on which we evaluate stories.

I

Before proceeding, it will be useful to note a few reasons why it may initially seem plausible to view histories as narrative structures.

In the first place, when an historian is ready to write his essay, book, or monograph, there are a number of respects in which he may be compared to a storyteller. Having done his research, and already possessing a great deal of knowledge concerning the past, he knows in general what he is going to say, and he will construct his account in a manner that permits his readers to follow, in a way that will be clear and intelligible to them, those events whose natures and connections he is attempting to portray. Since such events fit into a chronological order, he, like a storyteller, will normally attempt to follow that order in his exposition, rather than jumping backwards and forwards in time. Thus, the results of his research – which may have been reached in almost any order – are recast into what can be looked upon as narrative form.[3] Furthermore, like a storyteller, an historian may recount these relationships in a manner which is consciously designed to appeal in a particular way to some particular group or groups of persons, and, like a storyteller, he may also wish to point up moral or prudential lessons. Yet none of these resemblances is more than superficial when compared to the differences between "telling a story" and all of those activities in which historians must become involved when they set out to discover that which must be discovered if they are to have any story to tell.

A second and more important reason why the activity of the historian has been identified with that of the storyteller lies in the fact that there is a tropistic, or teleological, factor in historical writing. The historian already knows the particular outcome of the events with which he is to deal, or, with current history, a probable outcome is conjectured by him. Given an actual or conjectured outcome, only those events which are considered by him to be relevant to that outcome will find a place in his work. Now, it is undoubtedly true – as Gallie in particular has emphasized – that when we analyze the concept of "a story" this same teleological factor is found to be present. Therefore, in one respect at least, there is a similarity between any historical account and the characteristics of narrative stories. However, this similarity is insufficient to support the further claim that the historian's task is to provide us with narratives.[4] This should be clear from the fact that *any* explanation of a particular occurrence or set of occurrences has a similar teleological aspect: given the facts which one wishes to explain, only those other facts which are considered to be relevant to it will be included in that explanation. Therefore, what must be established by those who wish to assimilate history to narrative is that the particular connections which historians trace are primarily successive in character, so that the events which enter into an historical account can be regarded as forming a linear chain of episodes. This view is explicitly advocated by Danto and by White. While I shall later try to suggest that it is basically mistaken, for my present purpose it has been sufficient to show that, whether true or not, it is not entailed by the tropistic, or teleological, factor in historiography: any explanation, once given, has a similar tropistic factor in which the *explicandum* controls the *explicans*.

Nor should it be supposed that this teleological factor justifies one in holding that the various relationships which an historian purportedly *finds* within his materials are actually regulated by the story which he wishes to tell. Nonetheless, those who have recently claimed that history is to be understood as narrative have been willing to cede considerable territory to this form of historical relativism. For example, in discussing the alleged distinction between chronicle and narrative, both White and Danto are ready to hold that among the connections which are attributed to the chronicled facts at least some are to be construed as functions of the historian's choice of the particular story that he wanted to tell. And in Gallie's less restrained assimilation of history to storytelling, this teleological factor may be said to have become dominant. It is not my intention to debate the merits and limitations of relativism; however, if it can be shown that historiography is not to be construed as narrative, the tropistic, teleological factor which is always present in it will be less likely to be interpreted as an argument in favor of relativism.

I turn now to a third and even more important reason why contemporary philosophers find it plausible to take storytelling as a model of the historiographical enterprise. This reason lies in a presently dominant view of the general nature of the causal connections which are to be found in history. Following Collingwood and Dray (and in line with current philosophic interests), it is widely assumed that what occurs in history is to be construed as if its occurrence were primarily, or even exclusively, due to intentional human actions. Thus, it has become usual to analyze the processes of historical change in terms of what – given a particular social situation – one or more individuals regard as goals to be pursued; then, given the ensuing state of affairs, it is once again asked what human agents might be expected to set themselves to do, etc., etc. Thus, history is interpreted as a linear sequence of intelligible human actions, and tracing the course of these lines of action is regarded as constituting a proper reconstruction of the past. And this, indeed, would suggest that the historian's task is like that of a storyteller, since paradigm cases of what constitute "stories" do place emphasis on the choices made by human agents, stressing the changes in fortune which follow upon these choices.

It is not the concern of this paper to argue whether the materials with which historians are concerned should be construed as being predominantly instances of the intentional actions of individual human agents. However, I venture to suggest that this assumption has been primarily responsible for the present tendency to view historiography as a form of narrative. Whether or not this suggestion is correct would, of course, have to be decided by historical inquiry. And it is relevant to the theme of my paper to remark that such an inquiry would itself not be likely to be an instance of narrative explanation.

Be that as it may, I think that one can readily show that even in what might be considered the most favorable sorts of instance, a sequential or narrative view of historiography does not merit our adherence. It is to this that I now turn.

II

It is of course true that history is temporal, and that historians are interested in the temporal aspect of human affairs. No writer can be taken to be a writer of history if he is indifferent to matters of place, date, and influence. However, the crucial question which I wish to raise is what relationships must exist if a temporally related series of events is to be taken as constituting the elements which, together, form a single history. The theories which regard historiography as narrative would have us regard the events which form a unitary strand of history as a linear, sequential series: a leads to b, b to c, c to d, and so on. The historian then has the task of finding the proper continuous series by means of which he can trace how element a, at the beginning of the story, was connected through a series of steps to element t, which constituted the terminus, or point, of the story being told. However, the assumption that an historical account can be construed in terms of this linear model is not one which can withstand scrutiny even in those cases in which the specific events whose connections are to be traced are presumably determined by the decisions and actions of individual men.

Consider, for example, a particular election campaign, say, any United States presidential campaign of recent times. In a case of this sort it would be a gross distortion of the subject-matter with which the historian is concerned if one were to view the events which constitute the campaign as a linear series (or as a criss-crossing set of linear series) in which each event is causally related to a particular antecedent and itself leads to a specific consequent. In order to see the degree of oversimplification which would be involved in assuming that a campaign can be charted as a series of sequential steps, one need merely note the extent to which the strategy of an election depends upon an initial analysis of such factors as the stable voting habits of some segments of the population, and a recognition of the manner in which long-standing interests, disaffections, and needs in various geographic, economic, or ethnic groups will be relevant to eventual success or to failure. Thus, to understand the various stratagems which each political party will employ, one must grasp their relationships to longer enduring factors which are not themselves links in the sequential chain of events which constitute the "story" of the campaign. In other words, an election, unlike a chess match, is not won or lost by a series of neatly arranged moves and counter-moves, made in sequential order; the past is not wiped clean each time one makes a new move or commences a new game. For this reason, a sequential narrative, or "campaign story," is not likely to give a reader much insight into why the elements in that story did actually occur, nor why they had the effects which they did.[5]

The same point can be made with respect to biographical writing, a field within which it might be supposed that the straightforward sequential, narrative method might be most satisfactory. It is not difficult to show that even here the notion of history as narrative fails to conform with practice. In the first place, in order to understand recurrent patterns in the behavior of this subject, and changes in these recurrent patterns, a biographer must frequently take into account not merely the situations by which his subject was confronted, but must appeal to factors of intelligence, temperament, and personality which often cannot be accounted for in terms of specific episodes which enter into his narrative. Thus, among the important elements to which biographers make reference in their attempts to bring us to an understanding of the lives of their subjects will be dispositional properties which are not themselves specific episodic events which form part of the sequential chain. In the second place (and even more obviously), every biographer must appeal to a knowledge of the society in which his subject lives if the nature of that person's activities are to be explained. Or – putting the matter in another way – if we are to understand the choices open to a specific person and the goals which he sought to attain, we must make reference to social situations in which those choices took place. Thus, to understand the story of a man's life we must understand a great deal about his society and his place in that society, and this essential background is not itself formulated in terms of narrative.

The foregoing strictures on the narrative, linear-series model of historiographical explanation should serve to suggest that the task of the historian is not one of tracing a series of links in a temporal chain; rather, it is his task to analyze a complex pattern of change into the factors which served to make it precisely what it was.[6] The relationship which I therefore take to be fundamental in historiography is (as I have elsewhere argued) a relationship of part to whole, not a relationship of antecedent to consequent.[7]

This contention may at first seem paradoxical. However, the apparent element of paradox may be quickly resolved by noting that when we speak of the relationship of parts to whole we are often (and perhaps usually) inclined to think of wholes which are already complete, and we thus regard their parts as a set of elements all of which exist simultaneously. For example, a watch is a complex whole, each of whose parts coexists as a component in that whole. On the other hand, it is surely not stretching our view of the part-whole relationship to view a man's life as a whole, and to regard his successive activities and accomplishments as the component elements which served to make that life what it was. In the latter case, the parts of a whole need not all be simultaneously present: they may succeed one another and still be viewed as its actual constitutive elements. To make this point clearer, consider once again the task of a biographer.

For the biographer, his subject's life may have a unity and pattern which he seeks to render intelligible. It constitutes a whole, although not an "all-at-once" whole. To discover such a pattern, which may not be at all obvious, is not a matter of tracing a series of events, each related in linear fashion to the next; rather, it is a matter of analyzing the character of his subject, relating his traits of character to his specific activities and decisions, and to his various accomplishments and failures. And even if the biographer constructs an account of his subject in order to show how various factors led to a particular conclusion – to, say, a great political victory or defeat – it is not the sequential story which will be in the forefront of his attention, but the question of why those events which make up the framework of that story should in each case have followed as they did. To understand the linkage between these elements in the narrative, we must in most cases appeal to factors which are not themselves events in the biography of the person whose life is the subject of our interest. We must, for example, view his actions against the background of the particular society in which he lived, and this — though it influenced his actions — is not a part of the story of the actions which comprised his life.

It is almost embarrassing to note such trivialities. I do not for a moment suppose that those who have recently stressed the narrative element in historiography have been unmindful of them. In fact, in one passage Danto makes a related point, and Walsh's discussion of colligation also involves a recognition of the importance of the whole-part relationship in historical understanding.[8] I do however wish to suggest that the current fashion of viewing history as narrative sets up a model for historiography which is far too simplistic. And, as I noted at the very outset, the accompanying emphasis on history as being essentially similar to storytelling leads to a neglect of the role of inquiry in the historian's enterprise. For both of these reasons, it would seem to me that the present tendency to view history as narrative is unfortunate, and stands in need of correction.

Notes

1   W. B. Gallie, *Philosophy and the Historical Understanding* (New York, 1964); Arthur C. Danto, *Analytical Philosophy of History* (Cambridge, 1965); Morton White, *Foundations of Historical Knowledge* (New York, 1965). Danto originally formulated some of the main points in his position in a series of articles beginning in 1953. The relevant chapters of Gallie's book were published in almost identical form in *History and Theory* III (1964), 149–202. For an earlier formulation of White's view, see his contribution to *Philosophy and History*, ed. Sidney Hook (New York, 1963), 3–31.

2   Cf. William Dray, *Laws and Explanation in History* (Oxford, 1957), Ch. III *et pass.*; W. H. Walsh, *An Introduction to Philosophy of History* (London, 1951), Ch. II; Benedetto Croce, *History, Its Theory and Practice* (New York, 1923); R. G. Collingwood, *The Idea of History* (Oxford, 1946).

3   However, it would be false to assume that all of the relationships which historians seek to establish among the events with which they deal are sequential in character. Neither the sequential nature of historical exposition nor the chronological framework into which all historical events fit entails the truth of that view. As we shall see, it is in fact false.

4   In "The Historian's Business," Richard Pares discussed the fact that the general public looks to historians for stories, not for answers to questions. In his discussion it is clear that Pares rejected the legitimacy of that expectation (cf. the title essay of *The Historian's Business* [Oxford, 1961], 1–10). I am indebted to Professor Marvin Levich for this and other helpful references, as well as for his comments on the general theme of this paper.

5   Put in another and more general way, it appears to me that those who look upon history as narrative mistakenly draw a sharp line between "causes" and "conditions," and mistakenly believe that the historian's primary concern is with what they look upon as causes, not conditions.

6   In a non-tendentious example, Patrick Gardiner illustrated one of his arguments by raising the question why Louis XIV died unpopular. In speaking of the

explanation which he would give, he said: "I regard it as the outcome of a particular complex of factors, a complex which included Louis's expansionist foreign
policy and his wars, his heavy taxation, his court policy with its disastrous effects
upon the role of the nobility, his religious persecution of the Huguenots and his
attacks upon Jansenism. What in fact is historically important is to bring to light
the nature of the connexion which existed between Louis XIV's policy and his
unpopularity, and this is principally a matter of analysing in detail the particular
case before me." And shortly thereafter Gardiner significantly says: "When an
historian gives us an explanation of Louis XIV's unpopularity in terms of his
policy, we want to know more about the form which Louis XIV's unpopularity
took, more about the relationship between his unpopularity and those features
of his policy that accounted for it, more about the relative weight and importance of those features in determining it." (*The Nature of Historical Explanation*
[Oxford, 1955], 89–90.) Gardiner's example has been extensively used in the
literature, notably by Dray and by Danto, and his interpretation of what would
constitute an explanation of Louis XIV's unpopularity has not (to my knowledge)
been challenged by those who have used it. However, they have failed to note
the extent to which it would seem to cast very serious doubts on taking narratives to be the models for historical explanation.

7   Cf. *The Problem of Historical Knowledge* (New York, 1938), Chs 7 and 8. (This is
to be reissued by Harper & Row).

8   Cf. Danto, *Analytical Philosophy of History*, 235; Walsh, *Introduction to Philosophy
of History*, Ch. III, §3.

Chapter 4

Richard G. Ely

MANDELBAUM ON HISTORICAL NARRATIVE

A discussion

A FAMILIAR METHOD OF DISCREDITING a procedural recommendation in any field of inquiry is to show that it is based on a supposition which is false. In his "A Note on History as Narrative,"* Professor Maurice Mandelbaum has mounted an assault of this kind against the claim that: "If we are to understand what historians actually do, we should examine what features are characteristic of narratives, and should consider the manner in which a narrative may be said to explain the events included within it" (p. 413). This hypothetical claim, which he attributes to White, Danto, and Gallie, he regards as based upon the following assumption: "Historical inquiry and historical writing are essentially [that is, need only be] matters of constructing stories, narratives, or connected chronicles" (terms which he takes as designating a single concept or a cluster of inseparable concepts). His note is mainly devoted to the task of demonstrating that this assumption is in fact defective in two separate, but equally important ways: on the one hand it sets up a model for historiography – the narrative model – which "is far too simplistic;" and on the other hand, by identifying history with storytelling, it induces a neglect of the role of inquiry in the historians' enterprise. Clearly, if the assumption is defective in either of these ways, let alone both, it must be rejected as false; and any procedural recommendation whose correctness is dependent upon the truth of such an assumption must thereby stand discredited.

I

I first wish to consider whether the procedural recommendation which Mandelbaum has attributed to White, Danto, and Gallie really is based on the assumption which he has attempted to falsify. I am prepared to accept, for reasons to which I shall refer later, that Mandelbaum has sufficiently established the falsity of the view that historical writing and historical inquiry are essentially matters of constructing stories, narratives, or connected chronicles. My inquiry here is concerned, more modestly, with the *relevance* of this demonstration to the task of determining the correctness of that procedural recommendation.

Superficially, it might seem that the claim which Mandelbaum attributes to White, Danto, and Gallie must be false, provided it is false that "historical inquiry and historical writing are essentially matters of constructing stories, narratives, or connected chronicles." However, a closer analysis indicates that Mandelbaum's account of these theorists' position is susceptible of two quite distinct interpretations:

1   If we are to understand what historians actually do, we *need* to examine what features are characteristic of narratives, and so forth; and
2   If we are to understand what historians actually do, it *suffices* to examine what features are characteristic of narratives, and so forth.

Closer inspection reveals that it is the first interpretation which is by far the most natural; but that it is only the second interpretation which presupposes the truth of the proposition: "Historical inquiry and historical writing are essentially [that is, need only be] matters of constructing stories, narratives, or connected chronicles." Even if one concedes, as I am prepared to do, that Mandelbaum has effectively demonstrated that this proposition is false, it becomes suddenly unclear whether any demonstration of its falsity is, in fact, relevant to the task of falsifying the *actual* positions of White, Danto, and Gallie. It is to that question that I now turn.

II

I shall argue that Mandelbaum in fact refutes White and Danto, who both hold that historical writing is essentially narrative; but not Gallie, who, maintaining that histories always contain features other than sequences of events, asserts that historical writing is necessarily, but never solely, a narrative construction.

Morton White has stated that all the conclusions which he reached in his attempt to answer the question: "What is history?" have grown out of "reflection on narratives."[1] On his view, the task of the historian (whom he describes as "the narrator") is "to give a connected account" of some "entity."[2] This connected account (or explanatory or connected chronicle) is a "logical conjunction of explanatory assertions."[3] White provides the following brief example of a connected account – a history – of the development of an "entity." The entity he nominates is the reigning house of England during a certain period of time: "The King of England died, so the Queen of England died of grief. And because he worried so much about the Queen's death, the Prince of England committed suicide; and therefore the Princess of England died later of loneliness. And so endeth our lugubrious history."[4] In this, the simplest case, a history of some central subject S consists in asserting: "Because A was true of S at time t_1, B was true of S at time t_2, and because B was true of S at time t_2, C was true of S at time t_3, and so on."[5]

White is evidently committed to the following propositions: first, that historical writing is essentially and necessarily narrative; second, that the events which form a unitary strand of history are to be conceived of as forming a linear, sequential series: A leads to B, B to C, C to D, and so on; and third that, in consequence, causal effectiveness within such unitary strands of history is solely the property of *antecedents*.

Mandelbaum directs against this view an argument designed to show that such a narrative model of historiography is "too simplistic." He suggests that the assumption that an historical account can be construed in terms of this linear model (A leads to B, B to C, C to D, and so on) is not one which can withstand scrutiny, even in the most favorable instances. To establish this claim he examines two types of historical account, each of which, he claims, falls into the "most favorable" category. One is the type of historical account which would normally be given of an election campaign; the other type is biographical writing. He selects these types of historical account for analysis because the subject-matter of such accounts normally consists of specific events "whose connections . . . are . . . determined by the decisions and actions of individual men," and it is in precisely such accounts as these that historians are most likely to feel the need to narrate.

Mandelbaum attempts to show that an historian of an election campaign, such as a campaign to elect a particular candidate to the US Presidency, could not but hold a distorted view of his subject-matter, the campaign itself, if he regarded its constituent events simply "as a linear series (or a criss-crossing set of linear series) in which each event is causally related to a particular antecedent and itself leads to a particular consequent." For, what a politician does and what he decides are as much determined by what is happening concurrently, by prevailing factors in the political situation, as by what happened previously. In order "to understand the various stratagems which each party will employ, the historian must grasp their relationships to longer enduring factors which are not themselves links in the sequential chain of events which constitute the 'story' of the campaign." But — and in this lies the weakness of a merely sequential narrative — such a narrative makes no provision for the historian to refer directly to these "longer enduring factors." It must therefore inevitably provide a distorted and superficial view of the campaign itself.

In arguing against the adequacy of the linear model in the field of biographical writing Mandelbaum makes the additional point that "Among the important elements to which biographers make reference in their attempts to bring us to an understanding of the lives of their subjects will be dispositional properties which are not themselves specific episodic events which form part of a sequential chain."

His general point, however, and evidently his basic objection to the linear series model of historiography, is that those who adopt such a model "mistakenly draw a sharp line between 'causes' and 'conditions,' and mistakenly believe that the historian's primary concern is with what they look upon as causes, not conditions."[6]

If Mandelbaum's argument against the view that historical writing "is essentially a matter of constructing stories, narratives, or connected chronicles" is sound, White's position is untenable. The crucial question is of course: Is it sound? There are two points in the foregoing argument on which Mandelbaum could well be challenged: his view of what constitutes an historical narrative, and his position on causation in history.

It might be suggested that Mandelbaum's model of an historical narrative (A leads to B, B to C, etc.) is unnecessarily narrow, and that this is why he is able to make it seem unequal to the normal demands of a biographer, or of an historian writing the history of an election campaign. Narrative in the ordinary sense, so the objection might be developed, is never merely the tracing of a series (or a criss-crossing set of series) of sequential steps; in its normal form narrative incorporates reference to contemporaneous conditions, and often attributes to these conditions some causal significance. This is apparently a serious difficulty. It is not, I believe, an insuperable one.

In the first place, it is hard to see how such a critic could make his point that situational descriptions and analyses can be incorporated into historical narratives, without drawing a distinction – between situational descriptions and analyses on the one hand, and narratives on the other – which invalidates his point. That is, in order to make his point, he needs to use the term "narrative" in Mandelbaum's sense. A second, and more serious, reply to such a critic would consist in pointing out that while we do narrate actions, we do not narrate situations: we describe or analyze them. Even when historians incorporate situational reference into their narratives, they do not, normally, speak about narrating the situations therein referred to. And this suggests that a narrative which solely consisted of events which were narrated would not normally contain such situational references;[7] that is, it would in fact generally conform to Mandelbaum's definition of a narrative.

The other feature of Mandelbaum's argument which is open to criticism is Mandelbaum's not fully worked out view that a sharp line should not be drawn between "causes" and "conditions."[8] Implicit in the narrative, linear-series model of historical writing is a view of causality in history according to which the occurrence of an historical event is primarily or invariably due to an antecedent human action, or to a set of antecedent human actions. On this view, it would not usually be necessary for an historian who is seeking to discover the cause of an historical occurrence to refer beyond some antecedent set or series of human actions to (say) conditions contemporaneous with that occurrence. Given this view of causality, the only model of historical writing which would *not* provide a distorted view of the historian's subject-matter would be the narrative, linear-series model. However there are, in fact, good reasons for accepting Mandelbaum's view of causality. And this implies that the linear-series model of historiography, if relied upon exclusively, would only rarely be a satisfactory vehicle for the history of something.

An important, although not in itself decisive, consideration which lends support to Mandelbaum's claim that "conditions" as well as antecedent "causes" have causal significance is that this is a view which historians themselves feel the need to accept. It is historians who constantly stress that circumstances alter cases, that the question of what a person is able to do should he choose to do it, or unable to do even if he chooses to do it, cannot be settled without reference to what that person's situation "allows."

Nor, of course, is this view solely the preserve of historians; it is demonstrably the view of those whose activities they study: the history makers. The successful politician, for example, is successful because he manages to take advantage of some feature of his situation, or the situations of those with whom he has transactions.

Admittedly, such a politician is only able to take advantage of such situations if he does certain things, but, by the same token, doing those things will not bring him the success he seeks unless the situations in question really do possess certain determinate characteristics.

Probably, however, the most decisive argument against the view that "conditions" are not causally significant is what might be called the "experimental" argument. If "conditions" did not affect the consequences of human actions (or non-human actions for that matter), it would not be necessary for laboratory experiments to be conducted under "controlled" conditions. But, of course, it is necessary for such conditions to be controlled, as far as possible, for the simple reason that it can be shown that very often variations in conditions measurably affect experimental results.

Consequently, the view of causation in history which underlies Mandelbaum's rejection of White's narrative, linear-series model of historical writing is basically correct; as is also, for the reasons which have been detailed, Mandelbaum's view of what (for purposes of argument) constitutes an historical narrative. This, however, implies that White's view of the nature of historical writing is quite untenable.

A. C. Danto advances a position similar in many respects to that of White, but one which reveals the exercise of considerably more caution. Where White affirmed that his view of history was the product of his "reflection on narratives," Danto put forward the more careful thesis that "narrative sentences are so peculiarly related to our concept of history, that analysis of them must indicate what some of the main features of that concept are."[9]

Like White, Danto takes the view that a history is fundamentally a narrative, and that any genuine history is a history of some continuous subject. However, his view of the structure or skeleton of a narrative differs from that of White in one crucial respect. If Danto were to use the symbols White has employed, he would need to affirm that, in the simplest case, a history of some central subject S consists in asserting: Because H happened to S at t_2, S, which at t_1 was A, became, at t_3, B; because I happened to S at t_4, S, which at t_3 was B, became, at t_5, C, and so on.[10] In marked contrast to this, White holds a view of the structure of an historical narrative according to which A *led to* (or caused) B, and B *led to* (or caused) C.

When the accounts of Danto and White are juxtaposed in this way, one may readily discern the crucial difference between them. All we are entitled to say about the relationship between A, B, and C, on Danto's account, is merely that A was *followed by* B, and B was *followed by* C. In Danto's account, as contrasted with White's, the connection between A, B, and C is not a causal one.[11] They are connected, rather, as parts of a certain kinds of whole – namely the change: SA–SB–SC.[12] The whole point of the historian's narrative, on Danto's view, is to account causally for changes in some continuous subject. Narratives are used in history "to explain changes, and, most characteristically, large-scale changes taking place, sometimes, over periods of time vast in relation to single human lives. It is the job of history to reveal to us these changes, to organize the past into temporal wholes, and to explain these changes at the same time as they tell what happened – albeit with the aid of the sort of temporal perspective linguistically reflected in narrative sentences. The skeleton of a narrative has this form:

$$/./././\,\ldots\ldots\ldots/$$

[The vertical strokes represent the termini of successive changes in some continuous subject; the intervening dots represent whatever happened to the continuous subject to cause it successive changes]."[13]

Danto, then, is also committed to the view that historical writing is essentially and necessarily narrative; but, as we saw, his view of what constitutes an historical narrative differs in certain respects from the narrative model against which Mandelbaum directs his criticism: A led to B, B led to C, etc. On Danto's view, one would need to say that: Action H at t_2 led to S (which at t_1 was A) changing into B at t_3; Action I at t_4 led to S (which at t_3 was B) changing into C at t_5; and so on. But although Danto's model of historical narrative is more complex than the one which Mandelbaum actually describes, and although it entails a different view of the relations between A, B, and C, it does not differ in any important respect from the model which Mandelbaum criticizes so severely. It, also, presupposes that the events which form a unitary strand of history are to be envisaged as forming a linear sequential series: $/./././$ and so on; and it also presupposes the unsound view that causal efficacy in history is solely the property of *antecedents*. There is, further, no place in Danto's model for the specification of conditions, as distinct from causes.

In the last analysis, therefore, Danto's position is untenable. It is quite as vulnerable as is that of White to Mandelbaum's arguments.

In the preface to his *Philosophy and the Historical Understanding*, W. B. Gallie declares that: "What is new in my account of historical understanding is the emphasis that I have put on the idea of narrative."[14] But this remark should not be misunderstood: his claim with respect to the position of narrative in history is merely, as he himself puts it, that narrative is "essential" to all history.[15] He nowhere asserts the adequacy of a solely narrative history. In fact, he spends considerable time discussing the question of "the place and function of narrative vis-à-vis other features or aspects of works of history, e.g. the discussions, analyses, and explanations that they contain."[16]

Hence, to summarize the argument in this section: the refutation of the claim that history is essentially a narrative construction entails the untenability of those views concerning historical writing which have recently been advanced by White and Danto; but Gallie is not, unlike these two theorists, committed to the truth of this claim, so that its refutation has no bearing on the question of the correctness of his position.

III

I wish to conclude this paper by suggesting that although the claim that history is essentially narrative is false, it is the kind of false claim which is likely to be fruitful in discussions of the nature of the historian's enterprise. It is likely to be fruitful because it reflects — even if it only imperfectly expresses — a genuine insight into the practice of history.

It is possible that theorists like White and Danto, who have argued that history is essentially narrative, have recognized, but misunderstood and misapplied, an important characteristic of historical *thinking*.

When an historian describes a series of human actions which were intended to achieve, and did achieve, some goal, he will need to describe the actions constituting such a series with reference to the circumstances in which they were performed. In principle, the historian might describe and analyze the entrepreneur's situation at the very beginning of his account; and this would then leave him free, during the remainder of his account, solely to narrate. So that, under such special circumstances, it really is the case that an historian needs only to narrate. But in any historical study of an enterprise of some magnitude, the placement of such situational analyses and descriptions at the beginning would impose an almost impossible burden on the historian's memory, and on that of his readers. It would, moreover, make it extremely difficult for the historian's readers to envisage the entrepreneur, or the entrepreneurs, successively overcoming the practical problems created by a (probably) changing situation. It would not, of course, be hard in such a case for the historian and his readers merely to envisage the series of actions performed by some entrepreneur. What would be difficult and complicated would be the envisaging of such a series of actions as a succession of practical *solutions*. For this would require, further, a sustained recollection of the nature of the problems which such actions solved, something which would be especially tricky when the problems arising were created by changes in the situations facing the entrepreneur. Hence, it is a characteristic feature of the historical study of human projects and human achievements, that, as was noted in section II, historians link together their descriptions of purposeful human actions with their descriptions of the circumstances under which such actions were performed.

It is therefore unwise and unprofitable for an historian who is describing a series of purposeful actions to seek to create for himself opportunities solely to describe such a series of actions. But is neither unwise nor impossible for the historian *conceptually* to isolate such a series of actions from the often changing situations with which they were, individually, designed to deal. The conceptual isolation of a series of actions, even of a highly complex series of actions, is not, normally, very difficult. Furthermore, in the so-called "narrative histories," and most notably in the historical study of the self-aware and successful pursuit of tangible goals, the conceptual isolation of a series of purposeful human actions is a necessary ingredient in the sort of understanding of his subject-matter which the historian typically strives to obtain and communicate.

The truth of this claim is readily demonstrated by reference to the historical study of successful enterprise. The historian, in order to conceive of the actions of some entrepreneur as a successful means to a certain objective, must think of those actions as together constituting the solution to a certain kind of practical problem. That is, the historian must think of those actions as conceptually isolated (in the way that solution and problem are conceptually isolated) from the circumstances in relation to which they were performed. For circumstances alter cases; they affect the consequences of human actions. They must accordingly be specified in the statement of the entrepreneur's problem. The historian cannot possibly obtain, let alone convey, an understanding of why a particular successful enterprise was successful, unless he conceptually isolates – isolates from the circumstances in which they happen to be performed – a particular series of actions which, in those circumstances, actually ensured the attainment of the desired objective.

It is, perhaps, a recognition of this aspect of the historian's work – the historian's conceptual isolation of a series of intentional human actions from the situations with which they were designed to cope – which has induced theorists such as White and Danto to regard historical writing as essentially narrative. That is, such theorists may have recognized, correctly, that "narrative" historians (such as Macaulay and Trevelyan) have principally sought to narrate a complex series of actions which they have conceptually isolated from the various situations in relation to which such actions have needed to be understood. But where such theorists have been seriously mistaken is in assuming that what can be conceptually isolated can always be described and appropriately understood without reference to that from which it is isolated. Certainly one can describe the leg of a chair without making reference to the chair itself. But in the case of the historical study of successful enterprises the matter is more complex. It is admittedly true in such cases that, regarded as a series of physical motions, the set of actions which the narrative historian has conceptually isolated can be satisfactorily described without reference to the circumstances in which they were performed. But what is not true – and this may be the fundamental error of White and Danto – is that although such a series of actions can be conceptually isolated from the set of problems which they in fact solved, they cannot be narrated as *solutions* unless they are described in conjunction with the problems which they solved.

My suggestion is, therefore, that the deficiencies which Mandelbaum has noted in the views of White and Danto are basically the result of a failure on the part of these two theorists to distinguish clearly between the question of how historians *think*, and the question of how historians may, perforce, have to *communicate* what they think.

Notes

History and Theory 6 (1967), 413–19.
1   M. White, "The Logic of Historical Narration," in *Philosophy and History*, ed. Sidney Hook (New York, 1963), 3.
2   Ibid., 4.
3   Ibid., 6.
4   *Idem.*
5   Ibid., 6–7.
6   Mandelbaum, "Note," 416–17.
7   Such a narrative would contain no situation references, but this is not to say that it provides no clues regarding the situation in which the narrated actions were performed. The statement "Luther joined in the persecution of the Anabaptists," which could well appear in an historical narrative, indirectly conveys some information about Luther's situation – namely that the Anabaptists were being persecuted. But, drawing a distinction between what a statement *means* and what it *presupposes*, I would deny that: "The Anabaptists were persecuted" was part of the *meaning* of the statement "Luther joined in the persecution of the Anabaptists."

8   The view is not fully worked out in the "Note" under discussion. In *The Problem of Historical Knowledge* (New York, 1938), Mandelbaum has attempted a comprehensive analysis of historical causation, but I do not know whether he now accepts all the theses he there argued for. I refer in particular to his analysis of historical causation solely in terms of "existential dependence."

9   A. C. Danto, *Analytic Philosophy of History* (Cambridge, 1965), 143.

10   Ibid., Chap. XI, *passim*.

11   Ibid., 235.

12   *Idem*.

13   Ibid., 255.

14   W. B. Gallie, *Philosophy and the Historical Understanding* (New York, 1964), Preface.

15   Ibid., 65. His claim that narrative is "essential" to history (i.e. is a necessary ingredient in it) should be clearly distinguished from the claim that history is "essentially" (i.e. really only) narrative.

16   It is appropriate to note in passing a further unwarranted criticism. On p. 415 Mandelbaum refers, without elaboration but critically, to Gallie's claim that history is a species of the genus, story. Mandelbaum would, perhaps, argue that if historical writing is not essentially a matter of constructing stories, narratives, or connected chronicles, it necessarily follows that history cannot be a species of the genus, Story. But to this hypothetical argument Gallie could well reply that this conclusion would only follow if he were committed to a much stronger claim than that history was a species of the genus, Story; the claim, namely, that history was a species *only* of the genus, Story. Certainly, in *Philosophy and the Historical Understanding* Gallie spends very little time discussing history as a form of inquiry, but his omission is deliberate, and it is in no sense a recommendation to philosophers of history to refrain from analyzing such matters as the vindication of historical understanding, the testing of historical theses, and the avoidance of bias. Gallie's position is, rather, that questions concerning the nature of historical understanding tend to be of a different type from questions concerning the methods whereby such understanding can be obtained and authenticated; that questions of the former type have hitherto been poorly handled, at least partly through being run together with questions of the latter type; and that, therefore, questions of the former type, questions concerning the nature of historical understanding, can more profitably be considered in isolation from questions of the logical and methodological type (Gallie, ibid., 12).

PART TWO

Narrative and
human action

Chapter 5

Frederick A. Olafson

THE DIALECTIC OF ACTION

THE LAST CHAPTER DEALT WITH HISTORY as a distinctive kind of sequence of events; and although the role of historicity in making possible such a sequence was emphasized, almost no attention was given to history in its second main sense of historiography. History as record and as text must therefore form the subject-matter of this chapter; and an attempt will be made to build on the results achieved in the course of the preceding discussion of the historical process and to show their implications for the analysis of historiography. More specifically, attention will be concentrated on historical narrative as the form of historical writing which most directly reflects the features of the historical process that were distinguished in the last chapter. This characterization of historical narrative will have two principal aspects. First, since it is not my intention to claim that all historical writing must be narrative in character on pain of losing its status as historical, it will be necessary to clarify the position of narrative history vis-à-vis other forms of historical writing and historical inquiry, and to do so in a way that gives a clear sense to the notion of the centrality of narrative within history as a whole for which I will argue. The second part of the task of this chapter will be to propose a characterization of historical narrative itself and specifically of the mode of continuity it establishes among the temporally successive events it recounts. By contrast with the matters which were discussed in the last chapter, these topics relating to the status and nature of historical narrative have recently been the subject of active discussion; and it will therefore be useful to develop the theses which I am concerned to defend in much closer contact with opposing views that I have done hitherto. The interpretations of the nature of historical narrative which I will consider are for the most part theses about the logical structure of narrative. Although my own position is not conceived primarily in these terms, some of these views are deeply congenial to it while others, though often highly suggestive, appear to go in quite different directions. In both cases, my effort will be to show that what is missing is a satisfactory working conception of the wider context from which logical theses about historical narrative and explanation too often and too drastically abstract.

As the preceding chapter indicates, I believe that context to be the dialectic of action which constitutes the historical process; and in this chapter I plan to develop the implications of this conception for our understanding of historical narrative.

I

The variety of forms which historical writing can assume is very great; and there can, as already indicated, be no question of trying to reduce them all to the narrative form, no matter how broad a definition of the latter we may eventually adopt. For one thing, the form of historical writing is often of the kind which Droysen described as "untersuchende" rather than "erzählende Geschichte" and relates to the order of the historian's inquiry much more directly than it does to the order of the events in the past with which he is concerned. The presentation of evidence and the argumentation by which conclusions are drawn from this evidence are not usually cast in a narrative form. Ideally, one might argue, it should always be possible to effect a separation between the presentation and interpretation of evidence and whatever assertions about the past the historian is disposed to make on the basis of his scrutiny of that evidence. Even when this can be done, however, it would be a mistake to assume that the content of this assertion about the past must necessarily conform to the narrative mode. In a great many cases it might well do so or at any rate state some fact which would be readily incorporable into a narrative sequence as, for example, if the point to which the historical inquiry had been addressed were the date of a certain monarch's accession to power. But suppose that, instead, the concern of the historian were with the form of papal government in the Middle Ages and his conclusion were one that defined a certain relationship between ecclesiastical and secular authority. Such an assertion on the part of the historian would not in any obvious way recount a series of events. Instead, it would attribute a certain structure to the institutional life of the Middle Ages; and it would typically do so in a form of statement which would normally be described as being "analytical" rather than as "narrative" in character.

   This contrast of the narrative with the analytical mode is one which has achieved wide currency at the present time and its effect is to imply rather directly that the narrative mode in historiography is almost necessarily condemned to a certain shallowness and superficiality by comparison with the deeper insights that are accessible to the analytical mode. The implication here is that the narrative historian is most often one who goes on using the familiar but crude descriptive apparatus of our common-sense understanding of actions and events and that as a result he is sharply limited with respect to the dimensions of these events which his account can capture. The analytical historian, by contrast, concentrates not on the sequential ". . . and then . . . and then . . ." in which narrative history too often exhausts itself but on the complex imbedding of each of the episodes of this narrative schema in wider patterns of culture or institutional life. These are in the current idiom "synchronic" with one another and with the episodes they determine; they are also typically of a degree of complexity and abstractness that suggests a substantial independence from the "subjective" rationales of the human agents who live and act under them. In any case, there has been a strong tendency for analytical history either to absorb the contrasting diachronic dimension of events into the synchronic altogether or, where it resists such absorption, to treat it as an unintelligible caesura between systems of synchronicity. In either case, historical narrative with its commitment to the primacy of the diachronic mode and its traditional approach to the emergence of novelty through the schema of human agency must be sharply discounted.

If such views as these have become very influential among practicing historians, as they clearly have, that has been more a matter of the development of new research strategies than of philosophical argument designed to show the inadequacies of the narrative mode. Fortunately, however, the philosophical case against narrative has recently been made in a brief but powerful essay by Professor Maurice Mandelbaum, and it will be useful to review the main theses he propounds as a preliminary to the statement of my own view of the status of narrative within history as a whole. In that essay Mandelbaum is concerned to call into question an interpretation of history "as a linear sequence of human actions" that is in fact very similar to the one that was put forward in the preceding chapter. Against such an interpretation he argues that stories composed of successive episodes in this way require a good deal of initial analysis and explanation of "longer enduring factors which are not themselves links in the sequential chain of events which constitute the story." Even in biography, which might seem to be the form of historical writing which most closely conforms to the narrative model, Mandelbaum argues that it is frequently necessary to "take into account not merely the situations by which [the] subject is confronted" but also "dispositional properties which are not themselves specific episodic events which form part of a sequential chain," that is, "factors of intelligence, temperament, and personality which often cannot be accounted for in terms of specific episodes which enter [the] narrative." In other words, since stories are fully intelligible only if we know a good deal about relevant elements of structure and background and since the presentation of this information is not itself narrative in form and the factors so referred to are not themselves sequential episodes, historiography will necessarily have a non-narrative component. But beyond that, Mandelbaum suggests that the whole conception of history as a series of antecedent–consequent relationships is misleading and should be replaced by a part–whole model of explanation in which the subject's "specific activities and decisions" will be made intelligible by being related to dispositions and traits of character which are not episodes at all and are instead stable features of that individual's makeup through most or all of his life. These linkages between the story of a person's life and his psychological and physical makeup are to be supplied by a deeper and more theoretical kind of inquiry which would be discouraged if emphasis were placed exclusively on historical narrative.

The crucial assertion that underlies this critique of history as narrative is the claim that the account a historian gives of structure and background is not itself narrative in character and deals not with episodes or actions but with stable environmental or dispositional facts which may not be at all obvious to common sense. So stated, this thesis has a solid core of truth. For example, when Henry Adams wrote his *History of the United States of America*, he devoted his first chapters to a masterly survey of the state of the country at the beginning of Jefferson's administration, in which he laid particular emphasis upon the undeveloped and relatively primitive conditions that prevailed, and he made no attempt to give this account a narrative form. The features of the American scene he described were broadly synchronous rather than successive; and many of them related to permanent geographical features of the country. In a still more impressive example, Ferdinand Braudel's *Le Méditerranée et le monde méditerranéen dans l'âge de Philippe II*, the first two-thirds of that very long book are given over to an account of the structures – geographical, agricultural, economic, and so on – of the Mediterranean world before the "histoire événementielle" – in this case, the political and military history of the latter half of the sixteenth century – is reached. Again, and in this case quite consciously and deliberately, the narrative form is abandoned; and it really seems that Braudel is describing the state structures of life in the Mediterranean basin. These examples clearly give considerable plausibility to the claim that narrative history is not only not the substratum of all the other forms which historiography assumes but itself depends on a stratum of non-narrative description and analysis.

One may wonder, however, whether such an objection would not rest on a conception of narrative history that is so restrictive as virtually to lack application. If narrative history must always proceed from one event to another and never interrupt the sequence of "and thens" with broader characterizations of one kind or another, then even the most famous exemplars of narrative history will not satisfy this requirement. From Thucydides to Macaulay the great narrative historians have felt quite free to interrupt the story they were telling for the purpose of describing the character of a statesman or the topography of a battlefield. In a book like Braudel's, of course, excursuses of this type have become so much larger and so much more important that it is the narrative sections that seem to be appendages of the main body rather than the reverse; but the older narrative historians were also trying to provide the sort of background that would make their narrative more intelligible than it would otherwise be. We might, of course, try to reinterpret the distinction between narrative and non-narrative history by setting limits to these background characterizations and say that, when these limits are exceeded, the history in question is no longer of the narrative type. It is unlikely, however, that wide agreement could be achieved as to just how these limits should be defined; and in any case the deeper issue raised by Mandelbaum's objections would not be satisfactorily joined along such lines. That issue is not really whether narrative histories contain non-narrative sections or, if they do, how extensive these may be. It concerns rather the nature of the structures which these non-narrative sections reputedly deal with and the relationship of these structures to the events which make up the narrative portions of the history.

Although Mandelbaum does not discuss this issue in any detail, there are indications of the sort of view he is inclined to defend. Thus, he speaks disapprovingly of the widespread assumption "that what occurs in history is to be construed as if its occurrence were primarily, or even exclusively, due to intentional human actions" and that "history [is] a linear sequence of intelligible human actions" which it is the historian's job to trace. This seems to indicate that his deeper objection is not to the literary form of narrative or to mistaken claims that this form is the universal form of historiography, but rather to the claim that history derives its characteristic mode of ordering its materials from the teleological organization of human action. If this conjecture is correct, then he would be saying not only that historians must abandon the narrative form on occasion but also that, when they do so, they must talk about something besides human actions and employ an explanatory mode quite different from that suggested by the "linear sequence of intelligible human actions." In its non-narrative aspects, history will concern itself not with actions but with "traits," "dispositional properties," and "recurrent patterns (of) behavior" and these terms clearly designate, not episodes that occur at particular times, but stable and perduring features of the person or the situation which is under study. It is these lasting characteristics that are to give unity and pattern to the lives of the individuals whose decisions and actions are to be related to them. Mandelbaum does not say that these traits incorporate lawlike regularities or that an action's being related to a permanent trait involves its subsumption under some such laws; but references to "recurrent patterns of behavior" strongly suggest that something of this kind is intended.

Now when one says as Mandelbaum does that the "background" against which we view human actions is not itself "a part of the story of [those] actions," this statement is susceptible of two interpretations. It may mean that what is related by way of background is not part of the story because it is not an episode or event at all and therefore can find no place among the episodes which form the story; or it may mean that although the relevant background may consist of events, they are events of a kind which do not lend themselves to a narrative form of presentation. If one examines the examples which Mandelbaum offers, they seem to suggest now the one and now the other of these interpretations. Thus, when he states that "it would be a gross distortion of the events with which the historian is concerned if one were to regard the events which constitute an [election] campaign as a linear series . . . in which each event is causally related to a particular antecedent and itself leads to a particular consequent" and cites the need for attention to "such factors as the stable voting habits of some segments of the population and a recognition of the manner in which long-standing interests, disaffections and needs in various geographic, economic or ethnic groups will be relevant to eventual success or failure," he seems to be inclining to the second interpretation. There is, moreover, much support for such a view in the actual practice of historians who in the course of their non-narrative excursuses typically inform us as to patterns of life, whether in an individual or a society, that form a more or less uniform background against which the events of the story that is being told are thrown into sharp relief. These are, in other words, the things that people do over and over again — their habitual and familiar ways of making a living, worshipping, making war, or whatever. Precisely because there is little or nothing to differentiate one cycle in such routines from another and no clear sense in which the routine itself forms over time a dramatic unit with a beginning, a middle, and an end, it is scarcely surprising that background characterizations of recurrent patterns of action are usually given in non-narrative terms and that those patterns are referred to by means of dispositional predicates. In fact, such terms normally serve simply as economical summarizations of patterns of action which are relevant to the understanding of the main story line but may not by themselves have any interesting dramatic structure.

But if such a characterization of what one would expect to find in the background of a narrative is unexceptionable, it remains unclear why such a conception must tell against the view of history as a "linear sequence of intelligible human actions." In speaking of "patterns of action" one is, after all, still speaking of actions, and of actions that follow one another in time and that are intelligible in the sense of being performed for a reason. It is not as though by introducing the notions of such patterns of actions into his narrative the historian had moved to entirely new ground or abandoned his interest in rational human agency. What he has done instead is to "thicken" his working conception of such agency by recognizing that it has distinguishable strata and that the episodes with which he deals in his narrative must be presented in such a way as to give a sense of the context in which they took place. To take the example of an election campaign which Mandelbaum himself proposes, the fact that the Southern states regularly voted Democratic in the post-Civil War period would presumably be the "whole" and the corresponding "part" would be their doing so in a particular election year. But in referring that part to a pattern of political behavior over many years as its proper whole the historian would not have enriched our understanding very greatly unless he also exhibited this pattern of political statistics as a pattern of agency based on certain attitudes toward the competing political parties and, most importantly, on the still-fresh memory of the Civil War. The only conception of narrative that could not admit this degree of complexity in the kind of agency with which it deals would be one so impoverished that it could hardly deserve to be taken seriously. Historical narrative is not, after all, a series of self-contained episodes, linked only to those that precede and follow it. Each episode of agency typically takes into account a great many features of the situation in which it occurs as well as of those that precede and that may follow upon it; and these features can include the very regularities themselves under which Mandelbaum wishes to subsume the episodes in a narrative. At one point in fact he seems to come close to acknowledging this fact when he says that "to understand the various stratagems which each political party will employ, one must grasp their relationship to longer enduring factors which are not themselves links in the sequential chain of events." It is unclear, however, whether Mandelbaum would agree that these "longer enduring factors" are recognized and taken into account not just by the historian but also by the designers of the stratagems which the historian has to interpret and that the reason *why* the historian should pay attention to these regularities is precisely the fact that they characterize the patterns of agency of his subjects and thus may figure as premises in the counterstrategies of other such subjects. In any case, such patterns of action are typically so familiar to those who engage in them that among the latter there is no need to allude specifically to them for the purposes of making a story line intelligible. This need arises with increasing remoteness from this kind of familiarity with the context in which the actions of the story were performed; and the non-narrative excursuses which the historian or novelist undertakes are often designed to help the reader to avoid confusing his own assumed contexts of action with those of the agents in the story. But the relationship in which these contextual elements of information stand to the actional developments of the story *sensu stricto* are not therefore different from those that obtain within the story itself; they are, in fact, included in the background of the story because they form a part of the background of the actions with which the story deals.

As I have already noted, Mandelbaum offers other examples of the part–whole relationship which seem to favor the first interpretation suggested above and which exclude events and thus actions from the background characterizations of the historian. These are the examples in which the relevant elements of information have to do with "dispositions" such as "factors of intelligence, temperament, and personality." One can certainly agree with Mandelbaum that such matters are indeed included in what we need to know in order to construct or understand a narrative, but here again it does not seem that the part–whole schema can do justice to the complexity of the relationship in which they stand to the events of the narrative proper. This can be shown best by means of an example which Mandelbaum does not use but which is unquestionably relevant to historical understanding and even more remote from the "linear sequence of intelligible human actions" than are the dispositional properties he does cite. I have in mind here the various features of the geographical setting in which the events of some narrative occur. Typically, the facts contained in a "geographical" preface to a historical account – distances, types of terrain, quality of soil, climate, and so on – do not describe human actions, and could not well be described in narrative form. Although these natural circumstances are not wholly unalterable by human action – the course of a river can be changed – they do constitute the more or less permanent nonhuman framework within which human history takes place; and while this environment may be very different in different places and times, its presence and its relevance to the understanding of human activities is a constant of human history. But if it would be impossible to give a historical account of human doings that abstracted altogether from this natural setting, it is equally clear that the geography in question is human geography, that is, those features of the natural setting that block or facilitate human effort in one or another of its major areas. These features of the natural setting have to be described because they stand in some relationship to human need and effort; and they assume their full significance in a historical account only when they are set in the context of a certain level of technology and technical capabilities. Thus, distances have a quite different meaning for purposes of sixteenth-century history than for twentieth-century history because the "coefficient of adversity" they present is specifiable only for a stipulated level of technology. All too often this interdependence of natural setting and human activity has been forgotten or left implicit in the geographical sections of history books; but in a work like Braudel's the topography, the climate, the resources of the Mediterranean area are described in a manner that makes their role within the human scene so clear that Braudel can truly speak of the "Mediterranean world" as an indissoluble unity of natural setting and human agency. The natural setting is thus the material precondition for those routines of action referred to above; and although mountain ranges and climates are certainly not actions, the context in which they become elements in the background of some historical narration is normally that of those purposive routines of action to which reference has been made.

Even if the dispositions referred to in the background characterization were the psychological ones which Mandelbaum himself proposes, the appropriateness of the part–whole schema would not be very much greater. There can, of course, be no doubt that "traits" or "dispositions" like those Mandelbaum cites do have their place within a historical account. A historian may tell his readers about such attributes of his subjects as, for example, their degree of intelligence, the state of their health, their capacity for enduring suffering or for sympathetic identification with others, or their physical strength. To these the historian of the future may wish, if he is able, to add disquisitions on the central nervous system of his subjects. The abilities and disabilities that are thus attributed to historical personages by way of explanatory preface to an account of something they did do seem to be somehow more permanent and more unalterable than the actions they help explain; and so they appear to satisfy the requirement of an explanatory structure that is antecedent to the episodic events of the narrative account itself. But in what sense can such attributions of dispositions be said to replace the "linear sequence" of human actions in the narrative? Suppose we take one of Mandelbaum's own examples and consider intelligence as a relatively stable attribute of the historical agents with whom we are concerned and attempt to see how this "background" feature of human personality might serve to explain human action. How, to cite a specific case, does the undoubted fact that General de Gaulle was a highly intelligent man help us to understand his career as a statesman? We might agree that his intelligence enabled de Gaulle to carry out policies in a way that would have been impossible for, say, a senile Hindenburg and that in this sense the possession of a certain level of intelligence may be a necessary condition for a given level of accomplishment. But it seems equally clear that just as the features of a natural setting have to be related to the kind of use that human beings want to make of them and can make of them before they will have much relevance to the concerns of history, so too a quality like intelligence has constantly to be situated within the properly actional context of the uses a given individual wishes to make of whatever natural endowments he may be supposed to possess. Intelligence in other words would be the necessary or supporting or facilitating condition for a form of activity which it does not by itself in any way dictate; and this does not seem to be a role that is very aptly described as that of whole to part.

This brief review of the case against narrative as Mandelbaum presents it strongly suggests that the distinction between historical narrative and its non-narrative background can best be made *within* the domain of human agency that was marked out in the discussions of the last chapter and that the analytical functions of the historian can be adequately characterized without introducing a theory, like that of the part–whole relationships proposed by Mandelbaum, that breaks with the agency-based pre-suppositions of the narrative mode. The fundamental point here is that human agency has distinct strata. These were distinguished from one another as the "cyclical" and the "linear" and it was argued that a distinctively historical process is one that incorporates both kinds of agency: the kind that expresses itself in the more or less stable routines by which the business of life is regularly discharged and the distributive and collective actions that deviate from those routines or are addressed to situations that lie outside the prior organization of life within a given society. In an obvious sense, it is the latter that form the primary and most natural subject-matter for narrative history since they mark the entrance of a society or an institution into an area of novelty and uncertainty that transcends the familiar domain of its established routines. What is done over and over again in pretty much the same circumstances and with pretty much the same kinds of results can be rendered in a typifying account in which primary emphasis is placed not on the temporal succession of actions as such but rather on the complex relationships among different human agents and between such agents and their natural environment upon which these stable routines are predicated. In such

cases, although the element of novelty and uncertainty can never be wholly eliminated from any human action, enough stability and predictability is realized so that
one can say that the element of temporality and succession that is inseparable from
all human action is dominated by the organizing structures of social work; and
although one can imagine a narrative that would faithfully reproduce each occasion
on which these routines were deployed, it would be an incredibly redundant and
boring narrative. It is just these cases in which the new action repeats the pattern
of the prior ones and does not introduce any significant element of novelty that
can be most readily accommodated to the part–whole schema; and it is this fact,
more than anything else, which casts doubt on the suitability of that schema as a
general interpretation of the way historical narrative proceeds. Narrative in the
more usual and interesting sense is reserved for those singular events which do not
form part of an established routine and for which there is not the alternative of a
non-narrative treatment because they create new situations in which the old routines
on which a typifying account would rely may themselves be drawn into the process
of change.

There is another important conclusion with respect to historical narrative that
is suggested by the set of distinctions within the domain of human agency that were
proposed in the last chapter. This is that the "regularities" with which the historian
is typically concerned – the "stable factors of long-standing" of Mandelbaum's
account – cannot claim the kind of unrestricted universality that would make them
in principle independent of any spatial or temporal limits in the way that the
regularities formulated in scientific laws are usually held to be. When a regularity
is a pattern of action within some human community, there is not only no reason
to suppose that that regularity must hold beyond the limits of that society; there
is not even any reason to believe that it must always hold within that society. These
are in other words "local" regularities which are themselves historical in the sense
that they are in principle as subject to change as are the particular situations
which they "govern." The spatio-temporal "locales" in which they obtain may be as
extensive as mankind itself or as narrow as a single family. They may be passing
fads or they may be so deeply ingrained in the life of a society that its members
can hardly imagine what that life would be like if these regularities no longer held.
But neither their actual scope, in space or in time, nor the degree of firmness with
which they are established can affect their status as patterns of action; and it is
because these regularities are patterns of action that they are inescapably subject
to revision. Thus, if we say that the Greeks use oil instead of butter or that the
Portuguese do not kill their bulls at the end of the corrida whereas the Spaniards
do or that unlike the Germans the Russians tightly swaddle newborn infants, we
are not stating a law; we are describing a shared pattern of action which belongs
in the series of intelligible human actions although at a different stratum from particular episodes, and not in the domain of the nonhistorical regularities of natural
science. The latter, of course, impinge in their own way on properly historical
events whether as the necessity with which the victim of the assassin collapses or
as the principle which a bit of technology turns to advantage. But this ever-present
natural or cosmetic background is of comparatively little relevance to the work of
the historian. The proximate regularities under which the latter seeks to bring the
events with which he deals are actional in character; and while those inevitably take

the circumstances and limits posed by these natural regularities into account, there is no realistic prospect of our being able to extend the chain of derivation and establish a linkage between historical regularities and nonhistorical laws of unrestricted universality. When we try to ignore these discontinuities and assimilate the one kind of regularity to the other, we run into difficulties to which attention will be given in the course of this chapter.

It follows from what has been said that historical narrative constitutes the mode of understanding that is proper to events which for one reason or another are not just parts of wholes or new instances of a recurrent pattern and therefore require an individualizing rather than a typifying mode of treatment. It is important to understand, however, that this is not to deny that history incorporates forms of inquiry that address themselves to the past for the purpose of discovering those elements in the life of some human community which were for some period of time invariant. The results of such an inquiry which defines the life of the community under study in synchronic terms may be entirely adequate and satisfactory from the standpoint guiding the inquiry; and when this is so there is no need to ask whether they are obtained by means of a special abstraction from such forms of instability and change as may have been taking place within the community in question or whether the routines so uncovered in fact subsume the life of this community in a quite literal way. The point I am making is rather that this point of view is historical only in a limited sense and that historians are interested in *both* stability and change, in routines of life and in singular events that depart from those routines in such a way as to produce changes in them. There are also disciplines like anthropology that make use of historical methods of inquiry for the purpose of investigating a society in the past which in these aspects that are of interest to the anthropological inquirer may have been quite static. A historian in the full sense, however, is, I am assuming, defined not just by the reference of his inquiries to the past but by the conception of the historical process within which he works; and this is a conception within which there are, in varying proportions, elements of both sameness and change, of routines and singular events. What is to count as a singular event will of course depend to some extent on the scope of the historical inquiry itself and on the way in which the routines themselves are understood. But the important point here is that a sequence of events that breaks up an established routine or gives rise to another one cannot be understood as simply an instance of either the prior or the later routine; and it is in this sense a singular event and one that requires an individuating form of representation. This form of representation, when applied to a number of events that succeed one another in time, is what I will refer to as historical narrative.

II

Against the background of the conclusions reached in the course of the preceding section, it should now be possible to turn to the positive characterization of historical narrative. It is, to begin with, generally agreed that a narrative of whatever kind presents the events with which it is concerned in the temporal order in which they occurred. This does not mean that a narrative may never leap over events or return to an earlier point in the sequence; but rather that wherever it rejoins the movement of events it will proceed once more in a temporally sequential way. What is not so clear is whether a narrative must do more than report such events in their proper time order and whether it must exhibit them as being connected in ways that go beyond the relationship that derives from their position in that time order. Those philosophers of history who answer this question in the affirmative often use some such term as "chronicle" to designate a record of events which exhibits no supplementary form of continuity; and others who are not concerned to reserve the term "narrative" as such for a contrasting use make a distinction between "plain" and "significant" narrative. This is a terminological issue on which nothing very momentous depends; but unless calendars and almanacs are to be included among narratives, it seems unlikely that very many "plain" narratives can be identified in which events are connected only by virtue of the temporal positions which they occupy in relation to one another. A narrative does not, after all, report just any events that happen to satisfy this condition of temporal order. Instead it limits itself to events which have something to do with the chosen theme or subject-matter of the narrative; and when these events are human actions or utterances as they typically are, it becomes quite unlikely that the order in which they follow upon one another will be "nonsignificant" in the sense of contributing nothing to our understanding of why these events occurred. One may suspect that a narrative that really managed to report the sequence of events in such a way as to imply no further explanatory connection among them would also be one to which it would be hard to attribute any internal organizing structure – a beginning and an end, for example – in any sense that is not itself purely temporal in character. There is, of course, a difference between a narrative that does not go beyond the kind of common-sense connectedness that is virtually inseparable from anything we are likely to call a narrative and the narrative that stops to ask questions that cannot be answered without some sort of further inquiry; it may be that this is the distinction which those who have spoken of "plain" and "significant" narrative have had in mind. But even so it would still be the case that "plain" narratives suggest an explanation, however inadequate and superficial it may be, of the occurrence of the events they report; the criterion of significance, accordingly, would be one which all narratives would, however modestly, satisfy.

To assert that all narratives perform some explanatory function is to be brought face to face with issues relating to the nature of explanation and, more specifically, its logical structure. The most notable general conceptions of explanation are, as we have seen, the nomological-deductive theory and its teleological competitor; and the hypothesis upon which the philosophical analysis of historical narrative proceeds is that the logical structure of one of these will prove to be a reliable guide to the structure of narrative. I have examined elsewhere two current versions of the theory of narrative to which the nomological-deductive theory gives rise and have tried to identify its characteristic weaknesses. The most conspicuous of these is the failure of such theories of narrative to give adequate attention to the kind of connectedness among events that characteristically arises in a context of human action; and as a result of this failure it has been necessary for the exponents of this view of narrative to seek the source of the connectedness of events in lawlike regularities that are wholly independent of the organization of events which action effects. In these circumstances, one would naturally expect that a teleological theory of explanation would be ideally well suited to the requirements of historical narrative and that, in view of the strong natural affinities between the two, a teleological theory of historical narrative would already have been fully elaborated. And yet surprisingly enough this proves to be not really the case. In the two most substantial explorations of the concept of historical explanation from a teleological standpoint — those of Professor William Dray and Professor G. H. von Wright — historical narrative as such has not been very extensively discussed, perhaps because the main concern of their accounts has been with the logical structure of such explanations as such rather than with its implications for the analysis of narrative. As things stand, the closest thing we have to a teleological interpretation of narrative is the account presented by Professor W. B. Gallie; but in spite of its great suggestiveness the perspective from which it is constructed seems somewhat limiting. Too often the focus of interest seems to be the process of following as a reader a historical narrative rather than of analyzing the teleological principle on which such a narrative is constructed, much less the historical process itself with which the historian deals. At the same time, however, the interpretation of narrative that will be presented here draws extensively on the pioneering work of these writers, and its main effort will be to connect these (not always identical) conceptions of teleology with the theory of the historical process that was developed in the last chapter and with a conception of historical narrative that corresponds with the latter.

It will be convenient to begin by locating a little more precisely the inadequacies of the presently available theories of teleological explanation as these relate to the analysis of historical narrative; and I will use Dray's theory of rational explanation as my example. This theory undertakes to show, against the claims made by the exponents of the covering-law theory, that human actions can be explained without recourse at any point to universal causal laws. As Dray puts it, rational explanations are the historian's reconstruction "of the agent's *calculation* of means to be adopted toward his chosen end in the light of the circumstances in which he found himself;" and "to explain the action we need to know what considerations convinced him that he should act as he did." In this statement there is an explicit reference to the agent's future — "his chosen end" — which is said to govern his choice of means in the present; but otherwise there is no attention to the connections among events which might be implicit in the agent's "calculation." To be sure, the reference to "the circumstances in which he [the agent] found himself" does not exclude their being stated in a form which relates them to specific past events, but it does not require it either, and the whole bit of practical reasoning that is imputed to the agent might very well, for all Dray says here, be tied to actual events only through the one factual premise relating to circumstances at the time of the action. The point I am making is that with the exception of the reference to the end to be achieved there is little in such a conception of the explanation of human action that breaks out of the segmented conception of time discussed earlier and correspondingly little that suggests a mode of continuity among the events that compose a historical narrative.

What is most distinctive about the rational explanation theory, at least in Dray's version of it, is the emphasis it places on what it takes to be the *appraisive* character of the historian's judgment as to the reasons which led to the action he is trying to explain. The historian is trying to reach "a logical equilibrium at which point an action is matched with a calculation;" and when that point is reached the action is seen to be the appropriate one in the sense that "if the situation had been as the agent envisaged it (whether or not we from our point of vantage concur in his view of it) then what was done would have been the thing to do." As Dray himself points out, however, this kind of appraisal does not imply any endorsement by the historian of the action under consideration and really reduces to the characterization of the action as "rationalizable" given a certain combination of beliefs about the agent's situation and certain goals to which he is committed. Once it is understood that the agent's calculations and preferences are such as to make the action in question a suitable one, that action has been satisfactorily explained at least for historical purposes; and there is no need, in Dray's view, to explain the fact that the agent had just these beliefs and these preferences and certainly no need to do so in a way that involves the use of general laws. This amounts to the view that it is legitimate in certain contexts of explanation to treat the rational agent as the final term of our explanation beyond which we do not seek further causes; and this is a view which has much to recommend it. But in the form in which Dray presents it, it may seem to require too sharp a rupture in the tissue of events to be acceptable. Unless an agent's having the beliefs and desires he has is a fit subject for historical analysis, the result may be that these beliefs and desires and the actions they motivate will lack any comprehensible relationship to prior events. In fact, this impression is due in large part, I believe, to Dray's rather abstract way of conceiving the agent's calculations and his tendency to emphasize the fact that they satisfy certain logical criteria of rationality rather than that they establish their own distinctive form of continuity with prior events. It is one thing to repudiate the claim that the continuity of historical events always requires that these events be subsumed under general laws, and this Dray has done with great skill and cogency. But if the competing model of rational explanation is construed in such a way that the policies of action by reference to which actions are to be explained stand in a "vertical" and abstract relationship to events and thus fail to establish any alternative form of continuity with prior events, then it will be difficult to translate this theory of historical explanation into a theory of historical narrative and of the continuity which is usually thought to be the distinctive mark of such narrative.

This criticism of the theory of rational explanation which has just been sketched is closely related to another one which is addressed to what might be called the individualistic bias of that theory. There has been a tendency on the part of philosophers of all persuasions to assume that the actions with which historians deal can be analyzed in much the same way as individual or personal decisions and to forget that these actions are in fact typically such as are taken in a public context and in behalf of some group or institution and that as such they are subject to multiple constraints beyond those that operate in the case of personal decisions. Whatever the balance of effective power within the group or society in question, it seems fair to say that significant actions must be in some comprehensible relationship to the traditions and established expectations of some substantial fraction of the membership of that group. It is, of course, possible for a minority and sometimes even for an individual to resolve upon a course of action on the basis of considerations that prescind from such traditions; but much the more common case is the one in which at least an effort is made to present what is to be done as reflecting shared understandings as to what the policies of the society are to be. Such understandings can be represented in the form of general principles from which an application to present circumstances is then deductively derived; but it is doubtful whether this is in fact the form in which the tradition would be understood by the people in question. The more plausible view is that this tradition is maintained in the more highly particularized and concrete form of an account of what that society has done and suffered over the period of its existence. What I am suggesting then is not only that the "goals" which would figure in the major premise of a schematization of the rationale of a collective action are goals which command some degree of shared acceptance by the members of a single society, but also that such goals are not readily detachable from that society's understanding of what it has been doing over a longer period of time. If this is correct, then the statement of a policy of action for such a society would not involve a unilateral reference to a future change to be realized in a present situation. It would also and equally carry forward into its future a certain understanding of what that society has already done and suffered, and it would construe its present circumstances in terms of what they signify within the context of such a past. To the extent that schematizations of the rationale of historical action make it appear that having a goal on the part of some society or institution is simply a matter of deciding in the present to bring about some change in the future and to the extent that the reference these goals and these readings of present circumstances make to the past is thereby obscured, the illusion is created that all the operative reasons for such actions are located in the present and in the future.

The point I am making here is one that has to do with the comparative importance for historical purposes of different elements in the practical inference on the part of the historical agent which all these theories of teleological explanation in history postulate. It seems fair to say that the element in such practical inferences which has received least attention is the factual premise which describes the relevant features of the situation in which the agent finds himself (or supposes himself to be) and this neglect is doubtless explained by the fact that the function of this premise is simply to make the major premise dealing with goals or principles of action applicable to the given situation of the agent. Typical logical schematizations tend to suggest that the features of such situations to which reference is made in these "factual" premises are such as are readily describable in general terms and thus in terms that rather directly invoke the application of higher-order policies of the agent. It is the goals set by these policies that are controlling, and "situations" are simply classified according to the opportunities they present for the realization of these goals. But such a schema does not readily accommodate the case in which it may be something in the factual situation — an action by another party in that situation — which first creates the need for action and in which it may be another element in that situation — one's institutional affiliation and the traditions of that institution — that are centrally involved in the response that is forthcoming. Doubtless these cases could be accommodated to the schema of practical deliberation described above; but the fact remains that the tendency of that schema is to encourage a neglect by the philosophical analyst of the embeddedness of the agent himself and of his motives for action in the process which receives such scant recognition in the "factual" premise. The alternative would be to find ways of repre-senting the practical inference of the historical agent that would not allow the relevant prior events which he is taking into account to disappear under descrip-tions cast in general terms. If that were done then the practical inference of the historical agent would not have the effect of sealing off his action within its own self-sufficient rationality, but would ensure instead the continuity of that action with preceding events through the overlap between the practical inferences of different agents in which the conclusions of one such inference would provide the initial premise of that of another.

In this connection it may be worth noting that the usual counterpart to the neglect of continuity with prior events which I am attributing to the theory of rational explanation is a tendency to exaggerate the explicitness and degree of gener-ality of the agent's calculations and to set impossibly high standards of rationality for these actions to meet. In this connection it has been pointed out recently that there has been a tendency to make it a condition of an action's qualifying as rational that that action has been considered at a level of generality and in a context of alternatives which are in fact characteristic of only the most highly reflective decisions. These are extremely rare and yet we do not normally regard all other decisions as irrational whose ultimate justifying principles may never have been critically reviewed. Instead of enforcing such unrealistic conditions defining rationality upon actions that plainly cannot satisfy them, it seems more reasonable to interpret the rationality of action in terms of a congruence between one's goals and the predicted outcomes of actions taken on the occasion of opportunities that present themselves. For example, the rationality of Bismarck's action in revising the Ems dispatch would consist in the fact that the effect of the publication of the revised text upon the French public was to make the war Bismarck desired inevitable. To be sure, this goal formed part of a yet more comprehensive set of goals which Bismarck was trying to realize and so contributed to a systematic coherence within his policies. But this is quite different from saying that Bismarck methodically compared this course of action with others that may have been open to him and decided upon the action he took because he believed it would produce the optimal combination of benefits.

In more general terms the claim I am making is that human actions through their motivating reasons refer to a wide variety of events and circumstances in the past of the societies that undertake these actions. In some cases the feature of the past that is internalized in this way so as to become an element in the rationale of future action may be a specific event like the defeat of the Roman legions in the Teutoburger Forest by the Germanic tribes under Varus, an event which lived in the memory of both the Romans and the Germans and became a symbol of successful German resistance to Romanization. In other cases, the reference to the past would be more in the nature of a *reprise* as for example in the case of the re-establishment of the Roman Empire in 800 with the coronation of Charlemagne. In still other cases, a previous historical experience may serve as the model used by a society for interpreting a later one and for developing policies in the later situation; and here the case of the United States applying a concept of collective security based on the experience of Munich to Southeast Asia in the post-World War II world comes to mind. There is a host of other forms which this backward referencing of action can assume and in each of them a society may be said to act in a way which cannot be understood without a reference to its past because it makes that reference itself. In this way the action itself takes on a conceptual relationship to the past by which it is informed and it is by virtue of this relationship that events take on a retrospective as well as a prospective form of continuity. Whether this conceptual continuity should be understood as also a form of causal influence upon the present action is a question to which I will turn later, but it is already clear that the influence such events have on present action must be "routed through" the representations of them which human agents entertain. Events of various kinds can, of course, change the world in countless ways that are quite independent of our capacity to describe them. They cannot provide reasons for or against actions, however, otherwise than under a certain mode of conceptualization or description; and it is this same mode of conceptualization of them by the historical agents themselves which generates a form of meaningful connectedness among events over time and thus provides the basis for historical narrative. In other words, rational explanation, when freed from the model of individual decision and from the exclusive temporal orientation running from the present to the future – both stripped of descriptions that relate them to the past – reproduces the structure of action and the mode of temporal synthesis implicit in the latter; and in this temporal form the rational structure of action is the structure of narrative.

With regard to the structure or "logic" of historical narrative a number of general theses may now be enunciated. The first of these is fundamental to everything that has been said up to this point and it asserts that human actions are the primary events with which the historian deals and that historical narrative is to be understood as the reconstruction of a sequence of human actions within which one action and its consequences become the premise for a succeeding action and so on. The second thesis is that it is a condition of grasping this kind of action-based continuity of historical narrative that the actions themselves be identified by the historian under the descriptions which the agent may be supposed to have used as well as those used by those who were in some way affected by those actions. And finally I want to argue that the explanatory function of historical narrative is teleological in character in the sense that successive episodes are connected through the role assigned to them within the practical inferences of the agents involved in them. In fact, these theses are not as distinct from one another as this mode of statement may make it appear and are in fact successive restatements of a single thesis with the emphasis successively shifted from the priority of human actions within historical narrative to the centrality of the agent's description in the identification of actions and then to the teleological character of the continuity within a sequence of actions which take one another into account. Nevertheless, for the purpose of defending them, I will treat them as distinct theses and I will take them up in the same order in which I have introduced them. Wherever possible I will try to bring these theses into a realistic relationship to actual historical materials, but in the case of the third thesis, which is the most purely philosophical of the three, I will have to abandon historical ground almost entirely and argue the logical issues involved at their own quite abstract level.

III

The events that historians recount and seek to explain are extremely heterogeneous. They include wars and famines, rebellions and depressions, discoveries of
continents and declines of empires. If one wishes to argue, as I do, that history has
as its preferential subject-matter human actions, this thesis can evidently draw no
unambiguous support from the way in which historical events are — at least superficially and initially — named. Even in the short list above, there are designations
of types of historical events which plainly refer to them as actions of some kind
and there are others which just as plainly do not. Thus if a historian talks about
the execution of Charles I, this very way of referring to that event implies that
someone executed him and presumably also that someone ordered or authorized
that execution, that is, that two distinct but related acts were performed by assignable persons or groups of persons. But if the historian's interest focuses on the
depression of 1929 or the Irish famine of 1846–9 it is not at all obvious that these
concepts of "depression" and "famine" are names of actions; nor is it clear what
actions, if any, are necessarily included in what we mean when we speak of depressions and famines. We know of course that in the case of famine there is often, as
there was in Ireland in 1846, a crop failure that reduces the food supply to the
point where people go hungry and die. But a crop failure is a natural event, not
an action; and its consequences — people going hungry and dying — are not actions
either in the sense that is relevant here. It seems then that a history of the Irish
famine would have to be an account of certain natural events — the successive crop
failures in the 1846–9 period — and of the suffering and death they caused. How,
it may be asked, can one claim that such a history of the Irish famine would be in
any special sense an account of what men did, especially when the event itself is
named after that element within it which is simply a natural event?

Considerations of this kind have led many philosophers to assume that history
is not merely superficially heterogeneous but profoundly and unalterably so, and
that it is a mixture of actions and nonactions in which the former enjoy at best a
priority of interest and attention. In fact, however, even such examples as those
given above do not, under closer inspection, really support these conclusions. For
while the potato blight in Ireland certainly explains why the principal food supply
of the Irish people was reduced to a small fraction of its normal quantity, that fact
by itself does not explain the occurrence of a famine. If it did, the work of historians of the Irish famine would be easily done — much more easily and quickly than
it in fact is. To be sure, historians take due note of the destruction of successive
potato crops by the *Phytophthora infestans* fungus; but they are not satisfied to explain
the famine — the suffering and death that followed upon the crop failures — simply
by reference to the latter as their cause. As any reasonable person would, they ask,
"What could have been done in the circumstances to prevent starvation?" If nothing
could have been done by anyone at any time to prevent the deaths that occurred,
then the famine would have to be regarded as an act of God or as an event similar
to the collision of the earth with another planet. It is quite clear, however, that
the famine was not uncontrollable or unpreventable in that sense. Various things
could have been done by various persons and institutions; and the historian who
wishes to explain the famine and not just a crop failure must ask whether any of

these things were done and, if they were, why they failed to prevent large-scale starvation. If they were not even attempted, he must ask why this was so and whether they were considered and then rejected; and in the latter case why they were rejected. Accordingly Mrs Cecil Woodham-Smith in her admirable book, *The Great Hunger*, pays only passing attention to the causes of the crop failures and a great deal of attention to the attitude of the British government, especially as formulated and expressed by the permanent under-secretary of the Treasury, Charles Edward Trevelyan. Since that government was aware of the magnitude of the disaster and had direct responsibilities in the area, it was in the best position to take action if something was to be done. This fact explains and justifies Mrs Woodham-Smith's close attention to the attitude of the British government in spite of the fact that the latter did not intervene in any significant way. At the same time, Mrs Woodham-Smith shows why it would have been very difficult to distribute food on the required scale, even if a decision to make the effort had been made, by reason of the primitive system of communication and transportation in Ireland and the absence of a highly developed governmental apparatus for carrying out welfare functions. But she also shows why the British government was reluctant to make this effort at all and why in fact it did not. Now all of this is clearly in the nature of a consideration of the matter from the standpoint of a person — especially certain persons with the means to intervene — in the situation itself, and from this standpoint the Great Hunger cannot be explained until it has been shown what courses of action might have prevented starvation in spite of the crop failures, and also why they failed if they were undertaken and why they were or were not undertaken. Among these remedial courses of action are, of course, those that were open to the victims of the famine themselves, and Mrs Woodham-Smith very properly raises such questions as why the Irish did not take to fishing when potatoes were unavailable, although it is not clear that she really explains this.

It would appear then that in these cases at least the historian shows a certain a priori selectivity in his analysis of the causes of such an event as the Great Hunger and that this selectivity is based upon a priority assigned to actions — possible and actual — over nonactions. In a period in which plant bacteriology and related prophylactic measures did not yet exist, a potato blight and the resultant crop failure were clearly nonactions, that is, they were not actions even in the marginal sense of being partially attributable to someone's negligence or folly. The potato blight was, moreover, a necessary condition of the famine since if it had not occurred there is no reason to think there would have been a famine. At the same time, this occurrence and its likely effects were known to many persons inside and outside Ireland; and so the possibility of doing something to prevent a famine unavoidably suggested itself to those persons at the time as it does to the historian of the event. A famine follows necessarily upon the destruction of the food supply only if nothing effective is done to provide food from other sources. In the Irish case nothing effective was done; and the decision of the British government not to attempt to supply food on a large scale can properly be regarded as a further and necessary condition for the famine's occurrence. But it was not just another condition, at least from the standpoint of the historian. It has already been noted that the historian pays some attention to the causes of the potato blight; but he draws his explanations of this event from other, non-historical sources and it is not his responsibility to discover its causes if they are not such as are already clear to the relevant branch of natural science. The specific scientific explanation which the historian borrows in this way will very likely have little or no connection with the rest of his narrative; and if it were to be revised by the plant bacteriologists, that change, too, would very likely have no impact on the historian's work. Certainly the fact that a potato blight had an identifiable natural cause is important if only as a means of warding off explanations that appeal immediately to the will of God and also as an indication of the area in which long-range solutions to the problem were to be sought. But in the main the occurrence of a potato blight is simply a fact that serves as an essential premise in the kind of explanation which the historian is really concerned to give. What has to be explained is what human beings did in the situation in which they were in their different ways confronted by this fact which was also a premise of their practical deliberations and of their actions. Those actions, as it turned out, were such as to make it inevitable that famine would follow upon the potato blight; and the historian's problem is to explain not that natural event itself but the course of action and inaction by virtue of which that event was permitted to lead to a famine. My point is that it is not the primary job of the historian to explain the natural events which provide the premises of human action but those actions themselves, unless of course these premises deal with events which are themselves in some measure, at least, the result of human action.

The thesis that human actions are the primary events with which the historian deals has now been interpreted to mean that human actions are treated as the decisive causes of the events the historian studies. The suggestion is thus that the historian has reasons for being interested in actions as actions and that this choice of a standpoint for interpreting events carries with it a mode of organization that is fundamental to an understanding of historical narrative. It is accordingly of considerable interest to note that the kind of organizing influence on the form of historical narrative that I am attributing to human action has an analogue in the field of law which may cast light on the parallel case of history. In the law, as in history, it is necessary to explain what caused certain events. While it is accepted that the events of the type to be explained may stand in invariant relationships of succession to some set of the conditions that obtained at the time of the event's occurrence, this fact is not of any special relevance for purposes of determining the cause of the event in legal contexts. Usually the sufficient conditions for producing the event are not known; even if they were, that would not permit us to make the all-important distinction between normal or usual conditions and the abnormal or unusual events which are typically regarded as intervening in the normal course of events and are therefore designated as *the* cause of the event to be explained. More importantly, since the purpose of legal inquiries into causes is to fix responsibility as a preliminary to reward or punishment, voluntary human actions have a special place among the conditions that produced a certain effect. Especially when these actions are intended to produce the effect in question, they are treated as the decisive cause of that event, and all of the other conditions necessary for the production of that event are reduced to the status of means or background conditions which are utilized by the action or on which the action supervenes, as it were, from outside. But even when the action is not intended to produce the effect, as in the case of a match dropped in a forest, it may well be treated as *the* cause of the forest fire since the latter was among the results of such an action that a normal person might reasonably be expected to bear in mind and seek to avoid. On the other hand, if the result was produced only because of certain exceptional conditions that could not be anticipated, then the action of dropping the match may no longer be ranked as a cause but be demoted instead to the status of precondition. What is important in all these cases is the fact that a distinction is made among the conditions for the occurrence of an event – a distinction between cause and conditions – and it is made on the basis of an interest in the control of the outcome by human agency. As Professor H. L. A. Hart puts it, "a deliberate human act is . . . most often a barrier and a goal in tracing back causes . . .: it is something *through* which we do not trace the cause of a later event and something *to* which we do trace the cause through intervening events of other kinds."

The reason for this priority of interest within the law in human agency is, as just indicated, quite clear and has to do with the directly practical concern of the law with determining who is to be held responsible and, if appropriate, punished. That motive cannot without further ado be assigned to the historian in order to explain why he evinces the same priority of interest in human agency as does the lawyer or the judge. In this connection it is interesting to note that Hart does discuss this parallelism between history and the law and makes the observation that "the narrative of history is scarcely ever a narrative of brute sequence, but is an account of the roles played by certain factors and especially by human agents. History is written to satisfy not only the need for explanation, but also the desire to identify and assess the contribution made by historical figures to changes of importance; to disasters and triumphs and to human happiness and suffering." This has certainly been the case throughout most of the history of historiography, but it has the disadvantage of making it appear that this feature of his practice which the historian shares with the jurist is simply an "interest" and as such might or might not be shared by all historians. As Hart points out, even historians who share this interest need not be moralists; and it is not quite clear what answer Hart could give to those present-day historians who claim that their inquiries are motivated entirely by the "need for explanation" and therefore feel no reluctance to trace causes through and beyond deliberate human agency. The deeper question raised by this challenge must therefore be whether there is any obstacle stronger than a traditional orientation of the historian's interest that stands in the way of a form of historical inquiry that assigns no special or privileged position to human agency.

Let us return to the example of the Irish famine in order to answer this question. One can well imagine a historian who felt no interest in condemning or justifying the action or nonaction of Charles Edward Trevelyan and no disposition to treat his reaction to the famine as the final term in his explanatory account. What would such a historian's first step beyond the permanent under-secretary of the Treasury be? One can guess that his attention would be drawn either to the long-standing relationship between England and Ireland or to the prevailing assumptions as to the role of government in the economic sphere or to both and that in either case this historian's effort would be to represent Trevelyan's case as an instance of some much more widespread system of practice. But in what sense would such a procedure provide the basis for a distinction between the historian who is disposed to move through a deliberate human act in his search for causes and the one who is not? The latter after all is interested in the reasons why people act as they do and would certainly not neglect Trevelyan's own justification for his course of conduct which appealed to precisely the kind of laissez-faire principles on which the economic system of the day rested. In these circumstances it is a fair question whether in widening the inquiry so as to bring in such matters as the pattern of economic life one would really be moving beyond or through Trevelyan's action and not simply enlarging one's view of the system of practice within which his action could seem right and proper. This could be very useful particularly as a corrective for a view of Trevelyan's conduct as a purely individual act without any larger rationalizing context. But the fact remains that that larger context impinges upon a particular occasion of action only if it has been internalized by the prospective agent – in this case Trevelyan – so that it can inform his beliefs and intentions and through them find expression in action. The same observations apply in the case of the relationship between England and Ireland if that were to be the relevant larger context of explanation. Here again it is a question of certain beliefs or prevailing assumptions as to the way a subject people may be treated; and if one of those beliefs were, for example, that Irish lives do not count for very much, it would be less likely to be cited in justification of some action and might not even be acknowledged in this form by those who in fact hold it, but for all that it would be a belief and an implicit directive for action and as such it could be efficacious on a given occasion only if it were the belief of some person who had the opportunity or responsibility for the action that would bring it into play. One can of course imagine an official who unlike Trevelyan did not personally share either of these beliefs but who acted on them nevertheless on the grounds that he had no real alternative; and in such a case the "system" does take on an appearance of externality to the agent which might seem to justify the historian in holding that in citing that system as a cause he had moved beyond a deliberate human act to a larger and more impersonal cause. But there is not only no reason to view such a relationship between bodies of beliefs or rules and the persons through whose actions they find expression as typical; it is also quite clear that it is merely a special case of the relationship described above. What is different is simply the fact that because the agent does not really accept the belief on which he acts another reason of a narrower and most probably prudential kind has to be inserted between that belief and his action in compliance with it. In other words, it is the agent's own beliefs which both resist the socially accepted belief on which he is to act and which provide him with a reason for compliance; and if he had the required information, it is in these terms that the historian would have to account for the action this person finally took. As Professor Hart points out in the course of his analysis of "interpersonal transactions" it is not usual to speak of one person "causing" another to do something even when threats are used or other means that satisfy the criterion of externality to the agent's beliefs that was cited above. There seems even less justification for using such language in the case of compliance with a socially accepted belief for reasons other than those supplied by the belief itself.

These considerations provide the elements of a stronger argument for the centrality of human action within historical inquiry than did those predicated on a certain kind of interest on the historian's part. Such an argument would be designed to show that if a historian traces the events in which he is interested to human actions at all, he will not be able to move through them otherwise than for the purpose of more fully exploring the contexts of practice within which they find their place. Because these contexts are themselves defined in terms of a network of beliefs and policies and in terms of the relationships they establish among various potential agents, the historian may indeed move to higher levels of understanding than a (or perhaps any) individual agent could achieve; but he is moving within the same rationalizing medium as such agents do and he is under an obligation to show how these wider aspects of the actional context within which the latter function reach a particular agent or group of agents and inform the beliefs and purposes that find expression in their actions. No doubt such a story could be told about Charles Edward Trevelyan, although from Mrs Woodham-Smith's account it appears that he was very much an agent in his own right. The main point, however, remains that there is no exit from the kinds of considerations that are generically the same as those involved in the initial agent's own action once the historian has entered upon an analysis of the role of the latter in some sequence of events. There is, moreover, strong reason to think that the supposition that there might be such an exit is due to an influence of a misleading model of the relationship in which agents stand to the wider institutional and social auspices under which they act.

The example that has been used here – the Irish famine of the 1840s – has one disadvantage in that it does not as clearly illustrate as some others might the full complexity of the exchanges that take place when *two* or more coherently organized societies or institutions are engaged with one another. It may be useful, therefore, to characterize such situations a little more fully and especially to draw attention to the way a society that is involved in such transactions has to make judgments of the nature and import of the actions in which the other society is engaged in its regard and to do so from the standpoint of the undertakings in which it is itself engaged. At the same time, the society so judged will be forming from its own standpoint *its* judgment as to what the first society is or is not doing; and in both cases some actions will be predicated upon the judgments so formed – actions for which the belief that the other society is acting in a certain way serves as an essential premise. To these actions there will then correspond other actions that are similarly based on the part of the other society. A sequence of actions of this kind is one which may very appropriately be called a dialectic since in it each action responds to another which is imputed to the partner in the exchange, and it creates a new situation to which the latter then has to respond itself. As in conversation – the original model for the concept of dialectic – there is no guarantee that the partners involved in such a series of exchanges will understand one another correctly, but a response that is based on misunderstanding is no less a term in a dialectic than is one that is based on an accurate understanding. (Identification of such a move as one resting on a misunderstanding is, of course, itself a distinct matter and in relationships between institutions probably presents greater difficulties than in a conversation between individuals.) It should also be understood that a dialectic can be one of cooperation or of conflict or of some mixture of the two; and it may be one that is itself cyclical in nature, that is, is often repeated and thus familiar on both sides, or it may be one for which past experience offers no satisfactory model.

If one thinks of the history of a society as its sequence of movements through an option-tree, then the dialectical aspect of this movement would have to be represented by a kind of interlacing of the branches of two or more such trees. This means that, if at any given point a society conceives itself to have a number of alternative courses of action before it, each of these will have to be understood and evaluated in terms of the possible responses it might call forth on the part of another society. The situation produced by a society's choice of a certain alternative course of action will in other words be itself modified in some more or less significant way by the choice made by another society in the new situation produced for it by the action of the first society. The latter will thus find itself in a situation involving a new set of alternatives – a situation which is the result of the sequence of its own action and the response which that action met on the part of another society; and in this way the two (or more) societies move one another forward through an option-tree that belongs wholly to neither of them and place themselves at choice-positions which they would not have chosen for themselves and which they could not have predicted with any very great degree of accuracy. Relationships of this kind have been intensively studied from a formal point of view within the theory of games; and the goal of these studies has been to construct a normative theory of rational choice under conditions of conflict and cooperation as well as under conditions of certainty and uncertainty. My suggestion is that the concept of dialectic can be most profitably interpreted as a sequence of situations conceptualized in this way – situations which follow upon one another in time and which produce one another in such a way that neither party is in full control of the outcome at any given stage. I would also argue that the business of the historian involves in a quite central way the reconstruction of actual and particular sequences of this kind. If that is true, it is obvious that the concern of the historian is quite different from the normative intention of the games theorist and that he is making use of a conceptualization of historical situations which is very similar to that of the games theorist for purposes that are primarily descriptive and explanatory rather than normative. Whether *any* normative character at all attaches to the historian's use of such concepts is a question which must be deferred.

These considerations offer an opportunity to correct a serious misconception to which my discussion of the historical process as a dialectic of action may give rise. This is the tendency to suppose that such a conception must have the effect of rationalizing the historical process to a quite unrealistic degree by representing human beings with their goals and beliefs as being somehow in the driver's seat and in control of their fate. Since such a picture would strike most people as quite unrealistic, the inference may be drawn that in order to do justice to the irrationality and lack of freedom that characterize our situation as historical beings we must give up the whole intentionalistic conception of history to which this erroneous picture is apparently due and adopt instead some theory of history in which impersonal laws and forces represent the severe constraints under which we actually live. In fact, however, the "unfreedom" of man as a historical being is something which the dialectical conception I have been proposing is uniquely well-suited to express and it does so in a way that avoids the semimythological tendency of many accounts of historical forces. It is a prime assumption of that dialectical approach that, while human beings are indeed the sources of the intentions by which their actions are identified, they have neither the knowledge nor the power that would enable them to control the consequences that are produced by these actions. Even actions that do not have a human vis-à-vis, as for example clearing the land to raise crops, may have unintended consequences such as erosion which human beings may be helpless to arrest but with which they have henceforth to contend. The consequence of an action can thus be to restrict or otherwise change the range of options which one would otherwise have had, and successive actions may modify the latter still further so as to produce a cycle of adjustments that moves farther and farther away from the goals one had originally set oneself. When there is a human vis-à-vis, his reactions are likely to be even more unpredictable and uncontrollable and their effect can be to compel me to choose between alternative courses of action, all of which are deeply unwelcome. In this way human beings can and do imprison one another; and it is not surprising that human history as a whole has often struck observers as a grandiose act of self-frustration on the part of mankind. But if we are thus coerced by history it is important to remember that this coercion has an intentional structure and that it is as the result of our actions and those of others in dialectical interplay with one another that the only alternatives we have are so often self-defeating. This kind of coercion with its complex intentional presuppositions is very different from the kind that is simply a function of the fact that we are finite and mortal beings; and it seems to me that it has a good title to be regarded as the historical, as distinct from the generically human, form of unfreedom.

I have been arguing that the *kind* of limit which human beings impose upon one another is comprehensible only within the intentional and dialectical framework that has been outlined above. At the same time, however, one must not forget that none of these limitations would be more significant in our lives than is a checkmate in a game of chess if it were not for the role that force and violence play in the real-life dialectic of societies. When we speak of actions and counter-actions and of the complex network of assumptions about the attendant circumstances of these actions and the possible responses with which they will meet, it must be remembered that the ultimate mode of contestation of our actions is that of force, which thus becomes a kind of implicit coefficient of every action that a society undertakes. Nor is it difficult to understand why this is so. Even when the firmest and most equitable understandings govern the allocation of whatever advantages may be pursued by various competing societies, the possibility always remains that one or more of these societies will not be prepared to live with its share; and the alternative of a resort to violence for the purpose of achieving its goals can never be finally foreclosed. In its collective form, such a resort to violence takes the form of war; and it is not just some misguided preference on the part of bellicose historians which has made so much of human history a history of war. Once the kind of social organization that makes war possible is in existence and the availability of war as the ultimate form of action is established in the human repertory of responses, it dominates all the relationships of societies with one another in a way which no one has as yet found a way of significantly modifying. For even if a given society is pacific and reasonable in its mode of life, it cannot simply ignore the fact that its neighbor may be very differently disposed so that a war may have to be fought in order to remove a threat to its existence. In such relationships as these the possibilities of misperception and misinterpretation by one society of the actions and intentions of another are almost infinite and the fact that such enormous issues are at stake is not likely to make the parties concerned more amenable to reconsideration or revision of their estimates. The dialectic among societies is thus one in which violence is always in the background and the survival and the well-being of each society is at stake. This is not to suggest that political and military aspects of the life of a society are more interesting or worth-while than others but that they constitute the instrument of a kind of change of absolutely vital importance to all the interests of a society. To recur to the image of the life of a society as a combination of cyclical and linear forms of movement, a good argument can be made for the view that the new element in the situation of these societies – the element that requires a response and thus touches off a sequence of situations no one of which is stable – is typically the existence of another society that is at once a threat and an opportunity and that the nuclear history of these societies is the dialectic of violence in which they are involved. There may have been many things in both Rome and Carthage that were more admirable and more worthwhile than their capabilities in the area of national orga-nization and political and military activity; but if, as seems evident, all of these depended upon the outcome of the struggle between the two "superpowers" of the Mediterranean basin, then the history of that struggle was indeed the central history of Rome and Carthage for almost two centuries.

The discussion up to this point might seem to suggest that the ingredients in a choice-situation for a society consist of certain fairly specific goals toward which it can move by one or more routes which then have to be evaluated in terms of likely responses which they may elicit from other societies. This is true as far as it goes, but it leaves out altogether a dimension of such situations that is of the greatest importance for a historian. This is the element of tradition understood as a corpus of norms, interpretative principles, and background beliefs of a great variety of kinds which any society builds up over time and which it brings to new situations that arise and which are interpreted for purposes of action in terms of the affini-ties they show to one or another of the categories that are the precipitate of past experience. A tradition in this sense – a highly developed example would be that of the Roman curia – is presumably a set of formulae, some of which are general in form since they cover classes of cases and indicate how they are to be inter-preted and what form the response to them should take, and of others that refer to particular historical events which are the paradigm cases or the precedents or the confirming instances for the general rule of judgment and action that is to control a given situation. Insofar as it embraces explicit references to past cases in this way a tradition represents a kind of extended historicity that goes back farther than the beginning of the particular episode in which a society may be involved at a given time. Thus, if the society in question were the Roman church and it were involved in a jurisdictional struggle with a particular Christian monarch, the rele-vant portion of the tradition would include past cases of such struggles together with whatever lessons of wider application had been learned from those cases. These past cases would thus have an important role in identifying the kind of contest in which the church was engaged at the time and in projecting certain ways of dealing with it. In this sense a tradition is, as H. G. Gadamer has pointed out, a body of "prejudices" or anticipatory judgments of an event or situation, and these judgments would encompass the nature and range of the alternative modes of response to a given type of situation. It is quite possible that the range of responses so defined might not be the same as that embodied in the tradition of the society to which these responses are to be made; and it is also possible that this difference might be the source of serious misunderstanding between the two societies.

At the same time as tradition so conceived is an element within the dialectic of societies as described above, it is itself characterized by a form of change that is itself dialectical although in a somewhat different sense than that discussed previously. As a tradition is projected forward onto new cases which it assimilates to its available categories, it undergoes modifications which go beyond the mere addition of new confirming instances. If the new cases are very different from those that have arisen before, it will be possible to maintain a sense of continuity with the past only by modifying somewhat the respect in which this case and previous cases may be said to be "the same." This tendency will be reinforced by the attrition that a tradition undergoes in the course of its transmission from generation to generation. For a new generation that knows that more recent and (I am supposing) deviant cases well and the earlier "standard" cases only by report, this contrast of what is standard and what is nonstandard is likely to reverse itself with the result that the present case instead of being just barely incorporable into the tradition generates backward lines of continuity and sameness that capture the earlier cases or most of them but along a subtly different axis of identification. Since a premium is often set on the maintenance of continuity with the past as such, the fact that the mode of recapitulating the experience of a society has changed, and with it the respect in which continuity has been putatively maintained, will not normally be emphasized if indeed it is grasped at all. Such a process of change within a tradition is itself a kind of dialectic since in it a past understanding of past events is modified by an understanding that is, as I have said, projected backward out of a present that is importantly different. Of course, there is in this case the very important difference that his temporal location makes it impossible for one partner in such a dialectic to respond to this reinterpretation that supervenes on his original "statement;" and there is also the further difference that the fact of reinterpretation and change in the present is not objectified as such by those in the present who are in fact responsible for it.

At a later stage in the life of a society changes in a tradition become dialectical in a fuller sense. The temporally prior partner in the process of interpretation and reinterpretation cannot, of course, ever respond to the response that is made to him, much as we might like to know what Bach would have thought of Mozart and Shakespeare of Dickens. What can and does happen is that reinterpretation is eventually recognized for what it is and even assumes explicitly critical forms. In general, the relationship to tradition becomes much more self-consciously free and with this freedom comes a willingness to pick and choose and to appropriate elements in a tradition without any feeling of being obliged to reproduce it in its entirety. In its extreme forms this emancipated consciousness generates its own "tradition of the new" and often explicitly denies any meaningful continuity with the past; and in these circumstances it is the fact of residual continuity that becomes unconscious rather than that of change through implicit reinterpretation as previously. More generally, once tradition and departure from tradition become established as terms of thought that are available for self-understanding, a wide range of uses to which they can be put opens up; and, as Professor Pocock has shown, there are complex dialectical relationships among these.

An example of the two kinds of dialectic – the dialectic among societies and the dialectic of a society with its own tradition – is offered by a recent book by William Bouwsma, *Venice and the Defense of Republican Liberty*. The period under consideration in this study is the Italian Renaissance and the protagonists are in effect three cities, Florence, Rome, and Venice. Each of these is characterized by reference to the broad tradition of thought and practice relating to the conduct of civic affairs and these traditions are shown to reflect assumptions of quite different kinds about the nature of human society, the scope and proper function of human reason, and the locus of political and ecclesiastical authority. Rome is, of course, identified not only with the universalistic claims of the Catholic church which in turn go back to those of imperial Rome, but in the later sixteenth century it also represents the Counter-Reformation and the international effort to re-establish throughout Europe the authority of the *Respublica Christiana*. Florence, by contrast, is the city of the Renaissance par excellence in which a quite different conception – pluralistic and in important respects secularistic – of society and political authority had developed and been given effect in the institutions and political consciousness of the city. These two cities are thus presented by Bouwsma as defining themselves through their opposition to one another in a dialectic that is at once a matter of opposing beliefs and of very concrete political and military struggle. Venice, to which the central role in the book is assigned, is described as an independent republic without a strong tradition of political consciousness that would have committed it to one side or another of the struggle between Florence and Rome. But in the course of the mid-sixteenth century Venice is shown to have experienced a kind of awakening of political consciousness with the result that she took up the role of Florence within the Italian political world, after the latter's crushing defeat by imperial forces in 1529. As a result, Venice increasingly came into conflict with the claims of the papacy until the decisive struggle provoked by the interdict of 1609. This transformation of the political stance of Venice was at once a development in the domain of political thought and in the area of political action where a new party – *the giovani* – emerged as the bearers of this new orientation of Venetian policy. Bouwsma's claim is that in both areas the example of Florence was of great importance and that the result of this internal Venetian dialectic was to place Venice in a posture of opposition to Roman policy that was in its essence a continuation of the role Florence had played. The Italian political world of the sixteenth century is thus shown to be a field of force organized around three societies which define themselves both positively and negatively by reference to one another and which define themselves in terms of a tradition and a conception of their own past which they also, as in the case of Venice, are able to revise.

IV

The second thesis which I have undertaken to defend states that it is a condition of the kind of continuity I impute to historical narrative that the actions in question be identified under the descriptions which their agents and patients may be supposed to have used. Clearly this is a claim which flows quite directly from the conception itself of human action which has been set forth in the preceding discussion. In that conception the relationship of an action to its environment is in the first instance one which it stipulates itself through the organization of its situation which it effects. In other words it confers on some element in that situation the character of an "obstacle" or an "opportunity" in the light of the goal it proposes; and when this action is itself complete, the situation it will have produced becomes the occasion for another redescription in the light of the practical concerns of some other agent. The guiding assumption here is, thus, that the relationship between human agents and their environment and among such agents themselves is to be understood on the model of the practical inference; and from this it follows that the historian must be in a position to reconstruct these practical inferences if he is to understand the sequence of events in which they provide the principle of continuity or colligation.

There is a set of issues, much debated by philosophers of history, that have to do with the epistemological difficulties that are sometimes thought to be posed by this requirement; but these matters will be taken up in the next chapter. My concern here is with the role such descriptions and redescriptions play within a developing narrative and not with the mode of the historian's access to them. The nature of that role can perhaps be best suggested by drawing attention as Kenneth Burke has done to the "dramatic" character of history and to the "unending conversation" which it constitutes. This analogy is one which should need no explanation after the discussion in the last two chapters that was intended to bring out the semantic character of the actional events with which history deals. The point of this discussion was not, of course, to remind the reader of how much of history literally consists in the talk of the agents involved nor was it to suggest that the historian's first obligation must be to reproduce that talk as though he were a glorified court reporter. The point was rather that all actional events, whether they are accompanied by any form of public discourse or not, must involve an element of implicit discourse in which the significance of relevant events and states of affairs is determined from the standpoint of certain predominant interests and concerns on the part of the agent, and various possible courses of action are evaluated in terms of their consequences as they bear on those interests. This process might be described as an encoding of the elements in an action situation in terms of their practical significance through the assignment to them of positive and negative values reflecting their eligibility in the light of the norms, interests, and knowledge which the agent brings to this situation. The claim that is made by my second thesis is that when a sequence of events is actional in the sense described and thus involves this kind of practical construal of events and circumstances on the part of the agent as a necessary preliminary to action, a historical narrative of those events must reconstruct the agent's descriptions wherever it is possible to do so or at the very least present the materials which enable the reader to do so. Otherwise the narrative will not be in a position to delineate the relationship in which these actions stand to one another and its continuity will be broken.

In defending this thesis I am not for a moment denying that there are other ways of describing such sequences of events which abstract from the contexts of practical concern reflected in what I have called the agent's description. It is always possible to describe any event and the changes which it brings about in an idiom which carries no implications (or at best very faint ones) that relate to any purposes that may be achieved or partially achieved or not achieved at all through the change which these events bring about. When the consequences of the action are thus described in a way that abstracts from any larger system of purposes within which it may be situated, they may be called the "natural consequences" of that action and in the simplest cases these will be physical changes. Even such actions as a political assassination can after all be described in terms of the movements of the bodies of the persons involved, the action of the pistol, the trajectory of the bullet, its impact, and so on, and generally in such a way as to abstract entirely from the purposive and actional character of the event and thus from its identity as an assassination. It is quite another matter to describe an action in a way that relates it, positively or negatively, to the achievement of some purpose. In the example just used, the initial description "political assassination" was clearly of this type since even this summary designation indicates the capacity in which the victim became the target of the bullets which struck him and also suggests the general area in which the more specific ulterior purposes of the assassins are to be sought. From another point of view this same act or its consequences might be described as a threat to constitutional government in a given country or in some other way, depending on the context of purposes and intention within which it is envisaged. No one would describe an action in this way unless either he or someone else had a practical stake in it one way or another and had projected further goals of action that would be influenced one way or another by it. A purely contemplative observer of such events and their consequences would lack the indispensable context of purposes and concern that is characteristic of human commentators on the consequences of action. Again, if human beings were solitary and isolated creatures and if the resources of the earth that supplied their needs were not in scarce supply so that competitive relationships became inevitable, there would be no reason for us to evaluate the consequences of the actions of others in terms of our own practical concerns since ex hypothesi they would be most unlikely to make any difference. But as things are, we are thrust into one another's company; and since we compete for so many of the same things, what one of us does has fateful consequences for the undertakings of others. The character and consequences of an action, considered from this standpoint, may be called "practical;" and the description they receive reflects the interests and thus in some sense the decisions and choices of the agent whose characterization it is. As has often been pointed out, the difference between these two modes of description – "practical" and "natural" – is closely comparable to the difference between, on the one hand, the accounts that would be given of the actions or moves of the players in some rule-governed game by persons who are familiar with these rules and can appreciate the point of a particular maneuver, relate it to a certain strategy for "winning," or detect the opportunity it creates for an opponent, and, on the other hand, accounts of those actions given by persons who are not familiar with the rules of the game, who do not know what constitutes winning or losing, and who must therefore describe what they observe simply in terms of the physical movements made by the players.

There is however another mode of characterization for human actions that goes beyond their "natural" description and treats actions as actions and yet appears to have almost as little to do with the agent's intention as those just discussed do. I have in mind here certain actions that are tightly circumscribed by social conventions and rules. If for example I buy an automobile or fire a subordinate or vote in an election, the nature of my action is defined by a multitude of socially accepted conventions and understandings; as a result, a characterization of my action as, e.g. a purchase can be taken as self-sufficient and as not standing in any further need of characterization in terms of my intentions. It may be acknowledged that I probably had such intentions – for example, a desire to impress my friends by a show of affluence – but these will be treated as being my business and the public meaning of my action will be regarded as the one given it in its legal definition as the purchase of an automobile. Of course, I can be assumed to have known what I was doing when I purchased the car and I could certainly be said to have intended to purchase a car; but just because this fact is taken to be so obvious as not to require notice except in some unusual case, as for example if I were to believe I was renting a car when I was really buying one, this kind of intention is, as it were, swallowed up in the public definition of my action. Certainly, if after buying a car without any apparent misunderstandings on either side I were to say that I had intended to rent the car and not buy it, the public definition of what I in fact did might very well take precedence over my claimed intention. All of these considerations thus seem to reduce the intentional aspect of my act to the status of something private and peripheral and thus to confirm the view that such intentions need not be centrally involved in the explanation of an action and to make the latter appear a more eligible candidate for a position in the kind of explanation that treats it as a compact unit without the complicating affiliations that belief and intention carry with them.

The important thing to notice in such cases as these is that the diminished importance of intention is brought about by elements within the action-situation itself taken in its full social context. For social purposes it is extremely important that it be possible to abstract on certain occasions from whatever intentions a person may have had and to be able to identify what he did as an action of a particular socially recognized type on the strength of certain public criteria of what counts as an action of this type. In these contexts the only relevant intention of the agent is the intention to perform an action of this publicly recognized type. Outside such well-defined situations, however, we may be much less certain how to describe what a person has done; and in such cases we will normally be much more willing to treat intentions as having the kind of constitutive role in the action in question that has been attributed to them in this book. It is also important to recognize that even the intention that we feel is too obvious to require mention because it is so firmly imbedded in a well-established social routine remains an intention nevertheless and that these very routines would not be possible if it were not the case that human beings can understand the conditions defining the actions of which they are composed and can perform them "intentionally." Beyond that, if history, as I have argued, is a mixture of actions that are incorporated into such social routines and those that in various ways break out of the latter, one would expect that the apparent importance of intention would vary a good deal within its domain. On some occasions, the only relevant intention may be the one that is implicit in the public description of the action itself; in others much more attention to the individual agent's beliefs and desires will be required. Neither kind of case should be treated as the model to which the other must be forcibly accommodated; nor should the "public" character that attaches to the former be misinterpreted in a way that removes it from the special context of shared understandings in which it comes into being. This "publicity" is in other words a very useful abbreviation or standardization of the intentional dimension of human action, not a substitute for it.

These observations must now be related to the thesis set forth above according to which narrative continuity is essentially dependent upon the descriptions agents use for the actions that they (and others) perform and upon the beliefs and intentions that are implicit in these descriptions. Once again it will be useful to take an example from an actual historical text that illustrates this principle of continuity. The example is drawn from Hubert Jedin's *History of the Council of Trent* and it has to do with the entente concluded in 1545 between Pope Paul III and the emperor, Charles V. In essence this was an agreement between the two to wage war jointly against the Protestants in Germany. At the same time the pope announced the postponement of the opening of the Council of Trent, although he was very reluctant to take this action. Jedin explains that he took this step nevertheless because it was thought that the opening of the council might provoke a Protestant uprising in Germany before the emperor was in a position to deal with it; and he characterizes the pope's position more generally in the following terms:

> Paul III, on his part, concluded the alliance in the spirit in which every modern statesman enters upon similar compacts, viz. for one definite purpose, none other, in fact, than the overthrow of the Protestants. It was not his intention to issue a blank cheque out of sheer benevolence. The thought of yielding on any point in which the interests of the Papacy and his responsibility as head of the Church were at stake did not enter his mind for a moment. He never really trusted Charles V. He was prepared to do what he could in the hope that by means of the ultimate, bloody instrument of war the disrupted unity of the Church might yet be restored. It was this higher consideration that induced him to consent to the postponement of the opening of the Council. What a heavy burden he thus laid upon its presidents and its members was to be seen in the coming weeks and months.

The emperor's view of the arrangement he had made with the pope was, as Jedin points out, quite different. In his estimation,

> The alliance did not do more than restore the normal conditions which corresponded to his wholly medieval conception of the Christian commonwealth of Western nations and of his own position as its secular head. He had always resented the Pope's policy of neutrality and his

support of the "disturber of the peace" and "the friend of the Protestants and the Turks" as a violation of what he regarded as the normal political situation in the West. The feature of the alliance against the German Protestants to which he attached perhaps the greatest importance was the resumption of close collaboration with the Pope. The suggestion that what he proposed to the Pope implied nothing less than the pontiff's subordination to his plans, hence the sacrifice of his independence, would have appeared absurd to him. In his eyes victory over the disturbers of the established order in Church and Empire was also a triumph for the Church.

This passage illustrates many of the features of historical narrative to which attention has been drawn in the course of this chapter. It is clear, for example, that neither Paul III nor Charles V is represented as acting in his capacity as an individual human being but rather in his capacity as the occupant of an office and the head of a vast institutional structure whose interests he is concerned to defend. These institutional interests are themselves grasped by their representatives in historical terms and in terms of the traditions established within each of these institutions that define its proper relationship to the other. Each of the principals also has a view of the intentions of the other which he substantiates by references to more recent history and the policies followed by his vis-à-vis in the many-sided struggles of sixteenth-century Europe; and in both cases the predominant feature of these reciprocating estimates is distrust and a sense of interests that, although ideally harmonious, are in fact incompatible. But even though their interests as leaders of two great institutions were indeed very different, it is also clear from this passage that the conclusion of an alliance was adequately motivated on each side by the short-run and long-run goals in terms of which pope and emperor interpreted the practical import of events. Nevertheless, in the pope's case, the conclusion of the entente involved a very real sacrifice in the form of a postponement of the opening of the council and he had in effect to weigh the desirability of a prompt opening of the council against the danger of a Protestant victory in Germany with the unreliability of the emperor with his quite different ideas about the proper position of the Church in relation to imperial authority always in the background of these deliberations. Finally, there is an allusion at the end of the passage to the untoward consequences that were to be produced by the delay in the opening of the council; and this reference illustrates the constraining influence of past upon future action that was discussed in the preceding chapter.

Now if we concentrate on the two events mentioned above – the pope's forming an alliance with the emperor and his postponement of the opening of the Council of Trent, is there any way in which someone who was not in a position to reconstruct the "logic of the situation" as it emerges from the foregoing characterizations of the intentions and belief of the pope (or of "the papacy") could establish a connection between the one event and the other? According to Jedin, the pope agreed to postpone the opening of the council because he was convinced that otherwise an uprising might occur which could frustrate the purpose for which he had entered into the alliance to begin with, that is, the purpose of defeating the German Protestants. If he had not had the goal or if he had not held this belief about the possible consequences of opening the council as scheduled, the second event – the postponement of the council – presumably would not have occurred at all, and so it seems fair to conclude that the postponement was decided upon precisely *as* a means to prevent an uprising. This is what is meant by saying that this belief was integral to the agent's description of his own action and not that the description, "postponement of the opening of the Council of Trent," somehow magically carries within it a conceptual linkage with the description, "means to prevent an uprising of the German Protestants." Under the former description alone the action the pope took would have been unacceptable to him since he had the strongest reasons for wishing to get the work of the council under way. But under the second description which presents that unwelcome action as being also a means to another goal of vital importance, the action was one that the pope saw he had to take. The net effect of all this is a new practical encoding by the pope of several events in terms of their means-end relationships to one another. The historian's narrative account of these events, moreover, is essentially borrowed from the terms in which this encoding takes place and without the latter he would be left with the blank fact of temporal sequence between the two events, that is, with something much more like a chronicle than a narrative.

It is, of course, true that historical narratives contain a great many events that are not related to one another within practical syllogisms like the one I have implicitly attributed to Paul III; and not all of these are the natural events whose status in historical narrative I discussed in the last section. They are typically consequences of the actions that have been decided upon through such practical reasoning. Sometimes these are at least partially foreseen as were the negative consequences of the postponement of the opening of the council which, in the pope's mind, presumably centered on the continuing weakness of the Roman communion in the face of theological attack as long as its own dogmatic position had not been authoritatively redefined. In the account Jedin gives, this certainly very unwelcome consequence of the postponement is represented as being in effect accepted by the pope as an unavoidable cost associated with a decision which on other grounds he felt obliged to take; and to the extent that this was the case one can say that these consequences were drawn into the perimeter of his practical deliberations. But the more common case is that in which consequences are produced that no one may have envisaged in advance or assigned a place to within their way of setting up their own action-situation. Nevertheless, if these consequences are significant enough to merit inclusion in a historical narrative at all, one must assume it will be because they were to have a place within the practical construal of the situation on which subsequent actions, whether by the same agent or by another, were based. They will in other words provide the reason or part of the reason why such a subsequent action took the form it did. Such an unintended and unforeseen consequence of an action will, moreover, have to be taken into account by the historian in just that aspect in which it assumes this practical significance. The point is thus not that the practical calculations of human agents set the limits to the domain of fact with which the historian must deal, but rather that what escapes even such putative control by human agency – and a very great deal does – is reintegrated into that domain of agency whenever it has the kind of significance that qualifies it for inclusion in a historical narrative at all.

It was noted above that in the case of the pope's action in postponing the council there were two descriptions of his action, the one simply as a postponement and the other as a means to another end. It would be misleading to leave the impression that since narrative is dependent for its continuity upon descriptions like the latter, the former are somehow ideally eliminable from it. Not only is this not the case but action-descriptions like the former play an essential and often predominant role in such narrative. This is in the first instance due to the obvious fact that unless such descriptions were included one would not know *what* action had been performed. But the point here is a little more interesting than its obviousness suggests. It is that we would not know what had been done unless the action were described in a manner that conveys its public or socially identifiable character. I have commented above on the way certain rule-governed action-descriptions appear to abstract from whatever intentions their agent may be supposed to have had in performing them; and while my point in doing so was to argue that this elimination of intention is not to be taken at face value, it is also worth noting that this public or neutral mode of characterizing actions can also be found in historical narrative. Contrary to a good deal of what has been said on this subject and often from a standpoint congenial to that of the present study, the historian's description of actions does not normally require any form of impersonation of or identification with the agent in question. There is, in other words, not a full stop in the narrative while the historian as it were slips into the situation and into the intentions and beliefs of some historical agent; if this were the normal procedure it would constantly generate difficulties of the kind that are encountered by the reader of *Mrs Dalloway*, who must search for events that figure in the conscious life of distinct characters and are yet, like the tolling of Big Ben, unmistakably the same event. Instead, the historian for the most part takes up his position in a zone which is coextensive with the territory mapped by the knowledge, interests, or descriptive vocabulary of the agents concerned, but he has to survey it in a quite different manner. There is in fact a prima facie obligation for the historian not to accept any agent's description of his own action just as it stands since these descriptions often conflict and the espousal of one of them would make it impossible for him to accept and thus do comparable justice to the descriptions of the same events offered by other agents. The sheer plurality of agency makes any simple strategy of associating himself with an agent's system of descriptions impracticable for the historian. Where the same event can be set within more than one context of practical interest and is thus a candidate for sharply contrasting descriptions, the conscientious historian will typically try to cast his own initial description of the event in question into an idiom in which it would be at least recognizable to all the agents involved. For example, if he were describing the event in recent American history known as the Saturday Night Massacre, he would presumably not begin by saying either that Nixon was attacking the principle that the president is subject to the law of the land or that he acted to frustrate the schemes of a Kennedy-inspired clique in the special prosecutor's office, even though one of these statements might be true. Rather, he would say something to the effect that the president ordered one attorney general and then another to fire Archibald Cox, the special prosecutor, and that he was finally dismissed.

All of this may make it sound now as though the hallmark of the historian's mode of description were precisely an avoidance of the agent's description rather than the positive concern to reconstruct that description which was imputed to the historian in the preceding discussion. It might almost seem in fact that on the view I am proposing now the historian must pitch his description to the highest common denominator of description he can find among parties in conflict and that in some cases this requirement might have the effect of actually pushing his description down into the domain of the natural as distinct from the practical consequences of an action. That, however, is not what happens. Normally there will have been a prior account of the interests and goals and character of the agents in question which enables the reader to carry out a practical encoding of the elements in the action-situation and thus to place the action taken in an intelligible relationship to those goals. Sometimes the task of reconstructing such a practical inference will not be as straightforward as it sometimes is and the historian then intervenes directly to supply the missing steps. In both cases, however, the result is that the narrative moves back and forth between levels of description of a given event, one of which is concerned with what might be called the "brute facts" of the matter and the other with the same event under the descriptions that express its practical significance for the agents involved. It is of course by no means certain that the first kind of description can always be found without dropping below the level of descriptions that have any real relevance to a historical understanding of what occurred. It can happen that the disagreements between two parties are so profound that they extend to almost every description that might be offered of an event that involves both of them. But fortunately this does not always happen and when it does not, the historian is in a position to move in the manner described from a relatively neutral description of an event to the descriptions expressing the various forms of practical significance it has for the parties concerned. These descriptions are not thereby espoused or endorsed by the historian himself; they are rather imputed to their sponsors in the historical situation itself. But this does not mean that they are presented simply as opinions about an event which is objectively described only in the neutral language of the historian. As has been emphasized repeatedly, these practical descriptions are themselves part and parcel of the event with which the historian is concerned and they supply the essential element of colligation without which the event would stand isolated and unexplained. The objectivity of the historian's initial description is not the result of abstracting from the agents' descriptions as such but rather of fixing on elements that are common to all these descriptions and that can thus serve as a public term of reference to these events for those — the historian and his reader among them — who at least at this stage are concerned to learn what happened without thereby necessarily committing themselves to a particular partisan view of that event. Whether it is proper for the historian to assume any other more directly evaluative posture toward the events he recounts is a matter that will be taken up in the next chapter.

One other source of resistance to the role assigned here to the agent's description in the constitution of a narrative deserves at least passing attention. This is the strong feeling of suspicion that is often directed at "official" declarations of the reasons for some action that has been taken and at the "ideological" considerations to which these often appeal. To some extent this feeling may spring from an unwillingness to believe that the representatives of institutions ever really believe what they say, even when they say it in private. Such a view is naive to the extent that it rests on the assumption that unless such official persons "mean" what they say in some subjectively sincere way what they say does not mean what it seems to mean; and this is surely a mistake that is due to a failure to understand the independence of an institutional role from the personality of its incumbent. Misguided though it is, moreover, even this view of the public world would not license the historian to abstract altogether from the way an agent fits his actions into some larger practical design. If it were inspired by such a view as I have just outlined, the belief that there is a very different sort of alternative to such explorations as Jedin's of the actional logic of a situation is likely to be at the bottom a belief that the strategies which the historian discovers when he penetrates behind the screen of ideology conform to some basically very simple and universal logic of self-interest and that this is so powerful an explanatory tool that it dispenses the historian from the necessity to occupy himself for very long with the rhetorical dress which self-interest puts on for its public appearances. But whatever the degree of plausibility of this view – in my opinion not very great – it should be obvious that even the narrowest kind of self-interest has a means-end form of organization and that when one seeks to reconstruct a sequence of action that is assumed to be motivated in this way one can hardly afford to disregard information that casts light on the way the agent conceives the self-interest he pursues and how he perceives the means by which such ends can best be achieved.

V

The third thesis with respect to historical narrative set forth above was the claim that the explanatory function of narrative is discharged through a teleological ordering of the historical materials which is modeled on the practical inferences of the historical agent. Since the import of this claim has already been very extensively developed in the course of preceding discussions, it seems unnecessary at this stage to add to what has already been said by way of further characterization of what this teleological ordering involves. The underlying thought is simply that human action sets up its own form of continuity over time which it is the responsibility of the historian to retrace and that this continuity has a logical character that accrues to it through the agent's description of the goals and circumstances of his action.

Chapter 6

M. C. Lemon

THE STRUCTURE OF
NARRATIVE

What is a narrative?

W E WILL NOT GO FAR WRONG in equating a "narrative" with a "story," so long as we are not immediately insistent that a "story" is something with a beginning, middle, and end, in such a strong sense as to sustain its overall coherence. Perhaps the archetypal story is of this character, but not all stories begin on a new dawn and end with a satisfying completeness. Many, as we finish the last page or watch the last scene or film-roll, are simply adjourned; they are nonetheless stories. Alternatively (to concede to the strong sense of the term), they are incomplete, unfinished stories – but they remain *stories* for all that, rather than something else. And what makes them stories is that they are purposeful accounts of continuous events. It is true there are many types of story, one of the major distinctions being between factual and fictional ones. But what enables us to subsume them all under the term "story" is that at the minimum, and necessarily, they assume the narrative form. They narrate events.

Put another way, we can say that because *any* kind of story is necessarily structured on events ("happenings," "actions," "changing situations"), then its form of discourse must be capable of communicating events, of saying "what happened." That form of discourse (for there is only one), is *narrative*. The term denotes that kind of discourse which has the form or structure, "this happened, *then* that," or "this was the situation, *then* that occurred." Despite the obvious ubiquity and apparent simplicity of this form of discourse, reflection reveals it has epistemological implications of such complexity that they threaten to be intractable. Rather than approach the matter a priori, let us first raise some questions about the construction of stories as we conventionally know them.

Stories and chronicles

Stories are of course constructed by human beings, and obviously for a wide variety of reasons, ranging from the simple (for instance, the moral fable, the excitation of a few basic emotions, the joke), to the increasingly complex (as in most good literature, drama, and film-making). Further, some stories are purely fictional, others purely factual, whilst many combine both fact and fiction. Some are told in order to answer questions, others in order to raise them. In short, we should remark upon the flexibility of the story-form to suit an impressive variety of purposes. Yet in all cases the form remains the same at root – "this happened, *then* that" – whereby events, situations, or actions are presented as succeeding each other in such a manner as to appear to "follow on." The story "develops," "progresses," "evolves" – whatever term we use, we mean to indicate an essential continuity in a sequence of events.

The case is different with a mere chronicle of events, for a chronicle is a kind of calendar. It lists events (or other data) in the order of their dates. For example, one could produce a list of every Act of Parliament ordered (sequentially) according to their dates; or one could chronicle the offspring of a family over the generations. Insofar as their succession in time is the sole principle underlying their manner of presentation, it would appear continuity is the essence of the matter in the construction of a chronicle – and if so, then the chronicle is the narrative in its starkest, hence purest, form. But of course this is not the case. A chronicle's "continuity" is merely abstract, superimposed by the purely formal rationale of the numerical ordering of dates; it is a meaningless continuity. Put more formally, the chronicle is structured in terms of "this (then) that," whereas the narrative is structured in terms of "this *then* that." In the narrative form, the "then" has a peculiar, distinctive significance which transforms a succession of events into a meaningful sequence. Insofar as this transformation is somewhat mysterious and yet is the heart of the matter, it cries out for explication.

When we offer someone a story, a narrative account of "what happened" – it might be the story of the Falklands War or of my friend's arrival at the cinema late, soaking wet, and penniless – we cannot but structure this discourse in terms of a sequence of events. But unlike in a chronicle, this structuring is done intentionally by us, for our purposes, rather than being formally imposed by the anonymous requirements of dates succeeding each other. Our structuring is meaningful; it manifests the reasons we have in doing it; it constitutes a rationale. A computer can produce a chronicle, and do so more quickly, accurately, and hence efficiently, than can a human being. But only human beings can produce stories, because only they have reasons for doing something, whereby they endow what they do with meaning – and in proportion as that meaning is communicated by means of the story form, the story is more or less intelligible. At the minimum, intelligibility is the criterion of success for the construction of a story. It has to "make sense," whatever else it might also achieve.

How is it, then, that to put events into a sequence can *of itself* be to construct meaning, to communicate intelligibility? And *what* is made intelligible by the very form of narrative? The chronicle is a "sequence" but is not intelligible. It might imply a story; one might infer an intelligibility from or in it; but its form is not in itself meaningful. What is happening in a narrative which makes it so different?

Narrative explanation

First, then, *what* is explained by means of the narrative form? Mundanely enough it is already clear that, at the minimum, it is the nature and occurrence of events presented "subsequent" to "prior" events (or situations or circumstances). To present an event as "subsequent" to a "prior" event is to do more than narrate the event – it is to say why it happened. And the way we do this is to preface the statement that "x happened" with the term, "*then*". But this term must be meaningful rather than merely formal. "He began to feel the cold and then closed the window," is an example. Not only do we know he closed the window; we know why. He did it "because" he felt the cold. Alternatively one could say, "he closed the window because he felt the cold" – that is, narrate an event and then add its explanation, rather than use the narrative form to provide it. Thus on the face of it both statements mean the same thing despite the former taking the form of narrative, and the latter the form of analytic discourse. If they amount to the same thing, we can say the kind of explanation is identical despite the different forms of discourse. And insofar as to say, "this happened because of that," is to suggest a simple causal model of explanation, we could conclude that the kind of explanation inherent in narrative is causal. Were this so, there would be no special virtue, nor singularity, in writing factual narrative rather than straightforwardly causal explanations.

However, it is wrong to equate the kind of explanation achieved in narrative with causal explanation, even in the above example of "feeling the cold and then closing the window." Yet the difference is more a matter of intimation than of logic. To state, "he closed the window because he felt the cold," is to intimate the exclusion of alternative explanations; in intimating that his feeling the cold "caused" him to close the window, it is dogmatic. In other words, the mode of discourse structured in terms of "this happened *because* of that" is strongly suggestive of that mode of (causal) explanation employed by the natural sciences, whereby the necessary interdeterminations between natural phenomena are displayed, construed as the product of "laws." In short, to employ this mode of discourse is to intimate the human "behavior" under scrutiny is a "reaction" to "stimuli."

Those who take this view of human conduct may or may not be correct – at present the only point is that the narrative form of discourse does not bear the same dogmatic intimations. When we say, "he felt the cold and then closed the window" ("this happened and *then* he did that") we are leaving him some elbow-room to have behaved differently; nevertheless, elbow-room only, since we wish to account for his subsequent action as indeed his "next" action by using the term, "*then*;" that is, we wish to render his conduct intelligible, and this places parameters to what he can (intelligibly) do "*next*" (that is, subsequent to feeling the cold). He may have turned up the heater, or put on a cardigan, or left the room, or chosen to suffer the cold. But it would not make sense to present his "next" action as playing the piano, or standing on his head, or coming home from work.

In short, the narrative form presents his conduct as a response to situations rather than as the effect of causes, because it is intelligible to us in terms of our more or less hazy, or systematically reflective, view of "how the world works," especially of the factors which influence (but do not *determine*) human conduct. Now it is true the very form of narrative thus begs the question, "is human behavior a caused reaction or an intelligible response?" The form of narrative reflects the latter position (and in so doing is replete with tautology), but does not argue it. It is simply the most universal and therefore appropriate form of explanation adopted by those who, reflectively or not, draw a line (usually at the point where human beings are involved) between causally deterministic explanations of events and those which leave room for "human freedom," "human motivation," or "human reason." As a mode of explanation it is inherently "messy" for philosophical or scientific purposes. It lacks the coherence of a philosophy because it does not examine its premises – indeed, when exposed, the assumptions regarding "the way the world works" may vary so much that they are found to be contradictory. And it lacks the coherence of science for similar reasons – namely, it does not subsume events under tried and tested "laws" of causality, determinateness, and inevitability. Further, it lacks the *objectivity* of science insofar as its explanations depend perhaps just as much upon the way the narrator understands "the way things work" as upon the objective events available for verification. But at the moment none of this matters; the overriding point is that the narrative form *is* explanatory. It is necessary to identify it as such, and analyze how it works. Evaluation is a separate project best undertaken only after the topic to be evaluated is thoroughly understood.

What, then, can be said so far regarding narrative as a mode of explanatory discourse? It does not seem to offer an understanding of events as determinately caused. Rather, it seems to achieve an understanding in the sense that the reader can see an action as an appropriate response by an agent. He can say, "given that such-and-such was the situation at point *a* in time, I can see why the agent did *x* at point *b* in time." Certainly he could have done things other than *x* – for instance, *f*, *g*, or *h*; but he could not have done *m*, *n*, or *p*. Or at least, if he *had*, the action would be unintelligible to the reader. He would be unable to imagine why he did it, given the narrative so far. What this demonstrates, as already indicated, is that the narrator assumes a certain credulity in his readers. If the event in question is, "he closed the window," it is sufficient to say he did this subsequent upon feeling the cold. Thus the narrator is assuming, either himself and/or on behalf of his readers, certain notions about the way individuals behave. Whether he admits it or is even aware of it, he is implying a "theory" about individuals and about the world in general insofar as he selects (and omits) data on the basis of assumptions about what is reasonable, predictable, or appropriate for their conduct in different contexts.

Narrative, then, assumes a general theory about human conduct, meaning by this not an explicit, specific theory but a set of assumptions about how people behave and how the world works, which may even be contradictory. And the writing of narrative is itself a potent bulwark to these "ordinary," conventional assumptions since, if it does not establish them, it certainly reinforces them. They are not, then, derived from any particular theory – for instance, Marxian, or Freudian – but are taken to be common to all people of a similar culture, received through tradition, experience, and indeed the writing of history and fictional stories. To the extent these assumptions are thus unexamined rather than the product of reflection, some would argue they are the worst kind upon which to base any explanation or understanding. Hence we arrive at a claim encountered earlier – namely, that if there is such a thing as "narrative explanation," it is a weak, naive, and unreflective kind of explanation for the purposes of precise historical work.

But although a fuller refutation of this critique must emerge from deeper examination of the logic of narrative, we can even now retort that a mode of explanation which focuses upon human beings as responding agents rather than reacting animals, nor again as god-like masters of their conduct, can hardly be called weak. Moreover, that this mode of explanation does not need articulating on each occasion through explanatory and analytic discourse but is actually embedded in a *form* of discourse exclusive to itself (viz. narrative), suggests that narrative explanation is sophisticated rather than naive. Finally, as to its being unreflective let us for the moment at least concede that, whilst reflective theories come and go in profusion, it has stood the test of time all over the world.

I have argued up to now that the basic form of narrative is, "this happened *then* that;" that to put two occurrences as contiguous to each other is to achieve a kind of intelligibility; that in the absence of any extrinsic purpose governing the narrator's inevitable selection (and hence omission) of events, intelligibility is achieved through the economic establishment of continuity (viz. "*a* to *y* minus 1"). And what this amounts to is that the establishing of continuity is not only a necessary condition for the intelligibility of any kind of narrative, but can also be a sufficient condition. The latter is the case in "narrative for its own sake." Not only is this crucial relationship between continuity and intelligibility somewhat mysterious, but such is the pertinence of this case to our overall enquiry that it cries out for elaboration. This leads into an area of philosophy replete with paradoxes – namely, the concept of *change*.

Continuity, difference, and change

Of two things we treat as distinct from each other, we say they are "*different*" things. Mr Anon is a different individual from Mr Brown. They are different phenomena. "This differs from that," is the basic formulation of the logic of "difference," and we note that in no sense is temporal sequence relevant. Now suppose we perceive a thing at two points in time; at point 1 it is yellow, and at point 2, blue. Are we perceiving two *different* things, time again being irrelevant? For instance, in June we saw our neighbor's car, and it was yellow; in July we saw our neighbor's car, and it was blue. Is the June car a different car from the July one, or are we dealing with just one car which has changed (that is, has been resprayed)? Has our neighbor got two different cars or has he changed the colour of his car, such that we can say the car is the same one at points 1 and 2 in time, but that it has changed? In the absence of any further information we cannot say whether the two things in question are different things or whether it is the same thing which has changed. Are we dealing with a different thing, or with a changing (or changed) thing?

It is not hard to imagine circumstances where the answer to this general problematic is of practical as well as intellectual importance. Is that my girlfriend of years ago or someone different? Is this document a different will, to be invoked in alternative circumstances, or are you changing your will? Do these statistics indicate a different economic situation or has the recession simply changed its direction? Is marriage a dead, or a changing, institution?

One thing, then, differs from another thing; but a thing is said to "*change*" when it *now* differs from what it *was*. It is not a different thing – it is the *same* thing which is different now from how it was then; that is, it "has changed." As for the paradox, "how can it be the same thing if it is now different?," the reply is simply that in some respects it *is* different, but that in others the observer regards as dominant it is not different, such that the thing in question has not assumed a new identity. And as for the paradox, "can a thing change so much that it becomes a different thing?," the reply must be that it indeed can, inasmuch as a thing may be judged in the mind of the observer to have changed in respects which are dominant or "essential," such that it is now a different thing rather than one which has changed. But even here we can still say of the new, different thing, that it *was* the previous thing, whereas this cannot be said of two things which differ from each other at the same point in time. For instance, as we heat some water we say it is still the same water, although now different in some "inessential" respects (that is, its volume and temperature). But when it boils we say we are now confronted by a different thing, namely, steam. The point is, however, that unlike saying this water here differs from that oil there, we can say this steam here differs from that (previous) water, but it used to be that water.

This highlights that if the temporal sequence into which a thing or state of affairs falls is irrelevant to it, then it is difficult to see where the concept of "change" figures in anything we say about it. In short, if to say a thing differs is to say it changes, and to say it changes is to say it differs, then this is tantamount to saying change and difference are identical, which is nonsense. A thing differs *from* something else, whereas a thing changes *over* time. When a thing differs from something else, time is irrelevant. When a thing changes, however, time and the continuance of the single identity are essentially relevant. By "continuity," then, we do not mean the static persistence of a state of affairs, but something persisting through changing states of affairs. Thus it is as well to reserve the term, "persist," for changeless states of affairs and employ the term, "continue," for situations involving a sequence of occurrences where a thing changes (over time).

This brief exploration of the threateningly paradoxical concepts of difference, change, identity, and continuity, has prepared the way for an important general proposition regarding narrative; namely, what is common to all narrative is that continuity is a necessary condition of its intelligibility, and this demand for continuity itself generates a demand for an identity or "subject," which in its turn must undergo change.

In addition, the clarification of these principles affords further insight into what narrative explains, and how. Narrative is structured on what happened *next* – ("this happened *then* that"). We know there could be any number of "nexts" – today's scientists can measure time in millionths of a second – but where there is no extrinsic purpose or message to the narrative governing what to choose as "next" in terms of *relevance*, what is selected is that event or state of affairs penultimate to that which does *not* "follow on from," or can "reasonably" be construed as subsequent to, the initial situation. This – "*a* to *y* minus 1" – preserves continuity, and hence intelligibility. It supersedes mere chronicle (which is meaningless), because it endows the term, "then," in the formula, "this then that," with a power it lacks in the mere ordering of events according to dates. By saying a thing happened *next*, we know why it happens. However, the formula does *not* explain why it happens *next*. Neither does it explain why *it* happens rather than something else which might equally "reasonably" have happened next.

It is, then, confirmed as an "indeterministic" mode of explanation, and as noted is perhaps peculiarly defensible when dealing with human affairs – and therefore of special appropriateness for the historian, as will emerge. What we can say straight away, however, is that where the historian employs the narrative form, that form of itself imposes the above limitations on his scope for explanation – or, put in a positive light, allows him the freedom or "open-endedness" of explanation appropriate to human affairs. From the opposite side of the fence we can note the narrative form does not commonly appear in discourse regarding the (solely) physical world, nor in those sciences which seek to explain aspects of reality construed as consisting solely of material objects and states of affairs. Hence we again encounter the recurring intimation of some special link between narrative and the world of human beings. Pursuit of this intimation not only proves its validity but also reveals further principles underlying the narrative form which add to its significance.

Narrative agents

The considerations which throw light on this adumbrated connection between the narrative form and the specifically *human* world derive from what has already been uncovered regarding the need for "continuity" in a narrative, the manner in which that need generates the demand for something which "persists" through "change," and the way in which "explanation" is implicit in the logic of narrative structure. Given these principles, the question arises as to whether *anything* can constitute this "something which changes" in a narrative, or whether there are inherent constraints. For example, apart from a person, can a town, make of car, or even "*the* car," provide the focus of a narrative? Can an activity, such as wine-making, or governing? Can a religion, or a country?

On the face of it the answer to all these cases is yes, since not only can, for example, "the story of Birmingham" be told in common-or-garden terms, but there are numerous professional factual stories – called, indeed, "histories" – of cities, paintings, activities, universals such as "the motor car," and of such complex phenomena as "the British Empire" and "Christianity." However, we should note the story of Birmingham only becomes a *story* when the script ceases being simply a description of that city at successive points in time – that is, a chronicle – and achieves some continuity by Birmingham at one point in time being linked to Birmingham at "the next" point in time, such that one gets a sense of *change* (for instance, expansion, recession, or modernization). Now, at all such points we note the involvement of people who make things happen. The same is the case with, for example, "the story of the motor car" – it stops being an unintelligible succession of model names and designs only when individuals such as entrepreneurs, financiers, engineers, and designers play a role as agents.

Putting the matter a priori, if all we do is describe Birmingham at one point in time and describe a Birmingham different in some respects at a later point, then so far as we know we are presenting two different states of affairs unrelated to each other in time – and this is to give none of that special force or significance to the term, "*then*" (or "*next*"), which lies at the heart of narrative structure. Rather, for these two otherwise merely *different* states of affairs to be intelligibly connected into one *changing* state of affairs, there must be a *reason* why Birmingham is now different from how it was.

Now Birmingham, this piano, or that car, cannot change themselves – that is, make themselves different from how they are. As (merely) physical objects they cannot effect or do anything. They can only suffer being acted upon. They cannot change themselves; they can only be changed. And if the most we can offer as, for instance, "the story of Birmingham" is, "this happened to it, and then that happened to it," and so on, then we are confronted by a (necessarily unintelligible) chronicle of discrete happenings where what occurs next (or "*then*") is an arbitrary choice of the chronicler rather than the painstaking discovery of intelligible continuity by the narrator.

What narrative requires, then, is agents which are active, which, in responding to states of affairs, are *responsible* for their temporal sequentiality, thereby binding them together as, in fact, the *same* state of affairs changed (for a reason). Only thus are narrative's interrelated conditions of change, continuity, and intelligibility secured – and in *factual* narrative this points to the necessity for the agents to be *human* because, for it to be possible to employ the narrative form, there must be a reason why "this happened *then* that." So far as we know, only human beings (with the possible exception of animals), "have reasons" for what they do – or put another way, a necessary condition of *action* (as distinct from mechanistic "reaction") is "having a reason" to do something. Narrative, then, requires agents which have reasons for behaving as they do. In each case, this "reason" can only be the agent's reason, not someone else's. In other words, the agent must be self-moving, must generate its own behavior; and one of the perennial themes of philosophy is that it is precisely this capacity which distinguishes human beings from all other known phenomena.

Now, whether one agrees with this last proposition regarding the uniqueness of human beings or not, what is clear is that, in requiring subjects capable of reasoned agency, inanimate objects or abstract universals cannot play this role in (factual) narrative. In short, it is as impossible for "Birmingham," "the motor car," or "wine-making" to be the subjects in a narrative as it is for "blueness," "silence," or "intelligence." We are confronted by categorical distinctions on a priori grounds. Another way of demonstrating this is to develop these arguments where they imply a distinction between "scientific" and narrative explanation. This is all the more necessary since it may be objected that things do properly "change" *without* the agency of human beings. For example, "Mount Vesuvius erupted, and then (or 'next') Pompeii was engulfed in ashes," or, "the red billiard ball was near the pocket, then the white ball struck it, and the next thing was that the red ball rolled into the pocket." In other words, does not "science" frequently use the narrative form to convey an intelligibility to natural sequences rather than present them as meaningless chronicles of differing states of affairs which "happen to occur" at different points in time?

In reply it must be conceded that events where human agency is absent can of course be linked together in terms of "prior" and "subsequent" – namely, when we talk of *causal* sequences; *a* causes *b*, *b* causes *c*, and so on. This can be expressed as "*a* happens, then *b*, then *c*." Thus these different events or circumstances are genuinely related in time, such that the term, "then," in "*a* happened then *b*," is not merely formal as in a chronicle. Indeed, the concept of temporal succession is crucial, for *b* would not have occurred at all if *a* had not happened first.

But this is also where a difference is apparent between the narrative form and the relating of a causal sequence. In the latter, what happens "next" (or "then") happens necessarily, and happens necessarily "next;" "*a* caused *b*," or, "*a* happened, then *b*." The occurrence of *b* rather than of something else is (construed as) necessary, and its "nextness" is (construed as) literal rather than some events intervening between *a* and *b* having been omitted. In the narrative structure we have already noted that in saying, "he did this then that," *why* he did "that" rather than something else is not explained, nor why he did "that" *next*. All that is explained is "why he did that" (namely, "because" he had "just" done this). In a causal sequence, however, why *b* rather than *x* happened (next) *is* explained, and also why *b* happened *next*. Further, that what happens next in a causal sequence must occur *literally* next is crucial, for where *a* causes *b*, which causes *c*, which causes *d*, and so on, every moment of that sequence must be recounted to preserve intelligibility. In short, *a* does not cause *d*; to say, "*a* happened then *d* ," would not make sense. In a narrative, however, we have already observed a different principle at work, where what is presented as happening "next" is not presented because it *is* literally next, but because it precedes a situation which could not (conventionally) be construed as "next." The narrative is structured in terms of "*a* to *y* minus 1," whereas causal sequences are structured in terms of *a*, *b*, *c*, *d*, and so on.

The clarification of this fundamental difference in structure and logic between the narrative form and causal sequences (albeit one more intimated in, than articulated by, the ordinary use of language) thus helps substantiate (factual) narrative's need for agents which, in turn, must be *human*. All a causal sequence requires is a starting point; for instance, a thunderstorm, which (then) causes a flooding river, which causes the collapse of a section of river-bank, which causes the local otters to move habitat. Nowhere does a subject figure in this sequence, such that it is difficult to see how the concept of continuity is relevant. Rather than being taken through a changing situation, we are presented with a number of different, discrete situations, and are told what caused each. But there is nothing which persists throughout the causal sequence to allow the notion of one ongoing, changing state of affairs. The case is entirely different where we are taken through the various situations engendered by Mr Anon's agency in the world as he, for example, mends his fence. Urged by his wife to get on with it, he looks at the sky to check the weather, fetches his tool bag, studies the fence, digs away its crumbling supports, discovers he has misjudged the kind of brackets needed, changes his clothes, and goes down to the shop to buy the right kind. In this sequence of events or different situations, each is related to a *selected* "prior" event in terms of being an intelligible response by an agent who "has a reason" for what he does "next." To present this as a causal sequence in the strict sense would be absurdly difficult, involving exhaustive detail regarding each action the man took and relying on any number of laws of, for instance, physiology and psychology under which to subsume the causes at work.

The easy way out of these difficulties, of course, would be to treat the man's reason for doing something as a cause. But even were one to countenance this, it is to add something crucial to the notion of causality which it properly lacks in scientific discourse. Where a sequence of events can be explained causally – that is, be subsumed under general laws – human reason or response plays no part, and there is no "story" to be told.

Finally, we may be reminded of the manner in which in ancient times certain especially important or relevant sequences of natural events were made intelligible, not through particular causal explanations (of which they were ignorant), but by being made into stories. What this essentially required was a subject, or agent, who responded to situations, who had reasons for doing things; namely, one or other of "the gods." In this way what we now understand as causal sequences of events – for instance, terrible natural disasters, the origin and spread of plague, the geographical dispersion of species, and the revolution of the seasons – were converted from discrete states of affairs merely happening to succeed each other in time into an intelligible continuity where what occurred happened as a response by an "agent." In such a way did ancient myths make certain events meaningful, which is another way of saying they made events intelligible by presenting them as "meant" by a reasoning subject. However much we may scorn such explanations today, we must concede that their form, given the presence of familiar gods, had integrity. Where the form fails lamentably in its explanatory potential is, as Spinoza noted, where events are explained by referring them to "the will of God," God being inscrutable. What he castigated as "truly, a ridiculous way of expressing ignorance," we might gloss as "an abortive approach to narrative explanation."

Thus although the ordinary use of language can indeed disguise the differences in both logic and structure between causal and narrative explanations, analysis reveals their distinctness from each other, and perhaps no more pointedly than where the narrative form is demonstrated to necessitate, not merely agents, but (at least in factual narrative) *human* agents at that.

Narrative explication

Thus far, enquiry into narrative as an explanatory form of discourse has revealed the need for continuity, change, and agency. Further analysis of these interrelated conditions of the intelligibility of narrative has revealed that, for them to be met, the agents or subjects must be human beings, and this helped substantiate the recurring surmise that (factual) narrative explanation is somehow peculiarly appropriate when dealing with human affairs.

There is, however, a further and different sense in which the narrative form "explains" things, which we must now examine to do full justice to its explanatory potential. The foregoing has treated of the manner in which the narrative form explains *why* (what I have indifferently called) the separate "events," "states of affairs," or "happenings" *within* a narrative sequence take place. Now, to say why a thing happened is to *account for* its happening, and this is precisely one of the meanings of the term, "explain." But to "explain" a thing can also mean to make a thing intelligible – that is, to show its meaning – and where it is important to distinguish these different senses then the latter can be more closely denoted by the term, "explicate," meaning to "develop the notion of something," or to "unfold" or "make explicit the nature of something." Now it is in just these terms of being *explicatory* that there is an additional sense in which the narrative form is explanatory over and above its ability to account for things happening. What, then, is this additional "explicatory" sense in which the narrative form, of itself, achieves "explanations"?

In first distinguishing narrative from both descriptive and analytic discourse, we noted that what is immediately clear is that narrative is the form used to articulate "things happening." As put initially, the only way to articulate "something happening" is to narrate it, and this involves relating states of affairs into prior and subsequent, suggesting a genuine sequential interdependence. But this analysis has nevertheless kept silent so far about precisely that crucial ingredient, "things *happening*." What exactly is this link between narrative and "things happening"? Narrative feeds on "things happening." We can put states of affairs into a sequence of prior and subsequent but our analysis has already intimated that no *narrative* is involved unless something *happens* to make this link intelligible. Further, narrative feeds on explaining *why* things happen, through its formula, "this happened, *then* (or *next*) that happened." So necessarily is this an achievement of the narrative form that it is more correct to say narrative feeds, not on things happening, but on things happening "next." Nevertheless nothing can happen next if nothing happens in the first place, so there remains an obvious sense in which "things happening" is as important as things "happening next" for narrative to be possible at all.

This same problematic can be revealed in less abstract terms. To use an earlier example, we can talk of a "happening" such as someone getting out of bed, and intelligibly link this with a subsequent happening – for example, "he got out of bed and then put on his slippers." Insofar as there are now two happenings linked sequentially, we are engaged in the narrative form. However, as we follow subsequent happenings such as getting washed and then going downstairs, we recognize that all these sequentially linked happenings can, precisely insofar as they *are* linkable, be conceived and expressed as one happening – namely, "he got up" (after which, the "next" happening might be, "he had breakfast"). Are we, then, confronted with one happening, "he got up," or a sequence of happenings, "he got out of bed, then put on his slippers, then went to the bathroom and washed," and so on? In the latter case the narrative form comes into play, but not in the former case where we simply state the single happening, "he got up." In this former case his "getting out of bed" is simply an (implied, or conventionally understood) part of "getting up."

The same problem also extends backwards in time, for if "getting out of bed" can be seen as merely part of a "larger" happening – namely, "getting up" – then "getting out of bed" can itself be seen as constituting a "larger" happening made up of a sequence of happenings such as, "he moved his left leg to the side of the bed, then raised himself up on one elbow, and then put his left leg on the floor." Thus from both directions it becomes increasingly obscure as to whether, in talking of someone "getting out of bed," we are treating of one happening or of several in sequence – and if the latter, then *which* sequence?

Thus the distinction between "things happening" and "things happening *next*" seems elusive, even paradoxical; and so long as this remains the case the apparently obvious link between the narrative form and "things happening" must remain something of a mystery. Is the narrative form structured around things happening, or around *sequences* of things happening? Or do both amount to the same thing? How is it that a happening can be made up of other happenings, somehow connected, possibly *ad infinitum*? Or can we safely talk of happenings as if they have beginnings and endings? And if they do have such parameters, how do we proceed to nevertheless link up happenings which have "ended" with subsequent happenings, such that despite "endings" some kind of continuity is preserved?

In short, we will not attain a full understanding of narrative logic whilst such basic questions remain, and it is all the more important to pursue them since only such an investigation can set out what I have referred to as the "explicatory" potential of narrative. We need, then, a further grasp of the logic, grammar, and semantics of "happenings," and for purposes of exposition it is now necessary to find terms which will enable the pursuit of that elusive distinction within "happenings" to which I have just alluded. In order to make relevant distinctions which avoid unnecessary jargon, I will use two terms which are otherwise indifferently equated with "happenings" – namely, "occurrences" and "events" – but give them a narrower compass than has been necessary so far in this exposition.

Occurrences

There are occasions when the only way to say "what happened" is to give a "blow-by-blow" account – for instance, "the boy ran into the barn." There are other cases, however, where we can summarize "what happened" by using a single term, such as in "a theft took place" or "an avalanche occurred." What happened blow-by-blow is not spelt out, but a general term replaces an account, and the only verb required is (indifferently) one denoting the *general* condition of *anything* happening – that is, the theft "occurred," "happened," or "took place." In the former (blow-by-blow) case, however, a particularizing verb is used, as in "the boy ran." This draws attention to *verbs* in relation to the logic and grammar of what we have repeatedly pointed to as the business of narrative structure; namely, "things *happening*."

In dealing with "objects" or "things" we use nouns. A noun denotes a thing – "thinghood" is articulated through nouns. This noun rather than that one denotes this rather than that thing – for example, "a cat," meaning "any cat." Individual nouns, then, denote individual universals; and in the course of Chapter One we went on to draw a number of implications regarding the nature of "things" and the manner in which we "perceive" them or find them meaningful. In analyzing "occurrences" a parallel treatment is salutary for the sake of clarity.

Thus: in dealing with "occurrences" we use verbs. "Occurrings" are articulated through verbs. An individual verb denotes this rather than that kind of occurrence

– for instance, "to fall," meaning any falling. Thus, individual verbs denote individual universal occurrences; for example, the verb "to fall" denotes a class of occurrences, otherwise discrete, for what they have in common.

It is clear from this that "occurrence in general" is, so to speak, an irreducible datum. One may define as many individual verbs as one likes – (that is, specify what kind of occurrence is denoted in each case) – without getting any closer to breaking down into analytic form what "occurrence in general" is. That we experience the world in terms of occurrences is a given, as also is our experiencing it in terms of objects, qualities, and properties. Or at least, these matters are "given" in relation to the grammar of the respective modes in which we articulate them. Thus, although occurrences are articulated through verbs, that there are "occurrings" perhaps remains impenetrable.

The case is different, however, when we deal with individual occurrences. Here, the verb used tells us what *kind* of occurrence we are dealing with – for instance, to fall, estimate, love, dissolve; and we have only to consult a dictionary to find the meaning of these verbs. It tells us what *kind* of occurrence a verb denotes, as in, for example, the various meanings of "to swim;" "1. Float on or at surface of liquid; 2. Progress at or below surface of water by working legs, arms, tail, webbed feet, fins, flippers, wings, body, etc.; 3. Appear to undulate or reel or whirl, have dizzy effect or sensation; 4. Be flooded and overflow with." What the dictionary does not, need not, and cannot tell us is in what sense "to swim" (in any of its meanings) is an occurrence rather than, for example, an object or a quality. Rather, in drawing attention to those particular features which assist in distinguishing an individual kind of occurrence from others, the definition of a verb invariably involves other verbs, as is clear from the example just given. And the only relevant considerations here are the same we suggested regarding "things" or "objects" – not, then, "do trees really exist?," or, "do objects in general really exist?," nor, "do things really swim?," nor, indeed, "do occurrences actually occur?," but, "how far is this individual kind of occurrence a relevant abstraction from the world of occurrences in general, and how reliable and workable is it?" And just as nouns denoting things can come and go and change meaning, so can verbs, as with the emergence, for instance, of "to commute" (*re* travel). Again, just as with nouns denoting objects, verbs denote occurrences ranging from the precise, as in specialized contexts such as law – "conveyancing," "arraigning" – to the vague – "to go," "to move." Finally, different cultures can find different "occurrings" worth individuating; for example, German has the verb, "*spazieren*" and French, "*se promener*," whilst English has no equivalent individuation but makes do with phrases such as "to go for a walk," or "to take a stroll."

A further parallel between the world of objects and occurrences is worth pursuing, for it concerns the intelligibility of "occurrences." In relation to objects, it was argued earlier that the meaning of a noun (for instance, "chair"), manifests the reason we have for abstracting and individuating the object denoted; in that sense, objects are "meaningful," "reasonable," or "intelligible." Just so with occurrences. The intelligibility of an individual kind of occurrence (for instance, "falling"), is conveyed by nothing other than the definition of the verb denoting it, which exposes in what ways it is meaningful to us – or put another way, exposes the reason we have for abstracting and identifying it. Hence, just as "the reason this object has legs is that it is a chair, and all chairs have legs," so "the reason this is going down is that it is falling, and all things which fall go downwards." In this way we revert to the point that an individual occurrence (articulated by a verb) is made intelligible through other verbs – that is, through refining and differentiating it from other kinds of occurrences – but that "occurrencehood" itself is not thereby made intelligible. It remains a given – the ground, so to speak, of individual kinds of occurrences. *Their* intelligibility is specific to their definitions rather than being derived from some prior principle underlying the intelligibility of "occurrence in general."

Sufficient has been clarified, I hope, to sustain an observation which is both important and paradoxical; namely, although narrative is the form we use to tell of "things happening" or of "what occurred," and is essentially structured in terms of "this happened *then* (next) that" – involving concepts of time, continuity, change, *et. al.* – nevertheless the fundamental nature of occurrences is nothing to do with time, continuity, or temporal succession. An individual occurrence is articulated through an individual verb, and we have seen its intelligibility derives from the meaning or definition of that verb. But the meaning of an individual verb – that is, the intelligibility of the particular kind of occurrence – is *not* spelt out in terms of "this happened *then* that." This is the form narrative demands, but it is not the form of occurrences.

Thus, contrary to what we might expect when analyzing the world of events, or of "things happening," where we know we are dealing with one thing happening after another, what nevertheless lies at the core of this world (namely, the individual occurrence), is not intelligible in terms of temporal succession, or "this *then* that." Although it seems difficult to conceive of "time" when nothing happens, or conversely of something "happening" where time does not enter into the matter, this is nevertheless the case in this area of analysis. In dealing with occurrences we are not, unlike in a narrative, dealing in a "this *then* that" context. For instance, "to swim" is, after all, in one of its meanings, to "float on or at the surface of liquid" – no "then and now" is either stated or implied. If, then, one "is swimming," the explanation of what this means in no way rests upon the notion that one is doing this and then (or next) that. It is true "swimming" may *involve* doing one thing and then another in a purposeful sequence, as it does in another of its meanings, "to progress at or below surface of water by working legs, arms, tail, webbed feet, fins, flippers, wings, body, etc." – but this is to explain *how* to swim rather than what it *means* to swim (just as in our earlier example of "getting up," where it *involves*, but does not *mean*, "getting out of bed, washing," and so on). Time, change, continuity, and temporal succession are not relevant to the intelligibility of this occurrence. But they are the heart of the matter when it comes to the intelligibility of a narrative. Hence, and in short, we do not narrate occurrences; occurrences are not made intelligible through the narrative form; they are not structured narratively; they are not "narrative identities."

Finally, in discussing "occurrences" there remains the particular, "actual" occurrence; for instance, "the boy ran into the barn." Here our task is that of articulating *this* particular occurrence, akin to identifying *this* particular cat. This particular cat is identified by describing it – that is, stating what is particular rather than essential about it as a cat. Similarly with occurrences. In stating "the boy ran into the barn" we articulate not only the general kind of occurrence in question (by using the verb, "run"), but also what is particular about this instance of it. As such, we are *describing* this or that occurrence when we say, "the boy ran into the barn." Again, neither time, continuity, change, nor temporal succession enter the matter. It is not essentially a "this *then* that" context, despite appearances. Thus with a particular occurrence, we state it; we do not narrate it. To say, "the boy ran into the barn," is not to tell a story. The intelligibility of that particular occurrence is derived from principles entirely different from those we have set out as underlying the constructing of narrative.

Thus the question arises, what *does* narrative achieve if it is not the form in which we either define or describe "occurrences"? If narrative does not make occurrences intelligible, what *does* it make intelligible? The answer to this emerges from what can now be understood more clearly – namely, that although narrative neither defines nor describes occurrences, it does link them together. Indeed, occurrences are its essential ingredient. It is occurrences, in the stricter sense in which I have used the term, which narrative links up in its basic structure, "this *happened* and then that *happened*," or "this *occurred* and then that *occurred*." If nothing occurred, narrative would be impossible. Equally, if only one thing ever occurred, again narrative would be impossible. Narrative does not articulate particular occurrences, then; rather, it articulates something else *by means of* ordering occurrences sequentially in an intelligible manner. Thus we can state, "the boy ran into the barn," but this is to describe a single occurrence. We only begin a narrative, begin "telling a story," when we add a ("the") subsequent occurrence – for example, "the boy ran into the barn and then climbed into the hayloft."

Thus the formula, "this *then* that," can be given proper precision by extending it to, "this *occurred* and then that *occurred*," thereby making it clear that narrative is the form whereby we articulate, not occurrences, but the *ordering* of occurrences. Hence the connection between narrative and occurrences, between narrative and "things happening," is evident. To state, "the boy ran into the barn and *then* the boy was blue-eyed," does not make sense; nor, "the boy ran into the barn and *then* the barn belonged to Farmer Brown." Necessarily in every case, what is "next" or "then" in the narrative form must be an occurrence rather than a circumstance, state of affairs, or situation. Similarly regarding that which is "prior" to the "subsequent" occurrence – it must also be an occurrence. "The boy was blue-eyed and *then* ran into the barn," does not make sense, nor, "the barn belonged to Farmer Brown and *then* the boy ran into it."

Narrative identities

Narrative, then, links occurrences to one another in terms of "prior" and "subsequent." But, as already observed, this formula does not simply put occurrences into the temporal order in which they occur – indeed, in the teeming world of occurrences such a task seems beyond human ability and also peculiarly pointless. Rather, narrative links them up so that (or insofar as), they follow on from the "prior" to the "next." And we have already gone some way in exploring how this is worked and what is achieved – namely, the explanation of why the "next" occurrence took place. But this does not exhaust the function of the narrative form, for it would imply that the *sequencing* of occurrences (which it essentially constitutes), is no more than an abstract by-product, of no relevance to actuality – or put another way, to view narrative orderings of occurrences as merely (one) way in which we explain discrete occurrences is to lose that ordinary sense in which a narrative or "story" can have a completeness which, if cut short, leaves one curious to know, not what happened next, but what happened "in the end." And both observations amount to suggesting narrative can achieve something unitary in itself, over and above being the vehicle for explaining discrete occurrences.

Let us recall the salutary fact that narrative has to be narrated. It is not so much, then, a question of "what narrative can achieve," as of "what do narrators achieve by narrating a sequence of occurrences?" Insofar as they are narrating we know they are not chronicling occurrences but linking them up into an order which makes sense. And this is not a difficult thing to do; indeed, both the perceiving and the constructing of intelligible sequences of occurrences is a universal, instinctive human characteristic. By comparison, the production of some kind of chronicle is a painstaking, deliberate, artificial contrivance with far less immediate and obvious point to it.

People can tell or make stories, then, with an easy facility. We have already remarked in general terms upon the variety of purposes served by telling stories. In the case of fiction it was urged the story-teller must have some purpose beyond simply that of putting invented occurrences into an invented (albeit intelligible) order. And it was pointed out that the factual story-teller *may* share the same purposes. In the case of the discipline of history, however, our attention is focused on the exploitation of factual narrative solely for its informative and explanatory possibilities – that is, for the sole purpose of achieving and conveying knowledge. And the question we are approaching is, knowledge of *what*? When stripped of the numerous extrinsic purposes to which it can be put, what is it in general terms that narrative informs us of, and what is it that it explains in addition to why "things happened"?

There is an agreeable sense in which no special mystery looms here, inasmuch as ordinary language suggests that what narrative achieves is a story – narrative conveys knowledge of "a story," and closer analysis does not refute this. As we have seen, narrative links occurrences into an intelligible sequence, into an *order*; narrative orders occurrences intelligibly or meaningfully. Now this would remain an empty tautology – "it is an order because it is intelligible, and it is intelligible because it is an order" – were it not that "an order" of occurrences is, so to speak, an actual phenomenon. It has a unity, a particular identity; or at least this is what is proposed through the narrative form. Now, what is "a story" other than "an order" or sequence of occurrences? And what is this to say other than that "stories" articulate a distinct class of phenomena in the world; that is, that just as we perceive objects and occurrences as "real" things in the world, so we perceive "story-objects" as real things in the world? From a virtually infinite number of occurrences happening at a virtually infinite range of temporal points we extract or abstract lines of continuity. We posit some *real* sequential relationships within an otherwise undifferentiated, meaningless flux of occurrences happening at different times. This ordering of occurrences is proposed as constituting an identity in itself, over and above the discrete occurrences contained in it. This implies the ordering of occurrences achieved by the narrative *form* is itself the *content* of that form — that is, this specific form is the form of a specific content which has its own identity or unity. Hence, the contents within a narrative (that is, occurrences), are not the content the narrative itself constitutes. As Spinoza argued, dealing in the same general problematic when differentiating between *natura naturans* and *natura naturata*, a system can be more than a mere "thing of reason." It can, if it is a real system, be a unity — that is, constitute what we might refer to as an "organic unity" over and above, but inextricably determined by, its parts.

A story or narrative, then, is more than the sum of its parts. Its parts are occurrences, and intelligibility *within* a narrative relates to "the reason" for its occurrences, intimated through the "this occurred and *then* (or 'next') that occurred" formula. But insofar as something unitary is achieved through this formula we have yet to see in what sense a "story-as-a-whole" is intelligible. That is, there are two kinds of intelligibility with respect to narrative — that contained *within* it (which I have termed its explanatory potential), and that constituted *by* it as a whole, which I term its *explicatory* potential. In examining this latter, we are thus not concerned with how "this *then* that" is meaningful, but with how a *"this"* (this story-as-a-whole), is meaningful or intelligible. In short, narratives do more than show occurrences following on from each other — they articulate meaningful overall entities.

Hence the full understanding of the narrative form, especially in terms of its overall explanatory characteristics (often so glibly denied or under-estimated), must involve grasping in what sense this class of phenomenon — namely, the story as an entity in itself — is meaningful or intelligible. Now, if seeing a narrative as an entity in itself involves seeing it as more than the sum of its parts, the other side of the coin is that this involves seeing the entity it articulates as something distinct both from *other* kinds of entity, and from other "story-objects." To constitute a distinct identity it must have parameters, and to ask what these are is to ask in what sense a "story-object" or "narrative identity" is a meaningful or intelligible phenomenon. By analogy, we not only know what kinds of things make up a "city," we also know where the city stops and something else (even a different city), begins. Moreover we know a city is not a quality, nor an occurrence. Likewise we need to understand what principles underlie the distinction between one "narrative identity" and another, and the categorical distinction between "narrative identities" and objects, qualities, and other such classes of phenomena.

What, then, is the nature of the unitary identity the story-form articulates? Or put the other way around, in what sense is a story a unity? Clearly, the "identity" involved is that of an order or sequence of occurrences, and it is as well to point out straight away that the integrity of the entities articulated through narrative varies in different cases. Some stories articulate more strongly parametered phenomena than others. By analogy, we have seen the world of objects, and of occurrences, exhibit this same characteristic — respectively, "a building" articulates a vaguer object than "an abattoir;" "to move" articulates a vaguer occurrence than to "arraign." Reference to this analogy points to those same cardinal principles of the intelligibility or meaningfulness of any class of phenomenon — namely, relevance and workability. The case is no different respecting narrative entities. The narrator is the articulator of real lines of continuity between occurrences; he perceives them as "there" rather than inventing them. But this does not mean his own principles of perception, understanding or "reasoning" are not involved. He is not Marx's "contemplative materialist" whose perceptions simply mirror a given, meaningful reality; neither does he construct lines of continuity from logical categories indifferent to the external world. Rather, he abstracts a particular line of continuity between different occurrences for its relevance to him. From within the same general *mélange* of occurrences over a period, different individuals can extract or abstract different stories, different lines of continuity. But a line of continuity abstracted for its relevance to *us* must also be credible in relation to the world of narrative entities — that is, it must be a workable way of experiencing orderings of occurrences in the real world. There is, after all, a distinction between fanciful and absurd stories. Given our normal way of perceiving lines of continuity, or "stories," in the world, the fanciful story at least *could* be true. But the absurd story could not — or at least, the world has not yet taught us it could. We are not referring here, of course, to an absurd story proposing, for instance, that "the house swam across the river," since that is an absurd *occurrence*, and absurd stories do not essentially derive from absurd occurrences. Rather, its absurdity stems from an absurd line of continuity which is proposed; for example, "he made a cup of tea and then the house collapsed," or, "the House of Lords adjourned and then swam to the surface."

Additionally, that we understand there to be "stories" or "sequences of occurrences" in general, let alone this or that particular story, is explained along the same lines of relevance and workability. From the one side it seems such a way of experiencing the world has always been of relevance to human beings. From the other side, the world has not let human beings down, so to speak, in respect of the notion that there are "real" continuities of occurrences rather than merely potential or absurd ones. Thus the same can be said of the status of particular "narrative identities" as has been argued respecting particular "objects" and "occurrences" — namely, it is not a question of whether this or that connecting-up of occurrences into an intelligible line of continuity is "real" or "objective," but whether it is relevant and workable. Where such continuities are not found, perceived, or noticed, the temporal relationships between occurrences remain an abstract kaleidoscope of possible sequences of occurrences — a meaningless turmoil. Hence, that part of our understanding of the world is in terms of this and that story, tells as much about ourselves as it does about the world. One of our characteristics is that we are "story-perceiving" beings; one of the characteristics of the world is that it generates stories, that is, "story-objects."

Stories or narratives are, then, more than the sum of their parts. They articulate a valid class of things in the world I have variously called "story-objects," "story-entities," or "narrative identities," and the issue of the "external reality" of these phenomena has been shown to be no different from that in relation to other kinds of phenomena such as physical objects and occurrences. As entities which we perceive and/or abstract, particular "story-objects" are therefore intelligible; they are meaningful things. Although they are formed in terms of "this occurred and then that occurred and then that," *what* occurred "then" or "next" is not randomly selected from out of a hat containing all later occurrences. Rather, the "story-object" has parameters and it is up to the story-teller to ensure he gets them right, that he makes the story he tells correspond to the story to be told — that is, that he uses the narrative form to delineate correctly the narrative identity or "story-object." What, then, are these "story-objects" or "narrative identities" when translated into familiar phenomena?

Events

If presented with a completely unfamiliar object, what do we make of it? How do we understand it? It is not a cat, house, or bottle — in fact, we cannot give it a name. We can attempt to describe it, but because we cannot classify it as a particular type of object (for instance, "a house"), it remains a meaningless object — it is unintelligible. Or rather, its only intelligibility is that it is indeed "an object" rather than, for instance, an occurrence or a quality. And that is precisely what we call it — "an object." As such we have said something meaningful, but not very much. The class of things we have put it in to give it a minimum of meaning is that class of things we call "objects." It is "an object," and that is as far as it is an intelligible phenomenon.

But even in saying this, we may be wrong. The "it" we are dealing with may not be a single object; it may be two or more objects adjoining each other. In the real world, indeed, it is only because we have, for instance, already identified other objects on a table-top as individual things (the table-cloth, bottle, and ashtray), that *this* strange conglomeration of matter stands out as a (supposed) single object. But this *is* a supposition. As for an object we *do* recognize — for instance, the bottle — we know it *can* be viewed as a collection of many separate individual things, including the cork, the label, and the glass structure. And we know in turn that the cork, for instance, can be seen as a collection of particles; and so on until we arrive at the collection of otherwise discrete "objects" which make up what we call "atoms." Yet we collect all these things together, call the object, "a bottle," and thereby indicate a unity, a single object somehow parametered off from other objects such as the table-cloth and the ashtray. Theoretically every atom adjoins the next; but we do not experience, nor articulate, the world as a soup of atoms. We extract individual, separate objects; and as so frequently argued up to now, we do this in terms of relevance and workability. "Air-pockets" were recurrable and predictable, but were not recognized and individuated phenomena until they were relevant to us. Conversely, the phenomenon known as an "air-pocket" was not established by the first encounter. "It" had to be a recurring, reliable phenomenon. And the same applies to occurrences, denoted by such verbs as "to swim," "to hiccup," "to commute" — that is, we "individuate" particular occurrences through the same general principles of relevance and workability which apply in individuating particular objects.

These same principles of individuation also apply to "story-objects" or "narrative identities," and the most appropriate term for this type of entity or "individual thing" is "an *event*." If the world of objects is differentiated by the use of (different) nouns and the world of occurrences by (different) verbs, so there is a world of events differentiated by the use (where available) of different "event-nouns" (such as "a wedding") — otherwise, by the narration of their particulars.

By "an event," then, I mean a sequence of occurrences singled out for notice. As an individual ordering of occurrences it must, like an individual object, have parameters. In this case, however, the parameters are not to do with physical properties — "the bottle stops here and the table-top begins" — but with the succession of occurrences; that is, an event must have a beginning, an end, and thus some kind of "middle." And what is sandwiched, so to speak, between the beginning and the end must constitute a sequence of occurrences which not only make sense in terms of "following on," but also specifically contribute to the intelligibility of the event construed as a whole, over and above its constituent parts. Thus in the more precise sense of the terms necessary for proper analysis, an "event" is different from an "occurrence" despite what might appear as an impenetrably dialectical interdependence between them, and despite dictionaries usually equating the terms. An event is an individuated ordering of occurrences; it is not a single occurrence, nor a sequence of occurrences which follow on from each other as in the basic narrative form but have no beginning and ending — that is, constitute no overall individual phenomenon. In referring to "events," then, the kind of phenomena under consideration are those such as wars, arguments, holidays, divorces, births, deaths, examinations, parties, elections, revolutions, evenings-out, and journeys. In other words, the stricter meaning it has been necessary to give the term, "event," does not remove it from everyday associations, where it does generally refer to more than a single occurrence and is understood to have parameters.

We do, then, individuate, or classify, many events; others, it is true, are so individual as not to attract classification. They simply have to be narrated, which equates with describing them. But particular instances of the former, classifiable events, can of course also be described, and this is done by stating what is particular rather than essential about them as, for instance, wars or weddings. This involves narrating the event in individual detail — that is, "telling its story," or "saying what happened" *within* the context of that *kind* of event.

Thus we arrive at the formula that to tell a story is to describe an event. Put more formally, the narrative structure is that by which we apprehend events — or again, the "content" of an event has the "form" of a narrative. Events are no more nor less "real" or "objective" phenomena in the world than occurrences and physical objects; like them, they are classifiable through that same logic which individuates an otherwise teeming and meaningless world into separable, intelligible phenomena. Or we can put the matter the other way; namely, the fact that events are classifiable and describable on the same general principles which apply to, for example, physical objects and occurrences, indicates we are confronted by phenomena just as "real," "objective," and "individual" as any object or occurrence.

Thus we see what it is that narrative achieves through its *explicatory* potential, and hence what a substantive and significant role it plays in our perception or construction of a world made intelligible to us through the process of discrimination and classification. Part of our understanding of "the real world out there" is constituted by our awareness of events. For example, wars, revolutions, dinner parties, road accidents, and domestic arguments, actually take place; they are objective phenomena, not mere abstractions, imaginings or inventions. Or at least, as individual, intelligible phenomena, events have as much or as little integrity as do physical objects and occurrences, for their logical status as concrete phenomena (with corresponding functional modes of articulation) is the same. Thus if we were incapable of narrative that entire aspect of reality constituted by events would be beyond our awareness.

Correspondingly, then, we owe an enormous debt to those who involve themselves in the activity of discovering, establishing, and communicating (almost necessarily past) "events." They are exploring an aspect of reality no more nor less valid, and certainly no less important, than that of physical objects. Their work is factual, their standards rigorous, and their conclusions provisional. One always hopes they get events right; but in the first place and above all one hopes the nature and significance of what they strive to achieve – namely, the revelation of an entire dimension of reality otherwise only dimly perceived and so often held to be "merely a matter of interpretation" – is understood and appreciated. "They," of course, are the historians; and especially, then, the narrative historians, for although we have yet to relate these general principles of narrative to historical knowledge in particular, it follows from what has already been said regarding "story-objects," "narrative identities," or "events," that they are narrative phenomena which correspondingly require the narrative form in order to be perceived and communicated.

Summary

The previous chapter concluded that in the search for what, if anything, peculiarly distinguishes the discipline of history, there are good reasons for focusing upon narrative history despite its current unfashionability amongst some historians and philosophers. Four issues in particular stood out as needing examination – to what extent narrative is a specific mode of discourse in its own right; what it achieves; in what sense, if any, it is explanatory; and how satisfactory it is as a formal framework for historians to work within.

The first three of these issues largely converge into the general question with which this chapter began – namely, what *is* a narrative? – and hence their treatment has been subsumed under this more general inquiry. Thus: the essential nature and distinctness of narrative as a structure or form has been analyzed; it has been identified as that mode of discourse which puts otherwise discrete occurrences into an intelligible order. Throughout, the distinction between (mere) chronicles and (meaningful) narratives or "stories" has been of recurring relevance, drawing attention to the special function of the (often implied) terms, "then," or, "next," in the logic of a narrative. Regarding its explanatory power, narrative was shown to convey intelligibility (and in that sense constitute the form of an explanation), at two different levels. On the first, a treatment of the concepts of continuity and change clarified the manner in which the narrative form renders occurrences intelligible as regards their happening – that is, explains why they take place. At the second level, narrative was shown to achieve something additional, for in our disentangling of the paradoxical dialectics of "happenings" (by positing a distinction between "occurrences" and "events"), it was argued the narrative form is *explicative* of a distinct and familiar dimension of reality – namely, the world of "story-objects," or "events." This explicatory power of narrative was shown to consist in rendering its own class of phenomena intelligible through those same principles of meaning and identification (and the attendant logic of individuation).

The fourth issue — that of how adequate narrative is as a framework for historians in particular to work within — now remains. Although much of relevance has already been adumbrated, the issue has not been fully subsumed under the course of this general exposition of the principles of narrative. Given the centrality of the issue to our overall topic, such questions which do remain regarding *historical* narrative now need to be brought into direct focus. In short, given the logic of narrative generally, there is still the need to see where the narrative historian stands in all this. For instance, that the historian who engages primarily in narrative is doing something which has its own distinct identity, has already been shown to the extent that narrative itself has been uniquely individuated from other modes of discourse. But within the realm of narrative it is necessary to restrict the historian to *factual* narrative; further, within these confines it is necessary to examine more closely how historical narrative differs from other narratives which, although equally factual, can serve a variety of purposes. In other words, we cannot blandly fit the historian into his narrative jacket without further investigation; indeed, this evidences that, although we have set out how narrative in general proceeds, questions remain in any event regarding the actual practice of constructing them, and perhaps no more so than in the case of the historian.

Similarly, although much of relevance to the historian has already been said regarding narrative's explanatory and explicatory potential, again the need remains to focus more directly on that issue as it relates specifically to *historical* narrative. For example, given the twofold nature of narrative explanation in general, is the *narrative* historian thereby restricted to explaining only certain things because of the narrative form? In other words, to what extent is his *narrative* jacket a straitjacket? Or conversely, in what ways are the explanatory and explicatory possibilities of narrative perhaps limited or modified in *historical* narrative? What, for instance, are the "story-objects" or "events" which constitute the material of *historical* narrative?

In these ways and for these reasons, then, we need to clarify where the narrative historian stands in relation to narrative generally before we can properly determine the overriding issue of how adequate narrative is as a framework for history. As for this issue itself, our general inquiry into narrative has already uncovered some relevant intimations. In particular, we have had occasion to approach the notion that the dimension of the world articulated through narrative in some sense specifically involves human beings. It was argued, for example, that any narrative must have subjects who are agents — and that in factual narrative these must be (responding) human beings. In addition, the first level of explanation achieved through narrative was characterized as peculiarly appropriate to human affairs, in contrast to the causal mode of explanation employed when treating of "natural" (non-human), phenomena. And concerning that second level of explanation — narrative's power of *explication* — it would seem to follow that so-called "natural events," such as avalanches and earthquakes, are not "events" in the stricter sense of the term I have used. In this connection it is interesting to note the old-fashioned curricular distinction between "natural" and "civil" history, a discrimination even the materialist Thomas Hobbes was anxious to insist upon. These intimations of a necessarily "humanist" character to the discipline of history are interesting enough in themselves, but are worth pursuing all the more, as the occasion arises, as we now turn to explore where the historian in particular stands in relation to narrative, so we can properly assess its adequacy as a formal framework for his discipline.

Chapter 7

Geoffrey Roberts

GEOFFREY ELTON

History and human action

W HEN SIR GEOFFREY ELTON DIED in December 1994 the obit-
uaries naturally focused on his contribution to the history of Tudor England.
Elton's name will forever be identified with the Tudors and his numerous textbooks, monographs, and papers on early modern England must surely rank as one
of the greatest ever achievements of historical labor. But Elton left another, equally
important legacy: a vigorous defense of traditional, narrative history – history as
the reconstruction and telling of tales about past human experiences, actions,
thoughts and endeavors.

Elton's first and most famous foray into the philosophy of history was *The
Practice of History* (1967) – a manifesto, he said, setting out his experience of
studying, writing and teaching history. This was followed by *Political History:
Principles and Practice* (1970) in which he argued for the centrality and importance
of political action in the study of the past and further developed his views on the
nature of historical explanation. *In Which Road to the Past?* (1983) he debated the
merits of "traditional" versus "scientific" history with Robert Fogel, the American
economic historian. Then came the study of his hero, the great Victorian legal historian *F. W. Maitland* (1985) and, finally, *Return to Essentials: Some Reflections on the
Present State of Historical Study* (1991) – a restatement of his faith in those "old-
fashioned convictions and practices" that informed his work.

Elton presented his writings on the nature and methods of history not as philosophy, but as an account of what working historians like himself did. To make
such an account coherent and convincing, however, it was necessary to explicate
and defend the fundamental assumptions underpinning the discipline's traditional
practices. The cumulative result of Elton's efforts was a sustained defense of what
may be called a human action account of the past: the view that history was not
the result of social structures, objective forces or (as some postmodernists argue)
linguistic discourses, but of autonomous human agents and that to explain and
comprehend the past historians must provide an account of those agents' actions
in their own terms, as they were lived and played out at the time.

Elton's view of the nature of history and its study had a very simple starting point: in the past there were people like us, reasoning people with thoughts, feelings, ambitions, concerns and problems. These people lived and made choices and what they did produced the events, effects, creations and results which is history. When people acted in the past, exercised their will and made choices they made their futures and created our present.

History for Elton was explicable, but the varieties, complexities and vagaries of human reasoning and thinking in diverse situations made it unpredictable.

Elton was above all concerned to assert the responsibility of those who study the past to acknowledge its humanity: "The recognition that at every moment in the past the future was essentially unpredictable and subject to human choice lies at the heart of a study which respects the past and allows it a life of its own. If men (and women) are treated as devoid of choice, their reason is demolished; the product is a history which dehumanises mankind."

In Elton's concept of history as a story of human existence and activity there was little place for those large-scale forces, trends, structures, and patterns beloved by social scientists. Everything in history – the events of the past – happens to and through people. Sociological categories may be useful descriptive shorthands of movements and outcomes over the long-run, but they remained abstractions unable to explain specific actions and events – the details and particularities of past happenings created by real people doing something. "History deals with the activities of men, not abstractions," Elton wrote.

That did not mean that for Elton the past was a site of free agents doing as they will. All events happen in a context, in particular conditions and circumstances of thought and action. But that context constituted a set of influences and constraints on action, not a transcendent force directing or determining action. If there is any transcendent force in history, Elton argued, it is the human capacity to exercise reason and thought, which enables us to transcend context, to change things and so make history.

Elton developed his account of causation in history (what made things happen in the past) in *Political History: Principles and Practice*. The task of historians, he argued, was to explain the events of the past. They did this by working backwards from known effects to their causes. By "causes" he meant those "antecedent events, actions, thoughts and situations" relevant to the explanation of the event to be explained. Such causes he divided into two types: *situational causes* and *direct causes*.

Situational causes are those circumstances and conditions that make an event possible or influence a particular historical outcome. Direct causes are those human factors which make something happen. And it is the latter which are decisive: while situational causes (which are anyway largely human creations themselves) produce contexts, it is direct causes – the exercise of human will – which make history. "Direct causes explain why the event actually happened; situational causes explain why direct causes proved effective," he argued.

Elton illustrated his point with reference to the type of explanation he proposed in *Reformation Europe, 1517–1559* (1963). Situational causes such as the state of the church, nationalist resentment of Italian popes, spiritual dissatisfaction, the growth of humanism and the desire for ecclesiastical wealth allowed or encouraged a particular historical result (namely, the split in the Church of Rome). But that outcome was actually brought about by actions such as those of Luther and other reformers, the separatist moves by the German princes, Henry VIII's divorce petition, and Thomas Cromwell's program for a political break with Rome.

Elton had another reason to stress the importance of the direct, willed causes of historical events: these are the causes which an historian can (at least in principle) demonstrate. Direct causes in history are, fundamentally, human chains of action and reaction which can be reconstructed from evidence. And for Elton evidence was king, its use and interpretation was the linchpin of historical method and of the historian's claim to be able to discover and tell true stories about the past.

Elton claimed that what distinguished history from other approaches to the study of human affairs was the role of evidence in generating and limiting, as well as validating, the statements and conclusions of historians. By evidence Elton meant all the deposits (mainly written accounts or records) of past human thought and action and its results. In this evidence is contained the story (in so far as we are able to know it) of past human action. The historical method consists of the critical examination of this evidence, and, ideally, only this evidence to reconstruct the causes of historical events.

Elton called his approach to evidence the "empirical or thesis-free" method, meaning that historians must be committed to allowing interpretations of the past to emerge from the evidence. As an illustration of this approach, he was fond of citing his own famous interpretation of "The Tudor Revolution in Government" – Thomas Cromwell's transformation of England into a centralized, administered, sovereign state – which he claimed emerged from a reading of the documents.

In arguing for the primacy of evidence in historical work Elton had to contend with the argument that the intrusion of human subjectivity in the interpretation and selection of the "facts" vitiated what were claimed to be true accounts of the past. Historians are human and there is biased and subjective history as well as balanced and objective history. Furthermore, argued Elton, the process of historical research should not be a matter of selecting facts to prove a thesis or an argument (bad history) but the reconstruction of a real past peopled by real individuals who did things that actually happened (good history) – and the veracity of such reconstructions should be assessed and judged against all the known evidence not just that which is presented in a particular account.

Despite Elton's robust defense of "good history," he was acutely aware of how limited a knowledge of the past was provided by historians. It was not just a question of the often inadequate and fragmented nature of surviving evidence and the necessary recourse to speculation, inference and "filling in the gaps." He acknowledged there were also problems inherent in the nature of the historical enterprise as an evidence-driven but also rationally-based investigation of past action.

In a striking passage in *The Practice of History*, Elton commented:

> All assessment of evidence must be the work of the intellect, of the reasoning faculty. The historian cannot but work on the assumption that whatever happened is capable of rational explanation and that evidence is the product of an act discoverable by reason. And yet we all know that this is not quite true; that we act, react and reflect from motives

which have little to do with reason and under influences – such as ill-health, a quarrel with people not involved in the transaction, whim and lack of thought – that can but rarely appear in the . . . evidence.

Elton also perceived difficulties and limits in the manner in which the results of historical research are presented. Elton favored the writing of history in the form of "narratives thickened by analysis" – stories of human action and reaction over time punctuated by in-depth discussions and explanations of direct and situational causes. But no narrative, of necessity composed of a linear sequence of sentences, could adequately capture the simultaneity of thoughts and actions, the complexity and multiplicity of causes, and the interconnectedness of events. Life was a mess on which historians imposed order, shape, pattern, meaning and intelligibility. "In a very real sense history cannot be correctly written," Elton concluded.

The resolution of these problems, however, lay not in abandoning reason as a tool of research or in dropping the assumption of intelligible purpose, but in recognizing the limits of the truths offered by historians. Elton also took solace in his belief that while "the historian . . . must concede the limits of rationality . . . reason also exists and men do act upon it, consciously, much of the time." Because of this the meaning and order which exists in history is not the invention of historians – it arises from the nature of human beings as creatures of thought and reason who on the whole consciously strive to achieve intelligible goals.

The assertion of the role of reason in human affairs was also at the heart of Elton's conception of the purpose of studying history. The study of history is an exercise in reason whose purpose is to enlarge the area of individual experience by teaching about human behavior. "History," Elton wrote in *Return to Essentials*, "provides the laboratory in which human experience is analyzed, distilled and bottled for use. The so-called lessons of history do not teach you to do this or that now; they teach you to think more deeply, more completely, and on the basis of an enormously enlarged experience, about what it may be possible or desirable to do now . . . By enormously enlarging personal experience, history can help us to grow up – to resist those who, with good will or ill, would force us all into the strait-jackets of their supposed answers to the problems of existence."

How historians conducted this exercise in reason was, for Elton, crucial. Historians' rejection of all paradigms except the assumption of reason and human choice secured their freedom from all authorities except that of evidence. In preserving their intellectual freedom to insist on the primacy of evidence and simply to state what happened and why, historians contribute to freedom of thought and action of all. "The historian, trained to freedom, offers the gift of sceptical criticism, which is liberty," argued Elton in his 1976 presidential address to the Royal Historical Society on "The Historian's Social Function."

Elton, as he made plain, offered to historians and students not a treatise but a manifesto – a statement of faith in the founding assumptions of their craft and a guide to the differences separating them from colleagues in the social sciences.

On one occasion Elton wrote: "history is an unending search for the truth, with the only certainty at each man's end that there will be more to be said and that, before long, others will say it." In the case of Elton's "philosophy," much of what he said was said by others – one thinks of the likes of Isaiah Berlin, Carl Becker,

R. G. Collingwood, Pieter Geyl, and Jack Hexter – and sometimes said better. But as one of the greatest practitioners of his craft and as one of the few out-right defenders of what he saw as the "beleaguered bastion of empiricist and non-ideological history," Elton deserves more than most to be read and listened to.

Note on sources

The books cited in the text are the main source for Elton's views on the philosophy of history, but a number of other important papers are published in his *Studies in Tudor and Stuart Politics and Government*, vol. 4 (Cambridge 1992). There is also the transcript of an interview with Elton conducted by Bob Scribner, which may be found in the Institute of Historical Research, London. Elton's Presidential Address to the RHS is published in *Transactions of the Royal Historical Society* (1976).

Elton's work as a historian was assessed by an RHS conference on "The Eltonian Legacy" in March 1996. The conference papers are published in *Transactions of the Royal Historical Society* (1997). These include Quentin Skinner's paper on "Sir Geoffrey Elton and the Practice of History." Another assessment of Elton's historical work is B. L. Beer, "G. R. Elton: Tudor Champion" in W. L. Arnstein (ed.), *Recent Historians of Great Britain* (Iowa State University Press, 1990).

Critiques of Elton's philosophy of history include Keith Jenkins, *On 'What is History?': From Carr and Elton to Rorty and White* (London 1995) and Dominic LaCapra, *History and Criticism* (Cornell 1985). For a partial defense see G. Roberts, "Postmodernism versus the Standpoint of Action," *History and Theory*, vol. 36, no.2, 1997.

Elton's most systematic treatment of the question of narrative may be found in the concluding chapter ("The End Product") of his *Political History: Principles and Practice* (1970).

Chapter 8

Geoffrey Roberts

J. H. HEXTER

Narrative history and common sense

ACCORDING TO THE PHILOSOPHER Louis O. Mink: "in the second half of the twentieth century no historian in the United States has accomplished more in the way of sustained reflection on the practice of historiography than Jack Hexter." This comment appeared in a *festschrift* for Hexter published in 1980,[1] but 20 years later Mink's verdict still rings true. Hexter's philosophical exploration of the theory of historiography remains a unique contribution by a practicing historian to a field dominated by philosophers and literary theorists. It is a contribution, moreover, that has yet to be fully explored and assessed.[2]

Hexter's central preoccupation was with "historiography," by which he meant the craft of writing history. At the heart of this craft was "the rhetoric of history" – the language that historians use to convey the knowledge and truth of their texts. Such rhetoric, Hexter argued, "affects not merely the outward appearance of history . . . but its inward character, its essential function." The rhetoric of history, one might say, had the appearance of form but was in fact part of the content – a content which conveyed "knowledge, understanding and truth about the past as it actually was."

These quotes are from *The History Primer*, published in 1971, which was the culminating text in Hexter's oeuvre on the rhetoric of history.[3] Hexter's starting point in this book (whose alternative title was *(Some) First Principles of Historical Discourse*[4]) was a definition of history as "any patterned, coherent account, intended to be true, of any past happenings involving human intention or doing or suffering."[5] Typically, these patterned, coherent accounts took the form of narrative or, as Hexter preferred, "historical storytelling."

The prevalence of narrative in historical accounts was for Hexter a necessary prescription as well as a description of historiography. Telling a story facilitated historical reconstruction of the connectivity of past happenings, those patterns of human activities which form the basis of the coherence of historical accounts. This view contrasts with so-called "analytical" history, which with its search for the "causes" of history often resulted, Hexter believed, in a mere accumulation of causal "factors," obfuscating the connections and interrelations of "times, places, persons and circumstances."[6]

Hexter's focus on historical storytelling converged with – and was indeed partly prompted by – the interest in the explanatory content of historical narratives of analytical philosophers of history like Morton White and Arthur Danto.[7] Hexter agreed with the analytical philosophers that historical narratives were explanatory but differed over the analysis of the form and content of these narratives. Morton White detected a causal "logic of historical narration" in historiography, whereas Danto explored the function of "narrative sentences" as bearers of the explanatory content of historical accounts.

Hexter's alternative was an account of "processive explanation" in historical narrative. The idea was that in constructing stories about the past historians identified critical points of change or transition in the processes that interest them. To illustrate his point Hexter referred to a narrative of the last, deciding game of a baseball season, which turns on the scoring of a home run. This was the pivot point of the game, indeed of the whole season. The narrative (Hexter's own) is structured around this moment and is driven by a logic of historical rhetoric – the use of language to explain and impress upon the reader the importance of a particular act. Such pivot points are common in historical narrative and are selected by historians on the basis of the known outcomes that interest them. Knowledge of outcome is also crucial in determining the tempo of a narrative – where it begins and ends and the details and proportions of the sequencing of the story. "Unless the writer has the outcome in mind as he writes his historical story, he will not know how to adapt the proportions of his story to the actual historical tempo, since that is knowable only to one who knows the outcome."[8]

For Hexter, then, processive explanation and the role of retrospective knowledge were examples of the "large structures of historical discourse" or, alternatively, the "macrorhetoric of historical storytelling" – that is the driving force of the rhetorical strategies deployed by historians, including the selection of facts embraced within the narrative. On the much-vexed issue of selection Hexter argued that "the outcome defines the appropriate historical macro-rhetoric, and the macro-rhetoric in turn dictates the selection of 'facts' . . . Or to put it more bluntly, amid a mass of true facts about the past too ample to set down, historians choose not merely on logical grounds but on the basis of appropriate rhetorical strategies."[9]

Historical narratives are also characterized by "microrhetoric, the small details of the language and syntax by means of which historians seek to communicate what they know."[10] As examples of microrhetoric Hexter referred to the use in historical narratives of footnotes, quotations, lists and hypothetical subjunctives ("must" and "may"). He also formulated three rules for the deployment of microrhetoric in historical narrative: (1) the Reality Rule, i.e. adherence to the evidence; (2) the Maximum Impact Rule, i.e. how best to convey historical reality to the reader; and (3) the Economy of Quotation Rule, i.e. direct quotation only when necessary for the achievement of (2).

Throughout his discussion of the rhetoric of history – macro and micro – Hexter is insistent that the goal of this rhetoric is "to convey knowledge, understanding and truth about *the past as it actually was*."[11] (my emphasis) But Hexter's adherence to the Rankean dictum of *wie es eigentlich gewesen* was singled out for special criticism by Mink.[12] The philosopher pointed out that there was a contradiction between Hexter's assertion that narratives were constructed by historians deploying various rhetorical strategies and rules and his insistence on relating the past as it actually was. How could one ever know that the structure of the narrative represented the structure of historical actuality, asked Mink, especially given Hexter's equally strong emphasis on the role of a historian's subjectivity (his or her "second record" of actual and imagined experience) in the creation of narrative?[13]

There certainly seems to be a tension between Hexter's constant avowal of the subjective construction by historians of the patterns of the past and his insistence on telling it like it actually was. But, as Mink himself notes, while this tension presented a problem for a *theory* of historiography it did not greatly vex Hexter since in practice historians do use rhetoric to construct successful narratives which provide a practical, common-sense knowledge of the past as it actually was, at least arguably so.

Hexter used the story of a twelve year-old-boy who has to explain to his father why he has mud on his trousers to illustrate his point. Muddy Pants explains by telling a story:

> "Well, I had to stay late at school for Group Activities today. So I was in a hurry to get home, because I was late, so I took a shortcut through Plumber's Field. Well, some tough big kids hang around there, and a couple of them started to chase me – boy, they were really big – and yelled that they were going to beat me up. So I ran as fast as I could. Well you know it rained a lot Tuesday and there are still puddles in the field, and I skidded in one that I didn't see and fell; but they didn't catch me, and – well I'm sorry I got messed up. O.K.?"[14]

Clearly, this is a highly selective, extremely biased account of what happened, one in which Muddy Pants deploys various rhetorical strategies designed to impact on his father's reception of the narrative. Equally, the story would be meaningless in the absence of some experiential sense of what Muddy Pants was talking about[15] – which emphasizes further the inter-subjective nature of the relationship between the narrator and the narratee. But, assuming Muddy Pants to be a reasonably reliable witness, does it impart knowledge of what happened and why, as well as provide a sense of what it was like to live out the narrative? Common sense tells us that it does, that Muddy Pants has given us a good historical account of what happened to him, albeit only from his point of view (no doubt the big kids would have a different story to tell). And what of Mink's point concerning the homology between the structure of historical actuality and the structure of the narrative? That depends on what is meant by "structure." If structure refers to the components, relationship, sequencing and results of *action*, it is not unreasonable to conclude that there is, in this case at least, a reasonable fit between the past actuality and the offered historical narrative.

Of course, the Muddy Pants story was concocted by Hexter in order to make a point; actual historical narratives are usually a good deal more complex and questionable. Hexter argued, however, that there is an elemental continuity between the common-sense narratives of everyday life – as exemplified by Muddy

Pants — and historical storytelling. Like Carl Becker[16], Hexter believed that the efforts of "Everyman" to make sense of life was not that much different from historians' efforts to make sense of the past. In both cases common sense, common reasoning and common experience are deployed to pattern, interpret and explain the world. "Historians," argues Hexter, "owe to common sense most of what they can rightly claim to know and understand about the human past."[17]

There are, however, differences between the common sense deployed by Everyman and that deployed by historians. Historians often utilize different kinds of evidence and are guided by scholarly ethics as well as by practical concerns in their use of evidence. Above all there is a difference of aim. Historians aim to expand common sense by providing knowledge beyond the immediate and the everyday, including insights into what it must have been like to be another human being in a different time and place. Historical narratives typically attempt to explain what happened and why but also to explore "what was what happened like?"[18] To achieve this latter aim historians use what Hexter called "translational" language "to assist the reader to translate his experience from a familiar accepted context into a context strange and perhaps initially repugnant."[19] As well as being translational, historians' language is often "psychedelic" — aiming to expand the readers' consciousness and awareness of past human responses and experiences. Moreover:

> historians . . . use language translationally and psychedelically not merely because 'history is an art', but as an indispensable means for communicating knowledge about the past . . . As a result of the impact of the translational and psychedelic language on their second record, readers indeed learn things about what happened in the past that they could not learn otherwise.[20]

Although "common language is the special rhetoric of historical discourse"[21] and provides the main terminology for historical narrative the fact that historians' tales are texts not speech is of considerable rhetorical importance. Historians, says Hexter, use "common formal historical prose", which is characterized by the utilization of various substitutes for the non-verbal and dialogic elements that makes everyday speech such a powerful means of communication. Indeed, the ability to write good common formal historical prose is what distinguishes good history writers — or historical storytellers — from bad ones. Which is not to say that well-written history is necessarily good history. The quality of history is a matter of substance as well as rhetoric. Historians, says Hexter, "tell the best historical story that their knowledge of the record of the past, their command of subsequent studies of that record, the use of their second record, and their control of common-formal prose permit them to."[22]

Hexter's overall conclusion is that "history is a rule-bound discipline by means of which historians seek to communicate their knowledge of the past."[23] However, as Mink notes, Hexter's rules of narrative construction are more practical maxims than anything else. It is the exploration of how these maxims are applied by historians in the writing of narrative that constitutes Hexter's most important contribution to the philosophy of history.

Notes

1   L. O. Mink, "The Theory of Practice: Hexter's Historiography" in B. C. Malament, *After the Reformation: Essays in Honor of J.H. Hexter*, Manchester University Press, 1980, p. 5. The essays in this *festschrift* are mainly devoted to Hexter's work as an historian of early modern Britain and Europe. Hexter died in 1996.

2   But see the critical discussion of some of Hexter's central contentions in P. Munz, *The Shapes of Time*, Wesleyan University Press: Hanover, NH 1977; Richard T. Vann's assessment of Hexter in his "Turning Linguistic: History and Theory and History and Theory, 1960–1975" in F. Ankersmit and H. Kellner, *A New Philosophy of History*, London, 1995; and Peter Novick's scattered remarks on Hexter in *That Noble Dream: The "Objectivity Question" and the American Historical Profession*, Cambridge University Press, 1988.

3   J. H. Hexter, *The History Primer*, New York, 1971, p. 328. See also Hexter's "The Rhetoric of History," *History and Theory*, vol. vi, no.1, 1967 and his contribution on the same topic to D. L. Sills (ed.), *International Encyclopaedia of the Social Sciences*, vol. 6, London and New York, 1968.

4   Ibid., p. 369.

5   Ibid., p. 3.

6   Ibid., p. 156.

7   See W. H. Dray, "On the Nature and Role of Narrative in History" in this volume.

8   Ibid., p. 226.

9   Ibid., p. 251. Cf. Paul Veyne: "Facts exist only in and through plots in which they take on the relative importance imposed by the human logic of the drama". Cited by P. Ricoeur, *The Contribution of French Historiography to the Theory of History*, Clarendon Press: Oxford, 1980, pp. 34–5.

10   Ibid., p. 238.

11   Ibid.

12   Mink, op.cit, pp. 18–21.

13   "Historians write history, all men write what they write, say what they say, do what they do, on the basis of their own experience, because in fact there is no other possible basis for writing, or saying, or doing anything. And the experience of each man is inescapably of his own day or age or time". "Carl Becker and Historical Relativism," p. 20 in J. H. Hexter, *On Historians*, Harvard University Press, 1979.

14   *The History Primer*, pp. 31–2.

15   In this connection, see Munz's comment (pp. 55–8) in *The Shapes of Time* that the intelligibility of the Muddy Pants story depends on shared knowledge and understanding of "general laws" of everyday behavior and human psychology.

16   C. Becker, "Everyman His Own Historian," *The American Historical Review*, vol. xxxvii, no. 2, January 1932. For Hexter's assessment of Becker see the article cited in n. 13.

17   *The History Primer*, p. 395.

18   Ibid., p. 275.

19   Ibid., pp. 137–8.

20   Ibid., p. 141.

21   Ibid., p. 77.

22   Ibid., p. 189.

23   Ibid., p. 328.

PART THREE

Narrative and historical realism

Chapter 9

David Carr

NARRATIVE AND THE
REAL WORLD

An argument for continuity

W HAT IS THE RELATION between a narrative and the events it
depicts? This is one of the questions that has been debated by many contributors to the lively interdisciplinary discussion of narrative in recent years.

The debate concerns the truthfulness, in a very broad sense of that term, of narrative accounts. Traditional narrative histories claim to tell us what really happened. Fictional narratives portray events that of course by definition never happened, but they are often said to be true-to-life; that is, to tell us how certain events might have occurred if they had really happened. Some histories may be inaccurate and some stories *invraisemblable*, but nothing in principle prevents such narratives from succeeding at their aim. Indeed, we take certain exemplary cases to have succeeded brilliantly.

But against this common-sense view a strong coalition of philosophers, literary theorists, and historians has risen up of late, declaring it mistaken and naive. Real events simply do not hang together in a narrative way, and if we treat them as if they did we are being *un*true to life. Thus not merely for lack of evidence or of verisimilitude, but in virtue of its very form, any narrative account will present us with a distorted picture of the events it relates. One result for literary theory is a view of narrative fiction which stresses its autonomy and separateness from the real world. One result for the theory of history is skepticism about narrative historical accounts.

I want to argue against this coalition, not so much for the common-sense view as for the deeper and more interesting truth which I think underlies it. Narrative is not merely a possibly successful way of describing events; its structure inheres in the events themselves. Far from being a formal distortion of the events it relates a narrative account is an extension of one of their primary features. While others argue for the radical discontinuity between narrative and reality, I shall maintain not only their continuity but also their community of form.

Let us look briefly at the discontinuity view before going on to argue against it.

I

In the theory of history one might expect such a view from those, from the positivists to the *Annales* historians, who believe narrative history has always contained elements of fiction that must now be exorcized by a new scientific history. The irony is that skepticism about narrative history should have grown up among those who lavish on it the kind of attention reserved for an object of admiration and affection. Consider the work of Louis Mink. Though he speaks of narrative as a "mode of comprehension" and a "cognitive instrument," and seems at first to defend narrative history against reductionists like Hempel, in the end he comes to a similar conclusion, namely that traditional history is prevented by its very form from realizing its epistemic pretentions. Narrative structure, particularly the closure and configuration given to the sequence of events by a story's beginning, middle, and end, is a structure derived from the act of telling the story, not from the events themselves. In the end the term "narrative history" is an oxymoron: "As historical it claims to represent, through its form, part of the real complexity of the past, but as narrative it is a product of imaginative construction which cannot defend its claim to truth by any accepted procedure of argument or authentication."[1] "Stories are not lived but told," he says. "Life has no beginnings, middles, or ends.. . . . Narrative qualities are transferred from art to life."[2]

If Mink arrives only reluctantly at such skeptical conclusions, Hayden White embraces them boldly. Like Mink he raises the question of narrative's capacity to *represent*. Inquiring after "The Value of Narrativity in the Representation of Reality" he seems clearly to conclude that in this respect its value is nil. "What wish is enacted, what desire is gratified," he asks, "by the fantasy that *real* events are properly represented when they can be shown to display the formal coherence of a story?"[3] "Does the world really present itself to perception in the form of well-made stories . . .? Or does it present itself more in the way that the annals and chronicles suggest, either as a mere sequence without beginning or end or as sequences of beginnings that only terminate and never conclude?" For White the answer is clear: "The notion that sequences of real events possess the formal attributes of the stories we tell about imaginary events could only have its origin in wishes, daydreams, reveries." It is precisely annals and chronicles that offer us the "paradigms of ways that reality offers itself to perception."[4]

Mink and White are led in this skeptical direction in part by their shared belief in the close relation between historical and fictional narratives; and if we look at some of the most influential studies of literary narrative in recent years, we find a similar view of the relation between narrative and the real. It is shared by structuralists and non-structuralists alike. Frank Kermode, in his influential study *The Sense of An Ending*, puts it this way: "In 'making sense' of the world we . . . feel a need . . . to experience that concordance of beginning, middle and end which is the essence of our explanatory fictions.. . . ."[5] But such fictions "degenerate," he says, into "myths" whenever we actually believe them or ascribe their narrative properties to the real, that is, "whenever they are not consciously held to be fictive."[6] In his useful recent presentation of structuralist theories of narrative, Seymour Chatman, also speaking of the beginning-middle-end structure, insists that it applies "to the narrative, to story-events as narrated, rather than to . . . actions themselves, simply because such terms are meaningless in the real world."[7] In this he echoes his mentor Roland Barthes. In his famous introduction to the structural analysis of narrative, Barthes says that "art knows no static." In other words, in a story everything has its place in a structure while the extraneous has been eliminated; and that in this it differs from "life," in which everything is "scrambled messages" (*communications brouillées*).[8] Thus, like Mink, Barthes raises the old question about the relation between "art" and "life," and arrives at the same conclusion: the one is constitutionally incapable of *representing* the other.

Paul Ricoeur draws together the theory of history and of literature in his recent *Time and Narrative* to form a complex account of narrative which is supposed to be neutral with respect to the distinction between history and fiction. For Ricoeur, as for White, the problem of representation is of central importance: the key concept in his account is that of *mimesis*, derived from Aristotle's *Poetics*.

By retaining rather than rejecting this concept Ricoeur's theory seems at first to run counter to the emphasis we have found in others on the *discontinuity* between narrative and the "real world." But in elaborating his complete theory of the mimetic relation he reveals himself to be much closer to Mink, White, and the structuralists than he at first appears. He does not go so far as to say with them that the real world is merely sequential, maintaining instead that it has a "pre-narrative structure" of elements that lend themselves to narrative configuration.[9]

But this prefiguration is not itself narrative structure, and it does not save us from what Ricoeur seems to regard as a sort of constitutional disarray attached to the experience of time, which in itself is "confused, unformed and, at the limit, mute."[10] From a study of Augustine's *Confessions* he concludes that the experience of time is characterized essentially by "discordance." Literature, in narrative form, brings concord to this "aporia" by means of the invention of a plot. Narrative is a "synthesis of the heterogenous" in which disparate elements of the human world — "agents, goals, means, interactions, circumstances, unexpected results, etc."[11] — are brought together and harmonized. Like metaphor, to which Ricoeur has also devoted an important study, narrative is a "semantic innovation" in which something new is brought into the world by means of language.[12] Instead of describing the world it *re*describes it. Metaphor, he says, is the capacity of "seeing-as."[13] Narrative opens us to "the realm of the 'as if'."[14]

So in the end for Ricoeur narrative structure is as separate from the "real world" as it is for the other authors we quoted. Ricoeur echoes Mink, White, *et. al.* when he says, "The ideas of beginning, middle, and end are not taken from experience: they are not traits of real action but effects of poetic ordering."[15] If the role of narrative is to introduce something new into the world, and what it introduces is the synthesis of the heterogeneous, then presumably it attaches to the events of the world a form they do not otherwise have. A story *re*describes the world; in other words, it describes it *as if* it were what presumably, in fact, it is not.[16]

This brief survey of important recent views of narrative shows not only that narrative structure is being considered strictly as a feature of literary and historical *texts*, but also that that structure is regarded as belonging *only* to such texts. The various approaches to the problem of representation place stories or histories on a radically different plane from the real world they profess to depict. Ricoeur's is a fairly benign and approving view. He believes that fictional and historical narratives enlarge reality, expanding our notion of ourselves and of what is possible. Their mimesis is not imitative but creative of reality. Hayden White seems by contrast to hold a darker, more suspicious view – one which he shares with Barthes and poststructuralists such as Foucault and Deleuze. Narrative not only constitutes an escape, consolation, or diversion from reality; at worst it is an opiate – a distortion imposed from without as an instrument of power and manipulation. In either case narrative is a cultural, literary artifact at odds with the real.[17]

There have been some dissenters, such as the literary critic Barbara Hardy, the historian Peter Munz, and the philosopher Frederik Olafson.[18] Alasdair MacIntyre presents a very different view in *After Virtue*, and I shall have more to say about him later. It is clear, however, that what I have called the discontinuity theory is held by some of the most important people writing about narrative in history and fiction. I would now like to show why I think this view mistaken.

II

My first criticism is that it rests on a serious equivocation. What is it that narrative, on the discontinuity view, is supposed to distort? "Reality" is one of the terms used. But what reality is meant? Sometimes it seems that the "real" world must be the physical world, which is supposed to be random and haphazard, or, alternatively and contradictorily, to be rigorously ordered along causal lines; but in any case it is supposed to be totally indifferent to human concerns. Things just happen in meaningless sequence, like the ticking clock mentioned by Frank Kermode. When asked what it says "we agree that it says *tick-tock*. By this fiction we humanize it. . . . Of course, it is we who provide the fictional difference between the two sounds; *tick* is our word for a physical beginning, *tock* our word for an end."[19]

This ingenious example merely confused the issue, nonetheless, since it is not primarily physical reality but human reality, including the very activity of "humanizing" physical events, which is portrayed in stories and histories and against which narrative must be measured if we are to judge the validity of the discontinuity view. Can we say of human reality that it is mere sequence, one thing after the other, as White seems to suggest? Here we would do well to recall what some philosophers have shown about our experience of the passage of time. According to Husserl even the most passive experience involves not only the retention of the just past but also the tacit anticipation, or what he calls protention, of the future. His point is not simply that we have the psychological capacity to project and to remember. His claim is the conceptual one that we cannot even experience anything as happening, as present, except against the background of what it succeeds and what we anticipate will succeed it.[20] Our very capacity to experience, to be aware of what *is* – "reality as it presents itself to experience," in Hayden White's words – spans future and past.

Husserl's analysis of time-experience is in this respect the counterpart of Merleau-Ponty's critique of the notion of sensation in classical empiricism and his claim that the figure-background scheme is basic in spatial perception.[21] He draws on the Gestalt psychologists, who were in turn indebted to Husserl. The supposedly punctual and distinct units of sensation must be grasped as a configuration to be experienced at all. Merleau-Ponty concludes that, far from being basic units of experience, sensations are highly abstract products of analysis. On the basis of Husserl's analysis of time-experience, one would have to say the same of the idea of a "mere" or "pure" sequence of isolated events. It is this that proves to be a fiction, in this case a theoretical fiction: perhaps we can conceive of it, but it is not real for our experience. As we encounter them, even at our most passive, events are charged with the significance they derive from our retentions and protentions.

If this is true of our most passive experience, it is all the more true of our active lives, in which we quite explicitly consult past experience, envisage the future, and view the present as a passage between the two. Whatever we encounter within our experience functions as instrument or obstacle to our plans, expectations, and hopes. Whatever else "life" may be, it is hardly a structureless sequence of isolated events.

It might be objected that structure is not necessarily narrative structure. But is there not a kinship between the means-end structure of action and the beginning-middle-end structure of narrative? In action we are always in the midst of something, caught in the suspense of contingency which is supposed to find its resolution in the completion of our project. To be sure, a narrative unites many actions to form a plot. The resulting whole is often still designated, however, to be an action of larger scale: coming of age, conducting a love affair, or solving a murder. The structure of action, small-scale and large, is common to art and to life.

What can the proponents of the discontinuity view possibly mean, then, when they say that life has no beginnings, middles, and ends? It is not merely that they are forgetting death, as MacIntyre points out,[22] and birth for that matter. They are forgetting all the other less definitive but still important forms of closure and structure to be found along the path from the one to the other. Are they saying that a moment in which, say, an action is inaugurated is no real beginning simply because it has other moments before it, and that after the action is accomplished time (or life) goes on and other things happen? Perhaps they are contrasting this with the absoluteness of the beginning and end of a novel, which begins on page one and ends on the last page with "the end." But surely it is the interrelation of the events portrayed, not the story as a sequence of sentences or utterances, that is relevant here. What I am saying is that the means-end structure of action displays some of the features of the beginning-middle-end structure which the discontinuity view says is absent in real life.

Thus the events of life are anything but a mere sequence; they constitute rather a complex structure of temporal configurations that interlock and receive their definition and their meaning from within action itself. To be sure, the structure of action may not be tidy. Things do not always work out as planned, but this only adds an element of the same contingency and suspense to life that we find in stories. It hardly justifies claiming that ordinary action is a chaos of unrelated items.

There may, however, be a different way of stating the discontinuity view which does not involve the implausible claim that human events have no temporal structure. A story is not just a temporally organized sequence of events — even one whose structure is that of beginning, middle, and end. To our concept of story belongs not only a progression of events but also a story-teller and an audience to whom the story is told. Perhaps it may be thought that this imparts to the events related in a story a kind of organization that is in principle denied to the events of ordinary action.

Three features of narrative might seem to justify this claim. First, in a good story, to use Barthes's image, all the extraneous noise or static is cut out. That is, we the audience are told by the story-teller just what is necessary to "further the plot." A selection is made of all the events and actions the characters may engage in, and only a small minority finds its way into the story. In life, by contrast, everything is left in; all the static is there.

This first point leads to a second. The selection is possible because the story-teller knows the plot in a way both audience and characters do not (or may not). This knowledge provides the principle for excluding the extraneous. The narrative voice, as Hayden White says,[23] is the voice of authority, especially in relation to the reader or listener. The latter is in a position of voluntary servitude regarding what will be revealed and when. Equally importantly, the narrative voice is an *ironic* voice, at least potentially, since the story-teller knows the real as well as the intended consequences of the characters' actions. This irony is thus embodied primarily in the relation between story-teller and character; but it is related to the audience as well, since their expectations, like the characters', can be rudely disappointed.

The ironic stance of the story-teller can be seen as a function (and this is the third point) of his or her temporal position in relation to the events of the story. Conventionally this is the *ex post* position, the advantage of hindsight shared by the historian and (usually) the teller of fictional stories. As Danto points out, this position permits descriptions of events derived from their relation to later events and thus often closed to participants in the events themselves.[24] This standpoint after the story-events can just as well be seen, in Mink's preferred fashion, as a standpoint *outside* or *above* the events which takes them all in at a glance and sees their interrelation.[25] This apparent freedom from the constraints of time, or at least of following the events, sometimes expresses itself in the disparity between the order of events and the order of their telling. Flashbacks and flashforwards exhibit in no uncertain terms the authority of the narrative voice over both characters and audience.

In sum, the concept of story, as Scholes and Kellogg said, involves not just a sequence of unfolding events but the existence of three distinguishable points of view on those events: those of story-teller, audience, and characters.[26] To be sure, these may seem to coincide in some cases: a story may be told from the viewpoint of a character, or in a character's voice. Here even the audience knows no more or less than the character and all points of view seem identical; but even a first-person account is usually narrated after the fact, and the selection process still depends on the difference in point of view between participant and teller. In any case the very possibility of the disparity between the three points of view is enough to establish this point — that the events, experiences, and actions of a story may have a sense, and thus a principle of organization, which is excluded from the purview of the characters in the story.

As participants and agents in our own lives, according to this view, we are forced to swim with events and take things as they come. We are constrained by the present and denied the authoritative, retrospective point of view of the story-teller. Thus the real difference between "art" and "life" is not organization vs. chaos, but rather the absence in life of that point of view which transforms events into a story by *telling* them. Telling is not just a verbal activity and not just a recounting of events but one informed by a certain kind of superior knowledge.

There is, no doubt, much truth in this analysis, and as an argument for the discontinuity view it is certainly superior to the claim that human events form a meaningless sequence. Nonetheless this argument, like its predecessor, neglects some important features of "real life."

The key to this neglect is a mistaken sense of our being "confined to the present." The present is precisely a point of view or vantage point which opens onto or gives access to future and past. This I take to be the sense of the Husserlian analysis. Even in the relatively passive experience of hearing a melody, to use his example, we do not simply sit and wait for stimuli to hit us. We grasp a configuration extending into the future which gives to each of the sounding notes their sense. Thus present and past figure in our experience as a function of what will be.

The teleological nature of action, of course, lends it the same future-oriented character. Not only do our acts and our movements, present and past, derive their sense from the projected end they serve; our surroundings function as sphere of operations and the objects we encounter figure in our experience in furtherance of (or hindrance to) our purposes. Indeed, in our active lives it could be said that the focus of our attention is not the present but the future – as Heidegger says, not on the tools but on the work to be done.[27] It has been noted by Alfred Schutz that action has, temporally speaking, the quasi-retrospective character which corresponds to the future perfect tense: the elements and phases of an action, though they unfold in time, are viewed from the perspective of their having been completed.[28]

If this is true when we are absorbed in action, it is all the more true of the reflective or deliberative detachment involved – not only in the formulating of projects and plans but also in the constant revision and reassessment required as we go along and are forced to deal with changing circumstances. The essence of deliberative activity is to anticipate the future and lay out the whole action as a unified sequence of steps and stages, interlocking means and ends. In all this it can hardly be said that our concern is limited to the present. Nor can it be said that no selection takes place. To be sure, the noise or static is not eliminated, but it is recognized as static and pushed into the background.

The obvious rejoinder here, of course, is that the future involved in all these cases is only the envisaged or projected future, and that the agent has only a quasi-hindsight, an as-if retrospection at his or her disposal. What is essential to the story-teller's position is the advantage of real hindsight, a real freedom from the constraint of the present assured by occupying a position after, above, or outside the events narrated. The story-teller is situated in that enviable position beyond all the unforeseen circumstances that intrude, all the unintended consequences of our action that plague our days and plans.

Of course this is true; the agent does not occupy a real future with respect to current action. My point is simply that action seems to involve, indeed quite essentially, the adoption of an anticipated future-retrospective point of view on the present. We know we are in the present and that the unforeseen can happen; but the very essence of action is to strive to overcome that limitation by foreseeing as much as possible. It is not only novelists and historians who view events in terms on their relation to later events, to use Danto's formulation of the narrative point of view; we all do it all the time, in everyday life. Action is thus a kind of oscillation between two points of view on the events we are living through and the things we are doing. Not only do we not simply sit back and let things happen to us; for the most part, or at least in large measure, our negotiation with the future is successful. We are, after all, able to act.

What I am saying, then, is that we are constantly striving, with more or less success, to occupy the story-tellers' position with respect to our own lives. Lest this be thought merely a far-fetched metaphor, consider how important, in the reflective and deliberative process, is the activity of literally telling, to others and to ourselves, what we are doing. When asked, "What are you doing?" we may be expected to come up with a story, complete with beginning, middle, and end, an accounting or recounting which is description and justification all at once.

The fact that we often need to tell such a story even to ourselves in order to become clear on what we are about brings to light two important things. The first is that such narrative activity, even apart from its social role, is a constitutive part of action, and not just an embellishment, commentary, or other incidental accompaniment. The second is that we sometimes assume, in a sense, the point of view of audience to whom the story is told, even with regard to our own action, as well as the two points of view already mentioned – those of agent or character and of story-teller.

Louis Mink was thus operating with a totally false distinction when he said that stories are not lived but told. They are told in being lived and lived in being told. The actions and sufferings of life can be viewed as a process of telling ourselves stories, listening to those stories, acting them out, or living them through. I am thinking here only of living one's own life, quite apart from both the cooperative and antagonistical social dimension of our action which is even more obviously intertwined with narrative. Sometimes we must change the story to accommodate the events; sometimes we change the events, by acting, to accommodate the story. It is not the case, as Mink seems to suggest, that we first live and act and then afterward, seated around the fire as it were, tell about what we have done, thereby creating something entirely new thanks to a new perspective. The retrospective view of the narrator, with its capacity for seeing the whole in all its irony, is not in irreconcilable opposition to the agent's view but is an extension and refinement of a viewpoint inherent in action itself. Mink and the others are right, of course, to believe that narration constitutes something, creates meaning rather than just reflecting or imitating something that exists independently of it. Narration, nevertheless intertwined as it is with action, does this in the course of life itself – not merely after the fact, at the hands of authors, in the pages of books.

In this sense the narrative activity I am referring to is practical before it becomes cognitive or aesthetic in history and fiction. We can also call it ethical or moral in the broad sense used by Alasdair MacIntyre and derived ultimately from Aristotle. This is to say that narration in our sense is constitutive not only of action and experience but also of the self which acts and experiences. Rather than a merely temporally persisting substance which underlies and supports the changing effects of time, like a thing in relation to its properties, I am the subject of a life-story which is constantly being told and retold in the process of being lived. I am also the principal teller of this tale, and belong as well to the audience to which it is told. The ethical–practical problem of self-identity and self-coherence may be seen as the problem of unifying these three roles. MacIntyre is probably right to attack the ideal of self-*authorship* or authenticity as an idol of modern individualism and self-centeredness.[29] But the problem of coherence cannot always be settled, as he seems to think, by the security of a story laid out in advance by society and its roles. My identity as a self may depend on which story I choose and whether I can make it hang together in the manner of its narrator, if not its author. The idea of life as a meaningless sequence, which we denounced earlier as an inaccurate description, may have significance if regarded as the constant possibility of fragmentation, disintegration, and dissolution which haunts and threatens the self.

III

But what has all this to do with history? We have reproached the discontinuity theory for misunderstanding "human reality," but our sense of this latter term seems tailored, as the conclusion of the previous section indicates, to *individual* experience, action, and existence. Indeed, our recourse to certain phenomenological themes may suggest that what we have said is methodologically tied to a first-person point of view. History, by contrast, deals primarily with social units, and with individuals only to the extent that their lives and actions are important for the society to which they belong. Is the narrative conception of experience, action, and existence developed in the previous section at all relevant to "human reality" in its specifically social forms?

I think it is, and in this section I shall present a brief sketch of how this is so. There is an obvious sense, of course, in which our conception of narrative is social right from the start. The story-telling function, whether metaphorical or literal, is a social activity, and though we spoke of the self as audience to its own narration, the story of one's life and activity is told as much to others as to oneself. On our view the self is itself an interplay of roles, but clearly the individual is constituted in interpersonal transaction as well as intrapersonal reflection. It is one thing to speak of the social construction of the self, however, and another to inquire into the make-up of social entities as such.

To consider this question it is not necessary to take up the attitude of the social scientist or historian observing something from the outside. We are also participants in groups, and our best understanding of their nature may come from a reflection on what it means to participate. What strikes me about social life is the extent to which an individual takes part in experiences and engages in actions whose proper subject is not the individual himself or herself but that of the group. To inhabit a territory, to organize politically and economically for its cultivation and civilization, to experience a natural or human threat and rise to meet it – these are experiences and actions usually not properly attributable to me alone, or to me, you, and the others individually. They belong rather to us: it is not my experience but *ours*, not *I* who act but *we* who act in concert. To say that *we* build a house is not equivalent to saying that I build a house, and you build a house, and he builds a house, and so on. To be sure, not all linguistic uses of *we* carry this sense of concerted action, division of labor, distributed tasks, and a shared end. In some cases the *we* is just shorthand for a collection of individual actions. But social life does involve certain very important cases in which individuals, by participation, attribute their experiences and acts to a larger subject or agent of which they are a part.

If this is so, it may not be necessary to give up the first-person approach, but only to explore its plural rather than its singular form in order to move from the individual to the social. If we make this move, we find many parallels to our analysis of the individual's experience and action. *We* have an experience in common when *we* grasp a sequence of events as a temporal configuration such that its present phase derives its significance from its relation to a common past and future. To engage in a common action is likewise to constitute a succession of phases articulated as steps and stages, subprojects, means and ends. Social human time, like individual human time, is constructed into configured sequences which make up the events and projects of our common action and experience.

As before, I think the structure of social time can be called a narrative structure, not only because it has the same sort of closure and configuration we found at the individual level, but also because this very structure is again made possible by a kind of reflexivity which is comparable to that of a narrative voice. The temporal sequence must be brought under a prospective–retrospective grasp which gives it its configuration, and lends to its phases their sense of presenting a commonly experienced event or of realizing a common goal. In the case of groups, however, the division of labor, necessary for carrying out common projects, may be characteristic of the narrative structure itself. That is, the interplay of roles – narrator, audience, and character – may here be literally divided among participants in the group. Certain individuals may speak on behalf of, or in the name of, the group, and articulate for the others what "we" are experiencing or doing. The resulting "story" must of course be believed or accepted by the audience to whom it is addressed if its members are to act out or live through as "characters" the story that is told.

In the last section I spoke of the temporal–narrative organization not only of experiences and actions but also of the self who experiences and acts. As the unity of many experiences and actions, the self is constituted as the subject of a life-story. So too with the constitution of certain kinds of groups which outlive particular common experiences and actions to acquire a stable existence over time. Not all groups are of this sort: collections of individuals make up groups simply by sharing objective traits such as location, race, sex, or economic class. But groups of a very special and socially and historically important sort are constituted when individuals regard each other in just such a way that they use the *we* in describing what is happening to them, what they are doing, and who they are. This is, of course, the sort of group for which the word "community" is reserved. In some of the most interesting cases, merely objective traits like sex, race, or class become the basis for the transformation of the one sort of group into the other: individuals recognize that it is *as* a race, sex, or class that they are oppressed or disadvantaged. What is grasped as common experience can be met by common action.

A community in this sense exists by virtue of a story which is articulated and accepted, which typically concerns the group's origins and its destiny, and which interprets what is happening now in the light of these two temporal poles. Nor is the prospect of death irrelevant in such cases, since the group must deal not only with possible external threats of destruction but also with its own centrifugal tendency to fragment. Again we can say that the narrative function is practical before it is cognitive or aesthetic; it renders concerted action possible and also works toward the self-preservation of the subject which acts. Indeed, we must go even further and say that it is literally *constitutive* of the group. As before, narrative is not a description or account of something that already exists independently of it and which it merely helps along. Rather, narration, as the unity of story, story-teller, audience, and protagonist, is what constitutes the community, its activities, and its coherence in the first place.

In this essay I have begun with a discussion of the individual's action, experience, and identity and have proceeded from there to the community, treating the latter as an analogue of the former. Since the story-telling and story-hearing metaphor, as already remarked, is more directly appropriate to the group than to the individual, it could be said that our order might better have been reversed. We might have presented the individual self as a kind of community of tellers, listeners, and characters, fused in their comprehension and execution of a common story. I find this interesting, but it could prove misleading; it is a special kind of story that is relevant here – the autobiographical one in which the issue is the unity and coherence of a subject who is identical with both the teller and the hearer of the story. The unity and coherence of one's own self, with all its attendant problems, is a matter closest to all of us. For this reason it serves as the best point of departure for a comparison designed to cast light on social existence.

Some may feel uncomfortable with this revival of the notion of the collective subject. While the idea that the community is a person "writ large" has strong historical precedents, notably in Plato and Hegel, it is regarded with great suspicion today. Everyone recognizes that in ordinary speech we often attribute personal qualities and activities to groups, but few are willing to grant this more than the status of a *façon de parler*. Even those who favor holism over individualism in debates about the methodology of the social sciences generally give a wide berth to any notion of social subjectivity.[30] It is the individualists who insist on the purposeful, rational, and conscious subject as the key to what goes on in society, but they reserve this conception strictly for the individual person; holists stress the degree to which the individual's behavior is embedded in non-intentional contexts of a structural and causal sort.

There are no doubt many and very interesting sorts of reasons why the idea of social subjectivity is not taken seriously, especially by the Anglo-Saxon mind, but one reason is doubtless the way this idea has been presented, or is thought to have been presented, by some of its advocates. The well-known caricature of Hegel's philosophy of history has the world spirit single-mindedly pursuing its own career by cunningly exploiting individuals for purposes unknown to them and usually opposed to the ones they themselves pursue. More recently, Sartre envisages the transcendence of the "seriality" of individual existence in the "group-in-fusion," for which the storming of the Bastille serves as the paradigm.[31] Confronted with these cases, Anglo-Saxon individualists cry alarm, since individuals are either un-witting and manipulated dupes or they are swept up in an unruly mob which obliterates their individuality altogether. Viewed with a combination of disapproval and disbelief, these notions are denied any importance or usefulness for the understanding of society and history.

But what I am talking about is really very different from either of those notions, which I agree must be rejected as paradigms. In abandoning and subverting individual subjectivity, these views do not take us from the I to a *we* but merely to a larger-scale I. What I have in mind here fits not the caricature but the genuine insight behind Hegel's notion of *Geist*, which he describes, when he first introduces it in the *Phenomenology*, as "an I that is We, a We that is I."[32] In describing the community of mutual recognition, Hegel insists as much on the plurality as on the subjectivity and agency of the social unit, and the community is not opposed to the individuals who make it up but exists precisely by virtue of their conscious acknowledgement of each other and consequently of it. Heigel also has a very healthy sense of the fragility and riskiness of this sort of community: it is born as a resolution of the conflict among its independent-minded members, and it never really overcomes the internal threat to its cohesion which is posed by their sense of independence. The *Phenomenology* is the account of the resulting drama in many of its possible social and historical variations. This account has a *narrative* structure: a community exists not only as a development, but also through the reflexive grasp of that development, when its members assume the common *we* of mutual recognition.

For all the objections that may be raised against the idea of a plural subject, the fact is that in the sorts of cases I have described, we do say *we* to each other, and we mean something real by it. Moreover, much of our lives and much of what we do is predicated on its reality for us. By stressing our use of language and our sense of participation I hope to make it clear that I am advancing not a straight-forward ontological claim about the real existence of such social entities, but rather a reflexive account based on the individuals that compose and constitute them. Furthermore the term "community" as I am using it has a variable application, from the nation-states of modern history to the many economic, linguistic, and ethnic groups that often stand in conflict with them. I do not maintain, as Hegel may have thought or hoped, that such communities fit inside each other in some hierarchical order. Conflict may be inevitable, there may be no *us* without a *them*. As for individuals, obviously many of their personal conflicts may arise from conflicting loyalties to the different communities they may belong to.

To sum up: a community exists where a narrative account exists of a *we* which persists through its experiences and actions. Such an account exists when it gets articulated or formulated – perhaps by only one or a few of the group's members – by reference to the *we* and is accepted or subscribed to by others.

It may be thought that in saying this I have so watered down the idea of a plural subject that it loses its interest. It seems now to exist only as a projection in the minds of individuals, who are the real entities after all in my account. If I have said that the *we* is constituted as the subject of a story in and through the telling of that story, remember that I have said exactly the same thing about the I. If the narrative that constitutes the individual self is at least partly social in origin, then the I owes its narrative existence as much to the We as the We does to the I. Neither the We nor the I is a *physical* reality; but they are not *fictions* either. In their own peculiar senses they are as real as anything we know.

IV

To return to narrative texts as literary artifacts, whether fictional or historical, I have tried to make good on my claim that such narratives must be regarded not as a departure from the structure of the events they depict, much less a distortion or radical transformation of them, but as an extension of their primary features. The *practical* first-order narrative process that constitutes a person or a community can become a second-order narrative whose subject is unchanged but whose interest is primarily cognitive or aesthetic. This change in interest may also bring about a change in content – for example, an historian may tell a story about a community which is very different from the story the community (through its leaders, journalists, and others) tells about itself. The form, nonetheless, remains the same.

Thus I am not claiming that second-order narratives, particularly in history, simply mirror or reproduce the first-order narratives that constitute their subject-matter. Not only can they change and improve on the story; they can also affect the reality they depict – and here I agree with Ricoeur – by enlarging its view of its possibilities. While histories can do this for communities, fictions can do it for individuals. But I disagree that the narrative *form* is what is produced in these literary genres in order to be imposed on a non-narrative reality – it is in envisaging new content, new ways of telling and living stories, and new kinds of stories, that history and fiction can be both truthful and creative in the best sense.[33]

Notes

1   Louis O. Mink, "Narrative Form as a Cognitive Instrument," in *The Writing of History*, ed. R. H. Canary and H. Kozicki (Madison, 1978), 145.
2   Mink, "History and Fiction as Modes of Comprehension," *New Literary History* 1 (1970), 557ff. [Ch. 6, this volume].
3   Hayden White, "The Value of Narrativity in the Representation of Reality," in *On Narrative*, ed. W. J. T. Mitchell (Chicago, 1981), 4.
4   Ibid., 23.
5   Frank Kermode, *The Sense of An Ending: Studies in the Theory of Fiction* (London, 1966), 35ff.
6   Ibid., 39.
7   Seymour Chatman, *Story and Discourse: Narrative Structure in Fiction and Film* (Ithaca, 1978), 47.
8   Roland Barthes, "Introduction à l'analyse structurale des récits," *Communication* 8 (1966), 7.
9   Paul Ricoeur, *Temps et récit* (Paris, 1983), I, 113.
10   Ibid., 14.
11   Ibid., 102.
12   Ibid., 11.
13   Ibid., 13. See Ricoeur's *La Métaphore vive* (Paris, 1975), 305ff.
14   *Temps et récit*, 101.
15   Ibid., 67.
16   For a more detailed critical account of Ricoeur's book see my review–essay in *History and Theory* 23 (1984), 357–70.

17   In a recent article, "The Question of Narrative in Contemporary Historical Theory," *History and Theory* 23 (1984), 1–33, White himself gives a much more thorough account of these developments than I have given here. Concerning his presentation, which is otherwise a model of scholarship and synthesis, I have three reservations: modesty apparently prevents the author from documenting his own important role in the developments he describes; he generally approves of the trends I shall be criticizing; and he has not, I believe, properly assessed the position of Ricoeur, perhaps because *Temps et récit* was not available to him.

18   Barbara Hardy, "Towards a Poetics of Fiction: An Approach Through Narrative," in *Novel* (1968), 5ff; and *Tellers and Listeners: The Narrative Imagination* (London, 1975); Peter Munz, *The Shapes of Time* (Middletown, 1977); Frederick Olafson, *The Dialectic of Action* (Chicago, 1979). Several German theorists have stressed the continuity of experience and narrative. See Wilhelm Schapp, *In Geschichten Verstrickt* (Wiesbaden, 2nd edn, 1979); Hermann Lübbe, *Bewusstsein in Geschichten* (Freiburg, 1972); Karlheinz Stierle, "Erfahrung und narrative Form," in *Theorie und Erzählung in der Geschichte*, ed. J. Kocka and T. Nipperday (Munich, 1979), 85ff.

19   Kermode, *The Sense of an Ending*, 44ff.

20   Edmund Husserl, *The Phenomenology of Internal Time-Consciousness*, trans. J. S. Churchill (Bloomington, 1964), 40ff.

21   Maurice Merleau-Ponty, *The Phenomenology of Perception*, trans. C. Smith (New York, 1962), 3ff.

22   Alasdair MacIntyre, *After Virtue* (Notre Dame, 1981), 197.

23   Hayden White, "The Structure of Historical Narrative," *Clio* 1 (1972), 12ff.

24   Arthur Danto, *Analytical Philosophy of History* (Cambridge, 1965), 143ff.

25   Mink, "History and Fiction as Modes of Comprehension," 557ff.

26   Robert Scholes and Robert Kellogg, *The Nature of Narrative* (New York, 1966), 240ff.

27   Martin Heidegger, *Being and Time*, trans. J. Macquarrie and E. Robinson (New York, 1962), 99.

28   Alfred Schutz, *The Phenomenology of the Social World*, trans. G. Walsh and F. Lehnert (Evanston, 1967), 61.

29   MacIntyre, *After Virtue*, 191.

30   See Ernst Gellner, "Explanation in History," in *Modes of Individualism and Collectivism*, ed. J. O'Neill (London, 1973), 251; and Anthony Quinton, "Social Objects," in *Proceedings of the Aristotelian Society* 76 (1975–6), 17.

31   Jean-Paul Sartre, *Critique de la raison dialectique* (Paris, 1960), I, 391ff.

32   G. W. F. Hegel, *Phenomenology of Spirit*, trans. A. V. Miller (Oxford, 1977), 110.

33   The themes in this essay are developed at greater length in my *Time, Narrative, and History* (Bloomington, 1986).

Chapter 10

W. H. Dray

NARRATIVE AND HISTORICAL REALISM

ACENTRAL CONTENTION OF THE CASE offered by both Mink and White for denying a realistic interpretation to historical narratives is that the human world simply isn't *experienced* as a congeries of stories, the conclusion being drawn that the story form is therefore something imposed upon what *was* experienced. One of the most incisive and original of recent critics of the anti-realist position, David Carr, has challenged this central contention directly.[1] We do indeed experience life in the way narratives characteristically organize their subject-matters, Carr maintains, this being true not only of complex and higher-order experience but of all human experience down to the most elementary perception or action. And he offers analyses of experience at various levels designed to show that this is so. Carr doesn't claim that these analyses, in themselves, show that the narratives typically offered by historians in fact mirror the real world of the past. He does, however, represent them as removing a main prop of the kind of skepticism expressed by Mink and White. In what follows, I want, first, to recapitulate the argument that Carr elaborates for his position, and to indicate why, despite its penetration, I think it falls somewhat short of removing the kinds of worries these anti-realists have felt. I shall then suggest another way of meeting the Mink-White challenge that seems to me capable of dissolving it more directly and more effectively.

I

Carr's strategy is to show, by directing attention to certain features of our temporal experience at various levels of complexity and sophistication, that something at least significantly "akin" to a narrative structure characterizes all our dealings with the world, and that narration itself enters essentially into more of them than may at first be thought. In developing his position, he borrows usefully, first from Husserl and Heidegger, and then from Hegel, but I shall ignore this background of his thought, simply setting out what seem to me the main points he wants to make, although necessarily with something less than the subtlety of his own presentation.

Against anti-realists like Mink and White, who often insist that our actual experience of the world takes the form of meaningless sequences, the sort of structure ascribed to them in narratives thus being something "artificial" and "imposed," Carr argues that even in the most elementary perceptions and actions, an embryonic narrative-type structure can be discerned, such a structure therefore being about as natural, humanly speaking, as anything can be.[2] There is a temporal horizon, he maintains, even to hearing a single note of a melody or a single tone of a striking clock. The note or tone is heard *as* a member of a series, that is, with implicit backward reference to what it succeeds and forward reference to what is expected to follow. What is involved here is more basic than consciously remembering and predicting, the terms of art "retention" and "protention" therefore being used to characterize it. What Carr stresses is that these very elementary experiences require of the experiencer a retentive–protentive grasp which, in effect, finds structure in what is experienced: for example, a beginning-middle-end. Any perception of something *as* present has such a structure. The end, of course, is only an envisaged one; yet something like a synthesis from an anticipated retrospective standpoint, if a constantly corrected one, seems to be implicit in the experience as described. Much the same can be said of elementary actions like serving a ball in tennis. Although in such a case no deliberately means-end ratiocination may take place, this can hardly be performed as the kind of action it is without our conceiving it as possessing a means-end structure, once again with beginning-middle-end, and having some idea of what will count later as success. It should be noted that Carr is not simply reminding us that something like this does happen; he is saying that it *has* to happen if elementary experiences and actions of the most familiar kinds are to be possible.

If his argument this far is accepted, Carr has already, in a formal sense at least, rebutted a central claim of the anti-realists as it is often expressed; he has shown that at least some human experiences and actions exhibit, and necessarily exhibit, a kind of structure which, according to Mink and White, is never found *in* what is actually experienced, but is always projected onto the world *after* it has been experienced. Carr is willing to go as far as claiming that no human experience can be so elementary that it fails to exhibit the proto-narrative structure which examples like those just noted reveal;[3] and since those to whom he is responding do not generally show interest in what the world may be like *other than* as experienced, this is a relevant sort of claim. I don't think, however, that for present purposes we need to ask whether it is true. Carr has shown the allegedly problematic structure to be present at a very basic level indeed. The real interest, if that is granted, lies in whether he can use his analysis of the elementary cases to throw light on the understanding of those higher order human experiences and actions that are objects of study for historians, and whether he can find ingredients in actual experience something more like a fully developed narrative structure. His further argumentation does in fact work up a ladder of ever more complex sorts of case, each step being represented as in some sense an "extension" of what was found true of a previous one.

Beyond the elementary level, Carr considers, first, individual experiences and actions of a more complex and reflective kind, into which the elementary ones may enter as "building blocks:" for example, recognizing a melody as a theme in a sonata, or serving a tennis ball as part of an overall strategy for winning a game.[4] Here pre-reflective retention-protention is replaced by explicit recollection and planning: experiences and actions are grasped as wholes made up of many parts or phases; and larger-scale ones can survive through interruptions, as when someone returns to enjoying a performance after the intermission, or follows the fortunes of a favorite hockey team throughout a season. The recognition of the relation of each element to the still developing temporal whole — to what went before and what is expected to come after — is just as necessary to the existence of the complex experience or action as was the pre-reflective temporal horizon to the existence of its elements. The elements enter *structurally* into the more complex unit, helping thereby to constitute it the kind of experience or action it is. At this level, too, narrative in the sense of actually recounting what is being done may play a role. As Carr remarks, if someone performing an action of some complexity is asked: "What are you doing?," the answer very naturally takes the form of a story linking a present elementary action with similar actions already performed and others envisaged for the future. Indeed, in order to perform a complex action expeditiously, we sometimes need to tell *ourselves* a story about what we are doing — a consideration which suggests, *contra* Mink, that stories are not only told of what *has been lived*, but are told *in being lived*. Complex experiences and actions, so conceived, are possible on a considerable scale, as in witnessing the expansion of one's city, or in bringing up a family.

At still a third level of analysis, the structure Carr has in view shows itself not only in an individual's experiences and actions, but also in his awareness of himself as a subject experiencing and acting.[5] When we think of facing the question of how, in general, to live our lives — one that, as Carr points out, arises for everyone in a more or less reflective way — we see that the structure displayed by narrative is the principle of unity, not only of experience and action, but of selfhood as well. Personal identity could be said to be story-structured: we attain it to the degree that we succeed in integrating our lives; and that integration involves the same backward and forward sweep, the same relating of temporally separated parts to whole, that is found at other levels. The events entering into the constitution of the self must have more unity than their all having happened to the same individual: there must be a continual incorporation of a remembered past and a reaching for a hindsighted view of one's life taken as a whole. In actual experience, of course, only a quasi-hindsight is possible, by contrast with the real hindsight which historians claim. And few manage to live completely integrated lives even as far as their vision of a past and future reaches. Integration is a task, an ideal, not something that simply happens. Yet a person whose life becomes a matter of "mere sequence" is precisely one threatened by loss of selfhood. Thus although something like a narrative structure is more difficult to discern in whole lives, and a much more deliberate reflexive grasp may be needed to maintain it than is true of individual experiences, such a structure is still a principle of unity. Its complete absence entails one self's disintegration.

So far what has been considered is a form which is exhibited in the experience, action and self-awareness of individuals. If the analysis is ultimately to make a contribution to the understanding of historical inquiry, it must be shown also to have a bearing on our experience of social phenomena; and this Carr begins to do at his fourth level.[6] Individual experience and action, he points out, have a temporal horizon or meaning-conferring framework that is social as well as strictly individual. Individuals come to see that others are necessary to their own self-definition: they are indispensable elements in the life stories in which they locate themselves. Some individual endeavors, indeed, are in part socially constituted: those engaging in them build on the work of predecessors and assume that successors will carry their own contributions further – as in ongoing scientific inquiry or the maintenance of any sort of tradition – a form of social association that Carr calls the *relay-relationship*. The meaning of the single individual's contribution in such cases is dependent upon the place it finds in some larger story-like structure as a phase or stage of it, illustrating at a new level the way lower-order structures of this kind can become elements in higher-order ones of the same logical type. In such cases the structure will often stretch beyond the limits of a contributing individual's memory, and even of his lifetime. The move to a form of experience and action possessing an essentially social dimension Carr calls a transition from mere temporality to historicity. He concedes, however, that the analysis is still not in contact with truly historical concerns. For the way social relationships at this level are conceived as functioning identifies a way in which the social may enter into the lives of individuals, not a way in which individuals may enter into the life of society. And as Carr very properly insists, history is about the social, not about the individual.

It is his claim, however, that his analysis can be extended to apply to cases where the social is considered, not just from the standpoint of its place in some individual's life-story, but in its own right.[7] If we approach social groups simply as objects of inquiry existing in the world, as some kinds of social scientists attempt to do, Carr observes, we shall not be able to do this. If, on the other hand, we personify them, treating them as super-agents who act, suffer and have careers as human individuals do, we shall open up the possibility of understanding them through their "life-story" at an ontological cost that few will nowadays be willing to pay. But there is a third way in which social groups can be studied, Carr maintains, one that characterizes them not in third or second person terms, but in terms of the first person plural. The key to such an approach, he says, is to take seriously the fact that we have an entrée into at least some social groups through our being *members* of them, in which case we naturally and properly report much of what is experienced and done in them using the pronoun "we."

Indeed, there are some forms of social activity which can *only* be reported by participating individuals in this way. To use one of Carr's own examples: if a group of friends go to the store, each can truly say "I went to the store." What they collectively did is a simple sum of what they individually did. But if a house is built by a group of tradesmen, this way of talking becomes inappropriate: each must use the collective "we" to report an action in which they participated but which is ascribable, as characterized, only to the group as a whole. There are passive experiences, too, which, as described, are *of* individuals only *as* members of groups: for example, that of being insulted where in fact what was denigrated was one's country, class or religious community. Carr has already noted, in the relationship of predecessor and successor, a kind of social phenomenon needing to be under-

stood through reference to a story-like structure that reaches beyond what a particular individual did. He now reminds us that there is such a thing as essentially
co-operative activity involving more than one individual not only through time, but
at the same time. What makes such activity an activity of the group is the recognition, by those participating in it, of the collective goal and the need to achieve
it by concerted action: their willingness to say "we" and mean it. As Carr puts it,
"saying we" brings into existence a new subject; and as in the case of human individuals, the experiences, actions and career of that subject are to be understood
through a narrative-style synthesis of its past, present and envisaged future. The
bearer of meaning has altered, but the mode of understanding has not. And the
element of necessity remains: the socially characterized phenomena cannot exist as
such except by virtue of the synthesis.

In response to anticipated objections that all this represents social relations
rather too idealistically or abstractly, Carr rounds out his notion of a plural social
subject in various ways.[8] He notes that the degree of group-awareness of participants in a collective enterprise or experience, and hence the degree of group
integration, may vary; but that is true also of individual subjects. He notes that
the individuals composing many social groups of the envisaged sort – for example,
business firms or churches – may be widely dispersed geographically, and in many
cases may not know each other personally. He points out that the same person may
participate at a given time in a number of groups criss-crossing each other in complicated ways. And he concedes that for many, membership in a social group like a
nation or cultural community comes gradually: one is born into a set of relationships which one gradually comes to accept, a process which he calls "ratification."
What is essential to the group's existence is a sufficient degree of acceptance by a
sufficient number of prospective members.

Since the articulation of the group's identity through telling and retelling
its "story" is functionally tied to it, Carr notes also the importance of spokesmen
for groups, especially the larger and more complex ones, a paradigmatic case being
Lincoln's speech at Gettysburg, which recapitulated (and perhaps reformulated)
for Americans of the time what they meant (or were to mean) when they said
"we."[9] Carr concedes that what may sometimes be at issue is not just recognition
and acceptance by particular individuals, but by *all* the individuals concerned:
for example, where a social group which previously enjoyed existence only as a set
of objective relations becomes capable of saying "we" in consequence of some
"consciousness raising" experience, such as the reception of Marx's message by
the European proletariat.[10] He allows also that there may sometimes be a fine line
between saying "we" in a genuinely participatory way, and saying it rhetorically
as an instrument of persuasion, as when Hegel, as Carr sees it, tried and failed to
evoke in his fellow Europeans, through his philosophy of history, a determination
to become anything closer to a true community than an agglomeration of warring
national states.[11] He wonders in this connection whether conflict itself – presumably conflict recognized and embraced as identity-affording – might not sometimes
constitute a group of people a plural subject, a "we-saying" community. Since even
a shared sense of deprivation is seen as capable of doing so, I see no reason why
it should not.

III

Carr's analysis seems to me to have shown without question that our experience of the world, both natural and human, is commonly of something that, in basic outline at any rate, is structured in very much the way the anti-realists said actual experience never was or could be. We do not ordinarily experience mere sequences of discrete occurrences; the world does not always, or even usually, come to us in the form of "scrambled messages." Any reservations I have about this response of Carr's to Mink and White relate either to points of detail, or to just how far what he says throws light on the epistemological status of narrative in historiography. In the present section, I shall consider three interconnected points of detail before passing to the larger issue in the next.

The first concerns the extreme caution shown by Carr about being taken as advancing any ontological claim when, at various points in his ascent through the five levels, he stresses the way a narrative-like structure enters into the constitution of the experience, action or subject he considers. He talks of "constitution" even in his analysis of our most basic retentive-protentive grasp of things, and still more explicitly and emphatically in characterizing our perception of community, the group subject which comes into existence when we say "we." Yet he insists that he makes no "simple, straightforward claim that group-subjects objectively exist." What matters, he says, is that individuals who say "we" *take* them to exist, and thus "in a sense" make it so.[12] The implication he seems to want to avoid is that something can be brought into existence simply by "thinking" – or, to put it another way, that group subjects might exist only "in the minds" of those who see themselves as members of them. He therefore represents himself as making only a methodological, not an ontological point: his purpose, he says, is simply to call attention to a fruitful way of investigating human life in groups. This makes it look as if he ascribes a purely heuristic role to "saying we" in setting up a community – as if it is just too difficult, in practice, to form and maintain one unless we constantly support, clarify and strengthen our resolve in this way. But unless I badly misunderstand Carr's analysis, what he calls "saying we" is regarded by him as necessary to community life in a *constitutive*, not merely a *causal* sense: it is what defines a human agglomeration as a community, not a mere technique for maintaining in existence something otherwise defined. I therefore do not see how he can deny that his views on narrative express an ontological thesis.

Nor do I see why he wants to do so. Ascribing real existence to a social group need not imply that it exists independently of its members as some kind of super-agent – what Carr calls "a person 'writ large'" – or that it somehow determines its members' behavior.[13] And there is nothing especially puzzling, surely, about the idea of communities, in Carr's special sense, being given existence by what their members "think," so long as this includes, as on his account it clearly does, their attitudes and tendencies to behave in the ways required for the collective action and experience under consideration. A further source of Carr's ontological reticence may perhaps reveal itself in the contrast he draws between his own "inside" approach to social reality and that of social scientists who are suspicious of anything they cannot observe as "objects" and subject to empirical verification.[14] His own communal subjects, he says, are not "entities in the world" in the latter's sense;

what he is talking about is something found only in communal experience. Yet, as he points out himself, his conception of how *social* subjects are constituted is, in logic, identical to his conception of how *individual* subjects come to be;[15] and there is no suggestion that attributing existence to the latter raises ontological problems. Both kinds of subject could be said to exist "in the mind." Both exist to the extent that relevant attitudes, beliefs and actions exhibit certain kinds of coherence. As for verification: if one wishes to verify the existence of a communal subject, as Carr has characterized it, one has to test for coherence precisely as is done in the case of individual subjects. One has to ascertain the extent to which data can be narrativized as the experience and action of a subject of the appropriate kind. There is, of course, another sense, but not the one at issue, in which a communal subject, like anything else, might be said sometimes to exist only "in the mind." This is wryly illustrated by Carr himself when he entertains the possibility that the community of intelligent readers of his own book, whom he frequently addresses as "we," exists only in his, the author's, mind.[16]

The second, and related point concerns Carr's insistence that what we find at all his levels except the first is not just narrative-like structures in what is experienced — for example, beginnings-middles-ends — but *narration itself*. Having the experience or performing the action and "telling" it, we are constantly informed, are inextricably interwoven.[17] Perhaps because of this, Carr often uses the term "narrative" in a way that is ambiguous as between a structure in experience that it would require a narration to make clear, and the actual articulation of that structure. Sometimes, indeed, he seems to blur the distinction deliberately, as when he declares that "the temporal structure or organization of experience and of action is not different from a story that is told about it; rather, the experience or action is embodied in and constituted by the story . . ."[18] And he blurs it from the other end when he claims that "what is essential to narration is not that it is a verbal act of telling, as such, but that it embodies a certain point (or points) of view on a sequence of events" — which presumably means that what is essential to it is that experience have the kind of structure that *could* be narrated, the allegedly constitutive function of the actual telling in this case being put aside.[19] It reappears, however, in Carr's declaration that "a community exists wherever a [relevant] narrative account exists," by which is meant, he says, that it "gets articulated or formulated" by at least some of the group's members and is "subscribed to" by the rest.[20]

Given a concern about the epistemological status of a recounted narrative's claim to convey genuine knowledge of what it is about, the important question is whether what it refers to in fact possesses the structure the narrative ascribes, not whether narration actually goes on. It thus seems to me irrelevant, from an epistemological standpoint, when Carr reports that at level two, for the first time, "narration itself" can be discerned, an agent being envisaged as recapitulating what he is doing as he does it with a view to filtering out extraneous "noise." The same can be said of the emphasis he places on the fact that, in telling my story to someone else, or even to myself, I may make sense of my life in a way that I couldn't do before. That something frequently happens which it would be natural to describe in this way is true enough, and doubtless important, too, for any general theory of the role narration may play in practical life. But we can get things out of focus, and also raise difficulties for any eventual application of the analysis to historical inquiry, if, with Carr, we say, without qualification, that in such a case a narrative is not "reflecting or imitating something existing independently of it."[21] When I tell my story, whether to myself or to others, with a view to getting clearer who I am, I am either "stock-taking," and hence getting clearer about a narrative-like structuring that is ingredient in my life already but has not been sufficiently recognized, or I am doing for myself what Carr represented Hegelian rhetoric as doing for others: encouraging myself to bring my life into conformity with an articulated narrative structure that is evocative and prescriptive, not imitative. In actual fact, I may, of course, be doing a bit of one and a bit of the other. But unless the two enterprises are distinguished conceptually, the epistemological status of narrative in inquiry will be made more difficult to determine. It is particularly important to resist Carr's tendency to speak of narration, rather than narrative structuring, as "constitutive" – as if what does the trick is actually *saying* "we."[22] What does the constituting, as I have noted and as Carr himself also sometimes says, is an appropriate set of "we-saying" attitudes and dispositions to act.

A third point, and again a connected one, relates to the use Carr makes throughout his discussion of a three-voice analysis of narration derived from literary theory: the notion that, to understand how meaning is conveyed by a narrative, one must take account of the different "roles" to be assigned with respect to it of the characters whose experience and action the story is about, the audience or readership to which it is addressed, and the story-teller or narrator himself.[23] Carr constantly adverts to this idea. He draws attention, for example, to the levels of experience at which the roles of agent, audience and narrator become more clearly discriminable; he represents the problem of personal identity as the problem of assuming all three of these roles at the same time vis-à-vis oneself; he treats it as significant for the transition to the social level that narration has already involved the self-explaining individual with the social in the form of an audience; he stresses the extent to which the "voice" of the narrator is the voice of authority, and an ironic one at that, since he alone knows the end from the beginning.[24] The concept of narrative, Carr declares, may seem "badly miscast as a key to understanding the experience of time in general and historical time in particular," unless "some semblance" of a teller and an audience, as well as a story told, can be identified – narrative being in this sense a more complex notion than that of "configuration alone."[25]

For a theory of narrative as a literary performance, or as a practical exercise, it may be useful to talk this way, as White also does. But for an appraisal of the knowledge status of what a narrative conveys about its object, for an epistemological consideration of a claim to have discerned a narrative structure in events rather than an actual narrational performance, the whole analysis in terms of different narrative "voices" seems to me a distraction. Carr sometimes seems to be telling us that there cannot be a narrative without a narrator, someone who keeps it "on plot;" but this is only so if by narrative he means an actual narration. What matters for present purposes is whether experienced reality, and especially social reality, can possess the kind of structure that it takes narration to display without there being a narrator. Since what the narratives envisaged by Carr are about is something constituted by the cooperative commitments of agents, not the linguistic performances of narrators, the answer to this question seems to me clearly to be "yes." Perhaps this much can be said for the approach in terms of "voices:" what is actually *said* by a narrator in a particular context may well be a function of what he assumes his likely audience or readers know already: one doesn't labor the obvious. But what is taken for granted as well as what is actually said is part of the structure being conveyed and is an aspect of the knowledge claimed. It is true, too, that part of what a narrator must make clear is why the agents concerned did what they did, which may require motive explanations setting forth only what *they* believed or intended, not what was in fact true or what they ought to have intended, the explanations in that sense being given from their standpoint. But it hardly seems necessary to conjure up a babel of "voices" to make this point.

IV

When Carr turns to showing the applicability of his analysis to what historians actually write, he deals with the problem in stages, and I shall do the same. As he points out, the most promising application is to the case of an historian writing the recent history of his own nation-state or cultural community, assuming it to be a truly "we saying" social group. In such a case, he says, "historical narrative is an extension by other means, and to some extent with different attitudes, of historical existence itself. To tell the story of a community . . . is simply to continue, at a somewhat more reflective and usually more retrospective level, the story-telling process through which the community constitutes itself and its actions . . ."[26] Here the roles of historian and of spokesman for the community shade into each other, as is well illustrated, Carr aptly remarks, by the way historians of the French Revolution have contributed to ongoing debates about the nature of French society.[27] The relationship also goes the other way, historians not constructing their own narratives *ex nihilo*, as Carr likes to say, but typically taking up a traditional or pre-thematic view of their society's relation to its past and to an envisaged future, then revising and extending it.[28] This case comes nearest to exemplifying Carr's reiterated claim that there is no difference of form, only of content, between practical and historical narratives.

There are difficulties, however, about pushing such a conception of historiography very far. For one thing, there is and always must be a certain amount of tension between the practical viewpoint of a social spokesman and the theoretical, cognitively-oriented viewpoint even of an historian of his own society's recent past. Carr tries to minimize this by pointing out that spokesmen and agent-members of a community, as well as historians, have a commitment to discovering the truth about the past: they do not normally want to arrive at a view of themselves and their activities that is cognitively indefensible.[29] And, certainly, self-conceptions that are practice-oriented do not *have* to be delusive. But that does not reach to the heart of the problem raised by the likeness Carr sees between historians and spokesmen. Historiography which is continuous with a society's own process of self-definition is, as Carr himself notes, thoroughly present-centered: it is what practicing historians often call "whiggish." But historians are not supposed to interpret the past, even of their own communities, only as the past of their own present.

They are not supposed to see it only as something "radiating out" from that present, something whose main interest lies in its having led to that present, something which has practical significance in and for that present.[30] All this seems to be positively required, however, by the notion of a community "appropriating" its past through its members' acceptance of an identity-expressing narrative. In other words, the approach of a spokesman would project upon the work of any historian who adopted it a principle of narrative selection that would exclude, as it ought not to do, whatever in a community's past could *not* be appropriated.[31] The problem may be held to decrease to the extent that the investigator restricts himself to his society's *very* recent past. But it would be odd to regard as setting forth a paradigm for historiography a theory that applied only, or at any rate best, to this variety of history, a variety which, under the name of "contemporary history," has often been an object of suspicion in the profession, and might even be regarded as a necessarily defective form.

A main reason why it is frequently so regarded raises a further problem for Carr's analysis. Most historians accept the Collingwoodian principle that, at any rate for the purposes of their inquiry, history ends in the present. They concede that they have no business reconstructing the past from the standpoint of something that has not yet happened, no matter how true it may be that, if it happens, some presently-accepted accounts may have to be revised in its light. That is, historical accounts ought not to be elaborated in relation to a merely envisaged future, and still less to a projected one. As Carr himself notes, practice-oriented social narration, which not only allows such an investigative standpoint but positively embraces it, can enjoy only quasi-hindsight, a feature of every one of the five levels of experience which he treated. As was noted earlier, however, history, as generally conceived, must be written from a standpoint which claims real hindsight, this being the reason why a truly historical account of the present, in which importance-conferring consequences are only beginning to unfold, is often said to be impossible. Carr insists that the hindsight of the historian is less than absolute, this making his work more like that of the quasi-hindsighted social narrator than may at first appear.[32] But if the historian may not, as a matter of principle, take into account anything that has not yet happened and the social narrator not only may but should, the difference between their enterprises seems to be quite fundamental. The only obvious sense in which the historian's hindsight is not absolute is that his retrospective judgments, like judgments made in any sort of empirical inquiry, can be mistaken.

When Carr turns to his second case, that of an historian investigating the more remote past of his own society,[33] further difficulties arise for any attempt to treat the self-identifying narrative of a "we-saying" community as paradigmatic for the epistemological assessment of narratives in historiography. If we regard such investigation as an attempt by the historian to appropriate a still more comprehensive past into the present self-understanding of his own community, it needs to be asked whether the general idea of fellow workers in a joint enterprise, the basic idea of Carr's narratively constituted community, will really stretch this far. Can the ancient Britons be plausibly thought of as standing in that relationship to Margaret Thatcher's England, for example, or Jacques Cartier to the Canadian Confederation? Are they not, at most, predecessors, rather than partners, a form of relationship which Carr himself dismissed as too thin and too lacking in reciprocity to bring a genuine social subject into view? Indeed, even to speak of predecessors, rather than just ancestors, might often be to fall into myth-making. So quite apart from the question of whether an historian *ought* to adopt the "appropriating" approach of a spokesman to the early history of his own community, seeking to represent it in ways that enlarge its present capacity to "negotiate with its future," there is real doubt about whether such an approach can in fact cogently be taken.[34]

The other possibility is that the historian should approach the problem of narrating the history of his own society's remote past as he would that of a community which is not his own, and for which he *cannot* therefore act as a spokesman. The latter is Carr's third case, and he prepares the way for bringing it under his theory, suitably extended, by pointing out that, in so far as the social units studied were true communities, "the reality [to be] recounted is already one lived as narrative," historians thus finding themselves "dealing with and evaluating narratives from start to finish."[35] What this suggests, although Carr doesn't explicitly say so, is that a good narrative historian will try to get "inside" the narratively structured life of a social group other than his own with a view to relating its past to its present in the same appropriating way that we do our own past, but vicariously. In other words, he will try to understand that society *as if* he were a member of it looking back on its past from a certain vantage point. What isn't clear is how far Carr thinks such vicarious appropriation could legitimately go beyond what was consciously effected by the original agents. To what extent may an historian say "we" for other people after the fact? Not at all, I should have thought, although it may often be of interest to point to missed opportunities in the past for plural-subject-making. This seems to be what Carr himself was doing when he interpreted Hegel's philosophy of history as aimed at persuading Europeans to see themselves as members of a hitherto unrecognized community with shared experience of the French Revolution, the Napoleonic Empire, and so on.[36] His hearers' refusal of the proffered vision would surely imply, however, that, on the view of historical narrative explicated and defended by Carr, a narrative history of Europe, by contrast with narrative histories of its stubbornly discrete parts, is out of the question. Thus, even if no difficulty is made about the notion of vicarious appropriation – about writing history in terms of a vicarious or empathetic "they" rather than a directly participatory "we"[37] – the scope allowed by Carr's theory to legitimate narrative-construction in historiography seems to exclude much of what we should ordinarily regard as narrative history.

The point perhaps deserves further elaboration. Suppose an historian goes beyond what was consciously lived as such by the original agents: what is the epistemological status of the account he gives? Carr argues that when a lived narrative is articulated, there is no reason to say, with the anti-realists, that what the historian tells us wasn't *there*. But what of an alleged structuring of the past – say Europe itself as a developing social entity – that an historian claims to discern despite the fact that those whose actions and experiences he sees as composing it refused it as a way of making sense of their lives? On Carr's theory, the original agents could have made the structure real by adopting it; but how can the historian do that after the fact, even vicariously, without undertaking to *change* the past?[38] If the story he tells about a community's past stops short of vicarious appropriation, however, while at the same time not pointing merely to a meaning which that past might have had, on what theory of narrative are we to determine its acceptability? Not on Carr's, as far as I can see, since what we are told was not consciously lived by the agents. Yet if an historian studying another community deliberately restricts himself to reconstructing what Carr would consider its lived narrative, the same problem arises in another form. For we must then ask with reference to what point in that community's retrospectively appropriating past something properly to be called "its history" is to be elaborated. Presumably, the historian will not want simply to repeat, as privileged, the narrative account that happens to be accepted in it in his own present (or, if the society is no longer extant, was accepted in it just before its demise). But if we say, instead, that he should consider each stage of its past, vicariously, from the appropriative standpoint peculiar to that stage, the only *overall* history of the community he will be able to offer may reduce to a series of visions it has had of its past. And these may have no narrative-style connections with each other in Carr's sense. To adapt Carr's own language, there may be no narrative of narratives.[39]

Carr's fourth case is an historical account of a social group which was at one time not a community, but which became one – perhaps through the kind of consciousness-raising experience noted earlier. The application of his analysis to this sort of case follows naturally from what he has said about the apparently more easily assimilated ones. No fresh problem arises about seeking a narrative understanding of such a group's career once it has gone through its transformation. But what sort of understanding can be had of its past while it was still a group "by external classification alone," a mere set of "objective relations," rather than an expression of mutual recognition, shared experiences and objectives, and interlocking roles?[40] And what of groups like Marx's lumpenproletariat that, as Carr himself points out, never passed beyond this state? Or groups like lapsed Roman Catholics – again one of Carr's own examples – composed of persons who were participants in genuine communities at an earlier stage but no longer are?[41] Carr may well be committed, and not unplausibly, to the idea that almost no human individuals lack some degree of integration into genuine communities of some kind, these existing at every level of generality, in varying degrees, and in overlapping relations to each other. But historians will often be interested even in the members of such communities as they fall into larger, more objectively defined units, with respect to which "what happened" went on largely over their heads. Carr does say that historians characteristically *rewrite* the narratives that actual participants in a community articulate about themselves – discerning causal relations and motives that were hidden from the original agents, for example. But even if the problem of how such further information is to be related to a *lived* narrative could be overcome, we seem here to be envisaging a kind of re-writing which could not yield a narrative in Carr's sense – which, in overall conception, would go well beyond the ideas of joint enterprise and knowingly shared experience.

This is even more obviously true with regard to groups that not only fail in fact to manifest mutual recognition and genuine "narrativity," but are not, so far as we can see, of a sort that could conceivably do so. When the course of early Stuart politics is described as a "drift towards civil war," for example, or a huge concatenation of economic and technological initiatives in the nineteenth century is described as an "industrial revolution," these characterizations are essentially retrospective ones expressing a degree of hindsightedness the content of which is simply out of the range of any consciousness-raising that might conceivably have been experienced by the individuals concerned. The object of interest in such cases is simply a *resultant* of the kinds of experience and activities Carr has chiefly in mind; it is not itself such an experience or activity. Even more clearly is this so of population trends or the gyrations of the stock market. Yet historians "tell the story" of such developments as freely as they do of the experiences and activities of true communities. If Carr's analysis does not stretch this far, this is perhaps not surprising given its starting point in the problem of an individual trying to make sense of his experience for the purpose of getting on with his life: the surprising thing is that it stretches as far as it does. It has more than disposed of the Mink-White claim that the human world is never experienced in story-form, and it has done this at the social as well as the individual level. But a great deal of what narrative historians write about is not, and perhaps could not be, experienced this way. It takes the historian's reconstructive ingenuity to see the story in it. Must such cases – a very large part of what historians actually do – be abandoned to the argument of the anti-realists?

V

If they are not to be so abandoned, I think we need to take a different, a more direct, perhaps even a more simple-minded approach than Carr's to the problem of the nature and role of narrative in historiography. At the same time, we need also to respond to a broader range of anti-realist arguments: for example, to the complaints that we lack criteria of relevance for narrative construction in history, or that different narratives written by historians about the same thing make it difficult to regard any of them as representative of reality, although Carr *has* begun to put in question Mink's contention that narratives do not aggregate. In the present section I shall sketch the more direct sort of approach that I think should be taken. In the next, I shall consider *seriatim*, although necessarily rather briefly, three or four further difficulties raised by Mink and White.

The anti-realist argument that Carr chiefly responds to is that the narrative form cannot be representative of the structure of reality because it is an intellectual "artifice" rather than something "natural." The burden of his rejoinder is that, on the contrary, it is very natural indeed, thrusting itself upon us even at the level of the most elementary experience and action. But why should such a counter-claim be needed to meet the arguments of the anti-realists? Why shouldn't one instead question the assumption on which it rests: that an intellectual form – a "cognitive instrument" – needs to be "natural," something found ready-made in experience, in order to be capable of conveying the true nature of reality? In making their case against narrative realism, Mink and White do not give the impression of wanting to question human conceptualization as such. Neither of them, for example, evinces any theory-induced worry about the possibility that they may project an intellectual form upon the world in making judgments of cause and effect; and both seem to regard the notion of offering a chronicle of past happenings as entirely unproblematic so far as the capacity of a form to represent reality is concerned. Yet I see no reason, any more than did Hume, to say that the world actually presents itself to us in experience in the form of cause and effect. Causal diagnoses are things to be won by *thinking* about what is experienced, not read off it as it comes. Nor, strictly speaking, is the world experienced in the form of chronicles. As Hayden White himself points out in contrasting chronicle with annals, chronicles involve an organization of a subject-matter at least in the sense of ascribing successive items to a central subject: they have to be "of" something – to which he might have added that, like narratives proper, they are necessarily selective, if on more rudimentary principles.[42] Yet neither Mink nor White talk, in consequence, of "imposing" these forms upon what is actually experienced. Not is it plausible to do so. The relevant principle is surely: "if the shoe fits, wear it." Such forms may perhaps be said to be imposed in the sense that we have to look actively for their exemplification in what is being studied. But they are *discovered*, too, in the sense that, sometimes at least, we find that what happened did exemplify them. Which is precisely the sort of thing narrative historians often claim to do with respect to what may not, in the first instance, have been experienced as narratively structured.

I think that Carr may do the cause of narrative realism a disservice when, in seeking to counter the Mink-White sort of skepticism, he emphasizes so much the *origin* of the idea of narrative in ongoing experience and action rather than what is involved in finding it retrospectively exemplified in what may not have come narrativized to the agents in the first place.[43] From the very beginning of his discussion, he takes aim at what he regards as the distorting effects of "abstract" analysis, complaining, for example, of the "analytical dismemberment" indulged in by theorists who talk of "discrete momentary experiences" or "mere sequences," thus according real existence to "theoretical fictions."[44] He regards as equally abstract and misleading an epistemological approach to history as inquiry which, as he says, pictures historians as reconstructing the past *ex nihilo*, moving from "total ignorance" to making warranted knowledge claims about the past by applying rules of evidence to documents and relics. What they do rather, he avers, is take up a "prethematic" narrative already central to a social group's conception of itself and gradually modify it by a process not unlike that which its members went through in producing it. What such an emphasis obscures is that an existing narrative of this kind, even if the historian makes some use of it in the way envisaged, has no *authority* for him. The question whether the past reality studied really assumed the narrative form ascribed is one which he is obliged ultimately to answer without reference to it.[45] Carr's tendency to represent cognition-oriented narratives as really continuous with and developing naturally out of the practice-oriented kind gives the impression, at times, indeed, that he holds the tentative acceptance of a preexisting socially generated narrative to be a *precondition* of an historian's being able to compose a narrative at all, thus greatly exaggerating the extent to which historians, especially of remote periods, in fact begin with existing accounts. He even argues, implausibly, that all historical work is done against a pre-thematic background view of world history.[46] The latter, if so, must be an abstraction indeed, something whose necessary character could hardly consist of more than an empty spatio-temporal form to be filled in, a structure without content. Carr's arguments in this connection seem to me to place quite an unacceptable limitation upon what historical inquiry can accomplish.

The question, then, is not where our idea of narrative as an intellectual form comes from, but whether, in historical studies, we sometimes have good reason to say that it is exemplified. Any well-conceived attempt to show that we do have presupposes some analysis of narrative *as* an intellectual form. Apart from their concern about closure, neither White nor the later Mink (by contrast with the earlier) pays much attention to this when questioning the capacity of narratives to represent. They would nevertheless probably agree that a narrative is expected to make clear such things as the following.[47] It must, first, display the true temporal succession of its elements, as in chronicle, although the elements need not be cited in their order of occurrence. It must ascribe them to a central subject, also as in chronicle, a narrative having to be about something which undergoes changes of some kind. It must relate at least some of its elements to others in such a way that they explain the others, in any of a number of senses of "explain" that may be judged appropriate to the particular subject-matter. It must relate at least some of them, not just to elements preceding them, as in most kinds of explanation, but to ones that succeed, with a view to displaying their significance. And it must show by means of these and perhaps other ways of displaying connectedness, that the various elements were parts, phases, or stages of a developing whole of some kind, a feature of narrative that the earlier Mink said required "synoptic judgment" or "synthesis."[48] This entails the narrative's indicating a beginning and an ending, and hence also a middle, of what it brings into view, so that we could add, although it is already implicit, that the story told will have the formal characteristic referred to as "closure." If particular happenings relevant to the course of a political campaign, the rise of a literary style, or the course of an economic depression are conceded in fact to manifest all of these interrelationships, then there would seem to be little logical room for refusing the conclusion that they collectively exemplify the narrative form.

Carr's reservation about such a claim would apparently be that it transfers the problem too much into the "logical domain." Both narratives themselves and what narratives are about, he stresses, are *temporal* structures, developments taking place through time, from which he seems to draw the conclusion that we shall misunderstand them if we study them simply as exemplifying a *logical* form – although, curiously, he does concede that narrative "partakes of the logical."[49] He criticizes Mink, especially, in this connection, for having pictured the achievement of narrative understanding as, in the end, the taking of an "aerial view" of the process under study, in which all its elements are seen together, and all at once, in their multifarious interrelationships. I cannot see that Mink's metaphor is such an inappropriate one. What it emphasizes in such a striking way is in fact something that Carr also wants to stress: the holistic aspect of what a narrative is designed to convey. And it is surely to misread it to interpret it as denying the essential role of temporal ordering in narrative understanding. Carr himself, furthermore, makes statements that are not so unlike Mink's: for example, that what is constantly sought in narratives as lived is retrospective "synthesis," the full meaningfulness of the story depending upon a sense of always being on the brink of achieving closure. And even he describes such striving for an "authorial overview" as an attempt to "dominate the flow of events" and to "transcend time."[50] What the overview requires is a grasp of the configuration *as* a configuration. And what is aimed at by a logical analysis of narrative form in history is a characterization of the species of configuration appropriately looked for in that kind of inquiry.

Such an approach has a much broader range of application than does Carr's. No problem arises, for example, about its applying to a subject-matter where the agents involved had no awareness of the configurational pattern being instantiated, as might be true of a retrospectively discerned emergence of a large-scale economic state. And it could apply not only to human subject-matters which exist only as a set of objective relations – common location, sex or race, for example – but also to natural objects and processes completely lacking in "subjectivity," like the formation and development of the Great Glacier or the progressive cooling of the earth, about both of which narratives not only can be, but have been composed. It might perhaps be objected that, even in the latter sort of case, a residually subjective approach will be discernible in the fact that when we write stories about natural objects, we tend to humanize them – as Kermode insisted we do even in claiming to hear a clock say "tick-tock"[51] – thus implicitly giving credence to something like Carr's analysis of narrative, which ties closure in it to the idea of ending an experience or an enterprise. The modicum of truth in this contention, however, is not enough to sustain the desired conclusion; for any humanization there may be need involve nothing close to making honorary human beings of the natural objects studied. There is no need for our approach to them to be *anthropomorphic*; it will be enough that it is *anthropocentric*, stressing aspects of their "careers" which are relevant to human concerns, or at least to human interests. In other words, narratives of natural objects need not involve us in empathizing (and still less in vicarious appropriation). They need only involve our making judgments of relative importance from a human point of view.

About most of the relationships which I have identified as belonging to the logical form of narrative the anti-realists generally make no difficulty. They agree that these are often instantiated: explanatory and consequential relations, for example. Why, then do they single out narrative closure as such a problem? We hardly need to consider further the ostensible reason given by both Mink and White, namely, that there is no closure in the world, no "real" series of events ever coming to an end.[52] Quite apart from the rest of his argument, Carr has utterly scotched this with the reminder that even the most ordinary events and processes in nature end – although, curiously, putting this aside as irrelevant to his case against the anti-realists. In both the human and natural worlds, many things continue to happen, of course, after the occurrence of whatever closes a story being recounted. Things go on happening, for example, after what historians call the end of World War I. What continues to happen, however, if the historian has got it right, is not further events *of the war*. That the end of an historical narrative is not the end of the world is simply irrelevant.

If a more substantial anti-realist argument for regarding narrative closure, in particular, as somehow distancing the historian's account from the reality he supposedly characterizes, it is to be sought, I think, in what White, especially, has had to say about the allegedly moral significance of identifying beginnings and endings. Narrative closure, he tells us, is always a means of expressing a moral meaning, or even a moralizing purpose, the conveying of which he sees as a main reason why narratives get composed and related.[53] A narrative, he maintains, imposes a moral meaning on a subject-matter by virtue of its very form, the form itself therefore having a moral content – hence the title of his most recent book, *The Content of the Form*. This seems to me to get things exactly upside down. It is true that if an historian represents the arrival of Cromwell in Ireland as the end of freedom in that land, or the reform bill of 1832 as the beginning of truly democratic politics in England, certain value-judgments are implied about the subject-matter. But the presence of these judgments is not attributable to the fact that the historian is discerning beginnings and endings of a story being told; it is traceable rather to the kind of thing he is telling the story about: in the cases noted, freedom and democracy – phenomena which are, in themselves, partly value-constituted. It is *what* begins and ends, not *that* it begins and ends, which, in such cases, makes the historian's work the conduit for a moral vision of the past. So far as its formal properties are concerned, narrative is value-neutral: there is no "content of the form." Contrast the sorts of historical case just noted, for example, with narrative histories of the stagecoach as a form of transportation or the bow and arrow as a weapon of war. Pointing out that, at certain points, these were replaced by other forms of transportation or of weaponry need express no judgment as to whether this was, in either case, a good or bad thing, morally speaking. The anti-realists would find even greater difficulty in maintaining that the way a natural historian's story of the Great Glacier began and ended imposed a moral significance upon the subject-matter.

It will be clear that none of this questions in the least the view that historical inquiry is, in a number of dimensions, a thoroughly moralistic enterprise, and perhaps is necessarily so. However, this fact, or necessity, reveals itself just as clearly in non-narrative history as it does in history of the narrative variety. What goes into a cross-sectional study, for example, will also be determined, at least in part, by the historian's judgment of what was important in the state of affairs he is trying to characterize. And this will require value-judgments on his part in no way related to judgments of beginnings, middles and ends. Although both Mink and White apparently believe otherwise, even the causal judgments which enter so naturally and normally into narratives may not be value-neutral – not, at any rate, according to some plausible current analyses of the way true causes are to be contrasted with the myriad of equally necessary conditions that are not so regarded, and by contrast with which they are accorded a place in a narrative designed to be explanatory. The same may be true of conclusions drawn about consequences, reference to which may be needed for assessing the significance of what is believed to have generated them. If one is an objectivist about values, none of this will count against the claim that a given narrative, full of such judgments, tells us the way a selected portion of the past really was. If one is not, the denial that historical narratives truly represent what they are ostensibly about will simply be one aspect of a general denial that what historians tell us about the past can be interpreted realistically.

VI

What is to be said, finally, in response to other arguments of the anti-realists – for example, Mink's complaint that while, as accounts of a single past human world, historical narratives, unlike fictional ones, should aggregate, they typically do not, and by virtue of their very nature as narratives. As we pointed out earlier, a partial rebuttal of this objection is already available in Carr's demonstration that, from the second of his levels up, more elementary narrative configurations are constantly incorporated *structurally* into more comprehensive ones, as setting forth phases and stages of experiences and actions which the latter elaborate, these not being conceivable as the experiences and actions they are commonly taken to be except as thus aggregated. What Carr has in view, however, is only the incorporation of shorter narratives into longer ones by agents determined to make narrative sense of their lives. It needs to be asked whether there is a general problem with regard to aggregating narratives that might show up more clearly in cases where they were not first "lived."

The main reason for the affirmative answer given by Mink to this question is that if we attempt to put two narratives together, we destroy the beginning-middle-end structure of both of them, the ending of the first losing the status of an ending, and the beginning of the second losing that of a beginning.[54] But that is a strange argument. It is true that the beginning of the second is no longer the beginning of the narrative in which it now finds a place; but it is still the beginning of a phase of the larger development which the aggregated narrative is about. There are, of course, many reasons why particular narratives, as written, may not aggregate in the sense of combining happily from a literary point of view. Differences of scale could cause problems, or differences of style, as is notoriously true of cooperative historical works which divide a large task of historical narration into more easily handled parts. Such cooperative enterprise, furthermore, is the ideal case, the authors deliberately writing with aggregation in view. Yet even where straightforward coupling raises problems, readers generally manage to put things together. It should be emphasized, too, that, so far as the epistemological appraisal of historiography is concerned, the question of the combinality of narratives is not one of their compatibility from a literary standpoint, but of the cumulativeness of what they assert. The difference stressed earlier between narrative as an ingredient structure and as a performance is relevant here. Nor can one reasonably expect two narratives to aggregate simply because one ends at the place and time that the other begins: their central subjects may not make sufficient contact. In such a case, however, the problem of aggregation would not arise from the nature of narrative itself. Mink's worry about the difficulty of aggregating narratives thus seems to me more than a little overblown.

What, then, about the concern expressed by both Mink and White about the fact that different historical narratives get written about the same thing?[55] It is important to determine exactly what is intended by this complaint. No implication about a departure from reality is to be derived, for example, from the mere fact that two histories of the Napoleonic wars tell us different things about them, one perhaps concentrating upon elites and the other on infrastructures, or one on military incidents and the other on a broader social stratum of what happened.

It is only when historical accounts of the same thing *contradict* each other that the giving of different ones raises a problem for the contention that historians tell us what really happened. Different historical accounts may, of course, sometimes contradict each other simply by expressing incompatible value-judgments. Representing the rise and fall of Napoleon as a glorious episode in French history makes a value-judgment with which not all historians would agree. And more subtle differences of values might show themselves in the different selections made by different historians into works dealing with the same topic. But if this is the sort of thing Mink sees as the difficulty, what he is pointing to is, once again, a general problem about history as a humanistically-oriented, value-judging type of inquiry, not one specifically attributable to the fact that the accounts in question may be in narrative form. Much the same could be said of an associated concern he expresses: the fact that the same event may be seen as having a different significance in different narratives. Since, to a considerable extent, to find something significant means to find it significant for something at issue, this is surely more a banality than a problem.

Mink's worry about not being able to state objective criteria for narrative construction needs to be appraised in the light of similar considerations.[56] The criteria for narrative inclusion and exclusion are, in fact, a miscellaneous lot. The central subject – what the narrative is about – obviously affords one such criterion, and if that subject is itself partly value-constituted, this already makes the historian's value-judgments relevant to deciding what should be said. What constitute the most important episodes in changes represented as taking place in the chosen subject, whether or not it is itself value-constituted, is another consideration necessarily governing selection; and this is no more value-free than the first. The search for details that offer explanation or ascribe importance, as was noted earlier, may similarly show value-oriented selective principles at work. And the same can be said of the determination of turning points, the recognition of stages and phases, judgments that a lot or a little was happening at particular times, or estimates of a policy's success or failure. One may certainly conclude from all this that narrative construction in history does not proceed on "objective" criteria of inclusion and exclusion if by this is meant simply that the ones normally and properly applied are not value-free. Again, however, no problem is raised that is peculiar to *narrative* history.

In White's hands Mink's concern about criteria is transmuted into something approaching the claim that historians, once their basic research is done, are free to arrange what they have discovered about the past into whatever stories they like. "Any given set of real events," White maintains, "can be emplotted in a number of ways," no real event, for example, being "intrinsically tragic, comic, farcical, and so on."[57] Like Mink in some moods,[58] White here represents story-construction as essentially a literary problem, a matter of taste, imagination, and poetic inventiveness, although there still lurks in the background the idea that choosing one way of emplotting rather than another may have moral and even political significance.[59] Since I have already conceded that historical narration is not value-free, although not specifically because of its form, what needs comment is White's strongly expressed historiographical aestheticism, a recurring theme in all his theoretical writings on history. Especially to be challenged is the assumption both he and the later Mink often appear to make that two aspects of historical inquiry are easily separated: first, an investigative, empirical part which establishes what actually happened in a certain region of the past — discrete events, and possibly causal and some other kinds of connections between them; and, second, an inventive, literary part, in which the historian takes on the task of arranging his discoveries into stories, much as a painter might first gather his materials and then, within the limits they set, proceed to "create" a work of art, which could quite legitimately have taken a very different form. Declares White: "it is the choice of the story type and its imposition upon the events that endows them with meaning," a sentiment echoed by Mink.[60]

Even at the very general level of analysis that White seems to find most congenial, that at which a set of happenings is brought under one or other of the basic poetic tropes, this is a doctrine that is not easy to make plausible. Does the historian really have carte blanche with regard to how a set of events like Stalin's decimation of the kulaks or the demise of the North American Indian should be emplotted? If he "chooses" to represent it as comic, should those who find this unacceptable regard it simply as a poetic *gaucherie* or should they resist it as morally obtuse? One's specifically literary judgment would seem, in fact, to have little to do with it. There are also difficulties with regard to the application of White's doctrine below the very general level of analysis just illustrated. The historian cannot write a certain *kind* of story without writing a *particular* story; and this will have to be one that his data, his connectional conclusions and his moral and other value-judgments allow. These impose *constraints* upon the story that can legitimately be told, constraints not deriving from the historian's poetic imagination. White may be trying to take this into account when, in hailing "recent theories" which "dissolve the distinction between realistic and fictional discourses based on the presumption of an ontological difference between their respective referents, real and imaginary," he makes it clear that he has only the specifically *narrative* aspect of what the historian tells us in mind, not the *elements* which the narrative incorporates.[61] The latter, because of their evidential base, are still seen as offering a way of distinguishing history from fiction. But can realistic elements and non-realistic structures be so easily distinguished? White sometimes maintains that, by contrast with narrative, annals and chronicle are representative of reality. But even chronicle, as was noted earlier, attributes an elementary structure to its subject-matter; and annals, on White's own showing, include elements which express judgments of precisely the kind that he often finds problematic in narrative.

I turn finally to Mink's objection that if we think that historical narratives tell us what the historical past was really like, we shall commit ourselves to an unintelligible notion: that of a real past consisting of "stories waiting to be told."[62] Stories are not discovered, Mink insists; they are composed. Reality *could not* consist of untold stories; the very idea is as incoherent as, say, the idea of "unknown knowledge." All there can be before the historian goes to work is "past facts not yet described in a context of narrative form." Mink associates what he considers to be the unacceptable notion of the past as untold stories with a hankering after an outmoded conception of universal history — something, he says, which we no longer think it feasible for historians to try to write, but which lingers on as a *presupposition* of much of what we say about historical inquiry in theoretical contexts.

The idea of universal history is the idea that all the particular stories historians tell are ultimately parts of one as yet untold super-story.

But the comparison between untold stories and unknown knowledge seems to me misleading. The terms "story" or "narrative" do not stand for a kind of knowledge; they stand for a set of relationships – those sketched earlier by way of a preliminary analysis of the idea of narrative as an intellectual form or cognitive instrument. A better parallel would be between untold stories and unstated facts or undiscovered explanations. That the explanation of the outbreak of World War I lay in pre-war balance-of-power politics is something that may be true whether or not anyone discovers it. And if it is discovered, it does not only at that moment become the explanation. Neither did President Nixon's cover-up become a fact only when Congressional investigators discovered it: it was a fact all along, if an unknown one. And the same might be said of the brutality of trench warfare in the 1914–18 war, if something the perception of which requires value-judgment can be called a fact. If we do not feel as comfortable with the claim that the task of historians (as of reporters) is to "find the story," implying that it exists before the historian (or reporter) is in a position to tell it, this may be due to some extent to our feeling that stories are, after all, generally *defined* as things told, narratives *defined* as things narrated; and certainly if one insists on such definition, there are no untold stories. It might be preferable, therefore, although in most contexts it would be an unnecessarily technical way of putting it, to speak of there being unknown narrativizable configurations – "tellables" – already there for the discovering. That, at any rate, is all that need be meant, and all that would generally be meant, by the claim that there are untold stories in the past.

The case against the anti-realists could, in sum, be put this way. The configurations brought into view in historical narratives are often such that it takes a narrative adequately to characterize them – this despite White's apparent suggestion that what can be expressed by a narrative can just as well be expressed by an analysis, a meditation or a report.[63] The separation of historical discovery from the aesthetic or moral task of "writing up" what has been discovered in narrative form is based on a simple but serious error: it implicitly, but falsely, denies that part of what the historian discovers is the configuration the narrative displays. Mink and White try to contrast the form in terms of which narratives convey knowledge of the facts with the facts they see historians as arranging in those forms. But the form, the configuration, is itself the most important fact that historians discover. And facts can exist unknown.

Notes

1   *Time, Narrative and History*, Bloomington: Indiana University Press, 1986. I am grateful to Professor Carr for very helpful discussions of the thesis of this book. He offers a summary of his position in "Narrative and the Real World: An Argument for Continuity," *History and Theory*, 15, 1986, pp. 117–31.
2   Ibid., pp. 18ff.
3   Ibid., pp. 45, 66.
4   Ibid., pp. 47ff.
5   Ibid., pp. 73ff.

6   Ibid., pp. 100ff.

7   Ibid., pp. 119ff. To illustrate the distinction, Carr contrasts the significance of the Great Depression as a bar to my getting an education and as a crisis in the economic development of my country.

8   Ibid., pp. 133, 154–7, 160.

9   Ibid., p. 156.

10   Ibid., p. 133.

11   Ibid., p. 159.

12   Ibid., pp. 124, 133.

13   Ibid., p. 150.

14   Ibid., pp. 118, 124, 149ff.

15   Ibid., p. 161.

16   Ibid., p. 157.

17   Ibid., pp. 46, 111, 149.

18   Ibid., p. 149.

19   Ibid., p. 62.

20   Ibid., p. 163.

21   Ibid., p. 62.

22   For example: "narration constitutes something, creates meaning." Ibid., p. 62.

23   Ibid., pp. 5, 46, 111.

24   Ibid., pp. 57, 97, 111–12.

25   Ibid., pp. 45–6.

26   Ibid., p. 177.

27   Ibid., p. 170.

28   Ibid., p. 169.

29   Ibid., pp. 171–2.

30   Ibid., p. 168.

31   Thus, although Carr plausibly rejects the view that historical narratives are to be distinguished from practical ones by their claim to express knowledge, he appears not to see how important in this connection is his concession that they aim to express *disinterested* knowledge, Ibid., p. 171.

32   Ibid., pp. 172–3.

33   Ibid., pp. 173ff.

34   In response to an imagined objection that an historical account of a remote period of one's own society's past is not "an extension of social existence," Carr replies only that its form will at any rate be the same as that of a lived narrative. Ibid., pp. 173–4. But the problem, in the context of Carr's theory, is to say precisely what this alleged community of form consists in.

35   Ibid., pp. 174, 177. The way Carr develops this point makes his position look like a more sophisticated version of Collingwood's theory of historical understanding.

36   Ibid., pp. 151, 159. Carr observes, illuminatingly, that Hegel's hearers' failure to seize the opportunity for self-constitution thus called to their attention makes his philosophy of history a practical failure, not the theoretical one it is sometimes taken to be.

37   In his argument recommending the first person plural (we) approach to understanding social reality, by contrast with a first person singular (a super-agent), a second person (I-thou), or a third person (I-it) approach, Carr strangely neglects the claims of the *personal* third person (I-they). Ibid., pp. 119–20, 124.

38   It is clear that narrative-style structures discerned retrospectively cannot be

constitutive of groups either ontologically or causally in the sense that, on Carr's theory, lived social narratives are. They may be constitutive of them nevertheless (the structures, not their articulation), but not in any way that his theory seems capable of explaining.

39 None of this questions the more modest claim Carr sometimes makes that the narrative-style structures in terms of which past agents made sense of their lives is "part of the human reality of the past about which historians write." But his theory throws little light on what the historian is to do with them when he has found them. Ibid., p. 176.

40 Ibid., pp. 150–1.

41 Ibid., pp. 160–1, 176.

42 H. White, *Content of the Form*, Baltimore, 1987, pp. 5ff. Carr recognizes that chronicles select on principle: chroniclers, he says, "anticipate possible stories." *Time, Narrative and History*, p. 90.

43 Literary narratives, according to Carr (and he means to include historical ones), "get their narrative structure from the human world in which they have their origin. It is to this origin that they owe . . . their capacity to represent the real world." Ibid., p. 72.

44 Ibid., pp. 24–5, 66.

45 Carr observes, no doubt correctly, that the historian can "hardly be unaffected by existing pre-thematic narratives," whether or not they think they should be. But a theory of likely distractions in inquiry is not the same as a theory of how knowledge claims are to be warranted in it.

46 Ibid., pp. 174–5. Like space, Carr observes, historical time "extends in all directions about us." One cannot argue from this formal presupposition, however, that "the larger panorama of history" reaches into "the remotest regions and times," its "narrative contours" being known to the historian before he begins.

47 See, for example, *Content of the Form*, p. 6.

48 L. Mink, "The Autonomy of Historical Understanding," in W. H. Dray (ed.), *Philosophical Analysis and History*, New York, 1966, p. 185. I leave undiscussed the problem of whether the whole which a narrative brings into view must be a whole of a certain *kind* (for example: a revolution, a decline) or whether it may simply be the whole story *as configurated*. The first alternative would seem to imply the superimposition of what Mink, in his later essay, called categoreal understanding upon understanding of the configurational sort. The second appears to be seen, in the earlier one, not only as acceptable but as characteristic of historiography, where he speaks of historians' conclusions as being "undetachable" from the works that body them forth.

49 *Time, Narrative and History*, pp. 50–2.

50 Ibid., p. 62.

51 Ibid., p. 19.

52 *Content of the Form*, p. 23.

53 Ibid., pp. xi, 6, 14, 21, 24–5.

54 L. Mink, "Narrative Form as a Cognitive Instrument," pp. 137, 143.

55 Ibid., p. 140.

56 Ibid., p. 134.

57 *Content of the Form*, p. 44.

58 "Narrative Form as a Cognitive Instrument," in R. H. Canary and H. Kozicki (eds), *The Writing of History*, Madison, 1978, pp. 140, 145.

59   The exact relationship White sees holding between the moral and the aesthetic in historical narration is not easy to determine. One way he puts it, however, is that the historian's aim is "to represent the moral under the aspect of the aesthetic." *Content of the Form*, pp. 24–5.

60   Ibid., p. 44. Mink, "Narrative Form as a Cognitive Instrument," p. 140.

61   *Content of the Form*, p. x.

62   "Narrative Form as a Cognitive Instrument," pp. 135ff.

63   *Content of the Form*, p. 2. White somewhat confuses the issue, however, by remarking that some historians, of whom he clearly approves, refused narrative because "the meaning of the events with which they wished to deal did not lend itself to representation in the narrative mode."

Chapter 11

Andrew P. Norman

TELLING IT LIKE IT WAS

Historical narratives on their own terms

I

SOMETHING IS ROTTEN in state-of-the-art narrative theory. Time has done nothing to correct it, and philosophers have managed even less. At issue is the epistemic legitimacy of the historical narrative, and the debates it generates are as protracted as they are confounding. What epistemic status does the kind of stories historians tell claim, and what have they any right to claim, in virtue of their narrative form? – that is the question. Both positive and negative answers have been backed by arguments that can seem quite compelling, at least for a time. Stepping back a bit, however, can make both positions appear strange and un-natural. Sweeping denials of the story's capacity to reflect the past accurately are ever catalyzing equally misleading global affirmations, which in turn and again make the more skeptical stance appear quite attractive. The contortions that both critics and defenders of narrative go through, and the instability of the convictions they generate, should in the end, I believe, make us suspicious of the question. Narrative histories should be taken on their own terms, and their epistemic adequacy assessed on a case-by-case basis.

The issue arises because the constructive activity of the narrator is seen to be in tension with history's professed aim to tell truths about the past. Louis Mink put the problem well: "So we have a . . . dilemma about the historical narrative: as historical it claims to represent, through its form, part of the real complexity of the past, but as narrative it is a product of imaginative construction, which cannot defend its claim to truth by any accepted procedure of argument or authentica-tion."[1] Mink's doubts about the possibility of such a defense have of course not deterred philosophers from trying to provide them. Recent years have seen some rather sophisticated dialectical defenses of the narrative mode. I intend to examine these arguments in some detail, and try to make both their virtues and their short-comings stand out clearly. More importantly, however, I aim to question the skepticism that inspires such attempts.

Thus recent efforts to defend the epistemic honor of the story should be understood as a response to pervasive worries about its representational adequacy. Such worries are by no means new to our day and age. For Descartes, for example, "even the most faithful histories, if they do not alter or embroider things to make them more worth reading, almost always omit the meanest and least illustrious circumstances, so that the remainder is distorted."[2] Alasdair MacIntyre sees Sartre's *La Nausée* as advancing this idea in its most radical form. For its character Roquentin, "to present human life in the form of a narrative is always to falsify it."[3]

The revival of such sentiments in recent years is owing in part, no doubt, to the fact that philosophers have assailed narrative repeatedly over the last quarter century. Hempel's influential theory of explanation as deduction from physical "covering laws" entailed, as he pointed out, that history practiced as narrative is not genuinely explanatory.[4] History's "narrativist" defenders have struggled to counter this charge, and for the most part seem to have forgotten that the best defense is often a good offense. For one can simply reverse the entailment here: since stories evidently *do* explain, so much the worse for Hempel's theory of explanation.

Narrative historiography was also impugned for being improperly scientific. Maurice Mandelbaum, for instance, argued that historical narratives "ensure explanatory incompleteness," and inevitably constitute a "gross distortion of the subject-matter."[5] Even Mink, who was in many ways narrative's most ardent and able defender, seems to David Carr to conclude that "the very form of historical discourse undermines its epistemic pretensions."[6] The same conclusions were being reached on the continent, where narrative was caught between the "social-scientific" historians, like those of the French *Annales* school, and theorists like Roland Barthes, who claimed that "we can see, simply by looking at its structure, and without having to invoke the substance of its content, that historical discourse is in its essence a form of ideological elaboration."[7]

And although the question of narrative's cognitive legitimacy is not new, the recent controversy has given the issue its own peculiar formulation. The concern these days is whether "narrative structure" is "imposed" by the historian upon a "pre-narrativized" past. What I will call "impositionalism" is the idea, raised (or lowered) to the level of a philosophical position, that telling a story about the past necessarily involves a certain kind of interpretative violence. The contemporary theorist who has pushed the impositionalist line hardest is Hayden White:

> Since no given set or sequence of real events is intrinsically tragic, comic, farcical, and so on, but can be constructed as such only by the imposition of the structure of a given story type on the events, it is the choice of the story type and its imposition upon the events that endow them with meaning.[8]

Constructing a narrative, for White, always involves the "projection onto the facts of the plot structure of one or another of the genres of literary figuration." The "real" past is devoid of meaning and order, on this view, for "in the historical narrative, the systems of meaning production peculiar to a culture or society are tested *against* the capacity of any set of "real" events to yield to such systems."[9] Positivist attacks on the narrative mode, it seems, have left scars on its epistemic reputation that have never fully healed.

Several forms of interpretive violence, or "imposition of structure," are commonly pointed to as endemic to story-construction. To begin with, an historian must always *select* the facts he or she will use, often on the basis of some identifiable criterion, interest, or bias. This is commonly held to insure a story's radical incompleteness, if not guarantee its falsehood. Artificial *closure* is created by the choice of beginning and end. The facts must then be integrated or configured in a way that creates a unity and coherence that are, strictly speaking, foreign to the past itself. "Imposition," then, signifies the activity wherein criteria of relevance are applied, closure is attained, and coherence and unity are created – a process, in short, that generates an *emplotted* account of the past.

Entering the 1980s, the issue of narrative's epistemic legitimacy had assumed the contours of the realism–constructivism controversies that philosophers of science and ethical ontologists, for example, know all too well. Do we, in constructing a narrative history, impose a narrative order on the past, or do we simply read off an order that is already there? What I will call "historical realism" is the idea that history exists as a determinate, untold story until discovered and told by the historian. Such a position naturally inclines in the direction of a high regard for narrative's epistemic legitimacy. Although seldom explicitly defended, it or something like it is often inveighed against.[10]

The important point for our purposes is that those arrayed against this realism have included narrative's supporters as well as its detractors. Narrativist affirmations of storytelling as a selective, creative activity have understandably done little to further its epistemic standing, for such affirmations give rise immediately to suspicions of misrepresentation. Without intending to inpugn the epistemic status of the story, narrativist contributions to the recent debate have in fact had that effect. In short, with the battle-lines thus drawn, the blatantly constructed character of the historical narrative has put narrativists on the defensive, and given impositionalists the upper hand.

A number of philosophers have come to the defense of narrative, however, offering innovative arguments for its cognitive validity. There are at least two quite distinct approaches that can be discerned in the literature. One grows out of a phenomenological understanding of the world as "already" structured in certain definite ways. It argues that narratives do not impose order or intelligibility where there is none, but instead merely give voice to a past that is already narratively structured. The second has its roots in the speech-act theory that is trying to situate and delimit truth-seeking discourse within a wider and more diverse set of language-games. The idea here is that historical narratives have wrongly been assumed to be making *truth* claims, and consequently judged by the wrong standard.

The first approach, in defending narrative's representational adequacy, amounts to a kind of moderated realism. The second, in challenging the very ideal of representational adequacy, tacitly admits narrative's representational *in*adequacy, and thus falls out as a sort of radicalized impositionalism. Although both develop important insights that must be retained, it will be shown that they misdescribe the way we construct and treat historical narratives and remain inadequate answers to the problem of their epistemic status.

II

The work of Alasdair MacIntyre, David Carr, and Frederick Olafson suggests a way of defending historical narrative against the charges brought against it by the impositionalists.[11] The impositionalist claim was that recounting the past in the form of a story inevitably imposes a false narrative structure upon it. By exploiting the phenomenological insight that the lived world of everyday experience is "already" structured in a number of ways, the response is made that that about which we tell stories is already *narratively* structured. The argument is that, because life, experience, and the past as lived are coherent and intelligible *before* we begin telling stories about them, the skeptical worries about imposing false coherence are ill-founded.

This line differs significantly from that of the (naive) "historical realism" mentioned earlier, in that both story and past are now taken to be thoroughly and inescapably interpreted: the "objectivity" of neither is presupposed. More precisely, neither the naive metaphysical posit of a past-in-itself, nor the problematic claim of epistemological access to such a past is taken for granted or defended. Rather than worry about our lack of access to a "real" past, independent of human acts of interpretation and cognition, the defenders of this line get on with the task of describing and thinking about the lived world: a world that is for them already narratively structured.

MacIntyre's account of the "narrative structure of a human life" is a small but important part of the argument of his book *After Virtue*, "Narrative," he claims, "is not the work of poets, dramatists and novelists reflecting upon the events which had no narrative order before one was imposed by the singer or the writer; narrative form is neither disguise nor decoration." He goes on to say,

> It is because we all live out narratives in our lives and because we under-
> stand our own lives in terms of the narratives we live out that the form
> of narrative is appropriate for understanding the actions of others. Stories
> are lived before they are told – except in the case of fiction. . . . What
> I have called a history is an enacted dramatic narrative in which the
> characters are also the authors.[12]

MacIntyre, then, would have us believe that our lives, and human history more broadly, are "enacted narratives." Both *our* pasts, and *the* past have a "narrative structure," for MacIntyre, prior to and independently of any explicit act of story-telling. Now this is not just the claim that we constantly and ordinarily understand ourselves and our past in the narrative mode; that is, with the aid of stories told with greater or lesser degrees of explicitness. MacIntyre wants to be taken quite literally when he says that our lives actually *are* enacted narratives, that human history actually *is* a dramatic enactment of some story or set of stories. He needs to make this stronger claim in order to give his account of the moral life the determinacy, continuity, and rootedness it needs in the face of the fact that disparate practices give rise to conflicting virtues.[13]

In any case, it is only because this stronger claim is made that the position articulated here represents an answer to impositionalism – a defense of the epistemic status of narrative. Because narrative structure actually inheres in that about which we write narrative histories, telling the story of the past is not a matter of imposing such a structure upon it. As Carr puts it:

> For if I am right in thinking that narrative structure pervades our very experience of time and social existence, independently of our contemplating the past as historians, then we shall have a way of answering the charge that narrative is nothing but window-dressing or packaging, something incidental to our knowledge of the past.[14]

The idea of the narrative structure of human experience (MacIntyre uses "life" where Carr speaks of "experience")

> permits us to correct the view that structure in general and narrative structure in particular is imposed upon a human experience intrinsically devoid of it, so that such structure is an artifice, something not natural but forced, something that distorts or does violence to the true nature of human reality.[15]

This view has several virtues atop its simple, homely appeal. To begin with, it goes a long way towards correcting a certain "atomistic prejudice" that has long been part of the analytic approach to the philosophy of history. The argument here is that, contrary to what many analytic philosophers (especially the impositionalists) have assumed, the past is not initially or primarily given to us in the form of separate, isolated incidents that are then given a false narrative coherence by an historian. Doing history is as much the breaking up of an initially seamless whole as it is the bringing together of initially unrelated events. World War II was no less real, no more a fiction, than was D-Day. And the D-Day of the historian is not just the events that happened during a certain twenty-four hour period. We understand the battle in terms of its being a pivotal episode of the war, and its boundaries and significance are set accordingly. The individuation of constitutive events is seldom unproblematic, and is usually guided by concerns informed by a prior understanding of the larger historical context.

Now I think that this objection cuts pretty deep. There does not seem to be any reason why the individuated "event" should enjoy epistemic priority over broader or more extended historical structures. In history, the parts are no more unproblematically "given" than is the whole. Impositionalism, it seems, has given unreflective priority to the "atomic" event (a questionable notion at best), and based its critique of narrative in large part upon this misleading supposition. Unity, coherence, and structure cannot be viewed as mere artifacts of the historian's work. The appearance of coherence should not by itself arouse skeptical suspicions, any more than should disjointed incoherence. Either can be an imposition of a false order (or lack thereof), but neither need be.

A second virtue of the plot-reifier's account is that it seems to explain how historical narratives can be true. A story about the past is true, on such an account, when it accurately maps the real narrative structure of the lived past. This is not an insignificant result, given that we *do* speak of histories as claiming and attaining truth, and that it is difficult to see how else we might explain the capacity of a history to be true, in light of the impositionalist charge that stories contain structures that do not appear in the past itself.

In an earlier work, MacIntyre had expressed an interest in defending the truth-claims of narratives. "To raise the question of truth," he wrote, "need not entail rejecting myth or story as the appropriate and perhaps the only appropriate form in which certain truths can be told."[16] The conclusion he reaches in *After Virtue* seems to have been forced by a need to explain how this can be so. The apparent reasoning is not difficult to trace. If stories about the past have a certain narrative structure, and some of them at least are true, then the past itself (on a correspondentist view of truth, it seems) must have that structure also. The thought that our lives are already narratively structured, then, represents a solution to what has been a long-standing problem for MacIntyre, and indeed, narrative theorists more generally.

I do not think we need to go to such extremes to affirm the epistemic status of the narrative history. Histories can be true without their being isomorphic structures in the past. Nor need we invoke or presuppose "correspondence" theories of truth to make sense of such claims. To call a story true is just to say that what it tells us about the past did happen – that what it says once was, was. It is when we go beyond this homely understanding that we run into problems. For accounts of truth in terms of correspondence (or some other sort of structural isomorphism) seem to require that "narrative structure" belong to both true stories and that which they are about. What history tells stories about is the past, and quite frankly, I do not think we can make sense of the notion of a past that is "already" narratively structured. To focus this critique, let us ask first what "narrative structures" are supposed to be, and then inquire into whether they are the kind of thing that even *can* belong to the past.

How are we to understand this crucial notion of "narrative structure"? I have not been able to find a clear account of it anywhere in the literature.[17] I think that it is crucial to MacIntyre and Carr that this central notion remain unexplicated, for as soon as we begin to spell it out, we run into difficulties. I should note, initially, that I do not think the same is true of other "structures" that serve as a model for this type of claim. To say that the past has a *temporal* structure, for example, strikes me as relatively unproblematic. I think we can also grant that the lived past is at least for the most part meaningfully arranged.[18] We might even say that the past as we know it is criss-crossed by the kind of intelligibility and significance structures that story-lines must trace out in portraying that past.

My point here is that, whatever it is a *narrative* structure is supposed to be, it must be more than just these things. To deserve the modifier "narrative," a structure must have the characteristics that are peculiar to and definitive of stories. And stories are discursive entities that display at least the traces of a plot. I can think of no account of narrative structure that does not come back, in the end, to the idea of plot. Even a discursive entity without a plot has an extremely tenuous claim to be called a story. Something that is neither discursive nor emplotted, it seems to me, has even less. But suppose we go along with the metaphorical extension of "narrative" to nondiscursive things. Such entities would still have to have something resembling a plot even to begin to count as "narratively structured." Thus something's not having a narrative structure would seem to follow pretty directly from its not having a plot.

But can the past have a plot? The notion of an already emplotted past is not an idea I think we can understand. For to speak of something as having a plot is to raise questions of its emplotment: of who authored it, how, when, and for whom. The notion entails not just that the past has an author, but implies also the occurrence of a prior storytelling. The "already," of course (on MacIntyre's own admission), means: prior to its story ever being told.[19] Putting aside questions of authorship and audience, we can ask: how and when did the past come to be emplotted? Either the storytelling that emplots the past never occurred, in which case the claim that it is actually emplotted is dubious or metaphorical at best, or it occurred prior to its story ever being told, which seems like a conceptual impossibility. The point, of course, is neither more nor less than this: that talk of a narratively structured past is, *strictly speaking*, nonsense.

It will be objected that this rebuttal relies upon a relatively straightforward denial of what MacIntyre and Carr assert. For MacIntyre's claim was that "stories are lived before they are told," and the suppressed premise of the above argument is clearly that, in order to *be*, a story must first be told. If one bare assertion is as good as another, what reason do we have for preferring either?

The bare implausibility of an emplotted past, I contend, places the burden of proof squarely on MacIntyre and Carr. This is a burden they tacitly accept by providing arguments for their central claim. Unfortunately, these arguments do not work. Carr's argument takes the form of a chapter-long excursus that never addresses the primary objection, which I have given above. That Carr's argument begs the central question at issue is made clear by his own formulation of his argumentative strategy: "Unless we can find some *semblance* of this complex relationship (that of story, story-teller, and audience) in the ordinary *experience* of time, it may be thought that the concept of narrative is badly miscast."[20] One reply, of course, is that it is not enough to show, as Carr proceeds to do, a *semblance* in this respect, and that, because of this, the concept *is* badly miscast.

But more to the point, it is not enough to show that our ordinary *experience* has this form. For noting a structural similarity between narrative histories and our experience of the past does not allow us to explain how those histories can be true. On the concept of truth that motivates this line, it is what histories are *about* that must be shown to have narrative structure, and the fact is, such stories purport to be about the past, not just our experience of it. If an historical narrative recounts our ordinary experience of the past, but does not report what actually happened, we rightly do not call it true. Hence it does not suffice to defend this far weaker claim.

The only gesture MacIntyre makes by way of argument here is quite clever, but it relies on a trick. The inference to the past's narrative structure is carried by the idea that it is "historical."[21] But this move only gets MacIntyre where he needs to go by exploiting the double sense of the term "history." If we spell out the argument, we find that its major premise is a falsehood disguised as a tautology: since history (in the sense of "our stories") has a narrative structure, history (in the sense of "the past") has a narrative structure. But when we recognize this ploy for what it is, the plot-reifiers are left without an argument for their central claim.

Quite simply, our concept of narrative is not as radically separable from that of discourse as this approach to defending narrative hopes and/or presupposes. Plot or narrative structure appears for the first time, if not exclusively, in the realm of discourse. The fact that a true historical account has a plot structure does not imply that the past it articulates has a plot structure, any more than the fact that "the sky is blue" has a grammatical structure implies that the sky has a grammatical structure.[22] The past need not have a narrative structure for a story about it to be true. To deny this is to confuse discursive form with semantic content: the presentation of a story with what it tells us. A plot, like grammar, is a structure that belongs to discursive entities. The past, like the sky, is not a discursive entity.

We have found no warrant, then, for the claim that the past is narratively structured. Taken literally, it is a flat out contradiction in terms — a simple category mistake. Of course it could quite properly be objected here that this rebuttal relies upon an uncharitably literal construal of the plot-reifier's central premise. The account fares better if simply accepted as the metaphor it is. Now this reply is well, true, and good as far as it goes. The plot-reifier's line *does* build on an instructive and worthwhile metaphor. But unless it is taken literally, the plot-reifier's thesis simply does not explain how stories can be true. Nor does it constitute a solution to the problem of narrative history's epistemic status. To eliminate the worry that narrative construction involves an interpretative violence, this defense of narrative must reify the structures that properly belong to stories, and project them onto the past. For then they can be "found" there, thus making narrative true. But, as we have seen, at least one of those structures — that of plot — is to be found only in stories.

And it seems to me that the plot-reifier's account suffers in another respect as well. It does not adequately acknowledge the truly constructive nature of the historian's work. If narrative structure is already there, prior to the historian's arrival, it begins to look as if the historian's task is simply a matter of finding and more or less passively (and literally!) *reading* narrative structures off of the past. What is already emplotted requires no emplotment, and the historian's creative skills never even come into play. On such an account, the past has its own story to tell, and the historian becomes a mere stenographer! This is misleading, however, for (except in rare cases) narrative histories must be hunted out and pieced together, arranged and articulated, worked and reworked in a constructive and often painstaking process. The plot-reifier's account does not do justice to the creative, actively configuring character of narrative construction.

I think, then, that we can follow the plot-reifiers in their attempt to affirm the truth-claims of (some) narratives, and still reject the strategy of reifying narrative structures in order to validate narratological representation. No matter how integrated, coherent, and structured our experience of the past "already" is, one cannot deny that the historian must piece together, interpret, articulate, and configure remnants of the past in constructing a narrative about it. And this will always leave room for suspicions of misrepresentation. There is no global defense of the narrative form that will insulate it, once and for all, from skeptical doubts.

III

The second approach to defending narrative as a respectable discursive tool is not as concerned that its representational adequacy be vindicated. It involves throwing into radical question the assumption that narrative histories even *purport* to be true, and amounts to the demand that we look at narrative histories as seeking something other than referential legitimacy. Histories must be seen, not as simple representations of what once was, but as practically oriented attempts to reshape our effective collective understanding of the past.[23] The rallying-cry of this movement has been that truth-claims belong to one language game, and historical narratives to another.

Anti-referentialism, then, may be seen as part of the movement – running from Wittgenstein through Austin to contemporary speech-act theory – to correct for the oversights and misperceptions that come from a view of language as a purely representational medium. It aims to bring to light the often obscured normative, performative, and practical dimensions of narrative language use.

The placing of narrative and the "criterion of truth" into separate realms also creates a fissure between the natural and human sciences that is intended to block the methodological imperialism of positivism. Habermas conceives this move in even broader terms. It is for him part of the attempt to halt the steady encroachment of instrumental rationality upon the symbolic-interactive realm that includes the historical–hermeneutical sciences.[24] On the anti-referentialist view, the criterion of truth as accurate representation has been wrongly imported across a fundamental divide, and used to dismiss historical narratives as epistemologically inadequate.

Narrative, on this account, should not be regarded as a mimetic mode. Rather than looking at historical narratives as referential, or candidates for truth, anti-referentialists would have us see them as striving to attain other discursive virtues such as coherence, comprehensiveness, and followability. If the function they serve is to foster comprehension, for example, then they must be evaluated according to whether or not (or to what degree) they achieve this end, not according to whether or not they correspond to what was once reality.[25]

Of course, in order to count as history rather than fiction, narratives must attend to the facts, but by and large this is reconceived to be a side issue. John McCumber, for example, defines narrative for his own purposes as the "reconstruction of a progress" that "aims at coherence" as opposed to "accuracy." "The 're-' in 'reconstruct,' to be sure, means that [one is] not engaged in fiction . . . but this does not mean that narrative aims at historical truth."[26]

Now I would like to applaud the motives of this attempt to protect history from the imposition of foreign standards, and I think that the need to correct an imbalance caused by a disproportionate attention to the representational function of language indeed calls for strong measures. My concern, however, is that the anti-referentialists have gone too far, and introduced arbitrary and pernicious distinctions in order to further these worthy ends. To point out the dimensions of storytelling that accounts of them as purely representational leave out is surely worthwhile, but to deny the referential function of narrative is likewise to miss something important. To argue that narratives ought not to be evaluated on their truth-content *alone* is one thing, but to develop a dichotomy that places narratives in a language game wholly apart from truth is another thing again.

The fact is, historical narratives for the most part *do* purport to tell us what the past was like. They consist of assertions *about* the past, and they attempt to tell us what actually occurred. This means precisely that narrative histories purport to refer — that they claim truth. Furthermore, they are generally offered for critical scrutiny on the understanding that entitlement to assert them can be revoked for inability to defend them successfully against significant challenges. Histories do belong — and properly — to language games wherein evidence must be given for novel claims, challenges to the truth of a given account are often appropriate, and confirmation and disconfirmation do in fact occur. It is highly artificial, not to mention outright dangerous, to claim that the question of whether or not an historical narrative is true is not a good question, or a category mistake of some kind. This is often a perfectly appropriate question, and at times it is of the utmost importance that it be answered. The recent revisionist histories that claim that the Holocaust never occurred, for example, challenge the truth of received accounts, and themselves call for immediate disconfirmation. It just would not do to exempt such stories from "the criterion of truth." As MacIntyre puts it: "It matters enormously that our histories be true."[27]

IV

The breakdown of both the plot-reifier's and the anti-referentialist's defenses of narrative casts us back upon the question of the epistemic legitimacy of the story. How can the impositionalist charge be answered short of reifying plot-structures or pulling narratives out of the truth-game entirely? The charge, again, was that casting the past into the form of a narrative falsifies that past by imposing a foreign structure upon it. I do not think that a knock-down argument against the skeptic is possible. But I do think we can indicate, in a preliminary manner, a way in which the impositionalist's skeptical conclusion can be reasonably avoided.

The first thing to note is that an argument advanced earlier (to block the inference to real narrative structures) can be used again here against the impositionalist charge. The fact that a discursive representation has a structure that that which it represents does not, does not itself entail that a falsifying imposition has taken place. To make this inference reflexively is again to confuse discursive form and semantic content. Discursive structure is not inherently falsifying, for its constitutes the positive condition of the possibility of language having *any* semantic content — of its being able to represent or be true at all. (This is as true of simple descriptive claims as it is of narratives. Without the grammatical structures that are a necessary part of any language, there would not even be any candidates for truth or falsity, and "true" would be meaningless. It follows from this that we must accept such structure as non-falsifying if the idea of truth is to remain meaningful.) A narrative certainly *may* impose a false coherence, or simply get the past wrong, but it *need* not.

The second argument against impositionalism, quite briefly, is that it does not adequately characterize the process of doing history. It is undeniable that historians must select, piece together, interpret, arrange, and so on, but to say that this constitutes an *imposition* on the past is to imply a violence that "misses the properly dialectical character" of historical inquiry.[28] A good historian will interact dialogically with the historical record, recognizing the limits it places on possible construals of the past. Although the traces of the past *underdetermine* the stories that can be told about that past, it is simply not the case that an historian must invent and impose to achieve a concrete determination. Historians are accountable for their choice of facts, wording, arrangement, and cast, and generally make these choices with an eye towards what the historical record will support. Characterizing what a good historian does as imposition — that is, in terms that suggest violence — is on a par with attempts to portray the process as simple transcription — a description that misleadingly implies passivity.

And those specific skeptical worries that were mentioned above can be answered, briefly, in turn. *Of course* historians select their facts, and obviously the stories they tell are incomplete. But by itself this does not mean that the result is distorted or false. To say so is to posit implicitly an evaluative ideal of a history that is complete and non-perspectival. But this very idea is incoherent. I have never read a history that claimed perfect objectivity or completeness, nor do I expect to. We learn to read such histories as situated and discriminating; and eventually learn, too, that such general skeptical objections count for nothing.

Nor need the charge of artificial closure worry us unduly. It is certainly true that, as MacIntyre acknowledges, "in taking an event as a beginning or an ending we bestow a significance upon it which may be debatable."[29] That is why historians usually go out of their way to situate the stories they tell in the larger context of what came before and after. But the fact that a story must begin somewhere and end somewhere else does not necessarily mislead. It might, of course, but the critic must shoulder the burden of showing that it does in any given case. In some cases, it will be possible to make the case for a falsifying imposition, and in others the attempt to do so will seem like a trivial academic exercise.

Nor does the appearance of coherence, unity, or intelligibility in a told story about the past indicate that distorting forces were at work in its creation. To make this argument, one must assume that the past is initially without order, coherence, or intelligibility. But we have no evidence for this. What we do know is that the past as we experience it in memory often does have unity, coherence, and intelligibility. Even where our initial, inarticulate experience of the past does not exhibit this coherence, the process of constructing a coherent story about it need not, and often does not, have the violent character of an imposition. Quite simply, it often has the unobjectionable character of a disclosure.

V

I have argued that there is something strained and artificial in each of three major positions in the philosophy of history. Some theorists insist, in spite of numerous counterexamples, that historical narratives cannot be true. In opposition, there are those who are driven to make bizarre ontological claims in order to defend the epistemic honor of the story. Finally, yet another group of theorists have embraced the conclusion that narrative histories do not even *claim* truth.

Each of these claims grows out of what can be formulated as a paradox. If you accept that narrative histories *purport to be* true, and believe that some of them *are* true, then you must explain how they *can be* true, given that story-construction brings new narrative figures into existence. Common sense will acknowledge the constructive, configuring activity of narrativizing, and simultaneously want to affirm the truth of some narratives. With a little philosophical coaching, however, this view can be made to seem incoherent, or at least paradoxical: for how can a process that imposes a foreign structure on the past produce true stories? The task is then to decide which of the three premises that generate the paradox one is going to throw out.

Impositionalists, as I have described them, accept that historical narratives purport to refer. They also believe that telling a story inevitably imposes a falsifying narrative structure on the past, and come to the unhappy (and contrary to experience) skeptical conclusion that narratives cannot be true.

Anti-referentialists opt out of the problem by denying that narrative histories even claim truth. This position, of course, is motivated largely by the desire to foreground the other, non-referential functions of narrative discourse. But to the extent that it constitutes a solution to this problem, it must deny the seemingly evident fact that historical narratives ask to be taken as true.

Plot-reifiers agree with the impositionalists that history aims at truth, but differ with them in thinking that it sometimes succeeds. This puts pressure on the central premise that narratives inevitably falsify the past by imposing a narrative structure upon it. By pretending to have discovered that the past is already narratively structured, these theorists can claim unique epistemic merits for the story. In brief, they reify plots in order for there to be something in the world to which narrative structures can correspond in being true.

In conclusion I would like to sketch the outlines of a stance towards narrative that escapes this trilemma. I have argued that it is important to preserve an understanding of histories as claiming, and sometimes attaining, truth. This means getting used to the idea that constructing an historical narrative need not falsify the past. Now some will argue that there is an unresolved or unresolvable tension between historical narrative's constructed and its (purportedly) referential character. In response to such a view, I would like to point out that some narrative histories simply *are* true constructs. I am urging that we take this fact seriously, and come to grips with what it means for narrative theory. Quite simply, *construction does not entail falsification*. Narrative history may be *figural* in the sense of generating new discursive figures, and at the same time *literal* in the sense of asking (and deserving) to be understood literally, and *there is nothing contradictory in this*.

So far this line does not differ in any significant respect from that of the plot-reifiers. Both accounts assert that historical narratives claim and sometimes attain truth, and are confronted with the task of explaining how this can be so. Plot-reifiers met this demand with assertions of the past's narrative structure, an "explanation" that suggests a pronounced tendency to think of truth in correspondence-like terms.

The dialectical option I am trying to articulate here distinguishes itself, first off, by distancing itself from the correspondence theory of truth and all of its attendant problems.[30] Correspondence accounts are built on the paradigm of simple descriptive (observation-) statements, and above and beyond difficulties in this, their stronghold, they grow increasingly inadequate the further one gets from that paradigm. For example, it is difficult to see or say in what respect, if any, a scientific theory that posits unobservables "corresponds" to the world. Some say that for this or like reasons, we must cease speaking of such theories as being true.[31] Such recommendations draw upon arbitrary-seeming distinctions, however, and distort ordinary usage to no apparent end.[32] How a true ethical judgment or a moral theory can correspond to the world is perhaps even more puzzling. But that does not mean that it is not true to say: "Murder is wrong." The same, I think, goes for narrative histories: they can be true without our being able to make any sense of the claim that they correspond.

Closer to the heart of what separates this common-sense line from more traditional accounts, however, is the issue of whether we need or want *any* theory of truth. Realisms and anti-realisms alike are often inclined to accept the burden of explaining what it is that truth consists in. There is a reasoned alternative to shouldering this burden, however. It is based on a denial that we need any such thing. The felt need for such a theory may itself be questioned, and in fact has been the target of rather telling critique.[33] No doubt those who push theories of truth will use familiar marketing techniques to preserve the illusion that we need what they have. Without such an account, they will say, we do not really understand what truth-claims are saying. But this simply is not true. We do not typically experience a problem understanding such claims. Nor is this any less true in cases where truth is predicated of stories. Even philosophers, who cultivate an ability to have their understanding of such things lapse, show definite performative signs that they understand well enough what they profess to be mystified by.

Thus scientific attempts to *describe* an eternal present, ethical attempts to *prescribe* a better future, and historical attempts to *reinscribe* the past can each be true in their own way. For those with a hankering for generalities, perhaps we can say (colloquially and in lieu of any proper theory of truth) that the first can be true for *telling it like it is*, the second for *telling it like it ought to be*, and the third for *telling it like it was*. What this amounts to in specific cases will of course vary widely. We must not expect more precision at this level of generality than the subject-matter allows.

Of course much more than this is required to carve out this dialectical niche and show that it is viable. My purpose has merely been to motivate a closer look at an alternative that avoids some of the recurrent difficulties of traditional accounts. A more adequate treatment would include a thorough explanation of why a relatively simple alternative to such problematic positions has been so seldom taken up. I will not attempt such an explanation here. It is worth noting, however, that it is extremely easy to generate a sense that a narrative's being true requires some sort of explanation. (How is it that each narrative history can articulate the past uniquely, yet somehow entirely different stories can disclose one and the same past? How is it that it can be at the same time figural and literal?) It may seem difficult to understand how this can be so, but we are in a position now to see our very puzzlement here as questionable. Might not this perceived lack of comprehension be the artifact of a deep-rooted "descriptivist" prejudice — the mistaken idea that we don't really understand how language works until we can see it as "standing in" for something?

The fact that a narrative is the product of a creative process, a construct that articulates the past anew, does not by itself compromise its truth. It might do so badly or wrongly, of course, in which case that would have to be pointed out. But such critique must be carried out on a case-specific basis. Global judgments require some external measure, and narratives do not need to be treated as an approximation to some foreign ideal. Instead, we might try simply understanding narratives on their own terms. What more is there to such understanding, after all, than our respective abilities to construct, recount, enact, embellish, share, and enjoy them?

Notes

1   Louis O. Mink, "Narrative Form as a Cognitive Instrument," in *The Writing of History*, Robert H. Canary and Henry Kozicki (eds), (Madison, Wisc., 1978), 145.
2   René Descartes, *Discourse on Method* [1635], trans. Donald A. Cress (Indianapolis, 1980).
3   Alasdair MacIntyre, *After Virtue* (South Bend, Ind., 1984), 214.
4   Carl Hempel, "The Function of General Laws in History," *Journal of Philosophy* 39 (1942), 35–48, and "Explanation in Science and History," in *Frontiers of Science and Philosophy*, R. Colodny (ed.), (Pittsburgh, 1962).
5   Maurice Mandelbaum, "A Note on History as Narrative," *History and Theory* 6 (1967), 414–15.
6   David Carr, *Time, Narrative and History* (Bloomington, 1986), 11.
7   Roland Barthes, "Introduction à l'analyse structurale des récits," *Communications* 8 (1966).
8   Hayden White, "The Question of Narrative in Contemporary Historical Theory," *History and Theory* 23 (1984), 20, reprinted in *The Content of the Form* (Baltimore, 1987), 44.
9   Ibid., 47 (my italics).
10   Leon Goldstein is perhaps the notable exception. See his *Historical Knowing* (Austin, 1976). What I am calling "historical realism" Mink referred to as "universal history" – an idea, he says with deep roots in the moral project of the Enlightenment, and perhaps even deeper roots in common sense. Although "seldom explicitly held," he argues, this view is "almost universally presupposed," as is evidenced by the intelligibility to us of the idea of an objective chronicle of history. Mink, "Narrative Form," 137–41.
11   MacIntyre, n. 3; Carr, n. 6; and Olafson's *The Dialectic of Action* (Chicago, 1979).
12   MacIntyre, *After Virtue*, 212, 215.
13   For a convincing account of the contortions MacIntyre goes through to find determinacy for the ethical life, see Pablo DeGreiff's "MacIntyre: Narrativa y tradicion," *Sistema* 92 (Madrid, 1989), 99–116.
14   Carr, *Time, Narrative and History*, 9.
15   Ibid., 43.
16   Alasdair MacIntyre, "Epistemological Crises, Dramatic Narrative, and the Philosophy of Science," *The Monist* 60 (1978), 457.
17   Earlier attempts by M. White, A. Danto, and W. B. Gallie to cash out this notion in terms of causal chains, temporal sequence, and followability are unlikely to be of any use here, for White's and Danto's attempts to develop causal models

of narrative — that is, accounts in which the ordering principle of a story is that later events are caused by earlier ones — were undermined by Gallie's argument that antecedent events in an historical narrative seldom if ever amount to sufficient causal conditions for the occurrence of later events. Gallie's own account in terms of followability faces what seem to be insurmountable difficulties. In addition to being too vague to be of any real use, the notion of an unfollowable narrative does not seem to be a contradiction in terms. See Morton White, *Foundations of Historical Knowledge* (New York, 1965); Arthur Danto, *Analytical Philosophy of History* (Cambridge, 1965); W. B. Gallie, *Philosophy and Historical Understanding* (London, 1964).

18   "For the most part" because the past is not *always* already meaningfully arranged. As Paul Roth pointed out to me, patients in psychoanalysis often suffer precisely from an inability to find any meaningful arrangement to the past.

19   "Stories are lived before they are told . . ." MacIntyre, *After Virtue*, 212.

20   Carr, *Time, Narrative and History*, 46, and the rest of Chapter 2 (my italics).

21   MacIntyre, *After Virtue*, 212: "We render the actions of others intelligible in this way (with narrative histories) because action itself has a basically historical character." For the argument here to go, what MacIntyre claims explicitly about "action" must go, too, for the past.

22   For Aristotle, of course, the grammatical structure of subject–predicate mirrored the ontological structure of substance–property. We need not deny the similarity that supports this analogy, of course, to deny that the sky has a grammatical structure.

23   Gadamer's notion of effective historical consciousness, or *Wirkungsgeschichtsbewusstsein*, is useful for conceptualizing the ethico-political import of history. The idea seems to be that there is a "field" of overlapping narratives that shape a society's awareness of its historical situation. This consciousness is "effective" because it orients us practically. The historian, through research and storytelling, can help to reshape this field, and in so doing alter the field of possibilities we confront, both individually and as a society.

24   Jürgen Habermas, *Knowledge and Human Interests*, trans. Jeremy J. Shapiro (Boston, 1971), esp. the Appendix. I do not wish to include Habermas among the anti-referentialists, for he does not to my knowledge deny that truth is a standard appropriate for the evaluation of narratives.

25   Mink argued in the late 1960s that there were three irreducible modes of comprehension — the theoretical, the categoreal, and the configurational. Configurational comprehension, he argued, was the end for which storytelling was the proper means. Mink, "History and Fiction as Modes of Comprehension," *New Literary History* (1969), 549ff.

26   John McCumber, *Poetic Interaction: Freedom, Language, and the Situation of Reason* (Chicago, 1989), xv.

27   MacIntyre, "Epistemological Crises," 469.

28   Paul Ricoeur, *Time and Narrative* (Chicago, 1984), 70–3. Ricouer arrives at many of the same conclusions I reach here, though his argument seems a good bit more roundabout. What it lacks in directness, however, it more than makes up for in richness and suggestion.

29   MacIntyre, *After Virtue*, 212.

30   The basic problem is that of making sense of correspondence, of spelling out what it means in a nontrivial way.

31   I have in mind Bas van Fraasen, *The Scientific Image* (Oxford, 1980), 11ff. Van Fraasen urges that we stop speaking of theories that posit unobservables as being true, arguing that we have no warrant for asserting anything more than their empirical adequacy, or usefulness for explaining and predicting. The similarity here between the move made by van Fraasen to escape the scientific realism dilemma, and that made by the anti-referentialists to escape what is essentially the same dilemma in the philosophy of history is striking, and of course no accident. The major positions in the two fields correspond almost exactly, due to a common set of argumentative pressures. The solution offered here is self-consciously modeled on Arthur Fine's "overcoming" of the realism–anti-realism debate. *The Shaky Game* (Chicago, 1986), Chs 7 and 8.

32   Fine pokes fun at van Fraasen's distinctions, calling them "arbitrary" and "obnoxious." Fine, *The Shaky Game*, 142–4.

33   Ibid., 139–42, but see all of Chapters 7 and 8.

Chapter 12

David Carr

GETTING THE STORY STRAIGHT
Narrative and historical knowledge

A WIDELY HELD VIEW AMONG PHILOSOPHERS and literary theorists is that narrative is in principle incapable of "representing" real events because its very nature is to impose on those events a form which in themselves they do not and cannot have. Not just some narratives, but all narratives by nature, distort or misrepresent the events or actions they depict. If this is true it is a denial of the pretensions of those narratives like historical ones, but unlike fictional ones, which purport to be truth-telling in some sense.

Along with others I have argued against this skeptical view on the grounds that it rests on implicit and incorrect assumptions about the nature of the "reality" narratives are about. In the case of history (as in fiction), narratives are centrally about human reality, i.e. about people's actions and sufferings, projects and plans, feelings and experiences. And those can be shown to have an implicitly (and sometimes explicitly) narrative structure prior to and independently of their being recounted by a historian or other narrator. If this is so, the "representational" pretensions of history can no longer be denied on purely formal grounds: far from differing in form or structure from the "real world," narrative shares in that form, and can be viewed as an extension and refinement by other means of the very reality it is about.

An argument of this sort, since it is directed against a form of skepticism, can be seen as an effort to reaffirm the epistemic or truth-telling character of history. But, as some critics have pointed out, it only goes part-way. It may remove the formal obstacle which the skeptics have placed in the way of considering history as a form of knowledge. But it does not tell us any more than we knew before about how history lives up to its epistemic pretensions. If it is true that historical narrative and historical reality share a common structure, what does it mean for the one to be about the other and to be capable of telling the truth about it?

These are the questions I would like to address in this chapter. I will begin by summarizing the skeptics' position and the arguments against it. I will then try to develop a more positive account of historical knowledge in light of what has been said. I shall argue that the epistemology of history can profit from recent developments in the epistemology of science.

I

Louis Mink is often cited as the pivotal figure in the treatment of narrative by philosophers of history. It was he who drew on the work of Danto and Gallie in affirming that narrative, rather than mere surface presentation, is actually constitutive of history's search for and claim to knowledge. Thus he called narrative a primary "mode of comprehension" and a "cognitive instrument." But it was also he who expressed doubts about narrative's capacity to achieve its goal, at least in history: "as historical it claims to represent, through its form, part of the real complexity of the past, but as narrative it is a product of imaginative construction which cannot defend its claim to truth by any accepted procedure of argument or authentication."[1] In his much-quoted formulation: "stories are not lived but told. Life has no beginnings, middles and ends. . . . Narrative qualities are transferred from art to life."[2] This view has been elaborated and developed by Hayden White. Like Mink he characterizes the aim of history as the "representation of reality" and then argues that this aim can never be achieved: "no given set or sequence of real events" has intrinsically narrative features; they acquire these features "only by the imposition of the structure of a given story type on the events."[3]

Clearly the skeptical view expressed by these two thinkers involves three key conceptions: that of historical narrative, that of "representation," and that of the "real events" that historical narratives try to represent. Critics of this view, myself included, have taken aim primarily at the third of these.[4]

If the "real events" which interest historians are the actions and experiences of persons and groups of people, rather than mere physical events, then they have a distinctive structure and in particular a special sort of temporality. As philosophers like Husserl and Heidegger have insisted, human time is not an undifferentiated succession – one thing after another – but is structured into wholes which unite past, present and future. As human experiencers and especially as agents we organize temporal sequences into configurations involving beginnings, middles and ends. This is not just the way we tell about our plans and projects after the fact; it is the way they are lived right from the start. And because we are involved with others, these temporal structures can be seen as proto-narratives, stories we tell ourselves and others which have the practical function of organizing our experiences and actions. Our very lives are organized in this way: the unity of a life can be seen as the unity of a life-story, an implicit autobiography which each of us is always in the process of composing.

In this extended sense narrative has not merely as an epistemological but also as an ontological significance. That is, it is not only a "cognitive instrument" as Mink claimed – a primary way of seeking, organizing and expressing our knowledge of a part of reality. It is constitutive of our very being, it is our way of existing, of constituting ourselves.

Moreover, it is not merely as individuals that we exist in this way. Communities, large and small, can be said to have the same narrative form of self-constitution. A community, whose members refer to themselves as "we," exists in a reflexive form which draws together a remembered past and a projected future, and these jointly serve to make sense of the present that is being lived through. Again the quasi-narrative has a practical function: it holds the community together, gives it coherence. It exists not only in the legends and stories that often preserve the memory of a birth or foundation; it resides also in the plans and proposals of leaders and politicians. Thus, like the individual, the community has a perhaps dimly remembered birth, and it faces like the individual the prospect of its own demise. As if in the face of its own possible non-being it preserves itself by constructing and living out a coherent story. This story may actually be told only by a few or even by one person – this being one of the primary functions of leadership – but it must be addressed to all, told on behalf of all, and be largely accepted by all. To be sure, like the life-story of the individual, this communal story is under constant revision, and the manner of its revision may be subject to factional dispute. If radically differing versions of the story are ultimately irreconcilable, the community may succumb to fragmentation. Here again the community is like the individual, whose personality is susceptible to fragmentation under analogous circumstances of internal conflict.

Thus narrative can be seen as a principle of social or communal as well as individual ontology, quite apart from the specifically cognitive role narrative takes on in the case of historical knowledge. This permits us to say that the latter has essentially the same form or mode of being as the former, which is its object. I think some version of this view was held by older philosophers of history, even though they did not speak directly of narrative. Vico's view that we can understand history because we are the makers of history suggests the analogy of form between historical existence and historical knowledge. The same is true of Dilthey's statement that "we are historical beings first, before we are observers of history, and only because we are the former do we become the latter."[5] Hegel believed that it was no accident that the term *Geschichte* denotes both the *res gestae* and the *historia rerum gestarum*. "We must suppose historical narrations to have appeared contemporaneously with historical deeds and events. It is an internal vital principle common to both that produces them synchronously."[6]

At the social level historical knowledge and historical writing can be seen as extensions by other means of historical existence. Far from transforming "real events" into something else, far from distorting them by imposing some alien form upon them, historical narrative shares with those events a constitutive form. On this view narrative is a mode of being before it is a mode of knowing.

II

Clearly this "ontological" interpretation of narrative, as presented so far, has the advantage of removing the formal obstacle to the truthfulness or fidelity of narratives. That is, it undermines the claim that narratives are *in principle* incapable of "representing" the events they depict because the form of narrative itself is necessarily at variance with that of "reality." Contrary to the views or implied views of at least some narrative theorists, narrative does not *necessarily* give a distorted account of the events it relates, at least not for the reasons stated.

But of course the removal of the formal obstacle is not a material guarantee. We must still allow that stories sometimes are untrue to events, that they may indeed distort them. What this reminds us is that we have as yet no positive account of the specifically epistemic relation between narratives that purport to be truth-telling, like historical narratives, and the events and actions they are about. We have attempted to get beyond a narrow epistemological interpretation of narrative by moving to the ontological level. This issued in a certain characterization of historical narrating as an activity in its own right, with a social function in its own community, namely as an extension and refinement of the "practical narratives" that constitute the community. This is an ontological characterization which ignores the epistemic pretensions of a discipline like history. But our point was not to deny that narrative has a cognitive function, only to argue against a prevalent interpretation of that function. Assuming that we have succeeded, how do we now return to the epistemological dimension of narrative and make sense of it in light of our "ontologizing" interpretation? At the very most we can say that we understand historical agents because we are the same sorts of beings they are. But we need more than this.

One critic, Andrew P. Norman, has taken the view that the point of the ontological conception is to reinstate some version of a correspondence theory of truth. To consider the historical past as made up of narratives, i.e. of the implicit and explicit self-descriptions of historical agents, is not merely to remove the ontological gap between historical reality and historical narrative; it is to reduce the historian's function to that of simply *reporting* what those narratives were. "A story about the past is true, on such an account, when it accurately maps the real narrative structure of the lived past."[7]

This solution would, in fact, go beyond the correspondence theory of truth to something like an idealist identity theory. The main problem of the traditional correspondence theory is to explain what it means for "ideas" (or bits of language like statements or propositions) to "correspond" to a reality which is not made up of ideas (or bits of language). Notions like "picturing" and "isomorphism" are called upon for help, but usually just make matters worse. By transforming reality into ideas (or into something linguistic) the idealist spares himself these difficulties. In the case of history the historian would presumably simply *repeat* some past story, and her account would not merely correspond to but actually be identical with the reality to which it refers.

Now such a theory would naturally inherit all the difficulties of idealism generally. Applied to history it perhaps most resembles Collingwood's notion of re-enactment. But in its narrative form it would be subject to special objections. As Norman points out,[8] to characterize human actions and events as embodied narratives is at best a very useful metaphor: history does not literally tell stories about stories, at least for the most part; it tells stories about actions, sufferings and events. Only a literal construal of narrative would do for the identity theory.

But this would be the least of its problems. This construal of historical knowledge would be simplistic caricature of what historians actually do. For one thing they usually need to go beyond any single agent's narrative description of an action or event and compare it with other descriptions of the "same" event, thus having to deal with identity problems across multiple descriptions. (cf. Luther's description – or story – vs. the Pope's description of Luther's actions in 1519.) Most important, this view would ignore precisely what many theorists, from Dilthey to Danto, have seen as history's distinctive cognitive advantage, that of hindsight. The historian's retrospective stance permits her to view the self-descriptions and practical narratives behind historical actions in light of their actual outcomes. The ironic disparity between the envisioned or intended and the actual consequences of an action is practically the historian's stock-in-trade.

It is true that the "re-enactment" or revival of agents' own narratives is a vital part of this retrospective comparison, a point often forgotten by those like Danto who stress the retrospective point of view.[9] The historian is not only capable of but usually *cannot avoid* viewing past events in light of their actual consequences. The interest and value in historical accounts often lies precisely in retrieving a perspective on events which has been lost to us because of our hindsightful wisdom. Luther did not plan, envision or desire the Protestant Reformation that was unleashed by his actions. Seeing such a person's action just as he saw it, deliberately blocking out all that we know of what came later, must surely be one of the most difficult feats of the historical imagination. It should be pointed out in passing that this problem is not confined to narrative history, nor is it only a problem of "empathizing" with a remote historical individual. A history of mentalities or concepts, of the sort inspired by Foucault, similarly seeks to block out the vision of hindsight by refusing to see past events (including theories or writings) merely as precursors of what came later. Thus Newton's theories must be viewed in light of the religious cosmology of his time, not merely as precursors of the physical theories of our own day.

There is another sense in which this operation of re-enactment is important. Many historians, especially today, see their activity as one of redressing certain imbalances, of rediscovering or retrieving what has been lost, forgotten or covered over. The lives of those excluded from the stories of the past or relegated to their margins, those selected out of the standard narratives of both historical agents and later historians, are to be reinstated in our historical consciousness. And the first task is to give them back their own voice if possible, let them tell their own stories just as they are articulated in diaries, speeches, sermons, court testimony, folk art or other expressions. Here too the historian must in a sense block out hindsight and efface himself before the voice of the past.

For narrative history, however, important and difficult as this operation of retrieval is, it is but one element in a larger and even more difficult operation. And this operation can be characterized as choosing, among various descriptions of an event (e.g. reform, rebellion, apostasy, schism), and in light of its real consequences, the correct or at least the best description, or again, of moving through various inadequate stories of what went on to arrive at a version that is superior to all of them.

Thus any account of narrative history that would restrict its role to the repetition of past narratives of historical agents would overlook its distinctive feature, namely that it has in each case its *own* story to tell, that its purpose is to generate a narrative of its own which is different from the other narratives it may incorporate.

But this brings us back to the problem with which we began this section. What we have said so far tells us only that history as a discipline simply adds *more stories* to an already story-laden world. We still have to deal with the epistemic pretensions of history, which we can express by saying that history wants to offer its own account as the true story. Its story is not only different from the others; what makes it different is that it is true. If the correspondence theory, and its idealist counterpart the identity theory, have been ruled out, what is left?

Those familiar with standard epistemological "moves" will expect us to trot out the obvious remaining alternative at this point, namely a coherence theory, also favored by idealists. Then, of course, the obvious questions would arise: with what should a given historical account be expected to cohere? what are the criteria for coherence and incoherence? If the eyes of the reader begin to glaze over at this point, it is no wonder. Obviously we are beginning to sway to the well-known minuet of textbook epistemology. One is easily tempted into these well-worn paths, of course, since our whole discussion of historical narrative began with a formal critique of its capacity to *represent*. Returning to the epistemic pretensions of history, after our ontological detour, we might be expected to reaffirm history's *representational* character by appealing to general notions of representation, correspondence, realism, idealism and the like. Above all, we might be suspected of trying to provide historical knowledge with some kind of legitimation or foundation.

III

But this would be to ignore the lessons of post-empiricist and non-foundationalist theories of knowledge which have emerged from the general weariness with traditional epistemology. Here one is inclined to think first of the sweeping attacks on foundationalism, of the sort begun by Wittgenstein, of new developments in the philosophy of science, starting with Kuhn, and perhaps of Foucault's novel approach to diverse disciplines like medicine, penology, philology, biology and political economy. In keeping with these models, the new approach involves a sharp rejection of anything like a general or abstract "problem of knowledge" and a focus instead on the diverse disciplines in all their concreteness and particularity. It seems to me that our consideration of the epistemic character of history, building on our ontological reinterpretation of narrative, could well follow this example.

What would this mean? Historical knowledge must above all be considered in its concreteness. To be sure, the analytical or critical philosophy of history arose precisely in order to deal with the particular epistemic problems of this branch of knowledge. But it typically defined them in an exceedingly abstract fashion. An envious sidelong glance at natural science, as the paradigm of knowledge, set the tone. And of course the object of this envy was the natural science of the classical modern epistemologists, itself far removed, if we are to believe contemporary philosophers, from the real thing. Hence such questions as: how can history verify its theories, when its objects, being in the past, cannot be perceived? How can a historian, confronted with a few documents or a heap of ruins, reconstruct events that are in principle not available for direct inspection? How, in other words, does she move from ignorance of the past to knowledge of it, fashioning in her head a picture that corresponds to the past *wie es eigentlich gewesen?*

While there are many features of such an approach that are (in the bad sense) abstract, the most egregiously so is the notion of the "historian." As in most modern epistemology, this worthy is portrayed strictly as a representative of *homo sapiens* equipped with sense organs and the capacity for language and conceptual thought. What is forgotten is that she would not be in this odd situation of staring with puzzled mien at documents or ruins if she were not also equipped with the intentions, goals, values and problems of the discipline she represents, namely history. Traditionally we have been inclined to regard "history" (qua *historia rerum gestarum*) as that body of knowledge or set of beliefs which results from the cognitive activity of certain individuals. But clearly this cognitive activity also *presupposes* "history" in the sense of an ongoing discipline or inquiry. As such, history is more than just the general project of knowing the past; it exists at any given time, for any individual who steps into it, as a set of problems, interests, tendencies, and a stock of knowledge embodied in the existing literature and the general accumulated wisdom of the field. And in our day, of course, in the world we know best, it is for the most part firmly embedded in the academy as one of its traditional departments. It would be culpably abstract, indeed almost wilfully blind, to think that we could understand the cognitive activity of "the historian" apart from this disciplinary and institutional context.

You can easily see that I am attempting to view history as a discipline in roughly the way theorists like Joseph Rouse have begun to view the sciences.[10] If this means breaking down some of the traditional barriers between the sociology of knowledge and epistemology "proper," so be it. But in keeping with the emphasis on concreteness, we should be on our guard against overlooking the important differences between history and those sciences that have inspired this new treatment.

The first point has already been made, namely the stress on the role in knowledge of the discipline itself. Even if historians are less inclined than scientists to work in teams, their work is no less determined by the discipline conceived as a community of inquirers sharing certain goals, values, training and, more concretely still, certain substantive opinions about their subject-matter and about outstanding problems to be solved. It is the discipline in this sense which determines, at any given time, what counts as interesting, as useful, as an advance, as a novel perspective of things. As in natural science a certain relationship obtains between "the" discipline and its various subdivisions, a relationship involving the existence of subcommunities, their dependence on each other for results and methods, and notions of expertise. The existence and role of these communities is indicated in the historian's use of the term "we" to apply variously to the interlocking and overlapping groups she and her work belong to.

Lest our reference to the "we" and to communities of inquirers be thought too idealistic, it must be noted that another sort of "we" vs. "they" distinction crisscrosses all the other divisions, namely that involving different schools or approaches: cliometricians, Marxists, narrativists, anti-narrativists, etc. The "we" also has the rhetorical or persuasive sense found in many domains: when an author says "we have seen that" or "we may thus conclude" such-and-such, she is hopefully implicating her audience in her account, and while this audience is in theory indeterminate, what is usually implied is the community of experts, if only in the very weak sense of those who have followed the argument (or the story) so far.

The point is that any claim to historical knowledge, narrative or non-narrative in character, arises *out of* the intersubjective background of the discipline, consisting of both community and conflict, and is itself addressed *to* a community, primarily that of the discipline itself. As the historian William Cronon puts it, "We tell stories *with* each other and *against* each other in order to speak *to* each other."[11] This means that the *sense* of the claims made derives from their relation to what went before and from what is to be made of it by those to whom it is addressed. Described in these terms, historical knowledge can be seen to have the same dynamic and temporal character that Rouse ascribes to scientific knowledge: it is always a moment in an ongoing process, not so much a *state* or *body* of knowledge as a cognitive *situation*.[12] The metaphor of the "body" of knowledge, instead of evoking a living and developing body, has tended to suggest a lifeless corpse.

But this means that we have simply returned to our ontological sense of narrative as a way of characterizing historical knowledge itself. This should not surprise us: cognition is, after all, a human activity, and as such a project with a past, present and future. To make a contribution to a discipline like history is to be involved in the practical, ongoing and unfinished narrative of that discipline.[13] If it is "the discipline" which determines, as we have claimed, what counts as interesting, problematic, useful, what constitutes a field or domain, it does this very differently at different times. Thus, and again unsurprisingly, just as we cannot understand science apart from its history, so we cannot understand history apart from the history of history.

So far we have evoked this history as one that is *internal* to the discipline and can be quite restricted in its proportions: the sense of "where we stand" with respect to a particular domain or problem. But like science, history has the external context of its relation to the world outside the discipline and thus an external history of its role in the society. If the development of theory in physical science has been deeply affected by the demand for its technical applications, and by the development and availability of apparatus which serves its theorizing, the story of the relation between history and society is a very different one. As a tradition in the modern West, history-writing, both inside and outside the academy, has been dominated by a concern for the historian's own society and its historical background. And on the whole what historians write is intelligible, without intermediaries, to the general public. Thus history remains deeply tied to the self-image and the sense of identity of the larger community in which it is found. Its political relations with that larger community will be very different from and in some ways more intimate than those of the physical sciences, which concern the control and exploitation of the natural world, and which has a much more complex hierarchy of specialist intermediaries than does history. Society supports and influences historical research and writing not only by funding universities and awarding grants but also by buying and reading the results, and its motives for doing so will be very different, and perhaps more subtle, than those behind its support and control of science.

IV

This last point allows us to return to our epistemological concerns. We have ventured into the sociology, the politics and the history of history, which has permitted us to consider the discipline as an ongoing or practical narrative in our previous, ontological sense. This is interesting in its own right, but our purpose in doing it was to cast light on the epistemic pretensions of historical narrative. Since we have more or less abandoned the traditional notion of epistemology, it may seem entirely unclear at this point what it means to "cast light" in a philosophical way on an instance of knowledge. What I think we can do is come up with an interesting new description, in light of the foregoing observations, of the cognitive activity of at least some historians.

The first thing to be noted is a proliferation of narratives. Before, we described the historian as someone interested in past events and actions which, in virtue of their human temporal character, already exist in narrative or quasi-narrative form. Even at this first level, as we have noted, multiple narratives abound. But now we realize that, in virtue of her place in the discipline, the historian deals with a past reality that is probably already narrativized at the *second* level by her precursors. I am thinking not merely of attempts to supersede and correct the existing histories of some much-storied event like the French Revolution or the American Civil War. Even telling the story, say, of a hitherto unknown heretical sect in some remote corner of medieval Europe, on the basis of some newly discovered inquisitional records, presupposes an already-storied past: the historian could never recognize such records or know how to interpret them except on the basis of a received account of the place and period from which they derive.

Such a received account would of course in the first instance come from within the discipline, broadly or narrowly conceived, but this may in turn be set in the larger background of a public or popular account, which may be more or less explicit and may at the limit consist only of scattered beliefs and attitudes. The importance of this larger popular background would be greater the closer to home – temporally, geographically and socially – the historical events in question. As we said earlier, every community has a popular, quasi-mythical narrative account of its own history, usually one that allows for rival versions. But even in the case of the remote heretical sect, such terms as "heretical," "medieval," and "inquisition," have meanings, at least among the moderately educated public, linked to a vague narrative account of the past.

All of this permits us to conjure up a picture of the workworld of the narrative historian: it is a world composed largely of narratives. This is not surprising: the scientist works in a world of theories, puzzles and anomalies, outstanding problems, experimental findings and their interpretations. These are the environments in which – through which – these theorists view the ultimate objects of their respective domains: for scientists, some part of nature; for historians, some part of the historical past. To be sure, theories and narratives are not the only kinds of things that make up their workworlds. Both must deal with equipment, funding, sometimes students and courses, and above all colleagues (assistants, rivals, peer reviewers, superiors). Each works, then, in an environment that is physical, financial, institutional, and human. But it consists of ideal entities as well – in the sense that theories, narratives, problems and questions exist primarily in linguistic or symbolic form. It is these last that are most important, it seems to me, because they "mediate" between the knower and his object in the pregnant sense of that term. That is, unlike computers or colleagues, they refer to or describe, more or less directly, the cognitive object itself.

Now I would like to suggest that the cognitive activity of the narrative historian be described as that of grappling with other narratives of various sorts and at different levels: explicit prior narrative accounts of the events she is interested in, or of events closely related to them; less explicit background narratives of the public or popular sort; and the events themselves as implicitly or explicitly narrativized by the participants in them. My emphasis on this field of multiple narratives is meant to replace the view of knowledge as a dual relation between knower and object known, and I choose the word "grappling" in order to emphasize the vigorously active character of cognition and the resistant and sometimes recalcitrant character of the things it deals with.

But what sort of grappling is this? Comparison, contrast and, of course, critical evaluation. It is at this point that we must make reference to the attitude of healthy skepticism and concern for "objectivity" that constitutes a guiding value for all forms of inquiry in our tradition. The translation of this guiding value into epistemological terms has more often than not resulted in a portrayal of the knowing subject relating contemplatively to a static object "in itself;" whereas in fact these values are embodied almost entirely in caveats and negative injunctions: we know what it means to be biased, one-sided, affected by ideology or wishful thinking; we look for these faults in others' accounts and seek to avoid them in our own. We are brought back to the intersubjective context. To quote Cronon again:

> being a scholar, I write also for a community of other scholars . . . who know nearly as much about my subject as I do. They are in a position instantly to remind me of the excluded facts and wrong-headed interpretations that my own bias, self-delusion and lack of diligence have kept me from acknowledging.[14]

Whether we or anyone can ultimately succeed at this is another question; the point is that the desire to avoid the abuses of inquiry, in this case the abuse of history, is constitutive and regulative of the *activity* of telling stories about the past, at least in the context of history as a discipline. Moreover such notions as objective, unbiased, unslanted, etc., must be seen in the particular context in which they occur, i.e. not only within the discipline as a whole (objectivity means something very different in history and in physics), but even in the context of particular inquiries – e.g. the slants and biases that threaten the history of American slavery are very different from those that may be involved in accounting for the origins of World War II or the nature of the medieval papacy.

Understanding the truth-telling capacity of narrative history thus requires a proper appreciation of the concrete milieu in which it operates – the many-layered world of narratives as I have described it – in a sense of the values and rules which guide its operations within that milieu. In this way the mistake of trying to subsume historical knowledge under some general paradigm of cognition can be avoided.

At the same time one should not overlook the links between the operations of historians and the activities of some other spheres of life. Sifting through rival accounts, being on the lookout for their biases and misperceptions, trying to get the story straight, distinguishing real from intended outcomes – these are activities that belong to many practical contexts of extra-scientific life: the juridical context, for example, or the political or sometimes the medical.

In these contexts, as in the sorting out of our own individual lives and practices, we know that we and others are often tempted to view the past as we would like it to be, or as we wish it had been. We also know that in some important sense this won't work, that we cannot make it so, that we must come to terms with it as it is or was. This is ultimately a practical value, not just a cognitive one.

It is terribly important to emphasize this value, in speaking of history especially, however much we may wish to avoid the categories of traditional epistemology or the ghosts of positivism. Isolated voices which deny the Holocaust may not seem dangerous. But we know that powerful regimes have succeeded for decades in distorting history, injuring its victims a second time over by denying their suffering. Rather than speaking in abstract terms of objectivity and correspondence, however, we can, it seems to me, make more sense of history's capacity and obligation to truth-telling by considering it in concrete terms as the activity of getting the story straight.

Notes

1   "Narrative Form as a Cognitive Instrument," in Louis Mink, *Historical Understanding*, B. Fay, E. O. Golob and R. T. Vann (eds), (Ithaca and London: Cornell University Press, 1987), p.199.

2   "History and Fiction as Modes of Comprehension," in Mink, op. cit., p. 60.

3   "The Question of Narrative in Contemporary Historical Theory," in H. White, *The Content of the Form* (Baltimore: Johns Hopkins University Press, 1987), p. 44. See further H. Kellner, *Language and Historical Representation: Getting the Story Crooked* (Madison: University of Wisconsin Press, 1989) and the review essay on it by J. L. Gorman in *History and Theory* 30, No. 3 (1991), pp. 356–68.

4   See my *Time, Narrative and History* (Bloomington: Indiana University Press, 1986), and "Narrative and the Real World: An Argument for Continuity," *History and Theory* 25, 2 (1986), pp. 117–31.

5   W. Dilthey, *Gesammelte Schriften*, vol. vii, 5th edition, B. Groethuysen (ed.), (Stuttgart: B. Teubner, 1968), pp. 277–8.

6   G. W. F. Hegel, *The Philosophy of History*, tr. J. Sibree (New York: Dover Publications, 1956), p. 60.

7   A. P. Norman, "Telling It Like It Was: Historical Narratives on their Own Terms," *History and Theory* 30, 2, p. 124.

8   Ibid., p. 127.

9   A. Danto, *Analytical Philosophy of History* (Cambridge: Cambridge University Press, 1965).

10 See J. Rouse, *Knowledge and Power: Toward a Political Philosophy of Science* (Ithaca: Cornell University Press, 1987).

11   W. Cronon, "A Place for Stories: Nature, History and Narrative," *The Journal of American History*, March (1992), pp. 1373f.

12   See J. Rouse, "The Dynamics of Power and Knowledge in Science," *The Journal of Philosophy*, 88, 11, Nov. (1991).

13   See J. Rouse, "The Narrative Reconstruction of Science," *Inquiry*, 33, 2 (1990).

14   W. Cronon, op. cit., p. 1373.

PART FOUR

Narrative history and the linguistic turn

Chapter 13

Louis O. Mink

NARRATIVE FORM AS A
COGNITIVE INSTRUMENT

One hears about life, all the time, from different people, with very
different narrative gifts.

(Anthony Powell, *Temporary Kings*)

PHILOSOPHY DOES BEGIN WITH WONDER, as Aristotle said, but
in popular culture this is usually misunderstood as meaning that the occasions
for philosophical speculation are miracles and mysteries, the apparently inexplicable intrusions on quotidian experience. On the contrary, nothing is more
wonderful than common sense. The comfortable certainties of what "everybody
knows" have been since Socrates a more natural field for philosophical reflection
than eclipses, prophecies, monstrosities, and the irruption of intelligible forces. The
common sense of an age, we recognize when we compare that age with others,
may well be for different times or places beyond the limits of comprehension or
even of fantasy. A primary reason for this is that common sense of whatever age
has presuppositions which derive not from universal human experience but from a
shared conceptual framework, which determines what shall count as experience for
its communicants. For experience centered on one conceptual framework, there
are literally sermons in stones or vengeance in the thunderbolt. But for other experience these perceptions seem poetic fancies, and for yet other experience they are
simply unintelligible.

The distinction between history and fiction is as universally shared an item in
"common sense" as any distinction in Western culture, at least since the rise of
popular literacy. "Everyone knows," as certainly as everyone knows that two bodies
cannot occupy the same space at the same time, that history claims to be a true
representation of the past while fiction does not, even when it purports to describe
actions and events locatable in particular times and places. At the most, fiction
demands a temporary suspension of disbelief. Everyone knows that what makes a
story good is different from what, if anything, makes it true. Fiction may indeed

be accurate in reporting some events, actions, and the details of life in a certain period, but we know this (and know that we know it), only because we can compare fiction with history, without doubting in principle which is which. Many of the details of life in the fictional Dublin of 16 June, 1904, in Joyce's *Ulysses* are also details of the historical Dublin. A horse named Throwaway did win the Gold Cup, and the newspapers did report the *General Slocum* disaster in America. Yet while no work of history captures as well as *Ulysses* the feel of some Dublin life on that day or in that time, we know perfectly well that there are true stories about the careers of Throwaway and of the Dublin newspapers which happen to intersect with *Ulysses*, while there is no such true story about Leopold Bloom. Whether or not he had breakfast in bed on the morning of 17 June is not a historical question, although, as a problem for literary critics, it is crucial to one's interpretation of the fiction.

Histories are of course full of things that are not so, just as fiction is full of things that are so. But this can be said only because for shared common sense there is no problem *in principle* about the distinction between history and fiction. To say that something in a history "isn't so" is to say that it did not happen or was not that way. This acknowledges what history and fiction have in common as well as how they differ. Both the similarity and the difference are, for common sense, clear and uncomplicated. History and fiction are alike stories or narratives of events and actions. But for history both the structure of the narrative and its details are representations of past actuality; and the claim to be a true representation is understood by both writer and reader. For fiction, there is no claim to be a true representation in any particular respect. Even though much might be true in the relevant sense, nothing in the fictional narrative marks out the difference between the true and the imaginary; and this is a convention that amounts to a contract to which writer and reader subscribe. In the absence of this contract we should not be able to play the enchanting games with the verisimilitude of fiction that depend on pretending that the contract does not exist although we know that it does – as in the recreations of the Baker Street Irregulars, which have made Sherlock Holmes a more vividly "historical" figure than Gladstone.

These observations are so far elementary, but even so historians might object. The difference between history and fiction, they might well say, is less a matter of truth than of evidence. One may well disclaim any privileged access to "truth" except as truth-claims are reformulated in terms of the assessment of evidence, a process which historians know well makes all claims inferential and tentative. Of course it is salutary to be reminded that historiography is a matter of fallible inference and interpretation, but the reminder does not touch the point of the common-sense distinction between history and fiction. For that distinction, it is still a matter of what "everyone knows" that the events and actions of past actuality happened *just as they did*, and there is therefore something for historiography, however fallible, to be about, something which makes it true or false even though we have no access to that something except through historical reconstruction from present evidence. The determinateness of the past is part of common-sense ontology; it is not a theory but a presupposition of unreflective common experience. Historians might object, too, to the emphasis on narrative historiography. Professional history, a historian might say, is largely "analytic;" it does not exclude the construction of narrative accounts, but that is a literary art quite independent of professional skill in actual research. Now this objection would be telling if historiography were *defined* as narrative exposition. But the common-sense distinction between history and fiction does not depend on such a tendentious definition. It only acknowledges that a great deal of historiography has been and continues to be narrative in form. Even histories that are synchronic studies of the culture of an epoch inevitably take into account the larger process of development or change in which that epoch was a stage. Huizinga's *The Waning of the Middle Ages*, for example, or Peter Laslett's *The World We Have Lost*, neither of which has a narrative structure, nevertheless indicate even in their titles the narrative relevance of their cross-sectional accounts. The most "analytic" historical monograph, one might say and could show, presupposes the historian's more general understanding, narrative in form, of patterns of historical change, and is a contribution to the correction or elaboration of that narrative understanding. That is what phrases like "pre-industrial society" and "decline and fall" express to our narrative imagination.

Historians would in fact be ill-advised to relegate skill in managing narrative complexity to the status of a merely literary grace irrelevant to the hard cognitive stuff of historical research. Even though narrative form may be, for most people, associated with fairy tales, myths, and the entertainments of the novel, it remains true that narrative is a primary cognitive instrument – an instrument rivaled, in fact, only by theory and by metaphor as irreducible ways of making the flux of experience comprehensible. Narrative form as it is exhibited in both history and fiction is particularly important as a rival to theoretical explanation or understanding. Theory makes possible the explanation of an occurrence only by describing it in such a way that the description is logically related to a systematic set of generalizations or laws. One understands the operation of a spring-powered watch, for example, only insofar as one understands the principles of mechanics, and this requires describing the mechanism of the watch in terms, and *only* in terms, appropriate to those principles. One could not, so to speak, understand the operation of a watch but fail to understand the operation of a mill wheel, or vice versa, unless one had given the wrong description of one or both. But a particular watch also has a historical career: it is produced, shipped, stored, displayed, purchased, used; it may be given and received, lost and found, pawned and redeemed, admired and cursed, responsible for a timely arrival or a missed appointment. At each moment of its career, that is, it is or may be a part of a connected series of events which intersects its own history, and at each such moment it may be subject to a particular description, which is appropriate only because of that intersection. Now from the standpoint of theoretical understanding, the type of appropriate description is a given; it is not problematic. But the particular *history* of the watch escapes theoretical understanding simply because to envision that history requires the attribution of indefinitely many descriptions of it as they are successively relevant or irrelevant to the sequences that intersect its career. This is what narrative form uniquely represents, and why we require it as an irreducible form of understanding. On the one hand, there are all the occurrences of the world – at least all that we may directly experience or inferentially know about – in their concrete particularity. On the other is an ideally theoretical understanding of those occurrences that would treat each as nothing other than a replicable instance of a systematically interconnected set of generalizations. But between these extremes, narrative is the form in which we make comprehensible the many successive interrelationships that are comprised by a career. Both historians and writers of imaginative fiction know well the problems of constructing a coherent narrative account, with or without the constraint of arguing from evidence, but even so they may not recognize the extent to which narrative as such is not just a technical problem for writers and critics but a primary and irreducible form of human comprehension, an article in the constitution of common sense.

I

Particular narratives express their own conceptual presuppositions. They are in fact our most useful evidence for coming to understand conceptual presuppositions quite different from our own. It is, for example, through the plots of Greek tragedy that we can best understand an idea of Fate that was never explicitly formulated as a philosophical theory and that is far removed from our own presuppositions about causality, responsibility, and the natural order. But while the structure of stories bodies forth a particular conceptual scheme necessary to any understanding of the story, there are also at a more general level conceptual presuppositions of the very idea of narrative form itself, and these supervene on its many varieties. Aristotle's comment that every story has a beginning, a middle, and an end is not merely a truism. It commands universal assent while failing to tell us anything new, simply because it makes explicit part of the conceptual framework underlying the capacity to tell and hear stories of any sort. And in making a presupposition explicit it has implications that are far from banal; it makes clear that our experience of life does not itself necessarily have the form of narrative, except as we give it that form by making it the subject of stories. That this implication is surprising should not be surprising. It merely reflects the difference between the deliverances of common sense and its presuppositions. The former are the comfortable certainties that we know; the latter, though sine qua nons, yield themselves up only to reflection, which finds them wonderful as their implications come to light.

Until recently, the concept of narrative form seemed straightforward and un-problematic (as everything does to common sense). After all, although *kinds* of stories vary widely and significantly from culture to culture, story-telling is the most ubiquitous of human activities, and in any culture it is the form of complex discourse that is earliest accessible to children and by which they are largely accul-turated. *How* we understand a story has never seemed a problem. But in recent years the concept of narrative has been increasingly subjected to sophisticated analysis, and with less than satisfactory results. In the critical philosophy of history, narrative has increasingly come to be regarded as a type of explanation different from and displacing scientific or "covering-law" explanation of actions and events. But one result has been the emergence of problems not even recognized before. There is, for example, the problem of explicating how a narrative structure deter-mines what is or is not relevant to it; this problem has no analogue in the explication of the structure of theories. We ordinarily recognize, and in certain clear cases with no uncertainty at all, whether in the recounting of a coherent narrative a specific incident or detail is relevant or irrelevant to *that* narrative. (If I am telling the story of an encounter and its outcome that took place last Wednesday, I might become preoccupied with the incidental fact that it occurred on Wednesday and begin to add other details of what otherwise happened to me on Wednesday, for no better reason than that.) Since we do recognize that a given incident is relevant or irrelevant to a certain narrative, it would seem that we must be in possession of implicit *criteria* of relevance. Just as logic makes explicit the criteria of valid inference, which are implicit in the unreflective recognition of arguments in ordinary discourse as good or bad, so it would seem that we should be able to make explicit in a systematic way the criteria implicit in our recognition of relevance and irrelevance. Yet in fact no one has been able to state in general form any criterion of narrative relevance other than that of causal connection with events already established in the narrative, and not even this is adequate as a criterion. Not all of the causes or effects of an occurrence will be relevant to the story of which it is a part, and therefore an additional criterion is necessary to distinguish those that are from those that are not – and this criterion cannot be that of causal connection. In general, we know that there are many different ways in which an incident may be relevant to a story, but are unable to list the kinds of relevance. Yet one could not accept the alternative that every part of every story is relevant in its own unique way – that is, that there are no *kinds* of relevance.

One conceptual problem about narrative, therefore, is to make explicit the criteria by which in fact we recognize a narrative as coherent or incoherent. But this is a problem for narrative form in general, whether it purports to be history or fiction. I mention it, although I have no criteria of relevance to propose for examination, to illustrate the idea of conceptual problems about narrative as such. There are other problems, more amenable to a solution even though a radical one, which arise, I believe, for the following reason. Just as one conceptual presupposition of common sense has been that historiography consists of narratives which claim to be true, while fiction consists of imaginative narratives for which belief and therefore truth-claims are suspended, so another presupposition has been that historical actuality itself has narrative form, which the historian does not invent but discovers, or attempts to discover. History-as-it-was-lived, that is, is an untold story. The historian's job is to discover that untold story, or part of it, and to retell it even though in abridged or edited form. It is because of this presupposition that historians have not been inclined to value literary skill, or to find instructive the comparison of the historian with the novelist. The presupposition gives the force of self-evidence to the difference between history and fiction. The novelist can make up his story any way he wishes, subject only to the requirements of art. The historian, on the other hand, finds the story already hidden in what his data are evidence for; he is creative in the invention of research techniques to expose it, not in the art of narrative construction. Properly understood, the story of the past needs only to be communicated, not constructed.

But that past actuality is an untold story is a presupposition, not a proposition which is often consciously asserted or argued. I do not know a single historian, or indeed anyone, who would subscribe to it as a consciously held belief; yet if I am right, it is implicitly presupposed as widely as it would be explicitly rejected. (The situation is as it were a mirror image of the explicit belief that the *future* is an untold story, held by those whose controlling presuppositions in all other areas of belief and action are logically incompatible with that belief.) And it is the conflict between implicit presupposition and explicit belief which generates characteristic conceptual problems about the form of narratives to each other.

II

As we know most clearly from the history of science, the most difficult and interesting conceptual problems arise when one theory is replaced by another although the presuppositions (or "metaphysics," or "paradigm") of the former theory persist, unconsciously as it were. The dissonance between new ideas and old presuppositions characteristically produces conceptual confusion and felt discomfort, which only gradually can be brought to formulation as conceptual or epistemological problems. It is always a problem to identify the area of dissonance which might reward rather than resist efforts at analysis. My central thesis is that the questions we should ask are about narrative *form* as a cognitive instrument. It may not seem that this is problematic at all. After all, we commonly and often successfully undertake to explain something by telling the story of how it came to be that way; in this respect a fictional narrative may be as explanatory as a historical narrative although in the one case it is an imaginary event and in the other an actual (or evidenced) event which is explained. Just because such narrative understanding is so common and apparently transparent, my strategy is to create perplexity about the concept of narrative, to make some ambiguities of the concept a discomfort which can be felt.

   The first problem arises if we ask how narratives can be related to each other: can two narratives be combined (under suitable restrictions on chronology and coincidence of characters and events) to form a single more complex narrative? In narrative fiction, we ordinarily regard it as possible but not necessary for two or more self-contained narratives to aggregate into a complex whole. Even though *Oedipus Rex* and *Antigone* are plays in the same trilogy, we do at any reasonable level of sophistication regard them as individual works of imagination, and therefore do not count it as a failure on Sophocles' part that the conventional and sagacious Creon of *Oedipus Rex* is not intelligibly continuous with the willful and even blasphemous Creon of *Antigone*. When individual narrative fictions do aggregate, as in Faulkner's record of Yoknapatawpha County or in Trollope's Barsetshire novels, we most naturally construe it as the borrowing, for imaginative and artistic purposes, of the conventions of historical representation. For historical narratives, *should* aggregate; insofar as they make truth-claims about a selected segment of past actuality, they must be compatible with and complement other narratives which overlap or are continuous with them. Even if there are different ways of emplotting the same chronicle of events, it remains true that historical narratives are capable of *displacing* each other. This happens, for example, when a narrative makes sense of a series of actions by showing them to be decisions reflecting a consistently held policy, where received accounts could only describe them as arbitrary and surprising reactions, or as irrational responses. But narrative fictions, though they may be more or less coherent, do not displace each other; each, so to speak, creates the unique space which it alone occupies rather than competing with others for the same space as historical narratives may.

Yet while historical narratives ought to aggregate into more comprehensive narratives, or give way to rival narratives which will so aggregate, in fact they do not; and here is where conceptual discomfort should set in. The traditional way of avoiding it, and very analgesic it has been, too, is to distinguish between "objectivity" and "subjectivity." Narrative histories *would* combine into more comprehensive wholes to the extent that they achieve complete objectivity; unfortunately, however, historians have been prone to introduce their individual idiosyncrasies and values both in the selection and in the combination of facts. It is because of the differences in these subjective elements that one historian's narrative does not comport with another's. My purpose is not to decide whether historical objectivity is possible; it is rather to point out that the claim that it is clearly presupposes what I have called the idea of Universal History — that past actuality is an untold story and that there is a right way to tell it even though only in part.

But while objectivity is conceivable for a cumulative *chronicle*, it cannot really be translated into terms of narrative history (and in general the belief in historical objectivity fails to distinguish between narrative and chronicle, which has no form other than that of chronology and no relations among events other than temporal relations.) A narrative must have a unity of its own; this is what is acknowledged in saying that it must have a beginning, middle, and an end. And the reason why two narratives cannot be merely additively combined — in the simplest case, by making them temporally continuous as the parallel chronicle is continuous — is that in the earlier narrative of such an aggregate the end is no longer an end, and therefore the beginning is no longer *that* beginning, nor the middle *that* middle. The more comprehensive narrative may be given its own formal unity, but this is a new unity, which replaces the independent coherence of each of its parts rather than uniting them. Sophocles' trilogy is not itself a play; if it were, its constituents would be not plays but acts.

The point we have reached, therefore, is that narrative histories should be aggregative, insofar as they are histories, but cannot be, insofar as they are narratives. Narrative history borrows from fictional narrative the convention by which a story generates its own imaginative space, within which it neither depends on nor can displace other stories; but it presupposes that past actuality is a single and determinate realm, a presupposition which, once it is made explicit, is at odds with the incomparability of imaginative stories.

Inseparable from the question of how narratives aggregate is a second problem about the sense in which a narrative may be true or false. This question arises only if a narrative as such does have holistic properties, that is, if the *form* of the narrative, as well as its individual statements of fact, is taken as representing something that may be true or false. One can regard any text in direct discourse as a logical conjunction of assertions. The truth-value of the text is then simply a logical function of the truth or falsity of the individual assertions taken separately: the conjunction is true if and only if each of the individual propositions is true. Narrative has in fact been analyzed, especially by philosophers intent on comparing the form of narrative with the form of theories, as if it were nothing but a logical conjunction of past-referring statements; and on such an analysis there is no problem of *narrative truth*. The difficulty with the model of logical conjunction, however, is that it is not a model of narrative form at all. It is rather a model of *chronicle*.

Logical conjunction serves well enough as a representation of the only ordering relation of chronicles, which is ". . . and then . . . and then . . . and then . . ." Narratives, however, contain indefinitely many ordering relations, and indefinitely many ways of *combining* these relations. It is such combination that we mean when we speak of the coherence of a narrative, or lack of it. It is an unsolved task of literary theory to classify the ordering relations of narrative form; but whatever the classification, it should be clear that a historical narrative claims truth not merely for each of its individual statements taken distributively, but for the complex form of the narrative itself. Only by virtue of such form can there be a story of failure or of success, of plans miscarried or policies overtaken by events, of survivals and transformations which interweave with each other in the circumstances of individual lives and the development of institutions. But narrative form, to paraphrase what Wittgenstein said of the logical form of a proposition, cannot be "said" but must be "shown" – in the narrative as a whole. We recognize that a narrative cannot be summarized, or restated as an inventory of conclusions or "findings;" not that conclusions may not be drawn, but if one asks for reasons for accepting or rejecting them, the answer is not simply a recital of pieces of evidence (of the sort that would be advanced to support a generalization), but rather the repetition of the way in which the narrative has ordered the evidence. The situation is not unlike the apocryphal story told of many composers, for instance of Schubert: when asked what a sonata he had just played "meant," he responded only by sitting down and playing it again. The difference, of course, is that a historical narrative claims to be true, in a way that music does not.

The cognitive function of narrative form, then, is not just to relate a succession of events but to body forth an ensemble of interrelationships of many different kinds as a single whole. In fictional narrative the coherence of such complex forms affords aesthetic or emotional satisfaction; in historical narrative it additionally claims truth. But this is where the problem arises. The analysis and criticism of historical evidence can in principle resolve disputes about matters of fact or about the relations among facts, but not about the possible combinations of kinds of relations. The same event, under the same description or different descriptions, may belong to different stories, and its particular significance will vary with its place in these different – often very different – narratives. But just as "evidence" does not dictate which story is to be constructed, so it does not bear on the preference of one story to another. When it comes to the narrative treatment of an ensemble of interrelationships, we credit the imagination or the sensibility or the insight of the individual historian. This must be so, since there are no *rules* for the construction of a narrative as there are for the analysis and interpretation of evidence, and historians have acknowledged this in making no attempt whatever to teach the construction of narrative as part of the professional apprenticeship of the historical guild.

So narrative form in history, as in fiction, is an artifice, the product of individual imagination. Yet at the same time it is accepted as claiming truth – that is, as representing a real ensemble of interrelationships in past actuality. Nor can we say that narrative form is like a hypothesis in science, which is the product of individual imagination but once suggested leads to research that can confirm or disconfirm it. The crucial difference is that the narrative combination of relations is simply not subject to confirmation or disconfirmation, as any one of them taken separately might be. So we have a second dilemma about historical narrative: as historical it claims to represent, through its form, part of the real complexity of the past, but as narrative it is a product of imaginative construction, which cannot defend its claim to truth by any accepted procedure of argument or authentication.

Finally, a third and last question in this budget of paradoxes. In everything I have presented up to this point I have used the terms "event" and "succession of events," and written as if there were no difficulty in distinguishing between a chronicle, or series of statements about events ordered in temporal sequence, and a narrative, which presumably in all cases contains a chronicle but adds to it other forms of ordering, for example causal relations. But hardly any concept is less clear than that of "event." For consider, we may speak of a war as an event, but a war consists of battles, and battles of engagements by units, and engagements by units of actions by individuals; and when the shoe is lost for want of a nail, that is an event too. Now there is no particular difficulty about the concept of a complex event whose parts are themselves events. Uncertainty sets in when we consider the limits of application of the concept. Are there simple or unit-events, that is, events which are not further divisible into events? At the other extreme, what is the maximum complexity and span of time beyond which the application of the term is inappropriate? Is the Renaissance an event? Moreover, it is clear that we cannot refer to events as such, but only to events *under a description*; so there can be more than one description of the same event, all of them true but referring to different aspects of the event or describing it at different levels of generality. But what can we possibly mean by "same event"? Under what description do we refer to the event that is supposed to sustain different descriptions? It seems that the ordinary use of the term "event" presupposes both an already existing division of complex processes into further irreducible elements, and some *standard* description of each putative event; then, to say that there are different descriptions of the "same" event is to say that they are selected from or inferred from that standard and preeminent description.

But in fact we have no idea whether there are minimal or maximal events, and no knowledge of any standard or preeminent descriptions of any events. I am speaking here, of course, of the actual and imaginary events described in the ordinary language of narrative accounts. In the development of natural science, a major function of theory construction and the development of specialized languages has been to establish what *counts* as a unit-event and to provide standard descriptions of events – e.g. the emission of a particle, or one operation of the lever in a Skinner box. In normal science, the uncertainties I have suggested about the concept of event do not arise at all. They are settled by the catechism that every student learns as his induction into the science. But to furnish historiography, or any of our story-telling activities, with an inventory of types of basic events, with standard descriptions of each, could not improve the intelligibility or cognitive value of narratives. This is not because such a project is impossible or undesirable, even if it were both. It is rather because if it were successful it would render narrative form wholly superfluous for the understanding of events; for in stipulating standard descriptions of events (combined with the body of theory that such descriptions are designed to serve) it would rule out the redescriptions that are required in the construction of narrative.

It is not my purpose to create confusion about the concept of "event" but rather to reveal that the confusion has been there all along. Even though we ordinarily think of a narrative as a story about successive and simultaneous events, there is something incompatible about our concept of "event" and our concept of "narrative," which might be put as follows: the concept of event is primarily linked to the conceptual structure of science (and to that part of common sense that has adopted the language and methods of science); but in that conceptual structure it is purged of all narrative connections, and refers to something that can be identified and described without any necessary reference to its location in some process of development – a process which only narrative form can represent. Therefore, to speak of a "narrative of events" is nearly a contradiction in terms. That it is not perceived as such, I suggest, again reflects the extent to which the idea of Universal History survives as a presupposition. To the extent that historical actuality is regarded as an untold story, then in that untold story our conceptual problems disappear. We can just as well suppose (so long as we do not reflect on it) that it contains the standard descriptions of events to which our descriptions more or less closely approximate, and that it is neatly organized into simple and complex events. Yet all our experience of narratives suggests that there is no way of settling on standard descriptions other than by arbitrary enforcement, and that therefore we cannot without confusion regard different narratives as differently emplotting the "same" events. We need a different way of thinking about narrative. "Events" (or more precisely, descriptions of events) are not the raw material out of which narratives are constructed; rather an event is an abstraction from a narrative. An event may take five seconds or five months, but in either case whether it is one event or many depends not on a definition of "event" but on a particular narrative construction which generates the event's appropriate description. This conception of "event" is not remote from our ordinary responses to stories: in certain stories we can accept even something like the French Revolution as a simple event, because that is the way it is related to characters and plot, while in other stories it may be too complex to describe as a single whole. But if we accept that the description of events is a function of particular narrative structures, we cannot at the same time suppose that the actuality of the past is an untold story. There can in fact be no untold stories at all, just as there can be no unknown knowledge. There can be only past facts not yet described in a context of narrative form.

Chapter 14

Hayden White

THE HISTORICAL TEXT AS
LITERARY ARTIFACT

O NE OF THE WAYS THAT a scholarly field takes stock of itself is
by considering its history. Yet it is difficult to get an objective history of a
scholarly discipline, because if the historian is himself a practitioner of it, he is
likely to be a devotee of one or another of its sects and hence biased; and if he is
not a practitioner, he is unlikely to have the expertise necessary to distinguish
between the significant and the insignificant events of the field's development. One
might think that these difficulties would not arise in the field of history itself,
but they do and not only for the reasons mentioned above. In order to write the
history of any given scholarly discipline or even of a science, one must be prepared
to ask questions *about* it of a sort that do not have to be asked in the practice
of it. One must try to get behind or beneath the presuppositions which sustain a
given type of inquiry and ask the questions that can be begged in its practice in
the interest of determining why this type of inquiry has been designed to solve the
problems it characteristically tries to solve. This is what metahistory seeks to do.
It addresses itself to such questions as, What is the structure of a peculiarly *historical*
consciousness? What is the epistemological status of historical *explanations*, as
compared with other kinds of explanations that might be offered to account for
the materials with which historians ordinarily deal? What are the possible *forms* of
historical representation and what are their bases? What authority can historical
accounts claim as contributions to a secured knowledge of reality in general and
to the human sciences in particular?

Now, many of these questions have been dealt with quite competently over
the last quarter-century by philosophers concerned to define history's relationships
to other disciplines, especially the physical and social sciences, and by historians
interested in assessing the success of their discipline in mapping the past and determining the relationship of that past to the present. But there is one problem that
neither philosophers nor historians have looked at very seriously and to which
literary theorists have given only passing attention. This question has to do with
the status of the historical narrative, considered purely as a verbal artifact purporting

to be a model of structures and processes long past and therefore not subject to either experimental or observational controls. This is not to say that historians and philosophers of history have failed to take notice of the essentially provisional and contingent nature of historical representations and of their susceptibility to infinite revision in the light of new evidence or more sophisticated conceptualization of problems. One of the marks of a good professional historian is the consistency with which he reminds his readers of the purely provisional nature of his characterizations of events, agents, and agencies found in the always incomplete historical record. Nor is it to say that literary theorists have *never* studied the structure of historical narratives. But in general there has been a reluctance to consider historical narratives as what they most manifestly are: verbal fictions, the contents of which are as much *invented* as *found* and the forms of which have more in common with their counterparts in literature than they have with those in the sciences.

Now, it is obvious that this conflation of mythic and historical consciousness will offend some historians and disturb those literary theorists whose conception of literature presupposes a radical opposition of history to fiction or of fact to fancy. As Northrop Frye has remarked, "In a sense the historical is the opposite of the mythical, and to tell the historian that what gives shape to his book is a myth would sound to him vaguely insulting." Yet Frye himself grants that "when a historian's scheme gets to a certain point of comprehensiveness it becomes mythical in shape, and so approaches the poetic in its structure." He even speaks of different kinds of historical myths: Romantic myths "based on a quest or pilgrimage to a City of God or classless society;" Comic "myths of progress through evolution or revolution;" Tragic myths of "decline and fall, like the works of Gibbon and Spengler;" and Ironic "myths of recurrence or causal catastrophe." But Frye appears to believe that these myths are operative only in such victims of what might be called the "poetic fallacy" as Hegel, Marx, Nietzsche, Spengler, Toynbee, and Sartre — historians whose fascination with the "constructive" capacity of human thought has deadened their responsibility to the "found" data. "The historian works inductively," he says, "collecting his facts and trying to avoid any informing patterns except those he sees, or is honestly convinced he sees, in the facts themselves." He does not work "from" a "unifying form," as the poet does, but "toward" it; and it therefore follows that the historian, like any writer of discursive prose, is to be judged "by the truth of what he says, or by the adequacy of his verbal reproduction of his external model," whether that external model be the actions of past men or the historian's own thought about such actions.

What Frye says is true enough as a statement of the *ideal* that has inspired historical writing since the time of the Greeks, but that ideal presupposes an opposition between myth and history that is as problematical as it is venerable. It serves Frye's purposes very well, since it permits him to locate the specifically "fictive" in the space between the two concepts of the "mythic" and the "historical." As readers of Frye's *Anatomy of Criticism* will remember, Frye conceives fictions to consist in part of sublimates of archetypal myth-structures. These structures have been displaced to the interior of verbal artifacts in such a way as to serve as their latent meanings. The fundamental meanings of all fictions, their thematic content, consist, in Frye's view, of the "pre-generic plot-structures" or *mythoi* derived from the corpora of Classical and Judaeo-Christian religious literature. According to this theory,

we understand *why* a particular story has "turned out" as it has when we have identified the archetypal myth, or pregeneric plot structure, of which the story is an
exemplification. And we see the "point" of a story when we have identified its theme
(Frye's translation of *dianoia*), which makes of it a "parable or illustrative fable."
"Every work of literature," Frye insists, "has both a fictional and a thematic aspect,"
but as we move from "fictional projection" toward the overt articulation of theme,
the writing tends to take on the aspect of "direct address, or straight discursive
writing and cease[s] to be literature." And in Frye's view, as we have seen, history
(or at least "proper history") belongs to the category of "discursive writing," so that
when the fictional element – or mythic plot structure – is *obviously* present in it, it
ceases to be history altogether and becomes a bastard genre, product of an unholy,
though not unnatural, union between history and poetry.

Yet, I would argue, histories gain part of their explanatory effect by their
success in making stories out of *mere* chronicles; and stories in turn are made out
of chronicles by an operation which I have elsewhere called "emplotment." And by
emplotment I mean simply the encodation of the facts contained in the chronicle
as components of specific *kinds* of plot structures, in precisely the way that Frye
has suggested is the case with "fictions" in general.

The late R. G. Collingwood insisted that the historian was above all a story-
teller and suggested that historical sensibility was manifested in the capacity to make
a plausible story out of a congeries of "facts" which, in their unprocessed form,
made no sense at all. In their efforts to make sense of the historical record, which
is fragmentary and always incomplete, historians have to make use of what
Collingwood called "the constructive imagination," which told the historian – as it
tells the competent detective – what "must have been the case" given the available
evidence and the formal properties it displayed to the consciousness capable of
putting the right question to it. This constructive imagination functions in much
the same way that Kant supposed the a priori imagination functions when it tells
us that even though we cannot perceive both sides of a tabletop simultaneously,
we can be certain it has *two* sides if it has one, because the very concept of *one side*
entails at least *one other*. Collingwood suggested that historians come to their
evidence endowed with a sense of the *possible* forms that different kinds of recognizably human situations *can* take. He called this sense the nose for the "story"
contained in the evidence or for the "true" story that was buried in or hidden behind
the "apparent" story. And he concluded that historians provide plausible explanations for bodies of historical evidence when they succeed in discovering the story
or complex of stories implicitly contained within them.

What Collingwood failed to see was that no given set of casually recorded
historical events can in itself constitute a story; the most it might offer to the historian are story *elements*. The events are *made* into a story by the suppression or
subordination of certain of them and the highlighting of others, by characterization, motific repetition, variation of tone and point of view, alternative descriptive strategies, and the like – in short, all of the techniques that we would
normally expect to find in the emplotment of a novel or a play. For example, no
historical event is *intrinsically tragic*; it can only be conceived as such from a particular point of view or from within the context of a structured set of events of which
it is an element enjoying a privileged place. For in history what is tragic from one

perspective is comic from another, just as in society what appears to be tragic from the standpoint of one class may be, as Marx purported to show of the 18th Brumaire of Louis Bonaparte, only a farce from that of another class. Considered as potential elements of a story, historical events are value-neutral. Whether they find their place finally in a story that is tragic, comic, romantic, or ironic – to use Frye's categories – depends upon the historian's decision to configure them according to the imperatives of one plot structure or mythos rather than another. The same set of events can serve as components of a story that is tragic *or* comic, as the case may be, depending on the historian's choice of the plot structure that he considers most appropriate for ordering events of that kind so as to make them into a comprehensible story.

This suggests that what the historian brings to his consideration of the historical record is a notion of the *types* of configurations of events that can be recognized as stories by the audience for which he is writing. True, he can misfire. I do not suppose that anyone would accept the emplotment of the life of President Kennedy as comedy, but whether it ought to be emplotted romantically, tragically, or satirically is an open question. The important point is that most historical sequences can be emplotted in a number of different ways, so as to provide different interpretations of those events and to endow them with different meanings. Thus, for example, what Michelet in his great history of the French Revolution construed as a drama of Romantic transcendence, his contemporary Tocqueville emplotted as an ironic Tragedy. Neither can be said to have had more knowledge of the "facts" contained in the record; they simply had different notions of the kind of story that best fitted the facts they knew. Nor should it be thought that they told different stories of the Revolution because they had discovered different *kinds* of facts, political on the one hand, social on the other. They sought out different kinds of facts because they had different kinds of stories to tell. But why did these alternative, not to say mutually exclusive, representations of what was substantially the same set of events appear equally plausible to their respective audiences? Simply because the historians shared with their audiences certain preconceptions about how the Revolution might be emplotted, in response to imperatives that were generally extra-historical, ideological, aesthetic, or mythical.

Collingwood once remarked that you could never explicate a tragedy to anyone who was not already acquainted with the kinds of situations that are regarded as "tragic" in our culture. Anyone who has taught or taken one of those omnibus courses usually entitled Western Civilization or Introduction to the Classics of Western Literature will know what Collingwood had in mind. Unless you have some idea of the generic attributes of tragic, comic, romantic, or ironic situations, you will be unable to recognize them as such when you come upon them in a literary text. But historical situations do not have built into them intrinsic meanings in the way that literary texts do. Historical situations are not *inherently* tragic, comic, or romantic. They may all be inherently ironic, but they need not be emplotted that way. All the historian needs to do to transform a tragic into a comic situation is to shift his point of view or change the scope of his perceptions. Anyway, we only think of situations as tragic or comic because these concepts are part of our generally cultural and specifically literary heritage. *How* a given historical situation is to be configured depends on the historian's subtlety in matching up a specific plot structure with the set of historical events that he wishes to endow with a meaning of a particular kind. This is essentially a literary, that is to say fiction-making, operation. And to call it that in no way detracts from the status of historical narratives as providing a kind of knowledge. For not only are the pregeneric plot structures by which sets of events can be constituted as stories of a particular kind limited in number, as Frye and other archetypal critics suggest; but the encodation of events in terms of such plot structures is one of the ways that a culture has of making sense of both personal and public pasts.

We can make sense of sets of events in a number of different ways. One of the ways is to subsume the events under the causal laws which may have governed their concatenation in order to produce the particular configuration that the events appear to assume when considered as "effects" of mechanical forces. This is the way of scientific explanation. Another way we make sense of a set of events which appears strange, enigmatic, or mysterious in its immediate manifestations is to encode the set in terms of culturally provided categories, such as metaphysical concepts, religious beliefs, or story forms. The effect of such encodations is to familiarize the unfamiliar; and in general this is the way of historiography, whose "data" are always immediately strange, not to say exotic, simply by virtue of their distance from us in time and their origin in a way of life different from our own.

The historian shares with his audience *general notions* of the *forms* that signifi-cant human situations *must* take by virtue of his participation in the specific processes of sense-making which identify him as a member of one cultural endowment rather than another. In the process of studying a given complex of events, he begins to perceive the *possible* story form that such events *may* figure. In his narrative account of how this set of events took on the shape which he perceives to inhere within it, he emplots his account as a story of a particular kind. The reader, in the process of following the historian's account of those events, gradually comes to realize that the story he is reading is of one kind rather than another: romance, tragedy, comedy, satire, epic, or what have you. And when he has perceived the class or type to which the story that he is reading belongs, he experiences the effect of having the events in the story explained to him. He has at this point not only successfully *followed* the story; he has grasped the point of it, *understood* it, as well. The original strangeness, mystery, or exoticism of the events is dispelled, and they take on a familiar aspect, not in their details, but in their functions as elements of a familiar kind of configuration. They are rendered comprehensible by being subsumed under the categories of the plot structure in which they are encoded as a story of a partic-ular kind. They are familiarized, not only because the reader now has more *information* about the events, but also because he has been shown how the data conform to an *icon* of a comprehensible finished process, a plot structure with which he is familiar as a part of his cultural endowment.

This is not unlike what happens, or is supposed to happen, in psychotherapy. The sets of events in the patient's past which are the presumed cause of his distress, manifested in the neurotic syndrome, have been defamiliarized, rendered strange, mysterious, and threatening and have assumed a meaning that he can neither accept nor effectively reject. It is not that the patient does not *know* what those events were, does not know the facts; for if he did not in some sense know the facts, he would be unable to recognize them and repress them whenever they arise in his consciousness. On the contrary, he knows them all too well. He knows them so well, in fact, that he lives with them constantly and in such a way as to make it impossible for him to see any other facts except through the coloration that the set of events in question gives to his perception of the world. We might say that, according to the theory of psychoanalysis, the patient has overemplotted these events, has charged them with a meaning so intense that, whether real or merely imagined, they continue to shape both his perceptions and his responses to the world long after they should have become "past history." The therapist's problem, then, is not to hold up before the patient the "real facts" of the matter, the "truth" as against the "fantasy" that obsesses him. Nor is it to give him a short course in psychoanalytical theory by which to enlighten him as to the true nature of his distress by cataloging it as a manifestation of some "complex." This is what the analyst might do in relating the patient's case to a third party, and especially to another analyst. But psychoanalytic theory recognizes that the patient will resist both of these tactics in the same way that he resists the intrusion into consciousness of the traumatized memory traces in the *form* that he obsessively remembers them. The problem is to get the patient to "re-emplot" his whole life history in such a way as to change the *meaning* of those events for him and their *significance* for the economy of the whole set of events that make up his life. As thus envisaged, the therapeutic process is an exercise in the refamiliarization of events that have been defamiliarized, rendered alienated from the patient's life-history, by virtue of their overdetermination as causal forces. And we might say that the events are detraumatized by being removed from the plot structure in which they have a dominant place and inserted in another in which they have a subordinate or simply ordinary function as elements of a life shared with all other men.

Now, I am not interested in forcing the analogy between psychotherapy and historiography; I use the example merely to illustrate a point about the fictive component in historical narratives. Historians seek to refamiliarize us with events which have been forgotten through either accident, neglect, or repression. Moreover, the greatest historians have always dealt with those events in the histories of their cultures which are "traumatic" in nature and the meaning of which is either problematical or overdetermined in the significance that they still have for current life, events such as revolutions, civil wars, large-scale processes such as industrialization and urbanization, or institutions which have lost their original function in a society but continue to play an important role on the current social scene. In looking at the ways in which such structures took shape or evolved, historians *re*familiarize them, not only by providing more information about them, but also by showing how their developments conformed to one or another of the story-types that we conventionally invoke to make sense of our own life-histories.

Now, if any of this is plausible as a characterization of the explanatory effect of historical narrative, it tells us something important about the *mimetic* aspect of historical narratives. It is generally maintained — as Frye said — that a history is a verbal model of a set of events external to the mind of the historian. But it is wrong to think of a history as a model similar to a scale model of an airplane or ship, a map, or a photograph. For we can check the adequacy of this latter kind of model by going and looking at the original and, by applying the necessary rules of translation, seeing in what respect the model has actually succeeded in reproducing aspects of the original. But historical structures and processes are not like these originals; we cannot go and look at them in order to see if the historian has adequately reproduced them in his narrative. Nor should we want to, even if we could; for after all it was the very strangeness of the original as it appeared in the documents that inspired the historian's efforts to make a model of it in the first place. If the historian only did that for us, we should be in the same situation as the patient whose analyst merely told him, on the basis of interviews with his parents, siblings, and childhood friends, what the "true facts" of the patient's early life were. We would have no reason to think that anything at all had been *explained* to us.

This is what leads me to think that historical narratives are not only models of past events and processes, but also metaphorical statements which suggest a relation of similitude between such events and processes and the story-types that we conventionally use to endow the events of our lives with culturally sanctioned meanings. Viewed in a purely formal way, a historical narrative is not only a *reproduction* of the events reported in it, but also a *complex of symbols* which gives us directions for finding an *icon* of the structure of those events in our literary tradition.

I am here, of course, invoking the distinctions between sign, symbol, and icon which C. S. Peirce developed in his philosophy of language. I think that these distinctions will help us to understand what is fictive in all putatively realistic representations of the world and what is realistic in all manifestly fictive ones. They help us, in short, to answer the question. What are historical representations *representations of*? It seems to me that we must say of histories what Frye seems to think is true only of poetry or philosophies of history, namely that, considered as a system of signs, the historical narrative points in two directions simultaneously: *toward* the events described in the narrative and *toward* the story-type or mythos which the historian has chosen to serve as the icon of the structure of the events. The narrative itself is not the icon; what it does is *describe* events in the historical record in such a way as to inform the reader *what to take as an icon* of the events so as to render them "familiar" to him. The historical narrative thus mediates between the events reported in it on the one side and pregeneric plot structures conventionally used in our culture to endow unfamiliar events and situations with meanings, on the other.

The evasion of the implications of the fictive nature of historical narrative is in part a consequence of the utility of the concept "history" for the definition of other types of discourse. "History" can be set over against "science" by virtue of its want of conceptual rigor and failure to produce the kinds of universal laws that the sciences characteristically seek to produce. Similarly, "history" can be set over against "literature" by virtue of its interest in the "actual" rather than the "possible," which is supposedly the object of representation of "literary" works. Thus, within a long and distinguished critical tradition that has sought to determine what is "real" and what is "imagined" in the novel, history has served as a kind of archetype of the "realistic" pole of representation. I am thinking of Frye, Auerbach, Booth, Scholes and Kellogg, and others. Nor is it unusual for literary theorists, when they are speaking about the "context" of a literary work, to suppose that this context — the "historical milieu" — has a concreteness and an accessibility that the work itself can never have, as if it were easier to perceive the reality of a past world put together from a thousand historical documents than it is to probe the depths of a single literary work that is present to the critic studying it. But the presumed concreteness and accessibility of historical milieux, these contexts of the texts that literary scholars study, are themselves products of the fictive capability of the historians who have studied those contexts. The historical documents are not less opaque than the texts studied by the literary critic. Nor is the world those documents figure more accessible. The one is no more "given" than the other. In fact, the opaqueness of the world figured in historical documents is, if anything, increased by the production of historical narratives. Each new historical work only adds to the number of possible texts that have to be interpreted if a full and accurate picture of a given historical milieu is to be faithfully drawn. The relationship between the past to be analyzed and historical works produced by analysis of the documents is paradoxical; the *more* we know about the past, the more difficult it is to generalize about it.

But if the increase in our knowledge of the past makes it more difficult to generalize about it, it should make it easier for us to generalize about the forms in which that knowledge is transmitted to us. Our knowledge of the past may increase incrementally, but our understanding of it does not. Nor does our understanding of the past progress by the kind of revolutionary breakthroughs that we associate with the development of the physical sciences. Like literature, history progresses by the production of classics, the nature of which is such that they cannot be disconfirmed or negated, in the way that the principal conceptual schemata of the sciences are. And it is their nondisconfirmability that testifies to the essentially *literary* nature of historical classics. There is something in a historical masterpiece that cannot be negated, and this nonnegatable element is its form, the form which is its fiction.

It is frequently forgotten or, when remembered, denied that no given set of events attested by the historical record comprises a *story* manifestly finished and complete. This is as true as the events that comprise the life of an individual as it is of an institution, a nation, or a whole people. We do not *live* stories, even if we give our lives meaning by retrospectively casting them in the form of stories. And so too with nations or whole cultures. In an essay on the "mythical" nature of historiography, Lévi-Strauss remarks on the astonishment that a visitor from another planet would feel if confronted by the thousands of histories written about the French Revolution. For in those works, the "authors do not always make use of the same incidents; when they do, the incidents are revealed in different lights. And yet these are variations which have to do with the same country, the same period, and the same events – events whose reality is scattered across every level of a multilayered structure." He goes on to suggest that the criterion of validity by which historical accounts might be assessed cannot depend on their elements – that is to say – their putative factual content. On the contrary, he notes, "pursued in isolation, each element shows itself to be beyond grasp. But certain of them derive consistency from the fact that they can be integrated into a system whose terms are more or less credible when set against the overall coherence of the series." But his "coherence of the series" cannot be the coherence of the *chronological* series, that sequence of "facts" organized into the temporal order of their original occurrence. For the "chronicle" of events, out of which the historian fashions his story of "what really happened," already comes pre-encoded. There are "hot" and "cold" chronologies, chronologies in which more or fewer dates appear to demand inclusion in a full chronicle of what happened. Moreover, the dates themselves come to us already grouped into classes of dates, classes which are constitutive of putative domains of the historical field, domains which appear as problems for the historian to solve if he is to give a full and culturally responsible account of the past.

All this suggests to Lévi-Strauss that, when it is a matter of working up a comprehensive account of the various domains of the historical record in the form of a story, the "alleged historical continuities" that the historian purports to find in the record are "secured only by dint of fraudulent outlines" imposed by the historian on the record. These "fraudulent outlines" are, in his view, a product of "abstraction" and a means of escape from the "threat of an infinite regress" that always lurks at the interior of every complex set of historical "facts." We can construct a comprehensible story of the past, Lévi-Strauss insists, only by a decision to "give up" one or more of the domains of facts offering themselves for inclusion in our accounts. Our *explanations* of historical structures and processes are thus determined more by what we leave out of our representations than by what we put in. For it is in this brutal capacity to exclude certain facts in the interest of constituting the very constitution of a set of events in such a way as to make a comprehensible story out of them, the historian charges those events with the symbolic significance of a comprehensible plot structure. Historians may not like to think of their works as translations of fact into fictions; but this is one of the effects of their works. By suggesting alternative emplotments of a given sequence of historical events, historians provide historical events with all of the possible meanings with which the literary art of their culture is capable of endowing them. The real dispute between the proper historian and the philosopher of history has to do with the latter's insistence that events can be emplotted in one and only one story form. History-writing thrives on the discovery of all the possible plot structures that might be invoked to endow sets of events with different meanings. And our understanding of the past increases precisely in the degree to which we succeed in determining how far that past conforms to the strategies of sense-making that are contained in their purest forms in literary art.

Conceiving historical narratives in this way may give us some insight into the crisis in historical thinking which has been under way since the beginning of our century. Let us imagine that the problem of the historian is to make sense of a hypothetical *set* of events by arranging them in a *series* that is at once chronologically *and* syntactically structured, in the way that any discourse from a sentence all the way up to a novel is structured. We can see immediately that the imperatives of chronological arrangement of the events constituting the set must exist in tension with the imperatives of the syntactical strategies alluded to, whether the latter are conceived as those of logic (the syllogism) or those of narrative (the plot structure).

Thus, we have a set of events

$$a, b, c, d, e, \ldots, n, \qquad (1)$$

ordered chronologically but requiring description and characterization as elements of plot or argument by which to give them meaning. Now, the series can be emplotted in a number of different ways and thereby endowed with different meanings without violating the imperatives of the chronological arrangement at all. We may briefly characterize some of these emplotments in the following ways:

$$A, b, c, d, e, \ldots, n \qquad (2)$$
$$a, B, c, d, e, \ldots, n \qquad (3)$$
$$a, b, C, d, e, \ldots, n \qquad (4)$$
$$a, b, c, D, e, \ldots, n \qquad (5)$$

And so on.

The capitalized letters indicate the privileged status given to certain events or sets of events in the series by which they are endowed with explanatory force, either as causes explaining the structure of the whole series or as symbols of the plot structure of the series considered as a story of a specific kind. We might say that any history which endows any putatively original event (a) with the status of a decisive factor (A) in the structuration of the whole series of events following after it is "deterministic." The emplotments of the history of "society" by Rousseau in his *Second Discourse*, Marx in the *Manifesto*, and Freud in *Totem and Taboo* would fall into this category. So too, any history which endows the last event in the series (e), whether real or only speculatively projected, with the force of full explanatory power (E) is of the type of all eschatological or apocalyptical histories. St Augustine's *City of God* and the various versions of the Joachite notion of the advent of a millennium, Hegel's *Philosophy of History*, and, in general, all Idealist histories, are of this sort. In between we would have the various forms of historiography which appeal to plot structures of a distinctively "fictional" sort (Romance, Comedy, Tragedy, and Satire) by which to endow the series with a perceivable form and a conceivable "meaning."

If the series were simply recorded in the order in which the events originally occurred, under the assumption that the ordering of the events in their temporal sequence itself provided a kind of explanation of why they occurred when and where they did, we would have the pure form of the *chronicle*. This would be a "naive" form of chronicle, however, inasmuch as the categories of time and space alone served as the informing interpretive principles. Over against the naive form of chronicle we could postulate as a logical possibility its "sentimental" counterpart, the ironic denial that historical series have any kind of larger significance or describe any imaginable plot structure or indeed can even be construed as a story with a discernible beginning, middle, and end. We could conceive such accounts of history as intending to serve as antidotes to their false or overemplotted counterparts (nos 2, 3, 4, and 5 above) and could represent them as an ironic return to mere chronicle as constituting the only sense which any cognitively responsible history could take. We could characterize such histories thus:

$$\text{``}a, b, c, d, e \ldots, n\text{''} \qquad (6)$$

with the quotation marks indicating the conscious interpretation of the events as having nothing other than seriality as their meaning.

This schema is of course highly abstract and does not do justice to the possible mixtures of and variations within the types that it is meant to distinguish. But it helps us, I think, to conceive how events might be emplotted in different ways without violating the imperatives of the chronological order of the events (however they are construed) so as to yield alternative, mutually exclusive, and yet, equally plausible interpretations of the set. I have tried to show in *Metahistory* how such mixtures and variations occur in the writings of the master historians of the nineteenth century; and I have suggested in that book that classic historical accounts always represent attempts both to emplot the historical series adequately and implicitly to come to terms with other plausible emplotments. It is this dialectical tension between two or more possible emplotments that signals the element of critical self-consciousness present in any historian of recognizably classical stature.

Histories, then, are not only about events but also about the possible sets of relationships that those events can be demonstrated to figure. These sets of relationships are not, however, immanent in the events themselves; they exist only in the mind of the historian reflecting on them. Here they are present as the modes of relationships conceptualized in the myth, fable, and folklore, scientific knowledge, religion, and literary art, of the historian's own culture. But more importantly, they are, I suggest, immanent in the very language which the historian must use to *describe* events prior to a scientific analysis of them or a fictional emplotment of them. For if the historian's aim is to familiarize us with the unfamiliar, he must use figurative, rather than technical, language. Technical languages are familiarizing only *to* those who have been indoctrinated in their uses and only *of* those sets of events which the practitioners of a discipline have agreed to describe in a uniform terminology. History possesses no such generally accepted technical terminology and in fact no agreement on what kind of events make up its specific subject-matter. The historian's characteristic instrument of encodation, communication, and exchange is ordinary educated speech. This implies that the only instruments that he has for endowing his data with meaning, of rendering the strange familiar, and of rendering the mysterious past comprehensible, are the techniques of *figurative* language. All historical narratives presuppose figurative characterizations of the events they purport to represent and explain. And this means that historical narratives, considered purely as verbal artifacts, can be characterized by the mode of figurative discourse in which they are cast.

If this is the case, then it may well be that the kind of emplotment that the historian decides to use to give meaning to a set of historical events is dictated by the dominant figurative mode of the language he has used to *describe* the elements of his account *prior* to his composition of a narrative. Geoffrey Hartman once remarked in my hearing, at a conference on literary history, that he was not sure that he knew what historians of literature might want to do, but he did know that to write a history meant to place an event within a context, by relating it as a part to some conceivable whole. He went on to suggest that as far as he knew, there were only two ways of relating parts to wholes, by metonymy and by synecdoche. Having been engaged for some time in the study of the thought of Giambattista Vico, I was much taken with this thought, because it conformed to Vico's notion that the "logic" of all "poetic wisdom" was contained in the relationships which language itself provided in the four principal modes of figurative representation: metaphor, metonymy, synecdoche, and irony. My own hunch – and it is a hunch which I find confirmed in Hegel's reflections on the nature of nonscientific discourse – is that in any field of study which, like history, has not yet become disciplinized to the point of constructing a formal terminological system for describing its objects, in the way that physics and chemistry have, it is the types of figurative discourse that dictate the fundamental forms of the data to be studied. This means that the *shape* of the *relationships* which will appear to be inherent in the objects inhabiting the field will in reality have been imposed on the field by the investigator in the very *act of identifying and describing* the objects that he finds there. The implication is that historians *constitute* their subjects as possible objects of narrative representation by the very language they use to *describe* them. And if this is the case, it means that the different kinds of historical interpretations that we have of the same set of events, such as the French Revolution as interpreted by Michelet, Tocqueville, Taine, and others, are little more than projections of the linguistic protocols that these historians used to *pre*-figure that set of events prior to writing their narratives of it. It is only a hypothesis, but it seems possible that the conviction of the historian that he has "found" the form of his narrative in the events themselves, rather than imposed it upon them, in the way the poet does, is a result of a certain lack of linguistic self-consciousness which obscures the extent to which descriptions of events *already* constitute interpretations of their nature. As thus envisaged, the difference between Michelet's and Tocqueville's accounts of the Revolution does not reside only in the fact that the former emplotted his story in the modality of a Romance and the latter his in the modality of Tragedy; it resides as well in the tropological mode – metaphorical and metonymic, respectively – which each brought to his apprehension of the facts as they appeared in the documents.

I do not have the space to try to demonstrate the plausibility of this hypothesis, which is the informing principle of my book *Metahistory*. But I hope that this essay may serve to suggest an approach to the study of such discursive prose forms as historiography, an approach that is as old as the study of rhetoric and as new as modern linguistics. Such a study would proceed along the lines laid out by Roman Jakobson in a paper entitled "Linguistics and Poetics," in which he characterized the difference between Romantic poetry and the various forms of nineteenth-century Realistic prose as residing in the essentially metaphorical nature of the former and the essentially metonymical nature of the latter. I think that this characterization of the difference between poetry and prose is too narrow, because it presupposes that complex macrostructural narratives such as the novel are little more than projections of the "selective" (i.e. phonemic) axis of all speech acts. Poetry, and especially Romantic poetry, is then characterized by Jakobson as a projection of the "combinatory" (i.e. morphemic) axis of language. Such a binary theory pushes the analyst toward a dualistic opposition between poetry and prose which appears to rule out the possibility of a metonymical poetry and a metaphorical prose. But the fruitfulness of Jakobson's theory lies in its suggestion that the various forms of both poetry and prose, all of which have their counterparts in narrative in general and therefore in historiography too, can be characterized in terms of the dominant trope which serves as the paradigm, provided by language itself, of all significant relationships conceived to exist in the world by anyone wishing to represent those relationships in language.

Narrative, or the syntagmatic dispersion of events across a temporal series presented as a prose discourse, in such a way as to display their progressive elaboration as a comprehensible form, would represent the "inward turn" that discourse takes when it tries to *show* the reader the true form of things existing behind a merely apparent formlessness. Narrative *style*, in history as well as in the novel, would then be construed as the modality of the movement from a representation of some original state of affairs to some subsequent state. The primary *meaning* of a narrative would then consist of the destructuration of a set of events (real or imagined) originally encoded in one tropological mode and the progressive restructuration of the set in another tropological mode. As thus envisaged, narrative would be a process of decodation and recodation in which an original perception is clarified by being cast in a figurative mode different from that in which it has come encoded by convention, authority, or custom. And the explanatory force of the narrative would then depend on the contrast between the original encodation and the later one.

For example, let us suppose that a set of experiences comes to us as a grotesque, i.e. as unclassified and unclassifiable. Our problem is to identify the modality of the relationships that bind the discernible elements of the formless totality together in such a way as to make of it a whole of some sort. If we stress the similarities among the elements, we are working in the mode of metaphor; if we stress the differences among them, we are working in the mode of metonymy. Of course, in order to make sense of any set of experiences, we must obviously identify both the parts of a thing that appear to make it up and the nature of the shared aspects of the parts that make them identifiable as a totality. This implies that all original characterizations of anything must utilize *both* metaphor and metonymy in order to "fix" it as something about which we can meaningfully discourse.

In the case of historiography, the attempts of commentators to make sense of the French Revolution are instructive. Burke decodes the events of the Revolution which his contemporaries experience as a grotesque by recoding it in the mode of irony; Michelet recodes these events in the mode of synecdoche; Tocqueville recodes them in the mode of metonymy. In each case, however, the movement from code to recode is narratively described, i.e. laid out on a time-line in such a way as to make the interpretation of the events that made up the "Revolution" a kind of drama that we can recognize as Satirical, Romantic, and Tragic, respectively. This drama can be followed by the reader of the narrative in such a way as to be experienced as a progressive revelation of what the *true* nature of the events consists of. The revelation is not experienced, however, as a restructuring of perception so much as an illumination of a field of occurrence. But actually what has happened is that a set of events originally encoded in one way is simply being decoded by being recoded in another. The events themselves are not substantially changed from one account to another. That is to say, the data that are to be analyzed are not significantly different in the different accounts. What is different are the modalities of their relationships. These modalities, in turn, although they *may* appear to the reader to be based on different theories of the nature of society, politics, and history, ultimately have their origin in the figurative characterizations of the whole set of events as representing wholes of fundamentally different sorts. It is for this reason that, when it is a matter of setting different interpretations of the same set of historical phenomena over against one another in an attempt to decide which is the best or most convincing, we are often driven to confusion or ambiguity. This is not to say that we cannot distinguish between good and bad historiography, since we can always fall back on such criteria as responsibility to the rules of evidence, the relative fullness of narrative detail, logical consistency, and the like to determine this issue. But it is to say that the effort to distinguish between good and bad interpretations of a historical event such as the Revolution is not as easy as it might at first appear when it is a matter of dealing with alternative interpretations produced by historians of relatively equal learning and conceptual sophistication. After all, a great historical classic cannot be disconfirmed or nullified either by the discovery of some new datum that might call a specific explanation of some element of the whole account into question or by the generation of new methods of analysis which permit us to deal with questions that earlier historians might not have taken under consideration. And it is precisely because great historical classics, such as works by Gibbon, Michelet, Thucydides, Mommsen, Ranke, Burckhardt, Bancroft, and so on, cannot be definitely disconfirmed that we must look to the specifically literary aspects of their work as crucial, and not merely subsidiary, elements in their historiographical technique.

What all this points to is the necessity of revising the distinction conventionally drawn between poetic and prose discourse in discussion of such narrative forms as historiography and recognizing that the distinction, as old as Aristotle, between history and poetry obscures as much as it illuminates about both. If there is an element of the historical in all poetry, there is an element of poetry in every historical account of the world. And this because in our account of the historical world we are dependent, in ways perhaps that we are not in the natural sciences, on the techniques of *figurative language* both for our *characterization* of the objects of our narrative representations and for the *strategies* by which to constitute narrative accounts of the transformations of those objects in time. And this because history has no stipulatable subject-matter uniquely its own; it is always written as part of a contest between contending poetic figurations of what the past *might* consist of.

The older distinction between fiction and history, in which fiction is conceived as the representation of the imaginable and history as the representation of the actual, must give place to the recognition that we can only know the *actual* by contrasting it with or likening it to the *imaginable*. As thus conceived, historical narratives are complex structures in which a world of experience is imagined to exist under at least two modes, one of which is encoded as "real," the other of which is "revealed" to have been illusory in the course of the narrative. Of course, it is a fiction of the historian that the various states of affairs which he constitutes as the beginning, the middle, and the end of a course of development are all "actual" or "real" and that he has merely recorded "what happened" in the transition from the inaugural to the terminal phase. But both the beginning state of affairs and the ending one are inevitably poetic constructions, and as such, dependent upon the modality of the figurative language used to give them the aspect of coherence. This implies that all narrative is not simply a recording of "what happened" in the transition from one state of affairs to another, but a progressive *redescription* of sets of events in such a way as to dismantle a structure encoded in one verbal mode in the beginning so as to justify a recoding of it in another mode at the end. This is what the "middle" of all narratives consist of.

All of this is highly schematic, and I know that this insistence on the fictive element in all historical narratives is certain to arouse the ire of historians who believe that they are doing something fundamentally different from the novelist, by virtue of the fact that they deal with "real," while the novelist deals with "imagined," events. But neither the form nor the explanatory power of narrative derives from the different contents it is presumed to be able to accommodate. In point of fact, history – the real world as it evolves in time – is made sense of in the same way that the poet or novelist tries to make sense of it, i.e. by endowing what originally appears to be problematical and mysterious with the aspect of a recognizable, because it is a familiar, form. It does not matter whether the world is conceived to be real or only imagined; the manner of making sense of it is the same.

So too, to say that we make sense of the real world by imposing upon it the formal coherency that we customarily associate with the products of writers of fiction in no way detracts from the status as knowledge which we ascribe to historiography. It would only detract from it if we were to believe that literature did not teach us anything about reality, but was a product of an imagination which was not of this world but of some other, inhuman one. In my view, we experience the "fictionalization" of history as an "explanation" for the same reason that we experience great fiction as an illumination of a world that we inhabit along with the author. In both we recognize the forms by which consciousness both constitutes and colonizes the world it seeks to inhabit comfortably.

Finally, it may be observed that if historians were to recognize the fictive element in their narratives, this would not mean the degradation of historiography to the status of ideology or propaganda. In fact, this recognition would serve as a potent antidote to the tendency of historians to become captive of ideological preconceptions which they do not recognize as such but honor as the "correct" perception of "the way things *really* are." By drawing historiography nearer to its origins in literary sensibility, we should be able to identify the ideological, because it is the fictive, element in our own discourse. We are always able to see the fictive element in those historians with whose interpretations of a given set of events we disagree; we seldom perceive that element in our own prose. So, too, if we recognized the literary or fictive element in every historical account, we would be able to move the teaching of historiography onto a higher level of self-consciousness than it currently occupies.

What teacher has not lamented his inability to give instruction to apprentices in the *writing* of history? What graduate student of history has not despaired at trying to comprehend and imitate the model which his instructors *appear* to honor but the principles of which remain uncharted? If we recognize that there is a fictive element in all historical narrative, we would find in the theory of language and narrative itself the basis for a more subtle presentation of what historiography consists of than that which simply tells the student to go and "find out the facts" and write them up in such a way as to tell "what really happened."

In my view, history as a discipline is in bad shape today because it has lost sight of its origins in the literary imagination. In the interest of *appearing* scientific and objective, it has repressed and denied to itself its own greatest source of strength and renewal. By drawing historiography back once more to an intimate connection with its literary basis, we should not only be putting ourselves on guard against *merely* ideological distortions; we should be by way of arriving at that "theory" of history without which it cannot pass for a "discipline" at all.

Chapter 15

F. R. Ankersmit

SIX THESES ON NARRATIVIST PHILOSOPHY OF HISTORY*

1.   Historical narratives are interpretations of the past.

1.1.   The terms *historical narrative* and *interpretation* provide better clues for an understanding of historiography than the terms *description* and *explanation.*

1.2.   We interpret not when we have too few data but when we have too many (see 4.3). Description and explanation require the "right" amount of data.

1.2.1. Scientific theories are underdetermined since an infinite number of theories may account for the known data; interpretations are underdetermined since only an infinite number of interpretations could account for all the known data.

1.3.   Interpretation is not translation. The past is not a text that has to be *translated* into narrative historiography; it has to be *interpreted.*

1.4.   Narrative interpretations are not necessarily of a sequential nature; historical narratives are only contingently stories with a beginning, a middle, and an end.

1.4.1. Historical time is a relatively recent and highly artificial invention of Western civilization. It is a cultural, not a philosophical notion. Hence, founding narrativism on the concept of time is building on quicksand.

1.4.2. Narrativism can explain time and is not explained by it (see 2.1.3 and 4.7.5).

1.5.   Twenty years ago philosophy of history was scientistic; one ought to avoid the opposite extreme of seeing historiography as a form of literature. Historism is the *juste milieu* between the two: Historism retains what is right in both the scientistic and the literary approaches to history and avoids what is hyperbolic in both.

F. R. ANKERSMIT

1.5.1. Historiography *develops* narrative interpretations of sociohistorical reality; literature *applies* them.

1.6.   There is no precise line of demarcation between historiography and narrativist philosophy of history (see 4.7.5 and 4.7.7).

2.   Narrativism accepts the past as it is. In the form of a tautology: it accepts what is unproblematic about the past. What is unproblematic is a historical fact. Both senses of the latter statement are true (see 3.4.1 and 3.4.2).

2.1.   It is necessary to distinguish between historical research (a question of facts) and historical writing (a question of interpretation). The distinction is similar, though by no means identical, to the distinction in philosophy of science between observation statement and theory.

2.1.1. The results of historical research are expressed in statements; narrative interpretations are sets of statements.

2.1.2. The interesting distinction is not that between the singular and the general statement but between the general statement and historical narrative. The singular statement may serve both masters.

2.1.3. Temporal determinations are expressed *in* statements and not *by* statements and are therefore not of particular interest to narrativist philosophy of history. Narrativist philosophy of history deals with statements and not with their parts (like temporal indications).

2.2.   There is an affinity between philosophy of historical research and the components (statements) of a historical narrative. Philosophy of historical writing and the historical narrative in its totality are similarly related.

2.2.1. With a few exceptions (W. H. Walsh, H. V. White, L. O. Mink), current philosophy of history is interested exclusively in historical research.

2.2.2. Its distrust of (narrativist) holism prevents current philosophy from understanding historical narrative.

2.3.   The most crucial and most interesting intellectual challenges facing the historian are found on the level of historical writing (selection, interpretation, how to see the past). The historian is essentially more than Collingwood's detective looking for the murderer of John Doe.

2.4.   Since it deals only with the components of historical narrative, philosophy of action can never further our insight into historical narrative.

2.4.1. Philosophy of action can never speak the language of the unintended consequences of human action. As a philosophy of history, philosophy of action is only suited to prehistorist historiography. Being unable to transcend the limitations of methodological individualism, it is historiographically naive.

2.4.2. Von Wright's and Ricoeur's attempts to solve this problem for philosophy of action are unsuccessful. Historical meaning is different from the agent's intention.

2.4.3. The language of the unintended consequences is the language of interpretation (there ordinarily is a difference between the historian's perspective and that of the historical agent).

2.4.4. The *logical connection argument* is a special case of narrativism (in that it provides a logical scheme in which knowledge of the past is organized).

3. Narrativism is the modern heir of historism (not to be confused with Popper's historic*i*sm): both recognize that the historian's task is essentially interpretative (i.e. to find unity in diversity).

3.1. Interpretations strive for the unity that is characteristic of things (see 4.4).

3.1.2. Historists attempted to discover the essence, or, as they called it, the *historische Idee*, which they assumed was present in the historical phenomena themselves. Narrativism, on the contrary, recognized that a historical interpretation *projects* a structure onto the past and does not *discover* it as if this structure existed in the past itself.

3.1.3. Historism is an unexceptionable theory of history if it is translated from a theory about historical phenomena into a theory about our speaking about the past (that which was metaphysical must become linguistic).

3.1.4. Insofar as the notion of plot or intrigue is suggestive of a structure or story present in the past itself, this notion is an unwarranted concession to historist, or narrativist, realism.

3.2. Historical narratives are not projections (onto the past) or reflections of the past, tied to it by translation rules which have their origin either in our daily experiences of the social world, in the social sciences, or in speculative philosophies of history.

3.2.1 Narrative interpretations are theses, not hypotheses.

3.3. Narrative interpretations *apply* to the past, but do not *correspond* or *refer* to it (as [parts of] statements do).

3.3.1. Much of current philosophy of historical narrative is bewitched by the picture of the statement.

3.3.2. Narrative language is autonomous with regard to the past itself. A philosophy of narrative makes sense if, and only if, this autonomy is recognized (see 4.5).

3.3.3. Since narrative interpretations only apply and do not refer (cf. the point of view from which a painter paints a landscape), there is no fixity in the relation between them and the past. The requirement that there should be such a relationship results from a category mistake (i.e. demanding for historical narrative what can only be given to the statement).

3.3.4. Narrative interpretations "pull you out of historical reality" and do not "send you back to it" (as the statement does).

3.4. In narrative language the relation between language and reality is systematically "destabilized" (see 5.1.2).

3.4.1. Epistemology is of relevance to philosophy of historical research, but of no importance to philosophy of historical writing or philosophy of narrative interpretation.

3.4.2. Epistemology, studying the relation between language and reality insofar as this relation is fixed and stable, disregards all the real problems of science and of historiography which only arise after that which bothers epistemology has been accepted as unproblematic. *Foundationalism* is interested in what is fundamentally uninteresting.

3.4.3. The philosophical investigation of "what justifies historical descriptions" is an implicit denial and denigration of the historian's intellectual achievements.

4. Narrative language is not object language.

4.1. Narrative language *shows* the past in terms of what does not *refer* or *correspond* to parts or aspects of the past. Narrative interpretations in this regard resemble the models used by fashion designers for showing the qualities of their gowns and dresses. Language is used for showing what belongs to a world different from it.

4.1.1. Narrativism is a constructivism not of what the past might have been like, but of narrative interpretations of the past.

4.1.2. Narrative interpretations are *Gestalts*.

4.2. Logically, narrative interpretations are of the nature of proposals (to see the past from a certain point of view).

4.2.1. Proposals may be useful, fruitful, or not, but cannot be either true or false; the same can therefore be said of historical narratives.

4.2.2. There is no intrinsic difference between speculative systems and history proper; they are *used* in different ways. Speculative systems are used as *master-narratives* to which other narratives should conform.

4.2.3. The writing of history shares with metaphysics the effort of defining the essence of (part of) reality, but differs from metaphysics because of its nominalism (see 4.7.1).

4.3.   Narrative interpretations are not knowledge but *organizations* of knowledge. Our age, with its excess of information – and confronted with the problem of the organization of knowledge and information, rather than of how knowledge is gained – has every reason to be interested in the results of narrativism.

4.3.1. Cognitivism, with regard to narrative interpretations, is the source of all realist misconceptions of historical narrative.

4.4.   Logically, narrative proposals are of the nature of things (not of concepts); like things they can be spoken about without ever being part of the language in which they are *mentioned*. Language is used here with the purpose of constructing a narrative interpretation which itself lies outside the domain of language, though the interpretation is "made out of" language (similarly, the meaning of the word *chair* cannot be reduced to the letters in the word).

4.4.1. Narrative interpretations cross the familiar border between the domain of things and the domain of language – as does metaphor.

4.5.   A historical discussion about the crisis of the seventeenth century, for example, is not a debate about the actual past but about narrative interpretations of the past.

4.5.1. Our speaking about the past is covered by a thick crust not related to the past itself but to historical interpretation and the debate about rival historical interpretations. Narrative language has no transparency and is unlike the glass paperweight through which we gain an unobstructed view of the past itself.

4.6.   The autonomy of narrative language with regard to the past itself does not in the least imply that narrative interpretations should be arbitrary (see 5.3, 5.6).

4.6.1. Facts about the past may be arguments in favor of or against narrative interpretations but can never determine these interpretations (facts only [dis]prove statements about the past) (see 1.2.1). Only interpretations can (dis)prove interpretations.

4.7.   Narrative interpretations may have proper names (like the General Crisis of the Seventeenth Century, the Cold War, Mannerism, or the Industrial Revolution). Mostly, however, this is not the case.

4.7.1.   Narrative logic is strictly nominalist.

4.7.2.   Names like *Mannerism* refer to historical interpretations and not to past reality itself ("What Mannerism do you have in mind?" "Pevsner's Mannerism.").

4.7.3.   This does not imply that these names are floating in a domain unrelated to historical reality itself (example: the name *Mannerism* refers to the statements of a narrative interpretation, and in these statements, reference is made to historical reality itself).

4.7.4.   Narrative interpretations have no existential implications (for example: *the Industrial Revolution* is not a vast impersonal force in historical reality, unnoticed and undiscovered until 1884 when Arnold Toynbee wrote *The Industrial Revolution in England*, but an interpretative instrument for understanding the past).

4.7.5.   Nevertheless, if a narrative interpretation goes unquestioned for a long time, is accepted by everybody, and becomes part of ordinary language (thereby losing its historiographical nature), it may turn into the notion of a (type of) thing. A *narrative thing* (see 4.4) has become a *thing in reality*. This is how our concepts of (types of) things originate. Typification procedures decide what is still merely interpretative and what is real; there is nothing fixed and absolute about the demarcation between what is interpretation and what belongs to the inventory of reality.

4.7.6.   Concepts of (types of) things (like *dog* or *tree*) are logically more complicated than narrative interpretations, since they presuppose a typification procedure still absent in the case of the latter. Interpretation logically precedes our (notions of) types of things. Ontology is a systematization of interpretation.

4.7.7.   Metaphor and narrative interpretation form the basis of our language.

4.7.8.   Without a theory of types, narrativism is impossible. Without it, we inevitably look in the wrong direction. (Types of) things are then more fundamental than narrative interpretations.

4.7.9.   To require fixed meanings for words like *the Cold War* or *Mannerism* would amount to requiring that historical debate should stop. Historical writing does not presuppose, but results in definitions.

4.7.10. Notions like *the Cold War*, being sets of statements, are logically distinct from theoretical concepts.

4.8.   Causal explanation – for instance, along the lines of the *covering law model* (CLM) – has its function exclusively on the level of historical research (and on that of the components of historical narrative): we should not ask for the cause of the Cold War since what this term refers to is a narrative interpretation. It makes no sense to ask for the cause of a historical interpretation. Anyone who asks for the cause of the Cold War is really asking for a vigorous interpretation of events between 1944 and the early 1990s and not for a causal tie between two separate sets of events.

5.   The statements of a historical narrative always have a *double* function: (1) to describe the past; and (2) to define or individuate a specific narrative interpretation of the past.

5.1.   Logically, both historical narratives and metaphor consist of two operations only: (1) description; and (2) the individuation of a (metaphorical) point of view. Historical narrative is a sustained metaphor.

5.1.1. Metaphor shows what the metaphorical utterance is about in terms of something else (e.g. "John is a pig"); similarly, historical narrative shows the past in terms of what is not the past, (i.e. a narrative interpretation) (see 4.1).

5.1.2. Thanks to its autonomy with regard to historical reality – in historical narrative the relation between language and reality is constantly destabilized – historical narrative, like metaphor, is the birthplace of new meaning. Accepted, literal meaning requires a fixed relation between language and reality.

5.2   The discrepancy between the (literal) meaning of the individual statements of a historical narrative – if taken separately – and the (metaphorical) meaning of historical narrative – if taken in its totality – is the *scope* of historical narrative. This shows the difference between the chronicle (corresponding to the separate statement) and historical narrative (corresponding to the totality of a narrative's statements). A set of statements arbitrarily jumbled together has no scope.

5.2.1. A historical narrative is a historical narrative only insofar as the (metaphorical) meaning of the historical narrative in its totality transcends the (literal) meaning of the sum of its individual statements. Being a historical narrative, therefore, is a matter of degree.

5.2.2. The historical narrative resembles a belvedere: after having climbed the staircase of its individual statements, one surveys an area exceeding by far the area on which the staircase was built.

5.2.3. The historian's capacity to develop (metaphorical) narrative scope is the most formidable asset in his intellectual arsenal.

5.3.   The best historical narrative is the most metaphorical historical narrative, the historical narrative with the largest scope. It is also the most "risky" or the most "courageous" historical narrative. In contrast, the non-narrativist has to prefer an unmeaning historical narrative without internal organization.

5.3.1. The narrative scope of a historical narrative cannot be established by considering only *that* historical narrative. Narrative scope only comes into being when one compares narrative interpretations with rival interpretations. If we have only *one* narrative interpretation of some historical topic, we have *no* interpretation.

5.3.2. Historical insight, therefore, is only born in the space *between* rival narrative interpretations and cannot be identified with any specific (set of) interpretations.

5.3.3. *Cognitive knowledge* is to be identified with the linguistic means used for expressing it (singular statements, general statements, theories, etc.); *historical insight* lies in the empty narrative space between the narrative interpretations (it is stereoscopic, so to speak).

5.3.4. Historical insight is constituted in and by historiographical controversy and not by the individual phases of historiographical controversy, hence not by individual narrative interpretations in isolation from others.

5.3.5. Historiographical debate, ultimately, does not aim for agreement but for the proliferation of interpretative theses. The purpose of historiography is *not* the transformation of narrative things into real things (or their type concepts) (see 4.7.5). On the contrary, it attempts to bring about the dissolution of what seems known and unproblematic. Its goal is not the reduction of the unknown to the known, but the estrangement of what seems so familiar.

5.3.6. This emphasis on disagreement and historiographical controversy requires us to reject the notion of a Cartesian or Kantian, interchangeable, transcendental knowing subject. The Aristotelian view is to be preferred. For Aristotle, experience and knowledge *are* the interaction between us and the world and not an abstraction from it determined by a transcendentalist, formal scheme. Similarly, historic interpretation arises from the interaction of interpretations and should not be attributed to either a concrete individual nor to a transhistorical, transcendental subject.

5.4.   Narrative scope is logically independent of the realm of values; therefore, historical narrative need not be value-free in order to have a large scope – that is, in order to be objective (for example, the notion of the totalitarian state proposed by K. Popper, J. L. Talmon, H. Arendt, and others was not value-free but had a very large scope).

5.4.1. The historian is the professional "outsider:" the gap between himself and historical reality, which he is always attempting to bridge, is identical to the gap between the individual and society, which ethics and political philosophy attempt to bridge. The ethical dimension must therefore be ubiquitous in historiography. Modern historiography is based on a political decision.

5.4.2. Metaphor and narrative are the *trait d'union* between the *is* and the *ought* — the *is* of the constative statements of a historical interpretation may suggest what *ought* to be done.

5.5. Leibniz's predicate in notion principle is the crucial theorem of the logic of historical interpretation. All statements about a historical narrative are *analytically* either true or false.

5.5.1. The fashionable view that the variables of quantification will take the place of the subject term in statements (Russell, Quine) is incorrect for narrative statements (i.e. statements about historical narratives). The subject term in narrative statements is unvoiceable, precisely because it merely "collects" the statements contained by a historical narrative.

5.5.2. Narrative interpretations have explanatory force since the description of historical states of affairs can be analytically derived from them.

5.6. There is no room for historical skepticism. We can see the rationality of why historians in a certain phase of historical debate preferred one view of the past to another. Skepticism only results if one is not content with the rationality of historical debate and absolute *foundations* are required. But, in practice, this requirement can never be more than an exhortation to historians to do their job carefully and conscientiously.

6. The roots of historicity go deeper than is suggested by either modern historiography or current philosophy (of history).

6.1. The notion of the self is a historical, narrative interpretation — the narrative interpretation that is presupposed by *all* other historical interpretations. This is the kernel of truth in Anglo-Saxon hermeneutics.

6.1.1. Consequently, the fact that narrative interpretations already play a role on the level of the life of the human individual can never be an argument in favor of a certain variant of narrative realism (i.e. the view that historical knowing should be modeled on our experiences of daily reality). It is the reverse: interpretative narrativism has already invaded our daily reality.

6.1.2. The concepts of (types of) individual things are logically dependent upon narrative interpretations (identity). Thus: identity precedes individuality, not the reverse, as positivism suggests (see 4.7.5).

Note

* These theses summarize the views I expounded in my *Narrative Logic: A Semantic Analysis of the Historian's Language*, The Hague, 1983.

Chapter 16

Noël Carroll

INTERPRETATION, HISTORY
AND NARRATIVE

I Introduction: historical narratives as fictions and as metaphors

AT PRESENT, ONE OF THE MOST recurrent views in the philosophy
of history claims that historical writing is interpretive and that a primary
form that this interpretation takes is narration. Furthermore, narration, according
to this approach, is thought to possess an inevitably fictional element, viz. a plot,
and, in this regard, the work of the narrative historian is said to be more like that
of the imaginative writer than has been admitted heretofore. The upshot of this
philosophically, moreover, is the assertion that historical narrations, *qua* narrative
interpretations, are to be assessed, in large measure, in terms of the kind of criterion of truth that is appropriate to literary works. And a subsidiary, though far less
tendentious, consequence is that our understanding of historical interpretation can
profit from literary or "discourse" analysis.

This position, which was perhaps anticipated by Nietzsche,[1] is suggested in
varying degrees by Roland Barthes[2] and Louis Mink;[3] it has been developed most
extensively by Hayden White;[4] and it commands a following among historians,
literary critics, and philosophers of history.[5]

For White, historical writing is interpretive in several separable, though interrelated, registers. Historical argumentation in the dissertative mode involves a
paradigm choice; second, in a broad sense, a historical tract requires the choice of
an ideological perspective; and, also, a historical narrative itself enjoins a choice of
a plot structure, which, in turn, is related to the discursive tropes that "figure" the
writing of the text.[6] For the purposes of this essay, it is White's conclusions about
the specific status that he assigns to narrative interpretation which preoccupy us.[7]

Stated roughly, White identifies historical discourse with interpretation and
historical interpretation with narrativization. A historical narrative is not a *transparent* representation or copy of a sequence of past events. Narration irreducibly
entails selecting the events to be included in its exposition as well as filling in links

that are not available in the evidential record. The historian does not find or discover her narrative; she constructs it. This process of construction involves distortion[8] and the imposition of generic plot structures (such as Romance, Tragedy, Comedy, and Satire) on the sequence of past events. The plot structures that are culturally available to the narrative historian are inherently fictional; they are not merely neutral, formal armatures on which events are displayed; they have a content – hence, White's emphasis on the notion of the *content of form*. Moreover, that content is fictional.

This conclusion, however, does not lead White to argue that historical interpretations cannot be truthful. Rather they are truthful, but in the way that White takes fictions to be truthful. That is, historical narratives, like fictional narratives, are, by virtue of their plot structures, true in the ways that metaphors are true.

Marx's characterization of the Eighteenth Brumaire of Louis Bonaparte as a farce is assessable in the same way that the sentence "our last faculty meeting was a farce" is assessable. Here, the presiding idea is that there is a variety of metaphorical truth, in contradistinction to literal truth, and that fictions and that historical narratives (with plot structures derived ultimately from myths) are a subspecies thereof.

In according historical narrative this means, albeit fictional in nature, of characterizing reality, White stands at odds with various Continental theorists, such as Lévi-Strauss[9] and the *Annales* school,[10] who disparage narrative history as regressively unscientific, alternatively mythic and fantastic. White, in contrast, grants historical narration cognitive purchase, specifically in terms of metaphor (though sometimes he also uses the notion of allegory to make this point).

White summarizes his position succinctly by saying:

> To emplot real events as a story of a specific kind (or as a mixture of stories of a specific kind) is to trope these events. This is because stories are not lived; there is no such thing as a "real" story. Stories are told or written, not found. And as for the notion of a "true" *story*, this is virtually a contradiction in terms. *All* stories are fictions which means, of course, that they can be "true" in a metaphorical sense and in the sense in which any figure of speech can be true. Is this true enough?[11]

Though as a slogan this is quite pointed, it does require some care in order to understand what White is asserting. Contra Paul Ricoeur's analysis of White,[12] White is not entirely erasing the distinction between fiction and historical writing. Historical writing does refer to past events and those references must be supportable on the basis of the evidential record. In virtue of this evidential requirement, historical writing can be assessed in terms of a literal criterion for truth in a way that fictional exercises should not be. However, in addition to this standard of truth, the historical narrative – i.e. the selection, combination, and arrangement of events attested to by the record – is to be evaluated by another criterion, one shared with fictional narratives – to wit: metaphorical aptness.

In this regard, there is a superficial resemblance between the structure of White's account of historical interpretation and Joseph Margolis's notion of robust relativism. For Margolis, the descriptions that ground interpretations are susceptible to evaluation in terms of truth and falsity, whereas the overall interpretation requires some other sort of assessment, say in terms of plausibility.[13] For White, the notation of the events by the historian is responsible to literal canons of evidence, whereas the narrative constructions themselves are metaphorically true. The historian promotes understanding in her reader by casting a sequence of historical events in the form of a culturally shared and familiar narrative pattern (e.g. tragedy), and we assimilate the past under a common myth. This pattern of meaning – embodied in the plot structure, which itself has a kind of mythic content – illuminates insofar as it is a serviceable analog for the past.

So far, I have merely offered a sketch of historical constructivism à la White. In the next section, I will try to refine the various arguments that he uses to advance this position, and, in the concluding section, I will review the problems that confront White at almost every turn, along with offering a diagnosis of certain of the deep presuppositions that I believe lead White astray.

2 White's arguments

White characterizes his approach as concerned with a *specifically* historical kind of writing[14] and he explicitly aligns himself with the narrativist, as opposed to a *scientific*, conception of historiography.[15] This seems extravagant to me, for clearly science can be narrative in form – e.g. the geological account of the disposition of the continents – without ceasing to be scientific, and, therefore, narrative cannot be the quiddity of history as differentiated from science.[16] However, even if White's commitment to narrativism is sometimes overzealous, his position is still a challenging one. For, obviously, history is often (most often?) presented in narrative form – even if narration is not the essence of historical exposition – and, thus, the finding (if it is that) that historical narrative is always in fundamental ways fictional remains a significant epistemological thesis.[17]

White's leading idea is that historical interpretation is a construction or an imposition on a sequence of past events insofar as it involves narration. The coherence that narration supplies to a sequence of events is an imaginative invention. The historical series of events is not coherent – despite the claims of speculative philosophers of history like Hegel; rather, historical events begin to take coherent shape only through the historian's narrative efforts.

In this respect, White is not thoroughly anti-realist; he does not deny that the past existed. He is only opposed to the notion that there are "real stories," that is, that narratives of the past reflect the structure of ongoing, successive, past events. The past, in other words, is not storied, and representing sequences of events in story form is, strictly speaking, adding something to them.

Furthermore, even if the reference to past events in the historical account are assessable in terms of truth or falsity, that added "something" – the narrative configuration or pattern (which is more than the conjunction of all the truth-functional references in a historical account) – is not. It must be evaluated as metaphor or allegory. That is, narrative histories must be thought of in terms of something called *narrative truth* which involves more than establishing the truth-values of the conjunction of the atomic sentences that comprise them and which is spoken of as a different kind of truth.[18]

On White's account, typical historiographic practice proceeds under the assumption that narrative historians are discovering the structure of past processes – that is to say, "real stories." But for White stories are invented, not found, and their invention by historians is structurally continuous with the efforts of authors of fiction. Thus, historical narratives are on a par with fictional narratives in this respect, and their cognitive value, *qua* narration, is of a piece with things like novels – viz. they are sources of metaphorical insight.

White attempts to support his view with a wide range of considerations, involving slogans, contrasts, and analyses of the nature of narrative. These different forms of argumentation build on and segue with each other in various ways. Their effect, one supposes, is meant to be cumulative, though one also suspects that White thinks that each has force independently of the others. So for the purposes of this presentation, I will introduce them as separate considerations, while also taking note of the ways in which later analyses and arguments build on and flesh out earlier ones.

White's often repeated[19] core slogan, which he shares with Louis Mink,[20] is that lives are lived and stories are told. Our lives do not come packaged as stories; we invent stories about them retrospectively through imaginative effort. Thus, the historians' narrative cannot be taken as a reflection of the lives lived by historical agents. If historians think this way – as White believes they do, despite what they may say – then narrative historians are woefully mistaken.

Though the invocation of "lives" here, as we shall see, is too restrictive as well as infelicitous in other ways, what is intended can be put more rigorously and comprehensively: "Histories, then, are not only about events but also about the possible sets of relationships that those events can be demonstrated to figure. These sets of relationships are not, however, immanent in the events themselves; they exist only in the mind of the historian reflecting on them."[21]

This slogan is fleshed out in terms of various, further contrasts. Since the past is not storied, historical narratives are not *found* or *discovered*; rather they are *invented*.[22] In this sense, historical narratives are *constructions*[23] – constructions that give a sequence of events, such as one might find notated in a historical chronicle or annal, a *meaning*.[24] Historical narratives, in this regard, are also said to *constitute* meaning.[25]

But events, as lived, do not have meanings. They only get meanings by being invested with a function in a narrative. That the Battle of Stalingrad was the *turning point* of World War II, for example, acquires this significance by being a complication in a narrative plot about World War II. The Battle of Stalingard, *qua* event, had no meaning; and, indeed, it could figure in other stories in which it would have a different meaning. (In an architectural history, for example, the significance of the battle might be that it occasioned the destruction of important buildings.)

Related to the meaning/real event contrast is a contrast between meaning and a copy of an event. Putatively, practicing historians have the naive view that their narratives could be *copies* of events past – by which I understand White to mean something like a perfect replica or mirror-image.[26] But historical writing cannot afford a perfect simulacrum of the past. It involves selection and filling in; so it is actually a deviation from an exact copy or representation of the succession of events.

In fact, White does not hesitate to call it a *distortion*,[27] presumably a distortion in contrast to whatever would count as a perfect replica or mirror-image of a succession of past events.

Narration has its own conditions of intelligibility. Narrative coherence requires features like beginnings, middles, and ends — ends, particularly in the technical sense of closure. But, on what must be ontological grounds, White thinks it is obvious that events do not emerge from the flux of history closured. Closure is a product of narrative coherence. It is the aim of achieving narrative coherence that leads to the selection and hierarchical ordering that imbues the relevant events with meaning, while also *distorting* them in the sense at play in the preceding paragraph.

Narrative coherence, then, is an *imposition*[28] on the historical past. Moreover, the patterns of narrative coherence thus imposed upon (or constructed out of) a collection of historical events are *conventional* (rather than, say, realistically motivated).[29] This inventing, distorting, constructing, imposing, constituting, meaning-making (signifying), and convention-applying activity are all acts of the imagination (in contrast, one supposes, to some more literal information-assimilating process). Moreover, this imaginative activity on the part of narrative historians is not different in kind from the activity of the literary fabulist and should be treated as telling us about the world in the same way.

White runs his various foils to actual sequences of events (and perfect replicas thereof) together rather indiscriminately. That is, imagining, constructing, distorting, signifying, constituting, and so on are never scrupulously and differentially defined, and they are all used to serve roughly the same purpose: to underpin the animating distinction between living (the succession of real events) and telling (narrating). One would think that signifying, imagining, distorting, conventionalizing, and so on — not to mention selecting — (though potentially interrelated in interesting ways) should not be lumped together so cavalierly. However, in White's brief they serve as "intuition pumps"[30] directed at consolidating the reigning slogan that distinguishes between living (history as process) and telling (history as narrative *artifact*). Each contrast, that is, is meant to convince us of a disjunction between a sequence of real events or a perfect replica thereof (whatever that might be) and a narrative structure which introduces fictional elements into the flow of events.

White expands upon and concretizes his slogans and intuition pumps by exploiting analyses of narrative by literary theorists — both those of the recent structuralist/poststructuralist dispensation, and that of Northrop Frye.

From Continental literary theory, White derives the idea of what he calls "narrativizing discourse."[31] This is putatively discourse that gives the impression that there is no narrator. It is the discourse that in contemporary literary circles is often called "transparent," that is, writing which presents itself to the reader as unmediated and full — a transcription of reality without gaps: "the whole unvarnished truth and nothing but," so to speak. Such discourse, ostensibly appearing without a narrator, presents itself as if "the events seem to tell themselves."[32] The property of "events telling themselves" is called narrativity, and discourse that imbues the events it recounts with this property is narrativizing.

The transparency or narrativizing effect is the hallmark of what many literary theorists call the realist text, such as is supposedly found in the form of the nineteenth-century novel. In adopting the narrating strategies of the realist text, the historian, likewise, presents events as if they were "telling themselves." For White, this implies that naive, narrative historians really have a deep, though unacknowledged and even disavowed, affinity with substantive philosophers of history, like Marx and Hegel, who see the historical process as a single unfolding story – history speaking through the acts of humankind. Thus, if substantive philosophers of history are open to criticism, then less grandiose but nevertheless still narrativizing historians should be vulnerable to the same kind of criticisms.

So, both ordinary narrativizing historians and philosophers of history can be charged with distortion and with masking their highly selective procedures with an imaginary aura of coherence, integrity, and fullness that exploits our desires (for coherence, etc.), but which misrepresents reality.[33] White writes, "Does the world really present itself to perception in the form of well-made stories, with central subjects, proper beginnings, middles and ends, and a coherence that permits us to see 'the end' in every beginning?"[34] Any form of narrativity – which is the presupposition that narrative structure literally corresponds to something in the historical past – amounts to the belief that "events tell themselves." But "real events should not speak, should not tell themselves. Real events should simply be."[35] Or, to return to White's earlier slogan: stories can't be found because *real stories* aren't out there in the world of the past to be found.. . .

3 Resisting White's constructivism

According to White, lives are lived and stories are told. The putative consequence of this is that insofar as historical narratives represent the lives of the past in story form, they do not correspond to what existed in the past and are, therefore, fictional. This is not compelling comprehensively. For it is often the case that we plan – if not our entire lives, at least important episodes therein – by means of telling or visualizing stories to ourselves, and, then, we go about enacting them. That is, lives can be storied; indeed there is a branch of psychology that uses this idea as a research hypothesis.[36] Consequently, with certain life episodes – and, in some cases, perhaps with some monomaniacal lives – there are stories, hatched by historical agents, that had causal efficacy in the past and which could be discovered and written up by historians. Thus, to the extent that the contrast between lives and stories is not thoroughly exclusive, the conclusion that any historical narrative must be fictional is not without exception; there could be historical narratives of storied lives, or, at least, of storied episodes in the lives of historical agents.

Of course, this is not the real issue that the lives/stories dichotomy is meant to broach. For historians are not merely biographers in search of life stories. The contrast between lives and stories is meant to call to mind colorfully the idea that historical narratives are not found or discovered in the past, but are constructions or inventions. The notion of *invention* here is a bit tricky and open to equivocation. In one sense, historical narratives are inventions, viz. in the sense that they are made by historians; but it is not clear that it follows from this that they are *made-up* (and are, therefore, fictional).

Narratives are a form of representation, and it is true that historians do not go about finding their representations as one might find a lost picture, a lost photo, or a lost piece of film footage. Photos and film strips are made (invented) and they are not found. We could say that lives are lived, and home movies are invented. But this doesn't entail that a stretch of film footage cannot record the past or yield accurate information about it. Similarly, narratives are a form of representation, and, in that sense, they are invented, but that does not preclude their capacity to provide accurate information. Narratives can provide accurate knowledge about the past in terms of the kinds of features they track, namely, the ingredients of *courses of events*,[37] which include: background conditions, causes and effects, as well as social context, the logic of situations, practical deliberations, and ensuing actions.

Recently, for example, on 3 July 1989, the United States Supreme Court announced a decision that delegated responsibility for regulating the availability of abortions to the discretion of individual states. This decision was the result, in significant respects, of the success of the Reagan regime in appointing a series of like-minded, conservative judges to the Supreme Court. The appointment of those judges, including O'Connor and Scalia, in the context of a background project of contesting the perceived past liberalism of the Supreme Court, was part of a real historical process, a course of events, that culminated on 3 July 1989.

This is not to say that there will not be further consequences to the court's decision nor that this is the *final* culmination of Reagan's successful efforts to reorient the court. But the fact that there is more to come does not vitiate the fact that the Reagan administration's decisions and appointments were significant ingredients in a real historical process which had as one result — *one*, for there will be more — the decision on 3 July 1989. The historian who tracks these decisions and appointments, situating them in their social contexts, will make something — something that may take imagination to accomplish — namely, a historical representation. But there is no reason to suppose that such historical representations are necessarily *made-up* or invented unless, for some as yet undemonstrated reason, courses of events must be excluded from our ontology. Moreover, if courses of events are admissible ontologically, then they are there to be discovered and represented.

That my counterexamples so far often rely on the idea of deliberations and decisions implemented in ensuing actions may appear open to the objection that they presuppose a commitment on the part of historians to recreating the internal perspective of historical agents. This, in turn, would be criticized as problematic for two related reasons. First, that historians are not simply concerned with narrating events in terms of how the agents saw them *and* that, even if historians were so disposed, they should not be so exclusively preoccupied since it is often (most often?) the unintended consequences of people's deliberations and decisions about which we most care.

These objections, however, require two remarks. First, if there are courses of events that did issue as planned from the agent's perhaps storied deliberation, this would be enough to show that there is a sense in which the thesis that stories are never found fails to be fully comprehensive. But a second and more important point is that in speaking of courses of events, we are not committed to rendering them solely in terms of the original intentions of the agents involved in them. A course of events may involve failed attempts, like Reagan's nomination of Bork to the Supreme Court, which will result in more deliberative activity which may have further unintended consequences. Or, the agent's deliberative activity may involve miscalculations that call for the historian to illuminate the prevailing conditions that made the attempt misfire. That practical reasoning and its implementation in action provide some of the ingredients that make a course of events cohere in no way implies that the representation of a course of events will be a string of successful practical syllogisms. That practical, deliberative activity will supply some measure of cohesiveness to the narratives of human events does not restrict us to a form of historical intentionalism nor does it preclude discussion of corporate entities like states or classes.[38]

Of course, in speaking of courses of events, I do not mean to imply that any given event is only a member of one course of events. The appointment of Sandra Day O'Connor to the Supreme Court is part of the course of events that led to the decision alluded to above. But that event also undoubtedly figured in various other courses of events — some in the history of the O'Connor family and some concerning the social advancement of women in the United States. And, equally, the event of O'Connor's appointment will also figure in courses of events still in the making. The same event can be part of different courses of events, and, there-fore, can be represented in different stories. But the fact that different events can figure in different stories in no way indicates that the stories are fictional. For this suspicion to counterfeit plausibility, we would have to assume that in order to be nonfictional, there would have to be only one relevant story, perhaps of the sort proposed by speculative philosophers of history, and that each event in it would be significant in one and only one way. That is, if there is more than one story, then stories are invented, and, therefore, fictional. But the presumed disjunction that either there is one real story or a multiplicity of fictional ones fails to accom-modate the fact that courses of action intersect and branch off from shared events, which intersections and branches can be found or discovered.

In White's way of speaking, when a given event is situated in different narra-tives it can acquire a different meaning. That events have these differential meanings indicates that they are imposed and, therefore, fictional. But talk of meanings here may be a little misleading. Events have different significances in different courses of events.[39] Antonin Scalia's appointment to the Supreme Court has one signifi-cance in terms of the great abortion debate and another, though perhaps not completely unrelated, significance in the history of Italian-Americans. In these exam-ples, the idea of significance can be cashed in causally. If *meaning* here amounts to playing a role in a network of socially significant causation, then there should be no problems in admitting that Scalia's appointment may have a different meaning in different courses of events. This simply allows that a single event can play a different role in different causal chains. This does not indicate that a meaning has been imposed on the event. Again, the event may occur in different stories because the different stories track different courses of overlapping events.[40]

White's use of the notion of meaning in his arguments gives his thesis a semantic flavor, which perhaps suggests a level of arbitrariness that would warrant talk of imposition. However, it is important to stress that the kind of *meaning* that an event has in a narrative is a matter of its significance with respect to subsequent events, often in terms of causation and/or practical reasoning. And whether significance in this sense obtains is not arbitrary or imposed. That the historian wants to know what caused the American entry into World War II does not make her citation of the attack on Pearl Harbor an imposition on the historical train of events nor is her imputation of causal efficacy to the attack arbitrary in any way. This is not to deny that events in historical narratives will be events under a description; but within the context of a given research project, the description of a pertinent event is not arbitrary in the way that on some views of language the relation between a signifier and a signified is arbitrary. Similarly, it is not helpful to think of the historian's description of an action in terms of its significance in a course of events as constitutive of the event in any strong sense; whether Pearl Harbor, for example, was a cause of World War II is a fact even if it were not asserted in historical accounts.

White contrasts historical narratives replete with meanings to copies of the past. The historical narrative, involving selection and abduction, is not a copy of the past, and, therefore, is fictional. The contrast here seems forced; the visual references to copies and mirrors is particularly strained though revelatory of an empiricist residue in White's thinking. Obviously, historical narratives are not mirror-images of the past; in general (save things like cinematic documentaries) they are not even pictorial, let alone perfect pictorial replicas of anything. But why should the fact that they are not pictures imply they are fictions?

However, the preceding worry misses the point. The idea of a copy of the past should probably be understood metaphorically. A copy of the past would be a perfect reflection of everything that transpired in the relevant time span with nothing added or subtracted. It would bear an exact correspondence to all and only what came about, or even more strictly, to what could have been perceived as past events unfolded. Anything that falls short of this is said to be fictional.

Of course, it is difficult to imagine that practicing historians pursue the production of such copies in their work, or that, informed as they are of the historical evidence, they construe their narratives as perfect replicas of the past. But White, it seems, wants to confront them with a dilemma. Either historical narratives are copies in the relevant sense or they are fictional. The way to deal with this dilemma is to reject it – to maintain that historical narratives are not and, in fact, should not be copies in the mirror sense while also maintaining that this does not make them fictional.

The notion that only copies in the mirror sense would not be fictional presupposes something like a narrowly empiricist, correspondence criterion of truth. White explicitly denies the viability of this approach in one sense – he denies that historical narratives could meet it. However, this does not seem to lead him to reject the criterion entirely. That is, he appears to continue to regard it as the ideal criterion for nonfictional historical exposition, even if it is an unrealizable ideal. And, to the extent that it is unrealizable, he consigns historical narration to the realm of fiction. But what is strange here is that White doesn't take the inapplicability of this ideal of truth as a grounds for advancing alternative criteria of nonfictional truth for historical narratives.

Confronted by the inapplicability of the copy ideal of an empiricist view of correspondence truth, it seems to me that the line one should take is to search for some other grounds for accommodating the truth of historical narratives construed as nonfictional. That is, we should hold onto the intuition that historical narratives can be truthful in the way that nonfictional discourse is true, drop the expectation that this is explicable in terms of a naive view of correspondence to the past as a whole, and explore alternative models. White, in effect, maintains the criteria of empiricist correspondence, which leads him to reassigning historical narration to the realm of fiction. In this respect, oddly enough, he turns out to be a closet empiricist – presupposing that anything that falls short of the correspondence standard is fictional.[41]

Undoubtedly, there is a parallel between White's strategy here and that of many deconstructionists. When they note the failure of certain theories of language on the grounds that no language is an absolute mirror of the world, they conclude that meaning is an arbitrary, infinitely fluctuating construct rather than surmising that the expectation that a language might absolutely mirror the world was a theoretical error to begin with, and that a better view of the way in which a language is objectively constrained should be sought. That is, they remain in the thrall of a bad theory of language, employing it to motivate their skepticism, at the same time that they agree that no language squares with the idealization. This is akin to reasoning that either existence has an absolute meaning ordained by God or it has no meaning; since there is no God, there is no meaning. This way of thinking shares the theistic assumption that only something like God could serve as a source of meaning. An alternative would be to search for other sources of meaning once the hypothesis that there is no God is endorsed. Similarly, in consigning historical narration to the realm of fiction on the grounds that it is not a perfect replica of the past, White remains implicitly in the very empiricist camp from which he explicitly wishes to part company.

Armed with the copy ideal of nonfictionality, White recycles the issue of selectivity, which must be the most perennial pretext for suspecting the objectivity of historical narration. Obviously, a narrative selects a subset of events and event relationships from the historical flow; thus, if candidacy for nonfictionality depends on correspondence to the whole past, or the whole past within certain stipulated time parameters, a historical narrative will be discounted. But, again, this should lead us to drop the copy ideal of nonfictionality and not to jettison the idea that historical narratives are nonfictional. This is not the place to review all the arguments that are designed to show that the selectivity of historical narratives need not be epistemologically problematic in any way that warrants special attention. Some historians may select the events they highlight in dubitable ways, but there are procedures for ascertaining whether the processes of selection a given historian employs are questionable. That is, historians may produce distortive representations of the past because of biased procedures, but this only goes to show that the selective attention of a given narrative may be distorting, and not that selectivity, in and of itself, is problematic. If it were, then scientific findings, which are also selective, would also, by parity of reasoning, be fictional.

White, himself, may remain unmoved by our last argument. For he is apparently convinced of the constructivist/conventionalist view of science. Thus, he seems to gain confidence by analogizing historical narratives with scientific theories, as construed by constructivists. Surmising that scientific theories are constructed on the basis of observational data that underdetermine theory choice, which data themselves are theory-laden, White thinks of narratives as similarly constructed, in contexts where the data would support alternative stories, and he thinks of narrative events as, so to speak, story-laden. Thus, if the adoption of a scientific theory is conventional, given the putative fact that it is one construction of the data within a range of equally acceptable ones, then historical narratives, assuming the analogy to scientific theories, are equally conventional. Their selective organization of the data does not correspond to reality, but is an invention developed within conventional choice procedures. Thus, one dispels the argument of the preceding paragraph by maintaining that scientific selectivity forces us to concede that scientific theories are imaginative constructions – and in that sense fictions – and, therefore, no incongruity is engendered by maintaining that comparable processes of selection with respect to historical narratives render them fictional as well.[42]

A major problem with this invocation of the philosophy of science is that it presumes that the facts of scientific theorizing pointed to by constructivists entail anti-realism. But a solid case for the compatibility of scientific realism with the facts of the history of science, upon which constructivists rely, is available,[43] thereby blocking any facile attempt to derive historical anti-realism with respect to narrative from scientific anti-realism with respect to theories. That is, the selective procedures and inferred nature of theoretical entities does not commit us to anti-realism; it does not force us to deny that scientific theories are approximately true. Therefore, even if suitable analogies could be drawn between constructivism in science and constructivism in historiography,[44] we would not have to regard historical narratives as fictional.

A course of events transpiring between t1 and t5 need not comprise every event or state of affairs in its temporal neighborhood. Therefore, a narrative representation that tracks that course of events need not refer to every occurrence in the stipulated time span. Narratives are selective but this is appropriate given the nature of courses of events. Nor is it useful to call the reconstruction of a course of events distortive just because it involves selection. Indeed, from the perspective of attempting cognitively to assimilate a representation of the past, the portrayal of a course of events that chronicled all of the events in the temporal neighborhood would distort insofar as it would muddy the links between the pertinent elements in the sequence.

Likewise, our narrative accounts may have to be revised in the light of subsequent events; this does not show that historical narratives are fictional, but only that there are always more stories to tell. Moreover, that some historical narratives may be superseded by ones that are more fine-grained no more shows that the earlier ones were fictional than the adjustment of one approximately true scientific theory with further details (atomic theory amplified by the characterization of subatomic particles) shows that the earlier viewpoint must now be evaluated according to a different standard of truth.

No historical narrative says everything there is to say, not even about all of the events within the time frame that it discusses. The historian exercises choice in the sense that the linkage between some events and not others will be given salience in order to illuminate a given course of events. It is true, as White repeatedly emphasizes, that in charting these linkages and in making the relevant selections, the historian uses her imagination. But, pace White, it is quite a long throw from the historian's use of her imagination in discerning said linkages to the inference that the historian's narrative is on a par with that of the imaginative writer (i.e. the writer of fiction). White appears to presume that there is a correlation between the use of the imagination and fiction. But this is illicit. On many views of the imagination, such as Kant's, the imagination plays a role in perception, but my perception of my house is in no way fictional.

Many of White's arguments for the fictionality of historical narrative hinge on contrasting said narratives with copies of the past. Any addition (imaginative construction) or subtraction of detail (selection) from such a copy, conceived of on the model of a mirror, is evidence of fictionality. But the foil is inadmissible. Not only is the visual metaphor inapplicable – it is not the case that not being an exact copy of x entails being a fictional representation of x; but it indicates a residual commitment to a very radical version of an empiricist expectation of exact "perceptual" correspondence between a representation and its referent, which is not only philosophically bogus but is at odds with White's own suspicion of empiricism. Like the skeptic who arrives at her position by accepting a phenomenalist account of perception and who, therefore, remains effectively an empiricist, White regards historical narration as fictional, because he continues to employ something as implausible as perceptual correspondence as the standard of nonfictionality.

White's emphasis on the verbal dimension of historical narration sends him to contemporary discourse theory for insight. There he encounters the idea that narration in what is called the realist text gives the reader the impression that the text is transparent – that it is unmediated, for example, by a narrator exercising selectivity – indeed, that it is as if the text were reality narrating itself. This corresponds to White's own view that historians write as if they were discovering real stories, stories immanent in the historical process, whereas they are really fitting pre-existing story templates onto past events. The ideas that "events narrate themselves" and that the historian, so to speak, records them as a dictaphone might, ostensibly shows acceptance of the disreputable assumption of speculative philosophers of history to the effect that the historical process is storied – i.e. that historical events have a single significance in some overarching historical narrative.

This is a very perplexing argument. It begins by attributing transparency – or narrativity, as White calls it – to realist texts. But to whom does the text appear transparent? Presumably, to naive readers and to the naive historians who write under the supposedly misguided faith that they could track a historical course of events. These naive readers and writers are somehow possessed by the idea that reality is narrating itself. Stated this way, the belief attributed to them is at least obscure and, on a number of readings, absurd.

It is absurd to think of events as telling or narrating their own story in any literal sense, as White notes. But, in fact, it is so absurd on a literal reading that it is hard to believe that any readers or writers, no matter how naive, can be taken in by it. No one could believe that reality literally narrates itself, so it is an inadequate starting point from which to field a dialectically alternative account. It is, so to say, an argumentative red herring, rather than a genuine competing theory whose defeat gives way to White's alternative, fictional account of historical narration. That is, faced with a transparency account of historical narration and White's account, we are not moved to White's theory by the all-too-easy defeat of the attributed transparency view, but rather suspect that we have not started with a viable field of competing accounts.

Stated nonabsurdly, but still obscurely, the transparency effect might be thought of as the impression on the part of naive readers and naive historians that the text is unmediated, that it is without gaps, that it renders a full account of the past. However, this too seems to be such a bizarre conviction to attribute to anyone that it is a non-starter. Historians obviously know that they are selecting a series of events from a larger sequence, and readers have only to look at the title page of the book to learn the identity of the narrator/mediator. No one, in short, believes that historical texts are unmediated; or, to put it positively, any informed reader or writer is aware that a text involves selection. In this, everyone agrees with White, and the view that some do not is a straw man. Where there is undoubtedly disagreement is in the assumption that selection implies fictionality. But the burden of proof is on White to show this, and, in my opinion, the only means at his disposal is the dubious, implicit assumption that nonfiction requires exact correspondence.[45]

Associated with White's implicit presumption of a standard of exact correspondence is his apparent view that if one assumes that there are "real stories," then said stories would have to be of the nature of what we can call absolute stories. For any series of events, an event emplotted in a narrative structure that is immanent in the historical process will have one and only one fixed significance. Something like this view is what leads him to believe that the narrative exploits of practicing historians correspond to those of substantive philosophers of history. I suppose that White is prompted to this intuition on the grounds that if one actually composed a nonfictional narrative in accordance with the exact correspondence standard, one would have a unitary picture of the past in which every event had a determinate place. Of course, White, and perhaps everyone else, thinks that this is impracticable. But White goes on to argue from the infeasibility of absolute stories to the fictionality of all historical narratives.

That is, given an event or a series of events, we can develop a number of stories. No event or event series has one final, i.e. *single*, fixed significance for reasons rehearsed above. Events and event series can, through narration, be connected with alternative events and event series. A collection of events, in a manner of speaking, underdetermines the stories in which they can play a role. From this, White infers that there can be no "real stories;" if there were "real stories," immanent in the historical process, events would fall into one and only one train of events, said train inscribed in events like the evolution of Hegel's world spirit. Historical narrative presumes that the historical process is narrativized and if the historical process is narrativized and there are real stories, the significance of each event fits into one and only one story. So, since there is always more than one derivable story, there are no real stories.

But once again, the argument proceeds on the basis of a straw man. The requirement that "real stories" be absolute stories is exorbitant from the outset. Stories will be nonfictionally accurate insofar as they track courses of events. But courses of events overlap and branch, and there is no need to presume – as perhaps Hegel did – that there is only one course of events. Thus, events and series of events may play different roles in different stories. But that events and series of events figure in different stories is no obstacle to those stories being nonfictional. There are different stories because there are discrete courses of events whose interest is relative to the questions the historian asks of the evidence. This relativity, which precludes the possibility of an absolute story, however, does not make the historical narrative fictional. Rather it makes the accuracy of the nonfictional account assessable in terms of what questions are being directed to the relevant courses of events.[46]

Like innumerable poststructuralist commentators, White appears to believe that agreement that there is no absolute interpretation, no final word, so to say, with respect to x, should impel us to avoid the imputation of truth to an interpretation of x. That is, if there is a multiplicity of interpretations available for x, then the question of literal truth goes by the boards. A true interpretation would have to be an absolute interpretation; an absolute interpretation would have to be the final word on its subject; but since there are no such absolute interpretations – here with respect to historical narratives – there is no question of literal truth.

Needless to say, this is a bad argument with respect to literary criticism. To say a literary interpretation is true if and only if it is the only acceptable account of a text is absurd; one does not deny the truth of a literary interpretation by showing that another interpretation is possible. For the other interpretation may be compatible with the interpretation under scrutiny. That a text supports a multiplicity of interpretations does not disallow the possibility that all of them are literally true; the epistemological issue with respect to a collection of interpretations of texts only becomes live when they are inconsistent.

But here it is important to keep two very different arguments separate: one says that truth is inapplicable to interpretations because there is always a multiplicity of acceptable interpretations of x available; the other says that truth is inapplicable to interpretations because there is always, at least in principle, a multiplicity of equally acceptable but inconsistent interpretations of x available. The former view is based on the truism that there may be no absolute interpretation of x, but from that truism it does not follow that several different interpretations of x cannot be conjointly true, for example, that *1984* is about totalitarianism *and* that it is about Stalinism. The pressure to abandon the question of truth with respect to interpretations only impinges when it can be argued that we are always confronted by a multiplicity of incompatible interpretations.

Turning from literary interpretation to historical narration, the pressing question is which of the preceding arguments can be sustained. Here, it seems to me that it is obvious that there are multiple stories that can be derived from a given set of events, but, without buying into White's confidence in generic emplotment, there is no reason to presume that these different stories must conflict, and, therefore, no reason to believe that they cannot be assessed in terms of literal truth.[47] Sandra Day O'Connor's appointment to the Supreme Court is part of the narrative of recent abortion decisions and part of the narrative of women's social empowerment. These stories need not conflict and both could be true. Insofar as White's arguments about historical narration, unlike Joseph Margolis's arguments about literary interpretation, do not show that different historical narratives can always in principle be nonconverging and inconsistent, historical narrations remain assessable in terms of literal standards of truth.

Again, the recognition that an event or an event series affords an ingredient for more than one story is a truism. It does not force us to concede that historical narratives cannot be assessed in terms of literal truth. Nor does it seem compelling to suppose that ordinary historians must buy into the presuppositions of substantive philosophers of history in order to regard their narratives in terms of truth. For there is no logical requirement that true narratives be absolutely true. Historians can trace alternative courses of events without presupposing that some one course of event is privileged because history is *the* story of human emancipation or class struggle.

Underlying White's overall view, it seems to me, is a picture of the following sort: a narrative, specifically a nonfiction narrative, is a collection of sentences ordered in a certain way. Narratives, however, are not simply evaluated in terms of the truth or falsity of their constituent sentences. The way in which the sentences are ordered is also epistemically crucial. But this dimension of epistemic evaluation would not be assessed if the narrative were evaluated solely in terms of the conjunction of the truth-values of its individual, fact-asserting sentences. Moreover, it seems to be presumed that saying a narrative's epistemic adequacy for White would have to be reducible to the assessment of the truth-value of the conjunction of the constituent atomic sentences in the narrative. But since the adequacy of the narrative – with respect to its structure of ordering relations – involves something beyond the truth of the sum of the truth-values of its atomic sentences, the narrative as a whole must, at least in part, be assessible in terms of some other standard.

Furthermore, White also appears to presuppose that the sole epistemic category relevant to the assessment of historical narratives is truth – either literal truth construed on the model of some picture theory in which each atomic sentence corresponds to some past fact (or facts), or to some kind of truth construed in other terms. White then worries that whatever governs the selective structure of a narrative may not correspond to anything in the past. Thus the truth of that structure must be assessable in other terms, such as metaphorical accuracy.

Now if this diagnosis of White's presuppositions is correct, it is easy to avoid his conclusions. First of all, too much is being made of the idea of atomic sentences.[48] Narratives are typically written in sentences. But nothing of great importance should hinge on this. For where the relevant narrative linkages are of the nature of relations between background conditions, causes, effects, reasons, choices, actions, and the like, the text can be reconstructed perspicuously in terms of propositions which can, in turn, be straightforwardly evaluated with respect to truth. In some cases, these reconstructions will be a matter of paraphrasing the individual sentences in such a way as to make the relevant narrative relations obtaining between them evident. In other cases, the sentences found in the text will have to be expanded so as to make narrative linkages that are presupposed or conversationally implied explicit. But paraphrases and expansions of this sort in nowise mandate some special criteria of truth.

Undoubtedly, White might concede the preceding point, but still maintain that it does not get at the heart of his misgivings. For even allowing the paraphrases and expansions adverted to above, he will argue that narratives still add something and that this added something – the principles that guide the narrator's selections – is not to be literally found in the past. To the extent that that something is a matter of linkages like causes and reasons, White's argument is not compelling. However, he is right to point out that we will assess a given narrative as a good

narrative in terms of criteria over and above the truthfulness of all of its propositions even when suitably expanded and/or paraphrased. Should this drive us toward
regarding narration as fictional and as assessable as metaphor?

I think not. To be an adequate narrative, indeed to be an adequate historical
account of any sort, a candidate needs to do more than merely state the truth
(indeed, a historical account could contain only true statements and yet be adjudged
unacceptable).[49] It must also meet various standards of objectivity. For example, a
historical narrative should be comprehensive; it should incorporate all those events
which previous research has identified to be germane to the subject that the historian
is seeking to illuminate.[50] A narrative of the outbreak of the American Revolution
that failed to recount the debates over taxation could include only true, chronologically intelligible statements, and still be regarded as an inadequate standard.
Like any other cognitive enterprise, historical narration will be assessed in terms
of rational standards which, though they are endorsed because they appear to be
reliable guides to the truth, are not reducible to the standard of truth.

Obviously, the selective procedures that historians respect in composing their
narratives will be evaluated in terms of all sorts of rational standards, like comprehensiveness, that do not correspond to anything found in the past. However, this
does not mean that the selections and deletions in a historical narrative are divorced
from literal questions of truth or falsity. For the selections and deletions are assessed
in terms of those sorts of standards that experience indicates reliably track the truth.

White's deepest problem seems to be that he believes that truth is the only
relevant grounds for the epistemic assessment of historical narratives. And, since
narrative selectivity cannot be epistemically assessed without remainder in terms
of truth on his correspondence model, it must be assessed in terms of some other
standard of truth, such as metaphorical truth. But we can dodge this dilemma by
noting that the selections and deletions of a historical narrative are subject to objective standards, which though not unrelated to ascertaining truth, are not reducible
to truth. Such standards may be considered our best means for discovering the
truth. Desiderata like comprehensiveness are, so to speak, truth-tracking. Thus, in
evaluating the selections and deletions the narrative historian makes, we need not
feel that we must embrace some special standard of truth, like metaphorical truth.
Rather, our concern with historical narratives is that they be true in the ordinary
sense of truth and that our assessments of their adequacy in terms of standards like
comprehensiveness are keyed to determining truth. That principles governing the
inclusion of an event in a narrative, like comprehensiveness, are not reducible to
the standard of truth in no way implies that the narrative is fictional, nor that it
should be understood as some kind of metaphor. This alternative only presents
itself if one mistakenly circumscribes the options for epistemically evaluating non-
fiction narratives in the way White does.[51]

White believes that the selections and deletions in a historical narrative are to
be explained in terms of literary exigencies. Events are included or excluded with
respect to whether they can function as beginnings, middles, and ends in come-
dies, tragedies, romances, and satires. I doubt that every historical narrative falls
or must fall into one of White's generic types, and I even doubt that historical
narratives require middles, and ends, in the technical sense of closure. A historical
course of affairs may have a turning point and it may have results, but these need

not be taken to be mere literary artifacts. Similarly, White writes as though the coherence of a historical narrative is solely a function of a literary imposition. But events in human life very often appear coherent, unfolding in terms of causes, reasons, complications, and consequences, and elucidating these relations between actions and their background conditions need not be exercises in fiction.

White and his followers regard historical interpretation as fictional insofar as it relies on narrative. This follows from their conviction that narrative, as such, is fictional. However, neither the philosophical considerations nor the empirical theses advanced in behalf of these views seem persuasive. At the very least, the reduction of all narrative to the status of fiction seems a desperate and inevitably self-defeating way in which to grant the literary dimension of historiography its due.

Notes

1 See Friedrich Nietzsche, *On the Advantage and Disadvantage of History for Life*, translated by Peter Preuss (Indianapolis, IN: Hackett Publishing Company, 1980). Speaking of "monumental history," for example, Nietzsche claims that this venture risks distorting the past by reinterpreting it according to aesthetic criteria and, thereby, brings it closer to fiction (p. 17). Nietzsche's specific reason for this belief is that insofar as monumental history functions to provide models for emulation, it will occlude attention to sufficient causes in order to produce representations available for imitation.

2 Roland Barthes, "The Discourse of History," in *Comparative Criticism: A Yearbook*, edited by E. S. Shaffer, translated by Stephen Bann (Cambridge: Cambridge University Press, 1981), pp. 7–20.

3 Louis Mink, "Narrative Form as a Cognitive Instrument," in his *Historical Understanding*, edited by Brian Fay, Eugene Golob, and Richard Vann (Ithaca, NY: Cornell University Press, 1987), pp. 183–203.

4 See Hayden White, *Metahistory: The Historical Imagination in Nineteenth-Century Europe* (Baltimore, MD: Johns Hopkins University Press, 1973); White, *Tropics of Discourse: Essays in Cultural Criticism* (Baltimore, MD: Johns Hopkins University Press, 1978); White, *The Content of the Form* (Baltimore, MD: Johns Hopkins University Press, 1987); "White," in *Future Literary Theory*, edited by Ralph Cohen (New York: Routledge, 1989), pp. 19–43.

5 For its impact on literary critics and historians see the essays by K. Egan, L. Gossman, and R. Reinitz in *The Writing of History: Literary Form and Historical Understanding*, edited by Robert H. Canary and Henry Kozicki (Madison, WI: University of Wisconsin Press, 1978). For an example of a philosopher of history influenced by this view, see F. R. Ankersmit, "The Dilemma of Contemporary Anglo-Saxon Philosophy of History," in the journal *History and Theory*, Beiheft 25 (1986), pp. 1–27. The view is also endorsed in Stephen Bann, "Toward a Critical Historiography: Recent Work in Philosophy of History," *Philosophy*, 56 (1981), pp. 365–85.

6 See White, "Interpretation in History," in *Tropics*, pp. 51–80. The interrelation between these different interpretive registers is also discussed in the "Introduction" to *Metahistory* (pp. 1–42), among other places. That White continues to regard historical narrative as interpretive is evident in his recent "'Figuring

the Nature of Times Deceased'; Literary Theory and Historical Writing;" see, for example, p. 21.

7   Here it is important to note that our reservations about White have less to do with his view that historical narratives are interpretive and more to do with his claims that such interpretive narratives are, in decisive respects, fictional.

8   See White, "Historicism, History and the Figurative Imagination," in *Tropics*, for example, pp. 111–12.

9   Claude Lévi-Strauss, *The Savage Mind* (Chicago: University of Chicago Press, 1966).

10 See, for example, Fernand Braudel, "The Situation of History in 1950," in his *On History* (Chicago: University of Chicago Press, 1980), and François Furet, "From Narrative History to History as a Problem," *Diogenes*, spring 1975. W. H. Dray criticizes the latter article in his "Narrative Versus Analysis in History," in *Rationality, Relativism and the Human Sciences*, edited by Joseph Margolis, Michael Krausz, and R. M. Burian (Dordrecht, Netherlands: Martinus Nijhoff, 1986).

11 White, "'Figuring the Nature of Times Deceased,'" p. 27. I take the gnomic, rhetorical question at the end of this quotation to signify that narratives as metaphors (in virtue of their generic plot structures) are true in the way analogies are true – do they provide an insightful fit; are they true *enough*?

12 Paul Ricoeur, *The Reality of the Historical Past* (Milwaukee, WI: Marquette University Press, 1984), pp. 33–4.

13 Joseph Margolis, *Art and Philosophy* (Atlantic Highlands, NJ: Humanities Press, 1980), p.158.

14 White, "'Figuring the Nature of Times Deceased,'" p. 18.

15 White, "'Figuring the Nature of Times Deceased,'" p. 21.

16 For a discussion of the failure of both the narrative and the covering-law models to pith the essence of history, see Gordon Graham, *Historical Explanation Reconsidered* (Aberdeen: Aberdeen University Press, 1983).

17 This is the case even if we accept Maurice Mandelbaum's distinction between inquiry and narrative for it would remain a question as to what kind of knowledge (if any) readers could derive from historical narratives. See Maurice Mandelbaum, "A Note on History as Narrative," in *History and Theory*, VI, 1967; and Mandelbaum, *The Anatomy of Historical Knowledge* (Baltimore, MD: Johns Hopkins University Press, 1977).

18 White, "The Question of Narrative in Contemporary Historical Theory," in *Content*, p. 46. White derives this argument from Louis Mink, "Narrative Form as a Cognitive Instrument," pp. 197–8.

19 See, for example: White, "The Historical Text as Literary Artifact," in *Tropics*, p. 90; "Historicism, History and The Figurative Imagination," in *Tropics*, p. 111; "Preface," in *Content*, pp. ix–x; "'Figuring the Nature of Times Deceased,'" p. 27; among others.

20 See Louis Mink, "History and Fiction as Modes of Comprehension," and "Narrative Form as a Cognitive Instrument" in his *Historical Understanding*.

21 White, "The Historical Text as Literary Artifact," in *Tropics*, p. 4.

22 For example, White, "The Historical Text as Literary Artifact," in *Tropics*, p. 82. Here, *invention* seems to follow from the verbal nature of the historical text.

23 For example, White, "The Burden of History," in *Tropics*, pp. 28–9.

24 For example, White, "The Question of Narrative in Contemporary Historical Theory," in *Content*, p. 42.

25   For example, White, "The Burden of History," in *Tropics*, p. 47.

26   For example, in "Interpretation in History," White uses the metaphor of the mirror of a whole for what narrative *passes* as (*Tropics*, p. 51). Also note the analogies to replicas like model airplanes in "The Historical Text as Literary Artifact," in *Tropics*, p. 88.

27   See White, "Historicism, History and the Figurative Imagination," in *Tropics*, pp. 111–12.

28   See, for example, White, "The Question of Narrative in Contemporary Historical Theory," in *Content*, p. 42.

29   That is, for White, narrative forms are the culture's patterns of story-telling and a given event can be plotted in accordance with more than one such structure (which White sometimes refers to as *codes* [*Content*, p. 43]). And in his "The Value of Narrativity in the Representation of Reality," White says that the relation between historiography and narrative is conventional (*Content*, p. 6).

30   For an account of the argumentative function of intuition pumps, see Daniel Dennett, *Elbow Room* (Cambridge, MA: MIT Press, 1984).

31   See especially, White, "The Value of Narrativity in the Representation of Reality," in *Content*, pp. 1–25.

32   Gerard Genette as quoted by White in *Content*, p. 3.

33   Though White flirts with the notion of the *imaginary* as that figures in Lacanian literary theory, he does not accept it whole cloth. He does apparently agree that narrative seduces us through our desire for the kind of coherence and completeness that it counterfeits. However, narratives are also imaginary for him in the sense of being products of the imagination. And, as we have already noted, White does not regard the imagination as discredited epistemically; it has its own realms of veracity, such as the metaphorical. Thus, unlike many contemporary literary theorists, White is not committed to the view that the imaginary structures of narrative necessarily coerce us into misrecognizing reality. They can, rather, reveal reality if they are construed metaphorically.

34   White, "The Value of Narrativity in the Representation of Reality," in *Content*, p. 24.

35   White, "The Value of Narrativity in the Representation of Reality," p. 3.

36   See Roger Schank and R. P. Abelson, *Scripts, Plans, Goals and Understanding* (Hillsdale, NJ: Lawrence Erlbaum Associates, 1977).

37   I've derived this term from John Passmore, "Narratives and Events," in *History and Theory*, Beiheft 26 (1987), p. 73.

38   For an expansion of these points, see Frederick A. Olafson, *The Dialectic of Action: A Philosophical Interpretation of History and the Humanities* (Chicago: University of Chicago Press, 1979). In his *Time, Narrative, and History* (Bloomington, IN: Indiana University Press, 1986), David Carr attempts to defend the notion of "real stories" with reference to corporate entities like nations in terms of the shared myths that serve in practical deliberations. For my objections to this way of confronting historical constructivism, see my article-review of Carr's book in *History and Theory*, vol. XXVII, no. 3, 1988.

39   The idea of significance here is derived from Arthur Danto, *Knowledge and Narration* (New York: Columbia University Press, 1985).

40   Of course, if the meaning of events is to be conceptualized at the level of comedy or tragedy, then the issue of fiction cannot be dealt with in the above fashion.

But remobilizing the argument in this way depends on the viability of White's theory of generic emplotment which we will take up shortly.

41   In his reliance on the "copy" standard of truth, one suspects that White is endorsing the myth of the Ideal Chronicler which Danto attacked so persuasively in *Narration and Knowledge*, pp. 142–82.

42   White's analogies to science, as comprehended by the constructivist dispensation, sit uncomfortably with his claims to be concerned with the specificity of history.

43   See, for example, Richard N. Boyd, "The Current Status of Scientific Realism," in *Scientific Realism*, edited by Jarrett Leplin (Berkeley, CA: University of California Press, 1984), pp. 41–82.

44   This may be a big *if* since the "unobservables" the historian deals with are categorically disanalogous to the "unobservables" of scientific theories.

45   For further criticism of the notion of transparency as it is used in contemporary literary theory see Noël Carroll, "Conspiracy Theories of Representation," *Philosophy of the Social Sciences*, vol. 17, 1987.

46   Moreover, the fact that in one story, told for one reason, a causal relation between events A and B is cited while in another story, undertaken for other purposes, that causal relation is not cited does not imply that the causal narrative linkage in the first story is an "imposition."

47   A related point is made against Louis Mink by William Dray in his review of *Historical Understanding* in *Clio*, vol. 17, no. 4 (summer, 1988), p. 397.

48   Leon Goldstein attacks the atomic sentences model for other reasons in his "Impediments to Epistemology in the Philosophy of History," in *History and Theory*, Beiheft 25 (1986), pp. 82–100.

49   See J. L. Gorman, *The Expression of Historical Knowledge* (Edinburgh: Edinburgh University Press, 1982), Ch. 3. See also, J. L. Gorman, "Objectivity and Truth in History," in *Inquiry*, 17 (1974), pp. 373–97.

50   See C. Behan McCullagh, "The Truth of Historical Narratives," *History and Theory*, Beiheft 26 (1987), pp. 33–40.

51   It seems to me that Paul Ricoeur makes a similar error in his *Time and Narrative* (Chicago: University of Chicago Press, 1984), vol. I. Pressed to account for historical narrative, he opts for a correspondence theory of truth and maintains that narrative corresponds to temporality. White justifiably rejects this view for its obscurity, but stays with the commitment to truth, modifying it in terms of metaphorical truth. Both White and Ricoeur on my view would do better to recognize that truth is not the only relevant epistemic standard for evaluating narratives. Granting that, they could avoid commitments to strange correspondents (temporality) and special standards of truth.

PART FIVE

Narrative and structure

Chapter 17

François Furet

FROM NARRATIVE HISTORY TO PROBLEM-ORIENTED HISTORY

HISTORY IS THE CHILD OF NARRATIVE. It is not defined by an object of study but by a type of discourse. To say that history studies time is just another way of saying that it arranges all of its objects of study in a temporal framework: to produce history is to tell a story.

A narrative, then, is an account of "what happened:" to someone or something, to an individual, to a country, to an institution, to the people who lived before the moment of the narrative, and to the products of their activity. Narrative history brings to life the tangle of events that make up the fabric of an existence, the thread of a lifetime. Its model is naturally biography, because the latter describes something that man can view as the quintessential image of time: the clean-cut duration of a lifetime from birth to death and the identifiable dates of the major events that took place between its beginning and end. The choice of a chronological segment is inseparable here from the empirical nature of the "subject" of the story.

A history of France or of any other country basically follows the same logic: it can begin only with the country's origins, followed by an account of the stages of its growth and the adventure of the nation, illustrated by chronological divisions. The only difference is that such a history leaves the future open; however, the narration of the past – the description of the nation's patrimony – is also intended to give some indication of this future and thus to freeze time.

Historical narrative, therefore, must follow a division of time inherent in the raw datum of experience. Essentially, it records the recollections of individuals and communities. It keeps alive what they have chosen of their past, or of the past in general, without taking apart or reconstructing the objects within that past. In other words, it deals with moments, not objects. Even when it discusses or tries to discuss, "civilizations," this kind of history cannot avoid the rule. When Voltaire compares the age of Pericles or of Augustus to that of Louis XIV, the concrete incarnations of these successive periods of greatness are proof enough that he is comparing periods, not concepts.

No doubt that is one of the reasons why narrative history has been primarily, although not exclusively, biographical or political. Within the collective experience of humanity, what witnesses have found most fascinating and what lends itself best to narrative is the saga of great men and of states. Little wonder, then, that history, first in Greek and Roman antiquity, then in modern Europe, developed into chronicles of power and war. The divisions of the narrative tended to underline the misfortunes and victories of mankind – the great moments of history.

The events in such a history consist precisely of moments. Their ephemeral nature is what characterizes them above all else. Events are the unique points in time in which something happens that cannot be assimilated to what has come before it or what will come after it. That "something" – the historical fact promoted to the rank of event – can never be compared, strictly speaking, to a preceding or subsequent fact, since it is its empirically unique nature that determines its importance. The battle of Waterloo and Stalin's death occurred only once; they cannot be likened to any other battle or any other death, and they have transformed world history.

And yet an event, if considered in isolation, is unintelligible. It is like a pebble picked up on a beach – meaningless. For it to acquire significance, it must be integrated into a pattern of other events, in relation to which it will become meaningful. That is the function of narrative. Waterloo can acquire significance in the context of a history of Napoleon's life, the First Empire, or nineteenth-century Franco-British rivalry. Stalin's death becomes important in the context of the history of twentieth-century Russia, international communism, or any other imaginable chronological constellation of facts. Thus, in narrative history, an event, even though it is by definition unique and not comparable, derives its significance from its position on the axis of the narrative, that is, on the axis of time.

Since an event is not an object intellectually created to be studied, it cannot acquire significance by means of an analysis of its relationship to other comparable or identical objects within a system. As it belongs to the realm of experience, of what has happened, it cannot be organized or even simply named except in relation to the external and general significance of the historical period of which it is one of the features. All narrative history is a succession of origin events, or, if one prefers, a history of events. And all history of events is teleological history: only the "ending" of the history makes it possible to choose and understand the events that compose it.

That ending can differ considerably from one historian to another and according to their chosen topics. For a long time endings were enveloped in religious apologetics or moral edification, which is no longer fashionable. The same cannot be said for the glorification of national power or national consciousness, which is still one of narrative history's most important functions, after having been, no doubt, its initial mainspring. All peoples need an account of their origins and a memorial to their times of greatness that can serve at the same time as guarantees of their future. Just as the ability to write brings power, so our archives are the memories or symbols of power. Not even transnational history, generally referred to as history of civilizations, can escape the inevitable obligation to assign a prior meaning to time. In our secular world, narrative history, apart from emphasizing national consciousness, more often than not embodies the other great collective experience of mankind since the eighteenth century: the feeling of progress. Progress assumes different names and aspects; it sometimes refers to the development of material goods, but more often to the problematic advent of reason, democracy, freedom, or equality. Confronted with the uncertainties that such a list brings to mind, we must recognize at the same time the full ambiguity of the deeds and values that characterize the contemporary world and the impossibility of not summoning them up as implicit foundations of a particular history. The narrator must, after all, place his own world at the end of the period he is describing.

In short, narrative history reconstructs an experience along a temporal axis. This reconstruction requires some conceptualization, but the latter is never made explicit. It is concealed within the temporal finality that structures and gives meaning to all narrative.

Yet the recent evolution of historiography seems to me to be characterized by the possibly definitive decline of narrative history. While it still flourishes in productions destined for mass consumption, it is being increasingly abandoned by professionals in the field. In my view, there has been a sometimes unconscious shift from narrative history to problem-oriented history, at the cost of the following changes:

1. The historian has surrendered before the immense indeterminacy of the object of his knowledge: time. He no longer claims to describe past events, not even important events, whether in the history of mankind or in that of a part of mankind. He is aware that he is choosing what to examine of the past and that in the process he is raising certain problems relative to a particular period. In other words, he constructs his own object of study by defining not only the period – the complex of events – but also the problems that are raised by that period and by those events and need to be solved. He therefore cannot avoid a minimal amount of explicit conceptual elaboration: a good question or a well-formulated problem is becoming more important – and is still less common! – than the skill or patience needed to bring to light an unknown but marginal fact.

2. As he breaks away from narrative, the historian also breaks away from his traditional source material: the unique event. If, instead of describing a unique, fleeting, incomparable experience, he seeks to explain a problem, he needs historical facts less vague than those to be found in human memory. He must conceptualize the objects of his inquiry, integrating them into a network of meanings and thus making them nearly identical, or at least comparable within a given period of time. Quantitative history provides the easiest – though not the only – means for this kind of intellectual task.

3. In defining his object of study, the historian must also "invent" his sources, for, in their original form, historical sources are usually unsuited to his inquiry. Naturally, he may come across a set of records that not only will be usable in themselves but will lead him to new or more valuable ideas and theories. History does provide such blessings, but the opposite is more often the case. Yet the historian who is trying to formulate and solve a problem must find pertinent sources and organize them into comparable and interchangeable units in order to be able to describe and interpret the phenomenon he is studying on the basis of a certain number of conceptual hypotheses.

4.   The fourth change in the historian's profession derives from the above. The conclusions of a study are becoming ever more closely bound up with the verification procedures upon which they are based and with the intellectual constraints imposed by those procedures. Narration's particular kind of logic – *post hoc, ergo propter hoc* – is no better suited to the new type of history than the equally traditional method of generalizing from the singular. Here the phantom of mathematics takes form. Quantitative analysis and statistical procedures, provided they are suited to the problem and sensibly applied, are among the most rigorous methods for "testing" data.

Before proceeding further, one ought to look at the possible reasons for these changes in historiography. They are probably related to factors external to the discipline itself, such as the general crisis affecting the idea of progress – a crisis that is challenging not only the concept of an evolution dominated by the nineteenth- and twentieth-century European model but the very notion of an all-embracing and linear history. However, the changes in historiography are also related to internal, intellectual factors such as the widespread influence of Marxist theory on the social sciences; the brilliant development of the social sciences dealing with limited and defined objects (economics, demography, anthropology); or the impact of computer technology, which makes it possible to carry out hitherto unimaginable calculations, provided the problems to be solved and the hypotheses to be tested have been rigorously formulated beforehand. Instead of discussing this vast problem at length, I should like to confine myself here to examining a few of the consequences of these changes on our profession and our historical knowledge.

The archives that serve as the basis for historiography are no longer collections of documents but data constructed in series. If historians are to work on conceptually clear objects of inquiry while remaining faithful to the specific character of their discipline – the study of the evolution of phenomena over time – they will need pertinent data (seldom available ready-made) that can be compared over a relatively long period. Historical facts no longer consist of the explosion of important events that shatter the silence of time but of chosen and constructed phenomena whose regularity makes them easier to identify and examine by means of a chronological sequence of identical data comparable within given time intervals. Such data no longer exist independently but as parts of a system that also includes earlier and later data. An examination of their internal consistency (by establishing their comparability within the system to which they belong) is a better test of their validity than an external assessment of their probability (by comparing them to other sources for the same period).

The intellectual process for defining the data is thus twofold. First, one must determine their significance in order to apply them correctly. For example, the major pre-nineteenth-century sources available to the historian interested in literacy are signature counts. But what significance does the ability to sign one's name have in relation to the usual criteria for measuring literacy: the ability to read and write? To take another example, the historian who studies crises – particularly the different kinds of economic crises of modern times – makes considerable use of price series. However, he must first answer the question, What does a price mean? For what movements or levels of economic life does it serve as an indicator? Once the significance of the data has been established, the historian must arrange them in serial form, make them comparable to one another, decide what time unit they concern, what statistical methods are appropriate to use, and so on. All these procedures are more than mere techniques; they require methodological choices at each step of the process.

One can raise a preliminary objection to this view of historical research, namely, that the historian's sources often contain gaps, are fragmentary, or simply do not exist, depending on the hazards of survival. In any case, the difference between history and other social sciences is not one of principle but of situation. There are undoubtedly problems, particularly relating to the more remote periods of the past, for which source material has disappeared. However, it must be stressed that such material was not developed once and for all in the public archives in the nineteenth century. On the contrary, the range of potential sources is almost infinite, and quite often their existence is revealed by the nature of the historian's curiosity or by the problem he sets himself. The classic example in this field is parish registers, which lay dormant for centuries in French towns until the advent of historical demography in the 1950s led to the discovery of their immense value. Moreover, a historian who is unable to find immediately pertinent data to answer the question he has set himself can, in most cases, get around the obstacle by treating whatever data are available in such a way as to be able to use them indirectly.

From this point of view, there is always the possibility of a "substitutional" use of historical data. In a recent article, I distinguished three kinds of serial data. The first kind is the simplest and the easiest to manipulate. It consists of the available quantitative data organized in a way that provides a direct answer to the question at hand. Births, marriages, and deaths listed in parish registers can be used in this way by the demographic historian. The classic demographic rates can be calculated from such data by means of minimal and standardized treatment (the technique used to reconstruct families). The historian of political attitudes can use the same technique with election results. The second kind of source also includes quantitative data. These, however, are used in a substitutional way to answer questions quite different from those for which the data had been originally assembled. An example is the historian's use of the calculation of time intervals between births to study the spread of contraception and the patterns of sexual behavior in the past. The specialist of economic growth also uses this method when examining price series. In these cases the main problem involved in handling the data is their relevance and the possibility of reorganizing them in relation to the problem examined. Finally, there is a third type of source, which requires even more careful handling: nonnumerical data that the historian nevertheless wants to treat quantitatively. In order to do so, he must not only establish the relevance and value of the data, as in the preceding case, but also rearrange them systematically into conceptually and chronologically comparable units. Two examples are the use of notarized marriage contracts to study endogamy, social mobility, fortune, or literacy; and the use of wills to analyze attitudes toward death.

Thus, if one wanted to classify the most recent advances in contemporary historiography according to their mathematical rigor, one would have to take into account both the type of conceptualization applied to the problems studied and the quality of the sources used to study those problems. For example, it is clear that historical demography and economic history are, on those two counts and at least for the so-called modern period, the best-equipped fields. First, they can draw on concepts developed in specific disciplines, such as demography and political economics – concepts that can be readily imported into history at a cost of only minor adaptations; second, the objects of those studies are easier to abstract, define, and measure than most products of human activity. Furthermore, most European states have been creating and preserving data in these fields for many centuries.

Nevertheless, even within these "advanced" sectors of history, the situation is not as simple as one might deduce from the ranking above, which is based on the academic classification of our disciplines. History, by virtue of its open-endedness, always tends to overflow the boundaries of the sectional advances in these specialized fields. The question that arises is whether, and to what extent, by borrowing some of those advances and integrating them into its own practices, history has established a knowledge of the past that could qualify as scientific.

The best way to tackle this very old problem is to study some examples, in increasing order of complexity and uncertainty. I shall borrow them from the field of historical demography, one of the most studied areas of French historiography in the past twenty years. It is also one of the fields that provide the greatest opportunities for formulating problems mathematically. This special position is due to the particular nature of the discipline and to the sacrifices it has made for the sake of defining its object clearly. Demography is entirely predicated on the principle of abstract equality, according to which Napoleon's birth has exactly the same importance as that of any one of his future soldiers. Having adopted a hypothesis that sacrifices all the particular aspects in the life of individuals – in other words, the essence of their history – it transforms historical individuals into interchangeable and measurable units, by means of unvarying and comparable events: birth, marriage, and death. Stripped of the layers of meaning that each civilization has in its own way given them, these events are reduced to their most fundamental characteristic: the stark fact that they took place.

I am deliberately describing them all as "events," since I do not see, a priori, what distinguishes one particular historical fact from another – for example, a birth, however anonymous, from a battle, however famous. In this respect, the current distinction between structural and narrative history is irrelevant to historical data themselves: there is no such thing as a difference between facts that are events and facts that are not events. History is a permanent event. However, some classes of events can be more easily conceptualized than others, that is, integrated into an intelligible system – as in the case of demographic events.

The raw and particularly simple data on births, marriages, and deaths have become the object of a specific discipline: demography. They can thus form the basis for a certain number of calculations and analyses, which themselves are prefabricated objects of historical research. In other words, they are objects or concepts elaborated by a discipline other than history – in this case, demography, for which history, however, also supplied primary material in the form of birth, marriage, and death records. To the limited degree that it works with reliable or verified data – though that "limited" degree is actually a considerable one, since the verification of numerical sources is no easy task – historical demography produces results comparable to those of demography itself: the set of relationships that allow one to measure the elements of a given population and the way in which they are evolving.

These elements, measured year by year, provide results that are unambiguous and certain – unlike their interpretation. Let us examine a century-long decline in the general mortality rate, for example in eighteenth-century France. In order to determine when the definitive drop in the mortality rate occurred, the rate must be calculated by age cohort, particularly to obtain the infant or juvenile mortality rate. Let us assume then there was a spectacular increase in the survival of newborns (from birth to one year). Such a phenomenon could be explained by any number of hypotheses, from an increase in the number of midwives throughout the countryside to a transformation of the nursing system, not to mention a sudden victory of medicine over a children's disease. How can one choose without testing each of these theories as well as several others?

Admittedly, one can proceed otherwise, starting not from a single variable but from the set of variables of a demographic system. Such an approach is more properly demographic than historical. It uses or constructs a reproduction model for a population that is considered stable, with the time factor provisionally set aside. Let us suppose that all the "blanks" in the model have been filled; one is left with the question that the historian must examine: How did the system evolve? Admittedly, by studying what happened or even simulating what might have happened if a given variable of the system had been missing or had been quite different, one can diagnose at what point the system changed – for example, how it expanded or regressed. However, the analysis of these strategic variables refers back, as in the previous case, to elements that are exogenous to the system and at the same time influence it: in other words, to hypotheses that lie outside the demographic field. These hypotheses involve not only concepts that have not yet been organized into a scientific discipline, but also indicators most of which remain to be invented.

Let us examine the problem of age at marriage, the main variable of demographic control in preindustrial Europe between the twelfth and nineteenth centuries. Although I cannot go into the question in detail here, the postponement of marriages seems to have been the basic endogenous factor that contributed to stabilizing the size of populations. External agents (such as famine, epidemics, and wars) also took their toll. However, their impact diminished during the period. The regulatory mechanism worked in two ways. In the long term, the gradual rise in the age at marriage, up to its classic "plateau" of twenty-five or twenty-six (for women), eliminated ten years of potential fertility and, independently of any recourse to contraception, reduced the number of children per "complete" family. In the short term, the considerable variation in mortality rates conditioned by particular historical situations was made up for by variations in the age at marriage. When a population experienced a demographic crisis (whatever the cause), marriages were put off and the age at marriage increased; but, once the crisis was over, marriages in younger age cohorts were added to delayed marriages. Thus, the temporary lowering of the age at marriage brought the population back to its precrisis size. It is therefore easy to devise and apply a demographic model enabling one, on the basis of variations in the age at marriage (all other factors being equal), to study population changes: in what conditions a population grows, and in what conditions it diminishes.

With this type of simulation one can isolate the role of a variable within a system, and even in the evolution of that system, but one cannot identify the causes at work. In other words, simulation allows one to describe, not to interpret, and still less to explain. As soon as one goes beyond it to ask which factors are capable of influencing a cultural behavior pattern such as age at marriage, one is confronted with any number of possible interpretations. In the long run, the rise in the age at marriage in seventeenth- and eighteenth-century Europe, up to twenty-five or twenty-six years, can be interpreted as an optimal adjustment of population density to available resources: witness Chaunu and Le Roy Ladurie rediscovering Malthus! In the rich, "developed" Europe of the period – a belt of high agricultural productivity extending from the London basin to northern Italy, passing through the Low Countries, open-field France, and the Rhine valley – the population density apparently stabilized at about forty inhabitants per square kilometer. But this statement, even if approximately true – which is not certain, since data on productivity and agrarian output for that period are difficult to handle – tells us nothing about the modes in which the adjustment of the age at marriage was experienced. To the extent that it was not accompanied by an increase in births of illegitimate children, did it mean a greater acceptance, during a longer adolescence, of the rules of sexual austerity? Or should one speak primarily of a socioeconomic adaptation – children waiting to get married and settle down until the preceding generation had turned over the family landholding to them?

It might be argued that one should begin by the easiest phenomena to interpret and that short-term variations in the age at marriage involve fewer uncertainties. Why, in a period of crisis, does a population postpone marriages? The answer is relatively clear: because of doubts about the future, which stem from the sight of the present. Historical awareness is determined by events in the short term; optimism or pessimism about the future is conditioned by the immediate situation. When a historian encounters reactions of this kind, which are conscious responses to specific events, it is fairly easy for him to reconstruct their progression by means of the traces they left behind; he is, after all, merely exposing the motives expressed by the historical agents themselves. Unfortunately, such redundancy does not lead very far. A crisis will delay marriages, prosperity will increase marriages, and the next crisis will cause a new drop – that much is clear. But one is left with the basic problem of understanding how, over a period of successive upward or downward adjustments, the age at marriage increased to such an extent that it slowed "natural" demographic growth in preindustrial Europe.

At this point a descriptive discovery such as the one above necessarily leads the historian to venture explanatory hypotheses that are fragile in two ways: first, because they were by nature out of reach of the people whose behavior he is studying, so that there are no directly usable written traces; second, because he will have to abandon a purely demographic analysis, and with it the factual and conceptual precision it requires. He will have to understand the mechanism by which the probability of collective behavior indicated in the analysis of data concerning age at marriage is embodied in the multiplicity of individual behavior.

Let us return to the two hypotheses mentioned earlier. As they are of a different nature, they are not incompatible. Their common feature is that the behavior patterns they describe would have made it easier for the people who lived in that period to harmonize their expectations with their actual opportunities. This process is one of the conditions of social life; it is the somewhat melancholy mechanism by which men predict and construct the most probable future for themselves. But the first hypothesis is of a psychological nature, the second of an economic nature. The first indicates a morality, the second a strategy. The first cannot be measured; the second can be, for the historian can establish a relationship between the demand represented by younger generations and the supply of farm estates or job vacancies generated by deaths in the ranks of older generations. If he does not have enough data at hand to work on a macroeconomic scale, he can at least tackle the problem through a series of monographs on family estates, which will enable him to see how generations succeeded one another on a single estate. This is an objective process that can lead, at least theoretically, to a clear conclusion. In contrast, the notion of the spread of a puritanical superego (on a sexual level) throughout seventeenth- and eighteenth-century Europe is a hypothesis that can lead only to ambiguous answers. It is easy enough to identify the factors that make it plausible: the Protestant ethic, the Counter-Reformation, or Norbert Elias's "civilization." However, it cannot actually be verified or invalidated.

Why is that so? To begin with, the superego is an indemonstrable psychological concept. It is used to interpret behavior that could be interpreted in any number of other ways. For example, Weber's notion of individual self-control can be replaced by that of a reinforcement of external constraints imposed, in this case, by church and clergy. But there are no appropriate data — nor will there ever be — that can provide answers to hypotheses concerning the psychology of historical agents. The agents are dead, and very few of them, even among the fraction who wrote about themselves, bothered with the part of their being that, before Freud, they had neither the means nor even the curiosity to explorer. Thus the historian of what is now referred to by the very vague term of *mentalités* must either base his investigation on scattered or ambiguous texts or find an indicator not of his subjects' psychology but of their behavior in order to deduce the psychological roots of this behavior.

In the first approach, the historian encounters the difficulty of assessing the significance of a both subjective and exceptional piece of evidence. Admittedly, all historical data (except the vestiges of men's material existence) are to a certain extent subjective. Even the registration of a birth or the accounts of an estate were, at a certain moment in time, put down on paper by an individual. But the constraints that govern the recording of an event differ considerably according to the phenomenon observed, the nature of the observation, and that of the observer; according to whether the event is normal and repetitive — that is, comparable to an earlier one — or extraordinary and therefore recorded precisely because it lies outside the norm of habit; according to whether one is dealing with a systematic observation governed by certain rules or with a chance testimony, a census, or an impression; finally, according to whether the relationship linking the observer to the object observed is or is not in the nature of knowledge.

With regard to my example, the historical evidence that can tell us about the psychological roots of behavior dating back several centuries is naturally of a literary nature. I use *literary* in the broad sense to include certain texts that posterity has not elevated to that rank: the handful of unpublished private diaries and of old manuscripts that can cast some light on the subject. But such evidence is scarce, impossible to use in systematic temporal series, and limited to a very narrow social environment. In order to bypass its random character, one will have to consult a different kind of documentation, this time of a normative type: manuals of good manners or specialized treatises on religious morality, such as penitentials. However, texts of this kind present the same ambiguity as government legislation. They prescribe an optimal conduct, but one can never determine to what extent it was accepted, obeyed, or internalized. Is the reiteration of rules of conduct over a long period a sign of their having penetrated into society or, rather, of the resistance they have provoked? The second hypothesis is as probable as, if not more probable than, the first. In this case, the normative text is more interesting for its "preamble" and whatever observations of actual behavior it may contain than for what it forbids or orders. But it serves primarily as evidence about the institutional environment in which it was produced, the state or the church.

That is why the historian of *mentalités*, who is trying to investigate the more common forms of behavior, cannot be content with the traditional literature of historical testimony, which is inevitably subjective, untypical, and ambiguous. He must examine behavior itself, that is, the objective indications of behavior. The hypothesis discussed above concerning a "Weberian" superego extending its control over the souls of seventeenth- and eighteenth-century Europe can be tested for many of the signs of a given behavior; for instance, the number of illegitimate births, the number of premarital conceptions, or the use of contraception. A decrease in, or a low incidence of, illegitimate births or premarital conceptions in a society characterized by a delayed age at marriage is indeed a sign of a long period of accepted chastity. However, for these indications to be meaningful, one would have to prove that the use of contraceptives in Europe during that period was not widespread. How can that be proved? Not by means of literary evidence – which is very rare in this realm par excellence of the unexpressed – but by measuring the spacing of children's births during the married life of couples. The statistical technique for measuring the behavior of this variable is well known. For a population of married women old enough to give birth, a ratio is established between the number of births and mothers' ages. If the fertility of couples decreases very rapidly after the first children and in relation to the mothers' ages, then the use of contraception can be deduced. Otherwise, one finds a succession of births, slowed down only by the nursing period for the latest-born child and the biological decrease in fertility as the potential mother grows older.

The conditions for this kind of experiment seem clear and simple. For example, graphs unambiguously prove that eighteenth-century Canadians were ignorant of contraception, while French dukes and peers of the same period practiced it. However, between these two extremes, the conclusions remain ambiguous. Precisely because the spacing of births during the life of a couple is also influenced by factors other than contraception, it is impossible to assess the specific role of contraception. An increased interval between births, if it is not abrupt, could be due to a change in nursing methods and a later weaning of the latest-born child. That is why categorical conclusions are difficult to reach, as witnessed by the discussions concerning this problem that have been going on since the mid-1960s.

To summarize the methodological aspects of the discussion, it seems to me that we are faced with insuperable difficulties on three levels. First, the concept of the superego as a sort of austere collective moral conscience governing individual behavior cannot be actually proven. Second, the subjective historical data and first-hand accounts are scarce, unrepresentative, and ambiguous. Third, the objective indicators are equally ambiguous. The hypothesis put forward is more in the realm of plausibility than in the realm of truth.

It would therefore be incorrect to believe that the passage from narrative history to problem-oriented history (or, if one prefers, to conceptualized history) suffices to enter *ipso facto* into the scientific domain of the demonstrable. From the episte-mological point of view, conceptualized history is probably superior to narrative history because it replaces an understanding of the past based on the future by explicitly formulated explanatory factors. It also unearths and constructs historical facts intended to support the proposed explanation; thus, while carving out specific entities within the realm of history, conceptual historiography expands it consid-erably. Perhaps Max Weber chose the wrong path with his *Protestant Ethic*, but what a landmark it was! A conceptual discovery can be judged by the areas of research it opens up and by the traces it leaves behind.

Nevertheless, we still have not arrived at a scientific history. First, there are some questions and concepts that do not lead to clear, unambiguous answers. Second, there are some questions that in principle lead to clear-cut answers yet cannot be solved, either because of lack of data or because of the nature of the data: the indicators may be ambiguous or impossible to subject to rigorous analyt-ical techniques.

As we have seen — and one could give many more examples — these techniques are suitable to handling data that are clear (or have been made clear), available in chronological series, and capable of answering unambiguous questions generally formulated by the most advanced contemporary social sciences, such as demog-raphy and economics. To that extent, even history can lead to definite conclusions. For example, one can calculate the major variables in demographic behavior in western Europe since the seventeenth century. One can measure the increase in prices in eighteenth-century France or the takeoff of agrarian productivity in the nineteenth century. In other words, this kind of history, with its potential for extrapolating into the past a number of very specific questions usually formulated in other disciplines, is both highly profitable and very limited. It enables one to arrive at clear-cut conclusions and to obtain a good description of the particular phenomenon chosen for study.

However, the interpretation of these findings does not offer the same degree of certainty as the findings themselves. In problem-oriented history, interpretation is basically the analysis of the objective and subjective mechanisms by which a prob-able pattern of collective behavior — the very one revealed by data analysis — is embodied in individual behavior in a given period; interpretation also studies the transformation of these mechanisms. Thus, it goes beyond the level of described data in order to relate it to other levels of historical reality. It generally requires additional data that belong to another field and are neither necessarily available nor necessarily clear. Interpretation more often than not involves hypotheses that are not proven or not provable.

The problem posed by recent historiographical developments, particularly by the use of strict demonstration procedures, is not to determine whether history itself can become a science. Considering the indeterminacy of history's object of study, the answer to that question is undoubtedly negative. The problem is to determine the limits within which those procedures can be of use in a basically unscientific discipline. Although these limits are obvious, one should not deduce that history should revert to its former function as the fortune-teller. Instead, the unreasonable ambitions of "total history" should be lowered and, in our exploration of the past, we should make the utmost use of the sectorial discoveries and methods of certain disciplines and of the conceptual hypotheses emerging from the great contemporary potpourri called the human sciences. The cost of this change is the breakup of history into many histories and the renunciation by historians of their role as social authorities. However, the epistemological gains may be worth such sacrifices. History will probably always oscillate between the art of narrative, conceptual understanding, and the rigor of proofs; but, if its proofs are more solid and its concepts more explicit, knowledge will stand to gain and narrative will have nothing to lose.

Chapter 18

Lawrence Stone

THE REVIVAL OF NARRATIVE

Reflections on a new old history*

I

HISTORIANS HAVE ALWAYS TOLD STORIES. From Thucydides and Tacitus to Gibbon and Macaulay the composition of narrative in lively and elegant prose was always accounted their highest ambition. History was regarded as a branch of rhetoric. For the last fifty years, however, this story-telling function has fallen into ill repute among those who have regarded themselves as in the vanguard of the profession, the practitioners of the so-called "new history" of the post-World-War II era.[1] In France story-telling was dismissed as "l'histoire événementielle." Now, however, I detect evidence of an undercurrent which is sucking many prominent "new historians" back again into some form of narrative.

Before embarking upon an examination of the evidence for such a shift and upon some speculations about what may have caused it, a number of things had better be made clear. The first is what is meant here by "narrative."[2] Narrative is taken to mean the organization of material in a chronologically sequential order and the focusing of the content into a single coherent story, albeit with sub-plots. The two essential ways in which narrative history differs from structural history is that its arrangement is descriptive rather than analytical and that its central focus is on man not circumstances. It therefore deals with the particular and specific rather than the collective and statistical. Narrative is a mode of historical writing, but it is a mode which also affects and is affected by the content and the method.

The kind of narrative which I have in mind is not that of the simple antiquarian reporter or annalist. It is narrative directed by some "pregnant principle," and which possesses a theme and an argument. Thucydides's theme was the Peloponnesian wars and their disastrous effects upon Greek society and politics; Gibbon's the decline and fall of the Roman empire; Macaulay's the rise of a liberal participatory constitution in the stresses of revolutionary politics. Biographers tell the story of a life, from birth to death. No narrative historians, as I have defined them, avoid analysis altogether, but this is not the skeletal framework around which their work is constructed. And finally, they are deeply concerned with the rhetorical aspects of their presentation. Whether successful or not in the attempt, they certainly aspire to stylistic elegance, wit and aphorism. They are not content to throw words down on a page and let them lie there, with the view that, since history is a science, it needs no art to help it along.

The trends here identified should not be taken to apply to the great mass of historians. All that is being attempted is to point to a noticeable shift of content, method and style among a very tiny, but disproportionately prominent, section of the historical profession as a whole. History has always had many mansions, and must continue to do so if it is to flourish in the future. The triumph of any one genre or school eventually always leads to narrow sectarianism, narcissism and self-adulation, contempt or tyranny towards outsiders, and other disagreeable and self-defeating characteristics. We can all think of cases where this has happened. In some countries and institutions it has been unhealthy that the "new historians" have had things so much their own way in the last thirty years; and it will be equally unhealthy if the new trend, if trend it be, achieves similar domination here and there.

It is also essential to establish once and for all that this essay is trying to chart observed changes in historical fashion, not to make value judgments about what are good, and what are less good, modes of historical writing. Value judgments are hard to avoid in any historiographical study, but this essay is not trying to raise a banner or start a revolution. No one is being urged to throw away his calculator and tell a story.

II

Before looking at the recent trends, one has first to attempt to explain the abandonment by many historians, about fifty years ago, of a two-thousand-year-old tradition of narrative as the ideal mode. In the first place, in spite of impassioned assertions to the contrary, it was widely recognized, with some justice, that answering the *what* and the *how* questions in a chronological fashion, even if directed by a central argument, does not in fact go very far towards answering the *why* questions. Moreover historians were at that time strongly under the influence of both Marxist ideology and social science methodology. As a result they were interested in societies not individuals, and were confident that a "scientific history" could be achieved which would in time produce generalized laws to explain historical change.

Here we must pause again to define what is meant by "scientific history." The first "scientific history" was formulated by Ranke in the nineteenth century and was based on the study of new source materials. It was assumed that close textual criticism of hitherto undisclosed records buried in state archives would once and for all establish the facts of political history. In the last thirty years there have been three very different kinds of "scientific history" current in the profession, all based not on new data, but on new models or new methods: they are the Marxist economic model, the French ecological/demographic model, and the American "cliometric" methodology. According to the old Marxist model, history moves in a dialectical process of thesis and antithesis, through a clash of classes which are themselves created by changes in control over the means of production. In the 1930s this idea resulted in a fairly simplistic economic/social determinism which affected many young scholars of the time. It was a notion of "scientific history" which was strongly defended by Marxists up to the late 1950s. It should, however, be noted that the current generation of "neo-Marxists" seems to have abandoned most of the basic tenets of the traditional Marxist historians of the 1930s. They are now as concerned with the state, politics, religion and ideology as their non-Marxist colleagues, and in the process appear to have dropped the claim to be pursuing "scientific history."

The second meaning of "scientific history" is that used since 1945 by the *Annales* school of French historians, of whom Emmanuel Le Roy Ladurie may stand as a spokesman, albeit a rather extreme one. According to him, the key variable in history is shifts in the ecological balance between food supplies and population, a balance necessarily to be determined by long-term quantitative studies of agricultural productivity, demographic changes and food prices. This kind of "scientific history" emerged from a combination of long-standing French interest in historical geography and historical demography, coupled with the methodology of quantification. Le Roy Ladurie told us bluntly that "history that is not quantifiable cannot claim to be scientific."[3]

The third meaning of "scientific history" is primarily American, and is based on the claim, loudly and clearly expressed by the "cliometricians," that only their own very special quantitative methodology has any claim to be scientific.[4] According to them the historical community can be divided into two. There are "the traditionalists," who include both the old-style narrative historians dealing mainly with state politics and constitutional history, as well as the "new" economic and demographic historians of the *Annales* and *Past and Present* schools — despite the fact that the latter use quantification and that for several decades the two groups were bitter enemies, especially in France. Quite separate are the "scientific historians," the cliometricians, who are defined by a methodology rather than by any particular subject-matter or interpretation of the nature of historical change. They are historians who build paradigmatic models, sometimes counter-factual ones about worlds which never existed in real life, and who test the validity of the models by the most sophisticated mathematical and algebraical formulae applied to very large quantities of electronically processed data. Their special field is economic history, which they have virtually conquered in the United States, and they have made large inroads into the history of recent democratic politics by applying their methods to voting behavior, both of the electorate and the elected. These great enterprises are necessarily the result of team-work, rather like the building of the pyramids: squads of diligent assistants assemble data, encode it, program it, and pass it through the maw of the computer, all under the autocratic direction of a team-leader. The results cannot be tested by any of the traditional methods since the evidence is buried in private computer-tapes, not exposed in published footnotes. In any case the data are often expressed in so mathematically recondite a form that they are unintelligible to the majority of the historical profession. The only reassurance to the bemused laity is that the members of this priestly order disagree fiercely and publicly about the validity of each other's findings.

These three types of "scientific history" overlap to some degree, but they are sufficiently distinct, certainly in the eyes of their practitioners, to justify the creation of this tripartite typology.

Other "scientific" explanations of historical change have risen to favor for a while and then gone out of fashion. French structuralism produced some brilliant theorizing, but no single major work of history – unless one considers Michel Foucault's writings as primarily works of history, rather than of moral philosophy with examples drawn from history. Parsonian functionalism, which itself was preceded by Malinowski's *Scientific Theory of Culture*,[5] had a long run, despite its failure to offer an explanation of change over time and the obvious fact that the fit between the material and biological needs of a society and the institutions and values by which it lives has always been less than perfect, and often very poor indeed. Both structuralism and functionalism have provided valuable insights, but neither has come even near to supplying historians with an all-embracing scientific explanation of historical change.

All the three main groups of "scientific historians," which flourished respectively from the 1930s until the 1950s, the 1950s to mid-1970s, and in the 1960s and early 1970s, were supremely confident that the major problems of historical explanation were soluble, and that they would, given time, succeed in solving them. Cast-iron solutions would, they assumed, eventually be provided for such hitherto baffling questions as the causes of "great revolutions" or the shifts from feudalism to capitalism, and from traditional to modern societies. This heady optimism, which was so apparent from the 1930s to the 1960s, was buttressed among the first two groups of "scientific historians" by the belief that material conditions such as changes in the relationship between population and food supply, changes in the means of production and class conflict, were the driving forces in history. Many, but not all, regarded intellectual, cultural, religious, psychological, legal, even political, developments as mere epiphenomena. Since economic and/or demographic determinism largely dictated the content of the new genre of historical research, the analytic rather than the narrative mode was best suited to organize and present the data, and the data themselves had as far as possible to be quantitative in nature.

The French historians, who in the 1950s and 1960s were in the lead in this brave enterprise, developed a standard hierarchical arrangement: first, both in place and in order of importance, came the economic and demographic facts; then the social structure; and lastly, intellectual, religious, cultural and political developments. These three tiers were thought of like the storeys of a house: each rests on the foundation of the one below, but those above can have little or no reciprocal effect on those underneath. In some hands the new methodology and new questions produced results which were little short of sensational. The first books of Fernand Braudel, Pierre Goubert and Emmanuel Le Roy Ladurie will rank among the greatest historical writings of any time and place.[6] They alone fully justify the adoption for a generation of the analytical and structural approach.

The conclusion, however, was historical revisionism with a vengeance. Since only the first tier really mattered, and since the subject-matter was the material conditions of the masses, not the culture of the élite, it became possible to talk about the history of Continental Europe from the fourteenth to the eighteenth centuries as "l'histoire immobile." Le Roy Ladurie argued that nothing, absolutely nothing, changed over those five centuries, since the society remained obstinately imprisoned in its traditional and unaltered "éco-démographie."[7] In this new model of history such movements as the Renaissance, the Reformation, the Enlightenment and the rise of the modern state simply disappeared. Ignored were the massive transformations of culture, art, architecture, literature, religion, education, science, law, constitution, state-building, bureaucracy, military organization, fiscal arrangements, and so on, which took place among the higher echelons of society in those five centuries. This curious blindness was the result of a firm belief that these matters were all parts of the third tier, a mere superficial superstructure. When, recently, some scholars from this school began to use their well-tried statistical methods on such problems as literacy, the contents of libraries and the rise and fall of Christian piety, they described their activities as the application of quantification to "le troisième niveau."

III

The first cause of the current revival of narrative is a widespread disillusionment with the economic determinist model of historical explanation and this three-tiered hierarchical arrangement to which it gave rise. The split between social history on the one hand and intellectual history on the other has had the most unfortunate consequences. Both have become isolated, inward-looking, and narrow. In America intellectual history, which had once been the flagship of the profession, fell upon hard times and for a while lost confidence in itself;[8] social history has flourished as never before, but its pride in its isolated achievements was but the harbinger of an eventual decline in vitality, when faith in purely economic and social explanations began to ebb. The historical record has now obliged many of us to admit that there is an extraordinarily complex two-way flow of interactions between facts of population, food supply, climate, bullion supply, prices, on the one hand, and values, ideas and customs on the other. Along with social relationships of status or class, they form a single web of meaning.

Many historians now believe that the culture of the group, and even the will of the individual, are potentially at least as important causal agents of change as the impersonal forces of material output and demographic growth. There is no theoretical reason why the latter should always dictate the former, rather than vice versa, and indeed evidence is piling up of examples to the contrary.[9] Contraception, for example, is clearly as much a product of a state of mind as it is of economic circumstances. The proof of this contention can be found in the wide diffusion of this practice throughout France, long before industrialization, without much population pressure except on small farms, and nearly a century before any other western country. We also now know that the nuclear family antedated industrial society, and that concepts of privacy, love and individualism similarly emerged among some of the most traditional sectors of a traditional society in late seventeenth- and early eighteenth-century England, rather than as a result of later modernizing economic and social processes. The Puritan ethic was a by-product of an unworldly religious movement which took root in the Anglo-Saxon societies of England and New England centuries before routine work-patterns were necessary or the first factory was built. On the other hand there is an inverse correlation, at any rate in nineteenth-century France, between literacy and urbanization and industrialization. Levels of literacy turn out to be a poor guide to "modern" attitudes of mind or "modern" occupations.[10] Thus the linkages between culture and society are clearly very complex indeed, and seem to vary from time to time and from place to place.

It is hard not to suspect that the decline of ideological commitment among western intellectuals has also played its part. If one looks at three of the most passionate and hard-fought historical battles of the 1950s and 1960s — about the rise or decline of the gentry in seventeenth-century England, about the rise or fall of working-class real income in the early stages of industrialization, and about the causes, nature and consequences of American slavery — all were at bottom debates fired by current ideological concerns. It seemed desperately important at the time to know whether or not the Marxist interpretation was right, and therefore these historical questions mattered and were exciting. The muting of ideological controversy caused by the intellectual decline of Marxism and the adoption of mixed economies in the west has coincided with a decline in the thrust of historical research to ask the big *why* questions, and it is plausible to suggest that there is some relationship between the two trends.

Economic and demographic determinism has not only been undermined by a recognition of ideas, culture and even individual will as independent variables. It has also been sapped by a revived recognition that political and military power, the use of brute force, has very frequently dictated the structure of the society, the distribution of wealth, the agrarian system, and even the culture of the élite. Classic examples are the Norman conquest of England in 1066, and probably also the divergent economic and social paths taken by eastern Europe, north-western Europe and England in the sixteenth and seventeenth centuries.[11] Future historians will undoubtedly severely criticize the "new historians" of the 1950s and 1960s for their failure to take sufficient account of power: of political organization and decision-making and the vagaries of military battle and siege, destruction and conquest. Civilizations have risen and fallen due to fluctuations in political authority and shifts in the fortunes of war, and it is extraordinary that these matters should have been neglected for so long by those who regarded themselves as in the forefront of the historical profession. In practice the bulk of the profession continued to concern itself with political history, just as it had always done, but this is not where the cutting edge of the profession was generally thought to be. A belated recognition of the importance of power, of personal political decisions by individuals, of the chances of battle, have forced historians back to the narrative mode, whether they like it or not. To use Machiavelli's terms, neither *virtu* nor *fortuna* can be dealt with except by a narrative, or even an anecdote, since the first is an individual attribute and the second a happy or unhappy accident.

The third development which has dealt a serious blow to structural and analytical history is the mixed record to date in the use of what has been its most characteristic methodology — namely quantification. Quantification has undoubtedly matured and has now established itself as an essential methodology in many areas of historical inquiry, especially demographic history, the history of social structure and social mobility, economic history, and the history of voting patterns and voting behavior in democratic political systems. Its use has greatly improved the general quality of historical discourse, by demanding the citation of precise numbers instead of the previous loose use of words. Historians can no longer get away with saying "more," "less," "growing," "declining," all of which logically imply numerical comparisons, without ever stating explicitly the statistical basis for their assertions. It has also made argument exclusively by example seem somewhat disreputable. Critics now demand supporting statistical evidence to show that the examples are typical, and not exceptions to the rule. These procedures have undoubtedly improved the logical power and persuasiveness of historical argument. Nor is there any disagreement that whenever it is appropriate, fruitful and possible from the surviving records, the historian should count.

There is, however, a difference in kind between the artisan quantification done by a single researcher totting up figures on a hand-calculator and producing simple tables and percentages, and the work of the cliometricians. The latter specialize in the assembling of vast quantities of data by teams of assistants, the use of the electronic computer to process it all, and the application of highly sophisticated mathematical procedures to the results obtained. Doubts have been cast on all stages of this procedure. Many question whether historical data are ever sufficiently reliable to warrant such procedures; whether teams of assistants can be trusted to apply uniform coding procedures to large quantities of often widely diverse and even ambiguous documents; whether much crucial detail is not lost in the coding procedure; if it is ever possible to be confident that all coding and programming errors have been eliminated; and whether the sophistication of the mathematical and algebraic formulae are not ultimately self-defeating since they baffle most historians. Finally, many are disturbed by the virtual impossibility of checking up on the reliability of the final results, since they must depend not on published footnotes but on privately owned computer-tapes, in turn the result of thousands of privately owned code-sheets, in turn abstracted from the raw data.

These questions are real and will not go away. We all know of doctoral dissertations or printed papers or monographs which have used the most sophisticated techniques either to prove the obvious or to claim to prove the implausible, using formulae and language which render the methodology unverifiable to the ordinary historian. The results sometimes combine the vices of unreadability and triviality. We all know of the doctoral dissertations which languish unfinished since the researcher has been unable to keep under intellectual control the sheer volume of print-out spewed out by the computer, or has spent so much effort preparing the data for the machine that his time, patience and money have run out. One clear conclusion is surely that, whenever possible, sampling by hand is preferable and quicker than, and just as reliable as, running the whole universe through a machine. We all know of projects in which a logical flaw in the argument or a failure to use plain common sense has vitiated or cast in doubt many of the conclusions. We all know of other projects in which the failure to record one piece of information at the coding stage has led to the loss of an important result. We all know of others where the sources of information are themselves so unreliable that we can be sure that little confidence can be placed in the conclusions based on their quantitative manipulation. Parish registers are a classic example, upon which a gigantic amount of effort is currently being spent in many countries, only some of which is likely to produce worthwhile results.

Despite its unquestionable achievements it cannot be denied that quantification has not fulfilled the high hopes of twenty years ago. Most of the great problems of history remain as insoluble as ever, if not more so. Consensus on the causes of the English, French or American revolutions are as far away as ever, despite the enormous effort put into elucidating their social and economic origins. Thirty years of intensive research on demographic history has left us more rather than less bewildered. We do not know why the population ceased to grow in most areas of Europe between 1640 and 1740; we do not know why it began to grow again in 1740; or even whether the cause was rising fertility or declining mortality. Quantification has told us a lot about the *what* questions of historical demography, but relatively little so far about the *why*. The major questions about American slavery remain as elusive as ever, despite the application to them of one of the most massive and sophisticated studies ever mounted. The publication of its findings, far from solving most problems, merely raised the temperature of the debate.[12] It had the beneficial effect of focusing attention on important issues such as the diet, hygiene, health and family structure of American Negroes under slavery, but it also diverted attention from the equally or even more important psychological effects of slavery upon both masters and slaves, simply because these matters could not be measured by a computer. Urban histories are cluttered with statistics, but mobility trends still remain obscure. Today no one is quite sure whether English society was more open and mobile than the French in the seventeenth and eighteenth centuries, or even whether the gentry or aristocracy was rising or falling in England before the Civil War. We are no better off now in these respects than were James Harrington in the seventeenth century or Tocqueville in the nineteenth.

It is just those projects that have been the most lavishly funded, the most ambitious in the assembly of vast quantities of data by armies of paid researchers, the most scientifically processed by the very latest in computer technology, the most mathematically sophisticated in presentation, which have so far turned out to be the most disappointing. Today, two decades and millions of dollars, pounds and francs later, there are only rather modest results to show for the expenditure of so much time, effort and money. There are huge piles of greenish printout gathering dust in scholars' offices; there are many turgid and excruciatingly dull tomes full of tables of figures, abstruse algebraic equations and percentages given to two decimal places. There are also many valuable new findings and a few major contributions to the relatively small corpus of historical works of permanent value. But in general the sophistication of the methodology has tended to exceed the reliability of the data, while the usefulness of the results seems – up to a point – to be in inverse correlation to the mathematical complexity of the methodology and the grandiose scale of data-collection.

On any cost-benefit analysis the rewards of large-scale computerized history have so far only occasionally justified the input of time and money and this has led historians to cast around for other methods of investigating the past, which will shed more light with less trouble. In 1968 Le Roy Ladurie prophesied that by the 1980s "the historian will be a programmer or he will be nothing."[13] The prophecy has not been fulfilled, least of all by the prophet himself.

Historians are therefore forced back upon the principle of indeterminacy, a recognition that the variables are so numerous that at best only middle-range generalizations are possible in history, as Robert Merton long ago suggested. The macro-economic model is a pipe-dream, and "scientific history" a myth. Monocausal explanations simply do not work. The use of feed-back models of explanation built around Weberian "elective affinities" seems to provide better tools for revealing something of the elusive truth about historical causation, especially if we abandon any claim that this methodology is in any sense scientific.

Disillusionment with economic or demographic monocausal determinism and with quantification has led historians to start asking a quite new set of questions, many of which were previously blocked from view by the preoccupation with a specific methodology, structural, collective and statistical. More and more of the "new historians" are now trying to discover what was going on inside people's heads in the past, and what it was like to live in the past, questions which inevitably lead back to the use of narrative.

A significant sub-group of the great French school of historians, led by Lucien Febvre, has always regarded intellectual, psychological and cultural changes as independent variables of central importance. But for a long time they were in a minority, left behind in a remote backwater as the flood-tide of "scientific history," economic and social in content, structural in organization and quantitative in methodology, swept past them. Now, however, the topics they were interested in have quite suddenly become fashionable. The questions asked, however, are not quite the same as they used to be, since they are now often drawn from anthropology. In practice, if not in theory, anthropology has tended to be one of the most ahistorical of disciplines in its lack of interest in change over time. None the less it has taught us how a whole social system and set of values can be brilliantly illuminated by the searchlight method of recording in elaborate detail a single event, provided that it is very carefully set in its total context and very carefully analyzed for its cultural meaning. The archetypal model of this "thick description" is Clifford Geertz's classic account of a Balinese cock-fight.[14] We historians cannot, alas, actually be present, with notebooks, tape-recorders and cameras, at the events we describe, but now and again we can find a cloud of witnesses to tell us what it was like to be there. The first cause for the revival or narrative among some of the "new historians" has therefore been the replacement of sociology and economics by anthropology as the most influential of the social sciences.

One of the most striking recent changes in the content of history has been a quite sudden growth of interest in feelings, emotions, behavior patterns, values, and states of mind. In this respect the influence of anthropologists like Evans-Pritchard, Clifford Geertz, Mary Douglas and Victor Turner has been very great indeed. Although psycho-history is so far largely a disaster area – a desert strewn with the wreckage of elaborate, chromium-plated vehicles which broke down soon after departure – psychology itself has also had its effect on a generation now turning its attention to sexual desire, family relations and emotional bonding as they affect the individual, and to ideas, beliefs and customs as they affect the group.

This change in the nature of the questions being asked is also probably related to the contemporary scene in the 1970s. This has been a decade in which more personalized ideals and interests have taken priority over public issues, as a result of widespread disillusionment with the prospects of change by political action.

It is therefore plausible to connect the sudden upsurge in interest in these matters in the past with similar preoccupations in the present.

This new interest in mental structures has been stimulated by the collapse of traditional intellectual history treated as a kind of paper-chase of ideas back through the ages (which usually ends up with either Aristotle or Plato). "Great books" were studied in a historical vacuum, with little or no attempt to set the authors themselves or their linguistic vocabulary in their true historical setting. The history of political thought in the west is now being rewritten, primarily by J. G. A. Pocock, Quentin Skinner and Bernard Bailyn, by painfully reconstructing the precise context and meaning of words and ideas in the past, and showing how they have changed their shape and color in the course of time, like chameleons, so as to adapt to new circumstances and new needs.

The traditional history of ideas is concurrently being directed into a study of the changing audience and means of communication. There has sprung up a new and flourishing discipline of the history of the printing-press, the book and literacy, and of their effects upon the diffusion of ideas and the transformation of values.

One further reason why a number of "new historians" are turning back to narrative seems to be a desire to make their findings accessible once more to an intelligent but not expert reading public, which is eager to learn what these innovative new questions, methods and data have revealed, but cannot stomach indigestible statistical tables, dry analytical argument, and jargon-ridden prose. Increasingly the structural, analytical, quantitative historians have found themselves talking to each other and no one else. Their findings have appeared in professional journals, or in monographs so expensive and with such small print runs (under a thousand) that they have been in practice almost entirely bought by libraries. And yet the success of popular historical periodicals like *History Today* and *L'histoire* proves that there is a large audience ready to listen, and the "new historians" are now anxious to speak to that audience, rather than leaving it to be fed on the pabulum of popular biographies and textbooks. The questions being asked by the "new historians" are, after all, those which pre-occupy us all today: the nature of power, authority and charismatic leadership; the relation of political institutions to underlying social patterns and value systems; attitudes to youth, old age, disease and death; sex, marriage and concubinage; birth, contraception and abortion; work, leisure and conspicuous consumption; the relationship of religion, science and magic as explanatory models of reality; the strength and direction of the emotions of love, fear, lust and hate; the impact of literacy and education upon people's lives and ways of looking at the world; the relative importance attached to different social groupings, such as the family, kin, community, nation, class and race; the strength and meaning of ritual, symbol and custom as ways of binding a community together; moral and philosophical approaches to crime and punishment; patterns of deference and outbursts of egalitarianism; structural conflicts between status groups or classes; the means, possibilities and limitations of social mobility; the nature and significance of popular protest and millenarian hopes; the shifting ecological balance between man and nature; the causes and effects of disease. All these are burning issues at the moment and are concerned with the masses rather than the élite. They are more "relevant" to our own lives than the doings of dead kings, presidents and generals.

IV

As a result of these convergent trends a significant number of the best-known exponents of the "new history" are now turning back to the once despised narrative
mode. And yet historians – and even publishers – still seem a little embarrassed
when they do so. In 1979 the *Publishers' Weekly* – an organ of the trade – promoted
the merits of a new book, a story of the trial of Louis XVI, with these peculiar
words: "Jordan's choice of *narrative rather than scholarly treatment* [my italics] . . . is
a model of clarity and synthesis."[15] The critic obviously liked the book, but thought
that narrative is by definition not scholarly. When a distinguished member of the
school of "new history" writes a narrative, his friends tend to apologize for him,
saying: "Of course, he only did it for the money." Despite these rather shamefaced
apologies, the trends in historiography, in content, method and mode, are evident
wherever one looks.

After languishing unread for forty years Norbert Elias's path-breaking book
about manners, *The Civilizing Process*, has suddenly been translated into English and
French.[16] Theodore Zeldin has written a brilliant two-volume history of modern
France, in a standard textbook series, which ignores almost every aspect of traditional history, and concentrates on little other than emotions and states of mind.[17]
Philippe Ariès has studied responses over a huge time-span to the universal trauma
of death.[18] The history of witchcraft has suddenly become a growth industry in
every country, as has the history of the family, including that of childhood, youth,
old age, women and sexuality (the last two being topics in serious danger of suffering
from intellectual overkill). An excellent example of the trajectory which historical
studies have tended to take over the last twenty years is provided by the research
interests of Jean Delumeau. He began in 1957 with a study of a society (Rome);
followed, in 1962, by that of an economic product (alum); in 1971, of a religion
(Catholicism); in 1976, of a collective behavior (*les pays de Cocagne*); and finally, in
1979, of an emotion (fear).[19]

The French have a word to describe the new topic – *mentalité* – but unfortunately it is neither very well defined nor very easily translatable into English. In
any case story-telling, the circumstantial narration in great detail of one or more
"happenings" based on the testimony of eyewitnesses and participants, is clearly
one way to recapture something of the outward manifestations of the *mentalité*
of the past. Analysis certainly remains the essential part of the enterprise, which is
based on an anthropological interpretation of culture that claims to be both
systematic and scientific. But this cannot conceal the role of the study of *mentalité*
in the revival of non-analytical modes of writing history, of which story-telling
is one.

Of course narrative is not the only manner of writing the history of *mentalité*
which has been made possible by disillusionment with structural analysis. Take, for
example, that most brilliant reconstruction of a vanished mind-set, Peter Brown's
evocation of the world of late antiquity.[20] It ignores the usual clear analytical
categories – population, economics, social structure, political system, culture, and
so on. Instead Brown builds up a portrait of an age rather in the manner of a post-
Impressionist artist, daubing in rough blotches of colour here and there which,
if one stands far enough back, create a stunning vision of reality, but which, if

examined up close, dissolve into a meaningless blur. The deliberate vagueness, the pictorial approach, the intimate juxtaposition of history, literature, religion and art, the concern for what was going on inside people's heads, are all characteristic of a fresh way of looking at history. The method is not narrative but rather a *pointilliste* way of writing history. But it too has been stimulated by the new interest in *mentalité* and made possible by the decline of the analytical and structural approach which has been so dominant for the last thirty years.

There has even been a revival of the narration of a single event. Georges Duby has dared to do what a few years ago would have been unthinkable. He has devoted a book to the account of a single battle – Bouvines – and through it has illuminated the main characteristics of early thirteenth-century French feudal society.[21] Carlo Ginzburg has given us a minute account of the cosmology of an obscure and humble early sixteenth-century north Italian miller, and by it has sought to demonstrate the intellectual and psychological disturbance at the popular level caused by the seepage downward of Reformation ideas.[22] Emmanuel Le Roy Ladurie has painted a unique and unforgettable picture of life and death, work and sex, religion and custom in an early fourteenth-century village in the Pyrenees.[23] *Montaillou* is significant in two respects: first, because it has become one of the greatest historical best-sellers of the twentieth century in France; and second, because it does not tell a straightforward story – there is no story – but rambles around inside people's heads. It is no accident that this is precisely one of the ways in which the modern novel differs from those of earlier times. More recently, Le Roy Ladurie has told the story of a single bloody episode in a small town in southern France in 1580, using it to reveal the cross-currents of hatred that were tearing apart the social fabric of the town.[24] Carlo M. Cipolla, who has hitherto been one of the hardest of hard-nosed economic and demographic structuralists, has just published a book which is more concerned with an evocative reconstruction of personal reactions to the terrible crisis of a pandemic than with establishing statistics of morbidity and mortality. For the first time, he tells a story.[25] Eric Hobsbawm has described the nasty, brutish and short lives of rebels and bandits around the world, so as to define the nature and objectives of his "primitive rebels" and "social bandits."[26] Edward Thompson has told the story of the struggle in early eighteenth-century England between the poachers and the authorities in Windsor forest, in order to support his argument about the clash of plebians and patricians at that time.[27] Robert Darnton's latest book tells how the great French *Encyclopédie* came to be published, and in so doing has cast a flood of new light on the process of diffusion of Enlightenment thought in the eighteenth century, including the nuts and bolts of book production and the problems of catering to a national – and international – market for ideas.[28] Natalie Davis has presented a narrative of four *charivaris* or ritual public shame procedures in seventeenth-century Lyon and Geneva, in order to illustrate community efforts to enforce public standards of honor and propriety.[29]

The new interest in *mentalité* has itself stimulated a return to old ways of writing history. Keith Thomas's account of the conflict of magic and religion is constructed around a "pregnant principle" along which are strung a mass of stories and examples.[30] My own recent book on changes in the emotional life of the English family is very similar in intent and method, if not in achievement.[31]

All the historians mentioned so far are mature scholars who have long been associated with the "new history," asking new questions, trying out new methods, and searching for new sources. Now they are turning back to the telling of stories. There are, however, five differences between their stories and those of the traditional narrative historians. First, they are almost without exception concerned with the lives and feelings and behavior of the poor and obscure rather than the great and powerful. Second, analysis remains as essential to their methodology as description, so that their books tend to switch, a little awkwardly, from one mode to the other. Third, they are opening up new sources, often records of criminal courts which used Roman law procedures, since these contain written transcripts of the full testimony of witnesses under interrogation and examination. (The other fashionable use of criminal records, to chart the quantitative rise and fall of various types of deviance, seems to me to be an almost wholly futile endeavor, since what is being counted is not the number of perpetrated crimes, but criminals who have been arrested and prosecuted, which is an entirely different matter. There is no reason to suppose that the one bears any constant relationship over time to the other.) Fourth, they often tell their stories in a different way from that of Homer, or Dickens, or Balzac. Under the influence of the modern novel and of Freudian ideas, they gingerly explore the subconscious rather than sticking to the plain facts. And under the influence of the anthropologists, they try to use behavior to reveal symbolic meaning. Fifth, they tell the story of a person, a trial or a dramatic episode, not for its own sake, but in order to throw light upon the internal workings of a past culture and society.

V

If I am right in my diagnosis, the movement to narrative by the "new historians" marks the end of an era: the end of the attempt to produce a coherent scientific explanation of change in the past. Economic and demographic determinism has collapsed in the face of the evidence, but no full-blown deterministic model based on politics, psychology or culture has emerged to take its place. Structuralism and functionalism have not turned out much better. Quantitative methodology has proved a fairly weak reed which can only answer a limited set of problems. Forced into a choice between a priori statistical models of human behavior, and understanding based on observation, experience, judgment and intuition, some of the "new historians" are now tending to drift back towards the latter mode of interpreting the past.

Although the revival by the "new historians" of the narrative mode is a very recent phenomenon, it is merely a thin trickle in comparison with the constant, large and equally distinguished output of descriptive political narrative by more traditional historians. A recent example which has met with considerable scholarly acclaim is Simon Schama's book about Dutch politics in the eighteenth century.[32] Works such as this have for decades been treated with indifference or barely concealed disdain by the new social historians. This attitude did not have very much justification, but in recent years it has stimulated some of the traditional historians to adapt their descriptive mode to ask new questions. Some of them are no longer so preoccupied

with issues of power and therefore with kings and prime ministers, wars and diplomacy, but are, like the "new historians," turning their attention to the private lives
of quite obscure people. The cause of this trend, if trend it be, is not clear but the
inspiration seems to be the desire to tell a good story, and in so doing to reveal
the quirks of personality and the inwardness of things in a different time and culture.
Some traditional historians have been doing this for some time. In 1958 G. R. Elton
published a book consisting of stories of riot and mayhem in sixteenth-century
England, taken from the records of Star Chamber.[33] In 1946 Hugh Trevor-Roper
brilliantly reconstructed the last days of Hitler.[34] Just recently he has investigated
the extraordinary career of a relatively obscure English manuscript-collector, con-
man and secret pornographer, who lived in China in the early years of this century.[35]
The purpose of writing this entertaining yarn seems to have been sheer pleasure
in a story-telling for its own sake, in the pursuit and capture of a bizarre historical
specimen. The technique is almost identical to that used years ago by A. J. A. Symons
in his classic *The Quest for Corvo*,[36] while the motivation appears very similar to that
which inspires Richard Cobb to record in gruesome detail the squalid lives and deaths
of criminals, prostitutes and other social misfits in the underworld of revolutionary
France.[37]

Quite different in content, method and objective are the writings of the new
British school of young antiquarian empiricists. They write detailed political narratives which implicitly deny that there is any deep-seated meaning to history except
the accidental whims of fortune and personality. Led by Conrad Russell and John
Kenyon, and urged on by Geoffrey Elton, they are now busy trying to remove any
sense of ideology or idealism from the two English revolutions of the seventeenth
century.[38] No doubt they or others like them will soon turn their attention elsewhere. Although their premise is never explicitly stated, their approach is
pure neo-Namierism, just at a time when Namierism is dying as a way of looking
at eighteenth-century English politics. One wonders whether their attitude to political history may not subconsciously stem from a sense of disillusionment with the
capacity of the contemporary parliamentary system to grapple with the inexorable
economic and power decline of Britain. Be that as it may, they are very erudite
and intelligent chroniclers of the petty event, of "l'histoire événementielle," and
thus form one of the many streams which feed the revival of narrative.

The fundamental reason for the shift among the "new historians" from the
analytical to the descriptive mode is a major change in attitude about what is the
central subject-matter of history. And this in turn depends on prior philosophical
assumptions about the role of human free will in its interaction with the forces
of nature. The contrasting poles of thought are best revealed by quotations, one
on one side and two on the other. In 1973 Emmanuel Le Roy Ladurie entitled a
section of a volume of his essays "History without People."[39] By contrast half
a century ago Lucien Febvre announced. "My quarry is man," and a quarter of a
century ago Hugh Trevor-Roper, in his inaugural lecture, urged upon historians
"the study not of circumstances but of man in circumstances."[40] Today Febvre's
ideal of history is catching on in many circles, at the same time as analytical structural studies of impersonal forces continue to pour out from the presses. Historians
are therefore now dividing into four groups: the old narrative historians, primarily
political historians and biographers; the cliometricians who continue to act like

statistical junkies; the hard-nosed social historians still busy analyzing impersonal structures; and the historians of *mentalité*, now chasing ideals, values, mind-sets, and patterns of intimate personal behavior – the more intimate the better.

The adoption by the historians of *mentalité* of minute descriptive narrative or individual biography is not, however, without its problems. The trouble is the old one, that argument by selective example is philosophically unpersuasive, a rhetorical device not a scientific proof. The basic historiographical trap in which we are ensnared has recently been well set out by Carlo Ginzburg: "The quantitative and anti-anthropocentric approach of the sciences of nature from Galileo onwards has placed human sciences in an unpleasant dilemma: they must either adopt a weak scientific standard so as to be able to attain significant results, or adopt a strong scientific standard to attain results of no great importance."[41] Disappointment with the second approach is causing a drift back to the first. As a result what is now taking place is an expansion of the selective example – now often a detailed unique example – into one of the fashionable modes of historical writing. In one sense this is only a logical extension of the enormous success of local history studies, which have taken as their subject not a whole society but only a segment – a province, a town, even a village. Total history only seems possible if one takes a microcosm, and the results have often done more to illuminate and explain the past than all the earlier or concurrent studies based on the archives of the central government. In another sense, however, the new trend is the antithesis of local history studies, since it abandons the total history of a society, however small, as an impossibility, and settles for the story of a single cell.

The second problem which arises from the use of the detailed example to illustrate *mentalité* is how to distinguish the normal from the eccentric. Since man is now our quarry, the narration of a very detailed story of a single incident or personality can make both good reading and good sense. But this will be so only if the stories do not merely tell a striking but fundamentally irrelevant tale of some dramatic episode of riot or rape, or the life of some eccentric rogue or villain or mystic, but are selected for the light they can throw upon certain aspects of a past culture. This means that they must be typical, and yet the wide use of records of litigation makes this question of typicality very difficult to resolve. People hauled into court are almost by definition atypical, but the world that is so nakedly exposed in the testimony of witnesses need not be so. Safety therefore lies in examining the documents not so much for their evidence about the eccentric behavior of the accused as for the light they shed on the life and opinions of those who happened to get involved in the incident in question.

The third problem concerns interpretation, and is even harder to resolve. Provided the historian remains aware of the hazards involved, story-telling is perhaps as good a way as any to obtain an intimate glimpse of man in the past, to try to get inside his head. The trouble is that if he succeeds in getting there, the narrator will need all the skill and experience and knowledge acquired in the practice of analytical history of society, economy and culture, if he is to provide a plausible explanation of some of the very strange things he is liable to find. He may also need a little amateur psychology to help him along, but amateur psychology is extremely tricky material to handle successfully – and some would argue that it is impossible.

Another obvious danger is that the revival of narrative may lead to a return to pure antiquarianism, to story-telling for its own sake. Yet another is that it will focus attention upon the sensational and so obscure the dullness and drabness of the lives of the vast majority. Both Trevor-Roper and Richard Cobb are enormous fun to read, but they are wide open to criticism on both counts. Many practitioners of the new mode, including Cobb, Hobsbawm, Thompson, Le Roy Ladurie and Trevor-Roper (and myself) are clearly fascinated by stories of violence and sex, which appeal to the voyeuristic instincts in us all. On the other hand it can be argued that sex and violence are integral parts of all human experience, and that it is therefore as reasonable and defensible to explore their impact on individuals in the past as it is to expect to see such material in contemporary films and television.

The trend to narrative raises unsolved problems about how we are to train our graduate students in the future — assuming that there are any to train. In the ancient arts of rhetoric? In textual criticism? In semiotics? In symbolic anthropology? In psychology? Or in the techniques of analysis of social and economic structures which we have been practicing for a generation? It therefore remains an open question whether this unexpected resurrection of the narrative mode by so many leading practitioners of the "new history" will turn out to be a good or a bad thing for the future of the profession.

In 1972 Le Roy Ladurie wrote confidently: "Present-day historiography, with its preference for the quantifiable, the statistical and the structural, has been obliged to suppress in order to survive. In the last decades it has virtually condemned to death the narrative history of events and the individual biography."[42] It is far too early to pronounce a funeral oration over the decaying corpse of analytical, structural, quantitative history, which continues to flourish, and even to grow if the trend in American doctoral dissertations is any guide.[43] Nevertheless in this, the third decade, narrative history and individual biography are showing evident signs of rising again from the dead. Neither look quite the same as they used to do before their alleged demise, but they are easily identifiable as variants of the same genus.

It is clear that a single word like "narrative," especially one with such a complicated history behind it, is inadequate to describe what is in fact a broad cluster of changes in the nature of historical discourse. There are signs of change with regard to the central issue in history, from the circumstances surrounding man, to man in circumstances; in the problems studied, from the economic and demographic to the cultural and emotional; in the prime sources of influence, from sociology, economics and demography to anthropology and psychology; in the subject-matter, from the group to the individual; in the explanatory models of historical change, from the stratified and monocausal to the interconnected and multicausal; in the methodology, from group quantification to individual example; in the organization, from the analytical to the descriptive; and in the conceptualization of the historian's function, from the scientific to the literary. These many-faceted changes in content, objective, method, and style of historical writing, which are all happening at once, have clear elective affinities with one another: they all fit neatly together. No single word is adequate to sum them all up, and so, for the time being, "narrative" will have to serve as a shorthand code-word for all that is going on.

Notes

*I am much indebted to my wife and my colleagues, Professors Robert Darnton, Natalie Davis, Felix Gilbert, Charles Gillispie, Theodore Rabb, Carl Schorske and many others for valuable criticism of an early draft of this paper. Most of the suggestions I have accepted, but the blame for the final product rests on me alone.

1   These recent "new historians" should not be confused with the American "new historians" of an earlier generation, like Charles Beard and James Harvey Robinson.
2   For the history of narrative, see L. Grossman, "Augustin Thierry and Liberal Historiography," *History and Theory*, Beiheft, xv (1979); H. White, *Metahistory: The Historical Imagination in the Nineteenth Century* (Baltimore, 1973). I am indebted to Professor Randolph Starn for directing my attention to the latter.
3   E. Le Roy Ladurie, *The Territory of the Historian*, trans. B. and S. Reynolds (Hassocks, 1979), p. 15, and pt. i, *passim*.
4   An unpublished paper by R. W. Fogel, "Scientific History and Traditional History" (1979), offers the most persuasive case that can be mustered for regarding this as the one and only truly "scientific" history. But I remain unconvinced.
5   Bronislaw Malinowski, *A Scientific Theory of Culture, and Other Essays* (Chapel Hill, N.C., 1944).
6   F. Braudel, *La Méditerranée et le monde méditerranéen à l'époque de Philippe II* (Paris, 1949); P. Goubert, *Beauvais et le Beauvaisis de 1600 à 1730* (Paris, 1960); E. Le Roy Ladurie, *Les paysans du Languedoc* (Paris, 1966).
7   E. Le Roy Ladurie, "L'histoire immobile," in his *Le territoire de l'historien*, 2 vols. (Paris, 1973–8), ii; the article was written in 1973.
8   R. Darnton, "Intellectual and Cultural History," in M. Kammen (ed.), *History in Our Time* (forthcoming Ithaca, NY, 1980).
9   M. Zuckerman, "Dreams that Men Dare to Dream: The Role of Ideas in Western Modernization," *Social Science Hist.*, ii (1978).
10   F. Furet and J. Ozouf, *Lire et écrire* (Paris, 1977). See also K. Lockridge, *Literacy in Colonial New England* (New York, 1974).
11   I refer to the debate triggered off by Robert Brenner, "Agrarian Class Structure and Economic Development in Pre-Industrial Europe," *Past and Present*, no. 70 (Feb. 1976), pp. 30–75.
12   R. W. Fogel and S. Engerman, *Time on the Cross* (Boston, Mass., 1974); P. A. David *et al.*, *Reckoning with Slavery* (New York, 1976); H. Gutman, *Slavery and the Numbers Game* (Urbana, Ill., 1975).
13   Le Roy Ladurie, *Le territoire de l'historien*, i, p. 14 (my translation).
14   C. Geertz, "Deep Play: Notes on the Balinese Cock-Fight," in his *The Interpretation of Cultures* (New York, 1973).
15   D. P. Jordan, *The King's Trial: Louis XVI v. the French Revolution* (Berkeley, 1979); reviewed in *Publishers' Weekly*, 13 Aug. 1979.
16   N. Elias, *Uber den Prozess der Zivilisation* (Basel, 1939), trans. Edmund Jephcott as *The Civilizing Process*, 2 vols. (Oxford and New York, 1978).
17   T. Zeldin, *France, 1848–1945*, 2 vols. (Oxford History of Modern Europe ser., Oxford, 1973–7), trans. as *Histoire des passions françaises* (Paris, 1978). See also R. Mandrou, *Introduction à la France moderne, 1500–1640* (Paris, 1961).
18   P. Ariès, *L'homme devant la mort* (Paris, 1977).

19   J. Delumeau, *Vie économique et sociale de Rome dans la seconde moitié du XVIe siècle*, 2 vols. (Paris, 1957–9); *L'alun de Rome, XVe–XIXe siècle* (Paris, 1962); *Le catholicisme entre Luther et Voltaire* (Paris, 1971); *La mort des pays de Cocagne: comportements collectifs de la Renaissance à l'âge classique* (Paris, 1976); *L'histoire de la peur* (Paris, 1979).

20   P. Brown, *The World of Late Antiquity from Marcus Aurelius to Muhammad* (London, 1971).

21   G. Duby, *Le dimanche de Bouvines, 27 juillet 1214* (Paris, 1973).

22   C. Ginzburg, *Il formaggio e i vermi* (Turin, 1976).

23   E. Le Roy Ladurie, *Montaillou, village occitan de 1294 à 1324* (Paris, 1976), trans. B. Bray as *Montaillou: Cathars and Catholics in a French Village, 1294–1324* (London, 1978).

24   E. Le Roy Ladurie, *Le carnaval de Romans* (Paris, 1979).

25   C. M. Cipolla, *Faith, Reason and the Plague in Seventeenth-Century Tuscany* (Ithaca, N.Y., 1979).

26   E. J. Hobsbawm, *Primitive Rebels* (Manchester, 1959); E. J. Hobsbawm, *Bandits* (London, 1969); E. J. Hobsbawm and G. Rudé, *Captain Swing* (London, 1969).

27   E. P. Thompson, *Whigs and Hunters* (London, 1975).

28   R. Darnton, *The Business of the Enlightenment* (Cambridge, Mass., 1979).

29   N. Z. Davis, "Charivari, honneur et communauté à Lyon et à Genève au XVIIe siècle," in J. Le Goff and J.-C. Schmitt (eds), *Le charivari* (forthcoming).

30   K. V. Thomas, *Religion and the Decline of Magic* (London, 1971).

31   L. Stone, *The Family, Sex and Marriage in England, 1500–1800* (London, 1977).

32   S. Schama, *Patriots and Liberators: Revolution in the Netherlands, 1780–1813* (London, 1977).

33   G. R. Elton, *Star Chamber Stories* (London, 1958).

34   H. R. Trevor-Roper, *The Last Days of Hitler* (London, 1947).

35   H. R. Trevor-Roper, *A Hidden Life: The Enigma of Sir Edmund Backhouse* (London, 1976); US edn, *The Hermit of Peking* (New York, 1977).

36   A. J. A. Symons, *The Quest for Corvo* (London, 1934).

37   R. Cobb, *The Police and the People* (Oxford, 1970); R. Cobb, *Death in Paris* (Oxford, 1978).

38   C. Russell, *Parliaments and English Politics, 1621–29* (Oxford, 1979); J. P. Kenyon, *Stuart England* (London, 1978); see also the articles by John K. Gruenfelder, Paul Christianson, Clayton Roberts, Mark Kishlansky and James E. Farnell, in *Jl. Mod. Hist.*, xlix no. 4 (1977).

39   Le Roy Ladurie, *The Territory of the Historian*, p. 285.

40   H. R. Trevor-Roper, *History, Professional and Lay* (Univ. of Oxford, Inaugural Lecture, Oxford, 1957), p. 21.

41   C. Ginzburg, "Roots of a Scientific Paradigm," *Theory and Society*, vii (1979), p. 276.

42   Le Roy Ladurie, *The Territory of the Historian*, p. 111.

43   Darnton, "Intellectual and Cultural History," Appendix.

Chapter 19

Eric Hobsbawm

THE REVIVAL OF NARRATIVE

Some comments

L AWRENCE STONE BELIEVES that there is a revival of "narrative history" because there has been a decline in the history devoted to asking "the big *why* questions," the generalizing "scientific history." This in turn he thinks is due to disillusionment with the essentially economic determinist models of historical explanation, Marxist or otherwise, which have tended to dominate in the post-war years; to the declining ideological commitment of western intellectuals; contemporary experience which has reminded us that political action and decision can shape history; and the failure of "quantitative history" (another claimant to "scientific" status) to deliver the goods.[1] Two questions are involved in this argument, which I have brutally over-simplified: what has been happening in historiography, and how are these developments to be explained? Since it is common ground that in history "the facts" are always selected, shaped and perhaps distorted by the historian who observes them, there is an element of *parti pris*, not to say intellectual autobiography, in Stone's treatment of both questions, as in my comments on it.

I think we may accept that the twenty years following World War II saw a sharp decline in political and religious history, in the use of "ideas" as an explanation of history, and a remarkable turn to socioeconomic history and to historical explanation in terms of "social forces," as Momigliano noted as early as 1954.[2] Whether or not we call them "economic-determinist," these currents of historiography became influential, in some cases dominant, in the main western centers of historiography, not to mention, for other reasons, the eastern ones. We may also accept that in recent years there has been considerable diversification, and a marked revival of interest in themes which were rather more marginal to the main concerns of the historical outsiders who in those years became historical insiders, though such themes were never neglected. After all, Braudel wrote about Philip II as well as the Mediterranean, and Le Roy Ladurie's monograph on *Le carnaval de Romans* of 1580 is anticipated by a much briefer, but most perceptive, account of the same episode in his *Les paysans du Languedoc*.[3] If Marxist historians of the 1970s write entire books on the role of radical-national myths, such as the Welsh Madoc legend, Christopher Hill at least wrote a seminal article on the myth of the Norman Yoke in the early 1950s.[4] Still, there probably has been a change.

Whether this amounts to a revival of "narrative history" as defined by Stone (basically chronological ordering of the material in "a single coherent story, albeit with sub-plots" and a concentration "on man not circumstances") is difficult to determine, since Stone deliberately eschews a quantitative survey and concentrates on "a very tiny, but disproportionately prominent, section of the historical profession as a whole."[5] Nevertheless there is evidence that the old historical avant-garde no longer rejects, despises and combats the old-fashioned "history of events" or even biographical history, as some of it used to. Fernand Braudel himself has given unstinted praise to a notably traditional exercise in popular narrative history, Claude Manceron's attempt to present the origins of the French Revolution through a series of overlapping biographies of contemporaries, great and small.[6] On the other hand the historical minority whose supposedly changed interests Stone surveys, has not in fact changed over to practicing narrative history. If we leave aside deliberate historiographical conservatives or neo-conservatives such as the British "antiquarian empiricists," there is very little simple narrative history among the works Stone cites or refers to. For almost all of them the event, the individual, even the recapture of some mood or way of thinking of the past, are not ends in themselves, but the means of illuminating some wider question, which goes far beyond the particular story and its characters.

In short those historians who continue to believe in the possibility of generalizing about human societies and their development, continue to be interested in "the big *why* questions," though they may sometimes focus on different ones from those on which they concentrated twenty or thirty years ago. There is really no evidence that such historians – the ones Stone is mainly concerned with – have abandoned "the attempt to produce a coherent . . . explanation of change in the past."[7] Whether they (or we) also regard their attempt as "scientific" will no doubt depend on our definition of "science," but we need not enter this dispute about labels. Moreover I very much doubt whether such historians feel that they are "forced back upon the principle of indeterminacy,"[8] any more than Marx felt his writings about Louis Napoleon to be incompatible with the materialist conception of history.

No doubt there are historians who have abandoned such attempts, and certainly there are some who combat them, perhaps with a zeal increased by ideological commitment. (Whether or not Marxism has declined intellectually, it is hard to detect much muting of ideological controversy among western historians, though the participants and the specific issues may not be the same as twenty years ago.) Probably neo-conservative history has gained ground, at any rate in Britain, both in the form of the "young antiquarian empiricists" who "write detailed political narratives which implicitly deny that there is any deep-seated meaning to history except the accidental whims of fortune and personality,"[9] and in the form of works like Theodore Zeldin's (and Richard Cobb's) remarkable plunges into those strata of the past, to which "almost every aspect of traditionalist history" is irrelevant, including the answering of questions.[10] So, probably, has what might be called anti-intellectual leftist history. But this, except very tangentially, is not what Stone is concerned with.

How then are we to account for the shifts in historical subject-matter and interests, in so far as they have occurred or are occurring?

One element in them, it may be suggested, reflects the remarkable widening of the field of history in the past twenty years, typified by the rise of "social history," that shapeless container for everything from changes in human physique to symbol and ritual, and above all for the lives of *all* people from beggars to emperors. As Braudel has observed, this "histoire obscure de tout le monde" is "the history towards which, in different ways, all historiography tends at present."[11] This is not the place to speculate on the reasons for this vast extension of the field, which certainly does not necessarily conflict with the attempt to produce a coherent explanation of the past. It does, however, increase the technical difficulty of writing history. How are these complexities to be presented? It is not surprising that historians experiment with different forms of such presentation, including notably those that borrow from the ancient techniques of literature (which has made its own stabs at displaying *la comédie humaine*), and also from the modern audio-visual media, in which all but the oldest of us are saturated. What Stone calls the *pointilliste* techniques are, at least in part, attempts to solve such technical problems of presentation.

Such experiments are particularly necessary for that part of history which cannot be subsumed under "analysis" (or the rejection of analysis) and which Stone rather neglects, namely synthesis. The problem of fitting together the various manifestations of human thought and action at a specific period is neither new nor unrecognized. No history of Jacobean England is satisfactory which omits Bacon or treats him exclusively as a lawyer, a politician, or a figure in the history of science or of literature. Moreover even the most conventional historians recognize it, even when their solutions (a chapter or two on science, literature, education or whatnot appended to the main body of politico-institutional text) is unsatisfactory. Yet the wider the range of human activities which is accepted as the legitimate concern of the historian, the more clearly understood the necessity of establishing systematic connections between them, the greater the difficulty of achieving synthesis. This is, naturally, far more than a technical problem of presentation, yet it is that also. Even those who continue to be guided in their analysis by something like the "three-tiered hierarchical" model of base and superstructures which Stone rejects,[12] may find it an inadequate guide to presentation, though probably a less inadequate guide than straight chronological narrative.

Leaving aside the problems of presentation and synthesis, two more substantial reasons for a change may also be suggested. The first is the very success of the "new historians" in the post-war decades. This was achieved by a deliberate methodological simplification, the concentration on what were seen as the socio-economic base and determinants of history, at the expense of – sometimes, as in the French battle against the "history of events," in direct confrontation with – traditional narrative history. While there were some extreme economic reductionists, and others who dismissed people and events as negligible ripples on the *longue durée* of *structure* and *conjuncture*, such extremism was not universally shared either in *Annales*, or among the Marxists who – especially in Britain – never lost interest in events or culture, nor regarded "superstructure" as always and entirely dependent on "base." Yet the very triumph of works like those of Braudel, Goubert and Le Roy Ladurie, which Stone underlines, not only left "new" historians free to concentrate on those aspects of history hitherto deliberately set aside, but advanced their place on the "new historians" agenda. As an eminent *Annalist*, Le Goff, pointed out several years ago, "political history was gradually to return in force by borrowing the methods, spirit and theoretical approach of the very social sciences which had pushed it into the background."[13] The new history of men and minds, ideas and events may be seen as complementing rather than as supplanting the analysis of socio-economic structures and trends.

But once historians turn to such items on their agenda, they may prefer to approach their "coherent explanation of change in the past" as it were ecologically rather than as geologists. They may prefer to start with the study of a "situation" which embodies and exemplifies the stratified structure of a society but concentrates the mind on the complexities and interconnections of real history, rather than with the study of the structure itself, especially if for this they can rely partly on earlier work. This, as Stone recognizes, lies at the root of some historians' admiration for works like Clifford Geertz's "close reading" of a Balinese cock-fight.[14] It implies no necessary choice between monocausality and multicausality, and certainly no conflict between a model in which some historical determinants are seen as more powerful than others, and the recognition of interconnections, both vertical and horizontal. A "situation" may be a convenient point of departure, as in Ginzburg's study of popular ideology through the case of a single village atheist in the sixteenth century or a single group of Friulian peasants accused of witchcraft.[15] These topics could also be approached in other ways. It may be a necessary point of departure in other cases, as in Agulhon's beautiful study of how, at a particular time and place, French villagers converted from Catholic traditionalism to militant republicanism.[16] At all events, for certain purposes historians are likely to choose it as a starting-point.

There is thus no necessary contradiction between Le Roy Ladurie's *Le paysans du Languedoc* and his *Montaillou*, any more than between Duby's general works on feudal society and his monograph on the battle of Bouvines, or between E. P. Thompson's *The Making of the English Working Class* and his *Whigs and Hunters*.[17] There is nothing new in choosing to see the world via a microscope rather than a telescope. So long as we accept that we are studying the same cosmos, the choice between microcosm and macrocosm is a matter of selecting the appropriate technique. It is significant that more historians find the microscope useful at present, but this does not necessarily mean that they reject telescopes as out of date. Even the historians of *mentalité*, that vague catch-all term which Stone, perhaps wisely, does not try to clarify, do not exclusively or predominantly avoid the broad view. This at least is a lesson they have learned from the anthropologists.

Do these observations account for Stone's "broad cluster of changes in the nature of historical discourse"?[18] Perhaps not. However, they demonstrate that it is possible to explain much of what he surveys as the continuation of past historical enterprises by other means, instead of as proofs of their bankruptcy. One would not wish to deny that some historians regard them as bankrupt or undesirable and wish to change their discourse in consequence, for various reasons, some of them intellectually dubious, some to be taken seriously. Clearly some historians have shifted from "circumstances" to "men" (including women), or have discovered that a simple base/superstructure model and economic history are not enough, or –

since the pay-off from such approaches has been very substantial – are no longer enough. Some may well have convinced themselves that there is an incompatibility between their "scientific" and "literary" functions. But it is not necessary to analyze the present fashions in history entirely as a rejection of the past, and in so far as they cannot be entirely analyzed in such terms, it will not do.

We are all anxious to discover where historians are going. Stone's essay is to be welcomed as an attempt to do so. Nevertheless it is not satisfactory. In spite of his disclaimer the essay does combine the charting of "observed changes in historical fashion" with "value judgements about what are good, and what are less good, modes of historical writing,"[19] especially about the latter. I think this is a pity, not because I happen to disagree with him about "the principle of indeterminacy" and historical generalization, but because, if the argument is wrong, a diagnosis of the "changes in historical discourse" made in terms of this argument must also be inadequate. One is tempted, like the mythical Irishman, asked by the traveler for the way to Ballynahinch, to stop, ponder, and reply: "If I were you, I wouldn't start from here at all."

Notes

1   Lawrence Stone, "The Revival of Narrative: Reflections on a New Old History," *Past and Present*, no. 85 (Nov. 1979), pp. 3–24.
2   Arnaldo Momigliano, "A Hundred Years after Ranke," in his *Studies in Historiography* (London, 1966), pp. 108–9.
3   Fernand Braudel, *La Méditerranée et le monde méditerranéen à l'époque de Philippe II* (Paris, 1960); Emmanuel Le Roy Ladurie, *Le carnaval de Romans* (Paris, 1979); Emmanuel Le Roy Ladurie, *Les paysans du Languedoc*, 2 vols. (Paris, 1966), i, pp. 394–9, 505–6.
4   Christopher Hill, "The Norman Yoke," in John Saville (ed.), *Democracy and the Labour Movement: Essays in Honour of Dona Torr* (London, 1954), repr. in Christopher Hill, *Puritanism and Revolution: Studies in Interpretation of the English Revolution of the 17th Century* (London, 1958), pp. 50–122.
5   Stone, op. cit., pp. 3, 4.
6   Fernand Braudel, "Une parfaite réussite" [review of Claude Manceron, *La Révolution qui lève, 1785–1787* (Paris, 1979)], *L'histoire*, no. 21 (1980), pp. 108–9.
7   Stone, op. cit., p. 19.
8   Ibid., p. 13.
9   Ibid., p. 20.
10   Theodore Zeldin, *France, 1848–1945*, 2 vols. (Oxford History of Modern Europe ser., Oxford, 1973–7), trans. as *Histoire des passions françaises* (Paris, 1978); Richard Cobb, *Death in Paris* (Oxford, 1978).
11   Braudel, "Une parfaite réussite," p. 109.
12   Stone, op. cit., pp. 7–8.
13   J. Le Goff, "Is Politics Still the Backbone of History?," in Felix Gilbert and Stephen R. Graubard (eds), *Historical Studies Today* (New York, 1972), p. 340.
14   Clifford Geertz, "Deep Play: Notes on the Balinese Cock-Fight," in his *The Interpretation of Cultures* (New York, 1973).
15   Carlo Ginzburg, *Il formaggio e i vermi* (Turin, 1976); Carlo Ginzburg, *I benandanti: ricerche sulla stregoneria e sui culti agrari tra Cinquecento e Seicento* (Turin, 1966).

16   Maurice Agulhon, *La République au village* (Paris, 1970).
17   Le Roy Ladurie, *Les paysans du Languedoc*; Emmanuel Le Roy Ladurie, *Montaillou, village occitan de 1294 à 1324* (Paris, 1976), trans. B. Bray as *Montaillou: Cathars and Catholics in a French Village, 1294–1324* (London, 1978); Georges Duby, *Le dimanche de Bouvines, 27 juillet 1214* (Paris, 1973); E. P. Thompson, *The Making of the English Working Class* (London, 1963); E. P. Thompson, *Whigs and Hunters* (London, 1975).
18   Stone, op. cit., p. 23.
19   Ibid., p. 4.

Chapter 20

Peter Burke

HISTORY OF EVENTS AND THE REVIVAL OF NARRATIVE

Narrative versus structure

LIKE HISTORY, HISTORIOGRAPHY seems to repeat itself — with variations.[1] Long before our own time, in the age of the Enlightenment, the assumption that written history should be a narrative of events was already under attack. The attackers included Voltaire and the Scottish social theorist John Millar, who wrote of the "surface of events which engages the attention of the vulgar historian." From this point of view, the so-called "Copernican Revolution" in historiography led by Leopold von Ranke in the early nineteenth century looks rather more like a counter-revolution, in the sense that it brought events back to the center of the stage.[2]

A second attack on the history of events was launched in the early twentieth century. In Britain, Lewis Namier and R. H. Tawney, who agreed on little else, suggested at much the same time that the historian should analyze structures rather than narrate events. In France, the rejection of what was pejoratively called "event history" (histoire événementielle) in favor of the history of structures was a major plank in the platform of the so-called "Annales school," from Lucien Febvre to Fernand Braudel, who regarded events, like Millar, as the surface of the ocean of history, significant only for what they might reveal of the deeper currents.[3] If popular history remained faithful to the narrative tradition, academic history became increasingly concerned with problems and with structures. The French philosopher Paul Ricoeur is surely right to speak of the "eclipse" of historical narrative in our time.[4]

Ricoeur goes on to argue that all written history, including the so-called "structural" history associated with Braudel, necessarily takes some kind of narrative form. In a similar way, Jean-François Lyotard has described certain interpretations of history, notably that of the Marxists, as "grand narratives."[5] The problem with such characterizations, to my mind at least, is that they dilute the concept of narrative until it is in danger of becoming indistinguishable from description and analysis.

I shall not pursue this argument here, however, preferring to concentrate on the more concrete question of the differences in what one might call the degree of narrativity between some contemporary works of history and others. For some years now there have been signs that historical narrative in a fairly strict sense is making another comeback. Even some of the historians associated with *Annales* have been moving in this direction – Georges Duby, for example, who has published a study of the battle of Bouvines, and Emmanuel Le Roy Ladurie, whose *Carnival* deals with the events which took place in the small town of Romans during 1579 and 1580.[6] The explicit attitude of these two historians is not very far from Braudel's. Duby and Le Roy Ladurie focus on particular events not for their own sake but for what they reveal about the culture in which they took place. All the same, the fact that they devote whole books to particular events suggests a certain distance from Braudel's position, and in any case Le Roy Ladurie has discussed elsewhere the importance of what he calls the "creative event" (*événement matrice*) which destroys traditional structures and replaces them with new ones.[7]

The new trend, which has begun to affect other disciplines, notably social anthropology, was discussed by the British historian Lawrence Stone in an article on "The Revival of Narrative" which has attracted much attention.[8] Stone claimed to be doing no more than "trying to chart observed changes in historical fashion" rather than making value judgments. In this respect, some of the best-known historical works which appeared in the 1980s confirmed his observations. Simon Schama's *Citizens*, for example, a study of the French Revolution published in 1989 and describing itself as a return "to the form of the nineteenth-century chronicles."[9]

All the same it is difficult not to sense Stone's regret at what he calls "the shift . . . from the analytical to the descriptive mode" of historical writing. The title of this article as well as its arguments has been influential. It has contributed to making historical narrative a matter for debate.[10]

More exactly, historical narrative has become a matter for at least two debates, which have been taking place independently, despite the relevance of each to the other. To link the two is a major aim of this chapter.[11] In the first place, there is the well-known and long-standing campaign opposing those who assert, like Braudel, that historians should take structures more seriously than events, and those who continue to believe that the historian's job is to tell a story. In this campaign, both sides are now entrenched in their positions, but each has made some important points at the expense of the other.[12]

On one side, the structural historians have shown that traditional narrative passes over important aspects of the past which it is simply unable to accommodate, from the economic and social framework to the experience and modes of thought of ordinary people.[13] In other words, narrative is no more innocent in historiography than it is in fiction. In the case of a narrative of political events, it is difficult to avoid emphasizing the deeds and decisions of the leaders, which furnish a clear story line, at the expense of the factors which escaped their control. As for collective entities – Germany, the Church, the Conservative Party, the People, and so on – the narrative historian is forced to choose between omitting them altogether or personifying them, and I would agree with Huizinga that personification is a figure of speech which historians should try to avoid.[14] It blurs distinctions between leaders and followers, and encourages literal-minded readers to assume the consensus of groups who were often in conflict.

In the case of military history in particular, John Keegan has pointed out that the traditional battle narrative is misleading in its "high focus on leadership" and its "reduction of soldiers to pawns," and needs to be abandoned.[15] The difficulty of doing so may be illustrated by the case of Cornelius Ryan's well-known study of D-Day.[16] Ryan set out to write about the soldier's war rather than that of the generals. His history is an extension of his work as a war correspondent: its sources are mainly oral. His book conveys very well the "feel" of battle on both sides. It is vivid and dramatic – indeed, like a classical drama, it is organized around the three "unities" of place (Normandy), time (6 June 1944) and action. On the other hand, the book is fragmented into discrete episodes. The experiences of the different participants do not cohere. The only way to make them cohere seems to be to impose a schema derived from "above" and thus to return to the war of the generals from which the author was trying to escape. Ryan's book illustrates the problem more clearly than most, but the problem is not his alone. This kind of bias may be inherent in narrative organization.

The supporters of narrative, on the other hand, have pointed out that the analysis of structures is static and so in a sense unhistorical. To take the most famous example of structural history in our time, although Braudel's *Mediterranean* (1949) finds room for events as well as structures, it has often been noted that the author does little to suggest what links there might be between the three time-scales with which he is concerned; the long, the medium and the short term. In any case, Braudel's *Mediterranean* is not an extreme example of structural history.[17] Despite his remarks in the preface about the superficiality of events, he went on to devote several hundred pages to them in the third part of his study. Braudel's followers, however, have tended to shrink his project (and not only in the geographical sense) in the course of imitating it. The now classic format of a regional study in the *Annales* manner includes a division into two parts, *structure* and *conjoncture* (in other words, general trends), with little space for events in the strict sense.

Historians in these two camps, structural and narrative, differ not only in the choice of what they consider significant in the past, but also in their preferred modes of historical explanation. Traditional narrative historians tend – and this is not exactly contingent – to couch their explanations in terms of individual character and intention; explanations of the type "orders arrived late from Madrid because Philip II could not make up his mind what to do," in other words, as philosophers would say, "the window broke because Brown threw a stone at it." Structural historians, on the other hand, prefer explanations which take the form "the window broke because the glass was brittle," or (to quote Braudel's famous example) "orders arrived late from Madrid because sixteenth-century ships took several weeks to cross the Mediterranean." As Stone points out, the so-called revival of narrative has a great deal to do with an increasing distrust of the second mode of historical explanation, often criticized as reductionist and determinist. Once again, Schama's recent book makes a good example of the trend. The author explains that he has "chosen to present these arguments in the form of a narrative" on the grounds that the French Revolution was "much more the product of human agency than structural conditioning."[18]

This protracted trench warfare between narrative and structural historians has gone on far too long. Some sense of the price of the conflict, the loss of potential historical understanding which it involves, may be felt by comparing two studies of nineteenth-century India which appeared in 1978 and focus on what used to be called the "Indian Mutiny" of 1857, and is now known as the "Great Rebellion."[19] Christopher Hibbert produced a traditional narrative, set-piece history in the grand manner, with chapters entitled "Mutiny at Meerut," "The Mutiny Spreads," "The Siege of Lucknow," "The Assault," and so on. His book is colorful, indeed gripping, but it is also superficial in the sense of failing to give the reader much idea of why the events took place (perhaps because it is written from the point of view of the British, who were themselves taken by surprise). On the other hand, Eric Stokes offers a careful analysis of the geography and sociology of the revolt, its regional variations and its local contexts, but draws back from a final synthesis. If one reads the two books one immediately after each other, one may be haunted, as I was, by the ghost of a potential third book, which might integrate narrative and analysis and relate local events more closely to structural changes in society.

It is time to investigate the possibility of a way of escaping this confrontation between narrators and analysts. One might begin by criticizing both sides for a false assumption which they have in common, the assumption that distinguishing events from structures is a simple matter. We tend to use the term "event" rather loosely to refer not only to happenings which take a few hours, like the battle of Waterloo, but also to occurrences like the French Revolution, a process spread over a number of years. It may be useful to employ the terms "event" and "structure" to refer to the two extremes of a whole spectrum of possibilities, but we should not forget the existence of the middle of the spectrum. The reasons for the late arrival of orders from Madrid need not be limited to the structure of communications in the Mediterranean or Philip II's failure to make up his mind on a particular occasion. The king may have been chronically indecisive, and the structure of government by council may have slowed down the decision-making process still further.

It follows from this vagueness of definition that we should do as Mark Phillips has suggested and "think of the varieties of narrative and non-narrative modes as existing along a continuum."[20] Nor should we forget to ask about the relation between events and structures. Working in this central area, it may be possible to go beyond the two opposing positions, to reach a synthesis.

Traditional narrative versus modern narrative

To this synthesis, the opinions expressed in the second debate may well have a useful contribution to make. This second debate began in the United States in the 1960s, and it has not yet been taken as seriously as it deserves by historians in other parts of the world, perhaps because it seems "merely" literary. It is not concerned with the question, whether or not to write narrative, but with the problem of what kind of narrative to write. The film historian Siegfried Kracauer seems to have been the first to suggest that modern fiction, more especially the "decomposition of temporal continuity" in Joyce, Proust and Virginia Woolf, offers a challenge and an opportunity to historical narrators.[21] A still more clear-cut example of this decomposition, incidentally, is Aldous Huxley's *Eyeless in Gaza* (1936), a novel composed of short dated entries over the period 1902–34 in an order which, whatever its logic, is determinedly non-chronological.

Hayden White attracted more attention than Kracauer did when he accused the historical profession of neglecting the literary insights of its own age (including a sense of discontinuity between events in the outside world and their representation in narrative form) and of continuing to live in the nineteenth century, the great age of literary "realism."[22] In similar vein, Lionel Gossman has complained that "it is not easy for us today to see who is, as a writer, the Joyce or the Kafka of modern historiography."[23] Perhaps. All the same, the historian Golo Mann seems to have learned something from the narrative practice of his novelist father. It is not entirely fanciful to compare Golo Mann's account of the thoughts of the ageing Wallenstein with the celebrated chapter in *Lotte in Weimar* evoking Goethe's stream of consciousness, apparently an attempt to go one better than Joyce. In his study, which he calls "an all too true novel," Golo Mann follows the rules of historical evidence and makes it clear that he is presenting a hypothetical reconstruction. Unlike most novelists, he does not claim to read his hero's mind, only his letters.[24]

In contrast to White and Gossman, I am not arguing that historians are obliged to engage in literary experiments simply because they live in the twentieth century, or to imitate particular writers because their techniques are revolutionary. The point of looking for new literary forms is surely the awareness that the old forms are inadequate for one's purposes.

Some innovations are probably best avoided by historians. In this group I would include the invention of someone's stream of consciousness, useful as it might be, for the same reasons that have led historians to reject the famous classical device of the invented speech. Other experiments, however, inspired by a wider range of modern writers than have yet been mentioned, may offer solutions to problems with which historians have long been wrestling, three problems in particular.

In the first place, it might be possible to make civil wars and other conflicts more intelligible by following the model of the novelists who tell their stories from more than one viewpoint. It is odd that this device, so effective in the hands of Huxley, William Faulkner, in *The Sound and the Fury* (1931), and Lawrence Durrell, in *The Alexandria Quartet* (1957–60) – not to mention the epistolary novels of the eighteenth century – has not been taken more seriously by historians, though it might be useful to modify it to deal with collective viewpoints as well as individual ones. Such a device would allow an interpretation of conflict in terms of a conflict of interpretations. To allow the "varied and opposing voices" of the dead to be heard again, the historian needs, like the novelist, to practice heteroglossia.[25]

Curiously enough, just as this essay was going to press, a historical work of this kind made its appearance. Richard Price presents his study of eighteenth-century Surinam in the form of a narrative with four "voices" (symbolized by four type-faces); that of the black slaves (as transmitted by their descendants, the Saramaka); that of the Dutch administrators; that of the Moravian missionaries; and finally that of the historian himself.[26] The object of the exercise is precisely to show as well as to state the differences in viewpoint between past and present, church and state, black and white, the misunderstandings and the struggle to impose particular definitions of the situation. It will be hard to imitate this *tour de force* of historical reconstruction, but Price deserves to inspire a whole shelf of studies.

In the second place, more and more historians are coming to realize that their work does not reproduce "what actually happened" so much as represent it from a particular point of view. To communicate this awareness to readers of history, traditional forms of narrative are inadequate. Historical narrators need to find a way of making themselves visible in their narrative, not out of self-indulgence but as a warning to the reader that they are not omniscient or impartial and that other interpretations besides theirs are possible.[27] In a remarkable piece of self-criticism, Golo Mann has argued that a historian needs "to try to do two different things simultaneously," to "swim with the stream of events" and to "analyze these events from the position of a later, better-informed observer," combining the two methods "so as to yield a semblance of homogeneity without the narrative falling apart."[28]

Here again Price's new book offers a possible solution to the problem by labeling his own contribution that of one "voice" among others, Alternative solutions are also worth considering. Literary theorists have lately been discussing the fictional device of "the unreliable first-person narrator."[29] Such a device may be of some use to historians too, provided that the unreliability is made manifest. Again, Hayden White has suggested that historical narratives follow four basic plots: comedy, tragedy, satire and romance. Ranke, for example, chose (consciously or unconsciously) to write history "emplotted as comedy," in other words, following a "ternary movement . . . from a condition of apparent peace, through the revelation of conflict, to the resolution of the conflict in the establishment of a genuinely peaceful social order."[30] If the way in which a narrative ends helps determine the reader's interpretation, then it might be worth following the example of certain novelists, such as John Fowles, and providing alternative endings. A narrative history of World War II, for example, will give one impression if the story ends at Versailles in 1919, another if the narrative is extended to 1933 or 1939. Alternative closures thus make the work more "open," in the sense of encouraging readers to reach their own conclusions.[31]

In the third place – and this is the main theme of this chapter – a new kind of narrative might cope better than the old with the demands of the structural historians, while giving a better sense of the flow of time than their analyses generally do.

Thickening narratives

A few years ago, the anthropologist Clifford Geertz coined the term "thick description" for a technique which interprets an alien culture through the precise and concrete description of particular practices or events, in his case, the description of cock-fights in Bali.[32] Like description, narrative might be characterized as more or less "thin" or "thick." At the thin end of the spectrum we have the bare remark in a volume of annals like the Anglo-Saxon Chronicle that "In this year Ceolwulf was deprived of his kingdom." At the other end we find stories (all too rare so far), which have been deliberately constructed to bear a heavy weight of interpretation.

The problem I should like to discuss here is that of making a narrative thick enough to deal not only with the sequence of events and the conscious intentions of the actors in these events, but also with structures – institutions, modes of thought, and so on – whether these structures act as a brake on events or as an accelerator. What would such a narrative be like?

These questions, though concerned with rhetoric, are not themselves rhetorical. It is possible to discuss them on the basis of texts, narratives produced either by novelists or by historians. It is not difficult to find historical novels which grapple with these problems. One might start with *War and Peace*, since Tolstoy may be said to have shared Braudel's view of the futility of events, but in fact many famous novels are concerned with major structural changes in a particular society, viewing them in terms of their impact on the lives of a few individuals. A distinguished example from outside western culture is Shimazaki Toson's *Before the Dawn* (1932–6).[33] The "dawn" of the title is the modernization (industrialization, westernization) of Japan, and the book deals with the years immediately before and after the imperial restoration of 1868, when it was far from clear which path the country was going to follow. The novel shows in vivid detail how "The effects of the opening of Japan to the world were making themselves felt in the lives of each individual."[34] To do this the author chooses an individual, Aoyama Hanzo, who is the keeper of a post-house in a village on the main road between Kyoto and Tokyo. His job keeps Hanzo in touch with events, but he does not merely observe them. He is a member of the National Learning movement, committed to an authentically Japanese solution to Japan's problems. The plot of the novel is to a large extent the story of the impact of social change on an individual and his family, a point emphasized by Toson's interruption of his story from time to time to narrate the main events in Japanese history from 1853 to 1886.

It is likely that historians can learn something from the narrative techniques of such novelists as Tolstoy or Shimazaki Toson, but not enough to solve all their literary problems. Since historians are not free to invent their characters or even the words and thoughts of their characters, they are unlikely to be able to condense the problems of an epoch into a story about a family, as novelists have often done. One might have hoped that the so-called "non-fiction novel," might have had something to offer historians, from Truman Capote's *In Cold Blood* (1965) to Thomas Keneally's *Schindler's Ark* (1982), which claims "to use the texture and devices of a novel to tell a true story." However, these authors do not grapple with the problem of structures. It looks as if historians have to develop their own "fictional techniques" for their "factual works."[35]

Fortunately, the authors of a few recent works of history have also reflected on problems like these and their studies sketch an answer, or more exactly several answers, of which it may be useful to distinguish four. One model is well on the way to becoming fashionable, while the other three are represented by little more than one book each.

The first answer might be described as "micronarrative" (along the lines of the new term "microhistory"). It is the telling of a story about ordinary people in their local setting. There is a sense in which this technique is commonplace among historical novelists, and has been since the age of Scott and Manzoni, whose *Betrothed* (1827) was attacked at the time (in the way that history from below and microhistory have been attacked more recently), for choosing as his subject "the miserable chronicle of an obscure village."[36]

It was only quite recently, however, that historians adopted the micronarrative. Well-known recent examples include Carlo Cipolla's story of the impact of the plague of 1630 on the city of Prato in Tuscany, and Natalie Davis's tale of Martin Guerre, a sixteenth-century prodigal son who returned to his home in the south of France to find that his place at the farm — and in his wife's bed as well — had been taken by an intruder claiming to be Martin himself.[37]

The reduction in scale does not thicken a narrative by itself. The point is that social historians have turned to narrative as a means of illuminating structures — attitudes to the plague and institutions for fighting it in the case of Carlo Cipolla, the structure of the southern French peasant family in the case of Natalie Davis, and so on. More exactly, what Natalie Davis wanted to do was to describe not so much the structures themselves as "the peasants' hopes and feelings; the ways in which they experienced the relation between husband and wife, parent and child; the ways in which they experienced the constraints and possibilities in their lives."[38] The book can be read simply as a good story, and a vivid evocation of a few individuals from the past, but the author does make deliberate and repeated references to the values of the society. Discussing, for example, why Martin's wife Bertrande recognized the intruder as her husband, Davis comments on the status of women in French rural society and on their sense of honor, reconstructing the constraints within which they maneuvered.

On the other hand, the comments are deliberately unobtrusive. As the author explains, "I . . . chose to advance my arguments . . . as much by the ordering of narrative, choice of detail, literary voice and metaphor as by topical analysis." The goal was that of "embedding this story in the values and habits of sixteenth-century French village life and law, to use them to help understand central elements in the story and to use the story to comment back on them."[39] The story of Martin may be regarded as a "social drama" in the sense in which anthropologists use the term; an event which reveals latent conflicts and thus illuminates social structures.[40]

Micronarrative seems to be here to stay; more and more historians are turning to this form. All the same, it would be a mistake to regard it as a panacea. It does not provide a solution to all the problems outlined earlier, and it generates problems of its own, notably that of linking microhistory to macrohistory, local details to general trends. It is because it tackles this major problem directly that I regard Spence's *Gate of Heavenly Peace* as an exemplary book.

Jonathan Spence is a historian of China who has long been interested in experiments in literary form. One of his first books was a biography of the emperor K'ang-Hsi, or rather a portrait of the emperor — indeed, a kind of self-portrait, an attempt to explore K'ang-Hsi's mind by making a sort of mosaic or montage out of the personal remarks to be found scattered among official documents, arranging them under headings such as "sons," "ruling," or "growing old." The effect is not unlike a Chinese *Memoirs of Hadrian*. It is difficult to think of a study which better deserves the description "history from above" than the self-portrait of the emperor, but Spence followed it with a moving essay in history from below. *The Death of Woman Wang* is a piece of microhistory in the manner of Cipolla or Davis, with four stories told, or images depicted, to reveal conditions in Shantung province in the troubled years of the later seventeenth century. More recently, in *The Memory Palace of Matteo Ricci*, Spence organized this account of the famous Jesuit missionary to China around a number of visual images, at the expense of chronological sequence, producing an effect reminiscent of Huxley's *Eyeless in Gaza*.

The Gate of Heavenly Peace, on the other hand, looks more like a piece of conventional history, an account of the origins and development of the Chinese Revolution from 1895 to 1980.[41] Once more, however, the author's interest in biography and in historical snapshots asserts itself and his book is built round a small number of individuals, notably the scholar Kang Youwei, the soldier- academic Shen Congwen and the writers Lu Xun and Ding Ling. These individuals did not play a leading part in the events of the revolution. From this point of view they may be compared with what the Hungarian critic Georg Lukács has called the "mediocre hero" in the novels of Sir Walter Scott; a hero whose ordinariness allows the reader to see the life and the social conflicts of the time more clearly.[42] In Spence's case the protagonists were selected because, as the author suggests, they "described their hopes and sorrows with particular sensitivity" and also because their personal experiences "help to define the nature of the times through which they lived." They are viewed as passive rather than active. Indeed, the author speaks of "the intrusions of outside events" on his characters.[43] His concern with different individuals implies an interest in multiple viewpoints or multivocality, but – in contrast to Price's book, discussed above – this multivocality remains below the surface of the story.

Presenting the history of China in this way does raise problems. The crosscutting from one individual to another risks confusing the reader, and so does the shift back and forth between what might be called "public" time, the time of events like the Long March or the 1949 Revolution, and the "private" time of the main characters. On the other hand, Spence does communicate in a vivid and moving way the experience of living (or indeed of failing to live) through these turbulent years. Among his most memorable passages are his account of a child's-eye view of the 1911 revolution, as remembered by Shen Congwen; Lu Xun's reaction to the massacre of student demonstrators in Beijing in 1926; and the official attacks on Ding Ling in 1957, following the suppression of the "Hundred Flowers" Movement.

There may be other ways of relating structure to events more closely than historians generally do. A possible method is to write history backwards, as B. H. Sumner did in his *Survey of Russian History* (organized by topics) or Norman Davies in his recent history of Poland, *Heart of Europe* (1984), a narrative which focuses on what the author calls "the past in Poland's present."[44] It begins with "The Legacy of Humiliation: Poland since the Second World War" and moves back through "The Legacy of Defeat," "The Legacy of Disenchantment" (1914–39), "The Legacy of Spiritual Mastery" (1795–1918), and so on. On each occasion the author implies that it is impossible to make sense of the events narrated in one chapter without knowing what preceded them.

This form of organization has its difficulties, most obviously the problem that even though the chapters are arranged in reverse order, each chapter has to be read forwards. The great advantage of the experiment, on the other hand, is to allow, or even force the reader to feel the pressure of the past on individuals and groups (the pressure of structures, or of events which have congealed, or as Ricoeur would say, "sedimented" into structures). Davies does not exploit this advantage as much as he might. He does not make any serious effort to relate each chapter to the one which comes "after" it. It is difficult to imagine his backward-walking approach becoming fashionable in the manner of microhistory. All the same, this is a form of narrative well worth taking seriously.

A fourth kind of analysis of the relation between structures and events can be found in the work of an American social anthropologist, yet it will complete the circle by bringing us back to *Annales*. The anthropologist is Marshall Sahlins, who works on Hawaii and Fiji, is extremely interested in modern French thought (from Saussure to Braudel, from Bourdieu to Lévi-Strauss), but takes the event more seriously than any of these thinkers do.[45] In his studies of encounters between cultures in the Pacific, Sahlins makes two different but complementary points.

In the first place, he suggests that events (notably Cook's arrival in Hawaii in 1778) "bear distinctive cultural signatures," that they are "ordered by culture," in the sense that the concepts and categories of a particular culture shape the ways in which its members perceive and interpret whatever happens in their time. The Hawaiians, for example, perceived Captain Cook as a manifestation of their god Lono because he was obviously powerful and because he arrived at the time of year associated with appearances of the god. The event can therefore be studied (as Braudel suggested) as a kind of litmus paper which reveals the structures of the culture.

However, Sahlins also argues (contrary to Braudel) that there is a dialectical relationship between events and structures. Categories are put at risk every time they are used to interpret the changing world. In the process of incorporating events, "the culture is reordered." The end of the *tabu* system, for example, was one of the structural consequences of contact with the British. So was the rise of intercontinental trade. It is true in more than one sense that Cook did not leave Hawaii as he had found it. Sahlins has told a story with a moral, or perhaps with two morals. The moral for "structuralists" is that they should recognize the power of "events," their place in the process of "structuration." Supporters of narrative, on the other hand, are encouraged to examine the relation between events and the culture in which they occur. Sahlins has gone beyond Braudel's famous juxtaposition of events and structures. Indeed, he has virtually resolved, or dissolved, the binary opposition between these two categories.

To sum up. I have tried to argue that historians such as Tawney and Namier, Febvre and Braudel were justified in their rebellion against a traditional form of historical narrative which was ill-suited to the structural history which they considered important. Historical writing was enormously enriched by the expansion of its subject-matter, and by the ideal of "total history." However, many scholars now think that historical writing has also been impoverished by the abandonment of narrative, and a search is under way for new forms of narrative which will be appropriate to the new stories historians would like to tell. These new forms include micronarrative, backward narrative, and stories which move back and forth between public and private worlds or present the same events from multiple points of view.

It they are looking for models of narratives which juxtapose the structures of ordinary life to extraordinary events, and the view from below to the view from above, historians might be well advised to turn to twentieth-century fiction, including the cinema (the films of Kurosawa, for example, or Pontecorvo, of Jancsó). It may be significant that one of the most interesting discussions of historical narrative is the work of a historian of the cinema (the piece by Kracauer, already cited). The device of multiple viewpoints is central to Kurosawa's *Rashomon*.[46] It is implicit in Jancsó's *The Red and the White*, a narrative of the Russian civil war in which the two sides take turns to capture the same village.

As for Pontecorvo, it might be said that he has made the historical process itself the subject of his films, rather than merely telling a story about individuals in historical costume.[47] It is interesting to see that Jonathan Spence uses the language of "montage," and that *The Return of Martin Guerre* appeared more or less simultaneously as history and as film, after Natalie Davis and Daniel Vigne worked together on the subject.[48] Flashbacks, cross-cutting, and the alteration of scene and story; these are cinematic (or indeed literary) techniques which may be used in a superficial way, to dazzle rather than to illuminate, but they may also help historians in their difficult task of revealing the relationship between events and structures and presenting multiple viewpoints. Developments of this kind, if they continue, may have a claim to be regarded as no mere "revival" of narrative, as Stone called it, but as a form of regeneration.

Notes

1   The paper originated as a lecture and the present version owes a great deal to the comments of various listeners, from Cambridge to Campinas and from Tel Aviv to Tokyo. My particular thanks to Carlo Ginzburg, Michael Holly, Ian Kershaw, Dominick LaCapra and Mark Phillips.
2   I try to support this argument in "Ranke the Reactionary," *Syracuse Scholar* 9 (1988), pp. 25–30.
3   F. Braudel, *The Mediterranean*, 2nd edn rev., tr. S. Reynolds (London, 1972–3), preface.
4   P. Ricoeur, *Time and Narrative*, tr. K. McLaughlin and D. Dellauer (3 vols, Chicago, 1984–8) 1, pp. 138ff.
5   J.-F. Lyotard, *La condition post-moderne* (Paris, 1979); *The Post-Modern Condition*, tr. C. Bennington and B. Macrumi (Manchester, 1984).
6   G. Duby, *The Legend of Bouvines*, tr. C. Tihanyi (Cambridge, 1990); E. Le Roy Ladurie, *Carnival*, tr. M. Fenney (London, 1980).
7   E. Le Roy Ladurie, "Event and Long-Term in Social History," tr. B. and S. Reynolds in his *Territory of the Historian* (Hassocks, 1979), pp. 111–32.
8   L. Stone, "The Revival of Narrative," *Past and Present* 85 (1979), pp. 3–24; cf. E. J. Hobsbawm, "Some Comments," *Past and Present* 86 (1980), pp. 3–8. Cf. J. Boon, *The Anthropological Romance of Bali* (Cambridge, 1977) and E. M. Bruner, "Ethnography as Narrative," in *The Anthropology of Experience*, V. Turner and E. Bruner (eds) (Urbana and Chicago, 1986), Chapter 6.
9   S. Schama, *Citizens* (New York, 1989), p. xv.
10 Cf. B. Bailyn, "The Challenge of Modern Historiography," *American Historical Review* 87 (1982), pp. 1–24.

11   Cf. Ricoeur; M. Phillips, "On Historiography and Narrative," *University of Toronto Quarterly* 53 (1983–4), pp. 149–65; and H. Kellner, *Language and Historical Representation* (Madison, 1989), esp. Chapter 12.

12   For a discussion from different points of view see *Theorie und Erzählung in der Geschichte*, J. Kocka and T. Nipperdey (eds) (Munich, 1979).

13   The last point is well made in E. Auerbach, *Mimesis*, tr. W. R. Trask (Princeton, 1953), Chapters 2 and 3 (discussing Tacitus and Ammianus Marcellinus).

14   J. Huizinga, "Two Wrestlers with the Angel" in his *Men and Ideas*, tr. J. S. Holmes and H. van Marle (London, 1960). Contrast the defense of personification in Kellner (esp. Chapter 5 on Michelet).

15   J. Keegan, *The Face of Battle* (1976: Harmondsworth, 1978 edn) pp. 61ff.

16   C. Ryan, *The Longest Day* (London, 1959).

17   Ricoeur (1983) goes so far as to claim that it is a historical narrative with a "quasi-plot" (pp. 298ff).

18   Schama (1989), p. xv.

19   C. Hibbert, *The Great Mutiny* (London, 1978); E. Stokes, *The Peasant and the Raj* (Cambridge, 1978).

20   Phillips, "On Historiography" (1983–4), p. 157.

21   S. Kracauer, *History: the Last Things before the Last* (New York, 1969), pp. 178ff.

22   H. V. White, "The Burden of History," *History and Theory* 5 (1966), reprinted in his *Tropics of Discourse* (Baltimore, 1983), pp. 27–50. For a philosophical defense of the continuity between narratives and the events they relate, see D. Carr, "Narrative and the Real World: an Argument for Continuity," *History and Theory* 25 (1986), pp. 117–31.

23   L. Gossman, "History and Literature," in *The Writing of History*, R. H. Canary and H. Kozicki (eds) (Madison, 1978), pp. 3–39.

24   G. Mann, *Wallenstein* (Frankfurt, 1971), pp. 984ff.; 993ff.; T. Mann, *Lotte in Weimar* (1939), Chapter 7. Cf. G. Mann, "Plädoyer für die historische Erzählung", 0in Kocka and Nipperdey (1979), pp. 40–56, especially his claim that historical narrative does not exclude awareness of theory.

25   Cf. G. Wilson, "Plots and Motives in Japan's Meiji Restoration," *Comparative Studies in Society and History* 25 (1983), pp. 407–27 which makes use of the terminology of Hayden White but is essentially concerned with the multiplicity of actors' viewpoints. N. Hampson, *The Life and Opinions of Maximilian Robespierre* (London, 1976) offers a dialog between diverse modern interpretations of the French Revolution.

26   R. Price, *Alabi's World* (Baltimore, 1990).

27   The problem was already discussed by Thierry and Michelet. See G. Pomata, "Overt and Covert Narrators in Nineteenth-Century Historiography," *History Workshop* 27 (1989), pp. 1–17.

28   Foreword to the English translation of his *Wallenstein* by C. Kessler (London, 1976). Mann confesses that "the first approach preponderates" in his own book. Another good example of what Mann advocates can be found in T. H. Breen, *Imagining the Past: East Hampton Histories* (Reading, Mass., 1989).

29   W. Riggan, *Picaros, Madmen, Naifs and Clowns: the Unreliable First-Person Narrator* (Norman, 1981).

30   H. White, *Metahistory* (Baltimore, 1973), pp. 176ff.

31   Cf. M. Torgovnick, *Closure in the Novel* (Princeton, 1981), and U. Eco, "The Poetics of the Open Work", in his *The Role of the Reader* (London, 1981), Chapter

1. A move in the direction of a more open historical narrative is predicted by Phillips, "On Historiography" (p. 153).

32 C. Geertz, "Thick Description: Towards an Interpretive Theory of Culture," and "Deep Play: Notes on the Balinese Cock-Fight" in *The Interpretation of Cultures* (New York, 1973).

33 Shimazaki Toson, *Before the Dawn* (Honolulu, 1987).

34 Ibid., p. 621.

35 W. R. Siebenschuh, *Fictional Techniques and Factional Works* (1983) discusses how this was done in the past, with special reference to Boswell's life of Johnson. Cf. R. W. Rader, "Literary Form in Factual Narrative: the Example of Boswell's Johnson," in *Essays in Eighteenth-Century Biography*, P. B. Daghlian (ed.) (Bloomington, 1968), pp. 3–42.

36 Quoted in *Letteratura Italiana*, A. Asor Rosa 5 (ed.) (Turin, 1986), p. 224.

37 C. Cipolla, *Cristofano and the Plague* (London, 1973); N. Z. Davis, *The Return of Martin Guerre* (Cambridge, Mass., 1973).

38 Davis, *Martin Guerre*, p. 1.

39 N. Z. Davis, "On the Lame," *American Historical Review* 93 (1988), pp. 573, 575.

40 On this concept, V. Turner, *Dramas, Fields and Metaphors* (Ithaca, 1974), Chapter 1.

41 J. Spence, *Emperor of China* (London, 1974); *The Death of Woman Wang* (London, 1978); *The Gate of Heavenly Peace* (London, 1982); *The Memory Palace of Matteo Ricci* (London, 1985).

42 G. Lukács, *The Historical Novel*, tr. H. and S. Mitchell (London, 1962), pp. 30ff.

43 Spence (1982), p. xiii.

44 N. Davies, *Heart of Europe: a Short History of Poland* (Oxford, 1984).

45 M. Sahlins, *Historical Metaphors and Mythical Realities* (Ann Arbor, 1981) and *Islands of History* (Chicago, 1985). Cf. P. Burke, "Les îles anthropologiques et le territoire de l'historien," in *Philosophie et histoire*, C. Descamps (ed.) (Paris, 1987), pp. 49–66.

46 The original story, by Akutawaga, did not adopt this device.

47 G. Pontecorvo, *La battaglia di Algeri* (1966); *Queimada* (1969).

48 N. Z. Davis, J.-C. Carrière, D. Vigne, *Le retour de Martin Guerre* (Paris, 1982).

Chapter 21

Edgar Kiser

THE REVIVAL OF NARRATIVE IN HISTORICAL SOCIOLOGY

What rational choice theory can contribute

MANY SOCIOLOGISTS HAVE recently begun to advocate a narrative methodology for historical analysis.[1] In contrast to more structuralist approaches, these sociological narrativists suggest that historical explanations should more fully incorporate human agency, particular events, and temporality (including path dependence). This article explores the strengths and weaknesses of the new sociological narrativism, focusing on the role of theory in narrative explanations. I argue that there are two current problems with the way most narrativists use theory: (1) they rely on *Historically defined scope conditions* and (2) they employ a "toolbox" approach to constructing *total explanations*. Rational choice theory provides one way of solving both of these problems. The central argument of the article is that most sociological narrativists have been too quick to reject rational choice theory, because it has much to contribute to narrative analyses.[2] Rational choice narrativism can incorporate human agency, particular events, temporality, and path dependence in ways that avoid the current problems with the use of theory in narrative explanations. Of course, rational choice theory will not be optimal for all types of narrative – I thus conclude with a discussion of the limitations of rational choice narrativism.

Two paths from structuralist historical sociology: narrative methods and rational choice theory

The resurgence of historical sociology that began in the 1960s was led primarily by structuralist analyses of long-term political and economic transformations.[3] This work has usually rejected both general theories (including functionalism, modernization theory, and much of Marxism) and traditional narrative historical accounts focusing on specific choices made by key historical actors. In place of general theory and particularistic narrative history, these scholars have usually developed "middle range" empirical generalizations focusing on the effects of various macrolevel structural factors on the development and transformation of capitalism and states. This work has tended to define the sociological (as opposed to purely historical) contribution to historical analysis in terms of the search for large-scale and long-term causal factors. Structuralist comparative-historical sociologists tended to pay less attention to the microlevel (individual choice and action) and the particular and short-term (events) aspects of the social world.

Many historical sociologists have recently begun advocating an alternative to this structuralist approach, based on narrative methods of analysis. Although narrativists certainly do not reject structuralist historical sociology entirely, the revival of narrative in sociology has been founded on a set of common criticisms of it. First, narrativists want to bring actors back into historical analysis. They argue that structuralist historical accounts are often incomplete because they lack sufficiently detailed accounts of how macrolevel causes produce macrolevel effects[4] and that the intervening mechanisms necessary to complete structural arguments are found at the microlevel.[5] For example, Aminzade criticizes "structural reductionism"[6] and argues that "by aggregating attributes of individuals or organizations at given points in time into seemingly enduring variables that are correlated with outcomes, sociologists divorce actors from actions."[7] Second, they suggest that structuralists often ignore the importance of particular events and of the sequences in which events occur.[8] Aminzade states the narrativists' position clearly: "The focus of macro-sociology on the study of large-scale structures and long-term processes has often discouraged close attention to temporally connected events."[9] Many studies of long-term processes, such as state formation, capitalist development, or the emergence of a world-system, are carried out at a level of abstraction that precludes attention to the temporal characteristics of events. As these criticisms indicate, narrativists advocate a reformulation of historical sociology focusing on human agency, temporality, and particular events. In many respects, the criticisms made by advocates of the new narrativism in sociology are similar to those made during the earlier revival of narrative in history. Stone also contrasts narrative history with "structural history" and argues that in the former the "central focus is on man, not circumstances," and that narrative "deals with the particular and specific, rather than the collective and statistical."[10]

There is also an emerging consensus among sociological narrativists about the type of theory that is optimal for doing narrative analysis. With only one notable exception,[11] sociological narrativists ignore or reject rational choice theory in favor of structuralist arguments combined with various forms of anthropological, cultural, and literary theories – many of which stress the importance of "identity" in determining action.[12]

Are narrativists right to reject rational choice theory, or does it have something to contribute to this type of work? At first glance, narrative methodologies and rational choice theory may seem to be unrelated or even incompatible, since the former focuses on particular historical details whereas the latter strives to build abstract general models. However, I will argue that in spite of some differences, there are several fundamental similarities in the approaches of narrativists and rational choice theorists that could form the basis of a productive synthesis. One strong indication of potential compatibility is that narrativists and rational choice theorists make similar criticisms of macrosociological historical and mainstream

quantitative work. Like narrativists, rational choice scholars have criticized structuralist historical sociologists for their lack of causal mechanisms and for paying
inadequate attention to the microfoundations of action.[13]

The new narrative methodology in historical sociology

Narrative is the traditional method used by historians (and in a more partial way
by most social scientists) to tell "stories" linking temporally ordered events. Most
structuralist historical work uses narrative, but relegates it to the background of
arguments that focus on more general macrolevel causes of major political and
economic transformations.[14] Narrative is used in structuralist historical work mainly
in two rather limited ways: (1) to describe and discuss the nature of the initial
conditions (factors exogenous to the causal model), in order to "set the stage" for
the causal argument, and (2) to describe in greater detail the relationship between
causes and effects, in order to make rather sparse structural arguments more
compelling. The revival of narrative analysis in sociology is an attempt to employ
narrative in a more central role than in most macrosociological history, and to do
it more systematically (and in some cases more formally) than most traditional
historians.

Narrativists argue that what distinguishes historical sociology from the rest of
the discipline is not its focus on the past, but its use of narrative to analyze temporally ordered events.[15] However, there is little consensus among sociological
narrativists about how to define these key terms, beginning with "narrative" itself.
Lawrence Stone, an historian often cited by sociological narrativists, provides the
most straightforward definition: "Narrative is taken to mean the organization of
material in a chronologically sequential order and the focusing of the content
into a single coherent story, albeit with sub-plots."[16] Griffin defines narrative as
"the portrayal of social phenomena as temporally ordered, sequential, unfolding,
and open-ended 'stories' fraught with conjunctures and contingency."[17] This definition stays fairly close to Stone, but with less stress on coherence and more on
complexity and indeterminacy. Other definitions of narrative, influenced more by
literary theory, see it as not only part of social science methodology, but part of
the social world as well. Thus narrative is both a method of study and a central
feature of the object of study. As Somers puts it, "The challenge of conceptual
narrativity is to devise a vocabulary that we can use to reconstruct and plot over
time and space the ontological narratives and relationships of historical actors, the
public and cultural narratives that inform their lives, and the crucial intersection
of these narratives with other relevant social forces."[18] This definition of narrative
is much more broad in that it includes an ontology and an implicit theoretical stance
(cultural and interpretivist, focusing on identity) that is not in the other definitions.

The two most important concepts in sociological narrative analysis are *events*
and *temporality*. Events are the main components of narrative sequences, and narrativists who focus on explanation are interested in events both as causes and effects.
Narrativists use the term *event* to refer to a broad and heterogeneous category of
entities, encompassing things as diverse as the Battle of Hastings, the Norman
Conquest, and the rise of capitalism.[19] Griffin defines an event as "a distinguishable

happening, one with some pattern or theme that sets it off from others, and one that involves changes taking place within a delimited amount of time."[20] Abrams defines an event as a "structuring of social action in time."[21] Abbott suggests that an event is a complex "combination of particular values of many variables;"[22] in other words, an event is a conjuncture. Although these definitions focus on different aspects, they all seem to view events as involving complex but patterned temporally ordered actions. In contrast to these definitions, Sewell defines events by their *effects*, as a "subclass of happenings that significantly transform structures."[23] Abrams's distinction between an event and a "happening" – the former is a "portentous outcome" whereas the latter is not – also seems to define events by their effects.[24] This way of defining events would seem to lead to tautological arguments, unless there is some way to distinguish events from less consequential happenings prior to the causal argument.

One of the key features of an event is its uniqueness. Griffin defines an event as "a historically singular happening,"[25] and for Abbott an event "is a matter of particular social actors, in particular social places, at particular social times."[26] However, unlike pure historicists, most sociological narrativists are willing to generalize to some extent, and their formal methods have been oriented toward discovering general features of events. Abbot wants to find "typical sequences,"[27] and Griffin tries to understand lynching as "both a historically singular event and as an instance of a class of historically repeated events."[28] Their interest in generalizing by creating theoretical "classes" of events indicates that sociological narrativists may be more open to general theory than traditional historicist narrativists.

All narratives are composed of *sequences* of events, and the temporal ordering of the events in the sequence is a central aspect of the analysis. Aminzade provides the most detailed analysis of the role of time and sequence in narrative analysis, distinguishing between four aspects of temporality: pace, duration, cycles, and trajectory.[29] The central claim narrativists make about temporality is that the order in which causal factors occur will affect outcomes. As Tilly puts it, "when things happen within a sequence affects how they happen."[30] This is an important point, and one too often ignored in sociological research.

Narrativists want not only to include temporality, but to do it in a fundamentally different way from that in most sociological research. Sewell argues that much macrosociological historical analysis is flawed due to its use of "teleological" or "experimental" notions of time, and argues instead for a more "eventful" temporality.[31] He notes that it is difficult for cases in "experimental time," such as the three revolutions in Skocpol's[32] analysis, to be both independent and equivalent. The more remote cases are from each other in space and time the more likely they are to be independent (and thus to avoid Galton's problem), but the less likely they are to be equivalent.[33] He thus concludes that it is difficult if not impossible to jointly satisfy these two necessary conditions for doing this type of study, and thus that "eventful" temporality is our only option. I am more sanguine about the possibility of getting equivalent cases that are remote in space and time (and thus successfully using experimental time), but I agree that jointly maintaining equivalence and independence is often difficult. If we think of equivalent not as meaning exactly the same but as similar on theoretically relevant dimensions (i.e. fit within the abstract scope conditions of the theory), then the problem seems less insurmountable. Second, the condition of independence of cases is not necessary if the theory includes an adequate model of diffusion. It may be easier to include models of diffusion in most historical analyses than to find cases that are both theoretically equivalent and totally independent.

Another aspect of the stress on temporality has been to limit theoretical arguments to particular time periods. Events are seen as only happening "in time" and "through time," and can only be fully understood within their temporal context. In other words, the scope of arguments is spatio-temporally defined. Their stress on the importance of temporal context leads most narrativists to define the scope of their studies in historical (spatio-temporal) terms. For example, Griffin wants to develop "temporally delimited causal generalizations" that are "relative to . . . particular historical contexts."[34] Quadagno and Knapp argue that "the universe to which generalizations or explanations apply must be time- and place-specific."[35] Isaac and Griffin have developed an empirical/inductive methodological procedure for setting historical scope conditions.[36] Although defining the scope of an argument historically is certainly better than not defining it at all, I will argue below that abstract scope conditions are preferable.

The focus on temporal order also leads many narrativists to emphasize the path-dependent nature of social processes. Although path dependence has been used in a wide variety of ways, the central thread seems to be an argument that some events in the distant past have effects on later historical periods. As Aminzade puts it, "for any given trajectory, past choices and temporally remote events can help to explain subsequent paths of development and contemporary outcomes."[37] Historical development is viewed as a branching process, in which key actions push history down one branch and foreclose others[38] (somewhat analogous to punctuated equilibrium analysis in evolutionary biology). In some cases, this is combined with a focus on small changes in initial conditions producing large effects – as stressed in chaos theory. Path dependence thus combines the narrative focus on action, events, and temporal sequence.

How theory is currently used in sociological narrative analysis

Sociological narrativists have concentrated more on methodology than on discussing the role of theory in narrative analysis. However, many of them are more interested in general, testable theory than traditional narrativists in history. This section explores the advances made in the use of theory by sociological narrativists, the remaining problems, and how they could be resolved.

One of the standard criticisms of traditional narrative analyses is that they contain too many unacknowledged explanatory devices – in other words, theoretical models and causal mechanisms are left implicit. Abrams has been the most articulate critic of this practice, noting that "the function of narrative in this enterprise is to carry – in a highly persuasive way not accessible to intellectual scrutiny – those bits of the argument the author does not choose to make available for direct critical examination on the part of his readers."[39] He further argues that "if knowledge and debate are to accumulate it is necessary to place one's explanatory design with all its connections and weightings of connections, assumptions of significance and inferences of structuring squarely before the reader."[40]

Sociological narrativists are not simply repeating the errors of historians – they are aware of the problems with traditional narrative and are attempting to resolve them. Most believe that some form of theory is necessary,[41] since narratives are not just sequences of events, but are tied together by a central theme or plot. Many sociological narrativists want to use theory to a greater extent than historical narrativists, and some of them want that theory to be more abstract, deductive, and testable.[42] For example, Griffin notes that the "distinction between a temporal antecedent and a causal one is too often obscured in narrative."[43] He argues that narrative must be merged with deductive reasoning and general theory to produce adequate causal arguments.[44] Abrams wants to combine "explanation in principle" and "explanation in detail."[45] Many narrativists also believe theory should be testable. Griffin wants to use narrative to "create theorized historical-sociological explanations that are replicable and verifiable" and argues that formal methods such as those he and Abbott use facilitate testing.[46] Finally, the attempts by Abbot and Griffin to develop classes of events and abstract narratives are also a movement toward the incorporation of general theory into narrative analysis.

Toward a rational choice narrativism

There is no one-to-one correspondence between particular theories and particular methodologies; thus many different types of theory have been used in narrative analysis. However, historical sociologists using narrative methods usually either ignore or criticize rational choice theory.[47] This section suggests that this premature rejection of rational choice is a mistake and that its incorporation could improve some types of narrative analysis. Contrary to what narrativists seem to think, rational choice theory does much of what they advocate – it links action and structure and facilitates the incorporation of temporal sequence, path dependence, and particular events. Moreover, it further advances some important goals of sociological narrativism by making theory more explicit, precise, and testable.

In order to build a clear foundation for rational choice narrativism, I will begin by providing definitions of narrative, event, and temporality that are consistent with rational choice theory. Of course, these definitions will not be acceptable to all narrativists – more historicist and culturally oriented narrativists will want to retain different assumptions and definitions. Rational choice theory will not be compatible with all forms of narrative analysis, it will simply be one type of narrativism among others.

The definition of narrative taken from literary theory, with its stress on the importance of "social narratives" in shaping outcomes, cannot be used here because the interpretivist/cultural theory embedded in it is inconsistent with most versions of rational choice theory. A definition that leaves the theoretical content of the narrative open is necessary. Narrative can be defined as a *method* – a form of data presentation that is optimal when the data are either too complex or too fragmentary for data reduction techniques (such as tabular presentation or quanti-tative analysis) to be used and when temporal sequence and particular details are important aspects of the data or the argument being made.[48] These two aspects of narrative are closely linked. When temporal sequence and particular details are important, data reduction techniques will usually be ineffective because too much information will be lost.

Rational choice narrativism must also define events somewhat differently. Events can be defined not by their effects, their duration, or the extent to which they are patterned, but by their relationship to theory. Events are complex historical partic-ulars and as such cannot be explained fully by any one theory. We can distinguish between two types of events: (1) combinations of processes, each of which can be theoretically explained separately, but their conjunctural occurrence (the complete event) cannot be theoretically explained,[49] and (2) happenings that are exogenous to theory, in the sense that not even their component processes can be theoretically explained, given the current level of development of theory. Defining events in this way stresses the distinction between the general and the particular in historical explanation, one that is too often blurred in current narrative analysis.[50] Moreover, it avoids the fallacy of the total explanation, since some aspects of the narrative are taken as exogenous – all explanations of complex historical particulars are nec-essarily partial.

The definition of temporality can also be narrowed. Temporality can be defined as the importance of the duration of causal processes and the order in which causal factors occur for the outcome of interest. A significant aspect of this definition is that *the importance of temporality is variable* – sometimes the duration and order of causal factors will affect outcomes, other times it will not. The problem with many current discussions of temporality by narrativists is that they polemically claim that temporality is always important in historical explanation (and that it in fact defines historical sociology). Although this is an understandable reaction to the tendency of most sociologists to ignore temporality (and narrativists deserve credit for stressing this important issue), it avoids the interesting and difficult question: under what conditions (abstractly defined) will changes in the duration of causal processes and the temporal order of causal factors alter outcomes? The same can be said of path dependence; the most significant issue to be addressed is, when will it be important in explanations? The empirical work done by narrativists is a rich source of information about this. Finally, temporality should not be defined as the temporal embeddedness of all causal arguments, because that precludes the use of abstract scope conditions in favor of historical ones and thus limits the explicitness and testa-bility of arguments in ways outlined above.

Given these definitions, how can rational choice theory contribute to narrative analysis? The most obvious basis for the elective affinity between narrative and rational choice is that both focus on individual choice and action. Abbott describes narrative as a processual, action-based approach.[51] Griffin notes that "narrativists generally try to emphasize agency and consciousness"[52] and that the proper data for narratives is "sequences of action."[53]

However, the approach taken by most narrativists to explaining action differs from the approach taken by most rational choice theorists. In order to combine rational choice theory and narrative methodology, it is necessary to reject the most radical version of the ontology of contingency, especially as it pertains to explaining action. I argue it is unproductive to begin with the assumption that contingency is global, and thus that action can be explained only by a large and heterogeneous toolbox of theoretical ideas. Instead, by initially attempting to find general patterns in human action, we an identify realms of contingency. Weber suggests one way of doing this. Because of its clarity and precision, he argues that a microlevel assumption of instrumental rationality can be used as an ideal type in historical analysis.[54] Certainly this model of action is oversimplified, but as Stinchcombe notes, "oversimplified mechanisms borrowed from the theory of lower-level phenomena are often useful when applied to upper-level phenomena."[55] The explicit and testable predictions produced by this ideal type will not only explain some action, they also serve to *highlight deviations* from instrumental rationality. Deviations from predictions are anomalies generated by the theory – resolving such anomalies is one important source of progress in science. The use of such general rational choice microfoundations is thus not contingent on a belief that all action is in fact rational in that sense.[56] Rational choice theory does not deny the complexity of action but reveals it and facilitates its explanation. Among other things, when studies taking this form begin to cumulate, the empirical information they generate could refine the scope of rational choice theory.

Narrativists are no doubt correct that the temporal sequence in which causal factors occur often affects outcomes, and theorists should certainly be aware of this. Both theoretical and historical analyses are often guilty of simply providing lists of important causal variables without specifying their temporal interrelations. This too is something to which rational choice theory can contribute. One set of rational choice models that can serve that purpose comes from game theory, especially extensive form games.[57] These models explain outcomes as the consequence of temporally ordered strategic interaction – *sequences* of action and reaction.[58] Abell's integration of game theory into narrative analysis is the most well-developed attempt to incorporate sequentiality in a theoretical manner, but there are other prominent examples.[59] Lindenberg outlines an ordered sequence of game structures that are likely to unfold as a revolutionary situation moves toward revolution – and then uses them to construct brief narratives of the French and Russian revolutions.[60] Heckathorn uses game theory to demonstrate the importance of collective sanctions in maintaining social control within groups.[61] Drawing on Heckathorn's work, Brown and Boswell analyze strike outcomes combining narrative, game theory, and qualitative comparative analysis – the sequence of "moves" by workers and unions is a critical determinant of the outcome.[62]

Game theory is not the only way in which rational choice models have incorporated termporality. Brinton shows that differences in the timing of human capital investments in Japan and the US result in different levels of gender stratification.[63] Barzel and Kiser demonstrate that the timing of factors affecting the insecurity of rule determines their effects on voting institutions – the Hundred Years War disrupted the development of voting institutions in France more than in England because their prior development (and thus the ability to withstand shocks) was greater in the latter.[64] Rational choice work on agenda setting also incorporates temporality, generally by demonstrating how moving first allows certain actors to shape outcomes.[65]

Temporality is also important at a more microlevel Aminzade suggests that narrativists should pay attention to how the time horizons of actors affect their actions.[66] Rational choice work on discount rates (the rate at which actors discount future costs and benefits relative to current ones) has contributed to our understanding of this. For example, Levi shows that discount rates increase with the insecurity of rule.[67] Most economists assume that discount rates are normally distributed in the populations they study, a reasonable assumption if one does not know what causes discount rates to vary. More sociological rational choice models have been attempting to discover the structural determinants of variations in discount rates.

Rational choice models are also useful for the study of path dependence. The concept of path dependence was initially developed by economists using rational choice microfoundations and focusing on the effects of sunk costs and transaction costs.[68] It emerged as an attempt to resolve an anomaly (the persistence of inefficiency, such as the QWERTY typewriter keyboard). The concept of path dependence combines specificity (the importance of particular initial conditions) and generality (abstract causal mechanisms that make it difficult to exit from particular paths). Both history and general theory are necessary to explain path dependent outcomes, and neither alone is sufficient – this is true of both evolutionary biology and historical sociology.[69]

Rational choice theory is especially important in explaining the conditions under which path dependence will be strong or weak. For example, although the QWERTY keyboard configuration has remained constant, other aspects of typewriting, such as the shift to electric typewriters and then computers, have changed dramatically.[70] General theory is necessary to explain why some aspects of typewriter technology seem to be strongly path dependent and others do not.[71] Path dependence arguments without general theory often lack sufficient causal mechanisms – they often take a *post hoc, ergo propter hoc* form in which continuity over time is posited as sufficient proof of causal path dependence. Baron and Hannan make a similar point when they note that "by articulating the sources of resistance to change in social systems, sociologists could help transform the study of path-dependent development from historicism into a field in which prediction and comparative assessments are possible."[72] Rational choice theory can help do this in two ways. First, Arthur has outlined four self-reinforcing mechanisms that produce and maintain path dependence (all of which assume rational action): (1) large fixed costs, (2) learning effects, (3) coordination effects, and (4) adaptive expectations.[73] Second, game theorists, by providing abstract models of the payoffs to relevant actors of various strategies, can show *why* something is path dependent – because it is not in the interests of any of the relevant actors to change it (or they lack the resources to do so). Path dependence is the result of low payoffs to actions that would lead to change – such actions are "off the equilibrium path."

Rational choice models can also facilitate the analysis of the role of events, in a way that keeps the distinction between general and particular clear and indicates the ways in which particular factors will enter into and affect the general model. Again game theory provides the most well-developed example. One feature of recent applications of game theory that increases its compatibility with narrative methodology is the incorporation of the effects of institutions and even particular events. Formal game theory models often do not produce precise predictions of outcomes. The models yield "multiple equilibria" and cannot predict which of these equilibrium outcomes will occur in a given situation. At best, these formal models can tell you what will not happen, which outcomes are "off the equilibrium path." In order to make their explanations more precise, game theorists have increasingly been attempting to integrate formal game theoretic models with particular features of the historical cases they study – since only these particular features can tell them why one of many possible equilibrium outcomes in fact occurred. The classic example of this is Schelling's discussion of the role of "focal points."[74] More recently, game theorists have been moving toward an integration of formal rational choice models with detailed narrative stories that incorporate events.[75] These models provide a way of constructing explanations that combine the general and the particular, while maintaining a clear distinction between the two.[76]

Other rational choice models have also begun to incorporate events in interesting ways. For example, Kiser and Barzel develop a general contracting model to explain the rise of voting institutions in medieval states, but also show how exogenous shocks (particular events outside the model, such as the plague or the death of the only heir to the throne) will affect the contracting process and thus the stability of democratic institutions.[77] The general model does not (and cannot) specify exactly when exogenous shocks will occur or what form they will take; it only predicts what their consequences will be if they do occur. Both general theory and history are thus necessary for the explanation. The narrative summary of the development of voting institutions in medieval England includes both general and particular causal factors (as any full explanation of a historical particular will), but the general rational choice theory clearly specifies their relationship.

Limitations of rational choice narrativism

Although I have focused on the positive features of a synthesis between rational choice theory and narrative analysis, it is important to understand two important limitations: (1) the rejection of total explanation may produce narratives with less literary elegance and (2) rational choice theory will not work well for all problems of interest to sociological narrativists.

Total explanations tend to work well rhetorically because they produce complete narratives. Every aspect of the story is tied together and every action is accounted for. If total explanation is rejected, the resulting story will be full of holes – not only will many things not be explained, but the narrative will call attention to these anomalies. This would certainly be considered a major flaw in fictional narratives. The use of one theoretical model such as rational choice instead of several may give a more coherent general plot and facilitate testing, but the trade-off is a loss of elegance due to the incompleteness of the explanatory account.

There are two additional limitations that result from the initial use of rational choice microfoundations as an ideal type. First, this strategy will not work well in circumstances in which most action is not based on instrumental rationality, but on values, identities, or emotions instead. Since these noninstrumental bases of action are very important in some situations, rational choice theory can never be expected to guide all narrative accounts. Although a full discussion of the conditions under which instrumental action might be the dominant form is beyond the scope of this article, two brief comments can be made. Rational choice theory will probably not be effective when either: (1) the costs and benefits of actions are very low or (2) uncertainty about costs and benefits of actions is very high. In the first situation, actors will not care much about acting instrumentally (because they will not "pay" much for acting on values, identities, etc.). This may explain the relative lack of success of rational choice theory in explaining low cost activities like voting. In the second situation they will not be able to make rational choices. To put the point more positively, rational choice theory should work well in narratives concerning actions that have high costs and benefits and are often repeated (the latter reduces uncertainty). Since many (although far from all) issues of interest to sociological narrativists meet these conditions, there should be some place for rational choice narrativism.

Of course, forms of narrative analysis other than rational choice will continue to have an important place, since rational choice theory will not be useful to all narrativists. Those who study "social narratives,"[78] practice "ontological narrativity,"[79] or draw heavily on cultural and literary theories[80] will want to begin from different foundational assumptions. In fact, in conditions in which instrumental action is not dominant, their alternative assumptions will often produce superior explanations. I have argued only that rational choice theory should have a place in narrative analysis, not that it should be hegemonic.

Notes

1   Andrew Abbott, "Conceptions of Time and Events in Social Science Methods: Causal and Narrative Approaches," *Historical Methods* 23 (1990): 140–50; Andrew Abbott, "From Causes to Events: Notes on Narrative Positivism," *Sociological Methods and Research* 20, no. 4 (1992): 428–55; Ronald Aminzade, "Historical Sociology and Time," *Sociological Methods and Research* 20, no. 4 (1992): 456–80; Ronald Aminzade, *Ballots and Barricades* (Princeton, NJ: Princeton University Press, 1993); Larry Griffin, "Temporality, Events, and Explanation in Historical Sociology," *Sociological Methods and Research* 20, no. 4 (1992): 403–27; Larry Griffin, "Narrative, Event-Structure Analysis, and Causal Interpretation in Historical Sociology," *American Journal of Sociology* 98, no. 5 (1993): 1094–133; William Sewell, "Introduction: Narratives and Social Identities," *Social Science History* 16, no. 3 (1992): 479–88; William Sewell, "Three Temporalities: Toward an Eventful Sociology," in *The Historic Turn in the Human Sciences*, Terrence J. McDonald (ed.) (Ann Arbor: University of Michigan Press, forthcoming); Margaret Somers, "Narrativity, Narrative Identity, and Social Action: Rethinking English Working Class Formation," *Social Science History* 16, no. 4 (1992): 591–630; Margaret Somers, "The Narrative Constitution of Identity: A Relational and Network Approach," *Theory and Society* 23 (1994): 605–49; George Steinmetz, "Reflections on the Role of Social Narratives in Working Class Formation: Narrative Theory in the Social Sciences," *Social Science History* 16, no. 3 (1992): 489–516.

2   For an interesting argument along similar lines, see Robert Bates, Avner Greif, Margaret Levi, Jean-Laurent Rosenthal, and Barry Weingast, *Analytical Narratives* (book manuscript in progress).

3   Perhaps the three most influential examples are Barrington Moore, *Social Origins of Dictatorship and Democracy* (Boston: Beacon Press, 1966); Theda Skocpol, *States and Social Revolutions* (Cambridge: Cambridge University Press, 1979); and Charles Tilly, (ed.), *The Formation of National States in Western Europe* (Princeton, NJ: Princeton University Press, 1975).

4   Abbott, "From Causes," 432.

5   Sewell, "Three," 42.

6   Aminzade, *Ballots*, 6.

7   Aminzade, "Historical Sociology and Time," 457.

8   Sewell, "Three."

9   Aminzade, "Historical Sociology and Time," 457.

10 Lawrence Stone, "The Revival of Narrative: Reflections on a New Old History," *Past and Present* 85 (1979): 3.

11 The exception among sociologists, to be discussed below, is Peter Abell. See *The Syntax of Social Life* (Oxford, UK: Clarendon Press, 1987); "Some Aspects of Narrative Method," *Journal of Mathematical Sociology* 18, no. 2–3 (1993): 93–134, "Narrative Method: A Reply," *Journal of Mathematical Sociology* 18, no. 2–3 (1993): 253–66. My debt to his pioneering work should be obvious – this article will be successful if it encourages others to follow his lead. However, Abell is not a historical sociologist and has not applied his narrative method to historical cases. There are also numerous exceptions to this generalization in other disciplines, including most economic historians, many political scientists, and some historians. For interesting arguments by political scientists and economists linking rational choice and narrative in historical analysis, see Bates *et al.*, *Analytical*, and Donald McCloskey, *If You're So Smart: The Narrative of Economic Enterprise* (Chicago: University of Chicago, 1990).

12 Andrew Abbott, "Measure for Measure: Abell's Narrative Methods," *Journal of Mathematical Sociology* 18, no. 2–3 (1993): 205–07; Larry Griffin and Charles Ragin, "Some Observations on Formal Methods of Qualitative Analysis," *Sociological Methods and Research* 23, no. 1 (1994): 7–8; Jill Quadagno and Stan Knapp, "Have Historical Sociologists Forsaken Theory?: Thoughts on the History/Theory Relationship," *Sociological Methods and Research* 20, no. 4 (1992): 481–507; Sewell, "Three," 29–30; Somers, "The Narrative;" Steinmetz, "Reflections." An analysis of the strengths and weaknesses of these cultural/interpretive/identity theories is beyond the scope of this article. My purpose is not to argue that rational choice theory is the only (or even necessarily the "best") way to do narrative analysis. My goal is much more modest – simply to suggest that rational choice has been too quickly rejected by most sociological narrativists and that it does have something to contribute to this type of work.

13 Michael Taylor, "Rationality and Revolutionary Collective Action," in *Rationality and Revolution*, Michael Taylor (ed.) (Cambridge: Cambridge University Press, 1988), 63–97; Edgar Kiser and Michael Hechter, "The Role of General Theory in Comparative-historical Sociology," *American Journal of Sociology* 97, no. 1 (1991): 7, 15–17, 19–23.

14 Moore, *Social*; Tilly, *The Formation*; Skocpol, *States*.

15   See Griffin, "Temporality," 405; Aminzade, "Historical Sociology and Time." This definition of historical sociology is problematic in two respects: (1) it includes things that do not seem historical at all, such as some types of ethnomethodological or symbolic interactionist analyses, and (2) it excludes all analyses of the past that do not use the narrative method. The definition thus both creates too much heterogeneity in the category "historical" and attempts to hegemonically exclude alternative methodological approaches.

16   Stone, "The Revival," 10.

17   Griffin, "Temporality," 405.

18   Somers, "The Narrative," 620.

19   Philip Abrans, *Historical Sociology* (Somerset: Open Books, 1982), 175.

20   Griffin, "Narrative," 1096.

21   Abrams, *Historical Sociology*, 192.

22   Abbott, "Conceptions," 141. This definition is Abbott's translation of the term into the language of what he calls the traditional "stochastic view." He argues that it is more parsimonious to view events as wholes than to translate them into values of several variables, because most of the cells in any such analytic decomposition will always be empty. Strictly speaking, this may be true. But if a general theory can be used to identify some small subset of features of an event (variables) as causally most important, the analytical strategy may be more parsimonious.

23   Sewell, "Three," 31.

24   Abrams, *Historical Sociology*, 191.

25   Griffin, "Temporality," 414.

26   Abbott, "From Causes," 428–9.

27   Ibid.

28   Griffin, "Narrative," 1096.

29   Aminzade, "Historical Sociology and Time."

30   Charles Tilly, *Big Structures, Large Processes, Huge Comparisons* (New York: Russell Sage, 1984).

31   Sewell, "Three."

32   Skocpol, *States*.

33   Sewell, "Three," 23–4.

34   Griffin, "Temporality," 407. See also Tilly, *Big*, 14; Somers, "Narrativity."

35   Quadagno and Knapp, "Have Historical Sociologists," 501–2.

36   Larry Issac and Larry Griffin, "Ahistoricism in Time-Series Analyses of Historical Process: Critique, Redirection, and Illustrations from U.S. Labor History," *American Sociological Review* 54 (1989): 873–90. See also Terry Boswell and Cliff Brown, "The Scope of General Theory: Methods for Linking Deductive and Inductive Comparative History," presented at the Annual Meetings of the American Sociological Association, Los Angeles, 1994, for an interesting attempt to use Qualitative Comparative Analysis to methodologically specify scope conditions.

37   Aminzade, "Historical Sociology and Time," 462.

38   One of the most difficult aspects of arguments stressing path dependence is the counterfactual analysis required to demonstrate the existence of foreclosed paths. On this point, see Jon Elster, *Logic and Society* (New York: John Wiley, 1978); Griffin, "Narrative;" and Edgar Kiser and Margaret Levi, "Using Counterfactuals in Historical Analysis: Theories of Revolution," in *Counterfactuals in International Relations*, Philip Tetlock and Aaron Belkin (eds) (Princeton, NJ: Princeton University Press, 1996).

39   Abrams, *Historical Sociology*, 307.

40   Ibid., 314.

41   Some formal narrative methodologies already contain some substantive theory. The ETHNO program developed by David Heise, "Modeling Event Structures," *Journal of Mathematical Sociology* 14 (1989): 139–69, and used by Griffin, "Narrative," contains "theoretical constraints." In fact, Griffin, "Narrative," 1105, notes that ETHNO was influenced by rational choice theory and contains some similar elements in its internal logic. However, ETHNO dos not contain a full causal theory, and Griffin, "Narrative," 1107–8, repeatedly circumvents the theoretical constraints it does have in his analysis of lynchings.

42   Other narrativists advocate the use of theory, but not general, deductive theory. Sewell, "Three," 49, thinks that sociologists "will increasingly have to look to historians and their narratives for theoretical inspiration." Aminzade, *Ballots*, 25–7, wants to develop "theoretically structured stories" using "historically grounded theory." Somers, "Narrativity," 594, worries that the use of abstract theory can result in "denarrativized" narrative (by which she seems to mean a narrative that lacks sufficient attention to time and space). Although Quadagno and Knapp, "Have Historical Sociologists," 505, are critical of general theory (as advocated by Kiser and Hechter, "The Role"), they too see a role for some type of theory in narrative analysis.

43   Griffin, "Narrative," 1100.

44   Ibid., 1102–3.

45   Abrams, *Historical Sociology*, 211–12.

46   Griffin, "Temporality," 420. See also Somers, "Narrativity," 601, on testing "plot hypotheses."

47   For criticisms, see Quadagno and Knapp, "Have Historical Sociologists;" Abbott, "From Causes," "Measure," 205–6; Somers, "Narrativity."

48   See Abell, "Some Aspects," 263, for a similar definition. This definition combines the traditional view of narrative as a discursive mode of representation with the more contemporary stress on temporality. McCloskey, *If You're so Smart*, also separates narrative (stories) from theory (models). He defines narrative as follows: "A story . . . sets down in chronological order the raw experience in one domain." Narrativists may object that this definition is too narrow, that narrative is not just a method but contains theoretical argument (that shapes "characters" and organizes "plots") as well. This is true in the sense that there are no totally atheoretical narratives; narrative is never just "data." However, since I want to explore the role that theory does and should play in narrative, it is useful to analytically separate the theoretical from the methodological aspect of narrative.

49   This is similar to Abbott's, "Conceptions," 141, definition of events as conjunctures.

50   For example, in Griffin, "Temporality," 417.

51   Abbott, "From Causes," 428–30.

52   Griffin, "Temporality," 425.

53   Griffin, "Narrative," 1251–2. See also Abrams, *Historical Sociology*, x, xv, 192; Aminzade, "Historical Sociology and Time," 467.

54   Max Weber, *Economy and Society* (Berkeley: University of California Press, [1922] 1968).

55   Arthur Stinchcombe, "The Conditions of Fruitfulness of Theorizing about Mechanisms in Social Science," *Philosophy of the Social Sciences* 21, no. 3 (1991): 367–88.

56   Stinchcombe, ibid., 384, notes that "'Assumption mongering,' showing that the theories of the mechanisms are not true, is therefore seldom a useful strategy in scientific theorizing at an aggregate level. Just as statistical mechanics is still useful even if molecules of gases are not little round elastic balls, so assumptions that all people can calculate at a level two standard deviations above the mean may not be far enough wrong *in relevant ways* to undermine assumptions of rationality in economics."

57   David Kreps, *Game Theory and Economic Modeling* (Oxford, UK: Clarendon Press, 1990), 13.

58   Abbott, "From Causes," 443–5, notes that game theory is one of the "most interesting of modeling techniques" that may serve as a "useful bridge" in moving toward a fully narrative method. However, he is critical of game theory because it is often difficult to know which of many different game theoretic models is appropriate in any analysis and because it has no way to explain preferences.

59   Abell, "Some Aspects." The extent of disagreement about the role of theory in narrative analysis is illustrated by contrasting reactions to Abell's work. In a recent symposium, he was criticized both for having too little theory and for having too much. David Willer, "A Critique of Abell's 'Paths of Social Determination,'" *Journal of Mathematical Sociology* 18, no. 2–3 (1993): 192–3, 200, and Thomas Fararo, "Generating Narrative Forms," *Journal of Mathematical Sociology* 18, no. 2–3 (1993): 154, criticize Abell for having an insufficient theory of structure and lacking an explanatory theory. On the other hand, Abbott, "Measure," 205–6, who has no substantive theory associated with his narrative method, criticizes Abell for including too much theory (and for using rational choice and game theory in particular).

60   Seigwart Lindenberg, "Social Production Functions, Deficits, and Revolutions: Pre-revolutionary France and Russia," *Rationality and Society* (July 1989): 50–76.

61   Douglas Heckathorn, "Collective Sanctions and the Creation of Prisoner's Dilemma Norms," *American Journal of Sociology* 94 (1988): 535–62; "Collective Sanctions and Compliance Norms: A Formal Theory of Group-Mediated Social Control," *American Sociological Review* 55 (1990): 366–84.

62   Cliff Brown and Terry Boswell, "Strikebreaking or Solidarity in the Great Steel Strike of 1919: A Split Labor Market, Game-Theoretic, and QCA Analysis," *American Journal of Sociology* 100, no. 6 (1995): 1479–1519.

63   Mary Brinton, "The Social-Institutional Bases of Gender Stratification: Japan as an Illustrative Case," *American Journal of Sociology* 94, no. 2 (1988): 300–34.

64   Yoram Barzel and Edgar Kiser, "The Development and Decline of Medieval Voting Institutions: A Comparison of England and France," *Economic Inquiry*, forthcoming.

65   See Barry Weingast and Michael Moran, "Bureaucratic Discretion or Congressional Control?: Regulatory Policy Making by the Federal Trade Commission," *Journal of Political Economy* 91 (1983): 765–800, on congressional committees, and David Mueller, *Public Choice II* (Cambridge: Cambridge University Press, 1989), 255, on bureaus proposing budgets.

66   Aminzade, "Historical Sociology and Time," 471.

67   Margaret Levi, *Of Rule and Revenue* (Berkeley: University of California Press, 1988).

68   Brian Arthur, "Self-Reinforcing Mechanisms in Economics," in *The Economy as an Evolving Complex System*, P. Anderson, K. Arrow and D. Pines (eds) (Reading, MA: Addison Wesley, 1988); Brian Arthur, "Competing Technologies, Increasing Returns, and Lock In by Historical Events," *Economic Journal* 99 (1989): 116–31; Paul David, "Clio and the Economics of QWERTY," *American Economic Review* 75 (1985): 332–7.

69   The case of evolutionary biology illustrates well the necessity of combining narrative methods with general theory. Although narrativists often like to point to the importance of path dependence and contingency in the narratives of evolutionary biologists such as Gould, it is important to note that in addition to these features, general theory such as natural selection and molecular biology guides these stories. The former provides macrolevel causal mechanisms and the latter microlevel causal mechanisms.

70   Oliver Williamson, "Transaction Cost Economics and Organization Theory," *Industrial and Corporate Change* 2, no. 2 (1993): 143.

71   Douglas North, *Institutions, Institutional Change, and Economic Performance* (Cambridge: Cambridge University Press, 1991), 92–5.

72   Paul Baron and Michael Hannan, "The Impact of Economics on Contemporary Sociology," *Journal of Economic Perspectives* 32 (1994): 1141–2.

73   Arthur, "Self-Reinforcing," 10.

74   Thomas Schelling, *Micromotives and Macrobehavior* (New York: Norton, 1960); see also Kreps, *Game*, 100–02.

75   Abell, *The Syntax*; "Some Aspects;" Bruce Bueno de Mesquita, "Counterfactuals in International Affairs: Some Insights from Game Theory," in *Counterfactuals in International Relations*, Philip Tetlock and Aaron Belkin (eds) (Princeton, NJ: Princeton University Press, forthcoming); Barry Weingast, "Off-The-Path Behavior: A Game-Theoretic Approach to Counterfactuals and Its Implications for Political and Historical Analysis," in *Counterfactuals in International Relations*, Philip Tetlock and Aaron Belkin (eds) (Princeton, NJ: Princeton University Press, forthcoming).

76   In contrast, Griffin's "Temporality," 417, view of the role of theory is complicated by an inability to separate it from historical particulars in his discussion of how narratives explain. "Events fuse the historically particular and the theoretically general so thoroughly that the distinction between the two is largely mute." A major problem with making this distinction mute is that it is not clear which arguments (or which parts of arguments) can be applied only to the case at hand, and which may be transportable to other cases (and, if so, to what types of other cases).

77   Edgar Kiser and Yoram Barzel, "The Origins of Democracy in England," *Rationality and Society* 3, no. 4 (1991): 396–422.

78   Steinmetz, "Reflections."

79   Somers, "Narrativity."

80   Sewell, "Three."

PART SIX

Narrative and the practice of history

Chapter 22

Kenneth C. Dewar

WHERE TO BEGIN AND HOW

Narrative openings in Donald Creighton's historiography

WAS DONALD CREIGHTON A NARRATIVE HISTORIAN? The question might be thought purely rhetorical, for surely it is a commonplace among historians not only that he was but that he was a master of narrative historiography. It is worth asking, nevertheless, in view of the renewed interest among philosophers and literary theorists in narrative as a form of prose discourse and of recent claims that contemporary historical writing is experiencing a "revival of narrative." In the former case, discussion has focused particularly on the epistemological import of narrative, in the latter on the practical implications of certain innovations observed in current historical study.[1] A reconsideration of Creighton's work in light of the new "narratology" may help to illuminate his historiographical practice and enhance our appreciation of his mastery. It may also assist in clarifying some of the issues with which all historians must deal in choosing the way they write their histories.

Debate in recent times concerning the value of narrative history has been confused by uncertainty as to its nature. There are those, on the one hand, for whom all history is narrative history and historiographical narration is the representation in prose form of what one has discovered about the past through the study of its remains. In this view, the term narrative history is a redundancy. On the other hand, there are those for whom the term evokes a set of distinctive characteristics, including descriptiveness, chronological organization, attention to individual character, and a focus on particular actions and events. In this view, narrative history is considered, often critically, to be history of a specific kind. In everyday usage, moreover, the term is often simply associated with a colorful prose style.

Disputes over what history ought properly to be about have further clouded the issue by identifying narrative with "political" or "traditional" history. The conception of history as past politics has been the model against which newer conceptions – social history, for example, or total history – have staked their claims as alternative or superior approaches to the study of the past. Critics have wedded the particular form in which political history has commonly been written to its contents and methods, in the interests of affirming the value of a different content and method. Narrative has thus served polemically as a code-word for "old-fashioned," while defenders of the old-fashioned have been content to accept the usage of their critics.[2]

By the same token, in postulating a "revival of narrative," Lawrence Stone used the concept as a catch-all to describe a wide-ranging reassessment of social history itself – of the role of individuality and consciousness, the meaning of culture, the determinacy of the past, and the importance of addressing a non-specialist reading public – in certain leading works of the 1970s. "No single word," he concluded, could sum up all the changes he observed, "and so, for the time being, narrative will have to serve as a shorthand code-word for all that is going on."[3] Stone's discussion was informative and provocative, but his use of the term narrative to denote changes in content, objective, methods, and style, and the ease with which he thereby shifted its connotation from political and traditional to cultural and innovative, without specific change in meaning, only highlights the need for clearer definition.

This confusion about the nature of narrative history derives, I believe, from our conventional approach to historiography. Historiography is usually conceived not in its original meaning, as the writing of history, but as the study of the history of historical study, including the development of different "schools" of interpretation and various conceptions of historical knowledge. As J. H. Hexter pointed out in an essay written some twenty years ago, historians have tended to be preoccupied by questions of content, method, procedure, and point of view when examining their discipline. Matters concerning the craft of writing have either been subsumed in debates over the scientific status of history or left to the creative intuitions of individual historians. For all the care that many exercise in writing their own histories, few have paid systematic attention to what Hexter called the "rhetoric of history," or historiography, properly speaking.[4]

In Creighton's case, for example, his writing, while much admired, is little studied. In what is now the standard history of English-Canadian historiography in the twentieth century, Carl Berger emphasizes Creighton's "artistry." Indeed, he says, "No other Canadian historian was so concerned with history as a literary art as Donald Creighton."[5] Yet Berger is more concerned with what Creighton wrote than the way he wrote it. He describes and analyzes Creighton's interpretations of Canadian history and traces their origins and impact, in relation both to the times and to the development of Canadian historical thought. He pays less heed to Creighton's writing as such, and, when he does, he considers it particularly in the context of contending views of history as art or science. Distinguishing between history seen as a type of imaginative literature and history seen as a branch of analytic social science, Berger situates Creighton in a romanticist tradition, in which research is conducted scientifically while its results are cast in an imaginative "mould."[6] Berger's method and argument throughout rely more on evidence derived from revelatory statements of programmatic intent than on that offered by Creighton's actual historiographic practice.

One result of this approach to historiography is that we have only an impressionistic awareness of the variety of modes in which history may be written, their possibilities, and their implications for historical understanding and the communication of meaning. My purpose here, then, is to examine Donald Creighton's historiography, in Hexter's sense, with a view to clarifying our understanding of the narrative mode in particular. I have found especially useful a distinction made by many narrative theorists between "discourse" and "story." In fiction, that is between the "order of telling" and a postulated "order of the told:" in history, between the historian's ordering of the past and the "real" order of the past, as recorded in documents, artifacts, photographs, and so on.[7] Narrative, in this view, is an order of telling that honors certain properties of temporal sequence, interconnectedness, and closure. It is neither assumed to be "found" in the aspect of the past to be recounted, nor is it assumed to be necessary to the recounting. The mode of a historiographical discourse, therefore, is in some measure optional. In the words of the philosopher Nelson Goodman, "although every narrative will survive some reordering, and some narratives will survive any reordering, not every narrative will survive any reordering. Some stories when reordered in certain ways are no longer stories but studies."[8]

This definition of narrative is not confining but allows for a degree of flexibility that is missing from definitions that rely more narrowly on content and chronological order. When examined from this perspective, Creighton's histories exhibit a variety of rhetorical strategies. While their mode is predominantly narrative, it is not, contrary to common opinion, uniformly so, nor are his narratives always narrativistic in the same way. The range of his historiographic practice may be observed in the different ways in which he begins his histories.

I propose to focus attention on what might be called Creighton's "inaugural motifs."[9] Needless to say, beginnings cannot be chipped off from prose structures, like bits of rock, and treated in isolation, any more than literary structural forms can be entirely separated from their contents. Beginnings, by their very nature, foreshadow middles and endings. Particular beginnings, however, initiate particular ways of ordering a discourse, and I hope to show that by studying Creighton's openings some of the distinctive properties of historiographical narrative will be revealed.

Consider, first of all, "classic" Creighton. In *The Empire of the St. Lawrence*, his first and perhaps most influential major work, we find what appears to be an archetypal narrative opening, the announcement of the fall of Quebec in September 1759. Here is a particular event, situated precisely in time. The collapse of French power that followed was "decisive," "definitive," "conclusive," and of "*apparently* unique importance."[10] On the one side lay the era of Anglo-French rivalry in North America, now terminated; on the other the age of British dominion. In the beginning, then, was the event, and Creighton's story is thus initiated. Yet, before the first paragraph is out, the significance of the word "apparently" is revealed. The event was unique and conclusive only in its European aspect, in the transfer of the sovereignty of Canada from France to England. Seen from North America, its significance as end and beginning was less decisive; it meant rather a "regrouping" of Americans and a "reorganization" of American economies.

The double-sidedness of Creighton's opening, signifying both change and continuity, is familiar enough to students of interpretations of the British conquest of Quebec. Its importance for the ordering of the discourse is twofold. In the first place, *The Empire of the St. Lawrence* is often said to be organized on the model of a drama in three acts, and Creighton himself introduces the metaphor of the stage play in his opening passages.[11] "For Europe," he writes, "the conquest was the conclusion of a drama; for America it was merely the curtain of an act" (1). The image here signals not so much that Creighton has constructed his story on the lines of a drama, but that the story he has to tell is inextricably part of a larger one. Only in European terms is there the beginning of a new play; in North America, it seems, the drama is of longer duration and the telling requires that both stories be established.

Equally important, and of formal relevance, the temporal and causal origins of the North American drama lie deep, indeed mysteriously, in the very essence of the continent. On one level, the North American struggle was between two colonial societies, distinguished partly by their European origins; fundamentally, it was between two geographic regions whose essential character Americanized their inhabitants and shaped the course of their conflict. These latter continental imperatives emerge as forces which expose the apparent finality of the imperial drama as superficial. The place they occupy in the opening pages of *The Empire of the St. Lawrence*, and their figurative treatment, challenge our conventional notions of what defines narrativity.

These structural implications will become apparent if we recognize the entirety of part I as the opening of the discourse. Readers will recall the book's tripartite division: part I, "The First Unity of the St. Lawrence," covers the period 1760–83; part II, "Transition in the Region of the Lower Lakes," 1783–1821; and part III, "The Struggle for the Second Commercial Empire," 1821–49. Expanding successively in size, each part follows a chronological order in a way that we commonly take to be a distinguishing feature of narrative. As students of narrative have shown, however, chronology by itself, understood as a linear order of actions or happenings, has never adequately described the sequential complexity found in narrative discourse. They point to the flashes forward and backward that break sequence, to the interweaving of miniature stories, and to the anticipation of endings – in short, to the reorderings – by which narrators give meaning to their stories.[12] Our concern, therefore, is less with chronology as such than with the way the narrator plays upon it to structure the discourse, and hence with the relationship between ordering principles and the object ordered, between the text of the discourse and the past it seeks to represent.

Considered in this light, Creighton's opening is striking for its thematic rather than its chronological ordering. The dominant theme is geographic, and geography is evoked in human terms: the continent compels, promises, seduces, and dictates; the Atlantic seaboard prohibits, invites, and directs "in a kindly fashion;" the Precambrian Shield's "wrinkled senility" is "touched by the curious appearance of youth;" the St Lawrence River system shouts and whispers and extends "acquisitive fingers" westward into the plains (4–6). Together, river and shield constitute a kind of leading motif, whose contrasting notes are registered in the bright opportunities offered for wealth and empire, and in the more somber colours of "imperious domination" and "portentous" intrinsic flaws and weaknesses. So represented, they shape the nature and progress of the northern economy – they were its "bone and bloodtide" (5) – and its rivalry with the south.

In the dramatic model, these seemingly humanized geographic features become the main actors in Creighton's play. Here again the analogy is slightly misleading, partly because it requires the continent to figure both as stage and as the actors upon it, more so because it masks the thematic significance of the geographic imperative. These actors do not act; they simply *are*. Conjoined with their anthropomorphic properties is their situation on a time-scale more geologic than human, extending back to the Ice Age, and their possession of inner qualities of impalpable meaning. The dream of western commercial empire, in Creighton's oft-quoted image, "rose, like an exhalation," from the great river itself (6). Personification here does not humanize; it excites mystery rather than identification. The river and shield are not personal; they are supra-personal.

No human being, in fact, is individually portrayed until the beginning of the second chapter of part I, and even here individuality is subordinated to thematic development.[13] The merchant Alexander Henry is introduced as the kind of man that "the northern economy began to select" as its "future servants" (23). Creighton quotes from Henry's journals, less to enliven Henry than to show his recognition of the economic potential of the north, and he follows with a list of other men similarly disposed. All, moreover, are immediately subsumed into the social group of which they became leading members. Just as the temporal specificity of the Plains of Abraham was overtaken, in Chapter 1, by geographic imperatives virtually extra-temporal in nature, so here individual human agency is no sooner introduced than it is collectivized into the commercial class. Referred to variously as "it" or "they," this class, as a class, rather than any particular individual or individuals, is the central subject of Creighton's narrative. Its fortunes are traced as, for better and for worse, it responds to and recoils from the dictates and constraints of North American geography.

Creighton goes on to analyze the merchant class in empirical terms – its social, spatial, economic, and political characteristics – and in so doing presents the kind of descriptive detail that conveys for the first time a sense of what it was like to live in eighteenth-century Canada. These characteristics, however, are represented primarily in relation to their thematic significance. The social relationship of French and English, for example, or the nature of fur-trade competition with both the southern colonies and the Hudson's Bay Company, or the political ambitions of the Montreal merchants, all "reflected" the demands of the Laurentian commercial system and answered to the requirements of its "destined" enmities and alliances (31, 34).

Furthermore, continental imperatives are now set against a secondary theme – that of imperial interest – for the merchant class finds itself beset, not only by the rivalries of North American trade, but by the political and commercial policies of London as well. The European aspect of the conquest is thus given thematic form, which finds ominous expression in the territorial restrictions of the Proclamation of 1763, in the feudal and military proclivities of the first British governors and their bureaucratic coteries, and in the Quebec Act's denial of political representation. Individuals appear (Murray, Carleton, Haldimand, or, more fleetingly, Peter Pond, Simon McTavish, Francis Maseres), events are recounted (the campaign for Murray's recall, the incident of Walker's ear, the failure of New York's initiative to regulate colonial trade), and policies are described (the formation of a western Indian reserve, the reorganization of the courts of common pleas, the various facets, above all, of the merchants' program). They have no autonomous interest or value, but serve as variations on and manifestations of the dominant and secondary themes, and as illustrations of their complex tensions.

The imperatives of continental geography, then, and the relationship of colony and empire are revealed as Creighton's inaugural motifs. They are brought to their initial fulfilment in the disastrous outcome of the American Revolution. The merchant class, having followed the dictates of the northern economy and rejected the path of independence – it could not, it seems, have done otherwise – was forced to embrace its imperial master, the ambiguous benefits of which were fast made apparent by the adverse boundary settlement of 1783. "The Treaty of 1783," Creighton writes, "is the ideal example, in Canadian history, of how a weak state can suffer alike from the ambitions of its competitors and the complaisant generosity of its supposed friends" (79). The note of catastrophe and betrayal here struck is significant, for the meaning of Creighton's inaugural motifs lies in their tonalities and rhythms as well as in their thematic contents. Part I, in other words, inaugurates not only the transcendent themes that order Creighton's discourse but the aura of tragedy and defeat that colors their elaboration, descending, ever more darkly, through the end of the western fur trade in the dying flame of an Indian campfire, at the conclusion of part II, to the final collapse of the northern commercial empire in 1849.

What conclusions may we draw from our analysis of this opening? In the first place, its content is at odds with that commonly said to be found in narrative histories. It is undeniably traditional history in some senses, yet can hardly be called political, concerned as it is with economic change and social relations as much as with political developments. Individuals are portrayed, yet the main focus of attention is the collective merchant class. The past is described in evocative prose, yet it is also explained by means of an interpretation well known as the Laurentian thesis. Finally, while Creighton depicts particular events, actions, and happenings, he does so with reference to the broad sweep of his general, overarching themes. Content, it would seem, is an uncertain test of narrativity.

Second, as I have already suggested, the analogy of the stage play falls short of adequately describing the book's structure, not because narrative accounts cannot be structured in ways analogous to dramatic presentations, but because the analogy here diverts attention from the merchant class to the river and shield as actors, and because it depends too simply on the congruence of a play's three acts and the book's three parts. Certainly, Creighton makes effective use of dramatic metaphor to punctuate his narrative, but so also does he draw musical analogies when appropriate. In the book's closing pages, he writes, "But, though the theme of the St. Lawrence continued, it was no longer stated with the old solemn simplicity. It was heard now through novel variations and through the loud beginnings of new movements" (383). Like the curtains of a play, musical imagery offers its own suggestive ways of describing certain aspects of the *Empire's* style and structure: its contrasting tones and colours, its rhythmic incantations of geographic qualities, its contrapuntal thematic development. In either case, however, the imagery reveals little about the book as a historiographical narrative.

How, then, does *The Empire of the St. Lawrence* manifest its narrativity? Part of the answer may be found in its treatment of chronology. In the opening, as we have seen, chronology fades from prominence, the temporal setting having been established. While the book's story is of the efforts of Montreal businessmen to build a commercial empire in northern North America during a specific time, it is told as a recounting of their struggles with conditions and forces that are at once the foundation and the curse of their existence and ambitions. Chronology is manipulated in the telling in various ways, sometimes to anticipate future events, as when Creighton calls the merchants of eighteenth-century Montreal "middle-class reformers who eventually became revolutionaries" (32), or to recall events past, as when he says that the Americans renewed, in 1775, the old struggle between river and seaboard, "which before 1763 had been magnified by the ambitions of Great Britain and France" (61). The narrator discloses his own temporal separation from his subject ("There were no commissariat services for the army of those days . . ." [22]) and his interrogatory status in the historiographic present ("Historians . . . have praised Jay and Shelburne . . ." [83]). He also makes interpretative assertions that transcend the chronological bounds of his story: "Transcontinentalism, the westward drive or corporations encouraged and followed by the super-corporation of the state, is the major theme in Canadian political life" (16). As Louis Mink, the philosopher of history, has observed, "in the understanding of a narrative the thought of temporal succession as such vanishes — or perhaps, one might say, remains like the smile of the Cheshire Cat."[14] Thus, rather than ordering the discourse, chronology underlies it.

A further point may be made arising from the way Creighton's thematic structure seems to imply a deterministic view of events. The literary theorist Jonathan Culler has noted the tension found in many fictional narratives between the priority of events and the priority of meaning. Events are recounted seemingly as they occur, he says, yet their telling is so ordered to give them meaning that they seem also to have been *meant* to occur.[15] This double logic of fictional narratives should be familiar to historians, who attempt to represent the past as contemporaries witnessed and experienced it, while simultaneously aware that their interpretations depend on their own knowledge of how things turned out. The meaning of historical narratives may therefore be immanent from their beginnings and seem to "determine" events, while their credibility hangs on the tension maintained between the immanence of meaning and the open-endedness of the human actions they represent.

In *The Empire of the St. Lawrence*, this tension is located in the relationship between thematic imperatives and the struggles of the Montreal commercial class. The Laurentian system is represented neither as actor nor as that which is acted upon, but rather as a verb, a prime mover so to speak, transcending thereby the very distinction between subject and object that "determinism" assumes.[16] The outcome of the merchants' struggles, foreshadowed in the promises and portents of the opening, is only fully comprehended through the unfolding of the narrative to its ultimate, tragic closure.[17]

The distinction employed here between discourse and story — between the order of telling and the order of the past — focuses particular attention on the element of choice in historiography. At the same time, if historians may choose among identifiable varieties of historiographical telling, they must also assess the appropriateness of different forms to the questions they ask, the interpretations they reach, and the aspect of the past they seek to recount. While the recently renewed debate concerning the ontological status of the historical record cannot be engaged here, my assumption is that the past as record exists as an autonomous reality and that histories are distinct from fictions precisely because of the fidelity they owe to the record that exists beyond them, on which the credibility of their interpretations depends.[18] One's choice of form is therefore neither arbitrary nor entirely free.

Clearly, different interpretative approaches to the same past may give rise to different formal representations. Fernand Ouellet's *Economic and Social History of Quebec 1760–1850*, for example, has as its object of inquiry a portion of the past almost identical to that examined in *The Empire of the St. Lawrence*, and shares with it certain concerns, with change as well as continuity, and with the relations of commerce and politics.[19] Even so, Ouellet's professedly empirical study of economic sectors, demographic patterns, and social relations finds expression in a synchronic form that contrasts sharply with Creighton's diachronic representation of the failure of the merchants' Laurentian ambitions. For all of his concern with periodization, and hence with chronology, Ouellet is not led to adopt a narrative ordering.

The past itself also exerts certain formal pressures and this is nowhere more evident than in biography, where the object of historical inquiry is the life of an individual. In biography, the literal sequence of birth, life, and death normally predetermines the unfolding of the subject's story from beginning to end. The basic framework of the "story" encourages a narrativistic form of "discourse." Other pressures derive from content. The delineation of character, the representation of individual action, the assessment of motive and effect, and the elucidation of background conditions and circumstances are all matters biographers normally address.[20] Their focus, therefore, is necessarily individual and human in the way commonly considered to be a mark of narrative. In turning to Donald Creighton's biography of Sir John A. Macdonald, then, we should expect to find a narrative discourse. At the same time, we might also ask whether the very coincidence of "story-form" and "discourse-form" does not present special problems for the narrator. If beginning, middle, and end are so obviously given, how does the discourse find its own coherence? How is it ordered so as to avoid the "and then, and then, and then" of simple chronological exposition?

Some answers to this question may be found in the opening of *John A. Macdonald: The Young Politician*, the first of the biography's two volumes.[21] More generally, by its treatment of space, time, and human action, it illustrates the role of sequence in the working out of narrative logic. The first thing we notice is that the beginning of the opening refers neither to John A. Macdonald nor to a precise time; it describes rather a general process, the arrival of immigrants in Upper Canada during the late eighteenth and early nineteenth centuries. More concretely, it describes their means of transport, the country through which they passed, the layout of the town of Kingston, its place in the colonial urban hierarchy, and its Janus-like situation at the head of the St Lawrence River and the foot of the Great Lakes system. The description is strikingly flat and spatial.

In a sense, of course, no one will find this surprising. The spatial background dimension of Creighton's discourse has always been recognized as a distinguishing feature of his art. Who has not remarked on his evocation of setting through descriptions of landscape, weather conditions, architecture, or the interior furnishings of the very rooms in which actions were taken and incidents occurred?[22] Yet space is represented in equally full and concrete detail and, sometimes, with an equal sense of immediacy, in the non-narrative discourse of historical geographers – in Harris's *The Seigneurial System in Early Canada*, say, or in Eric Ross's invented settler's guide, *Beyond the River and the Bay*.[23] In *The Empire of the St. Lawrence*, as we have seen, geography serves to order the narrative thematically rather than lend it a spatial dimension. The question, then, is what gives spatial description in *The Young Politician* its narrative stamp?

Here it will be useful briefly to consider the "microstructure" of the opening; the structure, that is, of Creighton's sentences, specifically those devices and constructions he uses to convey passage of time, temporal relations, and point of view, and which, in the normal course of reading, imperceptibly structure meaning.[24] These include verbal constructions, adverbs, adverbial phrases, and their contextual associations. The opening sentence, for example – "In those days they came usually by boat" (1) – refers to a time distant but unspecified, and to an action frequently repeated. The effect is to suggest duration. The immigrants referred to journeyed by various means, one of which was "the new steamers which in the last few years had begun" to travel the river (1). Nothing yet has indicated which "last few years" these might be, nor is the temporal vantage point of the past perfect "had begun" any more definite than "those days." Spatial description is interwoven, from the point of view of unspecified immigrants in indefinite time: "here the rocky formation of the Laurentian Plateau thrust a huge knotted fist southward . . . As the boats slipped at length past Howe Island . . . their destination was still hidden by a bulging promontory of mainland" (1). Although migration was a process occurring over time, it is represented, in space, as background.

Part way into the second paragraph we encounter the first verb in the simple past tense from the narrator's point of view: "In 1820," Creighton writes, "it was thirty-six years" since the settling of the town-site of Kingston (2). Here is where background intersects with the sequential ordering of the discourse. His own vantage point established, Creighton continues to develop his description of background, now specifying more precisely its temporal limits. Kingston "had not done badly" since 1784; it "had since 1789 been the British naval base on Lake Ontario" (2). Looping back to 1820, with the construction of the "stone frigate" at Point Frederick, he continues his survey: "West of the river, in the town itself, the commandant still kept up his fine house" (3). Duration is reasserted: some of the soldiers stationed at Kingston "were becoming citizens" and "were settling down" (3). Finally the nodal importance of 1820 is revealed: in July of that year, Macdonald's family arrived from Scotland. The opening thereby finds, at length, its temporal center of gravity.

No sooner is this point fixed than Creighton is off on another background loop, this time a description of the origins and family connections of Helen Shaw, John A.'s mother, to the time of her marriage to Hugh Macdonald; and then those of Hugh and the reasons for the family's migration – in 1820. Another description follows, first of Kingston as a commercial town, then of the opening of Hugh's first shop – in 1820. The children are then described, last of all John A. himself as he must have appeared at the age of about five and a half, when the family migrated – that is, in 1820. "Now," Creighton writes, "he was almost ready for school" (11). So, with this characteristic verbal construction – a temporal adverb in the discourse-present, "now," modifying a verb in the story-past, "was" – he introduces the subject of the biography.

It need hardly be said that no summary such as this can capture the full complexity of Creighton's manipulation of sequence, much less the nuances of his prose. Its purpose, rather, is to show that the narrativity of spatial description in the opening of *The Young Politician* derives from its relationship to the sequential order of the discourse. It has no autonomous significance. Together with other descriptions, including those depicting individual physical appearance and "character," spatial descriptions intersect with sequence and render it multidimensional, or "rounded." Discourse-sequence is not merely story-chronology; indeed, beginning with the introduction of John A., Creighton provides convenient chronological indicators in the upper corners of the text (1820–4, Age 5–9; 1825–28, Age 10–13; and so on), while the text itself roams widely around the ostensible benchmarks of "story-time." The "looping" effect noted above is the motor of the discourse, which moves, not year by year or day by day, but back and forth and overlapping around successive nodal points, accumulating bearings in time and space that serve to situate and explain successive actions.

Carl Berger makes a case for the continuing importance of the Laurentian theme in Creighton's interpretation of Macdonald. Although the river itself appears only fleetingly in the biography, he says, "images of it recur, like the lietmotif [sic] of an opera, sufficiently often to remind us that it is the ultimate source of the national design that Macdonald promoted." Its inspiration has become deeply embedded in the "instincts, emotions, and habits of men" and is now expressed in their very thoughts and actions: "The theme of the empire of the St. Lawrence is the same, but it is carried to a new movement and transformed."[25] We may note in this regard that the biography ends as well as begins with the river: "It was nearly seventy-one years since Hugh and Helen Macdonald and their small family of children had first set foot on the dock at Kingston. Beyond the dock lay the harbour and the islands which marked the end of the lowest of the Great Lakes; and beyond the islands the St. Lawrence River began its long journey to the sea."[26] In both opening and closing, aesthetic effect is derived from the river's associations, of arrival, promise and new beginning on the one hand, and of departure, death and return on the other. Even so, the theme does not act as a determinant of form as it did in *The Empire of the St. Lawrence*; instead, it is subordinated to the representation of human action. It is no accident that the explicit statements of the thesis that Berger offers in support of his case are drawn from sources other than the biography itself.[27]

Berger's interpretative insight is relevant, nevertheless, to our discussion. If the Laurentian theme is there, back of the discourse, as it were, what does this suggest about Creighton's use of the narrative mode? We know from his own testimony that he was attracted by Big Subjects: "There is an instinct in me for the grandiose," he once told Charles Taylor.[28] Searching for a subject in the mid-1940s, he was drawn to a life of Macdonald precisely because it might serve as a history of Canadian nation-making, with Macdonald at its center. The alternative he considered was a history of Anglo-French conflict in North America before the British conquest – no monographic intent there.[29] If Macdonald was a grand subject, however, biography was less susceptive of thematic execution than the rise and fall of the empire of the St Lawrence. It encouraged, if it did not actually prescribe, a different narrative treatment, which in turn required that Creighton discipline his instincts and his artistry to different narrative demands. The Laurentian theme might help to shape his interpretation; it could not show forth in all its preternatural grandeur.

P. B. Waite has said of Creighton, as Isaiah Berlin said of Tolstoy, that he was a fox who believed in being a hedgehog.[30] This is enormously suggestive of the tension in Creighton's work between the foxish depiction of diverse human actions firmly situated in time and place and the hedgehog impulse to locate meaning in transcendent, metahistorical forces. The analysis offered here suggests that Waite's formulation be reversed and slightly altered, to the effect that Creighton was a hedgehog who was led by his formal decisions to assume the outlook of a fox. Other indications of his hedgehog tendencies may be found in his attraction to Spengler's organicism or in the suspicions he harbored of the epistemological capacities of his own discipline. Novelists, he said, were better able to probe the mysteries of human behavior than were historians.[31] Narrative biography imposed constraints on these tendencies and, at the same time, offered Creighton an opportunity to write history on a human scale. Macdonald, as a man of vision, might embody history, but he had to do so without violating common-sense notions of human capacity.

A narrative, like any form of prose discourse, is composed of statements that may individually be abstracted from the whole for consideration of one kind or another: from a history, for example, to determine veracity in relation to cited evidence. At the same time, whatever truth a narrative claims to express derives from its coherence as a unit as well as from its components: a history, for example, from the way it sees things together as well as from its aggregation of successive verifiable statements. The "roundedness" conveyed by the intersection of background description and sequence is a feature not only of the narrative representation of individual actions and happenings but of the narrative in its entirety. To quote Louis Mink again, narratives construct a "single and concrete complex" or "ensemble" of relationships that communicates by the necessary means of consecutive sentences the narrator's comprehension of things together.[32] This explains why narrative histories cannot be additively combined to form a single story; each has its own beginning, middle, and end, and their stories can only be aggregated by telling a new story, with its own beginning, middle, and end. It also explains why narrative interpretations of the past are not contained *in*, but are rather expressed *by* the narrative as a unified entity.

The narrative depiction of things-together-in-a-whole is nowhere more instructively displayed in Creighton's historiography than in *The Road to Confederation: The Emergence of Canada, 1863–67*, a work that Roger Graham called an example of "narrative history at its best."[33] Again the opening sentence is revealing: "It was the enthusiasm of Gordon of New Brunswick that gave the movement its real start" (1). Here, conceivably, is a thesis statement, a proposition to be followed by proofs marshaled in demonstration of its validity. It is no such thing. Although we learn much in the course of the first chapter about Arthur Hamilton Gordon and the movement for Maritime Union, to which the sentence refers, that persuades us that he gave the movement its "real start," his enthusiasm is not represented as a link in a causal chain. It is an element in an interconnected story. We learn that, in the array of circumstances, conditions, actions, and happenings that constitute the story of the coming of Confederation, Gordon's actions as lieutenant-governor of New Brunswick are an appropriate place to begin.

Just as in *The Young Politician*, the opening sentence – or that to which the sentence refers – hovers indefinitely, its specificity withheld, and is succeeded by sentences that refer to things prior to it in time and distant from it in space. We are immediately told that Maritime Union "had long been" a subject of discussion. We learn further that one of its advocates, Lord Mulgrave, "had long before" moved on to his next colonial appointment and "was to return to England" in 1863. In a long second paragraph we are told of Gordon's arrival in New Brunswick in 1861, of his father's earlier prime ministership and still earlier adherence to Sir Robert Peel in the division over the Repeal of the Corn Laws, and of Gordon's service as private secretary to William Ewart Gladstone on the latter's mission to the Ionian Islands in 1858. Here Creighton tells us of how Gordon had embarrassed his superior, during their stopover in Brussels, by causing them to be late for a state dinner, forcing Gladstone, seated in one of the king's carriages, to await the young man's arrival: "Five minutes went by. No Arthur. Ten minutes. No Arthur." Finally, Arthur arrived for their departure, offering a trivial explanation and no apologies (1–2).

The impression created by the opening is of a beginning *in medias res*, yet the "real start" refers, in fact, to Gordon's dispatch to the colonial secretary of 6 July 1863, which sets in motion his plans for the convening of a conference to discuss the union of the Maritime colonies. Without it, Confederation would not have come about in the way that it did. The writing of the dispatch itself is only described about half-way into the chapter and its significance is only made apparent – and then partially – at the end. By withholding specificity, Creighton accomplishes two things. First, he begins at the beginning of *his* story, while indicating at the same time that *all* historical stories begin in the midst of things. Second, he lays the basis for his deployment of all those techniques by which he achieves roundedness: movement back and forth in time, variation of temporal extension, shifts in perspective between narrator and narrated, and the interweaving of miniature stories and stories within stories. By these means, sentences that, literally speaking, succeed one another on the page as discursive units communicate Creighton's understanding of the relationship among the things they describe, which, as we follow its development, we grasp as a whole.

The wholeness of a particular story communicated by narrative may perhaps be seen more clearly by comparing *The Road to Confederation* with *British North America at Confederation*, the study Creighton prepared for the Rowell-Sirois Commission in 1939.[34] The "story" in both cases is the same, the formation of the Dominion of Canada in 1867; the "telling," however, is different. In the earlier work, events are ordered according to their assigned significance in determining the constitutional structure of confederation and, particularly, its financial provisions. Creighton describes and analyzes external and internal influences, productive activities, economic changes, social patterns, and political problems. He treats colonies and regions as distinct units, devotes separate attention to their interrelations, and sums up his discussion by identifying the "forces" back of colonial unification. The ordering principle of *British North America at Confederation*, in short, is classificatory and analytic, rather than sequential and narrativistic.

This does not mean that time and chronology are unimportant in Creighton's earlier interpretation. On the contrary, he states plainly in his introduction that "the Confederation of the British North American provinces was achieved at a particular time, by a particular generation and in the midst of a peculiar conjuncture of circumstances" (7). Elsewhere in the text, chronology is prominent: "The year 1857 was the crisis year" (11); "In the period up to 1867, however, the changes were not conspicuous" (25); "In 1830 the Quebec and Halifax Navigation Company was founded . . . in 1836 the *Saint Andrews and Quebec Rail Road Association* was chartered . . . and in 1844 plans for the Intercolonial Railway began to take shape" (37). The chronology is not always straightforward: "By 1860 there were 172,000 inhabitants in Minnesota; in 1858 it became a state in the union; and several years before this had happened the transportation and communication system of the Hudson's Bay Company had already been directed southward" (29). (Here, in fact, the chronology is straightbackward.) In addition, to return to the introduction, the temporal relationship of author and subject is acknowledged by explicit reference to continuities as well as discontinuities between "then" and "now."

Yet, in each case statements denoting the time of an occurrence (or its location, or, more occasionally, its agent) are arrayed as components of an analysis rather than a story. The very plain-statedness of the introduction's reference to temporal particularity is a clue to the analytic nature of the discourse. In analysis, what is important is explicitly stated; in narrative, what is important is shown by the telling. Thus, the discourse of *British North America at Confederation* is susceptible to summary and disaggregation. After reading it, we can ask what, in Creighton's view, the external pressures were, what precipitated constitutional reorganization, why the constitution divided jurisdiction as it did, and arrive at an answer to each question without distorting the meaning of his work as a whole. By contrast, when we ask, after reading *The Road to Confederation*, how, in Creighton's view, Confederation came about, we can answer our question only by beginning again at page one.

Roger Graham said of Creighton's description of French-Canadian ladies at a ball, "There may be grumbles that all of this has nothing to do with Confederation."[35] Indeed, it has nothing to do with Confederation, considered as the constitutional result of certain economic, social, and political factors. Like other background descriptions of setting and character, however, it intersects with sequence to produce roundedness and is therefore integral, as Graham recognized, to the understanding of the coming of Confederation communicated by the narrative whole.

The answer to my opening question, then, is that of course Donald Creighton was a narrative historian – most of the time, in different ways. In posing the question, my purpose has been neither to recommend Creighton's historiographic practice as a model to be followed, nor to prescribe rhetorical techniques derived from it, however richly he exploited the possibilities of narrative history. Instead, I have sought to heighten our awareness of historiography in general, and to clarify our understanding of the narrative mode in particular. In criticizing our conventional notions of narrativity, I have shown them to be at once indefinite and unnecessarily restrictive. Conditions and circumstances, setting and character, and human actions, intentions, and experiences may all be elements of a story rendered as narrative. Yet they are seen together in manifold relationships – spatial, temporal, explanatory, genetic, and so on – by means of a discursive form constructed by the teller. The chronology of the story elements is established by the telling but does not order it, while the recounting of particular doings and events need not be at the sacrifice of collectivities and general processes.

Seen as a way of ordering a discourse, narrative has no necessary "political" content, nor does it require the use of particular kinds of evidence. Creighton's interests, the fullness of his sources, and his confidence in the pastness of the past allowed him to construct certain sorts of narratives, some of which were political in content. As Mark Phillips has argued, however, other sorts of narratives may well be constructed on more fragmentary sources and may give voice to more self-consciously subjective historical accounts of other matters.[36] One finds in Natalie Davis's *The Return of Martin Guerre*, for example, a discourse that derives narrative coherence from the story of the author's own efforts to piece together and find cultural meaning in the account of her subject, in the telling of which she acknowledges gaps, uncertainties, and her own historicity.[37] Phillips's own rendering of the story of Marco Parenti proceeds in a similar fashion, with similar intent.[38] Narrativity may be achieved in different ways, in the telling of different kinds of stories.

At the same time, narrative is only one among many ways of writing history. Character studies, interpretative essays, cross-sectional portraits, and so on offer alternative models of historiographical discourse. Adoption of the narrative mode is a matter of judgment. Such judgment, however, entails conceptual choices. When theorization or classification, for example, serves as the governing ideal of historical inquiry and understanding, some other kind of representation is called for, if only because the articulation of presuppositions required of these approaches cuts across the shared "common sense" of writer and reader on which narrative is commonly grounded. Such approaches, in applying theories, or in posing and testing hypotheses, or in manipulating data and abstracting factors and characteristics, will find a narrative order of telling inappropriate to their needs and purposes.

These conclusions should encourage a fresh consideration of the relationship of form and content. Historiographical narrative, in its structuring of human agency in the context of time and space, would seem to presuppose a domain of human choice and purposive action that is often neglected, hidden, or denied in theoretical and typological approaches to the study of the past. This may help explain its pejorative association with traditional political history and its more positive association, in putative revival, with the new cultural history. In both cases the underlying issue, for many, has been the extent to which people's lives are shaped by natural, structural, and systemic forces beyond their control. Narrative, in short, is a way of ordering a discourse; it may also be a way of thinking, whose virtues historians will need to reconsider if narrative is truly to experience a revival.

Notes

1   A useful guide to the narrative trend in the philosophy of history is Hayden V. White, "The Question of Narrative in Contemporary Historical Theory" [1984], in *The Content of the Form: Narrative Discourse and Historical Representation* (Baltimore: Johns Hopkins University Press, 1987), 26–57, while the narrativity of current historical writing is queried by Mark Phillips, "The Revival of Narrative: Thoughts on a Current Historiographical Debate," *University of Toronto Quarterly* 53 (winter 1983/4): 149–65.

2   Hayden White makes this point with respect to *Annaliste* criticisms of narrative history ("Question," 31–3); Gertrude Himmelfarb's liberal defense of political history is no more precise in its usage ("History with the Politics Left Out," in *The New History and the Old* (Cambridge, Mass.: Harvard University Press, 1987), 14, 25); while J. L. Granatstein simply claims narrative as the exclusive preserve of political history, "broadly defined" (*Toronto Star Saturday Magazine*, 24 June 1989).

3   Lawrence Stone, "The Revival of Narrative: Reflections on a New Old History," *Past and Present* 85 (1979): 24.

4   J. H. Hexter, "Historiography: The Rhetoric of History," *International Encyclopedia of the Social Sciences*, vol. 6 (New York: Macmillan and Free Press, 1972 [1968]), 369–93.

5   Carl Berger, *The Writing of Canadian History: Aspects of English-Canadian Historical Writing, 1900 to 1970* (Toronto: Oxford University Press, 1976), 208.

6   Ibid., 222–3. See also J. M. S. Careless, "Donald Creighton and Canadian History: Some Reflections," in John S. Moir (ed.), *Character and Circumstance: Essays in Honour of Donald Grant Creighton* (Toronto: Macmillan, 1970), 8–21, and George Woodcock, "The Servants of Clio: Notes on Creighton and Groulx," *Canadian Literature* 83 (winter 1979): 131–41.

7   The theoretical literature pertaining to fictional narrative is usefully summarized in Seymour Chatman, *Story and Discourse: Narrative Structure in Fiction and Film* (Ithaca: Cornell University Press, 1978), 15–42. For a humanist critique of the extremes to which recent theory has taken the "textuality" of the text see M. H. Abrams, "How To Do Things with Texts," *Partisan Review* 46 (1979): 566–88.

8   Nelson Goodman, "Twisted Tales; or Story, Study, and Symphony," in W. J. T. Mitchell (ed.), *On Narrative* (Chicago: University of Chicago Press, 1981), 111.

9   The term is Hayden White's, used in his *Metahistory: The Historical Imagination in Nineteenth-Century Europe* (Baltimore: Johns Hopkins University Press, 1973), 5.

10   Donald Creighton, *The Empire of the St. Lawrence* (Toronto: Macmillan, 1956), 1 (my emphasis). The book was first published as *The Commercial Empire of the St. Lawrence* (Toronto: Ryerson Press, 1937) in the series sponsored by the Carnegie Endowment for International Peace, "The Relations of Canada and the United States."

11   Berger, *Writing of Canadian History*, 213–14, 223–4. Creighton later described the structure of the book in this way, during an interview with Ramsay Cook; see Eleanor Cook (ed.), *The Craft of History* (Toronto: Canadian Broadcasting Corporation, 1973), 139.

12   Phillips, "Revival;" Hayden V. White, "The Value of Narrativity in the Representation of Reality" [1980], in *Content of the Form*, 1–25.

13   Cartier, Talon, Radisson, and La Salle are mentioned earlier by name only, in association with appropriate continental features.

14   Louis Mink, "History and Fiction as Modes of Comprehension" [1970], in *Historical Understanding* (Ithaca: Cornell University Press, 1987), 56.

15   Jonathan Culler, "Story and Discourse in the Analysis of Language," in *The Pursuit of Signs: Semiotics, Literature, Deconstruction* (Ithaca: Cornell University Press, 1981), 179.

16   Cf. John Ayre, *Northrop Frye: A Biography* (Toronto: Random House, 1989), 374. Discussing Frye's work on the Bible, Ayre writes, "Borrowing from Buckminster Fuller, Frye suggested that perhaps God was a verb, not simply a verb of asserted existence but a verb expressing a process fulfilling itself." So might Creighton be said to have naturalized the providential narrative.

17   For a suggestive discussion of tragedy in Creighton's works see William Westfall, "Creighton's Tragic Vision," *Canadian Forum* 50 (Sept. 1970): 200–2, a review of *Canada's First Century* (Toronto: Macmillan, 1970).

18   The debate is complex and often seems distant from the historian's practical concern with doing history. White's work, already cited, may be taken as representative of the extreme "self-referential" view of discourse in relation to record, which leads him to assimilate history to fiction. F. R. Ankersmit ("The Dilemma of Contemporary Anglo-Saxon Philosophy of History," *History and Theory, Beiheft* 25 (1986): 1–27) disputes certain aspects of White's formalism but, in his emphasis on the "intertextuality" of historical narratives, construed simply as historical interpretations, he shares White's aversion for epistemological questions. David Carr ("Narrative and the Real World: An Argument for Continuity," *History and Theory* 25 (1986): 117–31), at the other extreme, argues that narrative mirrors historical reality and is not, therefore, distinguishable as one mode of historiographical discourse, and is certainly not a "linguistic event." Helpful guides to the issues raised by "the semiotic challenge" are provided by two medieval historians: Nancy Partner, "Making Up Lost Time: Writing on the Writing of History," *Speculum* 61 (1986): 90–117, and Gabrielle M. Spiegel, "History, Historicism, and the Social Logic of the Text in the Middle Ages," *Speculum* 65 (1990): 59–86.

19   Fernand Ouellet, *Economic and Social History of Quebec, 1760–1850: Structures and Conjunctures*, Carleton Library No. 120 (Toronto: Macmillan, 1980).

20   Robert Craig Brown, "Presidential Address: Biography in Canadian History," *Historical Papers/Communications historiques*, 1980, 1–8.

21   *John A. Macdonald: The Young Politician* (Toronto: Macmillan, 1952); *John A. Macdonald: The Old Chieftain* (Toronto: Macmillan, 1955).

22   The epilog chapters of both volumes perhaps come first to mind in this regard.

23   Richard Colebrook Harris, *The Seigneurial System in Early Canada: A Geographical Study* (Kingston and Montreal: McGill-Queen's University Press, 1984 [1966]); Eric Ross, *Beyond the River and the Bay* (Toronto: University of Toronto Press, 1970).

24   See Chatman, *Story and Discourse*, Chap. 2, "Story: Events," 43–95, and Chap. 3, "Story: Existents," 96–145.

25   Berger, *Writing of Canadian History*, 223–4.

26   Creighton, *The Old Chieftain*, 578.

27   Berger, *Writing of Canadian History*, 217 n21, 224 n37; cf. *The Young Politician*, 383.

28   Charles Taylor, *Radical Tories: The Conservative Tradition in Canada* (Toronto: Anansi, 1982), 31–2.

29   Berger, *Writing of Canadian History*, 217, 222; Cook, *Craft of History*, 140.

30   Peter Waite, "A Point of View," in Moir (ed.), *Character and Circumstance*, 234. Berlin's famous essay starts from the maxim of the Greek poet Archilochus, "The fox knows many things, but the hedgehog knows one big thing." "The Hedgehog and the Fox," in *Russian Thinkers* (Harmondsworth, Eng.: Penguin Books, 1982 [1978]), 22–81.

31   Taylor, *Radical Tories*, 25, 32; see also Donald Creighton, "History and Literature," in *Toward the Discovery of Canada* (Toronto: Macmillan, 1972), 21–2. For an illuminating discussion of the challenge the novel presented to Thomas Babington Macaulay see Mark Phillips, "Macaulay, Scott, and the Literary Challenge to Historiography," *Journal of the History of Ideas* 50 (Jan.–March 1989): 11–33.

32   Mink, "History and Fiction," 52–3, and "Narrative Form as a Cognitive Instrument" [1978] also in *Historical Understanding*, 198. Mink distinguished among three "modes of comprehension:" theoretical, categoreal, and configurational. History, in this view, typically employs the configurational mode, though not exclusively; and while the form of discourse of the configurational mode tends to be narrative, it need not be so. A similar conception of historical understanding and communication may be found in Isaiah Berlin's discussion of "thick description" in "The Concept of Scientific History," *History and Theory* 1 (1960): 1–31, and in Hexter's account of "narrative explanation" in "Historiography," 373–80.

33   *The Road to Confederation: The Emergence of Canada, 1863–1867* (Toronto: Macmillan, 1964); Roger Graham, review of *The Road to Confederation*, *Canadian Historical Review* 46 (Sept. 1965): 251.

34   *British North America at Confederation: A Study Prepared for the Royal Commission on Dominion-Provincial Relations 1939* (Ottawa: Queen's Printer, 1963 [1939]).

35   Graham, review of *Road to Confederation*, 252.

36   Phillips, "Revival," 153.

37   Natalie Zemon Davis, *The Return of Martin Guerre* (Cambridge, Mass.: Harvard University Press, 1983).

38   *The Memoir of Macro Parenti: A Life in Renaissance Florence* (Princeton: Princeton University Press, 1987).

Chapter 23

Margaret R. Somers

NARRATIVITY, NARRATIVE IDENTITY, AND SOCIAL ACTION

Rethinking English working-class formation

THE NINETEENTH-CENTURY ENGLISH working class bears a most peculiar burden and embodies a most peculiar paradox. Like Auden's academic warriors who spar with "smiles and Christian names," historians, economists, and sociologists have pushed and prodded early nineteenth-century English working people into procrustean political positions to support or disconfirm Marx's predictions of revolutionary class conflict erupting from the contradictions of capitalism. A Manichaean concern locks the debate into an impasse. Were early nineteenth-century workers revolutionary or reformist? Was there a class struggle in the industrial revolution? The questions remain unsolved. Yet, surely it is the history of English working peoples that has suffered from this burden of praising or burying Marxism through competing interpretations of their early stories?

The burden has been made heavier, moreover, by the weight of continual excoriation from all sides of the ideological terrain for the "refusal" of English workers to precisely fit either of the categories of proper revolutionary or reformist behavior. Indeed, "why the peculiarities of the English?" has been an intellectual complaint since the birth of the theory of class. It is the paradox of this phenomenon, however, that is most striking: the yardstick against which the English working class is measured "peculiar" was constructed by classical sociological conceptions of class formation for which *English working people served as the putative historical model*. Surely, something is amiss when the original historical actors whose lives were appropriated for a theoretical schema of class formation are subsequently judged deviant by that same theory.

The paradox and the burden clearly point to a fresh agenda. Rather than asking yet again what explains the "peculiarities" of the English (or the "exceptionalism" of this or that national working class), the time has come to call into question the peculiarities of this *theory* that judges as deviant each empirical case it addresses.

These observations and claims are at the heart of this essay, which aims to offer a critical evaluation of class-formation theory — a theory that seeks to explain how and why the working class comes to *act* in the ways that it does. In this rethinking of class-formation theory I am joining with and benefiting from the critical and historical energies of many other students of class formation and social theory. My approach, however, will have a particular twist. I will argue that the means to achieve this revised conception must be through an engagement with the concept of *narrative* and, more generally, with the constitutive place of *narrativity* in social theory. My overall aim is to demonstrate the theoretical and historical significance of narrative and narrativity not only for studies of working-class formation, but for social science research more generally.

The relationship between narrative and the core problems of class-formation theory is twofold. First, I will argue that one particular *story* – the classical story of England's transition from traditional to modern society – is at the core of the problems of class-formation theory. This single *master-narrative* was the substantive vessel that carried the theoretical innovations of those we now recognize as founders of the social sciences – Adam Smith, Ricardo, Marx, Mill, Durkheim, Weber, Freud. Ultimately, this storied dimension of modern social science was lost from sight, but it did not lose its significance. In a curious inversion, the narrative of classical modernization became merely a subfield of the social science disciplines ("modernization theory" – which has been long discredited, especially in its 1950s–60s incarnation), while in an utterly fragmented form the story was abstracted into the foundations of class-formation theory. The conceptual and methodological vocabulary of this theory is built on these abstracted fragments of the classical narrative of English socioeconomic development. The implications are clear. Class-formation theory cannot be successfully revised on a theoretical basis alone. Instead, we must recognize, reconsider, and challenge the particular encoded narrative. But if we accept this as the case, it also seems unlikely that we can or should attempt to escape altogether from the narrative dimension of social explanation (Somers 1990, 1992a); thus, we must also rethink, rehistoricize, and ultimately *retell* that foundational story of the English.

This historical deconstruction, however, must be accompanied by a conceptual one. After all, the classical story of English socioeconomic development was constructed, like all narratives, through a particular *conceptual filter*. That filter was the social naturalism of the late eighteenth and nineteenth centuries – an attempted epistemological escape from all we associate with historicity. In social naturalism, temporality, spatiality, relationality, and concrete linkages all gave way to the abstract ideals of natural self-regulating entities. But nothing could have been more ironic and paradoxical: a master-narrative of modern English society was produced through the lens of a self-consciously – indeed, belligerently self-conscious – anti-historical, antinarrative, anti-relational, naturalistic conceptual frame. As a result, the foundational story deeply encoded within modern social science has all the formal components of an analytic narrative – a beginning (traditional society), a middle (crisis of the industrial revolution), and an end (resolution into modernity), as well as leading protagonists in action (classes in struggle) and causal emplotment (the engine of industrialization, proletarianization). The only thing missing is *conceptual narrativity* – social concepts that can embrace historicity, time, and space. The story's conceptual core – classes, society, tradition and modernity – comprises abstractions, unseen and atemporal.

The results are the strange hybrid we unconsciously live with today – a social science theory sprung from a vision of escaping the past (history) that is nonetheless constituted on a narrative framework. And in this paradoxical combination can be found the source of many of the problems of class-formation theory. In the task of recognizing and rethinking the master-narrative of this theory we must therefore reconstruct historical and relational concepts. In the following pages I will introduce the two central terms of this revision: *narrative identity* and *relational setting*. Part I examines recent theories of English class formation to demonstrate the presence of an encoded master-narrative and the paradoxical problem of this being a "denarrativized" (conceptually abstract) narrative. Part 2 addresses the concept of narrative in both its old and its new incarnations, and Part 3 examines the conceptual implications of narrative for social science research. Finally, Part 4 outlines a retold story of English class formation.

I. The denarrativized narrative of class-formation theory: the case of the English

Studies of English working-class practices are embedded and burdened by the *theory* of class formation. Yet the paradox is that encoded within the theory is a denarrativized master-narrative about the long-term processes of English socio-economic development. Such a naturalistic rendering of history is abstracted into a general model of the relationship between industrialization, proletarianization, the birth of class society, and the expected behavioral response of the working classes. Whether the term is worker, social actor, industrialization, culture, society, or class, each element of the theory bears within it the master-narrative. And from this obscured but powerful master-narrative comes the problem that drives all studies of working-class formation: why the failure (or incoherency, peculiarity, or deviance) of the "real" working classes?

This section argues that the incoherencies and peculiarities attributed to actual working-class practices are not those of the English or any other historical case. Rather, they are the incoherencies of class-formation theory. The incoherency stems from inferring a teleological prediction (class-in-itself–class-for-itself or working peoples' objective interests will eventually translate into revolutionary class consciousness) not from a genuine theoretical generalization but from a wrong-headed master-narrative based on an antihistorical conceptual framework. There are many new stories to be written; the work of renarrativization, however, first requires careful attention to the ways in which previous studies have been confined by class-formation theory.

The vast literature on English working-class formation in sociology and history is typically grouped around three explanatory paradigms. The English working class in the industrial revolution was either: (1) reformist (Smelser 1959; Perkin 1969; Thomas 1970; Musson 1976), (2) revolutionary in the 1830s but suppressed by the 1850s (E. P. Thompson 1966; Foster 1974; Saville 1988), or (3) "backward-looking" and composed of artisans (not factory workers) who were "reactionary radicals" (Calhoun 1981; Bauman 1982). With all injustice duly acknowledged, I am not going to address either the important complexities within or the differences among these three approaches; their common points, however, are of interest.

Each of these approaches is a different answer *to the same question*: why did the English working class in the industrial revolution either conform to or deviate from the revolutionary behavior predicted by class-formation theory? That is to say, why did the working class not act in "classlike" ways? And in all three paradigms, the question is addressed not to empirical cases of *variation*, but to *deviations* from a prediction. Why, in other words, did the class-in-itself–class-for-itself prediction fail? Each approach embodies the same prediction – namely, that under normal conditions there should be a causal link between the societal and economic changes of the industrial revolution (class in itself) and the emergence of a revolutionary class consciousness (class for itself).

The main difficulty with this prediction is that the English working class (and just about all working classes) have resolutely "refused" to behave properly. Yet when faced with divergences between observed behavior and theoretical predictions, scholars of class formation have all too rarely asked why workers did what they did *compared to other working classes*. Such a strategy would have led to a healthy multitude of competing empirical explanations to be tested and refined. Instead, the "nonrevolutionary" behavior of working people has been redefined into problems of *deviance* or *anomalousness*. Yet (as we know from Michael Polanyi [1958] and T. S. Kuhn [1970]), once an empirical finding has been defined as anomalous, *it cannot be used to test or falsify a theory*. Instead, it is the theory and the prediction that remain pristine (Polanyi has called this position of privilege one of "tacit knowledge"), while countless "alibis" are generated for the deviations. Thus, class-formation theory has been reduced to a measuring rod used to chastise the shortcomings of working peoples. The result has been a scholarly preoccupation with what I have elsewhere called an *epistemology of absence* (Somers 1989a).

Several scholars of working-class formation have criticized just this problem. Katznelson and Zolberg (1986), in particular, have tried to reframe the theory by jettisoning the constricting teleological expectation built into the concept of class consciousness and converting the explanandum to variations in class formation. Their efforts have been heroic but unsatisfactory. For the problem of failed expectations will not be solved by changing the dependent variable from revolutionary class consciousness to variations in working-class dispositions. The problem lies much deeper: *the tenacity of the prediction is inexorably grounded in the tenacity of a single representational narrative*. Indeed, most striking about all three theories of working-class formation is that they are in essence *three different versions of the same story*, that is, three different "endings" to the same beginning and middle of an encoded master-narrative.

There is, moreover, a ghostly familiarity to this narrative. Simply, it is the story of The Industrial Revolution – the emergence of an industrial capitalist society from a preindustrial past. It is, of course, a story told in many idioms – the transition from feudalism to capitalism, the emergence of market society, the emancipation of civil society from the state, the increasing division of labor, and the rationalization of the modern world. For each, the societal transformation – whether it is called industrialization, proletarianization or the division of labor

— ushers in the "birth of class society." It is a story that has economic, political, and cultural components. In the economic realm it is a process by which commercialization, an increasing division of labor, and technological development gradually break the bonds of relatively static preindustrial economies into industrial and capitalist growth. Politically, it is the story of the emergence of the liberal state that provides the framework and/or actively supports the new laissez-faire economy and its subsequent class relations. And it is a process by which "traditional" relations are transformed into class relations, and communitarian artisanal cultures organized by moral economies are supplanted by the force of new class alignments — from the "bread nexus to the wage nexus."

Rather than debating whether working-class behavior even *should* be explained by the "birth of class society," these different paradigms reflect only the different views about *how* the working class *responded* to a presupposed *causal primacy* of societal transformation. Here is the depth of the problem: each theory defines a priori the *same independent variable* — proletarianization and capitalist society. This leaves for empirical research only the historical variations of this process. Katznelson's (1986) theory, no less than the prevailing paradigms of English working-class formation, continues to build an a priori causal argument into the question and retains by assertion precisely that which requires demonstration, namely, the causal primacy of a social entity — proletarianization (or industrialization, or the transition from feudalism to capitalism, or modernization) — in explaining the social practices of working peoples. The different approaches, moreover, do not represent disagreement over the precise nature of the transformation. Each version follows the same sequence from traditional preindustrial to modern industrial society to make its case. And when all is said and done about the particular intervening influences on social action — religious, moral, cultural, political, and community factors — each explicitly makes the same point. First, Harold Perkin (1969): "At some point between the French Revolution and the Great Reform Act, the vertical antagonism and horizontal solidarities of class emerged on a national scale from and overlay the vertical bonds and horizontal rivalries of connection and interest. That moment . . . saw the birth of class." Now E. P. Thompson (1966): "When every caution has been made, the outstanding fact of the period between 1790 and 1830 is the formation of the working class. This is revealed, first, in the growth of class-consciousness: the consciousness of an identity of interests as between all these diverse groups of working people and as against the interest of other classes. And, second, in the growth of corresponding forms of political industrial organization" (pp. 212–13). Finally, Craig Calhoun (1981): "All were essentially movements of those [nineteenth-century "reactionary radicals"] who would fight against the coming of industrial society, who had traditional communities to preserve."

A sequential development from traditional preindustrial society to industrial capitalist society and a radical rupture of the late eighteenth and early nineteenth centuries are thus the essentially noncontested concepts at the heart of theories of class formation. The real linchpin that holds the theory and its prediction together is thus the *story* of the rupture and transformation from a preindustrial to an industrial/capitalist society. The chain of linkages is inexorable: only the presence of the prediction leads to the problematic of "failure" and "peculiarity" of behavioral outcome. Yet the *content* of the prediction – the expectation of class society producing class consciousness – is solely predicated on the explanatory master-narrative of classical modernity and its conceptual infrastructure. As long as the question of working-class social action is bound a priori to the societal transformations of industrialization and the birth of class society, the research task will be confined to elaborating different versions of a presumed (but not demonstrated) causality between the transformation of societal entities and a predicted working-class consciousness.

2. What is narrativity?

From contesting the master-narrative embedded in theories of class formation, it is only a short leap to suggest that new stories need to be constructed about the long-term history of the English. But new stories cannot merely be the product of one assertion against another. The original master-narrative of modernity, as I have argued, was itself constructed from a naturalistic, epistemological attempt to escape from historicity, time and space. The paradoxical consequence is that the master-"narrative" at the core of class-formation theory is conceptually both anti-narrative and ahistorical. From this odd hybrid comes the many incoherent predictions that so often render social life and social action fundamentally unintelligible. Indeed, class-formation theory exemplifies incoherence. Given the foundational role of the theory's master-narrative and the self-conscious expunging from that narrative of a conceptual narrativity, it is arguable that class-formation theory has been in a sorry state from the beginning. If our new stories are not to sound relentlessly like variations on the old, what we need is more than the deconstruction of the master-narrative of English modernization. We also need to develop a conceptual narrativity.

Narrative and the historians

While narrative has always been the nonexplanatory and non-theoretical "other" for the social sciences, historians themselves have had a conflicting and changing relationship to the concept. In France in the 1940s, the *Annales* historians rejected both traditional political history and narrative in favor of more anthropological, structural, and quantitative analysis (Stoianovich 1976; Bourde and Martin 1983; Hunt 1986, 1989). Meanwhile, instead of rejecting narrativity, a sector of Anglo-American historians led by Carl Hempel (1942, 1962) argued that narrative itself was a science of history and, if done correctly, would produce general laws capable of both explanation and prediction. In spite of two decades of vigorous debate, this particular view of narrative faded (Gardiner 1952; Gallie 1968; Dray 1957; Atkinson 1978). In the 1960s there was a new kind of rejection of narrative developing on both sides of the Atlantic. In this heyday of the social sciences, historians in North America produced "social science history," while the revival of Marxist and Weberian theory in Britain generated "social history" there (Kammen 1980; Stearns 1985). Social science methods and theories became favored, and narrative was rendered into nontheoretical storytelling about elites.

In the late 1970s, however, the leading social historian Lawrence Stone (1979) led a "return to narrative" movement. A vigorous auto-critique of social science historical methods allowed Stone to argue that the overbearing influence of these methods had eliminated any historical concern for meaning. Despite his terminology, however, Stone was not really advocating a return to the traditional notion of narrative. Newly influenced by Geertz (1973) and the emerging "anthropological turn," he was advocating an interpretative approach. By no means has the new "post-social" history returned to traditional narrative methods. In the present era where the central debates among historians take place among advocates of poststructuralist, interpretive approaches, and most recently advocates of the "linguistic turn," very few defenses can be found of what came to be defined as a nontheoretical mode of history writing (e.g. Scott 1988a; Megill 1989, 1991; Novick 1991).

But what exactly was it that was being rejected or rediscovered? Despite the broad debates, each of these positions shared a common definition of narrative as *a mode of representation* – discursive, rather than quantitative; nonexplanatory, rather than conditionally propositional; and nontheoretical, rather than the theoretically driven social sciences. The conflict among historians was solely over how to *evaluate* that representational form. For "traditional" historians, narrative was ideal because the accurate representation of history was the essence of the historian's craft; for the social science historians, traditional narrative representational form was inadequate to the task of explaining and interpreting the past.

Reframing narrativity

Despite historians debating and increasingly scorning the value of narrative over the past two decades, scholars from a wide spectrum of disciplines (including psychology, medicine, psychoanalytic theory, education, philosophy, political science, gender studies, and anthropology) have quietly appropriated the abandoned concept and often used it to produce major conceptual breakthroughs in their fields. But the concept employed by these disciplines is radically different from the older interpretation of narrative as simply a representational form. The new notion recognizes narrative and narrativity to be concepts of social epistemology and social ontology. These concepts posit that it is through narrativity that we come to know, understand, and make sense of the social world, and it is through narratives and narrativity that we constitute our social identities. It matters, therefore, not whether we are social scientists or subjects of historical research, but that we come to *be* who we *are* (however ephemeral, multiple, and changing) by our location (usually unconsciously) in social narratives and networks of relations that are rarely of our own making.

Common features of social narrativity

From diverse sources it is possible to identify four features of a reframed narrativity particularly relevant for the social sciences: (1) relationality of parts; (2) causal emplotment; (3) selective appropriation; and (4) temporality, sequence, and place. Above all, narratives are constellations of *relationships* (connected parts) embedded in *time and space*, constituted by what I call *causal emplotment*. Unlike the attempt to explain a single event by placing it in a specified category, narrativity precludes sense-making of a singular isolated phenomenon. Narrativity demands that we discern the meaning of any single event only in temporal and spatial relationship to other events. Indeed, the chief characteristic of narrative is that it renders understanding only by *connecting* (however unstable) *parts* to a constructed *configuration* or a *social network* (however incoherent or unrealizable). In this respect, narrative becomes an epistemological category.

The connectivity of parts is precisely why narrativity turns "events" into *episodes*, whether the sequence of episodes is presented or experienced in anything resembling chronological order. It is causal emplotment that gives significance to independent instances, not their chronological or categorical order. And it is emplotment that translates events into episodes. Without emplotment, events or experiences could be *categorized* only according to a taxonomical scheme. As a mode of explanation, then, causal emplotment is an accounting (however fantastic or implicit) of why a narrative has the story line it does (Veyne 1971; Ricoeur 1981, 1984-6). Causal narrativity allows us to test a series of "plot hypotheses" against actual events, and then to examine how – and under what conditions – the events intersect with the hypothesized plot. Polkinghorne (1988) implicitly addresses the difference between emplotment and categorization when he notes that social actions should not be viewed as a result of categorizing oneself ("I am 40 years old; I should buy life insurance") but should be seen in the context of a life-story with episodes ("I felt out of breath last week; I really should start thinking about life insurance"). Similarly, it is also apparent that serious mental confusion rarely stems from one's inability to place an event or instance in the proper category. Rather, we tend to become confused when it is impossible or illogical to integrate an event into an intelligible plot (MacIntyre 1981). To make something understandable in the context of what has happened is to give it historicity and relationality. This makes sense because when events are located in a temporal (however fleeting) and sequential plot, we then can explain their relationship to other events. Plot can thus be seen as the logic or syntax of narrative (Ricoeur 1979; Veyne 1971; Polkinghorne 1988).

The significance of emplotment for narrative understanding is often the most misunderstood aspect of narrativity. Without attention to emplotment, narrative's explanatory dimension can easily be overlooked and be misperceived as a non-theoretical representation of events. Yet it is emplotment that permits us to distinguish between narrative, on the one hand, and *chronicle* or *annales* (White 1987), on the other. In fact, it is emplotment of narrative that allows us to construct a *significant* network or configuration of relationships.

Another crucial element of narrativity is its *evaluative criteria* (Linde 1986; L. Polanyi 1985; Somers 1986). Evaluation enables us to make qualitative and lexical distinctions among the infinite variety of events, experiences, characters, institutional promises, and social factors that impinge on our lives. Charles Taylor (1989), for example, argues that the capacity to act depends to a great extent on having an evaluative framework shaped by what he calls "hypergoods" (a set of fundamental principles and values) (also see Calhoun 1991). The same discriminatory principle is true of narrative: in the face of a potentially limitless array of social experiences deriving from social contact with events, institutions, and people, the evaluative capacity of emplotment demands and enables *selective appropriation* in constructing narratives (Somers 1986). A plot must be thematic (Kermode 1984; Bruner 1987). The primacy of this narrative theme or competing themes determines how events are processed and what criteria will be used to prioritize events and render meaning to them. Themes such as "husband as breadwinner," "union solidarity," or "women must be independent above all" will selectively appropriate the happenings of the social world, arrange them in some order, and normatively evaluate these arrangements.

Four kinds of narrativity

These relatively abstract concepts, however, can also be expressed through four different kinds of narrative – ontological, public, conceptual, and metanarrativity.

Ontological narratives are the stories that social actors use to make sense of – indeed, in order to act in – their lives. We use ontological narratives to define who we *are*, not just to know what to do. Locating ourselves in narratives endows us with identities – however multiple, ambiguous, ephemeral or conflicting they may be (hence, the term *narrative identity* (Somers 1986)). To have some sense of social being in the world requires that our lives be more than different series of isolated events; ontological narratives, for instance, process events into episodes. People act, or do not act, in part according to how they understand their place in any number of given narratives – however fragmented, contradictory or partial. Charles Taylor (1989: 51–2) puts it this way: "because we cannot but orient ourselves to the good, and thus determine our place relative to it . . ., we must inescapably understand our lives in narrative form, as a 'quest.'"

But identity, like the self, is neither a priori nor fixed. Ontological narratives make identity and the self something that one *becomes* (Nehamas 1985). Narrative embeds identities in time, and spatial relationships; ontological narratives structure activities, consciousness, and beliefs (Carr 1985, 1986). Like all narratives, ontological narratives are structured by emplotment, relationality, connectivity, and selective appropriation. So basic to agency is ontological narrativity that if we want to explain – that is, to know, to make sense of, to account for, perhaps even to predict anything about the practices of social and historical actors, their collective actions, their modes and meanings of institution-building, and their apparent incoherencies – we must first recognize the place of ontological narratives in social life.

But where do ontological narratives come from? How are people's stories constructed? Above all, ontological narratives are social and interpersonal. Although psychologists are typically biased toward the individual sources of narratives, even they recognize the degree to which ontological narratives can only exist *interpersonally in the course of social and structural interactions over time* (Sarbin 1986, Personal Narratives Group 1989). To be sure, agents adjust stories to fit their own "identities," and, conversely, they will tailor "reality" to fit their stories. But the interpersonal webs of relationality sustain and transform narratives over time. Charles Taylor (1989) calls these "webs of interlocution;" others (MacIntyre 1981) call them "traditions;" I will call them "public narratives."

Public, cultural, and institutional narratives are those narratives attached to "publics," to a structural formation larger than the single individual, to intersubjective networks or institutions, however local or grand, micro or macro – stories about American social mobility, the "freeborn Englishman," the emancipatory story of socialism, and so on. Public and cultural narratives range from the narratives of one's family to those of the workplace (organizational narrativity), church, government, and "nation." Like all narrative, these stories have drama, plot, explanation, and selective appropriation. Families, for example, selectively appropriate events to construct stories about their descent into poverty. The mainstream media arrange and connect events to create "mainstream plots" about the origin of social disorders. The seventeenth-century church explains the theological reasons for a national famine. Government agencies tell us "expert" stories about unemployment. Charles Taylor (1989) emphasizes the centrality of public narrative to ontological narrative when he states: "We may sharply shift the balance in our definition of identity, dethrone the given, historical community as a pole of identity, and relate only to the community defined by adherence to the good (or the saved, or the true believers, or the wise). But this doesn't sever our dependence on webs of interlocution. It only changes the webs, and the nature of our dependence."

Conceptual/analytic/sociological narrativity refers to the concepts and explanations that we construct as social researchers. Because neither social action nor institution-building is solely produced through ontological and public narratives, our concepts and explanations must include the factors we call social forces – market patterns, institutional practices, organizational constraints. Herein lies the greatest challenge of analytic and conceptual narrativity: to devise a conceptual vocabulary that we can use to reconstruct and plot over time and space the ontological narratives and relationships of historical actors, the public and cultural narratives that inform their lives, and the crucial intersection of these narratives with other relevant social forces.

For our purposes, it is the conceptual dimension of analytic narrativity that is most important. To date, few if any of our analytic categories are in themselves temporal and spatial. Rather, our modern sociological use of terms such as "society," the "actor," and "culture" was for social science purposes intentionally abstracted from their historicity and concrete relationships. The conceptual challenge that narrativity poses is to develop a social analytic vocabulary that can accommodate the contention that social life, social organizations, social action, and social identities are narratively constructed through both ontological and public narratives.

Metanarrativity, the fourth level of narrativity, refers to the "master-narratives" in which we are embedded as contemporary actors in history and as social scientists (Foucault 1972, 1973; Jameson 1981; Lyotard 1984). Our sociological theories and concepts are encoded with aspects of these master-narratives – Progress, Decadence, Industrialization, Enlightenment, etc. – even though they usually operate at a presuppositional level of social science epistemology or beyond our awareness. These narratives can be the epic dramas of our time: Capitalism vs. Communism, the Individual vs. Society, Barbarism/Nature vs. Civility. They may also be progressive narratives of teleological unfolding: Marxism and the triumph of Class Struggle, Liberalism and the triumph of Liberty, the Rise of Nationalism, or of Islam. The example I discuss of the master-narrative of Industrialization/ Modernization out of Feudalism/Traditional Society is only one of many cases in which a presuppositional story gets in the way of historical social science. But I have also pointed to what is perhaps the most paradoxical aspect of master-narratives:

their quality of *denarrativization*. That is, they are built on concepts and explanatory schemes ("social systems," "social entities," "social forces") that are in themselves abstractions. Although master-narratives have all the necessary components of narrativity – relationality, transformation, major plot lines and causal emplotment, characters and action – they nonetheless miss the crucial element of a conceptual narrativity.

3. What are the new narrative's implications for social science history?

What, then, are the implications of this new conception of narrative for social and historical research? How can narrative help us do empirical research about social life and social practices? Although all four kinds of narrativity are relevant to social science research, if we are to adequately account for working-class formation and social action, the important one is the third: conceptual and analytic. A conceptual narrativity demands *temporality, spatiality*, and *emplotment* as well as *relationality, structure,* and *historicity*. *Narrative identity* and *relational setting* represent concepts that have worked best in my own research.

Narrative identity. I have argued that narrativity is a condition of social being, social consciousness, social action, institutions, and structures. If narrative is indeed a constitutive feature of social life, our first challenge is to develop concepts that allow us to capture the narrativity through which identities are constructed and social action mediated. The concept of a narrative identity is predicated on just this premise: narrativity is not a *form* imposed on social life, but social life and human lives are themselves "storied" (Carr 1986; Sarbin 1986). Social identities are constituted through narrativity, social action is guided by narrativity, and social processes and interaction – both institutional and interpersonal – are narratively mediated.

Class-formation theory, by contrast, explains action with the concept of interest. "Interest" is determined from the logic and stages of socioeconomic development. In this way the social analyst imputes a particular set of interests to people as members of *social categories* (e.g. traditional artisan, modern factory worker, peasant). For example, historians commonly argue that the decline of traditional domestic modes of production and the decline's concomitant threat to custom created an "artisanal interest." Although social science historians almost always demonstrate with subtlety how these interests are mediated through intervening factors (culture, gender, religion, residential patterns, etc.), the social interests derived from the socioeconomic entity are the foundational explanation for working-class practices and protests. Making sense of social action thus becomes an exercise in identifying social categories, deriving putative interests from them, and then doing the empirical work of looking at variations on those interests (e.g. Wright 1985; McNall *et al.* 1991).

To understand action, however, why should we assume that an individual or a collectivity has any particular set of interests simply because *one aspect* of their identity fits into one social category? Why should we assume that artisans have "artisanal" interests simply because they are members of the "declining artisanal mode of production" category? To let "class" stand for a determinative experience is to presume that which has not been empirically demonstrated – namely, that identities are foundationally constituted by categorization in the division of labor within a unified socioeconomic totality we call "society."

Substituting the concept of identity for that of interest circumvents this problem. An identity approach to action assumes that social action can only be intelligible if we recognize that people are guided to act by the relationships in which they are embedded rather than by interests we impute to them. Where interest is derived from how we as analysts categorize people's role in a division of labor, the identity approach focuses on how people *characterize* themselves. While a social category is an internally stable concept which assumes that under "normal" conditions, entities within that category will demonstrate appropriate "categorical" behaviors, characterization, by contrast, embeds the person within patterns of relationships that continually shift over time and space. These temporally and spatially shifting configurations form the relational coordinates of ontological, public, and cultural narratives. It is within these numerous and multi-layered narratives and social networks that identities are formed and challenged; hence, narrative identity.

The narrative dimension of identities presumes that action can be intelligible only if we recognize the one or many ontological and public narratives in which actors identify themselves. Rather than deriving from interests, narrative identities are constituted by a person's temporally and spatially specific "place" in culturally constructed stories that comprise (breakable) rules, (variable) practices, binding (and unbinding) institutions, and the multiple stories of family, nation, or economic life. People's experiences as workers, for example, were inextricably interconnected with the larger matrix of relations that shaped their lives – their regional location, the practical workings of the legal system, family patterns – and the particular stories (of honor, of ethnicity, of gender, of local community, of greed, etc.) used to account for the events happening to them.

Although social action is only intelligible through the construction, enactment, and appropriation of public narratives, this does not mean that individuals are free to fabricate idiosyncratic narratives at whim; rather, they must "choose" from a repertoire of stories. Which kinds of narratives will socially predominate is contested politically and will depend in large part on the actual distribution of power (Somers 1986). This is why the kinds of narratives people use to make sense of their situation will always be an *empirical* rather than a presuppositional question. The extent and nature of any given repertoire of narratives available for appropriation is always historically and culturally specific; the particular plots that give meanings to those narratives cannot be determined in advance.

Relational Setting. Social action and narrative identity are shaped through both ontological and public narratives, as well as by social environments. We thus need a conceptual vocabulary that can relate narrative identity to that range of factors we call social forces – market patterns, institutional practices, organizational constraints, and so on. Another challenge of analytic narrativity is therefore to *locate* the actors as characters in their social narratives and to *emplot* them in a temporal and spatial configuration of relationships and practices (institutions and discourses). We need concepts that will enable us to plot over time and space the ontological narratives of historical actors, the public and cultural narratives that inform their lives, as well as the relevant range of other social forces – from politics to demography – that configure together to shape history and social action.

Society is the term that usually performs that work for us in social analysis. When we speak of understanding social action, we simultaneously speak of locating the actors in their societal context. But society as a concept is rooted in a wholistic and falsely totalizing way of thinking about the world. If we want to be able to capture the narrativity of social life, we need a way of thinking that can substitute relational for totalizing metaphors. Here, I concur with Michael Mann (1986) who has written, "It may seem an odd position for a sociologist to adopt; but if I could, I would abolish the concept of 'society' altogether" (p. 2).

For virtually all practicing social science research, a society is a social *system*. As a system, it has a core essence – an essential set of social springs at the heart of the mechanism. This essential core, in turn, is reflected in broader, covarying societal institutions that the system comprises. Thus, when sociologists speak of feudalism, we mean at once "feudal society" as a whole, a particular set of "feudal class relations" at the core of this society, a "feudal manorial economy," and a concomitant set of "feudal institutions" such as feudal political units and feudal peasant communities. Most significantly for historical research, each institution within a society must covary with each other. Thus, in feudal societies, the state by definition must be a feudal state whose feudal character covaries with all other feudal institutions; feudal workers must all be unfree and extraeconomically exploited peasants. And in industrial society, a modern industrial/capitalist state must be detached from civil society and the industrial economy, and industrial workers must be individual and free. To be sure, the synchrony is not always perfect. In periods of transition from one society to another, there occurs a lag effect, and remnants of the old order persist against the pressures of the new. But despite these qualifications, the systemic metaphor assumes that the parts of society covary along with the whole as a single entity.

If understanding working-class formation is to be more than an exercise in extending a unifying core to the assumption of interest, these systemic typologies must be broken apart and their parts disaggregated and reassembled on the basis of empirical relational clusters. To make this possible, I am suggesting that we substitute the concept of a *relational setting* for "society." A relational setting is a pattern of relationships among institutions, public narratives, and social practices. Identity formation takes shape within this relational setting of contested but patterned relations among people and institutions. As such, it is a relational or structural matrix, similar to a social network.

One of the most important characteristics of a relational setting is that it has a history (MacIntyre 1981) and thus must be explored over time and space. Temporally, a relational setting is traced over time not by looking for the indicators of social development, but by empirically examining if and when the interaction among the institutions of the setting appears to have produced a decisively different outcome from its previous examinations. Social change, from this perspective, is viewed not as the evolution or revolution of one societal type to another, but by shifting relationships among the institutional arrangements and cultural practices that make up one or more social settings.

Spatially, a relational setting must be conceived with a geometric and morphological rather than a mechanistic metaphor; it is composed of a geometric matrix of institutions linked to each other in variable patterns contingent on the interaction of all points in the matrix. A setting crosses levels of analysis and brings together in one setting the effect of, say, the international market, the state's warmaking policies, the local political conflicts among elites, and a community's demographic practices. This cross-cutting character of a relational setting assumes that the effect of any one level (for example, the proto-industrial textile sector) can be discerned only by assessing how it is affected interactively with the other relevant levels. To do so requires that we first *disaggregate* the parts of a setting from any presumed covarying whole and then reconfigure them in their temporal and geographic relationality. In this way, for example, different regions of England are no longer cast as variants of a single society, but as different relational settings that can be compared.

4. Narrative identity, relational analysis, and class formation

So far, I have noted two implications of narrativity for engaging in social science: first, that we need to substitute the concept of narrative identity for that of interest, and second, that we need to substitute the concept of relational setting for that of society or social system. This new narrative and relational analysis can potentially liberate us as analysts from the overarching grand narratives that have constrained class-formation theory. In this final section, I will briefly note how this conceptual apparatus can be used to rethink research on working-class formation and retell the story of English class formation.

One important outcome of making relational settings and cultural narratives the basis of working-class social action is to eliminate class-formation theory's perenniel concerns about "inconsistency," "failed predictions," or "deviancy." The identity approach, in contrast, *expects absolute historical contingency* between social practices and the industrial revolution (or any other societal transformation). The effect of such historical interactions is what must be explored empirically, as must the question of whether these interactions will enable or constrain social action. The assumption of contingency thus challenges the assumptions that workers' behaviors which do not conform to categorical assumptions are anomalous, irrational, or "backwardlooking;" the settings in which identities are constituted have no endogenous directionality or a priori definition of rational action. If the contexts that give meaning, contingency, and historicity to identity have no teleology, no actions can be assessed as more objectively rational than others. All working-class behavior becomes potentially intelligible.

Another implication of the narrative identity approach is that our research must begin not from a single category but from the network of relationships and institutions in which actors are embedded; we then must emplot these actors and institutions in their varying relationships to each other — relationships that vary in social and political distances as well as interactive effects. Substituting a relational setting for the abstraction of society allows us to induce empirical connections among institutions rather than presupposing covariation. The positions and distances within a relational setting help to make sense of what kinds of social practices were possible, both at the level of structural opportunity and of purpose, identity, and meaning. Thus identity reconstitution becomes a two-step process. The first involves finding and interpreting the clues left by historical actors regarding the narratives that have guided their actions. The second step in the process involves using those clues as well as research on broader social and structural relationships to configure these elements and repertoires into geometric social networks.

My research on the English case can schematically illustrate these points. In the years from 1800 to 1850, English laboring people violently broke machines and marched peacefully to Parliament; they mobbed unpopular workhouses, and they petitioned to retain or reinstitute apprenticeship and wage regulations; they demanded new forms of state intervention into the length of the working day, and they tenaciously fought for the right to outdoor poor relief and for local control over its administration; they waged militant strikes, and they formed self-help and community-based educational organizations; families "huddled" and exercised political influence by boycotting selected merchants; and at critical periods they linked these practices to the political demand for working-class participation in Parliament and universal suffrage.

Let us leave aside the question of whether these were revolutionary, reformist, or "backwardlooking" goals. Who cares? Let us note, instead, the central narrative that ran like a thick thread through all the multiple social practices, goals, and movements. Simply, this narrative theme was that working people had inviolable *rights* to particular *political* and *legal* relationships. They claimed these rights as citizens and focused on a particular understanding of the law, a particular understanding of "the people" and their membership in the political community, and a particular conception of the legal relationship between the people and the law. This conception of rights defined independence and autonomy as inexorably linked to the property rights of working people (Prothero 1979; G. Stedman Jones 1983). But those rights were only in part the fruits of individual labor; they primarily rested on membership in the political community (Somers 1986, 1992b).

The most notable result of this narrative was that in the midst of the worst economic distress of their lives, English industrial families based their protests not on economic demands or those of a "moral economy," but on a broadly conceived claim to legal rights to participation, substantive social justice (Poor Laws), local government control, cohesive family and community relations, "modern" methods of labor regulation (trade unions), and the right to independence – be it from capitalists, the state, or on other workers. They relied on plot lines driven by a conception of justice and *rights in membership* to explain their distress and guide their action. Consistently, they aimed their protests toward the law, legal authorities, legal ideals of universality and equity, local political and legal institutions, and toward enhancing the solidarity of the community itself. The relationship between "the people and the law" was thus the prevailing public narrative of these working people, and the plot line which configured this narrative was that of a political culture of rights. The history and projected future of this rights' culture was the theme through which events were evaluated, explained, and given meaning. They provided the guides to action, the methods for the remedies of wrongs and distress.

This characterization does not prioritize either a language of class or of politics. There is no question that a language of class developed from the 1830s on, just as there is no question that that same language identified the state as controlling the levers of social power. But most significantly, the language of rights embraced both politics and class; it was the explanatory prism through which class issues and other aspects of social distress were mediated and made sense of. Rights' claims were thus political in the broadest sense; they established the claim to empowerment deriving not only from constitutional and "natural" rights, but from community cohesion and autonomy in membership. Because they conjoined artisanal conceptions of property-based citizenship rights, these claims also conjoined our usually separate notions of social and political rights. Rights-bearing identities included class rights as one part of a bundle of rights attached to political membership under law; they combined social power, politics, individual rights, and membership.

To explain these practices through narrative analysis means we must reconstruct the relational settings in which these identities unfolded. But in what did such settings consist? How do we know where to begin the task of reconstitution? After first recounting the prevailing narratives, we must follow their themes and plots – about the law, about the communities in which the law operated, and about the local interaction between communities and the law. And from these we can configure into geometric and temporal form the shifting and varied relational settings in which our actors lived. This is not the place to summarize such a massive project of identity-reconstitution; I will hint only programmatically at my findings.

The identities of nineteenth-century English working peoples can be traced to and compared among four roughly different relational settings: (1) pastoral, rural-industrial, later northern industrial communities; (2) agricultural laboring communities; (3) urban/artisanal communities; and (4) French pastoral and rural-industrial communities. Four different historical and geographical anthropologies (1300–1850) furthermore comprise (1) variations in productive activities and working relations; (2) variations among English and Continental legal institutions, doctrines, statutory claims, ideals, promises, and policies – especially the differing political and legal rights attached to property relations, statutory labor regulations, legal administrative procedures, and discursive ideals of jurisprudence; (3) variations among communities – kinship, demographic, inheritance, and migration patterns among England's urban and rural (both freeholder and laboring) popular communities; and (4) differences in the practical workings of English law and justice at the local levels of the contrasting English communities.

Doing comparisons via relational settings involves specifying linkages and constructing networks at two levels. In the setting as a whole, each institution forms a point, or a domain, in a geometric pattern. Connecting lines represent the actual interactive links between the institutions. Rather than imputing an a priori function to a type of production, for example, one asks what kinds of relationships it generated (or what kinds of relationships must have existed for it to have taken root in the first place?) and what the patterns of these connections were. Thus, for example, in the eighteenth-century rural domestic industries, I plotted the connections of merchant-capitalists to their family "employees" and followed the processes by which work was distributed, wages negotiated, infractions of contract dealt with, and payments organized. This led to plotting the daily treks of a middleman, as well as directly to local administrators of statutory labor law. This in turn led to the participatory mechanisms through which these laws were carried out, which would require an understanding of class relations in the community. Relational analysis therefore neither dismisses nor reduces production to "the economy" (with all the systemization invoked by that category), but rather it constitutes economic production as one institution among many; as merely one of a multiple network of competing institutions and practices that bear on identity-formation.

At a second level, relational analysis transforms each institution from a single entity to a set of relationships. The state, for example, may well be an instrument of coercion, but more important is its actual amalgam of suborganizations and their relationships with each other. The law is another example that as a category means little. The historical meaning of law begins to take shape only by charting its numerous institutional and discursive expressions, from the highest courts to the most trivial of local juries to the discourses of social justice and the statutory pre-ambles. This kind of network analysis makes it possible to study the continual shifts in the kinds and consequences of interactive patterns and institutional arrangements. Substituting the term *place* for that of "role" (part of the systemic metaphor) allows us to *locate* institutions and practices in their relational settings.

The significance for identity-formation of each relational setting emerges only by comparing patterns of power, economics, and culture over varying times and places. Thus, it would be a mistake to presume that the lives of seventeenth-century rural-industrial families can be understood by simply invoking the category "proletarianized unit of production." Instead, I asked what sorts of family and work ties had to exist, for example, to sustain certain kinds of inheritance practices. Inversely, what sorts of relationships did different inheritance practices produce and support? Similar questions can be addressed to institutional power relations (rather than relying on a priori categories of "strong" or "weak" states). What administrative power did the crown have available for certain policies? How was this power implemented in local communities?

My alternative story can be briefly summarized. The meaning of working-class formation cannot be found in the "birth of class society" but in the long-term conse-quences of the legal revolutions of medieval England. Alone among European state-builders, only the English created a national public sphere by appropriating from below and extending throughout the land the legal conventions of both the medieval cities and the public villages. In legal practices the state became the city "writ-large;" remedies of procedural justice ensuring rights in autonomy and inde-pendence coexisted with both national redistributive policies, as well as legal institutions that commanded community participation in the administration of law.

This mandatory participation in legal administration by all free-holders may have been the most crucial factor in English working-class formation. The most notable result of this participatory system was that which I have dubbed a system of *narrative justice* – the local contextualizing and negotiating of legal processes. This legal narrativity generated different patterns of justice – indeed, different legal cultures in different types of settings. Historically persistent patterns of difference existed in the structure of early labor markets, in the degree of popular participa-tion in political and legal institutions, in the character of corporate village institutions, and, above all, in popular conceptions and social narratives of justice and rights. Popular empowerment varied in the degree to which communities were able to appropriate the law into rights. Most remarkably, because local communities administered a formally uniform national law, the multiple narratives of community politics were institutionalized into the heart of the national legal and political apparatus.

Narrative analysis, thus, produces a different picture of English class formation. What we recognize as nineteenth-century working-class formation developed from patterns of protest almost exclusively in the northern industrial villages — the inheritors of those strong, popular legal cultures of early pastoral and rural-industrial relational settings. Working families carried with them into the nineteenth century a robust narrative identity based on a long culture of practical rights — a culture honed, revised, and adjusted over many centuries, and one they were not likely to dismiss at the crossing of an "event" dubbed by historians only years later as the industrial revolution.

5. Conclusion

The aim of this essay has been to explain why class-formation theory is so problematic and how it might be reconsidered. My definition of the problem is similar in part to that articulated by Katznelson and Zolberg (1986) in their influential volume on working-class formation. The theory, with its predictive teleology of class-in-itself–for-itself, forces an accounting not for actual patterns of variation, but for "an epistemology of absence" (Somers 1989). Ultimately, the theory has continually chastised and measured social action against a societal yardstick. These problems are reflected in the three prevailing approaches to nineteenth-century English class formation I discussed above; each defines working-class practices ("reformist," "revolutionary," "backwardlooking") against the presuppositional backdrop of the in-itself–for-itself theoretical prediction.

But there is a deeper problem to which I have called attention, namely, the a priori assumption that the rise of an entity called capitalism must be *the* foundational causal factor in shaping these practices. Regardless of its ideological persuasion, each paradigm roots the explanation of nineteenth-century working-class social action in the "birth of class society;" the *response* to that birth on the part of workers is what distinguishes the approaches. The conceptual limitations of Katznelson's (1986) own revisions show just how intractable a problem this is. Although he is able to avoid teleology through a comparative approach to the dependent variable (class dispositions and actions), he is unable to envision a theory that can escape from ultimately reducing these to the a priori causality of proletarianization and, more generally, the emergence of capitalism.

The true challenge for theorists of working-class formation is to be able to liberate the study of class action not only from the constraints of an a priori teleological outcome, as Katznelson has done, but, more importantly, to liberate it from the constraints of the a priori independent variable — the master-narrative of English proletarianization. I have tried to show, however, that freeing the theory from these constraints is no simple matter. The underlying problem is the conceptual vocabulary that is the universal parlance of existing discussions of class formation.

Contained within this vocabulary is the massively entrenched and conceptually encoded denarrativized story of the making of modern English class society.

Thus, explaining and recovering the meaning of working-class social action (which is, after all, the goal of class-formation theory) demands not only recognizing the centrality of the classical master-narrative but also systematically loosening its hold. It also requires *renarrativizing* our conceptual language of social action.

References

Atkinson, R. F. (1978) *Knowledge and Explanation in History: An Introduction to the Philosophy of History* (Ithaca, NY: Cornell University Press).

Bauman, Zygmunt (1982) *Memories of Class: The Pre-History and After-Life of Class* (London: Routledge and Kegan Paul).

Bourde, Guy, and Herve Martin (1983) *Les Ecoles Historiques* (Paris: Seuil).

Bruner, Jerome (1987) "Life as narrative." *Social Research* 54 (1): 11–32.

Calhoun, Craig (1981) *The Question of Class Struggle* (Chicago: University of Chicago Press).

—— (1991) "Morality, identity, and historical explanation: Charles Taylor on the sources of the self." *Sociological Theory* 9 (2): 232–63.

Carr, David (1985) "Life and the narrator's art," in Hugh H. Silverman and Don Idhe (eds) *Hermeneutics and Deconstruction* (Albany: State University of New York Press) 108–21.

—— (1986) "Narrative and the real world." *History and Theory* 25 (2): 117–31.

Dray, William H. (1957) *Laws and Explanations in History* (London: Oxford University Press).

Foucault, Michel (1972) *The Archeology of Knowledge* (New York: Pantheon).

—— (1973) *The Order of Things: An Archeology of the Human Sciences* (New York: Random House).

Gallie, W. B. (1968) *Philosophy and the Historical Understanding* (New York: Schocken Books).

Gardiner, Patrick (1952) *The Nature of Historical Explanation* (Oxford: Clarendon Press).

Geertz, Clifford (1973) *The Interpretation of Culture* (New York: Basic Books).

Hempel, Carl G. (1942, 1959) "The function of general laws in history," in Patrick Gardiner (ed.), *Theories of History* (New York: Free Press of Glencoe) 344–56.

—— (1962, 1966) "Explanation in science and history," in William H. Dray (ed.) *Philosophical Analysis and History* (New York: Harper and Row) 95–126.

Hunt, Lynn (1986) "French history in the last twenty years: The rise and fall of the Annales paradigm." *Journal of Contemporary History* 21: 209–24.

—— (ed.) (1989) *The New Cultural History* (Berkeley: University of California Press).

Jameson, Fredric (1981) *The Political Unconscious: Narrative as a Socially Symbolic Act* (Ithaca, NY: Cornell University Press).

Jones, Gareth Stedman (1983) *Languages of Class: Studies in English Working-Class History* (Cambridge: Cambridge University Press).

Kammen, Michael (ed.) (1980) *The Past Before us: Contemporary Historical Writing in the United States* (Ithaca, NY: Cornell University Press).

Katznelson, Ira (1986) "Introduction," in Ira Katznelson and Aristide R. Zolberg (eds) *Working-Class Formation: Nineteenth-Century Patterns of Western Europe and the United States* (Princeton, NJ: Princeton University Press) 3–41.

——— , and Aristide Zolberg (eds) (1986) *Working-Class Formation: Nineteenth-Century Patterns in Western Europe and the United States* (Princeton, NJ: Princeton University Press).

Kermode, Frank (1984) "Secrets and narrative sequence," in W. J. T. Mitchell (ed.) *On Narrative* (Chicago: University of Chicago Press).

Kuhn, Thomas (1970) *The Structure of Scientific Revolution*, 2nd edn (Chicago: University of Chicago Press).

Linde, Charlotte (1986) "Private stories in public discourse: Narrative analysis in the social sciences." *Poetics* 15: 183–202.

Lyotard, Jean-François (1984) *The Postmodern Condition: A Report on Knowledge* (Minneapolis: University of Minnesota Press).

MacIntyre, Alasdair (1981) *After Virtue: A Study in Moral Theory* (Notre Dame, IN: University of Notre Dame Press).

McNall, Scott G., Rhonda R. Levine, and Rick Fantasia (eds) (1991) *Bringing Class Back In: Contemporary and Historical Perspectives* (Boulder, CO: Westview Press).

Mann, Michael (1986) *The Origins of Social Power, vol. 1: A History of Power from the Beginning to AD 1760* (London: Cambridge University Press).

Megill, Allan (1989) "Recounting the past: 'Description,' explanation, and narrative in historiography." *American Historical Review* 94 (3): 627–53.

——— (1991) "Fragmentation and the future of historiography." *American Historical Review* 96 (June).

Musson, A. E. (1976) "Class struggle and the labour aristocracy, 1830–1860." *Social History* 3: 61–82.

Nehamas, Alexander (1985) *Nietzche: Life as Literature* (Cambridge, MA: Harvard University Press).

Novick, Peter (1991) "My correct views on everything." *American Historical Review* 96: 699–703.

Ortner, Sherry (1991) "Narrativity in history, culture, and lives." CSST Working Paper 66, (University of Michigan).

Perkin, H. L. (1969) *The Origins of Modern English Society, 1790–1880* (London: Routledge and Kegan Paul).

Personal Narratives Group (ed.) (1989) *Interpreting Women's Lives: Feminist Theory and Personal Narratives* (Bloomington: Indiana University Press).

Polanyi, Livia (1985) *Telling the American Story* (Norwood, NJ: Ablex).

Polanyi, Michael (1958) *Personal Knowledge* (Chicago: University of Chicago Press).

Polkinghorne, Donald (1988) *Narrative Knowing and the Human Sciences* (Albany: State University of New York Press).

Prothero, I. (1979) *Artisans and Politics in Early Nineteenth Century London: John Gast and His Times* (Baton Rouge: Louisiana State University; Folkstone, England: Dawson).

Ricoeur, Paul (1979) "The human experience of time and narrative." *Research in Phenomenology* 9: 25.

——— (1981) "Narrative time," in W. J. T. Mitchell (ed.) *On Narrative* (Chicago: University of Chicago Press) 165–86.

——— (1984–86) *Time and Narrative* 2 vols. Trans. Kathleen McLaughlin and David Pellauer (Chicago: University of Chicago Press).

Sarbin, Theodore R. (ed.) (1986) *Narrative Psychology: The Storied Nature of Human Conduct* (New York: Praeger).

Saville, John (1988) *The British State and the Chartist Movement* (Cambridge: Cambridge University Press).

Scott, Joan (1988a) Gender and the Politics of History (New York: Columbia University Press).

—— (1988b) "On language, gender, and working-class history," in Joan Scott (ed.) Gender and the Politics of History) 53–67.

Smelser, Neil (1959) Social Change in the Industrial Revolution (Chicago: University of Chicago Press).

Somers, Margaret R. (1986) "The people and the law: Narrative identity and the place of the public sphere in the formation of English working class politics – 1300–1850, a comparative analysis." PhD dissertation, Harvard University.

—— (1989) "Workers of the world, compare!" Contemporary Sociology 18 (May): 325–9.

—— (1990) "Narrativity, culture, and causality: Toward a new historical epistemology (or where is sociology after the historic turn?)." Paper presented at the conference, Historic Turn in the Human Sciences, University of Michigan, 5–6 October, CSST Working Paper 54, University of Michigan.

—— (1992a) "Where is sociology after the historic turn? Knowledge cultures and historical epistemologies," forthcoming in Terrence J. McDonald (ed.) The Historic Turn in the Human Sciences (Ann Arbor: University of Michigan Press).

—— (1992b) "A people without social relations is a people with property: property, relationality, and social networks in the formation of political rights," forthcoming in John Brewer (ed.) Early Modern Conceptions of Property (London: Routledge).

Stearns, Peter N. (1985) "Social history and history: A progress report." Journal of Social History 19 (1985): 319–34.

Stoianovich, Traian (1976) French Historical Method: The Annales Paradigm (Ithaca, NY: Cornell University Press).

Stone, Lawrence (1979) "The revival of narrative: Reflections on an old new history." Past and Present 85: 3–25.

Taylor, Charles (1989) Sources of the Self (Cambridge, MA: Harvard University Press).

Thomas, M. I. (1970) The Luddites (Newton Abbot, England: David and Charles).

Thompson, D. (1984) The Chartists: Popular Politics in the Industrial Revolution (New York: Pantheon).

Thompson, E. P. (1966) The Making of the English Working Class (New York: Vintage).

Veyne, Paul (1971, 1984) Writing History: Essay of Epistemology, translated by Mina Moore-Rinvolucri. (Middletown, CT: Wesleyan University Press).

Wright, Erik Olin (1985) Classes (London: Verso).

Chapter 24

Hayden White

HISTORICAL EMPLOTMENT AND THE PROBLEM OF TRUTH

THERE IS AN INEXPUNGEABLE RELATIVITY in every representation of historical phenomena. The relativity of the representation is a
function of the language used to describe and thereby constitute past events
as possible objects of explanation and understanding. This is obvious when, as in
the social sciences, a technical language is so used. Scientific explanations openly
purport to bear upon only those aspects of events – for example, quantitative and
therefore measurable aspects – which can be denoted by the linguistic protocols
used to describe them. It is less obvious in traditional narrative accounts of historical phenomena: first, narrative is regarded as a neutral "container" of historical
fact, a mode of discourse "naturally" suited to representing historical events directly;
second, narrative histories usually employ so-called natural or ordinary, rather than
technical, languages, both to describe their subjects and to tell their story; and
third, historical events are supposed to consist of or manifest a congeries of "real"
or "lived" stories, which have only to be uncovered or extracted from the evidence
and displayed before the reader to have their truth recognized immediately and
intuitively.

Obviously I regard this view of the relation between historical story-telling and
historical reality as mistaken or at best misconceived. Stories, like factual statements, are linguistic entities and belong to the order of discourse.

The question that arises with respect to "historical emplotments" in a study of
Nazism and the Final Solution is this: Are there any limits on the *kind* of story that
can responsibly be told about these phenomena? *Can* these events be responsibly
emplotted in *any* of the modes, symbols, plot types, and genres our culture provides
for "making sense" of such extreme events in our past? Or do Nazism and the Final
Solution belong to a special class of events, such that, unlike even the French
Revolution, the American Civil War, the Russian Revolution, or the Chinese Great
Leap Forward, they must be viewed as manifesting only one story, as being emplot-
table in one way only, and as signifying only one kind of meaning? In a word, do
the natures of Nazism and the Final Solution set absolute limits on what can be

truthfully said about them? Do they set limits on the uses that can be made of them by writers of fiction or poetry? Do they lend themselves to emplotment in a set number of ways, or is their specific meaning, like that of other historical events, infinitely interpretable and ultimately undecidable?

Saul Friedlander has elsewhere distinguished between two kinds of questions that might arise in the consideration of historical emplotments and the problem of "truth:" epistemological questions raised by the fact of "*competing* narratives about the Nazi epoch and the 'Final solution'" and ethical questions raised by the rise of "representations of Nazism . . . based on what used to be [regarded as] *unacceptable* modes of emplotment." Obviously, considered as accounts of events already established as facts, "competing narratives" can be assessed, criticized, and ranked on the basis of their fidelity to the factual record, their comprehensiveness, and the coherence of whatever arguments they may contain. But narrative accounts do not consist only of factual statements (singular existential propositions) and arguments; they consist as well of poetic and rhetorical elements by which what would otherwise be a list of facts is transformed into a story.[1] Among these elements are those generic story patterns we recognize as providing the "plots." Thus, one narrative account may represent a set of events as having the form and meaning of an epic or tragic story, and another may represent the same set of events — with equal plausibility and without doing any violence to the factual record — as describing a farce.[2] Here the conflict between "competing narratives" has less to do with the facts of the matter in question than with the different story-meanings with which the facts can be endowed by emplotment. This raises the question of the relation of the various generic plot types that can be used to endow events with different kinds of meaning — tragic, epic, comic, romance, pastoral, farcical, and the like — to the events themselves. Is this relationship between a given story told about a given set of events the same as that obtaining between a factual statement and its referent? Can it be said that sets of real events *are* intrinsically tragic, comic, or epic, such that the representation of those events as a tragic, comic, or epic story can be assessed as to its *factual* accuracy? Or does it all have to do with the perspective from which the events are viewed?

Of course, most theorists of narrative history take the view that emplotment produces not so much another, more comprehensive and synthetic factual statement as, rather, an *interpretation* of the facts. But the distinction between factual statements (considered as a product of object-language) and interpretations of them (considered as a product of one or more metalanguages) does not help us when it is a matter of interpretations produced by the modes of emplotment used to represent the facts as displaying the form and meaning of different kinds of stories. We are not helped by the suggestion that "competing narratives" are a result of "the facts" having been *interpreted* by one historian as a "tragedy" and *interpreted* by another as a "farce."[3] This is especially the case in traditional historical discourse in which "the facts" are always given precedence over any "interpretation" of them.

Thus for traditional historical discourse there is presumed to be a crucial difference between an "interpretation" of "the facts" and a "story" told about them. This difference is indicated by the currency of the notions of a "real" (as against an "imaginary") story and a "true" (as against a "false") story. Whereas interpretations are typically thought of as commentaries on "the facts," the stories told in narrative histories are presumed to inhere either in the events themselves (whence the notion of a "real story") or in the facts derived from the critical study of evidence bearing upon those events (which yields the notion of the "true" story).

Considerations such as these provide some insight into the problems both of competing narratives and of unacceptable modes of emplotment in considering a period such as the Nazi epoch and events such as the Final Solution. We can confidently presume that the facts of the matter set limits on the *kinds* of stories that can be *properly* (in the sense of both veraciously and appropriately) told about them only if we believe that the events themselves possess a "story" kind of form and a "plot" kind of meaning. We may then dismiss a "comic" or "pastoral" story, with an upbeat "tone" and a humorous "point of view," from the ranks of competing narratives as manifestly false to the facts – or at least to the facts that *matter* – of the Nazi era. But we could dismiss such a story from the ranks of competing narratives only if (1) it were presented as a *literal* (rather than *figurative*) representation of the events and (2) the plot type used to transform the facts into a specific kind of story were presented as inherent in (rather than imposed upon) the facts. For unless a historical story is presented as a literal representation of real events, we cannot criticize it as being either true or untrue to the facts of the matter. If it were presented as a figurative representation of real events, then the question of its truthfulness would fall under the principles governing our assessment of the truth of fictions. And if it did not suggest that the plot type chosen to render the facts into a story of a specific kind had been found to inhere in the facts themselves, then we would have no basis for comparing this particular account to other kinds of narrative accounts, informed by other kinds of plot types, and for assessing their relative adequacy to the representation, not so much of the facts as of what the facts *mean*.

For the differences among competing *narratives* are differences among the "modes of emplotment" which predominate in them. It is because narratives are always emplotted that they are meaningfully comparable; it is because narratives are differently emplotted that discriminations among the kinds of plot types can be made. In the case of an emplotment of the events of the Third Reich in a "comic" or "pastoral" mode, we would be eminently justified in appealing to "the facts" in order to dismiss it from the lists of "competing narratives" of the Third Reich. But what if a story of this kind had been set forth in a pointedly ironic way and in the interest of making a metacritical comment, not so much on the facts as on versions of the facts emplotted in a comic or pastoral way? Surely it would be beside the point to dismiss *this* kind of narrative from the competition on the basis of its infidelity to the facts. For even if it were not positively faithful to the facts, it would at least be negatively so – in the fun it poked at narratives of the Third Reich emplotted in the mode of comedy or pastoral.

On the other hand, we might wish to regard such an ironic emplotment as "unacceptable" in the manner suggested by Friedlander in his indictment of histories, novels, and films which, under the guise of seeming to portray faithfully the most horrible facts of life in Hitler's Germany, actually aestheticize the whole scene and translate its contents into fetish objects and the stuff of sadomasochistic fantasies.[4] As Friedlander has pointed out, such "glamorizing" representations of the phenomena of the Third Reich used to be "unacceptable," whatever the accuracy or veracity of their factual contents, because they offended against morality or taste. The fact that such representations have become increasingly common and therefore obviously more "acceptable" over the last twenty years or so indicates profound changes in socially sanctioned standards of morality and taste. But what does *this* circumstance suggest about the grounds on which we might wish to judge a narrative account of the Third Reich and the Final Solution to be "unacceptable" even though its factual content is both accurate and ample?

It seems to be a matter of distinguishing between a specific body of factual "contents" and a specific "form" of narrative and of applying the kind of rule which stipulates that a serious theme – such as mass murder or genocide – demands a noble genre – such as epic or tragedy – for its proper representation. This is the kind of issue posed by Art Spiegelman's *Maus: A Survivor's Tale*,[5] which presents the events of the Holocaust in the medium of the (black-and-white) comic book and in a mode of bitter satire, with Germans portrayed as cats, Jews as mice, and Poles as pigs. The manifest content of Spiegelman's comic book is the story of the artist's effort to extract from his father the story of his parents' experience of the events of the Holocaust. Thus, the story of the Holocaust that is told in the book is framed by a story of how this story came to be told. But the manifest contents of both the frame story and the framed story are, as it were, compromised as fact by their allegorization as a game of cat-and-mouse-and-pig in which everyone – perpetrators, victims, and bystanders in the story of the Holocaust and both Spiegelman and his father in the story of *their* relationship – comes out looking more like a beast than like a human being. *Maus* presents a particularly ironic and bewildered view of the Holocaust, but it is at the same time one of the most moving narrative accounts of it that I know, and not least because it makes the difficulty of discovering and telling the whole truth about even a small part of it as much a part of the story as the events whose meaning it is seeking to discover.

To be sure, *Maus* is not a conventional history, but it is a representation of past real events or at least of events that are represented as having actually occurred. There is nothing of that aestheticization of which Friedlander complains in his assessments of many recent filmic and novelistic treatments of the Nazi epoch and the Final Solution. At the same time, this comic book is a masterpiece of stylization, figuration, and allegorization. It assimilates the events of the Holocaust to the conventions of comic book representation, and in this absurd mixture of a "low" genre with events of the most momentous significance, *Maus* manages to raise all of the crucial issues regarding the "limits of representation" in general.

Indeed, *Maus* is much more critically self-conscious than Andreas Hillgruber's *Zweierlei Untergang: Die Zerschlagung des Deutschen Reiches und das Ende des europäischen Judentums* (Two kinds of ruin: the shattering of the German Reich and the end of European Jewry).[6] In the first of the two essays included in the book, Hillgruber suggests that, even though the Third Reich lacked the nobility of purpose to permit its "shattering" to be called a "tragedy," the defense of the eastern front by the Wehrmacht in 1944–5 could appropriately be emplotted – and without any violence to the facts – as a "tragic" story. Hillgruber's manifest purpose was to salvage the moral dignity of a part of the Nazi epoch in German history by splitting the whole of it into two discrete stories and emplotting them differently – the one as a tragedy, the other as an incomprehensible enigma.[7]

Critics of Hillgruber immediately pointed out: (1) that even to cast the account in the mode of a narrative was to subordinate any analysis of the events to their aestheticization; (2) that one could confer the morally ennobling epithet *tragic* on these events only at the cost of ignoring the extent to which the "heroic" actions of the Wehrmacht had made possible the destruction of many Jews who might have been saved had the army surrendered earlier; and (3) that the attempt to ennoble one part of the history of the "German Empire" by dissociating it from the Final Solution was as morally offensive as it was scientifically untenable.[8] Yet Hillgruber's suggestion for emplotting the story of the defense of the eastern front did not violate any of the conventions governing the writing of professionally respectable narrative history. He simply suggested narrowing the focus to a particular domain of the historical continuum, casting the agents and agencies occupying that scene as characters in a dramatic conflict, and emplotting this drama in terms of the familiar conventions of the genre of tragedy.

Hillgruber's suggestion for the emplotment of the history of the eastern front during the winter of 1944–5 indicates the ways in which a specific plot type (tragedy) can simultaneously determine the kinds of events to be featured in any story that can be told about them and provide a pattern for the assignment of the roles that can possibly be played by the agents and agencies inhabiting the scene thus constituted.[9] At the same time, Hillgruber's suggestion also indicates how the choice of a mode of emplotment can justify ignoring certain kinds of events, agents, actions, agencies, and patients that may inhabit a given historical scene or its context. There is no place for any form of low or ignoble life in a tragedy; in tragedies even villains are noble or, rather, villainy can be shown to have its noble incarnations. Asked once why he had not included a treatment of Joan of Arc in his *Waning of the Middle Ages*, Huizinga is said to have replied: "Because I did not want my story to have a heroine." Hillgruber's recommendation to emplot the story of the Wehrmacht's defense of the eastern front as a tragedy indicates that he wants the story told about it to have a hero, to be heroic, and thereby to redeem at least a remnant of the Nazi epoch in the history of Germany.

Hillgruber may not have considered the fact that his division of one epoch of German history into two stories – one of the shattering of an empire, the other of the end of a people – sets up an oppositional structure constitutive of a semantic field in which the naming of the plot type of one story determines the semantic domain within which the name of the plot type of the other is to be found. Hillgruber does not name the plot type which might provide the meaning of the story of "the end of European Jewry." But if the plot type of the tragedy is reserved for the telling of the story of the Wehrmacht on the eastern front in 1944–5, it follows that *some other* plot type must be used for the end of European Jewry.

In forgoing the impulse to name the kind of story that should be told about the Jews in Hitler's Reich, Hillgruber approaches the position of a number of scholars and writers who view the Holocaust as virtually unrepresentable in language. The most extreme version of this idea takes the form of the commonplace that this event ("Auschwitz," "the Final Solution," and so on) is of such a nature as to escape the grasp of any language to describe it or any medium to represent it. Thus, for example, George Steiner's famous remark: "The world of Auschwitz lies outside speech as it lies outside reason."[10] Or Alice and A. R.

Eckhardt's question: "How is the unspeakable to be spoken about? Certainly, we ought to speak about it, but how can we ever do so?"[11] Berel Lang suggests that expressions such as these must be understood figuratively, as indicating the difficulty of writing about the Holocaust and the extent to which any representation of it must be judged against the criterion of respectful silence that should be our first response to it.[12]

Nonetheless, Lang himself argues against any use of the genocide as a subject of fictional or poetic writing. According to him, only the most literalist *chronicle* of the facts of the genocide comes close to passing the test of "authenticity and truthfulness" by which both literary and scientific accounts of this event must be judged. *Only the facts* must be recounted, because otherwise one lapses into figurative speech and stylization (aestheticism). And *only a chronicle* of the facts is warranted, because otherwise one opens up oneself to the dangers of narrativization and the relativization of emplotment.

Lang's analysis of the limitations of *any* literary representation of the genocide and its *moral* inferiority to a sparse or denarrativized historical account is worth considering in detail, because it raises the question of the limits of representation in the matter of the Holocaust in the most extreme terms. The analysis hinges on a radical opposition between literal and figurative speech, the identification of literary language with figurative language, a particular view of the peculiar effects produced by any figurative characterization of real events, and a notion of "morally extreme" events of which the Holocaust is considered to be a rare, if not historically unique, instantiation. Lang argues that the genocide, quite apart from being a *real* event, an event that really happened, is also a *literal* event, that is, an event the nature of which permits it to serve as a paradigm of the kind of event about which we can be permitted to speak only in a "literal" manner.

Lang holds that figurative language not only turns or swerves away from literalness of expression, but also deflects attention from the states of affairs about which it pretends to speak. Any figurative expression, he argues, *adds* to the representation of the object to which it refers. First, it adds itself (that is, the specific figure used) and the decision it presupposes (that is, the choice to use one figure rather than another). Figuration produces stylization, which directs attention to the author and his or her creative talent. Next, figuration produces a "perspective" on the referent of the utterance, but in featuring one particular perspective it necessarily closes off others. Thus it reduces or obscures certain aspects of events.[13] Third, the kind of figuration needed to transform what would otherwise be only a chronicle of real events into a story at once personalizes (humanizes) and generalizes the agents and agencies involved in those events. Such figuration personalizes by transforming those agents into the kind of intending, feeling, and thinking subjects with whom the reader can identify and empathize, in the way one does with characters in fictional stories. It generalizes them by representing them as instantiations of the types of agents, agencies, events, and so on met with in the genres of literature and myth.

On this view of the matter the impropriety of any literary representation of the genocide derives from the distortions of the facts of the matter effected by the use of figurative language. Over against any merely literary representation of the events comprising the genocide Lang sets the ideal of what a literalist representation of the facts of the matter reveals to be their *true* nature. And it is worth quoting a longish passage from Lang's book in which he sets up this opposition between figurative and literalist speech as being homologous with the opposition between false and truthful discourse:

> If . . . the act of genocide is directed against individuals who do not motivate that act *as* individuals; and if the evil represented by genocide also reflects a deliberate intent for evil in principle, in conceptualizing [a] group and in the decision to annihilate it, then the intrinsic limitations of figurative discourse for the representation of genocide come into view. On the account given, imaginative representation would personalize even events that are impersonal and corporate; it would dehistoricize and generalize events that occur specifically and contingently.
>
> And the unavoidable dissonance here is evident. For a subject which historically combines the feature of impersonality with a challenge to the conception of moral boundaries, the attempt to personalize it — or, for that matter, only to *add* to it — appears at once gratuitous and inconsistent: gratuitous because it individualizes where the subject by its nature is corporate; inconsistent because it sets limits when the subject itself has denied them. The effect of the additions is then to *misrepresent* the subject and thus — where the aspects misrepresented are essential — to *diminish* it. In asserting the possibility of alternate figurative perspectives, furthermore, the writer asserts the process of representation and his own persona as parts of the representation — a further diminution of what (for a subject like the Nazi genocide) is its essential core; beside this, an "individual" perspective is at most irrelevant. For certain subjects, it seems, their significance may be too broad or deep to be chanced by an individual point of view, [and the significance may be] morally more compelling — and actual — than the concept of possibility can sustain. Under this pressure, the presumption of illumination, usually conceded *prima facie* to the act of writing (*any* writing), begins to lose its force.[14]

But literary writing and the kind of historical writing that aspires to the status of literary writing are especially objectionable to Lang, because in them the figure of the author obtrudes itself between the thing to be represented and the representation of it. The figure of the author must obtrude itself into the discourse as the agent of that act of figuration without which the subject of the discourse would remain unpersonalized. Since literary writing unfolds under the delusion that it is only by figuration that individuals can be personalized, "the implication is unavoidable," Lang says, that "a subject . . . could be represented in many different ways and as having no *necessary* and perhaps not even an *actual* basis. The assertion of alternate possibilities [of figuration] . . . suggests a denial of limitation: *no* possibilities are excluded," neither the possibility of figuring a real person as an imaginary or nonperson nor that of figuring a real event as a nonevent.[15]

It is considerations such as these that lead Lang to advance the notion that the events of the Nazi genocide are intrinsically "anti-representational," by which he

apparently means, not that they cannot be represented, but that they are paradigmatic of the kind of event that can be spoken about only in a factual and literalist
manner. Indeed, the genocide consists of occurrences in which the very distinction
between "event" and "fact" is dissolved.[16] Lang writes, "If there ever was a 'literal'
fact, beyond the possibility of alternate formulations among which reversal or
denial must always be one, it is here in the act of the Nazi genocide; and if the
moral implication of the role of facts needed proof, it is also to be found here,
again in the phenomena of the Nazi genocide."[17] It is the overriding actuality
and literalness of this event which, in Lang's view, *warrant* the effort on the part
of historians to represent real events "direct[ly] . . . immediately and unaltered" in
a language purged of all metaphor, trope, and figuration. Indeed, it is the literalness of this event which indexes the difference between "historical discourse" on
the one hand and "imaginative representation and its figurative space" on the other:
"However it may be conceived beyond [the distinction between history and fiction]
the *fact* of the Nazi genocide is a crux that separates historical discourse from the
process of imaginative representation, perhaps not uniquely, but as certainly as any
fact might be required or is able to do."[18]

I have lingered on Lang's argument because I think that it carries us to the
crux of many current discussions regarding both the possibility of representing
the Holocaust and the relative value of different ways of representing it. His objection to the use of this event as an occasion for a *merely* literary performance is
directed at novels and poetry, and it can easily be extended to cover both the
kind of belletristic historiography which features literary flourish and what the book
clubs identify as "fine writing." But it must, by implication, be extended also to
include any kind of narrative history, which is to say, any attempt to represent the
Holocaust *as a story*. And this is because, if every story must be said to have a plot,
and if every emplotment is a kind of figuration, then it follows that every narrative account of the Holocaust, whatever its mode of emplotment, stands condemned
on the same grounds that any merely literary representation of it must be
condemned.

To be sure, Lang argues that, although historical representation may "make use
of narrative and figurative means," it is not "essentially dependent on those means."
Indeed, in his view, historical discourse is posited on "the possibility of representation that stands in direct relation to its object – in effect, if not in principle,
immediate and unaltered."[19] This is not to suggest that historians can or should try
to occupy the position of the naive realist or mere seeker after information. The
matter is more complex than that. For Lang indicates that what is needed for anyone
writing about the Holocaust is an attitude, position, or posture which is neither
subjective nor objective, neither that of the social scientist with a methodology and
a theory nor that of the poet intent upon expressing a "personal" reaction.[20] Indeed,
in the introduction to *Act and Idea*, Lang invokes Roland Barthes's notion of "intransitive writing" as a model of the kind of discourse appropriate to discussion of the
philosophical and theoretical issues raised by reflection on the Holocaust. Unlike
the kind of writing that is intended to be "read *through*,. . . designed to enable
readers to see what they would otherwise see differently or perhaps not at all,"
intransitive writing "denies the distances among the writer, text, what is written
about, and, finally, the reader." In intransitive writing "an author does not write

to provide access to something independent of both author and reader, but 'writes himself' . . . In the traditional account [of writing], the writer is conceived as first looking at an object with eyes already expectant, patterned, and then, having seen, as representing it in his own writing. For the writer who writes-himself, writing becomes itself the means of vision or comprehension, not a mirror of something independent, but an act and commitment — a doing or making rather than a reflection or description."[21] Lang explicitly commends intransitive writing (and speech) as appropriate to individual Jews who, as in the recounting of the story of the Exodus at Passover, "should tell the story of the genocide as though he or she had passed through it" and in an exercise of self-identification specifically Jewish in nature.[22] But the further suggestion is that the product of intransitive writing, which is to say a distance-denying discourse, might serve as a model for *any* representation of the Holocaust, historical or fictional. And it is with a consideration of the ways in which the notion of intransitive writing might serve as a way of resolving many of the issues raised by the representation of the Holocaust that I would like to conclude.

First, I would note that Berel Lang invokes the idea of intransitive writing without remarking that Barthes himself used it to characterize the differences between the dominant style of modernist writing and that of classical realism. In the essay entitled "To Write: An Intransitive Verb?" Barthes asks if and when the verb "to write" became an intransitive verb. The question is asked within the context of a discussion of "diathesis" ("voice") in order to focus attention on the different kinds of relationship that an agent can be represented as bearing to an action. He points out that although modern Indo-European languages offer two possibilities for expressing this relationship, the active and the passive voices, other languages have offered a third possibility, that expressed, for example, in the ancient Greek "middle voice." Whereas in the active and passive voices the subject of the verb is presumed to be external to the action, as either agent or patient, in the middle voice the subject is presumed to be *interior* to the action.[23] He then goes on to conclude that, in literary modernism, the verb "to write" connotes neither an active nor a passive relationship, but rather a middle one. "Thus," Barthes says,

> in the middle voice of *to write*, the distance between scriptor and language diminishes asymptotically. We could even say that it is the writings of subjectivity, such as romantic writing, which are active, for in them the agent is not interior but *anterior* to the process of writing: here the one who writes does not write for himself, but as if by proxy, for an exterior and antecedent person (even if both bear the same name), while, in the modern verb of middle voice *to write*, the subject is constituted as immediately contemporary with the writing, being effected and affected by it: this is the exemplary case of the Proustean narrator, who exists only by writing, despite the references to a pseudo-memory.[24]

This is, of course, only one of the many differences that distinguish modernist writing from its nineteenth-century realist counterpart. But this difference indicates a new and distinctive way of imagining, describing, and conceptualizing the relationships obtaining between agents and acts, subjects and objects, a statement and its referent – between the literal and figurative levels of speech and, indeed, therefore, between factual and fictional discourse. What modernism envisions, in Barthes' account, is nothing less than an order of experience beyond (or prior to) that expressible in the kinds of *oppositions* we are forced to draw (between agency and patiency, subjectivity and objectivity, literalness and figurativeness, fact and fiction, history and myth, and so forth) in any version of realism. This does not imply that such oppositions cannot be used to represent some real relationships, only that the relationships between the entities designated by the polar terms may not be oppositional ones in some experiences of the world.

What I am getting at is expressed very well in Jacques Derrida's explication of his notion of *différance*, which also uses the idea of the middle voice to express what he means to convey. Derrida writes:

> *Différance* is not simply active (any more than it is a subjective accom-
> plishment); it rather indicates the middle voice, it precedes and sets up
> the opposition between passivity and activity . . . And we shall see why
> what is designated by *différance* is neither simply active nor simply
> passive, that it announces or rather recalls something like the middle
> voice, that it speaks of an operation that is not an operation, which
> cannot be thought of either as a passion or as an action of a subject on
> an object, as starting from an agent or a patient, or on the basis of, or
> in view of, any of these *terms*. And philosophy has perhaps commenced
> by distributing the middle voice, expressing a certain intransitiveness,
> into the active and the passive voice, and has itself been constituted by
> this repression.[25]

I cite Derrida as representing a modernist conception of the project of philosophy, founded on the recognition of the differences between a distinctively modernist experience of the world (or is it the experience of a distinctively modernist world?) and the notions of representation, knowledge, and meaning prevailing in the inherited "realist" cultural endowment. And I do so in order to suggest that the kind of anomalies, enigmas, and dead ends met with in discussions of the representation of the Holocaust are the result of a conception of discourse that owes too much to a realism that is inadequate to the representation of events, such as the Holocaust, which are themselves "modernist" in nature.[26] The concept of cultural modernism is relevant to the discussion inasmuch as it reflects a reaction to (if not a rejection of) the great efforts of nineteenth-century writers – both historians and fictioneers – to represent reality "realistically" – where *reality* is understood to mean *history* and *realistically* to mean the treatment, not only of the past but also of the present, *as* history. Thus, for example, in *Mimesis*, a study of the history of the idea of realistic representation in Western culture, Erich Auerbach characterizes "the foundations of modern realism" in the following terms: "The serious treatment of everyday reality, the rise of more extensive and socially inferior human groups to the position of subject-matter for problematic-existential representation, on the one hand; on the other, the embedding of random persons and events in the general course of contemporary history, the fluid background – these, we believe, are the foundations of modern realism."[27]

On this view, the modernist version of the realist project could be seen as consisting of a radical rejection of *history*, of *reality as history*, and of *historical consciousness* itself. But Auerbach was concerned to show the continuities as well as the differences between realism and modernism. Thus, in a famous exegesis of a passage from Virginia Woolf's *To the Lighthouse*, Auerbach identifies among the "distinguishing stylistic characteristics" of that "modernism" which the passage has been chosen to exemplify:

1.   The disappearance of the "writer as narrator of objective facts; almost everything stated appears by way of reflection in the consciousness of the *dramatis personae*;"
2.   The dissolution of any "viewpoint . . . outside the novel from which the people and events within it are observed . . .;"
3.   The predominance of a "tone of doubt and questioning" in the narrator's interpretation of those events seemingly described in an "objective" manner;
4.   The employment of such devices as "*erlebte Rede*, stream of consciousness, *monologue interieur*" for "aesthetic purposes" that "obscure and obliterate the impression of an objective reality completely known to the author . . .;"
5.   The use of new techniques for the representation of the experience of time and temporality, e.g. use of the "chance occasion" to release "processes of consciousness" which remain unconnected to a "specific subject of thought;" obliteration of the distinction between "exterior" and "interior" time; and representation of "events," not as "successive episodes of [a] story," but as random occurrences.[28]

This is as good a characterization as any we might find of what Barthes and Derrida might have called the style of "middle voicedness." Auerbach's characterization of literary modernism indicates, not that history is no longer represented realistically, but rather that the conceptions of both history and realism have changed. Modernism is still concerned to represent reality "realistically," and it still identifies reality with history. But the history which modernism confronts is not the history envisaged by nineteenth-century realism. And this is because the social order which is the subject of this history has undergone a radical transformation – a change which permitted the crystallization of the totalitarian form that Western society assumed in the twentieth century.

As thus envisaged, cultural modernism must be seen as both a reflection of and a response to this new actuality. Accordingly the affinities of form and content between literary modernism and social totalitarianism can be granted – but without necessarily implying that modernism is a cultural expression of the fascist form of social totalitarianism.[29] Indeed, another view of the relation between modernism and fascism is possible: literary modernism was a product of an effort to represent a historical reality for which the older, classical realist modes of representation were inadequate, based as they were on different experiences of history or, rather, on experiences of a different "history."

Modernism was no doubt immanent in classical realism – in the way in which Nazism and the Final Solution were immanent in the structures and practices of the nineteenth-century nation-state and the social relations of production of which *it* was a political expression. Looked at in this way, however, modernism appears, less as a rejection of the realist project and a denial of history, than as an anticipation of a new form of historical reality, a reality that included, among its supposedly unimaginable, unthinkable, and unspeakable aspects, the phenomena of Hitlerism, the Final Solution, total war, nuclear contamination, mass starvation, and ecological suicide; a profound sense of the incapacity of our sciences to *explain*, let alone control or contain these; and a growing awareness of the incapacity of our traditional modes of representation even to *describe* them adequately.

What all this suggests is that modernist modes of representation may offer possibilities of representing the reality of both the Holocaust and the experience of it that no other version of realism could do. Indeed, we can follow out Lang's suggestion that the best way to represent the Holocaust and the experience of it may well be by a kind of "intransitive writing" which lays no claim to the kind of realism aspired to by nineteenth-century historians and writers. But we may want to consider that by intransitive writing we must intend something like the relationship to that event expressed in the middle voice. This is not to suggest that we will give up the effort to represent the Holocaust realistically, but rather that our notion of what constitutes realistic representation must be revised to take account of experiences that are unique to our century and for which older modes of representation have proven inadequate.

In point of fact I do not think that the Holocaust, Final Solution, Shoah, Churban, or German genocide of the Jews is any more unrepresentable than any other event in human history. It is only that its representation, whether in history or in fiction, requires the kind of style, the modernist style, that was developed in order to represent the kind of experiences which social modernism made possible, the kind of style met with in any number of modernist writers but of which Primo Levi must be invoked as an example.

In *Il Sistema periodico* (The periodic table), Levi begins the chapter entitled "Carbon" by writing:

> The reader, at this point, will have realized for some time now that this is not a chemical treatise: my presumption does not reach so far — "ma voix est faible, et même un peu profane." Nor is it an autobiography, save in the partial and symbolic limits in which every piece of writing is autobiographical, indeed every human work; but it is in some fashion a history.
>
> It is — or would have liked to be — a micro-history, the history of a trade and all its defects, victories, and miseries, such as everyone wants to tell when he feels close to concluding the arc of his career and art ceases to be long.

Levi then goes on to tell the story of a "particular" atom of "carbon" which becomes an allegory (what he calls "this completely arbitrary story" that is "nonetheless true"). "I will tell just one more story," he says, "the most secret, and I will tell it with the humility and restraint of him who knows from the start that this theme is desperate, the means feeble, and the trade of clothing facts in words is bound by its very nature to fail."

The story he tells is of how an atom of carbon that turns up in a glass of milk which he, Levi, drinks, migrates into a cell in his own brain – "the brain of *me* who is writing, and [how] the cell in question, and within it the atom in question, is in charge of my writing, in a gigantic minuscule game which nobody has yet described." This "game" he then proceeds to describe in the following terms: "It is that which at this instant, issuing out of a labyrinthine tangle of yeses and nos, makes my hand run along a certain path on a paper, marks it with these volutes that are signs: a double snap, up and down, between two levels of energy, guides this hand of mine to impress on this paper this dot, here, this one."

Notes

1   Historical discourses consist also, obviously, of explanations cast in the form of arguments more of less formalizable. I do not address the issue of the relation between explanations cast in the mode of formal arguments and what I would call the "explanation-effects" produced by the narrativization of events. It is the felicitous combination of arguments with narrative representations which accounts for the appeal of a specifically "historical" representation of reality. But the precise nature of the relation between arguments and narrativizations in histories is unclear.

2   I have in mind here the farcical version of the events of 1848–51 in France composed by Marx in open competition with the tragic and comic versions of those same events set forth by Hugo and Proudhon respectively.

3   Unless, that is, we are prepared to entertain the idea that any given body of facts is infinitely variously interpretable and that one aim of historical discourse is to *multiply* the number of interpretations we have of any given set of events rather than to work toward the production of a "best" interpretation. Cf. work by Paul Veyne, C. Behan McCullagh, Peter Munz, and F. R. Ankersmit.

4   Saul Friedlander, *Reflets du Nazisme* (Paris: Seuil, 1982), pp. 76ff.

5   Art Spiegelman, *Maus: A Survivor's Tale* (New York: Pantheon Books, 1986).

6   Berlin: Siedler, 1986, p. 64.

7   Thus Hillgruber writes: "Das sind Dimensionen, die ins Anthropologische, ins Sozialpsychologische und ins Individualpsychologische gehen und die Frageeiner möglichen Wiederholung unter anderem ideologischen Vorzeichen in tatsächlich oder vermeintlich wiederum extremen Situationen und Konstellationen aufwerfen. Das geht über jenes Wachhalten der Erinnerung an der Millionen der Opfer hinaus, das dem Historiker aufgegeben ist. Denn hier wird ein zentrales Problem der Gegenwart und der Zukunft berührt und die Aufgabe des Historikers transzendiert. Hier geht es um eine fundamentale Herausforderung an jedermann." Ibid., pp. 98–9.

8   Most of the relevant documents can be found in *"Historikerstreit": Die Dokumentation der Kontroverse um die Einzigartigkeit der nationalsozialistischen Judenvernichtung* (Munich: Piper, 1989). See also "Special Issue on the *Historikerstreit*," *New German Critique*, 44 (Spring/Summer 1988).

9   The plot type is a crucial element in the constitution of what Bakhtin calls the "chronotope," a socially structured domain of the natural world that defines the horizon of possible events, actions, agents, agencies, social roles, and so forth of all imaginative fictions – and all real stories, too. A dominant plot type determines

the classes of things perceivable, the modes of their relationships, the periodicities of their development, and the possible meanings they can reveal. Every
generic plot type presupposes a chronotope, and every chronotope presumes a
limited number of the kinds of stories that can be told about events happening
within its horizon.

10   George Steiner, quoted in Berel Lang, *Act and Idea in the Nazi Genocide* (Chicago:
University of Chicago Press, 1990), p. 151.

11   Alice Eckhardt and A. R. Eckhardt, "Studying the Holocaust's Impact Today:
Some Dilemmas of Language and Method," in *Echoes from the Holocaust:
Philosophical Reflections on a Dark Time*, Alan Rosenberg and Gerald E. Myers (eds)
(Philadelphia: Temple University Press, 1989), p. 439.

12   Lang, *Act and Idea*, p. 160.

13   Ibid., p. 43.

14   Ibid., pp. 144–5.

15   Ibid., p. 146.

16   Ibid., pp. 146–7.

17   Ibid., pp. 157–8.

18   Ibid., pp. 158–9.

19   Ibid., p. 156.

20   Cf. Edith Milton, "The Dangers of Memory," *New York Times Book Review*, 28
January 1990, p. 27, for some perspicuous comments on the efforts of younger
writers who, lacking any direct experience of the Holocaust, nonetheless attempt
to make it "personal." This is a review of *Testimony: Contemporary Writers Make the
Holocaust Personal*, David Rosenberg (ed.) (New York: Times Books, 1990).
Milton remarks on the "obvious paradox at the heart of any anthology that offers
to recollect genocide in tranquility." She goes on to praise only those essays
which, "far from pretending to come to grips with the Holocaust, . . . emphasize their authors' necessary aloofness. Indeed," she says, "since subjectivity and
obliqueness are the only approaches possible," the best essays in the collection
are those which "make a virtue of being subjective and oblique."

21   Lang, *Act and Idea*, p. xii.

22   Ibid., p. xiii.

23   As in, for example, such "performative" actions as those of promising or swearing
an oath. In actions such as these in which the agent seems to act upon itself, the
use of the middle voice permits avoidance of the notion that the subject is split
in two, that is, into an agent who administers the oath and a patient who "takes"
it. Thus, Attic Greek expresses the action of composing an oath in the active
voice (*logou poiein*) and that of swearing an oath, not in the passive, but in the
middle voice (*logou poiesthai*). Barthes gives the example of *thuein*, to offer a sacrifice for another (active), versus *thuesthai*, to offer a sacrifice for oneself (middle).
Roland Barthes, "To Write: An Instransitive Verb?" in *The Rustle of Language*,
trans. Richard Howard (Berkeley: University of California Press, 1989), p. 18.

24   Ibid., p. 19.

25   J. Derrida, "Différance," in *Speech and Phenomena and Other Essays on Husserl's Theory
of Signs*, trans. David B. Allison (Evanston, Ill.: Northwestern University Press,
1973), p. 130.

26   Cf. Saul Friedlander's introduction to Gerald Fleming, *Hitler and the Final Solution*
(Berkeley: University of California Press, 1984), where he writes: "On the limited
level of the *analysis* of Nazi policies, *an answer* to the debate between the various

groups *appears to be possible.* On the level of global *interpretation,* however, the real *difficulties remain.* The historian who is not encumbered with ideological or conceptual blinkers easily recognizes that it is Nazi anti-Semitism and the anti-Jewish policy of the Third Reich that gives Nazism its *sui generis* character. By virtue of this fact, inquiries into *the nature of Nazism* take on a new dimension that renders it *unclassifiable* . . . If [however] one admits that the Jewish problem was at the center, was the very essence of the system, many [studies of the Final Solution] lose their coherence, and *historiography is confronted with an enigma that defies normal interpretative categories* . . . We know in detail what occurred, we know the sequence of the events and their probable interaction, but *the profound dynamics of the phenomena escapes us*" (my italics).

27 Erich Auerbach, *Mimesis: The Representation of Reality in Western Literature,* trans. Willard Trask (Princeton: Princeton University Press, 1953), p. 491.

28 Ibid., pp. 534–9.

29 This is the view held by Fredric Jameson and most explicitly argued in *Fables of Agression: Wyndham Lewis, the Modernist as Fascist* (Berkeley: University of California Press, 1979). It is a commonplace of leftist interpretations of modernism.

Chapter 25

Patrick Finney

INTERNATIONAL HISTORY, THEORY AND THE ORIGINS OF WORLD WAR II

IN THEORETICAL AND METHODOLOGICAL terms, international history is one of the most conservative discourses within our conservative discipline. This is not to deny that the best contemporary international history exhibits meticulous scholarship, conceptual sophistication, and vigorous interpretive pluralism, nor that it is almost unrecognizable from the Rankean diplomatic history which begat it. Yet the majority of practitioners still remain stubbornly devoted to empiricist methodologies grounded in realist assumptions about the accessibility of the past to objective inquiry, and committed to the goal of attaining reasonably secure and definitive historical truths. Moreover, these assumptions commonly remain unexamined – or at least unarticulated – since the international historians are ill-equipped by disciplinary training and disinclined by temperament to indulge in theoretical or philosophical debates: the predominant assumption is that "traditional historical methodology" continues to offer a secure foundation for historical practice (Watt 1992). The purpose of this discussion is to examine the relationship between international history and (in lieu of a better description) "postmodernist theory," through one particular case study, that of the origins of World War II. There is, of course, space here to discuss only a handful of recent books dealing with some aspects of that vast subject, which itself forms but part of the wider subdiscipline, but these works are sufficiently representative to serve as the basis for some broader generalizations. In particular, I will comment on the roots and consequences of international historians' general indifference or hostility to postmodernism, and speculate on some possible future directions within the discourse.

To begin, a narrative of the subdiscipline's own development is required. International history has its roots in the nineteenth-century Rankean revolution, when the study of political relations between states was established at the heart of the new, archive-orientated, scientific discipline. The rise of the modern nation-state and nationalism combined to create a conviction as to the primacy of foreign policy, diplomacy and war in determining human affairs; thus statecraft – the wielding of power by an elite handful of men – was deemed the quintessential stuff of history. Diplomatic history flourished at the turn of the century, encouraged by the growing tendency of governments to publish collections of diplomatic correspondence to justify their foreign policy to newly enfranchised electorates. These documents were revered as offering uniquely privileged access to fundamental human truths: diplomatic histories were considered "revelations both in the sensational and the biblical meaning of the word; they revealed the secret stratagems of monarchs and statesmen and they revealed the pattern of the past which explained the present" (Roger Bullen, quoted in Gardiner 1988: 135). Perhaps the pinnacle of the prestige of diplomatic history was reached between the wars, when explaining the origins of World War I acquired an urgent contemporary political importance through the interconnection between German war guilt and demands for the revision of the Treaty of Versailles. This controversy was largely played out through state publication of document collections and the construction from them of authorized historical interpretations, the patriotic cast of which only intensified their interpretive absolutism. Throughout this time diplomatic history occupied a privileged place in political discourse, and its basic methodological assumptions remained intact. Socialist and liberal critics of the international order urging the need to attend to the profound forces lying behind the actions of "great men," exerted some influence over the mainstream but the central preoccupation with diplomacy persisted.

It was only after World War II that sufficiently serious challenges arose to impel the wholesale Darwinian mutation of diplomatic into international history. In the 1950s, diplomatic history continued to be much practiced, but it increasingly came to be seen as "the most arid and sterile of all the sub-histories" (Marwick 1989: 94), obsessed by the irrelevant minutiae of what one clerk said to another. The increasingly evident complexity of contemporary international relations, in tandem with the rise of social and economic history and the accelerating diversification of the discipline, cast grave doubt on the continued validity of a specialism that was predominantly narrative in form, event-centered and preoccupied with the narrowly political activities of elite males. In response, over several decades, international history was created through a reconceptualization of international relations to embrace not merely diplomacy, but also economics, strategy, the domestic roots of foreign policy, ideology and propaganda, intelligence and the cultural, even recently the environmental, aspects of relations between states, as well as to acknowledge the roles of non-state actors and processes in international affairs.

Dramatic though these changes have been, international history has not escaped charges of "marking time," clinging to traditional categories of analysis and modes of explanation, and failing to keep pace with developments elsewhere in the discipline (Maier 1980). Crucially, any changes have not seriously impinged upon the fundamental realist epistemology and empiricist methodology which had underpinned diplomatic history. International historians may remain fiercely divided over particular conceptual and interpretive issues, and may argue vociferously as to which aspects of "the real" (and therefore which kinds of source materials) can be legitimately incorporated into – or should be privileged within – the historical study of international relations; but across the field as a whole, weighed down by a sense of the awesome gravity of their subject-matter, they continue to invest heavily in the solid reality and accessibility of the past. This commitment is also evident in the ambivalent relationship between international history and the social sciences, particularly international relations (IR). While some international historians have been prepared to borrow concepts from other, avowedly theoretical, disciplines (Thorne 1988), many others remain skeptical about any abstract theorizing, regarding it as a distortion of the particular reality of the historical record (Watt 1983). (These generalizations are, admittedly, largely based on international history within the United Kingdom, but they also hold broadly true, *mutatis mutandis*, with regard to practice in continental Europe and the United States (Combs 1983; Hogan 1995; LaFeber 1995).) In these circumstances, it is scarcely surprising that postmodernist theory has hitherto made little impact in the sub-discipline, and that examples of new international history are conspicuously absent from collections showcasing new perspectives on historical writing (Burke 1991).

Geoffrey Roberts's recent account of the Soviet Union and the origins of World War II offers a typical example of the hegemonic approach (Roberts 1995). Historical writing on the intensely controversial Soviet experiment has always been marked by conflict between radically different interpretations, corresponding to different ideological positions (Acton 1990; Ward 1993). This has been evident in the debate over Soviet policy in the 1930s since the first interpretations were forged during the early Cold War. Orthodox Soviet historiography, intended to legitimize the regime's past and present actions, stressed Moscow's unwavering principled commitment to anti-fascism and collective security in the 1930s and the sinister, pusillanimous machinations of the capitalist appeasers who had tried to divert Hitler eastwards and thus forced Moscow to conclude the Nazi–Soviet pact. The parallel Western interpretation offered historiographical justification for a contemporary anti-Soviet policy in the early Cold War: it demonized Stalin, emphasizing the long-term roots of his efforts to conclude a *rapprochement* with Hitler, dismissing Moscow's collective security orientations as a sham and concluding that the Nazi–Soviet pact revealed the inherently expansionist nature of communism. Subsequent mainstream Western historiography developed refined, less overtly ideological (but scarcely on that count objective), versions of these Cold War narratives, loosely identifiable as "collective security" and "German" school explanations, respectively crediting Moscow with sincerity and duplicitous Machiavellianism in its Popular Front policy. Both still retain adherents, although a third broad explanation has arisen attempting to bridge the gap between them – that of the so-called "internal politics" school – arguing that the often contradictory or ambiguous nature of Soviet policy was a function of debates within the policy-making establishment between partisans of pro-Western and pro-German policies.

From a postmodernist perspective skeptical about objectivity, these historiographical debates seem to offer a particularly graphic illustration of the necessarily interested, present-centered nature of historiography *tout court*. Each reading correlates with a particular ideological position (implicit or explicit) which precedes and shapes the interpretation. The archival record, while playing a limiting role, is not sovereign, since interpretations are always underdetermined by the evidence, their content invented as much as found: each is supportable on its own terms by reference to documentary materials, but "the evidence" can never decide between readings founded upon incompatible presuppositions external and prior to it. Rhetorically, historiographical debates revolve around "the evidence" but under the surface they are conflicts between the different ideological forces of which they are articulations. Of course, over time, in response to broader changes in the social world, particular interpretations become more or less plausible – thus Marxist–Leninist accounts no longer seem credible whereas conservative ones are resurgent – but there is a significant difference between plausibility and truth. (We can, incidentally, reserve the right to rule particular communist accounts out of court on the grounds that they involve gross and deliberate falsification of factual evidence, without deeming the whole Marxist–Leninist historical enterprise invalid.) Certainly, this paradigm offers a coherent and credible explanation of why, contrary to the logical implications of empiricist aspirations for definitive closure, the increasing availability of archival materials leads as often to the pluralization of (incompatible) readings as to the emergence of a single settled interpretation, as current controversies over the origins of the Cold War in the light of new Soviet archival evidence attest (*Diplomatic History* Symposium 1997).

These historiographical issues are systematically marginalized in Roberts's unabashedly empiricist treatment of the subject. True, he devotes an introductory chapter to them, but this is rather perfunctory (just under eight pages out of a total text of 150), and serves merely as the prelude to a chronological, largely narrative account, offering a sustained exposition of one particular interpretation, that of the "collective security" school. Moreover, this introduction's content conspires with the book's form to this end. In a crucial early move Roberts sets up a telling opposition between distorted representations of the past and history proper, when the orthodox Soviet interpretation is categorized as a "more ideological and less truthful version" of the "collective security" school explanation (Roberts 1995: 2). The latter – in this case the variant offered by A. J. P. Taylor – is thus immediately privileged as belonging to a truly historical realm of objective and value-free explanation. A little later, the point is reinforced when Roberts notes that the "German" school interpretation, "drew strength from the cold war atmosphere that pervaded post-war western Soviet Studies." This subtle move taints the "German" school interpretation as falling short of the objective ideal, thus marginalizing it, while simultaneously reaffirming that history proper, such as Roberts is about to offer, arises independently from social grounding.

In establishing this ideal of history as a disinterested, autonomous discursive practice, the obvious corollary is to bring in "the evidence" as the crucial determinant of – and the sovereign arbiter between – interpretations. The historiographical debate, we are told, "can only be settled by an analysis of the evidence," and, though on some issues we need more to facilitate "definitive conclusions," that evidence is now "of overwhelming weight." The divergence of other historians from Roberts's conclusions is attributed either to their use of the wrong or insufficient evidence (hence the "German" school rests on the "flimsiest of evidential bases," specifically fragments from the German archives) or their misinterpretation of the correct evidence (as in the case of the "internal politics" school): these other interpretations are therefore not merely different, but defective. Roberts thus completes a rhetorical maneuver setting up the conditions in which a single unreflexive narrative can be presented as incarnating the truth of the past. What he invokes as "the evidence" is of course actually the particular documentary traces he chooses to prioritize interpreted in the way he arbitrarily prefers, but through this strategy that subjective construct is objectified, and endowed with solidity and agency to enable him to marginalize other interpretations and to privilege his own as actually residing in the past.

The purpose of this rather heavy-handed textual exegesis is to illustrate the hegemonic international history approach, rather than to demonize Roberts. To do the latter would certainly be unfair. His book contains a crisply-told story summarizing much of the recent literature and new archival material, and thus has value as a student text. His reading of the Soviet past is also at least positive, and on that count infinitely preferable to the conservative, Cold War triumphalist readings in vogue since the ignominious collapse of the communist regime. Moreover, Roberts cannot be accused of failing to reflect upon theoretical issues, since he is unusual amongst international historians in having articulated a distinct philosophy of history, outlining a position which we can perhaps take (in the absence of other evidence) as representative of the silent masses in the subdiscipline. For Roberts, employing this narrative mode is not (as it is for many of us on occasions) a pragmatic or ironic move, but rather "a way of life" (Roberts 1996).

Roberts's arguments are, naturally, conservative and realist, drawing on an analytical philosophy tradition (cf. Lemon 1995) which is quite antithetical to the continental thought animating skeptical and relativist postmodernist critiques. For Roberts, "the dominant discourse of knowledge in history is coterminous with the common sense discourse of modern everyday life." The world consists of sovereign human individuals reacting rationally to external stimuli, and "the task of historians is to reconstruct the reasons for past actions" through reference to and interpretation of "the surviving evidence of past human thinking." These assertions are founded partly on "plain common sense" and "intuition of what the world is like," but also on more complex philosophical assumptions about the "narrative character of human existence," namely that people just do actually live stories to which historians' narratives (if they are good enough) will correspond (Roberts 1996: 221–4; cf. 1995: 8). Moreover, the traditional history built upon these assumptions has proved successful in practice and possesses a fundamentally democratic and popular character that contrasts favorably with the "elitist and intellectualist" understandings of postmodernism (Roberts 1997: 257–60).

There is no space here to subject this position to a comprehensive critique. Poststructuralists will feel that it rests on shaky assumptions about, for example, the centered and unified nature of human subjects and the transparency of language; that it begs a host of epistemological questions as to how we can empathize or engage with past actors; and that it depends upon some very dubious, totalizing generalizations about common sense. Equally, it seems like extreme sophistry to castigate the avowed pluralism of post-modern historiography as elitist, while lauding the absolutism of empiricist closure as conducive towards democratic emancipation. The fact is, however, that Roberts's neo-Collingwoodian philosophy and postmodernism are basically incommensurable discourses, and there is little prospect of resolving the differences between them through debate. The purpose of briefly outlining his position is rather to indicate the understandings which underpin his particular practice and, by extension, the discourse of international history as a whole, committed as it is to a belief that the stories of history are found and not made, and that the content of the past determines the shape of history.

Many international historians will doubtless find these observations erroneous and irrelevant, if not also impertinent, and will remain content to continue crafting scholarly and elegant conventional interpretations. It would certainly be an exaggeration to proclaim on the basis of an analysis of a single text that international history in general was in the throes of any kind of theoretical crisis or terminal morbidity. Even within the restricted area of the historiography of the origins of World War II, less central than it once was in international history now that attention has shifted to the post-1945 period, there remains scope for dynamic development. Over the last thirty years the subject has been driven forward by the opening of untapped archival resources, the exploration of new thematic issues beyond diplomacy and the engendering of fresh perspectives with the passage of time (Bell 1997; Finney 1997), and each of these retains a capacity to generate further changes.

But there are perhaps limitations to each of these avenues forward. First, although significant archival materials remain closed (particularly in Russia) or under-exploited, such resources are obviously finite. Second, the pursuit of thematic research, as with study of the deeper, profound causes of the war (another growth tendency over recent decades), might tend to lead international history towards the dissolution of its character as a distinctive discourse. This, at any rate, is one possible conclusion suggested by Richard Overy's recent text on the inter-war crisis. In the 1980s, Overy published a study on the origins of World War II which was a polished piece of orthodox international history offering a narrative account combined with consideration of the major thematic issues – economics, politics, strategy – prominent in the recent historiography. Revisiting the period seven years later, writing another book in the same series, he provided a wide-ranging interpretation of the same events as evidence of a crisis of modernization, capitalism and democracy which, while compelling, operates on a quite different level of explanation from mainstream international history (Overy 1987, 1994). There may well be a certain circularity of argument involved in refusing to admit work which does not conform to certain conservative norms as international history, and then defining international history as a conservative discourse, but I think Overy demonstrates that to remain a distinctive field of inquiry international history needs to be defined more narrowly than as simply the study of phenomena that transcend national boundaries. Third, while changing perspectives do indeed constantly alter our views of the past (albeit that historians differ as to how significant this factor is in determining interpretations), the history of historiography can be read as a warning that unless these changes are accompanied by occasional rather more radical paradigm shifts, there is a danger that particular fields may lapse into antiquarianism or sterility.

The recent historiography of British appeasement perhaps serves as testimony to this last point. Since the war, historical writing on appeasement has moved through several distinct, if not entirely neat and discrete, phases. The first interpretations, initially advanced in wartime polemics like *Guilty Men* and then refined and expanded in post-1945 Churchillian narratives, were fiercely critical, characterizing appeasement as the product of the purblind folly and misjudgment of a political clique. Interpretations began to soften in the transitional 1960s as a result of diverse politico-cultural, disciplinary and practical contingencies, before the elaboration from the 1970s onwards of a comprehensive and sympathetic revisionist interpretation. For the revisionists, appeasement was massively overdetermined, inevitable rather than stupid or wicked, the product of a host of objective constraints acting upon policy-makers as a consequence of secular imperial decline. This view, though it became dominant, was never universally accepted, and recently the historiographical wheel has turned almost full circle with the rise of a new, counter-revisionist critique which reaffirms many of the conclusions of *Guilty Men*.

The crucial work in crystallizing this view was *Chamberlain and Appeasement* (Parker 1993). For R. A. C. Parker, appeasement patently failed either to avert war or to prepare Britain adequately for it, and his argument refocused attention away from objective structural constraints and back onto the subjective choices made by the appeasers, especially Chamberlain. Decline did limit British options, but alternatives were open, and Chamberlain himself either artificially constructed many of the constraints or simply used them to justify pre-formed policies. The real roots of appeasement, therefore, lay in Chamberlain's flawed perception of Nazism, miscalculation of the prospects for a negotiated European settlement, and unrealistic conception of deterrence, all of which led him to reject robust policies to restrain Hitler. Parker's interpretation is obviously more nuanced and sophisticated than that of *Guilty Men*, from which he seeks to distance himself: his appeasers were not stupid or ignorant cowards pursuing peace at any price, but possessed a rational, albeit flawed, strategy to limit German expansion. (Equally, his account focuses much more upon the individual personality of Chamberlain than on his whole political class.) But the similarities are nonetheless striking, and other counter-revisionists have been more willing to present their views as entailing a return, with suitable refinements, to the interpretation first adumbrated in 1940 (Aster 1989: 261). Other recent work indicates that, even if countervailing arguments can still be found, Parker's study is part of a broader trend. Such at any rate is the conclusion to be drawn from Keith Robbins's revised edition of his short study of appeasement (Robbins 1997), from the changes evident in the position of particular scholars in recent years (McKercher: 1996; cf. 1991), and from hosts of recent detailed studies of diverse aspects of British foreign policy in the 1930s (Carley 1996; Murray 1994; Watt 1996a).

The question of what has motivated this and previous shifts in interpretation is extremely interesting. Historians' "professional ideology" disposes them to prioritize documentary factors, and the rise of the revisionist school is indeed often attributed to the opening of the British archives following the 1967 Public Records Act (Baxendale and Pawling 1996: 153). Yet the interpretation was already coalescing well before then, as a result of much broader factors, including shifting conceptions of British national identity, the vicissitudes of the Cold War and changes in disciplinary methodology. Such factors are often mentioned in historiographical surveys – since they have so obviously been important – but are usually swiftly marginalized since serious consideration of them sits very ill with the objectivity paradigm: once the door is opened to accepting history as an inherently contingent and relative cultural construct, then the solid ground of empirical foundation, and any kernel of unchallengeable truth, rapidly begins to dissolve.

Recent counter-revisionists have also foregrounded documentary factors, claiming either that records not used by revisionists – particularly Chamberlain's private papers – have now definitively proved their interpretation (Aster 1989: 240–1), or that revisionists misinterpreted those same materials (Parker 1993: 343–7, 364–5). The former claim cannot stand since the same papers – in some cases even the same sentences – were also used by revisionists in constructing their accounts. The latter claim – that historians have now finally got these documents "right" – conversely seems rather Whiggish and on that count inherently improbable. It seems much more plausible that it is again broader cultural forces conditioning how the documents are interpreted which have precipitated the rise of this interpretation, and though identification of these must remain speculative, they might include the rethinking of British national identity during the Thatcher decade and the reassertion of individual agency and responsibility entailed by the demise of collectivism. It is even tempting to prophesy that counter-revisionism is indicative of an imminent closure, that fifty years after the end of the war this subject is finally slipping out of our concerns and becoming an historical curiosity, but this may be premature.

What can be more confidently argued is that the return to ascendancy in modified form, after prolonged argument and the digestion of masses of documentary material, of an interpretation first articulated decades ago, indicates that new approaches are needed to revivify the subject and carry it forward: for all the elegance of counter-revisionist accounts, shifting perspectives without theoretical reformulation have left the subject in a cul-de-sac. This, at any rate, is what Wesley Wark has argued: why "write a history of British foreign policy based primarily on a study of the political leadership? . . . Great men performed their scripts; we have studied their parts for a half-century. We now have their characters in hand; we know their parts." Admittedly, some of Wark's suggested remedies to this problem – such as devoting more attention to the international system rather than individual states – do not involve any great theoretical innovation. But when he calls for the adoption of interdisciplinary approaches, for greater research into the mentalities of policy-makers, gender and perceptions of power (Wark 1995: 547, 561–2), then he is advocating approaches which are very much compatible with a postmodern turn in international history.

Defining precisely what this turn might involve poses problems. Postmodernism does not entail a single monolithic approach which can simply be picked up and applied. Rather, it bundles together many heterogeneous, conflicting, theoretical strands, and celebrates indeterminacy and contingency; thus it is scarcely possible to easily read off its implications for any discipline (Cahoone 1996: 4, 13–19). Some aspects of postmodernism are radically antihistorical, in that they question the possibility of achieving any meaningful or useful historicization at all. Consequently, the search for sustainable positions between (or beyond) the extreme relativist view that all history is entirely subjective ideological fantasy and the empiricist contention that it simply corresponds to the past lies at the heart of contemporary theoretical debates (Appleby et al., 1994; Berkhofer 1995; Poster 1997; Southgate 1996; Jenkins 1997b; McCullagh 1997). Certainly postmodernist historiography rests upon something of a paradox in that it problematizes our ability to gain access to the past while simultaneously setting out to make meaning from it (though of course empiricist historiography is scarcely any more securely grounded for failing to acknowledge the tenuous nature of its own foundations in "the real"). But while some anti-foundationalists advocate the Nietzschean solution of ceasing to bother with the past – closing the book on two centuries of modernist historiography and perhaps even abandoning historical consciousness altogether (Jenkins 1997a) – most theoretically-inclined historians have instead looked to the creative possibilities offered by postmodernism. Thus they have embarked on reflexive studies of the literary, linguistic and ideological dimensions of history as discourse, created new objects of study (by questioning received categories and by "resituating object after object from the realm of the ostensibly natural to the realm of the historical" (Kellner 1995: 18)), found new tools to read traditional documentary materials, and experimented with new forms of representation, some of which – fragmented, polyvocal, open-ended – constitute radical breaks with convention. Although there are undoubted tensions between these diverse enterprises, all are, in different ways, products of postmodernism.

Bearing in mind these general issues, the particular context of the subdiscipline, and the difficulties inherent in predicting the shape of "histories of the future" (Jenkins 1997b: 28–9), I would like to offer a few modest proposals to help delineate a "postist" international history, a new cultural history of international relations. In some senses these suggestions are very moderate, but they are offered merely as tentative opening gambits in the engagement between theory and an extremely traditional discourse, intended to open up spaces for future innovatory approaches. Of course, new approaches should be sufficiently radical to reflect postmodernism's anti-foundationalist epistemology and to minimize the already visible risk of trivialization through partial incorporation (Leffler 1995). But in so far as a genealogy can also be constructed that roots these suggestions in existing practice, it would be wrong to exaggerate their novelty; moreover, eschewing polemic may have tactical utility in persuading traditional practitioners of the efficacy of an open engagement with theory. (It is arguably also quite compatible with anti-foundationalism to acknowledge limits to our ability to break with the traditions and assumptions we critique.) Ultimately these suggestions may still fall between two stools, outraging traditionalists while failing to satisfy the expectations of the theoretically sophisticated (particularly, perhaps, post-positivist IR scholars who deal with the same subject-matter and whose work international historians could read with profit (Der Derian 1987, 1992; Der Derian and Shapiro 1989; Walker 1993)). But nevertheless, and without any claim to be providing an exhaustive discussion or seeking to set a rigid agenda, I would like to discuss three possible new approaches.

The first of these simply involves the elaboration of a more reflexive historiographical praxis. Far from entailing the propagation of a single authorized method, as some fearful critics assume, the postmodernist critique in history aims to promote methodological pluralism by "draw[ing] attention to the 'textual conditions' under which all historical work is done and all historical knowledge is produced." Thus all historians are quite free to "continue just as before, but with the proviso that none of them can continue to think that they gain direct access to, or 'ground' their textuality in, a 'reality' appropriated plain that they have an epistemology" (Jenkins 1995, 22). In other words, postmodernism's minimum demand is that historians should, while continuing to practice whatever history they like however they choose, be more open and humble about the status of the knowledge they produce, acknowledging its relativity, contingency and textuality. (Of course, many empiricists do acknowledge the provisional nature of their interpretations, and the inescapable role of some subjective influences, but the rhetoric and practice of the empiricist mode nevertheless implies the existence of a desirable goal transcending subjectivity.) This development – which could be construed as a return to pre-Rankean historiographical forms (Orr 1995) – might simply involve reflexive self-awareness – being "self-conscious and self-critical in theoretical outlook and practice" – and authors avowing their own subjective position, but can also lead to new reflexive forms of representation, "texts that refer to their own construction as they go about it" (Berkhofer 1995: 287), in the manner of "historiographic metafiction" (Hutcheon 1989: 32–92).

Robert Young's latest book on France and the origins of World War II consti-tutes an experiment in this direction (Young 1996). Superficially, it offers a straightforward international history account, comprising a narrative of events, an historiographical discussion, and thematic coverage of politics, diplomacy, strategy, economics and public opinion. But the tone Young strikes throughout is remarkable. Instead of maintaining the omniscient third-person viewpoint necessary to equate history with the past, he adopts a personalized, conversational, avowedly subjec-tive style – the text is littered with first-person pronouns, literary flourishes and philosophical digressions – and systematically draws attention to the constructed and therefore relative and contingent nature of his account. This is particularly evident in the introduction, where the motives behind particular interpretive choices are outlined (pp. 1–6); in the narrative chapter where, in confessing that "pure narration is next to impossible," a very relativist Sartre is approvingly quoted ("slow, lazy, sulky, the facts adapt themselves to the rigour of the order I wish to give them") (p. 36); and in the conclusion where we are reminded "that we have, at best, no more than an interpretation" (p. 149). The historiographical discussion, moreover, contrasts sharply with that offered by Roberts in his work on the Soviet Union (which is in the same series and therefore comparable). Rather than margin-alize historiography, Young takes it seriously, offering a substantial discussion (twenty-three pages out of 153) and frankly admitting how previous interpretations have governed his – and must shape our – engagement with the subject. Moreover, rather than exalting "the evidence" as leading progressively to the correct inter-pretation, Young revels in interpretive discord, and persistently emphasizes the subjective political, social, cultural and personal factors which have governed writing on the subject (pp. 37–59). Collectively these moves constituting an ironic running commentary highlighting the relativity of his own work, position Young at some considerable distance from traditional approaches.

Interpretively, Young's account also represents something of a departure from convention. For decades after 1940, France's catastrophic defeat, and by extension the French role in the origins of the war, was predominantly explained through the notion of decadence: gripped by a profound political, social and moral malaise the Third Republic staggered through the 1930s towards inevitable collapse. Since that paradigm began to fragment in the 1970s, historians have been and remain sharply divided as to whether France was actually weak or strong, declining or resurgent, well- or poorly-led, in the years before the war. In particular, according to Young, they have propagated two contradictory images, one of France smug and complacent behind the Maginot Line, the other of France fearful, lacking confidence and sensing defeat. To chart a course through this terrain Young deploys the interpretive device of ambivalence, refusing to resolve these contradictions or close them down but rather contending that they all contain elements of truth, reflecting part of the contradictory, ambiguous and messy reality of France in the 1930s (pp. 3–5, 59, 78, 149–53 and *passim*). The end result is intriguing: no doubt untidy and woolly by empiricist standards, but offering a portrait of complex reality that rings true.

Yet here we come up against the irony of Young's approach and the limits of his reflexive achievement. Despite his stress on the relativity of historical explanations, and the radical implications of the claim that historical reality is too messy to reduce to unambiguous accounts, he nevertheless implies that his own interpretation captures the reality of how things actually were better than any other. Thus an approach designed to undercut oversimplifying certainty, and affirm the value of ambivalence, itself falls prey to the lure of closure by producing and privileging its own (albeit qualitatively different) authorized narrative, thus reinscribing the epistemological assumptions it sets out to critique: narrating ambiguity still entails mastering the past. This irony could simply be a reflection of Young's own ambivalent current location on the road to relativism (although he has latterly become engaged with issues of culture and representation his initial interests were in the very traditional field of strategy). Alternatively, it could be a symptom of a broader problematic, specifically of the limits to what can be achieved through employing reflexive approaches without abandoning representational forms that still implicitly demand the production of a single reading of the past, however problematized it may be. These criticisms should certainly not detract from Young's refreshing achievement, however, nor discourage others from experimenting with an approach which offers a way forward that would permit international history to retain its traditional subject-matter and source base: while postmodernism certainly challenges the fetishization and sovereignty of "primary" documents, "postist" international history need not necessarily be entirely post-archival.

On the other hand, alternative approaches might prove more fruitful. The postmodern turn within history critically entails a loss of disciplinary innocence, a realization that historians have always been involved in fabricating subjective ideological constructs, interested representations rather than neutral reconstructions of the past. Concurrently, we have become aware that our engagement with the past is always mediated by subjective representations, that we can have no access to the past except through the sedimented layers of previous textualizations. Taken together these two developments suggest a new realm of historical inquiry, and have precipitated a vogue for "detailed historiographical studies to examine how previous and current histories have been constructed both in terms of their method and their content" (Jenkins 1991: 69). If history is not merely the objective reconstruction of the past for its own sake, then it becomes both significant and necessary to explore the factors (political, social, cultural, practical) which have conditioned past interpretations, the ideological conflicts which have been embedded within them and the ways in which they have served to ground political and cultural projects and to construct a whole range of social identities. This approach involves a fundamental shift of focus in our engagement with the past, away from seeking the essential meaning of past events and towards exploring how and why different significances have been imposed upon them over time: turning the urge to historicize upon the discipline itself, "the representation of history becomes the history of representation" (Hutcheon 1989: 58). Critical historiographical studies therefore constitute the second element in my envisioned reformulated praxis within international history.

Hitherto, despite the proliferation of diverse works broadly animated by this spirit (Novick 1988; Gildea 1994; Baxendale and Pawling 1996; Biel 1997; Noakes 1997), international history has remained impervious to it. Roberts and the appeasement counter-revisionists discussed above typify empiricist disdain for the historiographical dimension, and even Young, while acknowledging the role of previous interpretations in positioning subsequent historians, chooses to construct his own rather than subject that process to interrogation. Even more eloquent testimony is offered by *Forging the Collective Memory*, an edited collection exploring the political influences conditioning the publication of documentary collections and historical writing on the origins of the two world wars (Wilson 1996). The potential for nuanced case studies of the social construction of collective memories in this case is huge, given the intimate connections between the highly-charged politico-historical controversies over the origins of the 1914–18 conflict, the erosion of faith in the validity of Versailles, and the outbreak of war in 1939. But instead of realizing this potential and for all its exemplary scholarship this collection is hamstrung by its basic premise that the politicization of history in these instances was an undesirable and untypical deviation from "the objective and neutral study of the past." Permeating many of the essays is a very old-fashioned idealization of the full and complete archival record as a kind of holy grail, incarnating the truth of the past if only it can be accessed in its entirety. Thus the title is not intended to bring to mind the necessarily subjective construction of interested historical representations, but rather to hint at falsification, at misguided patriotic historians conspiring with governments in betrayal of their noble vocation.

A more promising portent is Richard Bosworth's eclectic, large-scale, study of the historicization of World War II (Bosworth 1993), as yet the only international history work (to my knowledge) to explore this historiographical approach. This ambitious, richly-textured, account traces how World War II has been comprehended historiographically in each of the major combatant societies over the years since 1945, exploring the role that particular understandings or representations of it have played in political and cultural discourse while also positing links between historiographical shifts and developments in the broader social world. While Bosworth is wary of aligning himself with postmodernism – professing to owe more to E. H. Carr than to Jacques Derrida – his insistence on the contingency and social grounding of historical explanation is profoundly relativist, as the splenetic ire aroused in some reviewers indicates (Kitchen 1994).

Of course, there are theoretical problems with this kind of project. Objectivist critics have tended to accuse Bosworth of failing to offer sufficient evidence to "prove" the links between changes in explanation and trends in politics and society (e.g. Lorenz 1996: 246–8), though a more telling criticism might be the converse, that it is reductive and mechanistic, if not naive, to attempt to assign specific cultural causes to certain textual effects (Hunt 1989: 8). (Connections suggest themselves here with the debates about the relationships between texts and contexts in literary studies in relation to the New Historicism (Veeser 1989).) Certainly, one inherent tension within this approach is that though it is predicated on the impossibility of objective historical explanation, it nevertheless formally offers just that: despite a novel focus and radical intent, representationally the method is quite conventional (Haskell 1990). Is this perhaps indicative of the inherent contradictions of contemporary postmodernist historiography, aware of its own contestability as just another reading yet typically deploying all the validating trappings of conventional scholarship (Samuel 1992: 233)? Alternatively, when first advancing provocative and unsettling ideas within a conservative discipline, is there not much to be said from a tactical point of view for "scrupulous adherence" to "its fetishized procedures and modes of discourse" in order to maximize their credibility (Novick 1991: 700–2)? In any case, with regards to the origins of World War II – only intermittently touched on by Bosworth – I have tried to demonstrate the potential of this critical historiographical approach in my recent reader (Finney 1997), but there remains almost limitless scope for future detailed studies.

Alternatively, a third possible new approach shifts the focus from representation back to past international relations, but seeks to conceptualize them in novel ways, building on existing cultural approaches in international history and drawing on a wide range of archival and other traces. For over two decades, a significant minority of international historians, led by pioneers like Akira Iriye, have explored myriad aspects of "international relations as intercultural relations" (Iriye 1979). Surveys show that an interest in culture does not mandate a particular theoretical position (Johnson 1994) and much of this work is resolutely empiricist, with culture simply representing a new thematic issue for traditional scholars sensitized to it by the growing salience of cultural issues in contemporary international relations (Iriye 1990: 106–7). On the other hand, the interest evinced by "culturalists" in representation and perception always posed a latent threat to the subdiscipline's fixation with the solid "realities" of military and economic power, just as their broad vision of what constituted international relations held the potential to destabilize the boundaries of the field. A new attentiveness to culture is of course central to postmodernist thinking – if reality is only accessible to us through discourse, everything is a cultural construct; culture is literally all we have – and so it seems likely that hitherto relatively marginal cultural approaches in international history will now flourish in new ways.

A possible focus for such approaches would be inquiry into the mentalities of policy-makers through discourse analysis, and exploration of the cultural construction of international subjectivities. Cultural historians' interest in mentalities – in the mind "as the site where identity is formed and reality linguistically negotiated" (Appleby et al. 1994: 218) – predates the articulation of postmodernism within the discipline, but it has been reinforced by the poststructuralist emphasis upon the determining power of language. Within the new cultural history this has led to the application of discourse analysis approaches which offer "a different measure of historical significance:"

> In search of meaning [this method] transfers attention from the study
> of "objective" reality to the categories in and through which it was
> perceived, from collective consciousness to cognitive codes, from social
> being to the symbolic order. In place of the Rankean project of showing
> the past "as it was," it asks us to piece together a social history of signi-
> fying practices and cultural modes.
>
> (Samuel 1991: 92)

For international history, this means shifting attention from the brute "realities"
of power onto how, to paraphrase Robert Darnton, policy-makers invested the
world with meaning and infused it with emotion (Samuel 1992: 225). Such
approaches build upon existing research into the "ideological or intellectual underpinnings" of international behavior (Iriye 1990: 101–3), and use new tools of analysis
to "look beneath the explicit meanings texts convey to the deeper structures of
language and rhetoric that both impart and circumscribe meaning," structures which
"help us understand what policy makers can and cannot say about the world" (Hunt
1990: 110).

Critics might argue that all this is nothing new, that international historians
have always indulged in sophisticated analysis of decision-making, attentive to the
significance of unspoken assumptions and matrices of perception. But making these
issues central, viewing the reality of international relations "not as a single, discov-
erable condition but as the product of situational vantage conditioned by location
within larger systems of power" (Rosenberg 1990: 123), as a field of clashing
mental and linguistic constructs, promises to lead us very far away from traditional
realist approaches which, by treating language as transparent, simply "reinscribe,
with little comment, the discourses of policymakers" (Costigliola 1997: 183). This
form of approach is particularly useful for studying the role of gendered understandings in international relations. It was long ago observed that gender is
"a primary way of signifying power" and that (unequal) power relations between
nations are commonly naturalized, "made comprehensible (and thus legitimate),"
in terms of relations between male and female (Scott 1988: 48). Analyzing how
this operates within policy-making discourses can therefore provide "deeper understanding of the cultural assumptions from which foreign policies spring:" "close
attention to symbolic and rhetorical structures can provide keen analytical insights
into systems of power, how they are constructed, described, challenged, legiti-
mated, and challenged again." International relations is a particularly masculine
discourse, saturated with "terms and images that represent gender differences" and
analyzing these can illuminate "the systems of thought that underlie constructions
of power and knowledge" (Rosenberg 1990: 119–21). Such approaches promise
to expand the field of study, by opening up new ways of conceptualizing the relationship between policy-making and its broader social and cultural context, and to go
far beyond "thematic" study of women in international history (though this has in
any case attracted criticism from traditionalists (Watt 1996b)). Little of this work
has yet centered on the inter-war period (*Diplomatic History* Symposium 1994;
Costigliola 1997), but there is no reason why (as suggested by Wark above) this
approach could not prove extremely fruitful there: particular gendered understandings were of course embedded in fascist ideologies, and telling gendered

metaphors are also evident in the discourse of British policy-makers (Adamthwaite 1977: 132).

It is true that these discourse analysis approaches – and the new cultural history generally – problematize the notions of causation and agency, being concerned with systems of meaning and the boundaries of what constitutes knowledge rather than cause and effect (or, indeed, origins). Hence they cannot be expected to provide new explanations for familiar diplomatic events, and are less conducive than the other two approaches discussed above to producing representationally familiar accounts. But these approaches can open up new horizons for our understandings of international relations by doing different things, in particular by questioning the foundational "givens" of international history through emphasis on the discursive construction of international subjectivities. IR scholar David Campbell's study of United States foreign policy since World War II is an exemplary study of this kind (Campbell 1992). His Foucaultian analysis – the methodology of which could fruitfully be applied to myriad other subjects including inter-war international relations – explores how foreign policy, "through the inscription of foreign-ness . . . helps produce and reproduce the political identity of the doer supposedly behind the deed" (p. vii). States exist only by virtue of their ability to constitute themselves as imagined communities, a process in which foreign policy discourses play a critical role:

> Central to the process of imagination has been the operation of discourses of danger which, by virtue of telling us what to fear, have been able to fix who "we" are. The effective discourses of danger which have led to successful instances of foreign policy are those which have been able to combine both extensive and intensive forms of power, so that the social identity of the community has been aligned with the political space of the state.
>
> (195–6)

Similar concerns are evinced by Peter Hansen in a path-breaking study of Anglo-Tibetan relations in the 1920s. Hansen combines analysis of formal policy-making discourses with the role of popular culture images and other forms of cultural exchange to explore how those relations were "reciprocal and mutually constitutive:" through complex intercultural exchanges subject positions were defined and redefined as "each influenced the other in complex and ambiguous ways" (Hansen 1996: 714, 717). These analyses are certainly very far from traditional linear narrative accounts, but then their value lies precisely in the ways in which they problematize the realist assumptions underpinning a discourse which valorized such accounts above all others.

Some words towards a conclusion seem necessary. I would not have the temerity to present the new approaches discussed above as constituting an exclusive agenda for the future of international history. They certainly do not represent "last words," or the projected "end product" of an engagement between international history and postmodernism: in many ways they are rather moderate compromises between the old and the new, as befits attempts to open up spaces for innovative approaches in a subdiscipline where claims to objectivity are still seriously entertained. Equally, within and between all these approaches, there are tensions and contradictions, which are at least in part a reflection of the youthful and still paradoxical condition of postmodernist historiography generally. What these suggestions do represent are my own personal ideas, drawn from reflection on existing practice, as to some ways forward which would enrich and expand the possibilities for international history. This is not to denigrate the achievements of previous generations of scholars, nor to suggest that international history is necessarily yet in a terminal crisis to which postmodernism offers the only answer, but I am animated by a conviction that any branch of academic inquiry which remains insulated from wider intellectual trends risks ossification. Whether international historians will choose to embrace postmodernism must remain a very moot point, and it would be naive not to acknowledge that there is a good deal at stake ideologically in the question of historians' authority over the past, and their privileged position as authorized producers of historical truth. Yet the very fact that examples of each of the new approaches which I advocated above could be drawn from existing practice gives me cause for optimism that international history does indeed contain within itself the potential for its own transformation.

References

Acton, Edward (1990) *Rethinking the Russian Revolution* (London: Arnold).

Adamthwaite, Anthony (1977) *The Making of the Second World War* (London: Allen & Unwin).

Ankersmit, Frank and Kellner, Hans (eds) (1995) *A New Philosophy of History* (London: Reaktion).

Appleby, Joyce, Hunt, Lynn and Jacob, Margaret (1994) *Telling the Truth about History* (New York: Norton).

Aster, Sidney (1989) "'Guilty men': the case of Neville Chamberlain," in Robert Boyce and E. M. Robertson (eds) *Paths to War* (London: Macmillan), pp. 233–68.

Baxendale, John and Pawling, Chris (1996) *Narrating the Thirties. A Decade in the Making: 1930 to the Present* (London: Macmillan).

Bell, P. M. H. (1997) *The Origins of the Second World War in Europe*, 2nd edn (London: Longman).

Berkhofer, Robert F. (1995) *Beyond the Great Story. History as Text and Discourse* (Cambridge, MA: Harvard University Press).

Biel, Steven (1997) *Down with the Old Canoe: A Cultural History of the Titanic Disaster* (New York: Norton).

Bosworth, R. J. (1993) *Explaining Auschwitz and Hiroshima. History Writing and the Second World War, 1945–1990* (London: Routledge).

Burke, Peter (ed.) (1991) *New Perspectives on Historical Writing* (Oxford: Polity Press).

Cahoone, Lawrence (ed.) (1996) *From Modernism to Postmodernism. An Anthology* (Oxford: Blackwell).

Campbell, David (1992) *Writing Security. United States Foreign Policy and the Politics of Identity* (Manchester: Manchester University Press).

Carley, Michael Jabara (1996) "'A fearful concatenation of circumstances': the Anglo-Soviet rapprochement, 1934–6," *Contemporary European History* 5: 29–69.

Combs, Jerald A. (1983) *American Diplomatic History. Two Centuries of Changing Interpretations* (Berkeley: University of California Press).

Costigliola, Frank (1997) "The nuclear family: tropes of gender and pathology in the Western alliance," *Diplomatic History* 21: 163–83.

Der Derian, James (1987) *On Diplomacy. A Genealogy of Western Estrangement* (Oxford: Blackwell).

—— (1992) *Antidiplomacy: Spies, Terror, Speed and War* (Oxford: Blackwell).

—— and Shapiro, Michael (eds) (1989) *International / Intertextual Relations. Postmodern Readings of World Politics* (Lexington: Lexington Books).

Diplomatic History Symposium (1994) "Culture, gender and foreign policy," *Diplomatic History* 18: 46–124.

—— (1997) "Soviet archives: recent revelations and Cold War historiography," *Diplomatic History* 21: 215–305.

Dockrill, Michael and McKercher, Brian (eds) (1996) *Diplomacy and World Power. Studies in British Foreign Policy, 1890–1950* (Cambridge: Cambridge University Press).

Finney, Patrick (ed.) (1997) *The Origins of the Second World War* (London: Arnold).

Gardiner, Juliet (ed.) (1988) *What is History Today?* (London: Macmillan).

Gildea, Robert (1994) *The Past in French History* (New Haven: Yale University Press).

Hansen, Peter (1996) "The dancing lamas of Everest: cinema, orientalism, and Anglo-Tibetan relations in the 1920s," *American Historical Review* 101: 712–47.

Haskell, Thomas (1990) "Objectivity is not neutrality: rhetoric versus practice in Peter Novick's *That Noble Dream*," *History and Theory* 29: 129–57.

Hogan, Michael (ed.) (1995) *America in the World. The Historiography of American Foreign Relations since 1941* (Cambridge: Cambridge University Press).

Hunt, Lynn (ed.) (1989) *The New Cultural History* (Berkeley: University of California Press).

Hunt, Michael (1990) "Ideology," *Journal of American History* 77: 108–15.

Hutcheon, Linda (1989) *The Politics of Postmodernism* (London: Routledge).

Iriye, Akira (1979) "Culture and power: international relations as intercultural relations," *Diplomatic History* 3: 115–28.

—— (1990) "Culture," *Journal of American History* 77: 99–107.

Jenkins, Keith (1991) *Rethinking History* (London: Routledge).

—— (1995) *On "What is History" From Carr and Elton to Rorty and White* (London: Routledge).

—— (1997a) "Why bother with the past?" paper delivered at a symposium on Taboo and Recollection, Gregynog, Wales, May 1997; published in *Rethinking History* 1(1): 56–66.

—— (ed.) (1997b) *The Postmodern History Reader* (London: Routledge).

Johnson, Robert (ed.) (1994) *On Cultural Ground. Essays in International History* (Chicago: Imprint).

Kellner, Hans (1995) "Introduction: describing redescriptions," in Ankersmit and Kellner (1995), pp. 1–18.

Kitchen, Martin (1994) Review of Bosworth (1993), *International History Review* 16: 189–91.

La Feber, Walter (1995) "The world and the United States," *American Historical Review* 100: 1015–33.

Leffler, Mervyn (1995) "New approaches, old interpretations and prospective reconfigurations," in Hogan (1995), pp. 63–92.

Lemon, M. C. (1995) *The Discipline of History and the History of Thought* (London: Routledge).

Lorenz, Chris (1996) Review of Bosworth (1993), *History and Theory* 35: 234–52.

Maier, Charles (1980) "Marking time: the historiography of international relations," in Michael Kammen (ed.) *The Past Before Us: Contemporary Historical Writing in the United States* (Ithaca: Cornell University Press) pp. 355–87.

Marwick, Arthur (1989) *The Nature of History*, 3rd edn (London: Macmillan).

McCullagh, C. B. (1997) *The Truth of History* (London: Routledge).

McKercher, Brian (1991) "'Our most dangerous enemy': Great Britain pre-eminent in the 1930s," *International History Review* 13: 751–83.

—— (1996) "Old diplomacy and new: the Foreign Office and foreign policy, 1919–1939," in Dockrill and McKercher (1996), pp. 79–114.

Murray, Williamson (1994) "The collapse of empire: British strategy, 1919–1945," in Williamson Murray, MacGregor Knox and Alvin Bernstein (eds) *The Making of Strategy: Rulers, States and War* (Cambridge: Cambridge University Press) pp. 393–427.

Noakes, Lucy (1997) *War and the British. Gender, Memory and National Identity, 1939–1991* (London: Tauris).

Novick, Peter (1988) *That Noble Dream. The "Objectivity Question" and the American Historical Profession* (Cambridge: Cambridge University Press).

—— (1991) "My correct views on everything," *American Historical Review* 96: 699–703.

Orr, Linda (1995) "Intimate images: subjectivity and history – Staël, Michelet and Tocqueville," in Ankersmit and Kellner (1995) pp. 89–107.

Overy, Richard (1987) *The Origins of the Second World War* (London: Longman).

—— (1994) *The Inter-War Crisis, 1919–1939* (London: Longman).

Parker, R. A. C. (1993) *Chamberlain and Appeasement. British Policy and the Coming of the Second World War* (London: Macmillan).

Poster, Mark (1997) *Cultural History and Postmodernity* (New York: Columbia University Press).

Robbins, Keith (1997) *Appeasement*, 2nd edn (Oxford: Blackwell).

Roberts, Geoffrey (1995) *The Soviet Union and the Origins of the Second World War. Russo-German Relations and the Road to War, 1933–1941* (London: Macmillan).

—— (1996) "Narrative history as a way of life," *Journal of Contemporary History* 31: 221–8.

—— (1997) "Postmodernism versus the standpoint of action," *History and Theory* 36: 249–60.

Rosenberg, Emily (1990) "Gender," *Journal of American History* 77: 116–24.

Samuel, Raphael (1991) "Reading the signs," *History Workshop Journal* 32: 88–109.

—— (1992) "Reading the signs II," *History Workshop Journal* 33: 220–51.

Scott, Joan W. (1988) *Gender and the Politics of History* (New York: Columbia University Press).

Southgate, Beverley (1996) *History: What and Why?* (London: Routledge).

Thorne, Christopher (1988) *Border Crossings: Studies in International History* (Oxford: Blackwell).

Veeser, H. A. (ed.) (1989) *The New Historicism* (London: Routledge).

Walker, R. B. J. (1993) *Inside/Outside: International Relations as Political Theory* (Cambridge: Cambridge University Press).

Ward, Chris (1993) *Stalin's Russia* (London: Arnold).

Wark, Wesley (1995) "Appeasement revisited," *International History Review* 13: 545–62.

Watt, D. C. (1983) *What about the People? Abstraction and Reality in History and the Social Sciences* (London: London School of Economics).

—— (1992) "Postmodernist history," *Times Literary Supplement* 30 October.

—— (1996a) "Chamberlain's ambassadors," in Dockrill and McKercher (1996), pp. 136–70.

—— (1996b) "Women in international history," *Review of International Studies* 22: 431–7.

Wilson, Keith (ed.) (1996) *Forging the Collective Memory. Government and International Historians through Two World Wars* (Oxford: Berghahn).

Young, Robert (1996) *France and the Origins of the Second World War* (London: Macmillan).

Chapter 26

William Cronon

A PLACE FOR STORIES

Nature, history and narrative

Children, only animals live entirely in the Here and Now. Only nature knows neither memory nor history. But man – let me offer you a definition – is the story-telling animal. Wherever he goes he wants to leave behind not a chaotic wake, not an empty space, but the comforting marker buoys and trail-signs of stories. He has to go on telling stories. He has to keep on making them up. As long as there's a story, it's all right. Even in his last moments, it's said, in the split second of a fatal fall – or when he's about to drown – he sees, passing rapidly before him, the story of his whole life.

Graham Swift, Waterland

IN THE BEGINNING WAS THE STORY. Or rather: many stories, of many places, in many voices, pointing toward many ends.

In 1979, two books were published about the long drought that struck the Great Plains during the 1930s. The two had nearly identical titles: one, by Paul Bonnifield, was called *The Dust Bowl*; the other, by Donald Worster, *Dust Bowl*. The two authors dealt with virtually the same subject, had researched many of the same documents, and agreed on most of their facts, and yet their conclusions could hardly have been more different.

Bonnifield's closing argument runs like this:

> In the final analysis, the story of the dust bowl was the story of people, people with ability and talent, people with resourcefulness, fortitude, and courage.. . . The people of the dust bowl were not defeated, poverty-ridden people without hope. They were builders for tomorrow. During those hard years they continued to build their churches, their businesses, their schools, their colleges, their communities. They grew closer to God and fonder of the land. Hard years were common in their past, but the

future belonged to those who were ready to seize the moment.. . .
Because they stayed during those hard years and worked the land and
tapped her natural resources, millions of people have eaten better,
worked in healthier places, and enjoyed warmer homes. Because those
determined people did not flee the stricken area during a crisis, the nation
today enjoys a better standard of living.[1]

Worster, on the other hand, paints a bleaker picture:

The Dust Bowl was the darkest moment in the twentieth-century life
of the southern plains. The name suggests a place – a region whose
borders are as inexact and shifting as a sand dune. But it was also an
event of national, even planetary significance. A widely respected
authority on world food problems, George Borgstrom, has ranked the
creation of the Dust Bowl as one of the three worst ecological blunders
in history. . . . It cannot be blamed on illiteracy or overpopulation or
social disorder. It came about because the culture was operating in
precisely the way it was supposed to. . . . The Dust Bowl . . . was the
inevitable outcome of a culture that deliberately, self-consciously, set
itself [the] task of dominating and exploiting the land for all it was
worth.[2]

For Bonnifield, the dust storms of the 1930s were mainly a natural disaster;
when the rains gave out, people had to struggle for their farms, their homes, their
very survival. Their success in that struggle was a triumph of individual and community spirit: nature made a mess, and human beings cleaned it up. Worster's version
differs dramatically. Although the rains did fail during the 1930s, their disappearance expressed the cyclical climate of a semiarid environment. The story of the
Dust Bowl is less about the failures of nature than about the failures of human
beings to accommodate themselves to nature. A long series of willful human misunderstandings and assaults led finally to a collapse whose origins were mainly cultural.

Whichever of these interpretations we are inclined to follow, they pose a
dilemma for scholars who study past environmental change – indeed, a dilemma
for all historians. As often happens in history, they make us wonder how two
competent authors looking at identical materials drawn from the same past can
reach such divergent conclusions. But it is not merely their *conclusions* that differ.
Although both narrate the same broad series of events with an essentially similar
cast of characters, they tell two entirely different *stories*. In both texts, the story is
inextricably bound to its conclusion, and the historical analysis derives much of its
force from the upward or downward sweep of the plot. So we must eventually ask
a more basic question: where did these stories come from?

The question is trickier than it seems, for it transports us into the much
contested terrain between traditional social science and postmodernist critical
theory. As an environmental historian who tries to blend the analytical traditions
of history with those of ecology, economics, anthropology, and other fields, I cannot
help feeling uneasy about the shifting theoretical ground we all now seem to occupy.
On the one hand, a fundamental premise of my field is that human acts occur within

a network of relationships, processes, and systems that are as ecological as they are cultural. To such basic historical categories as gender, class, and race, environmental historians would add a theoretical vocabulary in which plants, animals, soils, climates, and other nonhuman entities become the coactors and codeterminants of a history not just of people but of the earth itself. For scholars who share my perspective, the importance of the natural world, its objective effects on people, and the concrete ways people affect it in turn are not at issue; they are the very heart of our intellectual project. We therefore ally our historical work with that of our colleagues in the sciences, whose models, however imperfectly, try to approximate the mechanisms of nature.[3]

And yet scholars of environmental history also maintain a powerful commitment to narrative form. When we describe human activities within an ecosystem, we seem always to tell *stories* about them.[4] Like all historians, we configure the events of the past into causal sequences — stories — that order and simplify those events to give them new meanings. We do so because narrative is the chief literary form that tries to find meaning in an overwhelmingly crowded and disordered chronological reality. When we choose a plot to order our environmental histories, we give them a unity that neither nature nor the past possesses so clearly. In so doing, we move well beyond nature into the intensely human realm of value. There, we cannot avoid encountering the postmodernist assault on narrative, which calls into question not just the stories we tell but the deeper purpose that motivated us in the first place: trying to make sense of nature's place in the human past.

By writing stories about environmental change, we divide the causal relationships of an ecosystem with a rhetorical razor that defines included and excluded, relevant and irrelevant, empowered and disempowered. In the act of separating story from non-story, we wield the most powerful yet dangerous tool of the narrative form. It is a commonplace of modern literary theory that the very authority with which narrative presents its vision of reality is achieved by obscuring large portions of that reality. Narrative succeeds to the extent that it hides the discontinuities, ellipses, and contradictory experiences that would undermine the intended meaning of its story. Whatever its overt purpose, it cannot avoid a covert exercise of power: it inevitably sanctions some voices while silencing others. A powerful narrative reconstructs common sense to make the contingent seem determined and the artificial seem natural. If this is true, then narrative poses particularly difficult problems for environmental historians, for whom the boundary between the artificial and the natural is the very thing we most wish to study. The differences between Bonnifield's and Worster's versions of the Dust Bowl clearly have something to do with that boundary, as does my own uneasiness about the theoretical underpinnings of my historical craft.[5]

The disease of literary theory is to write too much in abstractions, so that even the simplest meanings become difficult if not downright opaque. Lest this essay wander off into litcrit fog, let me ground it on more familiar terrain. I propose to examine the role of narrative in environmental history by returning to the Great Plains to survey the ways historians have told that region's past. What I offer here will *not* be a comprehensive historiography, since my choice of texts is eclectic and I will ignore many major works. Rather, I will use a handful of Great Plains histories to explore the much vexed problems that narrative poses for all historians.

On the one hand, I hope to acknowledge the deep challenges that postmodernism poses for those who applaud "the revival of narrative;" on the other, I wish to record my own conviction — chastened but still strong — that narrative remains essential to our understanding of history and the human place in nature.

If we consider the Plains in the half millennium since Christopher Columbus crossed the Atlantic, certain events seem likely to stand out in any long-term history of the region. If I were to try to write these not as a *story* but as a simple *list* — I will not entirely succeed in so doing, since the task of *not* telling stories about the past turns out to be much more difficult than it may seem — the resulting chronicle might run something like this.

Five centuries ago, people traveled west across the Atlantic Ocean. So did some plants and animals. One of these — the horse — appeared on the Plains. Native peoples used horses to hunt bison. Human migrants from across the Atlantic eventually appeared on the Plains as well. People fought a lot. The bison herds disappeared. Native peoples moved to reservations. The new immigrants built homes for themselves. Herds of cattle increased. Settlers plowed the prairie grasses, raising corn, wheat, and other grains. Railroads moved people and other things into and out of the region. Crops sometimes failed for lack of rain. Some people abandoned their farms and moved elsewhere; other people stayed. During the 1930s, there was a particularly bad drought, with many dust storms. Then the drought ended. A lot of people began to pump water out of the ground for use on their fields and in their towns. Today, Plains farmers continue to raise crops and herds of animals. Some have trouble making ends meet. Many Indians live on reservations. It will be interesting to see what happens next.

I trust that this list seems pretty peculiar to anyone who reads it, as if a child were trying to tell a story without quite knowing how. I've tried to remove as much sense of *connection* among these details as I can. I've presented them not as a narrative but as a *chronicle*, a simple chronological listing of events as they occurred in sequence.[6] This was not a pure chronicle, since I presented only what I declared to be the "most important" events of Plains history. By the very act of separating important from unimportant events, I actually smuggled a number of not-so-hidden stories into my list, so that such things as the migration of the horse or the conquest of the Plains tribes began to form little narrative swirls in the midst of my ostensibly story-less account. A pure chronicle would have included every event that ever occurred on the Great Plains, no matter how large or small, so that a colorful sunset in September 1623 or a morning milking of cows on a farm near Leavenworth in 1897 would occupy just as prominent a place as the destruction of the bison herds or the 1930s dust storms.

Such a text is impossible even to imagine, let alone construct, for reasons that help explain historians' affection for narrative.[7] When we encounter the past in the form of a chronicle, it becomes much less recognizable to us. We have trouble sorting out why things happened when and how they did, and it becomes hard to evaluate the relative significance of events. Things seem less *connected* to each other, and it becomes unclear how all this stuff relates to us. Most important, in a chronicle we easily lose the thread of what was going on at any particular moment. Without some plot to organize the flow of events, everything becomes much harder — even impossible — to understand.

How do we discover a story that will turn the facts of Great Plains history into something more easily recognized and understood? The repertoire of historical plots we might apply to the events I've just chronicled is endless and could be drawn not just from history but from all of literature and myth. To simplify the range of choices, let me start by offering two large groups of possible plots. On the one hand, we can narrate Plains history as a story of improvement, in which the plot line gradually ascends toward an ending that is somehow more positive — happier, richer, freer, better — than the beginning. On the other hand, we can tell stories in which the plot line eventually falls toward an ending that is more negative — sadder, poorer, less free, worse — than the place where the story began. The one group of plots might be called "progressive," given their historical dependence on eighteenth-century Enlightenment notions of progress; the other might be called "tragic" or "declensionist," tracing their historical roots to romantic and anti-modernist reactions against progress.

If we look at the ways historians have actually written about the changing environment of the Great Plains, the upward and downward lines of progress and declension are everywhere apparent. The very ease with which we recognize them constitutes a warning about the terrain we are entering. However compelling these stories may be as depictions of environmental change, their narrative form has less to do with nature than with human discourse. Their plots are cultural construc-tions so deeply embedded in our language that they resonate far beyond the Great Plains. Historians did not invent them, and their very familiarity encourages us to shape our storytelling to fit their patterns. Placed in a particular historical or ideological context, neither group of plots is innocent: both have hidden agendas that influence what the narrative includes and excludes. So powerful are these agendas that not even the historian as author entirely controls them.

Take, for instance, the historians who narrate Great Plains history as a tale of frontier progress. The most famous of those who embraced this basic plot was of course Frederick Jackson Turner, for whom the story of the nation recapitulated the ascending stages of European civilization to produce a uniquely democratic and egalitarian community. Turner saw the transformation of the American landscape from wilderness to trading post to farm to boomtown as the central saga of the nation.[8] If ever there was a narrative that achieved its end by erasing its true subject, Turner's frontier was it: the heroic encounter between pioneers and "free land" could only become plausible by obscuring the conquest that traded one people's freedom for another's. By making Indians the foil for its story of progress, the fron-tier plot made their conquest seem natural, commonsensical, inevitable. But to say this is only to affirm the narrative's power. In countless versions both before and after it acquired its classic Turnerian form, this story of frontier struggle and progress remains among the oldest and most familiar narratives of American history. In its ability to turn ordinary people into heroes and to present a conflict-ridden invasion as an epic march toward enlightened democratic nationhood, it perfectly fulfilled the ideological needs of its late-nineteenth-century moment.[9]

The Great Plains would eventually prove less tractable to frontier progress than many other parts of the nation. Turner himself would say of the region that it constituted the American farmer's "first defeat," but that didn't stop the settlers themselves from narrating their past with the frontier story.[10] One of Dakota

Territory's leading missionaries, Bishop William Robert Hare, prophesied in the 1880s that the plot of Dakota settlement would follow an upward line of migration, struggle, and triumph:

> You may stand ankle deep in the short burnt grass of an uninhabited wilderness – next month a mixed train will glide over the waste and stop at some point where the railroad has decided to locate a town. Men, women and children will jump out of the cars, and their chattel will be tumbled out after them. From that moment the building begins. The courage and faith of these pioneers are something extraordinary. Their spirit seems to rise above all obstacles.[11]

For Hare, this vision of progress was ongoing and prospective, a prophecy of future growth, but the same pattern could just as easily be applied to retrospective visions. An early historian of Oklahoma, Luther Hill, could look back in 1909 at the 1890s, a decade that had "wrought a great change in Oklahoma territory:" in a mere ten years, settlers had transformed the "stagnant pool" of unused Indian lands into the "waving grain fields, the herds of cattle, and the broad prospect of agricultural prosperity [which] cause delight and even surprise in the beholder who sees the results of civilization in producing such marvels of wealth."[12] Ordinary people saw such descriptions as the fulfillment of a grand story that had unfolded during the course of their own lifetimes. As one Kansas townswoman, Josephine Middlekauf, concluded,

> After sixty years of pioneering in Hays, I could write volumes telling of its growth and progress.. . . I have been singularly privileged to have seen it develop from the raw materials into the almost finished product in comfortable homes, churches, schools, paved streets, trees, fruits and flowers.[13]

Consider these small narratives more abstractly. They tell a story of more or less linear progress, in which people struggle to transform a relatively responsive environment. There may be moderate setbacks along the way, but their narrative role is to play foil to the heroes who overcome them. Communities rapidly succeed in becoming ever more civilized and comfortable. The time frame of the stories is brief, limited to the lifespan of a single generation, and is located historically in the moment just after invading settlers first occupied Indian lands. Our attention as readers is focused on local events, those affecting individuals, families, townships, and other small communities. All of these framing devices, which are as literary as they are historical, compel us toward the conclusion that this is basically a happy story. It is tempered only by a hint of nostalgia for the world that is being lost, a quiet undercurrent of elderly regret for youthful passions and energies now fading.

If the story these narrators tell is about the drama of settlement and the courage of pioneers, it is just as much about the changing stage on which the drama plays itself out. The transformation of a Kansas town is revealed not just by its new buildings but by its shade trees, apple orchards, and gardens; the triumphant prosperity of Oklahoma resides in its wheat fields, cattle pastures, and oil derricks. As the literary critic Kenneth Burke long ago suggested, the scene of a story is as fundamental to what happens in it as the actions that comprise its more visible plot. Indeed, Burke argues that a story's actions are almost invariably consistent with its scene. "there is implicit in the quality of a scene," he writes, "the quality of the action that is to take place within it."[14]

If the way a narrator constructs a scene is directly related to the story that narrator tells, then this has deep implications for environmental history, which after all takes scenes of past nature as its primary object of study. If the history of the Great Plains is a progressive story about how grasslands were turned into ranches, farms, and gardens, then the end of the story requires a particular kind of scene for the ascending plot line to reach its necessary fulfillment. Just as important, the closing scene has to be different from the opening one. If the story ends in a wheat-field that is the happy conclusion of a struggle to transform the landscape, then the most basic requirement of the story is that the earlier form of that landscape must either be neutral or negative in value. It must *deserve* to be transformed.

It is thus no accident that these storytellers begin their narratives in the midst of landscapes that have few redeeming features. Bishop Hare's Dakota Territory begins as "an uninhabited wilderness," and his railroad carries future settlers across a "waste." Just so does narrative revalue nature by turning it into scenery and pushing to its margins such characters as Indians who play no role in the story – or rather, whose roles the story is designed to obscure. When Luther Hill's Oklahoma was still controlled by Indians, it remained "a stagnant pool," while Josephine Middlekauf perceived the unplowed Kansas grasslands chiefly as "raw materials." Even so seemingly neutral a phrase as this last one – "raw materials" – is freighted with narrative meaning. Indeed, it contains buried within it the entire story of progressive development in which the environment is transformed from "raw materials" to "finished product." In just this way, story and scene become entangled – with each other, and with the politics of invasion and civilized progress – as we try to understand the Plains environment and its history.

Now in fact, these optimistic stories about Great Plains settlement are by no means typical of historical writing in the twentieth century. The problems of settling a semiarid environment were simply too great for the frontier story to proceed without multiple setbacks and crises. Even narrators who prefer an ascending plot line in their stories of regional environmental change must therefore tell a more complicated tale of failure, struggle, and accommodation in the face of a resistant if not hostile landscape.

Among the most important writers who adopt this narrative strategy are Walter Prescott Webb and James Malin, the two most influential historians of the Great Plains to write during the first half of the twentieth century. Webb's classic work, *The Great Plains*, was published over half a century ago and has remained in print to this day.[15] It tells a story that significantly revises the Turnerian frontier. For Webb, the Plains were radically different from the more benign environments that Anglo-American settlers had encountered in the East. Having no trees and little water, the region posed an almost insurmountable obstacle to the westward march of civilization. After describing the scene in this way, Webb sets his story in motion with a revealing passage:

> In the new region — level, timberless, and semi-arid — [settlers] were thrown by Mother Necessity into the clutch of new circumstances. Their plight has been stated in this way: east of the Mississippi civilization stood on three legs — land, water, and timber; west of the Mississippi not one but two of these legs were withdrawn, — water and timber, — and civilization was left on one leg — land. It is small wonder that it toppled over in temporary failure.[16]

It is easy to anticipate the narrative that will flow from this beginning: Webb will tell us how civilization fell over, then built itself new legs and regained its footing to continue its triumphant ascent. The central agency that solves these problems and drives the story froward is human invention. Unlike the simpler frontier narratives, Webb's history traces a dialectic between a resistant landscape and the technological innovations that will finally succeed in transforming it. Although his book is over five hundred pages long and is marvelously intricate in its arguments, certain great inventions mark the turning points of Webb's plot. Because water was so scarce, settlers had to obtain it from the only reliable source, underground aquifers, so they invented the humble but revolutionary windmill. Because so little wood was available to build fences that would keep cattle out of cornfields, barbed wire was invented in 1874 and rapidly spread throughout the grasslands. These and other inventions — railroads, irrigation, new legal systems for allocating water rights, even six-shooter revolvers — eventually destroyed the bison herds, created a vast cattle kingdom, and broke the prairie sod for farming.

Webb closes his story by characterizing the Plains as "a land of survival where nature has most stubbornly resisted the efforts of man. Nature's very stubbornness has driven man to the innovations which he has made."[17] Given the scenic requirements of Webb's narrative, his Plains landscape must look rather different from that of earlier frontier narrators. For Webb, the semiarid environment is neither a wilderness nor a waste, but itself a worthy antagonist of civilization. It is a landscape the very resistance of which is the necessary spur urging human ingenuity to new levels of achievement. Webb thus spends much more time than earlier storytellers describing the climate, terrain, and ecology of the Great Plains so as to extol the features that made the region unique in American experience. Although his book ends with the same glowing image of a transformed landscape that we find in earlier frontier narratives, he in no way devalues the "uncivilized" landscape that preceded it. Quite the contrary: the more formidable it is as a rival, the more heroic become its human antagonists. In the struggle to make homes for themselves in this difficult land, the people of the Plains not only proved their inventiveness but built a regional culture beautifully adapted to the challenges of their regional environment.

Webb's story of struggle against a resistant environment has formed the core of most subsequent environmental histories of the Plains. We have already encountered one version of it in Paul Bonnifield's *The Dust Bowl*. It can also be discovered in the more ecologically sophisticated studies of James C. Malin, in which the evolution of "forest man" to "grass man" becomes the central plot of Great Plains history.[18] Malin's prose is far less story-like in outward appearance than Webb's, but it nonetheless narrates an encounter between a resistant environment and human ingenuity. Malin's human agents begin as struggling immigrants who have no conception of how to live in a treeless landscape; by the end, they have become "grass men" who have brought their culture "into conformity with the requirements of maintaining rather than disrupting environmental equilibrium." So completely have they succeeded in adapting themselves that they can even "point the finger of scorn at the deficiencies of the forest land; grassless, wet, with an acid, leached, infertile soil."[19] Human inhabitants have become one with an environment that only a few decades before had almost destroyed them.

The beauty of these plots is that they present the harshness of the regional environment in such a way as to make the human struggle against it appear even more positive and heroic than the continuous ascent portrayed in earlier frontier narratives. The focus of our attention is still relatively small-scale, though both the geographical and the chronological context of the plot have expanded. The story is now much more a regional one, so that the histories of one family or town, or even of Kansas or Oklahoma, become less important than the broader history of the grassland environment as a whole. The time frame too has advanced, so that the history of technological progress on the Plains moves well into the twentieth century. Because the plot still commences at the moment that Euroamerican settlers began to occupy the grasslands, though, there is no explicit *backward* extension of the time frame. The precontact history of the Indians is not part of this story.

Most interestingly, the human subject of these stories has become significantly broader than the earlier state and local frontier histories. Rather than focus primarily on individual pioneers and their communities, these new regional studies center their story on "civilization" or "man." The inventions that allowed people to adapt to life on the Great Plains are thus absorbed into the broader story of "man" and "his" long conquest of nature. No narrative centered on so singular a central character could be politically innocent. More erasures are at work here: Indians, yes, but also women, ethnic groups, underclasses, and any other communities that have been set apart from the collectivity represented by Man or Civilization. The narrative leaves little room for them, and even less for a natural realm that might appropriately be spared the conquests of technology. These are stories about a progress that, however hard-earned, is fated; its conquests are only what common sense and nature would expect. For Webb and Malin, the Great Plains gain significance from their ties to a world-historical plot, Darwinian in shape, that encompasses the entire sweep of human history. The ascending plot line we detect in these stories is in fact connected to a much longer plot line with the same rising characteristics. Whether that longer plot is expressed as the Making of the American Nation, the Rise of Western Civilization, or the Ascent of Man, it still lends its grand scale to Great Plains histories that outwardly appear much more limited in form. This may explain how we can find ourselves so entranced by a book whose principal subject for five hundred pages is the invention of windmills and barbed wire.

But there is another way to tell this history, one in which the plot ultimately falls rather than rises. The first examples of what we might call a "declensionist" or "tragic" Great Plains history began to appear during the Dust Bowl calamity of the 1930s. The dominant New Deal interpretation of what had gone wrong on the Plains was that settlers had been fooled by a climate that was sometimes perfectly adequate for farming and at other times disastrously inadequate. Settlement had expanded during "good" years when rainfall was abundant, and the perennial optimism of the frontier had prevented farmers from acknowledging that drought was a permanent fact of life on the Plains. In this version, Great Plains history becomes a tale of self-deluding hubris and refusal to accept reality. Only strong government action, planned by enlightened scientific experts to encourage cooperation among Plains farmers, could prevent future agricultural expansion and a return of the dust storms.

The classic early statement of this narrative is that of the committee that Franklin D. Roosevelt appointed to investigate the causes of the Dust Bowl, in its 1936 report on *The Future of the Great Plains*. Its version of the region's history up until the 1930s runs as follows:

> The steady progress which we have come to look for in American communities was beginning to reverse itself. Instead of becoming more productive, the Great Plains were becoming less so. Instead of giving their population a better standard of living, they were tending to give them a poorer one. The people were energetic and courageous, and they loved their land. Yet they were increasingly less secure in it.[20]

One did not have to look far to locate the reason for this unexpected reversal of the American success story. Plains settlers had failed in precisely the agricultural adaptations that Webb and Malin claimed for them. Radical steps would have to be taken if the Dust Bowl disaster were not to repeat itself. "It became clear," said the planners, describing their own controversial conclusions with the settled authority of the past tense, "that unless there was a permanent change in the agriculture pattern of the Plains, relief always would have to be extended whenever the available rainfall was deficient."[21]

Whatever the scientific or political merits of this description, consider its narrative implications. The New Deal planners in effect argued that the rising plot line of our earlier storytellers not only was false but was itself the principal cause of the environmental disaster that unfolded during the 1930s. The Dust Bowl had occurred because people had been telling themselves the wrong story and had tried to inscribe that story – the frontier – on the landscape incapable of supporting it.[22] The environmental rhythms of the Plains ecosystem were cyclical, with good years and bad years following each other like waves on a beach. The problem of human settlement in the region was that people insisted on imposing their linear notions of progress on this cyclical pattern. Their perennial optimism led them always to accept as "normal" the most favorable part of the precipitation cycle, and so they created a type and scale of agriculture that could not possibly be sustained through the dry years. In effect, bad storytelling had wreaked havoc with the balance of nature.

By this interpretation, the "plot" of Great Plains history rises as Euroamerican settlement begins, but the upward motion becomes problematic as farmers exceed the natural limits of the ecosystem. From that moment forward, the story moves toward a climax in which the tragic flaws of a self-deluding people finally yield crisis and decline. Although the geographical and chronological frame of this narrative are much the same as in the earlier progressive plots, the *scene* has shifted dramatically. For Webb and Malin, the Plains environment was resistant but changeable, so that struggle and ingenuity would finally make it conform to the human will. In this early New Deal incarnation of a pessimistic Great Plains history, the environment was not only resistant but in some fundamental ways unchangeable. Its most important characteristics – cyclical drought and aridity – could not be altered by human technology; they could only be accommodated. If the story was still about human beings learning to live in the grasslands, its ultimate message was about gaining the wisdom to recognize and accept natural limits rather than strive to overcome them. Although the close of the New Deal committee's story still lay in the future when its report was released in 1936, its authors clearly intended readers to conclude that the only appropriate ending was for Americans to reject optimistic stories such as Webb's and Malin's in favor of environmental restraint and sound management.

The political subtext of this story is not hard to find. Whereas the heroes of earlier Great Plains narratives had been the courageous and inventive people who settled the region, the New Dealers constructed their stories so as to place themselves on center stage. Plainspeople, for all their energy, courage, and love of the land, were incapable of solving their own problems without help. They had made such a mess of their environment that only disinterested outsiders, offering the enlightened perspective of scientific management, could save them from their own folly. In this sense, the New Deal narrative is only partially tragic, for in fact the planners still intended a happy ending. Like Webb and Malin, they saw the human story on the Plains as a tale of adaptation, but their vision of progressive modernization ended in regional coordination and centralized state planning. Federal planners would aid local communities in developing new cooperative institutions and a more sustainable relation to the land. This was the conclusion of Pare Lorentz's famous New Deal propaganda film, *The Plow that Broke the Plains* (1936), in which a seemingly inevitable environmental collapse is finally reversed by government intervention. Technology, education, cooperation, and state power – not individualism – would bring Plains society back into organic balance with Plains nature and thereby avert tragedy to produce a happy ending.

Seen in this light, James Malin's storytelling takes on new meaning. Malin wrote in the wake of the New Deal and was a staunch conservative opponent of everything it represented. His narratives of regional adaptation expressed his own horror of collectivism by resisting the New Deal story at virtually every turn. The planners, he said, had exaggerated the severity of the Dust Bowl to serve their own statist ends and had ignored the fact that dust storms had been a natural part of the Plains environment as far back as anyone remembered. Their scientistic faith in ecology had grave political dangers, for the ecologists had themselves gone astray in viewing the Plains environment as a stable, self-equilibrating organism in which human action inevitably disturbed the balance of nature.[23] Ecosystems were dynamic, and so was the human story of technological progress: to assert that nature set insurmountable limits to human ingenuity was to deny the whole upward sweep of civilized history. The New Dealers' affection for stories in which nature and society were metaphorically cast as organisms only revealed their own hostility to individualism and their flirtation with communist notions of the state. "Scientism," Malin declared, "along with statism, have become major social myths that threaten freedom."[24]

If the New Dealers' Great Plains was a constrained environment forcing inhabitants to accept its natural limits, Malin's was a landscape of multiple possibilities, a stage for human freedom. The story of the one began in balance, moved into chaos, and then returned to the wiser balance of a scientifically planned society. The story of the other had no such prophetic return to an organic whole but expressed instead a constant process of readaptation that continued the long march of human improvement that was the core plot of Malin's history. In both cases, the shape of the landscape conformed to the human narratives that were set within it and so became the terrain upon which their different politics contested each other. Malin's commitment to individualist freedom led him to probe more deeply into grassland ecology than any historian before him, but always in an effort to find human possibilities rather than natural limits. The scene he constructed for his story was an environment that responded well to human needs unless misguided bureaucrats interfered with people's efforts to adapt themselves to the land.

It is James Malin's anti-New Deal narrative that informs Paul Bonnifield's *The Dust Bowl*. Writing in the late 1970s, at a time when conservative critiques of the welfare state were becoming a dominant feature of American political discourse, Bonnifield argues less urgently and polemically than Malin, but he tells essentially the same story. For him, the Great Plains did pose special problems to the people who settled there, but no one grappled with those problems more successfully than they. When the Dust Bowl hit, it was the people who lived there, not government scientists, who invented new land-use practices that solved earlier problems. New Deal planners understood little about the region and were so caught up in their own ideology that they compounded its problems by trying to impose their vision of a planned society.

Rather than allow residents to come up with their own solutions, Bonnifield argues, the planners used every means possible to drive farmers from their land. They did this not to address the environmental problems of the Plains, but to solve their own problem of reducing the national overproduction of wheat. To justify this deceit, they caricatured Plains inhabitants as "defeated, poverty-ridden people without hope" in such propaganda as *The Plow that Broke the Plains* and the Farm Security Administration photographs, with their mini-narratives of environmental destruction and social despair.[25] In fact, Bonnifield argues, the Plains contained some of the best farming soil in the world. The landscape was difficult but ultimately benign for people who could learn to thrive upon it. Their chief problem was less a hostile nature than a hostile government. The narrative echoes Malin's scenic landscape but gains a different kind of ideological force when placed at the historical moment of its narration – in the waning years of the Carter administration just prior to Ronald Reagan's triumphant election as president. Bonnifield's is a tale of ordinary folk needing nothing so much as to get government off their backs.

If Bonnifield elaborates the optimistic Dust Bowl narrative of a conservative critic of the New Deal, Donald Worster returns to the New Deal plot and deepens its tragic possibilities. Worster, who is with Webb the most powerful narrator among these writers, accepts the basic framework of Roosevelt's planners – the refusal of linear-minded Americans to recognize and accept cyclical environmental constraints – but he shears away its statist bias and considerably expands its cultural boundaries. One consequence of the New Deal tale was to remove the history of the Plains from its role in the long-term ascent of cilivilization; instead, the region became merely an unfortunate anomaly that imposed unusual constraints on the "steady progress" that was otherwise typical of American life. Worster rejects this reading of Plains history and argues instead that the Plains were actually a paradigmatic case in a larger story that might be called "the rise and fall of capitalism."

For Worster, the refusal to recognize natural limits is one of the defining characteristics of a capitalist ethos and economy. He is therefore drawn to a narrative in which the same facts that betokened progress for Webb and Malin become signs of declension and of the compounding contradictions of capitalist expansion. The scene of the story is world historical, only this time the plot leads toward catastrophe:

> That the thirties were a time of great crisis in American, indeed, in world, capitalism has long been an obvious fact. The Dust Bowl, I believe, was part of that same crisis. It came about because the expansionary energy of the United States had finally encountered a volatile, marginal land, destroying the delicate ecological balance that had evolved there. We speak of farmers and plows on the plains and the damage they did, but the language is inadequate. What brought them to the region was a social system, a set of values, an economic order. There is no word that so fully sums up those elements as "capitalism." . . . Capitalism, it is my contention, has been the decisive factor in this nation's use of nature.[26]

By this reading, the chief agent of the story is not "the pioneers" or "civilization" or "man;" it is capitalism. The plot leads from the origins of that economic system, through a series of crises, toward the future environmental cataclysm when the system will finally collapse. The tale of Worster's Dust Bowl thus concerns an intermediate crisis that foreshadows other crises yet to come; in this, it proclaims an apocalyptic prophecy that inverts the prophecy of progress found in earlier frontier narratives. Worster's inversion of the frontier story is deeply ironic, for it implies that the increasing technological "control" represented by Webb's and Malin's human ingenuity leads only toward an escalating spiral of disasters. He also breaks rank with the New Dealers at this point, for in his view their efforts at solving the problems of the Dust Bowl did nothing to address the basic contradictions of capitalism itself. For Worster, the planners "propped up an agricultural economy that had proved itself to be socially and ecologically erosive."[27]

Given how much his basic plot differs from Webb's and Malin's, the scene Worster constructs for his narrative must differ just as dramatically. Since Worster's story concerns the destruction of an entire ecosystem, it must end where the frontier story began: in a wasteland. His plot must move downward toward an ecological disaster called the Dust Bowl. Whereas the frontier narratives begin in a negatively valued landscape and end in a positive one, Worster begins his tale in a place whose narrative value is entirely good. His grasslands are "an old and unique ecological complex" that nature had struggled for millions of years to achieve, "determining by trial and error what would flourish best in this dry corner of the good earth."[28] Delicate and beautiful, the Plains were an ecosystem living always on the edge of drought, and their survival depended on an intricate web of plants and animals that capitalism was incapable of valuing by any standard other than that of the market-place. From this beginning, the story moves down a slope that ends in the dust storms whose narrative role is to stand as the most vivid possible symbol of human alienation from nature.

The very different scenes that progressive and declensionist narrators choose as the settings for their Great Plains histories bring us to another key observation about narrative itself: where one chooses to begin and end a story profoundly alters its shape and meaning. Worster's is not, after all, the only possible plot that can organize Great Plains history into a tale of crisis and decline. Because his meta-narrative has to do with the past and future of capitalism, his time frame, like that of the frontier storytellers, remains tied to the start of white settlement – the moment when the American plot of progress or decline begins its upward or downward sweep. Although he acknowledges the prior presence of Indians in the region, he devotes only a few pages to them. They are clearly peripheral to his narrative. This is true of *all* the stories we have examined thus far, for reasons that have as much to do with narrative rhetoric as with historical analysis. In their efforts to meet the narrative requirements that define a well-told tale – organic unity, a clear focus, and only the "relevant" details – these historians have little to say about the region's earlier human inhabitants. They therefore ignore the entire first half of my original chronicle of "key events" in Great Plains history. If we shift time frames to encompass the Indian past, we suddenly encounter a new set of narratives, equally tragic in their sense of crisis and declension, but strikingly different in plot and scene. As such, they offer further proof of the narrative power to reframe the past so as to include certain events and people, exclude others, and redefine the meaning of landscape accordingly.

One can detect this process of inclusion and exclusion in the passing references that progressive frontier narrators make to the prior, less happy stories of Indians. Sometimes, the tone of such references is elegiac and melancholy, as in the classic image of a "vanishing race;" sometimes the tone is simply dismissive. As Webb put it, "The Plains Indians were survivals of savagery," and "when there was nowhere else to push them they were permitted to settle down on the reservations."[29] If progressive change was inevitable, then so too was the eventual death or removal of the Indians. Their marginalization is thus a necessary requirement of the narrative. The feature of the environment that served as the best scenic indicator of this inevitability was the American bison, whose destruction was among the most crucial steps in undermining Indian subsistence. Even if one did not feel favorably disposed toward Indians, one could still mourn the bison. Webb again: "The Great Plains afforded the last virgin hunting grounds in America, and it was there that the most characteristic American animal made its last stand against the advance of the white man's civilization."[30]

These passing references to Indian "pre-history" are essentially framing devices, the purpose of which is to set the stage for the more important drama that is soon to follow. Historians who focus more centrally on Indians in their narratives almost inevitably construct very different plots from the ones I have described thus far. Among such scholars, one of the most sophisticated is Richard White.[31] Although his work too can be seen as a metaplot about the expansion of capitalism, the landscape he constructs is defined by Indian stories. White's narrative of Pawnee history, for instance, begins with a people living in the mixed grasslands on the eastern margins of the Plains, dividing their activities in a seasonally shifting cycle of farming, gathering, and bison hunting. As one would expect of a declensionist plot, the initial scene is basically a benign and fruitful landscape, despite occasionally severe droughts. At the moment when the Pawnees began their encounter with Euro-american culture – first with the arrival of the horse, then with the fur trade – the Plains environment was furnishing them a comfortable subsistence. In narrative terms, its meaning was that of a much-loved home.

The downward line of White's narrative records the steady erosion of the Pawnees' landscape. European disease wiped out much of their population. The expanding Sioux tribes made it harder for them to hunt bison and raise crops. As hunting became more difficult, the material and spiritual underpinnings of Pawnee subsistence began to disintegrate. Pawnee life was increasingly in crisis, and by the 1870s – when the great herds were finally destroyed – the tribe was forced to abandon its traditional homeland and remove to Indian Territory. The story ends as a classic tragedy of exodus and despair: "When the Pawnees decided to leave the Loup Valley, it was in the hope that to the south in Indian territory lay a land where they could hunt the buffalo, grow corn, and let the old life of the earth-lodges flower beyond the reach of the Sioux and American settlers."[32] Unfortunately, this hoped-for ending to the Pawnee story would never be achieved, because the scene it required no longer existed. As White says, "Such a land had disappeared forever."[33]

The frame of this story differs from anything we have seen thus far. It ends at the moment most of the other plots began. It starts much further back in time, as European animals and trade goods begin to change the Plains landscape, offering opportunities and improvements in Pawnee life. Eventually a downward spiral begins, and the tragedy of the narrative becomes unrelenting as the Pawnees lose control of their familiar world. As for the scene of this plot, we have already encountered it in a different guise. The "wilderness" in which the progressive frontier narrators begin their stories is nothing less than the destroyed remnant of the Pawnees' home. It is less a wasteland than a land that has been wasted.

Narratives of this sort are by no means limited to white historians. Plenty Coups, a Crow Indian chief, tells in his 1930 autobiography of a boyhood vision sent him by his animal Helper, the Chickadee. In the dream, a great storm blown by the Four Winds destroyed a vast forest, leaving standing only the single tree in which the Chickadee – smallest but shrewdest of animals – made its lodge. The tribal elders interpreted this to mean that white settlers would eventually destroy not only the buffalo but also all tribes who resisted the American onslaught. On the basis of this prophetic dream, the Crows decided to ally themselves with the United States, and so they managed to preserve a portion of their homelands. Saving their land did not spare them from the destruction of the bison herds, however, and so they shared with other Plains tribes the loss of subsistence and spiritual communion that had previously been integral to the hunt. As Plenty Coups remarks at the end of his story, "when the buffalo went away the hearts of my people fell to the ground, and they could not lift them up again. After this nothing happened."[34]

Few remarks more powerfully capture the importance of narrative to history than this last of Plenty Coups: "After this nothing happened." For the Crows as for other Plains tribes, the universe revolved around the bison herds, and life made sense only so long as the hunt continued. When the scene shifted – when the bison herds "went away" – that universe collapsed and history ended. Although the Crows continued to live on their reservation and although their identity as a people has never ceased, for Plenty Coups their subsequent life is all part of a different story.[35] The story he loved best ended with the buffalo. Everything that has happened since is part of some other plot, and there is neither sense nor joy in telling it.

The nothingness at the end of Plenty Coups's story suggest just how completely a narrative can redefine the events of the past and the landscapes of nature to fit the needs of its plot. After this nothing happened: not frontier progress, not the challenge of adaptation to an arid land, not the Dust Bowl. Just the nothingness that follows the end of a story. It is this nothingness that carries me back to the place where I began, to my own awareness of a paradox at the heart of my intellectual practice as an historian. On the one hand, most environmental historians would be quite comfortable in asserting the importance of the nonhuman world to any understanding of the human past. Most would argue that nature is larger than humanity, that it is not completely an invention of human culture, that it impinges on our lives in ways we cannot completely control, that it is "real," and that our task as historians is to understand the way it affects us and vice versa. Black clouds bringing dust and darkness from the Kansas sky, overturned sod offering itself as a seedbed for alien grains sprouting amid the torn roots of dying prairie grasses, dry winds filled with the stench of rotting bison flesh as wolves and vultures linger over their feasts: these are more than just stories.

And yet – they are stories too. As such, they are human inventions despite all our efforts to preserve their "naturalness." They belong as much to rhetoric and human discourse as to ecology and nature. It is for this reason that we cannot escape confronting the challenge of multiple competing narratives in our efforts to understand both nature and the human past. As I hope my reading of Great Plains history suggests, the narrative theorists have much to teach us. Quite apart from the environmental historian's analytical premise that nature and culture have become inextricably entangled in their process of mutual reshaping, the rhetorical practice of environmental history commits us to narrative ways of talking about nature that are anything but "natural." If we fail to reflect on the plots and scenes and tropes that undergird our histories, we run the risk of missing the human artifice that lies at the heart of even the most "natural" of narratives.

And just what *is* a narrative? As the evidence of my Great Plains chronicle would imply, it is not merely a sequence of events. To shift from chronicle to narrative, a tale of environmental change must be structured so that, as Aristotle said, it "has beginning, middle, and end."[36] What distinguishes stories from other forms of discourse is that they describe an action that begins, continues over a well-defined period of time, and finally draws to a definite close, with consequences that become meaningful because of their placement within the narrative. Completed action gives a story its unity and allows us to evaluate and judge an act by its results. The moral of a story is defined by its ending: as Aristotle remarked, "the end is everywhere the chief thing."[37]

Narrative is a peculiarly human way of organizing reality, and this has important implications for the way we approach the history of environmental change. Some nonhuman events can be said to have properties that conform to the Aristotelian beginning-middle-end requirement of storytelling, as when an individual organism (or a species or a mountain range or even the universe itself) is born, persists, and dies. One *can* tell stories about such things – geologists and evolutionary biologists often do – but they lack the compelling drama that comes from having a judgeable protagonist. Things in nature usually "just happen," without raising questions of moral choice. Many natural events lack even this much linear structure. Some are cyclical: the motions of the planets, the seasons, or the rhythms of biological fertility and reproduction. Others are random: climate shifts, earthquakes, genetic mutations, and other events the causes of which remain hidden from us. One does not automatically describe such things with narrative plots, and yet environmental histories, which purport to set the human past in its natural context, all have plots. Nature and the universe do not tell stories; we do. Why is this?

Two possible answers to this question emerge from the work that philosophers and post-structuralist literary critics have done on the relationship between narrative and history. One group, which includes Hayden White and the late Louis Mink as well as many of the deconstructionists, argues that narrative is so basic to our cultural beliefs that we automatically impose it on a reality that bears little or no relation to the plots we use in organizing our experience.[38] Mink summarizes this position nicely by asserting that "the past is not an untold story." The same could presumably be said about nature: we force our stories on a world that doesn't fit them.[39] The historian's project of recovering past realities and representing them "truly" or even "fairly" is thus a delusion. Trapped within our narrative discourse, we could not do justice either to nature or to the past no matter how hard we tried – presuming, of course, that "nature" or "the past" even exist at all.

An alternative position, most recently defended by David Carr but originally developed by Martin Heidegger, is that although narrative may not be intrinsic to events in the physical universe, it is fundamental to the way we humans organize our experience. Whatever may be the perspective of the universe on the things going on around us, our human perspective is that we inhabit an endlessly storied world. We narrate the triumphs and failures of our pasts. We tell stories to explore the alternative choices that might lead to feared or hoped-for futures. Our very habit of partitioning the flow of time into "events," with their implied beginnings, middles, and ends, suggests how deeply the narrative structure inheres in our experience of the world. As Carr puts it, "Narrative is not merely a possibly successful way of describing events; its structure inheres in the events themselves. Far from being a formal distortion of the events it relates, a narrative account is an extension of one of their primary features."[40]

Carr's position will undoubtedly be attractive to most historians, since it argues that, far from being arbitrary, our narratives reflect one of the most fundamental properties of human consciousness. It also gives us a way of absorbing the lessons of narrative theory without feeling we have abandoned all ties to an external reality. Insofar as people project their wills into the future, organizing their lives to make acts in the present yield predictable future results – to just that extent, they live their lives as if they were telling a story. It is undoubtedly true that we all constantly tell ourselves stories to remind ourselves who were are, how we got to be that person, and what we want to become. The same is true not just of individuals but of communities and societies: we use our histories to remember ourselves, just as we use our prophecies as tools for exploring what we do or do not wish to become.[41] As Plenty Coups's story implies, to recover the narratives people tell themselves about the meanings of their lives is to learn a great deal about their past actions and about the way they *understand* those actions. Stripped of the story, we lose track of understanding itself.

The storied reality of human experience suggests why environmental histories so consistently find plots in nature and also why those plots almost always center on people. Environmental history sets itself the task of including within its boundaries far more of the nonhuman world than most other histories, and yet human agents continue to be the main anchors of its narratives. Dust storms have been occurring on the Plains for millennia, and yet the ones we really care about — those we now narrate under the title "Dust Bowl" — are the ones we can most easily transform into stories in which people become the heroes or victims or villains of the piece. In this, historians consistently differ from ecologists, who more often than not treat people as exogenous variables that fit awkwardly if at all into the theoretical models of the discipline. The historian's tendency is quite opposite. The chief protagonists and antagonists of our stories are almost always human, for reasons that go to the very heart of our narrative impulse.

Our histories of the Great Plains environment remain fixed on people because what we most care about in nature is its meaning for human beings. We care about the dust storms because they stand as a symbol of human endurance in the face of natural adversity — or as a symbol of human irresponsibility in the face of natural fragility. Human interests and conflicts create *values* in nature that in turn provide the moral center for our stories. We want to know whether environmental change is good or bad, and that question can only be answered by referring to our own sense of right and wrong. Nature remains mute about such matters. However passionately we may care about the nonhuman world, however much we may believe in its innate worth, our historical narratives, even those about the nonhuman world, remain focused on a human struggle over values. If these values are in effect the meanings we attach to judgeable human actions — nonhuman actions being generally unjudgeable by us — then the center of our stories will remain focused on human thoughts, human acts, and human values.

It is because we care about the consequences of actions that narratives — unlike most natural processes — have beginnings, middles, and ends. Stories are intrinsically teleological forms, in which an event is explained by the prior events or causes that lead up to it. This accounts for one feature that all these Great Plains histories have in common: all are designed so that the plot and its changing scene — its environment — flow toward the ultimate end of the story. In the most extreme cases, if the tale is of progress, then the closing landscape is a garden; if the tale is of crisis and decline, the closing landscape (whether located in the past or in the future) is a wasteland. As an obvious but very important consequence of this narrative requirement, opening landscapes must be different from closing ones to make the plot work. A trackless waste must become a grassland civilization. Or: a fragile ecosystem must become a Dust Bowl. The difference between beginning and end gives us our chance to extract a moral from the rhetorical landscape. Our narratives take changes in the land and situate them in stories whose endings become the lessons we wish to draw from those changes.

However serious the epistemological problems it creates, this commitment to teleology and narrative gives environmental history – all history – its moral center. Because stories concern the consequences of actions that are potentially valued in quite different ways, whether by agent, narrator, or audience, we can achieve no neutral objectivity in writing them. Historians may strive to be as fair as they can, but as these Plains examples demonstrate, it remains possible to narrate the same evidence in radically different ways. Within the field of our narratives we too – as narrators – are moral agents and political actors. As storytellers we commit ourselves to the task of judging the consequences of human actions, trying to understand the choices that confronted the people whose lives we narrate so as to capture the full tumult of their world. In the dilemmas they faced we discover our own, and at the intersection of the two we locate the moral of the story. If our goal is to tell tales that make the past meaningful, then we cannot escape struggling over the values that define what meaning is.

This vision of history as an endless struggle among competing narratives and values may not seem very reassuring. How, for instance, are we to choose among the infinite stories that our different values seem capable of generating? This is the question that lurks so threateningly at the intersections of the different Great Plains histories we have encountered. Are nature and the past infinitely malleable in the face of our ability to tell stories about them? The uneasiness that many historians feel in confronting the postmodernist challenge comes down to this basic concern, which potentially seems to shake the very foundations of our enterprise. If our choice of narratives reflects only our power to impose our preferred version of reality on a past that cannot resist us, then what is left of history?[42]

Most practicing historians, of course, do not believe that all stories about the past are equally good, even if we are not very articulate in explaining why one is better or worse than another. Usually we just declare that we recognize good history when we see it. If pressed, we may perhaps offer a few rules of thumb to help define what we are looking for. Some might argue for depth, saying that the narrative that explains more, that is richer in its suggestions about past causes, meanings, and ambiguities, is the better history. Others might seek breadth, preferring the historical narrative that accommodates the largest number of relevant details without contradicting any relevant facts.[43] Then again, less may be more: A simple story well told may reveal far more about a past world than a complicated text that never finds its own center. Inclusiveness is another virtue: a history is better, surely, when it incorporates many different voices and events to reflect the diversity of past human experiences. But maybe coherence is more important: we might demand of good history that its components be tightly enough linked that it contains no unnecessary parts of extraneous details, lest we call it antiquarian. We might ask that a good history reflect the full historiographical tradition that lies behind it while simultaneously pushing the boundaries of that tradition. We of course want it to offer a subtle and original reading of primary sources. It should surprise us with new perspectives and interpretations. We would prefer that it be lucid, engaging, a good read. And so the list goes on.

All of these are plausible criteria, and most of us would agree that they play a part in helping us recognize good history when we see it. The trouble, obviously, is that they themselves can all too easily become objects of disagreement and struggle. Indeed, many of them reflect the same sorts of aesthetic judgments that we make when encountering any narrative, historical or nonhistorical, fictional or nonfictional. It is not at all clear that they would help us very much in deciding whether Webb or Worster or Bonnifield or Plenty Coups is the better narrator of Great Plains history. If the criteria we use in deciding the relative merits of historical narratives are open to the same sorts of value judgments as the narratives themselves, then we have hardly escaped the dilemma that postmodernist theory has posed for us. We seem still to be rudderless in an endless sea of stories.

Before going any further, I should probably confess my own uncertainty about how to navigate from here to a safe harbor, wherever it might be. I first wrote this essay nearly five years ago in an effort to acknowledge the rich insights that postmodernism has given us into the complexities of narrative discourse. I assembled a small collection of stories about the Great Plains to see what narrative theory might tell me about the way those stories shape our sense of a landscape and the people who live upon it. The exercise persuaded me that plot and scene and character, beginnings and middles and ends, the rhetoric of storytelling, the different agendas of narrators and readers, all permeate our activities as historians. To deny the richness of this insight would be an evasion of self-knowledge, a willful refusal to recognize the power and the paradoxes that flow from our narrative discourse.

And yet despite what I have learned in writing this essay, it has also been a frustrating struggle, because I, like most practicing historians, am only willing to follow the postmodernists so far. The essay has gone through four radically different versions, each with a different title, each trying to make a different kind of peace with the dilemmas these Great Plains histories pose. My goal throughout has been to acknowledge the immense power of narrative while still defending the past (and nature) as real things to which our storytelling must somehow conform lest it cease being history altogether. Alas, I shared each new version of the essay with a different group of readers and critics, and each time they persuaded me that my efforts to find safe harbor had failed. Each new version of the essay, and each letter and conversation that critiqued it, returned me to where I began: each became a different story about the meaning of stories, a different argument about how narrative does and does not ground itself in nature and the past. The essay, in other words, recapitulated the very problems it set out to solve.

But perhaps there lies hidden in this seemingly frustrating fact a partial solution to the narrative dilemma. (Watch: I try one more tack to seek some shelter in this rhetorical storm.) The same process of criticism that shaped the different versions of this essay typifies the production and consumption of all historical texts. The stories we tell about the past do not exist in a vacuum, and our storytelling practice is bounded in at least three ways that limit its power. First, our stories cannot contravene known facts about the past. This is so much a truism of traditional historical method that we rarely bother even to state it, but it is crucial if we wish to deny that all narratives do an equally good job of representing the past. At the most basic level, we judge a work bad history if it contradicts evidence we know to be accurate and true. Good history does not knowingly lie. A history of the Great Plains that narrated a story of continuous progress without once mentioning the Dust Bowl would instantly be suspect, as would a history of the Nazi treatment of Jews that failed to mention the concentration camps. Historical narratives are bounded at every turn by the evidence they can and cannot muster in their own support.

Environmental historians embrace a second set of narrative constraints: given our faith that the natural world ultimately transcends our narrative power, our stories must make ecological sense. You can't put dust in the air — or tell stories about putting dust in the air — if the dust isn't there.[44] Even though environmental histories transform ecosystems into the scenes of human narratives, the biological and geological processes of the earth set fundamental limits to what constitutes a plausible narrative. The dust storms of the 1930s are not just historical facts but natural ones: they reflect the complex response of an entire ecosystem — its soils, its vegetation, its animals, its climate — to human actions. Insofar as we can know them, to exclude or obscure these natural "facts" would be another kind of false silence, another kind of lying.

In choosing to assign narrative meaning to "natural" events of this sort, we face a special problem, for nature does not tell us whether a dust storm is a good or bad thing; only we can do that. Nature is unlike most other historical subjects in lacking a clear voice of its own. The very fact that Great Plains historians can ascribe to the same landscape such different meanings is one consequence of this lack of voice. Still, nature is hardly silent. No matter what people do, their actions have real consequences in nature, just as natural events have real consequences for people. In narrating those consequences, we inevitably interpret their meaning according to human values — but the consequences themselves are as much nature's choice as our own. To just that extent, nature coauthors our stories. A Bonnifield and a Worster may draw radically different lessons from the Dust Bowl, but neither can deny the great storms themselves. The power of narrative does not extend nearly so far.

Finally, historical narratives are constrained in a third important way as well. Historians do not tell stories by themselves. We write as members of communities, and we cannot help but take those communities into account as we do our work. Being American, being male, being white, being an upper-middle-class academic, being an environmentalist, I write in particular ways that are not all of my own choosing, and my biases are reflected in my work. But being a scholar, I write also for a community of other scholars — some very different from me in their backgrounds and biases — who know nearly as much about my subject as I do. They are in a position instantly to remind me of the excluded facts and wrong-headed interpretations that my own bias, self-delusion, and lack of diligence have kept me from acknowledging.

The stories we write, in other words, are judged not just as narratives, but as nonfictions. We construct them knowing that scholars will evaluate their accuracy, and knowing too that many other people and communities — those who have a present stake in the way the past is described — will also judge the fairness and truth of what we say. Because our readers have the skill to know what is *not* in a text as well as what is in it, we cannot afford to be arbitrary in deciding whether a fact does or does not belong in our stories. Someone among our readers — a bemused colleague, an angry partisan, a wounded victim — will eventually inform us of our failings. Nature, of course, will not bother to construct such a critique, but plenty of others will step forward to speak on its behalf as we ourselves have done. We therefore struggle to anticipate criticisms, to absorb contradictory accounts, and to fit our narratives to what we already know about our subject. Criticism can sometimes do more harm than good — sapping the life from a story, burying strong arguments beneath nitpicking caveats, reinforcing conventional wisdom at the expense of new or radical insights, and murdering passion — but it can also keep us honest by forcing us to confront contradictory evidence and counternarratives. We tell stories *with* each other and *against* each other in order to speak *to* each other. Our readers, in short, play crucial roles in shaping the stories we tell. Just so has this essay gone through four separate incarnations to reach its present form, each of them responding in different ways to the critical communities that in a very real sense helped author them. No matter how frustrating this process of revision may be, the resulting text is in this case unquestionably better as a result.[45]

And what of my own story here? What kind of tale have *I* been telling about Great Plains history? My most visible narrative has of course been a story about storytellers who express their own times and political visions. Each told tales that embodied the values of a particular community. Each tried to be true to the "facts" as they then appeared. Each looked back to earlier storytellers, accommodating them when possible and trying to demonstrate their inadequacy when this was necessary to the success of the newer story. The result was a sequence of contesting stories, from tales of frontier progress to the New Deal tragedies, to Malin's and Bonnifield's stories of local resistance in the face of a hostile environment and bureaucracy, to Worster's tragedy of environmental crisis and capitalist self-destruction.

But the meaning of my story about stories also reflects that other, more personal, narrative, the one about my struggle to accommodate the lessons of critical theory without giving in to relativism. That story began with a question. If postmodernism is correct in arguing that narrative devices are deeply present even in such a field as environmental history, which takes for its subject the least human and least storied of worlds — nature — must we then accept that the past is infinitely malleable, thereby apparently undermining the entire historical project? Given my biases, the answer to this question has got to be no, and so my story has worked its way toward an ending about the ultimate justification of history in community, past reality, and nature itself. For me, there is something profoundly unsatisfying and ultimately self-deluding about an endless postmodernist deconstruction of texts that fails to ground itself in history, in community, in politics, and finally in the moral problem of living on earth. Against it, I would assert the virtues of narrative as our best and most compelling tool for searching out meaning in a conflicted and contradictory world.

The danger of postmodernism, despite all the rich insights it offers into the contested terrain of narrative discourse, is that it threatens to lose track of the very thing that makes narrative so compelling a part of history and human consciousness both. After all, the principal difference between a chronicle and a narrative is that a good story makes us *care* about its subject in a way that a chronicle does not.[46] My list of "significant Great Plains events" surely had no effect on anyone's emotions or moral vision, whereas I doubt anyone can read Donald Worster's *Dust Bowl* without being moved in one way or another. More powerfully still, the nothingness at the end of Plenty Coups's story suggests that even silence – the ability of narrative to rupture the flow of time in the service of its meaning – can touch us deeply with its eloquence. When a narrator honestly makes an audience care about what happens in a story, the story expresses the ties between past and present in a way that lends deeper meaning to both. This process, like everything else in history, is open to criticism, since the rhetorical devices for making an audience care can become all too manipulative and sentimental. At its best, however, historical storytelling helps keep us morally engaged with the world by showing us how to care about it and its origins in ways we had not done before.

If this is true, then the special task of environmental history is to assert that stories about the past are better, all other things being equal, if they increase our attention to nature and the place of people within it. They succeed when they make us look at the grasslands and their peoples in a new way. This is different from saying that our histories should turn their readers into environmentalists or convince everyone of a particular political point of view. Good histories rarely do this. But if environmental history is successful in its project, the story of how different peoples have lived in and used the natural world will become one of the most basic and fundamental narratives in all of history, without which no understanding of the past could be complete. Despite the tensions that inevitably exist between nature and our narrative discourse, we cannot help but embrace storytelling if we hope to persuade readers of the importance of our subject. As Aristotle reminded us so long ago, narrative is among our most powerful ways of encountering the world, judging our actions within it, and learning to care about its many meanings.

Notes

1   Bonnifield, *The Dust Bowl*, (Albuquerque, 1979), 202.
2   Worster, *Dust Bowl*, (New York, 1979), 4.
3   For a wide-ranging discussion that explores the emerging intellectual agendas of environmental history, see "A Round Table: Environmental History," *Journal of American History*, 76 (March 1990), 1087–1147.
4   Throughout this essay, I will use "story" and "narrative" interchangeably, despite a technical distinction that can be made between them. For some literary critics and philosophers of history, "story" is a limited genre, whereas narrative (or *narratio*) is the much more encompassing part of classical rhetoric that organizes all representations of time into a configured sequence of completed actions. I intend the broader meaning for both words, since "storytelling" in its most fundamental sense is the activity I wish to criticize and defend. I hope it is emphatically clear at the outset that I am *not* urging a return to "traditional" narrative history that revolves around the biographies of "great" individuals (usually elite white male politicians and intellectuals); rather, I am urging historians to acknowledge storytelling as the necessary core even of *longue durée* histories that pay little

attention to individual people. Environmental history is but one example of these, and most of my arguments apply just as readily to the others.

5   Much of the reading that lies behind this essay cannot easily be attached to a single argument or footnote. Among the works that helped shape my views on the importance and problems of narrative are the following: William H. Dray, *Philosophy of History* (Englewood Cliffs, 1964); Robert Scholes and Robert Kellogg, *The Nature of Narrative* (New York, 1966); Frank Kermode, *The Sense of an Ending: Studies in the Theory of Fiction* (New York, 1967); Hayden White, *Metahistory: The Historical Imagination in Nineteenth-Century Europe* (Baltimore, 1973); Hayden White, *Tropics of Discourse: Essays in Cultural Criticism* (Baltimore, 1978); Robert H. Canary and Henry Kozicki, eds, *The Writing of History: Literary Form and Historical Understanding* (Madison, 1978); W. J. T. Mitchell, ed., *On Narrative* (Chicago, 1981); Fredric Jameson, *The Political Unconscious: Narrative as a Socially Symbolic Act* (Ithaca, 1981); Jonathan Culler, *On Deconstruction: Theory and Criticism after Structuralism* (Ithaca, 1982); Terry Eagleton, *Literary Theory: An Introduction* (Minneapolis, 1983); Paul Ricoeur, *Time and Narrative* (3 vols, Chicago, 1984, 1985, 1988), trans. Kathleen Blamey and David Pellauer; Dominick LaCapra, *Rethinking Intellectual History: Texts, Contexts, Language* (Ithaca, 1983); Arthur C. Danto, *Narration and Knowledge: Including the Integral Text of Analytical Philosophy of History* (New York, 1985); James Clifford and George E. Marcus, eds, *Writing Culture: The Poetics and Politics of Ethnography* (Berkeley, 1986); Wallace Martin, *Recent Theories of Narrative* (Ithaca, 1986); Louis O. Mink, *Historical Understanding* (Ithaca, 1987); Hayden White, *The Content of the Form: Narrative Discourse and Historical Representation* (Baltimore, 1987); and Kai Erikson, "Obituary for Big Daddy: A Parable," unpublished manuscript (in William Cronon's possession).

6   This distinction between chronicle and narrative is more fully analyzed in White, *Metahistory*, 5–7; White, *Tropics of Discourse*, 109–11; Louis O. Mink, "Narrative Form as a Cognitive Instrument," in *Writing of History*, eds Canary and Kozicki, 141–4; David Carr, *Time, Narrative, and History* (Bloomington, 1986), 59; Danto, *Narration and Knowledge*; and Paul A. Roth, "Narrative Explanations: The Case of History," *History and Theory*, 27 (no. 1, 1988), 1–13.

7   There are deeper epistemological problems here that I will not discuss, such as how we recognize what constitutes an "event" and how we draw boundaries around it. It should eventually become clear that "events" are themselves defined and delimited by the stories with which we configure them and are probably impossible to imagine apart from their narrative context.

8   Frederick Jackson Turner, *The Frontier in American History* (New York, 1920), 12.

9   I have written about the rhetorical structure of Turner's work in two essays: William Cronon, "Revisiting the Vanishing Frontier: The Legacy of Frederick Jackson Turner," *Western Historical Quarterly*, 18 (April 1987), 157–76 and William Cronon, "Turner's First Stand: The Significance of Significance in American History," in *Writing Western History: Classic Essays on Classic Western Historians*, Richard Etulain, ed. (Albuquerque, 1991), 73–101. See also Ronald H. Carpenter, *The Eloquence of Frederick Jackson Turner* (San Marino, 1983).

10   Turner, *Frontier in American History*, 147.

11   William Robert Hare, ca. 1887, as quoted in Howard R. Lamar, "Public Values and Private Dreams: South Dakota's Search for Identity, 1850–1900," *South Dakota History*, 8 (Spring 1978), 129.

12   Luther B. Hill, *A History of the State of Oklahoma* (Chicago, 1909), 382, 385, 386.

13   Josephine Middlekauf, as quoted in Joanna L. Stratton, *Pioneer Women: Voices from the Kansas Frontier* (New York, 1981), 204.

14   Kenneth Burke, *A Grammar of Motives* (Berkeley, 1969), 6–7.

15   Walter Prescott Webb, *The Great Plains* (New York, 1931).

16   Ibid., 9.

17   Ibid., 508.

18   These terms appear, for instance, in Malin's magnum opus, James C. Malin, *The Grassland of North America: Prolegomena to Its History* (Gloucester, Mass., 1967), but this basic notion informs virtually all of his work on the grasslands. See also James C. Malin, *Grassland Historical Studies: Natural Resources Utilization in a Background of Science and Technology* (Lawrence, Kan., 1950); and the collection of essays, James C. Malin, *History and Ecology Studies of the Grassland*, Robert P. Swierenga, ed. (Lincoln, 1984).

19   Malin. *Grassland of North America*, 154.

20   *The Future of the Great Plains: Report of the Great Plains Committee* (Washington, 1936). 1. On this report, see Gilbert F. White, "*The Future of the Great Plains* Re-Visited," *Great Plains Quarterly*, 6 (Spring 1986), 84–93.

21   *Future of the Great Plains*, 1.

22   This image of colonial invaders seeking to "inscribe" their ideology on an alien landscape is one of the central notions of a fascinating monograph: Tzvetan Todorov, *The Conquest of America* (New York, 1984).

23   On the role of the Dust Bowl in reshaping the science of ecology itself, see Ronald C. Tobey, *Saving the Prairies. The Life Cycle of the Founding School of American Plant Ecology, 1895–1955* (Berkeley, 1981).

24   Malin, *Grassland of North America*, 168.

25   Bonnifield, *The Dust Bowl*, 202.

26   Worster, *Dust Bowl*, 5.

27   Ibid., 163.

28   Ibid., 66.

29   Webb, *Great Plains*, 508.

30   Ibid., 509. For a similar use of the bison story as the symbol of an earlier Indian world that in some sense "vanished" during the last third of the nineteenth century, see William Cronon, *Nature's Metropolis: Chicago and the Great West* (New York, 1991), 213–18.

31   Richard White, *The Roots of Dependency: Subsistence, Environment, and Social Change among the Choctaws, Pawnees, and Navajos* (Lincoln, 1983), 147–211.

32   White, *Roots of Dependency*, 211.

33   Ibid.

34   Frank Linderman, *Plenty-coups: Chief of the Crows* (1930; reprint, Lincoln, 1962), 311.

35   The danger in the way Plenty Coups ends his story, and in Richard White's ending as well, is that the close of these tragic narratives can all too easily be taken as the end of their protagonists' cultural history. The notion that Indian histories come to an end is among the classic imperialist myths of the frontier, wherein a "vanishing race" "melts away" before the advancing forces of "civilization." Plenty Coups's declaration that "after this nothing happened" conveys with great power the tragedy of an older Indian generation but says nothing about the generations of Indians who still live within the shadow of that narrative's punctuation mark.

36   Aristotle, *Poetics*, in *The Complete Works of Aristotle: The Revised Oxford Translation*, Jonathan Barnes, ed. (2 vols, Princeton, 1984), II, 2321.

37   Ibid. On the importance of a story's ending in determining its configured unity, see Kermode, *Sense of an Ending*; this can be usefully combined with Edward W. Said, *Beginnings: Intention and Method* (New York, 1975).

38   See White, *Tropics of Discourse*; White, *Metahistory*; Mink, "Narrative Form as Cognitive Instrument;" a less extreme position that ultimately leads toward a similar conclusion can be found in Ricoeur, *Time and Narrative*, 1. For a useful, if biased, explication of these debates, see Hayden White, "The Question of Narrative in Contemporary Historical Theory," *History and Theory*, 23 (no. 1, 1984), 1–33. A valuable survey can be found in Martin, *Recent Theories of Narrative*.

39   Mink, "Narrative Form as Cognitive Instrument," 148. See also Richard T. Vann, "Louis Mink's Linguistic Turn," *History and Theory*, 26 (no. 1, 1987), 14.

40   David Carr, "Narrative and the Real World: An Argument for Continuity," *History and Theory*, 25 (no. 2, 1986), 117.

41   See Robert Cover, "Nomos and Narrative," *Harvard Law Review*, 97 (Nov. 1983), 3–68. Carr's argument that all human experience is narrated does not address a deeper relativist claim, that there is no necessary correlation between the stories people tell in their own lives and the stories historians tell in reconstructing those lives. One this issue, see Noel Carroll, review of *Time, Narrative, and History* by David Carr, *History and Theory*, 27 (no. 3, 1988), 297–306.

42   This question, in a somewhat different form, is the chief topic of Peter Novick, *That Noble Dream: The "Objectivity Question" and the American Historical Profession* (Cambridge, Eng., 1988).

43   As with most of these criteria, there are deep problems here. To say that historical narratives must include all relevant details and contradict no relevant facts begs the most important question, for the tool we use to define relevance is narrative itself. Does this particular fact belong to this particular story? Only the story can tell us. To test a narrative by its ability to include facts – the relevance of which is defined by the narrative's own plot – is to slide rapidly into tautology.

44   I borrow this lovely epigram from a remark of Patricia Limerick's.

45   I owe this argument about the role of criticism in limiting historical narratives to Richard White's comments on an earlier version of this essay. His help, and the way it has reshaped the text you now read, precisely illustrates my point about the critical praxis of scholarly communities.

46   Jim O'Brien pointed me toward the importance of this insight.

Glossary of key concepts

Analytical philosophy of history   The critical examination of the concepts and methods used by historians, particularly with a view to uncovering typical modes of explanation. The first phase in the discussion of history and narrative was dominated by analytical philosophers searching for an account of narrative that identified or established it as a mode of explanation equivalent to those found in the natural sciences.

Discourse   The way something is talked about. The discourse of narrative history, for example, has a language and mode of discussion that is actionist, individualist, interpretive, empiricist and, of course, narrativist.

Emplotment   A concept associated with the work of Hayden White which refers to the story line/plot structure imposed on sequences of events. It is this act which creates the meaning embodied in a narrative, i.e. a romantic, tragic, epic, comic, satiric or ironic story. Indeed, White argues that, without emplotment, there is no narrative, only a chronology or some such primitive form of sequencing. On the other hand, in more recent pronouncements, he seems to admit the possibility of narration without emplotment, i.e. meaningful accounts of the human past which cannot be assimilated into a theory of tropology. *See also* Plot.

Epistemology   The study of what we can know of the world and how knowledge is created and validated. Arguably, the problem of knowing the world is inextricably tied to the problem of how we conceive the world, i.e. the question of ontology. Indeed, the practice of narrative history tends to be informed by a sense of ontology rather than by notions of epistemology. Much of the epistemological critique of narrative history misses the point that, for historians, the world is a particular, ontologically given object of inquiry with problems of knowledge which are quite ordinary and everyday.

Figuration   The linguistic creation of meaning through the deployment of figures of speech. Note that meanings can be prefigured (signed in advance), configured (arranged in different ways) and refigured (rearranged). *See also* Tropology.

Great story   Synonym for metanarrative. (But see Berkhofer's distinguishing of great story from metanarrative, and metahistory.)

Historical explanation   The answer to a "why" question about the past, particularly in relation to human action. *See also* Historical understanding.

Historical realism   The view that there is a continuity and a correspondence between the real world and the narration of that world in historians' stories.

Historical understanding   The interpretive, analytical and conceptual ability to follow and grasp a story. Even more of the same capacities are required to research and write history. *See also* Historical explanation.

Historiography   A word used in various senses to refer to (a) the history of historical writing; (b) the substantive history of historical interpretations and historical writings about past events and happenings; (c) the art and crafting of historians' texts; and (d) sources and methods in the study of history.

Linguistic turn   Refers in general to a turn in postwar philosophy to the study of the role of language in the creation of "meaning" and "truth." In the history and narrative debate the linguistic turn would be associated with notions of emplotment, tropology, figuration, metanarrative, postmodernism and so on.

Metahistory   The whole paradigm of presuppositions that create normal historical practice (Berkhofer).

Metanarrative   A big or overarching story or narrative thematization of a significant portion of the past, or indeed of the whole of human history. Alternatively, metanarrative is "narrative about narratives" (Munslow).

Narrative   An account of a connected sequence of actions, events and circumstances. Such accounts may contain varying amounts of description, analysis and explanation. There are numerous alternative definitions of narrative, most of which convey a point of view on the functioning and effects of narrative. (There are similar definitional debates about other concepts, for example, ideology.) *See also* Story.

Narrativists   A term variously applied to a diverse group of theorists — analytical philosophers, phenomenologists, pragmatists and postmodernists — who agree that the study of history is and/or should be primarily narrative in orientation.

Ontology   The study of the fundamental nature of reality and existence. All histories presuppose a view of what the world is like and how it works. Narrative history presupposes a narrative ontology, i.e. the existence and centrality of stories, or story-creating events and actions, and of individual and collective narrative identities. Narrative philosophers of history generally concentrate on the explication of various aspects of narrative ontology; the work of narrative historians instantiates, explores, and exemplifies that narrative world. *See also* Phenomenology.

Phenomenology   The philosophical study of how the world is perceived and experienced. One of the most powerful arguments in favor of narrative history is that it grapples directly with the narrativity of human perception and experience and with the narrative creation and constitution of the human world itself.

Plot   Plot, in effect, comprehends in one intelligible whole, circumstances, goals, interactions, and unintended results. (Ricoeur) *See also* Emplotment.

Postmodernism   In the history and narrative debate the postmodernists are those who highlight the role of language in creating the "meaning" and "truth" of stories about the human past. As in other domains, the postmodernists question the objectivity and representationality of historical narratives and conclude that historians' stories are in a very real sense fictions, i.e. artifacts of language and of the narrative strategies. At the same time, there is a large measure of agreement between postmodernists and narrative historians about the centrality of story-telling to the historical enterprise. The difference is that historians generally view their narratives as both real and true to a significant practical degree.

Story   Most often used as a synonym for narrative. But story is sometimes reserved as a term referring to actual sequences of human happenings, as opposed to narratives, which are tales told about those stories. Another point of view is that narrative conveys a stronger sense of the existence of the narrator of a story and of the audience to whom the story is told. *See also* Narrative.

Tropology   A trope is a figure of speech (e.g. a metaphor). Tropes create meaning. Emplotment is an act of troping to create a particular story-type: romance, tragedy, comedy, satire, etc. Figuration is an alternative label for this linguistic creation of meaning.

Further reading

Alan Munslow, *The Routledge Companion to Historical Studies*, London, 2000.

Further reading

Books

F. Ankersmit and H. Kellner (eds), *A New Philosophy of History*, Reaktion Books: London, 1995.

F. R. Ankersmit, *History and Tropology*, University of California Press: Berkeley, 1994.

F. R. Ankersmit, *Narrative Logic: A Semantic Analysis of Historian's Language*, The Hague, 1983.

R. Aron, *Politics and History*, Transaction Books: New Brunswick, 1978.

S. Bann, *The Inventions of History*, Manchester University Press: Manchester, 1990.

C. L. Becker, *Detachment and the Writing of History*, Cornell University Press: Ithaca, NY, 1958.

R. F. Berkhofer, *Beyond the Great Story: History as Text and Discourse*, Harvard University Press: Cambridge, Mass., 1995.

P. Burke (ed.), *New Perspectives on Historical Writing*, Polity Press: London, 1991.

A. Callinicos, *Theories and Narratives*, Polity Press: London, 1995.

R. H. Canary and H. Kozicki, *The Writing of History: Literary Form and Historical Understanding*, University of Wisconsin Press: Madison, 1978.

D. Carr, *Time, Narrative, and History*, Indiana University Press: Bloomington, 1986.

D. Carr *et al.* (eds), *La Philosophie De L'Histoire et La Pratique Historienne D'Aujourd'hui/Philosophy of History and Contemporary Historiography*, University of Ottawa Press: Ottawa, 1982.

A. Cook, *History/Writing*, Cambridge University Press: Cambridge, 1988.

A. C. Danto, *Narration and Knowledge*, Columbia University Press: New York, 1985.

W. H. Dray, *On History and Philosophers of History*, E. J. Brill: Leiden, 1989.

B. Fay, P. Pomper and R. T. Vann (eds), *History and Theory*, Blackwell: Oxford, 1998.

S. Friedlander (ed.), *Probing the Limits of Representation: Nazism and the "Final Solution,"* Harvard University Press: Cambridge, Mass., 1992.

F. Furet, *In the Workshop of History*, University of Chicago Press: Chicago, 1984.

W. B. Gallie, *Philosophy and the Historical Understanding*, Chatto & Windus: London, 1964.

J. H. Hexter, *The History Primer*, Allen Lane: London, 1972.

S. Hook (ed.), *Philosophy and History*, New York University Press: New York, 1963.

K. Jenkins, *On "What is History?,"* Routledge: London, 1995.

K. Jenkins (ed.), *The Postmodern History Reader*, Routledge: London, 1997.

K. Jenkins, *Why History?*, Routledge: London, 1999.

H. Kellner, *Language and Historical Representation*, University of Wisconsin Press: Madison, 1989.

M. C. Lemon, *The Discipline of History and the History of Thought*, Routledge: London, 1995.

S. Lottinville, *The Rhetoric of History*, University of Oklahoma Press: Oklahoma, 1976.

"Metahistory: Six Critiques," *History and Theory*, vol. 19, no. 4, Beiheft 19, 1980.

L. O. Mink, *Historical Understanding*, Cornell University Press: Ithaca, NY, 1987.

A. Munslow, *Deconstructing History*, Routledge: London, 1997.

A. Munslow, *The Routledge Companion to Historical Studies*, Routledge: London, 2000.

P. Munz, *The Shapes of Time*, Wesleyan University Press: Hanover, NH, 1977.

F. A. Olafson, *The Dialectic of Action: A Philosophical Interpretation of History and the Humanities*, University of Chicago Press: Chicago, 1979.

"The Representation of Historical Events," *History and Theory*, Beiheft 26, December 1987.

P. Ricoeur, *The Contribution of French Historiography to the Theory of History*, Clarendon Press: Oxford, 1980.

P. Ricoeur, *Time and Narrative*, 3 vols, University of Chicago Press, 1984–8.

A Rigney, *The Rhetoric of Historical Representation*, Cambridge University Press: Cambridge, 1990.

J. Rusen, *Studies in Metahistory*, Human Sciences Research Council: Pretoria, 1993.

M. Stanford, *A Companion to the Study of History*, Blackwell: Oxford, 1994.

J. Topolski (ed.), *Historiography Between Modernism and Postmodernism*, Rodopi: Amsterdam, 1994.

G. M. Trevelyan, *Clio, A Muse and other essays*, Longmans, Green: London, 1931.

P. Veyne, *Writing History*, Wesleyan University Press: Hanover, NH, 1984.

H. White, *The Content of the Form: Narrative Discourse and Historical Representation*, The Johns Hopkins University Press: Baltimore, 1987.

H. White, *Figural Realism: Studies in the Mimesis Effect*, The Johns Hopkins University Press: Baltimore, 1999.

H. White, *Metahistory: The Historical Imagination in Nineteenth Century Europe*, The Johns Hopkins University Press: Baltimore, 1973.

H. White, *Tropics of Discourse*, The Johns Hopkins University Press: Baltimore, 1978.

M. White, *Foundations of Historical Knowledge*, Greenwood Press: Westport, Conn., 1965.

Articles

C. J. Arthur, "On the Historical Understanding," *History and Theory*, vol. 7, no. 2, 1968.

B. Bailyn, "The Challenge of Modern Historiography," *American Historical Review*, vol. 87, 1982.

S. Bann, "Towards a Critical Historiography: Recent Work in Philosophy of History," *Philosophy*, vol. 56, 1981.

H. Butterfield, "Narrative History and the Spade-Work Behind It," *History*, vol. 53, no. 178, 1968.

D. Carr, "Review of Paul Ricoeur, *Temps et Récit*," *History of Theory*, vol. 23, no. 3, 1984.

N. Carroll, "Review of David Carr, *Time, Narrative and History*," *History and Theory*, vol. 27, no. 3, 1988.

N. Carroll, "Tropology and Narration" [review of Hayden White, *Figural Realism*], *History and Theory*, vol. 39, no. 3, 2000.

L. B. Cebik, "Understanding Narrative Theory," *History and Theory*, vol.25, Beiheft 1986.

S. G. Crowell, "Mixed Messages: The Heterogeneity of Historical Discourse," *History and Theory*, vol. 37, 1988.

A. C. Danto, "Narrative Sentences," *History and Theory*, vol. 2, no. 2, 1962.

A. Donagan, "Review of Dray, *On History and Philosophers of History*," *History and Theory*, vol. 30, no. 1, 1991.

W. H. Dray, "Mandelbaum on Historical Narrative," *History and Theory*, vol. 8, no. 2, 1969.

W. H. Dray, "Narrative versus Analysis in History," *Philosophy of the Social Sciences*, vol. 15, 1985.

W. H. Dray, "Review of Frederick Olafson, *The Dialectic of Action*," *History and Theory*, vol. 20, no. 1, 1981.

W. H. Dray, "Review of Hayden White, *The Content of the Form*," *History and Theory*, vol. 27, no. 3, 1988.

A. P. Fell, "'Epistemological' and 'Narrativist' Philosophies of History" in W. J. Van Der Dussen & L. Rubinoff (eds), *Objectivity, Method and Point of View*, E. J. Brill: Leiden 1991.

A. P. Fell, "Epistemological and Ontological Queries Concerning David Carr's *Time, Narrative and History*," *Philosophy of the Social Sciences*, vol. 22, no. 3, 1988.

J. L. Gorman, "Review of Kellner, *Language and Historical Representation*," *History and Theory*, vol. 30, no. 3, 1991.

R. Gruner, "Mandelbaum on Historical Narrative," *History and Theory*, vol. 8, no. 2, 1969.

T. L. Haskell, "Farewell to Fallibilism: Robert Berkhofer's *Beyond the Great Story* and the Allure of the Postmodern," *History and Theory*, vol. 37, no. 3, 1998.

D. L. Hull, "Central Subjects and Historical Narratives," *History and Theory*, vol. 14, no. 3, 1975.

K. Jenkins, "A Conversation with Hayden White," *Literature & History*, 3rd series, 7/1 (Spring 1998).

W. Kansteiner, "Hayden White's Critique of the Writing of History," *History and Theory*, vol. 32, no. 3, 1993.

C. Lorenz, "Can Histories Be True? Narrativism, Positivism, and the 'Metaphorical Turn,'" *History and Theory*, vol. 37, no. 3, 1998.

A. R. Louch, "History as Narrative," *History and Theory*, vol. 8, no. 1, 1969.

C. B. McCullagh, "Narrative and Explanation in History," *Mind*, vol. 78, no. 310, 1969.

C. B. McCullagh, "Review of Ankersmit, *Narrative Logic*," *History and Theory*, vol. 23, no. 3, 1984.

A. Megill, "Jorn Rusen's Theory of Historiography," *History and Theory*, vol. 33, no. 1, 1994.

A. Megill, "Recounting the Past: 'Description', Explanation and Narrative in Historiography," *American Historical Review*, vol. 94, June 1989.

P. Munz, "The Historical Narrative" in M. Bentley (ed.), *Companion to Historiography*, Routledge: London, 1997.

F. A. Olafson, "Narrative History and the Concept of Action," *History and Theory*, vol. 9, no. 3, 1970.

M. Phillips, "The Revival of Narrative: Thoughts on a Current Historiographical Debate," *University of Toronto Quarterly*, vol. 53, 1983–4.

G. Roberts, "Narrative History as a Way of Life," *Journal of Contemporary History*, vol. 31, no. 1, 1996.

G. Roberts, "Postmodernism versus the Standpoint of Action" [review of Keith Jenkins, *On 'What is History?'*], *History and Theory*, vol. 36, no. 2, 1997.

P. Roth, "Narrative Explanations: The Case of History," *History and Theory*, vol. 28, no. 1, 1988.

P. Roth, "How Narratives Explain," *Social Research*, vol. 56, no. 2, 1989.

P. Roth, "The Object of Understanding" in H. H. Kogler & K. R. Stueber (eds), *Empathy and Agency*, Westview Press: Boulder, Col., 2000.

A. Sayer, "The 'New' Regional Geography and Problems of Narrative," *Environment and Planning D: Society and Space*, vol. 7, 1989.

W. H. Sewell, "Narrative and Social Identities," *Social Science History*, vol. 16, no. 3, 1992.

H. Suganami, "Narratives of War Origins and Endings: A Note on the End of the Cold War," *Millennium*, vol. 26, no. 3, 1997.

J. E. Toews, "A New Philosophy of History? Reflections on Postmodern Historicizing" [review of Ankersmit & Kellner, *A New Philosophy of History*], *History and Theory*, vol. 36, no. 2, 1997.

J. Topolski, "Conditions of Truth of Historical Narratives," *History and Theory*, vol. 20, no. 1, 1981.

J. Topolski, "The Role of Logic and Aesthetics in Constructing Narrative Wholes in Historiography," *History and Theory*, vol. 38, no. 2, 1999.

R. T. Vann, "Louis Mink's Linguistic Turn," *History and Theory*, vol. 26, no. 1, 1987.

W. H. Walsh, "'Plain' and 'Significant' Narrative in History," *The Journal of Philosophy*, vol. 55, 1988.

P. Zagorin, "Historiography and Postmodernism: Reconsiderations" [and reply by F. R. Ankersmit], *History and Theory*, vol. 29, no. 3, 1990.

P. Zagorin, "History, the Referent, and Narrative: Reflections on Postmodernism Now," *History and Theory*, vol. 38, no. 1, 1999.

J. H. Zammito, "Ankersmit's Postmodernist Historiography: The Hyperbole of 'Opacity,'" *History and Theory*, vol. 37, no. 3, 1998.

Index